LET'S GO:
PACIFIC NORTHWEST, WESTERN CANADA & ALASKA

is the best book for anyone traveling on a budget. Here's why:

No other guidebook has as many budget listings.

In Seattle and Vancouver we list dozens of hostels for less than $40 a night. Outside of the city we found hundreds more. We tell you how to get there the cheapest way, whether by bus, plane, or thumb, and where to get an inexpensive and satisfying meal once you've arrived. There are hundreds of money-saving tips for everyone plus lots of information on student discounts.

LET'S GO researchers have to make it on their own.

Our Harvard-Radcliffe researchers travel on budgets as tight as your own—no expense accounts, no free hotel rooms.

LET'S GO is completely revised every year.

We don't just update the prices, we go back to the places. If a charming restaurant has become an overpriced tourist trap, we'll replace the listing with a new and better one.

No other budget guidebook includes all this:

Coverage of both the cities and the countryside; directions, addresses, phone numbers, and hours to get you there and back; in-depth information on culture, history, and the people; transportation between and within regions and cities; tips on work, study, sights, nightlife, and special splurges; city and regional maps; and much, much more.

LET'S GO is for anyone who wants to see The Pacific Northwest, Western Canada, and Alaska on a budget.

Books by the Harvard Student Agencies, Inc.

LET'S GO:

The Budget Guide to

THE PACIFIC NORTHWEST, WESTERN CANADA, and ALASKA

1991

James Samuel Rosen
Editor

Beth M. N. Quitslund
Assistant Editor

Written by Harvard Student Agencies, Inc.

PAN BOOKS
London, Sydney and Auckland

Helping Let's Go

If you have suggestions or corrections, or just want to share your discoveries, drop us a line. We read every piece of correspondence, whether a 10-page letter, a postcard, or, as in one case, a collage. All suggestions are passed along to our researcher/writers. Please note that mail received after June 1, 1991 will probably be too late for the 1992 book, but will be retained for the following edition. Address mail to: *Let's Go: Pacific Northwest, Western Canada, and Alaska;* Harvard Student Agencies, Inc.; Thayer Hall-B; Harvard University; Cambridge, MA 02138; USA.

In addition to the invaluable travel advice our readers share with us, many are kind enough to offer their services as researchers or editors. Unfortunately, the charter of Harvard Student Agencies, Inc. enables us to employ only currently enrolled Harvard students.

Published in Great Britain 1991 by Pan Books Ltd
Cavaye Place, London SW10 9PG
9 8 7 6 5 4 3 2 1

Published in the United States of America
by St. Martin's Press, Inc.

LET'S GO: PACIFIC NORTHWEST, WESTERN CANADA AND ALASKA. Copyright © 1991 by Harvard Student Agencies, Inc. All rights reserved.

Maps by David Lindroth, copyright © 1991, 1990, 1988 by St. Martin's Press, Inc.

ISBN: 0 330 31715 6

Let's Go: Pacific Northwest, Western Canada and Alaska is written by Harvard Student Agencies, Inc., Harvard University, Thayer Hall-B, Cambridge, Mass. 02138, USA.

Let's Go ® is registered trademark of Harvard Student Agencies, Inc.

Printed and bound in the United States of America.

ACKNOWLEDGMENTS

After researching and writing for *Let's Go: Pacific Northwest, Western Canada & Alaska* last summer, returning to the book this year as an editor has been a labor of love. This would not have been true, however, without my preternaturally gifted assistant editor, Beth Quitslund. Even when it seemed that the job was all labor and no love, Beth performed remarkably well—conquering mountains of paper and enduring tidal waves of copybatches. This book reflects her clever wit and vast knowledge of the region.

This book also reflects the work of the Gang of Four who walked, drove, bused, hitchhiked, skied, and parachuted across thousands of miles in the never-ending search for a better bargain. Singlehandedly researching the entire state of Alaska, Steve Cohn literally went to the ends of the Earth for *Let's Go*. Augmenting the chapter with new coverage of Prudhoe Bay and the Prince William Sound area, his copy was a delight to edit. Chris Salvaterra (overcoming the handicap of spotty research from the last two years) took time out from writing screenplays for *The Wonder Years* to write entertaining prose about two states and two provinces. Michael Raynour laboured on buses as he traveled thousands of kilometres between major centres in BC; his colourful writing flavoured the book with an unmistakably Canadian perspective. Lastly, Lori Smith, unfazed by deadlines, sent back detailed and thoughtfully written descriptions about her own neck of the woods in Washington and Oregon. We all anxiously awaited each installment.

I would also like to thank the office crew for making this summer great; I could not have been trapped underground with a more wonderful bunch of people. I only wish that I had more time to spend with Madeline Whalen, who has been a constant source of love and support.

—Jamie

I traveled a fair way in the Canaday grotto this summer, and had more help than I can acknowledge, both in Cambridge and from my neighbors and tribe at home. My friend and editor Jamie let me bully him and not myself; Alex managed warmth and wit; Chris deserves kudos for both being everything to everybody, and being Chris. My landlord had a share in making the office such a magnetic place, but more credit really goes to the other AEs and all the *Let's Go* hive. Thanks to them for sympathetic insanity; to Claire, Gunnar, and Liz for listening to my own; to Frances for quiet wisdom, long-suffering efficiency, and great cooking; Mel for love; Katharine for almost anything that I can think of; and my parents for the rest.

—Beth Quitslund

CARRY-ON RELIEF.

CONTENTS

x   **Contents**

LIST OF MAPS

About Let's Go

In 1960, Harvard Student Agencies, a three-year-old nonprofit corporation established to provide employment opportunities to Harvard and Radcliffe students, was doing a booming business selling charter flights to Europe. One of the extras HSA offered passengers on these flights was a 20-page mimeographed pamphlet entitled *1960 European Guide,* a collection of tips on continental travel compiled by the staff at HSA. The following year, students traveling to Europe researched the first full-fledged edition of *Let's Go: Europe,* a pocket-sized book with a smattering of tips on budget accommodations, irreverent write-ups of sights, and a decidedly youthful slant. The first editions proclaimed themselves to be the companions of the "adventurous and often impecunious student."

Throughout the 60s, the series reflected its era: a section of the 1968 *Let's Go: Europe* was entitled "Street Singing in Europe on No Dollars a Day;" the 1969 guide to America led off with a feature on drug-ridden Haight-Ashbury. During the 70s, *Let's Go* gradually became a large-scale operation, adding regional European guides and expanding coverage into North Africa and Asia. In 1981, *Let's Go: USA* returned after an eight-year hiatus, and in the next year HSA joined forces with its current publisher, St. Martin's Press. Now in its 31st year, *Let's Go* publishes 13 titles covering more than 40 countries.

Each spring, over 150 Harvard-Radcliffe students compete for some 70 positions as *Let's Go* researcher/writers. Those hired possess a rare combination of budget travel sense, writing ability, stamina, and courage. Each researcher/writer travels on a shoestring budget for seven weeks, researching seven days per week, and overcoming countless obstacles in the quest for better bargains.

Back in a basement in Harvard Yard, an editorial staff of 25, a management team of five, and countless typists and proofreaders—all students—spend four months poring over more than 50,000 pages of manuscript as they push the copy through 12 stages of intensive editing. In September the efforts of summer are converted from computer diskettes to nine-track tapes and delivered to Com Com in Allentown, Pennsylvania, where their computerized typesetting equipment turns them into books in record time. And even before the books hit the stands, next year's editions are well underway.

A Note to our Readers

The information for this book is gathered by Harvard Student Agencies' researchers during the late spring and summer months. Each listing is derived from the assigned researcher's opinion based on his or her visit at a particular time. The opinions are expressed in a candid and forthright manner. Other travelers might disagree. Those traveling at a different time may have a different experience since prices, dates, hours, and conditions are always subject to change. You are urged to check beforehand to avoid inconvenience and surprises. Travel always involves a certain degree of risk, especially in low cost areas. When traveling, especially on a budget, you should always take particular care to ensure your safety.

LET'S GO: PACIFIC NORTHWEST, WESTERN CANADA, & ALASKA

GENERAL INTRODUCTION

"How delightful it is, and how it makes one's pulses bound to get back to this reviving northland wilderness!" wrote naturalist John Muir in the journal of his 1880 expedition to Alaska. To travel to the Great Northwest is to experience the little ecstacies of sheer living in one of the freshest and most hospitable parts of the continent. In the last century, of course, the wilds have blossomed into rich urban clusters and quiet communities spangled across open fields. But reflected in the windows of the most gleamingly new sky-scrapers of the Northwest, you cannot avoid the reflected profiles of the mountains shored up against the Pacific Rim—and you wouldn't want to.

Hike through the majestic parks of Alberta and climb the peaks of Alaska, where time creeps at the geological pace of the glacial expanses. Stop over in the orchard towns of Washington and Oregon, where the frontier spirit is rooted despite the commercial revolution. Step out in the cities of Seattle, Portland, and Vancouver, whose faces turn toward international trade and the future. This hinterland has no dearth of civilized culture, either. Journey to the tiny town of Ashland, Oregon, and see the summer-long Shakespeare Festival in progress. Listen to a festival of jazz in Portland as the Columbia River churns. If you like your fun a little rough, go to Pendleton, Oregon, for the annual Round-Up, or to Calgary for the Stampede. Lose yourself in the largest shopping mall in the world—nay, the universe—in Edmonton. And seize every chance to indulge in the cornucopia of fresh fruits, fish, and vegetables along the way.

Let's Go: The Pacific Northwest, Western Canada, and Alaska is written especially for the budget traveler. Researchers travel on a shoestring budget, and their concerns are the same as yours: how to get from place to place, fill their stomachs, drink in the sights, enjoy the evenings, and get some sleep, all in the most economical way possible. Their numerous tips on how to experience more while spending less, and their honest appraisals of everything from hostels to hamburgers, will give you the freedom to experience the Northwest without getting bogged down in humdrum logistics.

The **General Introduction** provides information that you will need to know before you leave. **Planning Your Trip** contains a slew of details organized as a checklist: where to write for information about the region, how to maintain your supply of money, how and what to pack, and how to stay safe and healthy. **Getting There and Getting Around** sorts out the various modes of transportation to and around the region. **Accommodations** covers everything from cheap motels to youth hostels to bed and breakfasts. **Camping and the Outdoors** provides detailed information for those interested in camping, hiking, and sporting in the region's various systems of parks, forests, and waterways. **Life in the Northwest** surveys the history of the area and its culture, art, and climate. **For International Visitors** is a guide to visas, customs, inexpensive transportation to the Northwest from around the world, foreign exchange, and the postal and telephone systems in the U.S. and Canada.

1

State, provincial, regional and city introductions acquaint you with both the layout and the ambience of the area. Following these introductions are sections on **Practical Information,** listing such crucial resources and information as tourist centers, emergency numbers and crisis hotlines, local and intercity transport, post offices, and telephone area codes. Sections on Getting There and Getting Around, Accommodations, and Food help you get oriented, moved, settled, and fed. *Let's Go* lets you in on the most affordable entertainment and restaurants, and we point you toward the unique, the characteristic, the splendid, and the awe-inspiring wherever you go.

Keep in mind, though, that although the last explorers trekked this way a more than a century ago (and our researchers beat an annual trail through the region), not all has been discovered in the Great Northwest. Always keep an eye out for attractions and options that *Let's Go* doesn't list, and follow your spirit and your imagination. Be sure to check other sources; the tourist bureaus of states, provinces, and regions can always provide fresh and detailed information. And remember to write or call ahead!

If you intend to travel to other parts of North America as well, consult *Let's Go: USA* (which includes substantial coverage of Canada), *Let's Go: California and Hawaii,* and *Let's Go: Mexico.*

Enjoy your trip!

Planning Your Trip

Planning ahead is one of the keys to an enjoyable, anxiety-free vacation. Spend the time now rather than later getting in touch with travel resources in the region and figuring out how to handle the basic issues: when to go, how to have enough money on hand, how to stay in good health, and a variety of other concerns small or large. Set aside a few hours well before your trip to make calls and write letters to organizations with useful information, and to compile lists of things to consider and bring along. It'll save you time and frustration once you hit the road and will help you take the more unusual situations in stride.

When To Go

Traveling is like comedy—timing is everything. In the Pacific Northwest, your rival concerns will be the tourist season and the weather. In general, summer (June-Aug.) is high season; during those months, you can expect to share the warm weather with crowds of fellow tourists. If you prefer to experience the region as its human and animal residents do, go during the off-season, when crowds are smaller and rates are lower. Beware the disadvantages of winter travel in certain parts, however: slush, icy roads, and miserably cold weather will constrain your movement and outdoorsmanship. All things considered, May and September may be the best times to travel in the Northwest. See Climate below for details about the weather in different regions.

Official Holidays

Keep in mind the following dates when you plan your vacation. Government agencies, post offices, and banks are closed on certain holidays, and businesses may have special (shorter) hours. Many holidays are the occasions for parades and public celebrations. These are the dates for 1991:

New Year's Day:	Tues., Jan. 1
Martin Luther King Jr.'s Birthday:	Mon., Jan. 21 (observed; U.S. only)
Presidents' Day:	Mon., Feb. 18 (U.S. only)
Good Friday:	Fri., Mar. 29
Easter:	Sun., Mar. 31 (next day also a holiday in Canada)
Victoria Day:	Mon., May 20 (Canada only)

Memorial Day:	Mon., May 27 (U.S. only)
VJR Day:	Wed., June 12 (U.S. only)
Canada Day:	Mon., July 1 (Canada only)
Independence Day:	Tues., July 4 (U.S. only)
Heritage Day:	Sat., Aug. 3 (Alberta only)
British Columbia Day:	Mon., Aug. 5 (BC only)
Discovery Day:	Mon., Aug. 19 (Yukon only)
Labor Day:	Mon., Sept. 2
Thanksgiving Day:	Mon., Oct. 14 (Canada only)
Columbus Day:	Mon., Oct. 14 (U.S. only)
Alaska Day:	Fri., Oct. 18. (Alaska only)
Veterans Day (U.S.)/ Remembrance Day (Canada):	Mon., Nov. 11
Thanksgiving Day:	Thurs., Nov. 28 (U.S. only)
Christmas Day:	Wed., Dec. 25
Boxing Day:	Thurs., Dec. 26 (Canada except Yukon)

Getting More Information

As you plan your itinerary, it's a good idea to consult the listings (starting with *Let's Go*) for the specific destinations you intend to include. Chambers of Commerce for individual towns can send you information in advance that may help you to plan (see the Practical Information sections below for addresses). One general resource worth writing to is the **U.S. Government Printing Office.** Among the government's many publications are a wide variety concerning travel and recreation. *Let's Go* lists many of the most useful, but you can call or write for complete bibliographies. Bibliography #17 deals with outdoor activities in general, and #302 with travel to particular regions. The pamphlet "Travel and Tourism" covers travel within the U.S. To receive free bibliographies or to order a specific publication, write or call the Superintendent of Documents, U.S. Government Printing Office, Washington, DC 20402 (202-783-3238).

Tourism Bureaus

Each state and province has its own travel bureau, which can refer you to other useful organizations, send you travel brochures, and answer your specific questions about the region.

Alberta Tourism, Box 2500, Edmonton, AB T5J 2Z4 (800-661-8888; within AB, 800-222-6501).

Alaska Division of Tourism, P.O. Box E, Juneau, AK 99811 (907-465-2010).

Tourism British Columbia,, 1117 Wharf St., Victoria, BC V8W 2Z2 (604-387-1642).

Oregon Tourism Division, Dept. of Trade and Economic Development, 775 Summer St. NE, Salem, OR 97310 (800-547-7842; in OR, 800-543-8838).

Washington Tourism Division, Dept. of Trade and Economic Development, 101 General Administration Bldg., Olympia, WA 98504-0613 (800-544-1800 for free travel booklet; 206-586-2088 for general information).

Tourism Yukon, P.O. Box 2703, Whitehorse, YT Y1A 2C6 (403-667-5340).

Money

The best things in life are free. Inferior things abound, of course, and they all cost money. Your budget will be just that: a plan and a projection of how much you will spend. Overruns are to be expected. (This may be the only thing the budget traveler and the United States Federal government have in common.) Various kinds of surcharges will inflate your expenses on the road, as well. Prices in stores and restaurants (and thus in *Let's Go*) do not include a state or provincial **sales tax** of up to 14%, which will be added before you pay. Waiters, taxi drivers, and many others will expect you to add a **tip** to the bill: 15% is the general rule. Bellboys and airport porters expect about a dollar per piece of luggage.

No matter how low your budget, if you plan to travel for more than a couple of days you will need to keep handy a much larger amount of cash than usual. Carrying it around, even in a money belt, is risky; personal checks from home may not be acceptable no matter how many forms of ID you carry (even banks may shy away). Inevitably you will have to rely on some combination of the innovations of the modern financial world.

Cash, Banks, and Currency

Whatever forms of currency substitutes you carry, you will need to periodically refresh your cash supply. Don't get your hopes up about the electronic banking revolution. Automatic teller machine (ATM) networks are continually expanding across the continent, but you'll need to find out whether or not your bank belongs to a network with machines in the region. Don't rely on ATMs too much—service charges are steep, and there is generally a limit on how much you can withdraw on any given day ($250 for most banks). If a machine tells you that "your bank cannot process this transaction at this time," that's often the machine's polite way of saying your card won't work on that network.

In the U.S., banks are usually open weekdays 9am to 5pm, and some are open Saturdays 9am to noon or 1pm. Canadian banks are open Monday through Friday 10am to 3pm, in some areas with extended hours on Fridays and/or business hours on Saturdays. In northern Alaska, banks are scarce and may operate only a few days per week. All banks, government agencies, and post offices are closed on legal holidays (see Official Holidays above for a list). When you arrive in a major city, or if in a smaller town you know you will need to use a bank, find out the hours of the major bank(s); they may vary somewhat from place to place.

If you will be traveling between the U.S. and Canada, remember that a Canadian dollar and a U.S. dollar are identical in name only, and you will have to convert between them. Many Canadian shops accept U.S. coins at face value (which is a small loss for you), and some will even convert the price of your purchase for you. These tend to be located in more expensive tourist centers, though, and may not give a very favorable rate in any case. When possible, exchange larger amounts in major banks to avoid fees. The exchange rate hovers around CDN$6 to US$5.

Traveler's Checks

Traveler's checks are the safest way to carry large sums of money. Most tourist establishments will accept them and almost any bank will cash them. Usually banks sell traveler's checks for a 1% commission, although your own bank may waive the surcharge if you have a large enough balance or a certain type of account. In addition, certain travel organizations, such as the American Auto Association (AAA), offer commission-free traveler's checks to their members. Try to purchase traveler's checks in small denominations ($20 is best, never larger than $50)—otherwise, a small-to-medium purchase and you're back to carrying a large amount of cash. If the bank doesn't have small denominations available, try a larger institution or come back another day.

Always keep the receipts from the purchase of your traveler's checks, a list of their serial numbers, and a record of which ones you've cashed. Keep these in a separate pocket or pouch from the checks themselves, since they contain the information you will need to replace your checks if they are stolen. It's also a good idea to leave the serial numbers with someone at home as a back-up in case of wholes luggage loss.

American Express traveler's checks are perhaps the most widely recognized in the world, and the easiest to replace if lost or stolen—just contact the nearest AmEx Travel office or call the (800)-number below. Other well-known banks also market traveler's checks. Call any of the toll-free numbers below to find out the advantages of a particular type of check and the name of a bank near you that sells them.

Don't forget to write.

If your American Express® Travelers Cheques are lost or stolen, we can hand-deliver a refund virtually anywhere you travel. Just give us a call. You'll find it's a lot less embarrassing than calling home.

 **Travelers Cheques**

American Express: 800-221-7282 in U.S and Canada. From abroad, call their office collect in Brighton, Great Britain at (44) 273 57 16 00; from most countries this is toll-free, otherwise call collect.

Bank of America: 800-227-3460 in U.S.; from Canada and abroad, call collect 415-624-5400. Checks in US$ only. Free in CA. 1% commission for non-Bank of America customers. Checkholders may use the Travel Assistance hotline (800-368-7878 from U.S., 202-347-7113 collect from Canada), which provides free legal assistance, urgent message relay, lost document services, and up to $1000 advance for prompt medical treatment.

Barclay's: 800-221-2426 in U.S.; from Canada and abroad, call collect 415-574-7111. Connected with Visa. Checks issued in US$ in Canada and U.S., CDN$ as well in Canada. Barclay's charges a 1% commission. Any branch will cash Barclay's checks free Mon.-Fri.; surcharge on Sat.

Citicorp: 800-645-6556 in U.S and Canada; from abroad, call collect 813-623-1709. Checks available in four currencies. Commission of 1%. Checkholders enrolled automatically in Travel Assist Hotline (800-523-1199) for 45 days after purchase.

Mastercard International, (800-223-7373; from abroad, call collect 212-976-5496). In US$. Free from Mastercard, though bank commissions may run 1-2%.

Thomas Cook: 800-223-7373; from Canada and abroad, call collect 212-974-5696. Available at any bank displaying a Mastercard sign.

Visa: 800-227-6811 in U.S. and Canada; from abroad, call collect 415-574-7111 (San Francisco) or (01) 937 80 91 (London). No commission if purchased at Barclay's.

Credit Cards

Most places mentioned in *Let's Go* will not honor major credit cards. This is just as well—rely on them too much and your trip will soon no longer deserve the label "budget travel." However, credit cards have a variety of uses for economical traveling. Use them for large purchases to avoid depleting your cash on hand. Credit cards also make renting a car easier, and can be used often in lieu of a cash deposit. In addition, you can use credit cards to get a cash advance from a bank or electronic teller.

Visa and **MasterCard** are accepted in more establishments than other credit cards, and they are also the most useful for getting an instant cash advance. Visa holders can generally obtain an advance up to the amount of the credit line remaining on the card, while Mastercard imposes a daily limit. Be sure to consult the bank that issues your card, however, since it may impose its own rules and restrictions. At a bank, you should be able to obtain cash from a teller, who will essentially "charge" you as if you had made a purchase. Not all ATMs will honor your credit card; those that do require you to enter your personal code number. You will have the option to set up a personal code when you receive a new card; if you do not have a code number for an old account, contact the credit card company to establish one. Expect a service charge for electronic cash advances.

American Express offers a number of services to cardholders. Local AmEx offices will cash personal checks up to $1000 for Green Card holders ($200 in cash, $800 in traveler's checks) and $5000 of which $500 may be cash for Gold Card holders. You can do this once every seven days—note that the money is drawn from your personal checking account, not your AmEx account. Cash advances are available in certain places to Gold Card holders. At some major airports, American Express also operates machines from which you can purchase traveler's checks with your card. Cardholders can take advantage of the American Express Travel Service. Benefits include assistance in changing airline, hotel, and car rental reservations, as well as Global Assist (800-554-2639), a 24-hour helpline that provides legal and medical assistance. At any American Express Travel Service office you can pick up a copy of the *Traveler's Companion,* a list of full-service offices throughout the world. For more information, contact the American Express Travel Service office or affiliate nearest you.

If you're a student or your income level is low, you may have difficulty acquiring a recognized credit card. Some of the larger, national banks have credit card offers geared especially toward students, even those who bank elsewhere. Otherwise, you may have to find someone older and more established (such as a parent) to co-sign your application. If someone in your family already has a card, they can usually ask for another card in your name (this encourages travel economy, as they will see the bill before you do). When using your credit card, keep in mind that there is no free lunch—in addition to the annual fee that Amex and many Visa and Mastercard accounts charge, beware the hefty interest rate if you do not pay your balance each month.

Sending Money

If you run out of money on the road and have no credit card, you have several options. Most inexpensive is to have a **certified check** or a **postal money order** mailed to you. Certified checks are redeemable at any bank, while postal money orders can be cashed at any post office upon presentation of two forms of ID (one with photo). You lose only a miniscule fee (in all likelihood, whoever sends you the check will forget they paid it and you'll be off the hook) and the time that the check is in the mail.

Another alternative is cabling money. Through **Bank of America's** Global Seller Services (800-227-3333), money can be sent to any affiliated bank. Have someone bring cash, a credit card, or a cashier's check to the sending bank—you need not have an account. You can pick up the money three to five working days later with ID. To send $1000, someone will have to pay 1% plus a $15 telex charge. **American Express** offers a money transfer service, which takes only a day or two, but costs $45 per $1000 sent domestically and $70 per $1000 sent abroad. The first $200 may be received in cash, the rest in travelers' checks or as a money transfer check which may be cashed at a bank. Those who bank at **Barclay's** can get their money within two to four working days. Again, have someone bring cash or a cashier's check to the sending location, and you will need to present a driver's license or passport to receive the transfusion. The fee is $15 for sums under $3000 within the U.S.; otherwise, the you may pay as much as $35-40. To take advantage of a classic, time-honored, and expensive service, use **Western Union** (800-325-6000). You or someone else can phone in a credit card number, or else someone can bring cash to a Western Union office. As always, you need ID to pick up your money. Their charge is $47 per $1000.

If time is of the essence, you can have money wired directly, bank to bank. Contact your bank by telegram or phone and state the amount of money you need, whether you need American or Canadian dollars, and the name and address of the bank to which the money should be sent. You should receive your money in about a day, although it will take longer to reach smaller and more out-of-the-way locales, and the cost will be at least $25 for amounts under $1000.

Keeping Safe

Security

Even the minimal wares of the low-cost traveler have their allure for theives, but with an appropriate amount of caution and common sense, you can reduce the risk of losing your treasures. After protecting yourself, protecting your money should be your first concern. First the don'ts: don't carry your money in your back pocket, don't take out your money and count it on the street or in front of strangers, don't leave your money dangling from a bag or pouch that can easily be grabbed off your shoulder. You should always keep your important documents—ID, passport, traveler's check numbers and receipts—separate from the bulk of your belongings, along with a small amount of emergency cash and a credit card. What you need at your fingertips you should carry in a well-protected fashion. Most impervious to theft are **necklace pouches** that stay under your shirt; they are not easily accessible, though, and large ones can be quite uncomfortable. **Money belts** can be worn around your waist and buried under one or all your layers of clothing—these are more convenient and nearly theft-proof.

Wherever you stow your stuff, either for the day or for the evening, try to keep your valuables on your person and leave little other than clothing in your room. In the dorm-style rooms of some hostels, consider this rule ironclad. In general you may as well err on the side of caution and carry around a small daypack with your documents, credit cards, and camera. Lockers at bus and train stations are safe, and very useful if you want to sleep outside without most of your bulky possessions—or just want to sightsee for the day between accommodations. Label *all* your belongings (and maybe even yourself) with your name, address, and home phone. Label your luggage inside and out, including easy-to-drop items such as sleeping bags and tents; on your valuables, like cameras, write "call collect" and a trusted phone number at home. Try to memorize as many of your important numbers as possible in case they disappear (a good pretravel exercise): passport, ID, driver's license, health insurance policy, traveler's checks, credit cards. You should also leave all of this information with someone at home, in case your memory fails you mid-trip.

More important than your belongings is yourself. Avoid bus and train stations and public parks after dark. Walk on busy, well-lit streets, especially in the larger cities. When you're walking alone, walk as though you know where you're going, even if you don't; avoid passing too close to dark alleyways or doorways and stay in the light. Don't walk though parking lots at night. When you get to a place where you'll be spending some time, find out about its unsafe areas from tourist information, from the manager of your hotel or hostel, or from a local person you meet whom you trust. Both men and women may want to carry a small whistle to scare off attackers or attract attention, and it's not a bad idea to jot down the number of the police if you'll be in town for a couple days. (Remember that in an emergency, you may call 911 for help toll free on a public phone.) In addition, you may feel safer sleeping in places with either a curfew or a night attendant.

For more safe travel information, refer to *Travel Safely: Security and Safeguards at Home and Abroad,* from **Hippocrene Books, Inc.,** 171 Madison Ave., New York, NY 10016 (212-685-4371). Women or anyone traveling alone can see Special Concerns, below.

Insurance

Purchasing insurance against accident, sickness, or theft may make sense, although you will have to weigh the costs, benefits, and conditions carefully. Beware of unnecessary coverage. Check whether your own or your family's homeowners' insurance covers theft or accident during travel. Homeowners' insurance often covers the loss of travel documents such as passports, airplane tickets, and rail passes up to $500. If you are a student, your university's term-time medical plan may include insurance for summer travel. For U.S. residents, **Medicare** covers travel in the U.S., Canada, and Mexico. Canadians may be covered by their home provinces's health insurance plan for up to 90 days after leaving the country. Check with your provincial Ministry of Health or Health Plan Headquarters before buying additional coverage.

Before an insurance company will reimburse you for theft, you will have to provide a copy of the police report filed at the time of the theft. To be reimbursed for medical expenses, you will have to submit a doctor's statement and evidence that you actually paid the charges for which you are asking to be reimbursed; make sure you keep all receipts for conceivably reimburseable expenses. When you file for any kind of insurance reimbursement, make sure that you are filing within the time limit specified by the policy and that either you or someone at home can be in touch with your insurer if necessary.

If you are an ISIC cardholder, you automatically receive US$3000 of accident-related coverage and US$100 per day of in-patient health coverage, up to 60 days as well as generous compensation for death, dismemberment, or repatriation of remains. While good in Canada and Hawaii, these benefits do *not* cover the continental U.S. and Alaska. CIEE also offers the **Trip-Safe** plan, which *does* cover the entire U.S., to ISIC holders and nonholders alike. Trip-Safe includes the above package as well as insurance for medical treatment and hospitalization, accidents, baggage loss, trip cancellation, emergency evacuation and repatriation, and coverage for charter flights missed due to illness. Cost of the insurance varies with the length of your trip. Call or write CIEE (see Student Travel below) for information. **American Express** cardmembers automatically receive car-rental and flight insurance on purchases made with the card.

The following firms also specialize in travel insurance. You can buy a policy either directly from them or through an agent operating on their behalf:

Access America, Inc., 600 Third Ave., Box 807, New York, NY 10163 (800-284-8300). A subsidiary of Blue Cross/Blue Shield. Covers trip cancellation/interruption, on-the-spot hospital admittance costs, emergency medical evaluation, and a 24-hr. hotline.

Carefree Travel Insurance, P.O. Box 310, Mineola, NY 11501 (800-645-2424). Package includes coverage for baggage loss, accidents, medical treatment, and trip cancellation or interruption (which can also be purchased separately). 24-hr. hotline.

Edmund A. Cocco Agency, 220 Broadway, #201, P.O. Box 780, Lynnfield, MA 01940 (800-821-2488; in MA, 617-595-0262). Coverage against accident, sickness, baggage loss, and trip cancellation or interruption. Emergency medical evacuation covered as well. Payment of medical expenses "on-the-spot" anywhere in the world. Protection against bankruptcy or default of airlines, cruise lines, or charter companies. Trip cancellation/interruption coverage $5.50 per $100 of coverage. Group rates available. 24-hr. hotline.

The Traveler's Insurance Co., 1 Tower Sq., Hartford, CT 06183-5040 (800-243-3174; in CT, HI, or AK 203-277-2318). Insurance against accident, baggage loss, sickness, trip cancellation or interruption, and company default. Covers emergency medical evacuation as well. Available through most travel agencies.

Travel Guard International, P.O. Box 1200, Stevens Point, WI 54481 (800-782-5151). Basic ($19), deluxe ($39), and comprehensive "Travel Guard Gold" (8% of total trip cost) packages cover baggage delay, car rental, accidental death, and trip cancellation or interruption. 24-hour hotline for policyholders.

WorldCare Travel Assistance Association, Inc., 6505 Market St., #1300, San Francisco, CA 94105 (800-666-4993). Annual membership US$162 covers all trips under 90 days. Coverage for 1-8 day trips US$86; longer trips less per day. Free repatriation and medical evacuation. Trip cancellation/interruption coverage additional.

Health

Common sense is the simplest prescription for health while you travel: eat well, drink enough, get enough sleep, and don't overexert yourself. You will need plenty of protein (for sustained energy) and fluids (to prevent dehydration and constipation, two of the most common health problems for travelers). Carry a canteen or water bottle and make sure to drink frequently. Sunscreen is mandatory—clothes and a pack over sunburned skin can be torturous, and more importantly, dry skin doesn't keep the body as cool or retain moisture as well. Wear a hat (preferably a big, floopy one). And lavish your feet with attention; make sure your shoes are appropriate for extended walking, do not wear the same pair of socks for too long, use talcum powder frequently, and have some moleskin on hand to pad your shoes if they become uncomfortable. If possible, bring an extra pair of good walking shoes and alternate between the two pairs, both to vary the points of stress on your feet and to allow the shoes to dry thoroughly after a day of walking.

While you travel, pay attention to the signals of pain and discomfort that your body may send you. Expect some adjustment to a new climate, diet, water quality, or pace when you first arrive or after a couple of weeks—often this is nothing, but keep an eye on it. Once you get going, some of the milder symptoms that you can safely ignore at home may be signs of something more serious on the road, and your increased exertion may wear you out and make you more susceptible to illness.

Airplane travelers are often plagued by **jet lag.** Jet lag sufferers are generally uncomfortable and tired, but unable to sleep normally. To avoid or cure jet lag, the best thing to do is to adopt the new region's time as soon as you arrive and to try to sleep during the appropriate hours. Some studies caution sufferers against excessive eating and alcoholic drinking as well.

In the warmer parts of the Northwest, like Spokane in the summertime, be on the alert for **heatstroke.** This term is often misapplied to all forms of heat exhaustion, but in fact it refers to a specific ailment that can cause death within a few hours if it is not treated. Heatstroke can begin without direct exposure to the sun; it results from continuous heat stress, lack of fitness, or overactivity following heat exhaustion. In the early stages of heatstroke, sweating stops, body temperature rises, and an intense headache develops, soon followed by mental confusion. To treat heatstroke, cool the victim off immediately with fruit juice or salted water, wet towels, and shade. Then rush the victim to the hospital.

Out of doors, watch out for **poison oak,** which grows plentifully in forested areas along the Pacific Coast. Skin that comes in contact with poison oak becomes inflamed and fiercely itchy. If you do develop a poison oak rash, do not wash or scratch it: these actions will spread the rash. Instead, find a doctor who can tell you what kind of medication to apply. And be careful—the rash spreads on contact, so stay at (more than) arm's length from your loved ones and fellow travelers. Each stalk of the plant has three dark green leaves with serrated edges. In the fall, poison oak may turn red as well.

Hypothermia can strike in cold, windy, or wet conditions—and this can include temperatures well above freezing—when body temperature drops rapidly, resulting in a failure to produce body heat. Symptoms are easy to detect: uncontrollable shivering, poor coordination, and exhaustion followed by slurred speech, sleepiness, hallucinations, and amnesia. You can often save victims of hypothermia by making them warm and drying them off. *Do not* let victims fall asleep if they are in the advanced stages—if they lose consciousness, they might die. To avoid hypothermia, always keep dry. Wear wool, *especially* in soggy weather—it retains its insulating ability even when wet. Dress in layers, and stay out of the wind, which carries heat away from the body. Remember that most loss of body heat is through your head, so always carry a wool hat with you.

Frostbite is an obvious danger in really cold weather activities. The affected skin will turn white, then waxy and cold. To counteract the problem, the victim should drink warm beverages, stay or get dry, and gently and slowly warm the frostbitten area in dry fabric or with steady body contact. *Never rub* frostbite—the skin is easily damaged. Take serious cases to a doctor or medic as soon as possible.

For minor health hazards, a compact self-assembled **first-aid kit** should suffice. You should include any or all of the following, depending on your plans: bandaids, gauze, adhesive tape, aspirin, soap (both mild and antiseptic), antibiotic ointment, a thermometer in a sturdy case, multiple vitamins, decongestant (particularly important for clearing your ears if you find yourself needing to fly with a cold), antihistamine, motion sickness medicine (such as Dramamine), medicine for stomach problems and diarrhea, burn ointment, lip balm, an elastic bandage, and a Swiss Army knife (with tweezers). If you anticipate sexual activity during your travels, be aware of how to do it safely and carry your own condoms. Women taking oral contraceptives need to take time zone changes into account, as do diabetics who must have regular insulin injections. If you wear glasses or contact lenses, bring a prescription and/or an extra pair along with you. Lens wearers can avoid dried-out contacts by drinking sufficient fluids and switching to glasses where the air is dry or dirty. All travelers should be sure that their immunizations, such as tetanus shots, are up to date.

Before you leave, check and see whether your insurance policy (if you have one) covers medical costs incurred while traveling (see Insurance, above). If you choose to risk traveling without insurance, you still have avenues for health care that bypass hospitals and private practice. In an emergency, call the local hotline or crisis center listed in *Let's Go* under Practical Information for each area. Operators at these organizations have numbers for public health organizations and clinics that treat patients without demanding proof of solvency. Such centers charge low fees. University teaching hospitals usually run inexpensive clinics as well.

If you have a chronic medical condition that requires medication on a regular basis, consult your physician before you leave. Carry copies of your prescriptions and an ample supply of all medications; it might be difficult to find pharmacies in rural areas. Always distribute medication and/or syringes among all your carry-on and checked baggage in case any of your bags is lost. If you are traveling with a medical condition that cannot be easily recognized—such as diabetes, an allergy to antibiotics or other drugs, epilepsy, or a heart condition—you should obtain a **Medic Alert identification tag** to alert both passersby and medical personnel of your condition in case of emergency. Your tag is engraved with the name of your ailment, and you receive a wallet card with personal and medical information. The tag costs $25 for steel, $38 for silver, and, for the fashion-conscious, $48 for gold plate. Fee includes access to an emergency phone number as well. Contact Medic Alert Foundation International, Turlock, CA 95381-1009 (800-432-5378).

For more information, consult *The Pocket Medical Encyclopedia and First-Aid Guide* (Simon and Schuster, $5; write to Mail Order Dept., 200 Old Tappan Rd., Old Tappan, NJ 07675, or call 800-223-2348). Both **The Mountaineers Books** and **Wilderness Press** publish several books about travel medicine and mountaineering medicine in particular. Write or call for free catalogs—for their addresses and phone numbers, see Camping and the Outdoors below. In addition, the **International Association for Medical Assistance to Travelers (IAMAT)** provides members with free pamphlets and a directory of fixed-rate physicians throughout the world. Membership is free, although donations are encouraged. Contact IAMAT in the U.S. at 417 Center St., Lewiston, NY 14092 (716-754-4883), or in Canada at 40 Regal St., Guelph, Ont., N1K 1B5 (519-836-0102).

Alcohol and Drugs

In Oregon, Washington, and Alaska, the drinking age is 21 years of age and is strictly enforced. British Columbia and the Yukon Territory prohibit drinking below the age of 19, while in Alberta you can drink at 18.

Drugs and traveling, however, are mutually incompatible. Even where possession of marijuana no longer constitutes a misdemeanor in the state's reckoning, it is still a U.S. federal offense subject to imprisonment. At the Canadian border, if you are found in possession of drugs, you will be subject to an automatic seven-year jail term, regardless of how small an amount you are found with, and the foreign would-be visitor will be permanently barred from entering the country. Police attitudes towards drugs vary widely across the region. In some cities, police tend to ignore pot smokers who mind their own business. But don't be fooled by their seeming lack of interest; arrests are not uncommon. In Alaska, possession and use of up to four ounces of marijuana is legal only on private property, which does not include automobiles.

Officials at both the United States and Canadian borders also take drunk driving very seriously. No matter what kind of transportation you use for entry, if the customs guards discover a drunk driving conviction, you will be denied access.

Packing

Pack light—all the rest is commentary.

Traveling light will make your life easier in a number of ways. Obviously, the less you have to carry the less unpleasant it will be to go from place to place, and the less you will have to worry about belongings left somewhere while you step out (or forgotten until you've moved on). Furthermore, the fewer bags you have to lug around, the less you will look like (and thus be treated like) a tourist, and the more space you will have for gifts.

Your first decision is what kind of luggage you need: frame backpack, light suitcase, shoulder or duffle bag. If you'll be biking or hiking a great deal, a backpack may be in order. If you plan to stay in one city or town for awhile, you might prefer a suitcase. Large shoulder bags are good for stuffing into lockers, crowded baggage compartments, and all-purpose lugging. Whatever your main piece of baggage, be sure to have a small daypack. Daypacks are great for carrying a day's worth of food, camera, first-aid essentials, and valuables and documents. Anyone planning to cover a lot of ground on foot should have a sturdy backpack—see Tent Camping, Hiking, and Climbing below for advice on types of packs and good mail-order firms to buy from.

In the Northwest, be prepared for a wide range of weather conditions no matter what time of year you travel (see Climate for more details). To cover the most bases, stick with the "layer concept." Start with several T-shirts, over which you can wear a sweatshirt or sweater in cold or wet weather. Then pack a few pairs of shorts and a couple pairs of jeans. Add underwear and socks, and you've got your basic wardrobe. For winter, and depending on which regions you visit, you may want a few heavier layers as well. A good winter coat for travel in the Northwest should have a breathable, waterproof shell. Stick with darker colors to avoid showing wear, tear, and dirt. Natural fibers and lightweight cottons are the best materials. Make sure your clothing can be washed in a sink and will survive a spin in the dryer. And don't forget a towel, swimwear, and a raincoat. A rain poncho will cover both you and your pack, and can double as a groundcover for a night outdoors.

Shoes are very important whether you'll be doing serious hiking or not. Break your shoes in before you leave. Don't be caught without some type of rainproof footwear, from slipover rubbers to hiking boots, depending on your needs. Other odds and ends to consider bringing (in no particular order): first-aid kit (see Health), flashlight, pens and paper, travel alarm, canteen or water bottle, Ziplock bags, sewing kit, safety pins, pocketknife, earplugs for noisy hostels, waterproof matches, clothespins and a length of cord, sunglasses, and assorted toiletries. A rubber squash ball is a universal sink stopper, and either liquid soap or shampoo will do for hand-washing clothes.

Pack light! (It's worth repeating.) A convenient method of keeping organized is to pack items in different colored stuff sacks (found at camp stores)—shirts in one, underwear in another, etc. Wrap sharper items in clothing so they won't stab you or puncture your luggage, and pack heavy items along the inside wall if you're carrying a backpack. Carry your luggage around the block a few times to simulate real travel—if beads of sweat start trickling down your brow, go home and take some things out. The neighbors may guffaw, but it'll give you a sense of how heavy your luggage really is.

Cameras and Film

At every turn in the Northwest, you'll want to photograph your breaktaking surroundings. You will need to carefully consider before you leave, though, how much equipment you absolutely *need*: camera gear is heavy, fragile, and costly to replace. Make sure your camera is in good shape before you go—repair on the road is likely to be rare, inexpert, expensive, slow, or some combination of these hassles. Buy film before you leave, or in the big cities as you go. Often large discount department stores have the best deals. Avoid buying film in small towns or at tourist attractions, where prices are exorbitant. The sensitivity of film to light is measured by the ASA/ISO number: 100 is good for normal outdoor or indoor flash photography, 400 or (usually) higher is necessary for night photography. Consult a photo store for advice about the right film for special types of photography.

Even the greatest photographs cannot do the scenery perfect justice, so don't let the need to snap the perfect photo fill your every waking hour. Back home, sad to say, stacks of mountain or forest pictures without people in them will all start to look the same, regardless of how unique the angle or lighting at the time. Keep this in mind and don't shoot too much scenery. To preserve some of the grandeur (and to save on processing costs), consider shooting slides instead of prints, or at least opt for larger prints (4 by 6 in.).

Process your film after you return home; you will save money, and it's much simpler to carry rolls of film as you travel, rather than easily damaged boxes of slides or packages of prints and negatives. Protect exposed film from extreme heat and the sun.

Despite disclaimers, airport X-ray equipment can fog film, and the more sensitive the film, the more susceptible to damage: anything over ASA 1600 should not be x-rayed. Ask security personnel to inspect your camera and film by hand. Serious photographers should purchase a lead-lined pouch for storing film.

Alternatives to Tourism

Work

Your best leads in the job hunt often are from local residents. You should also try employment offices and Chambers of Commerce. Temporary agencies often hire for non-secretarial placement as well as for the standard typing-type assignments. Consult the local newspapers once you've arrived, or check out the want-ads before you leave (many university and public libraries subscribe to the Northwest's major dailies). Keep your eyes peeled for notices put up on streetlights and telephone poles. Local college bulletin boards can also be very helpful, particularly for finding short-term jobs.

Paid employment can occasionally be found through the **U.S. Forest Service.** For information, contact the Alaska Regional Office, Federal Office Building, P.O. Box 21628-PAO, Juneau 99802 (907-568-8806), or the U.S. Forest Pacific Northwest Region, P.O. Box 3623, Portland, OR 97208 (503-326-3816). Agriculture in the Northwest generates a huge variety of temporary unskilled jobs, but expect low wages and poor conditions. Fruit pickers are always needed in Oregon, Washington, and BC's Okanagan Valley, since shortages of workers cause tons of fruit to spoil each year. Those jobs that do pay well have their own drawbacks—seasonal fish cannery jobs on the coast of Alaska demand strenuous 16- to 18-hour days, non-stop for up to 45 days. As a crew member on an Alaskan fishing boat, you can make over $2000 per week baiting halibut hooks. However, the work is dangerous, and you can expect to sleep less than four hours per night. You may also be able to find more restful seasonal work at resorts in the region or with companies that organize hiking, climbing, and boat trips.

Volunteer jobs are readily available almost everywhere. Some jobs provide room and board in exchange for labor. Send $7 plus $1 postage to CIEE for *Volunteer! The Comprehensive Guide to Voluntary Service in the U.S. and Abroad* (see Student Travel above for address). If you would like to volunteer in the national forests of Washington or Oregon, contact the US Forest Service, Pacific Northwest Region, Attn: Volunteer Coordinator, P.O. Box 3623, Portland, OR 97208 (503-326-3651).

Many student travel organizations organize work-exchange programs. Both CIEE and the YMCA place students as summer camp counselors in the U.S. **American Youth Hostels** pays expenses and a small stipend to tour-group leaders in the U.S. and Europe. Applicants must be 21 years of age, and the nine-day training course costs $250. For more information, write or call AYH, P.O. Box 37613, Washington, DC 20013-7613 (202-783-6161). The **Association for International Practical Training (AIPT)** offers on-the-job training programs in agriculture, engineering, computer science, math, natural sciences, and architecture. The program is open to college students who have completed their sophomore year in a technical major. Internships generally last eight to twelve weeks. You must apply by December 10 for summer placement, six months in advance for other placements. There is a $75 non-refundable fee. Write to IAESTE Trainee Program (International Association for the Exchange of Students for Technology Experience), c/o AIPT, 10 Corporate Center, Suite 250, Columbia, MD 21044 (301-997-2200).

For placement in an international work-camp, you have several options. **Service Civil International** arranges placement in the U.S. and Canada as well as overseas. You must be 16 years of age to work in a U.S. camp, older elsewhere, and registration fees range from $25 to $70. COntact their U.S. office at Rte. 2, Box 506, Innisfree Village, Crozet, VA 22932 (804-823-1826) for more information. You can avoid the expense of a placement fee by contacting camps directly, but allow yourself plenty of time to work through the list. You can obtain a listing of "Work Camp Organizers" through **UNESCO, Coordinating Committee for International Voluntary Service (CCIVS)**, 1, rue Miollis, 75015 Paris, France.

If you are interested in working on an archaeological dig, contact the **Archaeological Institute of America,** 675 Commonwealth Ave., Boston, MA 02215 (617-353-9361) for a copy of their "Fieldwork Opportunities Bulletin".

International visitors should see Visas below for regulations concerning work in the United States.

Study

Many colleges in the Pacific Northwest welcome visiting students. The colleges and universities listed below all offer summer terms (3-11 weeks). Direct all correspondence to the Director of Admissions.

University of Alaska, Fairbanks, Fairbanks, AK 99775-0060 (907-474-7821).

University of Alaska, Anchorage, 3211 Providence Dr., Anchorage, AK 99508 (907-786-1525).

Lewis and Clark College, Portland, OR 97219 (503-293-2679).

University of Oregon, 240 Oregon Hall, Eugene, OR 97403 (503-346-3201).

Oregon State University, Corvalis, OR 97331 (503-737-4411).

University of Washington, 1400 NE Campus Pkwy., Seattle, WA 98195 (206-543-9686).

Washington State University, 342 French Administration Bldg., Pullman, WA 99164-1036 (509-335-5586).

University of Alberta, 1201 Administration Bldg., Edmonton, AB T6G 2M7 (403-492-3283).

University of Calgary, 2500 University Dr. NW, Calgary, AB T2N 1N4 (403-220-6640).

Simon Fraser University, Burnaby, BC V5A 1S6 (604-291-3224).

University of British Columbia, Vancouver, BC V6T 1Z2 (604-228-3014).

University of Victoria, Box 1700, Victoria, BC V8W 2Y2 (604-721-8111).

Many reference books revised each year provide summaries and evaluations of various colleges, describing their general atmosphere, fields of study, tuition, and enrollment data. Among the most useful are *The Insider's Guide to the Colleges* (St. Martin's Press, $12), the *Fiske Guide to Colleges,* by Edward Fiske (N.Y. Times Books, $11), and *Barron's Profiles of American Colleges* ($15).

International visitors interested in studying in the U.S. should also see For International Visitors below.

Keeping in Touch

Especially if they know where you will be when, your friends and families will be able to keep in touch with you easily by phone or mail. To speak with the folks back home, it may be easiest for you to call them collect or with a credit card. To save everyone some money, you can try calling from a pay phone and having the person on the other end call you back. Some pay phones do not receive incoming calls, however; when this is the case, they are usually so marked where the phone number is printed.

If you want to receive mail while you're on the road, it can be sent to you c/o General Delivery. Letters to you should be addressed with your name (last name capitalized and underlined, to ensure proper filing), the words "c/o General Delivery," the city/town and state/province, and the General Delivery ZIP or postal code for the town. *Let's Go* lists local ZIP and postal codes; for ZIP codes in the U.S. you can also call 800-228-8777. Make sure the code is correct, or else the letter will end up in oblivion at some other post office in town. The envelope should also say "Please hold until . . . ," the blank filled in with a date a couple weeks after your correspondent expects you to pick up the letter. When you claim your mail, you'll have to present ID, and if you do not claim a letter within two to four weeks, it will be returned to its sender.

American Express cardholders and checkholders can receive letters at those AmEx Travel Service offices that provide "Client Letter Service." When you come to pick up your mail, you'll need to show your American Express card or traveler's checks plus one more form of ID. Contact the AmEx Travel Service office or affiliate in your area for more details and for the addresses of offices in the towns you plan to visit where you can collect your mail.

For instructions on the intricacies of the U.S. and Canadian postal and phone systems, see Communication under For International Visitors.

Special Concerns

Student Travel

Students are often entitled to special discounts on admission prices, hotel rates, and airfares. Most places accept a current university ID or an **International Student Identity Card (ISIC)** as sufficient proof of student status. An ISIC for 1991 will cost you $14 and you can obtain one from the student travel office of your university (if it has one) or else from one of the organizations listed below. When you apply for an ISIC, be sure to have up-to-date proof of full-time student status, a vending-machine photograph with your name printed and signed in pencil on the back, and proof of your birthdate and nationality. In some places a university ID is enough to demonstrate student status, while in others an official school document is necessary. The ISIC card is good until the end of the calendar year in which it is issued, or up to sixteen months, from September to the end of December the following year. Note that you cannot purchase a new ISIC card in January unless you were in school during the previous fall, so if you are about to graduate, get the card now. Students must be at least 12 years old to be eligible. Non-students under 26 years of age should look into the International Youth Card from the **Federation of International Youth Travel Organizations (FIYTO)**, which may help you take advantage of discounts on the basis of age. Applicants must submit proof of birthdate, a photo, and a fee of $10. For further information, write to the FIYTO at Islands Bryyge 81, DK-2300 Copenhagen S, Denmark (tel. 31 54 32 97).

The following agencies specialize in travel for high school and university students. They sell ISIC cards and have tips on transportation discounts. For listings of similar organizations that serve foreign travelers, see For International Visitors.

Council on International Educational Exchange (CIEE) Travel Services: Advice on questions ranging from package tours and low-cost travel to work opportunities and long-distance hiking. Special academic and employment exchange programs. ISIC and International Youth cards. Ask for the free annual *Student Travel Catalog.* **Council Travel,** the budget travel division of CIEE, operates 30 offices throughout the U.S., including the following:

New York: 205 E. 42nd St., New York, NY 10017 (800-223-7402 or 212-661-1450). One of 3 offices in NYC.
Seattle: 1314 NE 43rd St., #210, Seattle, WA 98105 (206-632-2448).
Portland: 715 SW Morrison, #600, OR 97205 (503-228-1900).
San Francisco: 919 Irving St. #102, CA 94122 (415-566-6222). One of 2 offices in SF.
Los Angeles: 1093 Broxton Ave., #220, CA 90024 (213-208-3551).

Write or call the NY office for general information and for the address and phone of an office closer to you.

Let's Go Travel Services, Harvard Student Agencies, Inc., Thayer Hall-B, Harvard University, Cambridge, MA 02138 (tel. (617) 495-9649 or (800) 5-LETS-GO). Sells Railpasses, American Youth Hostel memberships (valid at all IYHF youth hostels), International Student and Teacher I.D. cards, International Youth Cards for nonstudents, travel guides and maps (including the *Let's Go* series), discount airfares and a complete line of budget travel gear. All items are available by mail.

Educational Travel Centre (ETC): 438 N. Frances St., Madison, WI 53703 (608-256-5551). IYHF membership cards, flight information. Write or call for their free travel pamphlet, *Taking Off*.

STA Travel, 7202 Melrose Ave., Los Angeles, CA 90046 (213-934-8722) or 17 E. 45th St. #805, New York, NY 10017 (800-770112 or 212-986-9470). A worldwide travel organization with 10 U.S. offices. Bargain flights, railpasses, accommodations, insurance, and ISIC cards.

Travel CUTS (Canadian Universities Travel Service, Ltd.): 44 George St., Toronto, Ont. M5S 2E4 (416-979-2406). Canadian distributor of the ISIC, IYHF, and International Youth Cards. Discounts on domestic and international flights. Canadian Wilderness trips. Write for address and phone of branches in Burnaby, Calgary, Edmonton, Halifax, Montreal, Ottawa, Quebec, Saskatoon, Sudbury, Victoria, Waterloo, Winnipeg, and London.

Senior Citizens

Senior citizens enjoy a tremendous assortment of discounts on public transportation, museum, movie, theater, and concert admissions, accommodations, and even dining. To take advantage of these savings, you usually need an acceptable piece of identification proving your age, such as a driver's license, a Medicare card, or a membership card from a recognized society of retired people.

There is a whole slew of organizations that cater to senior citizens in general and senior travelers in particular. Membership in the **American Association of Retired Persons (AARP)** is open to U.S. residents aged 50 and over. For the $5 annual membership fee (which will cover your spouse as well), AARP offers scores of services and can help members save a lot of money. AARP's Purchase Privilege Program arranges discounts at major hotel/motel chains throughout the nation. In addition, older travelers receive discounts from car-rental and sight-seeing companies. For more information on these benefits, write AARP National Headquarters, Special Services Dept., 1909 K St. NW, Washington, DC 20049 (202-662-4850 for Special Services; 800-227-7737 for membership).

Older travelers should also contact the **National Council of Senior Citizens,** 925 15th St. NW, Washington, DC 20005 (202-347-8800). Through this organization, anyone of any age can get hotel and auto rental discounts, a senior citizen newspaper, uses of a discount traval agency, and members over 65 years of age receive supplemental Medicare insurance. Fee are $12 per year or $150 for lifetime membership. Membership in the **September Days Club (SDC)** (800-241-5050 or 800-344-3636) costs $12 per year and is also open to people over 50. Members enjoy a 15-50% discount at all Days Inns, discounts in restaurants and gift shops run by the chain, and a quarterly magazine.

If you are academically inclined, look into **Elderhostel,** which offers residential academic programs for senior citizens at many colleges and universities in the Pacific Northwest. Participants pay a weekly sum to live in the dorms, take courses, and use the institution's various facilities. Programs are offered year-round, and you can register at any time. To participate you must be 60 or older; your companion may join you if he or she is over 50. Domestic Elderhostels cost $245 to $270 for the week-long program and $1500 to $5000 for the longer international sessions (scholarships are available). For a free catalog, contact Elderhostel, 80 Boylston St., #480, Boston, MA 02116 (617-426-7788).

People aged 62 and over can acquire a free **Golden Age Passport,** which entitles them to free entry into U.S. National Parks, Monuments, and Recreation Areas, as well as 50% off Federal use fees for facilities and services at these parks. You can obtain a Golden Age Passports on the spot wherever you can use them, or at Federal offices whose function concerns land, forests, or wildlife.

Helpful publications regarding travel for senior citizens abound. "Travel Tips for Older Americans," a pamphlet put out by the U.S. Government, may be useful. For a copy, send $1 to the Bureau of Consular Affairs, Superintendent of Documents, U.S. Government Printing Office, Washington, DC 20402 (202-783-3238). **Pilot Books** puts out two travel books for senior citizens: *Senior Citizen's Guide to Budget Travel in the United States and Canada* ($4), and *The International Health*

Guide for Senior Citizen Travelers ($5). Order from Pilot Books, 103 Cooper St., Babylon, NY 11702 (516-422-2225) and add $1 for postage.

Traveling Alone

The freedom to come and go at will, to backtrack or deviate from a schedule or route, is the solitary traveler's special prerogative. Traveling with even one other person can become stifling or even annoying at times, especially when separate desires and plans conflict. Pairs of travelers should consider splitting up for a few days, to satisfy personal whims and to meet other people. Often you'll stay fonder if you have been absent and have stories to tell. Traveling alone has its downside, though. Single accommodations are much more costly per person than doubles. In addition, if you do travel alone, you should be extremely careful about where you sleep: outdoor locations make the lone traveler an easy target.

Even if you're alone, chances are you won't be hurting for company along the way. If you carry your copy of *Let's Go,* you might be noticed by others doing the same (sympathetically, we hope—although they may ask you things like "What's a nice person like you doing with an ugly book like that?"). Another trick for finding people with whom you may have some connection is to wear a baseball cap or T-shirt from your home state or college. Striking up acquaintances in this fashion might allow you to visit somewhere you hadn't considered, or to pool your resources and rent a car to reach out-of-the-way sights or to get rides that you might otherwise have hitchhiked for.

Women Travelers

Women traveling alone must take extra precautions. Forgo cheap accommodations in city outskirts—the risks outweigh any savings—and stick to youth hostels, university accommodations, bed-and-breakfasts, and YWCAs. Religious organizations offering rooms for women only are another safe option. Hitching is dangerous and generally a bad idea.

If you find yourself the object of catcalls or propositions, your best answer is no answer. Always look as if you know where you're going (even when you don't), and maintain an assertive, confident posture wherever you go. If you feel uncomfortable asking strangers for information or directions, it may be easier to approach other women or couples. Always carry enough change for a bus, taxi, or phone call. And in emergencies, don't hesitate to yell for help. Know the emergency numbers for the area you're visiting; *Let's Go* lists them in the Practical Information section of each area. More information and safety tips can be found in the *Handbook for Women Travelers,* available from **Judy Piatkus (Publishers) Ltd.,** 5 Windmill St., London W1P 1HF, England (tel. (071) 631 07 10).

Gay and Lesbian Travelers

Generally, in the larger cities of the Pacific Northwest, you need not sacrifice much freedom or openness to enjoy your trip. Use more discretion, though, in rural areas: smaller communities may not be so receptive to gay and lesbian travelers. Wherever possible, *Let's Go* lists gay and lesbian information lines, community centers, bookshops, and special services. A more extensive directory of gay and lesbian bars, restaurants, accommodations, businesses, and medical services is available in the *Gayellow Pages* ($10), which covers both the United States and Canada. Order a copy from Renaissance House, P.O. Box 292, Village Station, New York, NY 10014 (212-674-0120). You can also contact Renaissance House for a copy of the *Spartacus Guide for Gay Men* ($25), a worldwide touring guide, or send a stamped, self-addressed envelope for a list of available publications.

Lesbians should consider buying a copy of *Gaia's Guide,* which lists local lesbian, gay, and feminist information numbers, as well as gay and lesbian hotels, restaurants, book stores, and publications, and women's cultural centers. If this guide isn't in your local bookstore, order by sending $12 to **Giovanni's Room,** 345 S. 12th St. NE, Philadelphia, PA 19107 (800-222-6996 or 215-943-2960 in PA). Giovanni's

Room also stocks all of the other books mentioned in this section, with the exception of the Gayellow Pages. Add $3.50 for shipping.

Other general guides for lesbian and gay travelers include: *Inn Places: USA Worldwide Gay Accommodations* ($15); *Bob Damron's Address Book,* a guide for gay men ($14); and *Places of Interest,* which covers major cities in the U.S. and Canada ($9 for women's guide, $11 for men's guide, $12.50 for gay/lesbian guide with maps). These are available from **The Bob Damron Company, Inc.,** P.O. Box 11270, San Francisco, CA 94101 (415-255-0404), or from **Ferrari Publications,** P.O. Box 35575, Phoenix, AZ 85069 (602-863-2408).

Travelers without published material on gay and lesbian services can contact the **Gay/Lesbian Crisisline** (800-SOS-GAYS, i.e. 800-767-4297) which provides information about clubs, local gay/lesbian hotline numbers, counseling and support services in the U.S. and Canada, legal and medical advice, resources concerning AIDS, and information on dealing with homophobia.

Disabled Travelers

Easy-access facilities on the road can be more or less rare. *Let's Go* indicates wherever possible if establishments are accessible to disabled travelers. Research the area you will be visiting before you leave. Call restaurants, hotels, parks, and other facilities to find out about the existence of ramps, the presence of easy trails, the width of doors, the dimensions of elevators, etc. Also inquire about restrictions on motorized wheelchairs.

Hotels and motels have become increasingly accessible to the disabled—consult the motel chains listed in Budget Chain Motels below. If you are planning to visit a national park you should obtain a free **Golden Access Passport,** available at all park entrances and from Federal offices whose functions relate to land, forests, or wildlife. The Golden Access Passport entitles disabled travelers and their families to enter the park for free and provides a 50% reduction on all campsite fees.

Arrange transportation well in advance to ensure a smooth trip. If you give sufficient notice, some major car rental agencies have hand-controlled vehicles at certain locations. Call **Avis** (800-331-1212, at least 24 hours notice), **Hertz** (800-654-3131, 2-3 days notice), or **National** (800-328-4567, at least 24 hours notice). Both **Amtrak** and the airlines are now required to serve disabled passengers if notified in advance—simply tell the ticket agent when making reservations which services you'll need. On Canada's **VIA Rail,** disabled passengers who can provide documentation that they need assistance may bring a companion on the price of their own fare. **Greyhound** or **Trailways** buses will also provide free travel for a companion; if you are without a fellow-traveler, call Greyhound (800-752-4841) at least 48 hours before you plan to go so that they can make arrangements to assist you. Seeing eye and hearing ear dogs also ride Greyhound without charge. Hearing-impaired travelers may contact Amtrak (800-345-3109, in PA 800-322-9537) using teletype printers. Many ferries that run up and down the Pacific coast can also accommodate disabled travelers; consult the companies listed below under By Ferry. For information on transportation availability for disabled people in any United States city, contact the **American Public Transit Association** (202-898-4000) in Washington, DC.

There are many special information services for disabled travelers. The **Travel Information Service** at the **Moss Rehabilitation Hospital,** 1200 W. Tabor Rd., Philadelphia, PA 19141 (215-329-5715, ext. 2233) is an excellent source of information on tourist sights, accommodations, and transportation for the disabled and charges only a nominal postage fee if you request any mailings. The **Society for the Advancement of Travel for the Handicapped,** 26 Court St., Penthouse Suite, Brooklyn, NY 11242 (718-858-5483), provides several useful booklets as well as advice and assistance on trip planning. Membership is $40 per year, $25 for senior citizens and students; non-members may obtain publications for $2. The **American Foundation for the Blind** recommends travel books and issues ID discount cards ($6) for the legally blind. For an ID application or for other information, contact the American Foundation for the Blind, 15 W. 16th St., New York, NY 10011 (800-232-5463).

Other organizations specialize in arranging tours. **Evergreen Travel Service,** 19505 (L) 44th Ave. W, Lynnwood, WA 98036 (800-435-2288) offers tour programs for travelers in wheelcharis, blind travlers, deaf travelers, and "slow walkers." **Directions Unlimited,** 720 N. Bedford Rd., Bedford Hills, NY 10507 (800-533-5343; in NY, 914-241-1700), also conducts tours for the physically disabled. To inquire about other organizations that plan tours for disabled travelers, write to the **Handicapped Travel Division, National Tour Association,** P.O. Box 3071, Lexington, KY 40596 (606-253-1036).

Read up in any of a number of books helpful to disabled travelers. One good resource is *Access to the World,* by Louise Weiss ($13). For a copy, contact Facts on File, Inc., 460 Park Ave. S., New York, NY 10016 (800-322-8755). **Twin Peaks Press** publishes three books: *Directory for Travel Agencies for the Disabled* ($13), *Travel for the Disabled* ($10), and *Wheelchair Vagabond* ($10), which discusses camping and travel in cars, vans, and RVs. Order from Twin Peaks Press, P.O. Box 129, Vancouver, WA 98666 (800-637-2256). Add $2 shipping per book for the first three ordered, $1 for each book after that. Twin Peaks also operates a worldwide traveling nurse network.

Traveling with Children

There are plenty of opportunities in the Pacific Northwest to keep both you and your kids entertained, even all of you at the same time. Consult local newspapers or travel bureaus to find out about events that might be of special interest for young children, such as the Cannon Beach Sandcastle Festival in Oregon or the annual Magicazam magic show that visits Portland in the summer.

Parents generally find it easier to travel with children by car than by bus, train, or just about any form of public transportation. With a car, you will have the freedom to make frequent stops, and children will have more room to spread out their toys, books, and selves in the back seat. Try to avoid areas with extreme climatic conditions, since children's bodies can be very sensitive, and they are more prone than you to frostbite, hypothermia, and heatstroke. (See Health for more information.) **Wilderness Press** (see Camping and the Outdoors for address and phone) publishes *Backpacking with Babies and Small Children* ($9), *Sharing Nature With Children* ($7), and the companion *Sharing the Joy of Nature: Nature Activities for All Ages* ($10). Written *for* children, the *Kidding Around* series ($10 each) includes a book about National Parks. Order from **John Muir Publications,** P.O. Box 613, Santa Fe, NM 87504 (800-888-7504). Include $2.75 shipping for the first book requested and 50¢ for each additional.

Vegetarian and Kosher Travelers

The Northwest heaps blessings on vegetarians and observers of the laws of *kashrut* alike. Fresh fish, fruits, and vegetables abound in both the larger cities and smaller towns of the region. Delicious apples and Chinook salmon are just a couple of the area's indigenous treats. Vegetarian travelers can obtain *The International Vegetarian Travel Guide* and *Vegetarian Times Guide to Natural Foods Restaurants in the U.S. and Canada* (each costs $10 plus $2 postage) from the **North American Vegetarian Society,** P.O. Box 72, Dolgeville, NY 13329 (518-568-7970).

Kosher travelers should contact synagogues in Seattle, Portland, Vancouver, Edmonton, and Calgary for information about kosher restaurants in those cities; your own synagogue or college Hillel should have access to lists of Jewish institutions across the continent. *The Jewish Travel Guide* ($11) lists Jewish institutions, synagogues, and kosher restaurants in over 80 countries. It is available in the U.S. from **Sepher-Hermon Press,** 1265 46th St., Brooklyn, NY 11219 (718-972-9010), with a shipping charge of $1.50. If you eat at nonkosher restaurants, you will have the most options available. Discuss eating with your own rabbi before you go. According to some rabbis, you may eat anything at a restaurant as long as it does not contain any meat, and you may use the restaurant's utensils. Others restrict eating out to cold items such as cheeses and salads. Often you can ask to have ingredients that you would not eat left out of prepared dishes. Check to see whether foods are fried in vegetable oil and whether soups and sauces are meat-based. If you are more strict, consider preparing your own food. Bring along some sturdy plasticware, a pan, a small grill, and lots of aluminum foil; buy fresh fish, fruits, and vegetables along the way. You may need to bring your own bread—if so, bags of pita last longer than loaves of bread.

Getting By and Getting Along

By Air

The simplest and surest way to find a low airfare is to have a knowledgeable travel agent guide you through the inferno with his or her computer flight listings. In addition, check the weekend travel sections of major newspapers for bargain fares.

Super Saver fares can save you hundreds of dollars over the regular coach price. On the average, you save more than half on a 14-day advance-purchase fare, and a still-considerable amount on the 7-day advance-purchase fare. To obtain the cheapest Super Saver fare, buy a round-trip ticket (not necessarily returning on the same route, if you want a stop-over) and stay over at least one Saturday. You will need to pay for the ticket within 24 hours of booking the flight, and you will not be able to change your flight reservation; the fare is also entirely non-refundable. By paying a bit extra, you can buy the ability to alter your plans, though there will still be some penalties for doing so. Also check with your travel agent for system-wide air passes and excursion fares.

There are a few principles to keep in mind when booking a flight. Traveling at night and during the wee hours of the morning is generally cheaper than during the day, and traveling on a weekday (between Monday and Thursday at noon) is cheaper than traveling on the weekend. Since airline travel peaks between June and August and around holidays, reserve a seat several months in advance for these times. Given the occasional appearance of sudden bargains and the availability of standby fares, advance purchase may not guarantee the lowest fare, but you will save some money and be assured a seat. The best deals usually appear between January and mid-May.

Many airlines offer special rates (usually 50% off regular fares) to children accompanied by an adult. These may still be higher than Super Savers, though. Very few airlines offer discounts for senior citizens. Chances of receiving discount fares increase on competitive routes. Flying smaller airlines instead of the national giants can also save money. Check for specials on **Alaska Airlines** (800-426-0333) or **Northwest** (800-225-2525).

If all you need is a short flight, scout local airfields for prospective rides on private, non-commercial planes. Some airfields have ride boards. If not, a good place to begin is the operations counter, where pilots file their flight plans. Ask where they are headed and if they'd like a passenger. Remember that propeller planes have a much higher accident rate than their larger commercial counterparts; if the pilots seem even slightly reluctant because of the weather, think about heading back out to the highway.

For information on reaching the Northwest from a country other than the United States, see Transportation under For International Visitors.

By Bus

Buses generally offer the most frequent and complete service between the cities and towns of the Pacific Northwest. Often they are only way to reach smaller locales without a car. The exceptions are some rural areas and more open spaces, particularly in Alaska and the Yukon, where bus lines are much sparser. Your biggest challenges when you travel by bus will involve scheduling. *Russell's Official National Motor Coach Guide* is an indispensible tool for constructing an itinerary. Updated each month, *Russell's Guide* contains schedules of literally every bus route between any two towns in the United States and Canada. Copies of the guide can be obtained for $8.35 plus 50¢ postage from Russell's Guides, Inc., P.O. Box 278, Cedar Rapids, IA 52406 (319-364-6138). Since schedules change frequently and the guide is updated monthly, a far better idea than purchasing the guide is to look at a copy in a library reference room.

In both the U.S. and Canada, **Greyhound** operates the largest number of lines, including those under the **Trailways** name (Greyhound acquired Trailways in 1987). Greyhound can get you both to and around the Northwest. Senior citizens receive a 5-10% discount, children ages 5-11 travel for half-fare, and younger children on laps travel free. If you plan to tour a great deal by bus within the U.S., you may save money with the **Ameripass.** Passes can be purchased for seven days ($189), 15 days ($249), or 30 days ($349), and each can be extended for $10 per day. Before you purchase an Ameripass, you should have a pretty good idea of your itinerary; total up the separate bus fares between towns to make sure that you will in fact do better with the pass. To contact Greyhound, call the local schedule and fare information number where you live.

Greyhound allows passengers to carry two pieces of luggage weighing up to 200 pounds in total at no charge. Whatever you stow in the compartments underneath the bus should be clearly marked; be sure to get a claim check for it. As always, keep your essential documents and valuables on you, and carry a small bag onto the bus with you.

For a more unusual and social trip, consider **Green Tortoise.** These funky-looking coaches are remodeled diesel buses done up with foam mattresses, sofa seats, stereos, and dinettes. Bus drivers operate in teams so that one can drive and the other can point out sites and chat with passengers. In addition to the fare, each passenger contributes about $3.50 per day ($7 on longer trips) to a group kitty that goes for food, park entrance and use fees, and supplies. Most meals are prepared communally, with some scheduled restaurant stops. Green Tortoise can get you to San Francisco from Boston, Hartford, and New York City in 11 days for $299. Buses run between San Francisco and Seattle (northbound on Monday and Friday, southbound on Thursday and Sunday), with additional service as far south as Los Angeles. Between Seattle and San Francisco the fare is $59, less for shorter trips. For an extra $10 you can stay for a while between legs of a round trip. Deposits ($100 most trips) are generally required since space is tight and economy is important for the group. For more information, write Green Tortoise, P.O. Box 24459, San Francisco, CA 94124 (800-227-4766, in CA 415-821-0803; in Boston, New York, Los Angeles, Santa Barbara, Santa Cruz, Vancouver, Seattle, Portland, and Eugene there are local agents).

By all means avoid spending the night in a bus station. Though generally guarded, bus stations can be hangouts for dangerous or at least frightening characters. Try to arrange your arrivals for reasonable day or evening times. This will also make it easier for you to find transportation out of the station and another place to stay.

By Train

A century ago, locomotion tied the Northwestern Coast into the arteries of the energetic young nations of North America. The train is still one of the cheapest and most comfortable ways to tour the area. The budget traveler should settle for a reclining seat, rather than paying unnecessarily for a roomette or bedroom. Trains cramp you less than buses—you can walk from car to car to stretch your legs. Avoid the temptation to stop at the snack bar, though—prices are sometimes double those at a station (which are inflated to begin with). Bring your own snacks on board instead.

Within the lower 48 states, **Amtrak** offers the **"All Aboard America"** fares for long distance travel. Dividing the U.S. into three regions, Amtrak charges the same rate for both one way and round-trip travel: $189 within one region, $269 between two regions, $339 between three. Along the West Coast, fares vary by time, day, and destination: a round trip between Seattle and Portland is $41. Amtrak discounts allow children ages 2-11 to travel for half-fare when accompanied by an adult. Senior citizens and disabled travelers may save up to 25%. Watch for special holiday packages as well. For information and reservations, call 800-872-7245 or look up Amtrak's local number in your area.

VIA Rail, Amtrak's counterpart in Canada, makes British Columbia, Alberta, and the Yukon accessible to the northwestern traveler. Routes are as scenic as Amtrak's and the fares are often more affordable. If you'll be traveling by train a great deal or across the rest of Canada as well, you may save money with the **Canrailpass,** which allows unlimited travel and unlimited stops for 45 days. Passes cost CDN$499 in peak season, $339 off-peak ($449 and $295 for youths under age 24). On regularly purchased tickets, a number of discounts apply. Students and seniors are entitled to a reduction of 10%, and children accompanied by an adult pay only half-fare. Disabled passengers and companions together are charged a single fare (see Special Concerns, above). For more information, call 800-561-7860.

Travel by train in Alaska with the **Alaska Railroad Company (ARC).** ARC runs between Anchorage and Fairbanks for $194 round-trip (with a stop in Denali National Park) and between Anchorage and Seward for $35 one way, $60 round-trip. ARC also arranges transportation from Portage to Whittier, depending on demand. For more information, contact ARC, P.O. Box 107500, Anchorage, AK 99510 (800-544-0552).

In addition to the major lines, local and regional lines still roar through some areas—check the yellow pages or inquire at the local train station. Trains reach many fewer towns in the Northwest than buses do, so plan accordingly. Regardless of which railway line you ride, always compare prices before purchasing a ticket.

By Car

If you plan to do a lot of driving within the U.S. during your trip, you might do well to join an automobile club. King of the hill, top of the heap is the **American**

Automobile Association (AAA), 811 Gatehouse Rd., Falls Church, VA 22047 (800-444-8008). Annual dues vary with the size and location of the local AAA club—call the toll-free number or contact your local club for details. Membership includes free maps and guidebooks, trip-planning services, emergency road service anywhere in the country, discounts on car rentals, the International Driver's License, and commission-free traveler's checks from American Express. Your membership card doubles as a $5000 bail bond (if you find yourself in jail) or a $200 arrest bond certificate (which you can use in lieu of being arrested for any motor vehicle offense except drunk driving, driving without a valid license, or failure to appear in court on a prior motor-vehicle arrest). Many clubs also have an "AAA Plus" membership program which provides more extensive emergency road service, insurance protection, and 100 miles of free towing (this is not as far as it seems in rural areas, where AAA-affiliated garages are few and farther between).

Other automobile travel service organization are affiliated with oil companies or other large corporations. These include:

AMOCO Motor Club, P.O. Box 9014, Des Moines, IA 50306 (800-334-3300). $40 annual membership enrolls you, your spouse, and your car. Services include 24-hour towing and emergency road service.

Mobil Auto Club, P.O. Box 5039, North Suburban, IL 60194 (800-621-5581, in IL 800-572-5572). $39 membership covers you and one other person. Benefits include locksmith and other services on the road, as well as car-rental discounts with Hertz, Avis, and National.

Montgomery Ward Auto Club (800-621-5151). $45 membership includes entire family with children (ages 16-23).

Learn a bit about minor automobile maintenance and repair before you leave, and pack an easy-to-read manual—it may at the very least help you survive long enough to reach a reputable garage. If you never have done it before, practice changing your tire once or twice without help, and spend an afternoon discovering what is under the hood.

In Canada, automobile insurance with coverage of CDN$200,000 is mandatory. If you are involved in a car accident and you don't have insurance, the stiff fine will not improve the experience. U.S. motorists are advised to carry the **Canadian Non-Resident Inter-Provincial Motor Vehicle Liability Card,** which is proof of coverage. The cards are available only through U.S. insurers. In Washington, British Columbia, and Alberta, everyone must wear seatbelts; in Oregon, children under 16 must wear them.

For information on the International Driver's License, see Documents and Formalities below under For International Visitors.

On the Road

Gas is generally cheaper in towns than at interstate service stops. Oil company credit cards are handy, but many stations charge for this service. MasterCard and Visa are not always accepted, and those stations that do accept them are often more expensive. In addition, you can often get about 4% of the price discounted for cash payment. Moral: always carry enough cash for gasoline emergencies.

When planning your budget, remember that the enormous travel distances of the Northwest will require you to spend more on gas than you might expect. Burn less money by burning less fuel. (To estimate roughly how much you'll spend on gas, figure 5¢ per mile or 3¢ per kilometre.) Tune up the car, make sure the tires are in good repair and properly inflated, check the oil frequently, and avoid running the air conditioner unnecessarily. Don't use roof luggage racks—they cause air drag, and if you need one, you're probably over-packed. Driving at 65 miles per hour is now legal on some rural interstates and tempting elsewhere, but believe it or not, traveling at 55 miles/90km per hour *does* save gas.

Unlike the more densely populated regions of the continent, the Northwest does not have an extensive system of quality secondary roads. Older highways predominate; they merge with the main street of each town in their path, and are slower to drive—but far more rewarding—than most interstate freeways. Venture down unpaved roads for some unforgettable vistas, but be sure to have plenty of gas and a healthy driving machine. And before you hit the road, particularly during the winter, check out the road conditions.

Alaska Northwest Books puts out three valuable guides which include maps, detailed car routes, and general travel information. Send for *The Milepost,* a guide to Alaska and Western Canada, *Northwest Mileposts,* a guide to the U.S. Pacific Northwest and southwestern Canada, or *Alaska Wilderness Milepost* (each US$15, CDN$19). Order from Alaska Northwest Books, GTE Discovery Publications, Inc., 22026 20th Ave. SE, P.O. Box 3007, Bothell, WA 98021-3007 (800-331-3510 or 800-343-4567).

The greatest difficulty posed by interstates is not the state troopers, the other drivers, or even bad road conditions (although these can be imposing)—it's the sheer boredom. For a normally active brain, license plate games only stave off the soporific monotony for so long. To prevent "frozen vision," don't keep your eyes glued to the road. If you feel drowsy, pull off the road to take a break, even if there are no official rest areas in the vicinity. To avoid overexhaustion, start driving in the wee hours of the morning and stop early in the afternoon (this way, you'll also have more time to find accommodations). When you're driving with companions, insist that one of them is awake at all times, and keep talking. If you're driving by yourself, be extra careful. If you can't pull over, try listening to an aggravating radio talk show (music can be as lulling as silence). A thermos of coffee is also helpful. And remember that turning the heat up too high in the car can also make you sleepy.

Never drive if you've had anything alcoholic to drink or if you've used drugs or any potentially impairing substance. Avoid the open road on weekend nights and holidays, when more drivers are likely to be drunk.

Renting

Although the cost of renting a car for days at a time can be prohibitively expensive, renting for local trips is often reasonable, especially if several people share the cost. In general, automobile rental agencies fall into two categories: national companies with thousands of affiliated offices across the country, and local companies that serve only one city or area.

Major rental companies usually allow cars to be picked up in one city and dropped off in another without any hitch. Their toll-free numbers enable customers to reserve a reliable car anywhere in the country. Drawbacks include steep prices and high minimum ages for rentals (21 or, frequently, 25). If you have a major credit card in your name, you can avoid having to leave a large cash deposit at a rental agency, and you may be able to rent where the minimum age would otherwise rule you out. Student discounts are occasionally available. Some major companies: **Alamo** (800-327-9633), **Avis** (800-331-1212), **Budget** (800-527-0700), **Dollar** (800-421-6868), **Hertz** (800-654-3131), **National** (800-328-4567), and **Thrifty** (800-331-4200).

While many local companies observe similar age requirements, they often have more flexible policies. Some require smaller cash deposits, on the order of $50-100. Others will simply accept proof of employment (check stubs, etc.). Local companies often charge less than major companies, although you'll generally have to return to your point of origin to return the car. Companies with confidence-inspiring names like Rent-A-Wreck supply cars long past their prime. Sporting dents and purely decorative radios, the cars sometimes get very poor mileage, but for the most part run. *Let's Go* gives the addresses and phone numbers of local rental agencies in most towns.

When dealing with any car rental company, make certain the price includes insurance against theft and collision. This may be an additional charge, though American Express automatically insures any car rented with the card. Although basic rental charges run from $20-35 per day for a compact car, plus 7-20¢ per mile, most companies offer special money-saving deals. Standard shift cars are usually a few dollars cheaper then automatics. All companies have special weekend rates, and renting by the week can save you even more. Most packages include a certain amount of free mileage that varies with the length of time you're renting for. If you'll be driving a long distance, ask for an unlimited-mileage deal. If you want to rent for longer than a week, look into automobile leasing. Leasing is cheaper than renting, but make sure the car is covered by a service plan, or you could end up stuck with outrageous repair bills.

Auto Transport Companies

If you don't have a car and can't afford to rent one for a long trip, you might consider registering with an automobile transport company. These outfits hire drivers on behalf of car owners who need their automobile moved from one city to another. You can let the companies know where you want to drive, and if one of them is asked to have a car driven there, you'll get a call. You are provided with the first tank of gas; all other expenses are yours (gas, food, lodging, tolls). Before you leave you have to pay a deposit, which is refunded to you when you deliver the car. If the car breaks down or is damaged, the insurance of the car transport company covers it. You must be at least 21 years old and have a valid driver's license.

If offered a car, look it over first. Think twice about accepting a gas guzzler, since you're the one paying for gasoline. Driving for an auto transport company is a more promising option if your schedule is flexible: you may find a car within a week, or it may take several. One firm to try is the **Auto Driveaway Co.** (800-346-2277), which serves the U.S. and Canada. As the arrival deadline can be negotiated, you may be able to detour along the way. Auto Driveaway requires a $250 deposit.

By Ferry

Along the Pacific coast, ferries are an exhilirating and occasionally unavoidable way to travel. Some Alaskan towns can only be reached by water or air—Juneau, the capital, for example. In addition to basic transportation, the ferry system gives travelers the chance to enjoy the wind in their faces and the beauty of the water and the coast, one of the most vital experiences of the Northwest. A deck or porthole frames the Columbia Glacier from Alaska's *MV Bartlett* or *Tustumena*, the San Juan Islands surround the Washington State ferry to Victoria, or Sitka's volcano, "The Mount Fuji of Alaska," rises over the *LeConte* ferry. Ferry travel, however, is quite expensive, particularly when you bring a car along with you.

Alaska ferry travel is run by the **Alaska State Ferry System,** better known as the **Alaska Marine Highway.** There are three routes in the system. The southeastern route cruises from Seattle, WA, to Skagway, AK, via Prince Rupert, BC; this ferry stops in Juneau and a number of other small towns along the Alaskan panhandle. The southcentral route runs between Cordova and Port Lions in Alaska. Much less frequent (only six scheduled voyages between May and October) is the southwestern route, which serves the Aleutian Islands. Alaska's ferry schedule is quite complicated, and changes every May and October. Fares are also subject to change. Fares are charged according to three categories: passengers (who ride on deck), cabins, and vehicle transport. Reservations are almost always required. Standby is available on a first-come, first-served basis, although the ferry still has the right to unload either vehicles or passengers before either reaches its intended destination. Senior citizens aged 65 and over can obtain passes that entitle them to free ferry travel (subject to certain restrictions); passes are issued at any port of embarkation. Some ships are equipped for disabled travelers, who can also obtain a pass for free ferry travel by writing the central office in Juneau. Ferries do not stop at each port every day; doublecheck your itinerary with care, or you may find yourself unexpectedly grounded for days. For information and reservations, contact the Alaska Marine Highway, P.O. Box R, Juneau, AK 99811, 800-642-0066. See also the sections on the Alaska Marine Highway later in this book under Seattle and Alaska.

Ferries traveling along the coast also serve the area between Seattle, Vancouver Island, and the northern coast of British Columbia. Contact these companies for further information:

BC Ferries, 1112 Fort St., Victoria, BC V8V 4V2 (206-624-6663 in Seattle, 604-669-1211 in Vancouver, 604-386-3431 in Victoria). Operates *Queen of the North* between Port Hardy and Prince Rupert year-round; during the summer, northbound and southbound routes on alternate days. Special facilities for disabled passengers.

BC Stena Line Ltd., 254 Belleville St., Victoria, BC V8V 1W9 (800-962-5984 in Seattle, 604-388-7397 in Victoria). Runs the *Crown Princess of Victoria* and the *Vancouver Island Princess* between Seattle and Victoria. Two ferries per day in each direction; 1 per day fall to spring.

Black Ball Transport, Inc., 430 Belleville St., Victoria, BC V8V 1W9 (206-622-2222 in Seattle, 206-457-4491 in Port Angeles, 604-386-2202 in Victoria). Ferries every day between Port Angeles and Victoria.

Washington State Ferries (206-464-6400). Ferries between Anacortes, WA, and Sidney, BC, and between Seattle and points on the Kitsap Peninsula and San Juan Islands.

The **Alaska Northwest Travel Service, Inc.,** 130 2nd Ave. S., Edmonds, WA 98020 (800-533-7381 or 206-775-4504), is an agent for Alaska and British Columbia ferries as well as a full service travel agency specializing in Alaska; they can book ferries and offer advice on itineraries. Ferry scheduling information can also be found in *The Milepost,* published by Alaska Northwest Publishing Co.; see By Car for information on how to obtain a copy.

Information about fares, reservations, vehicles, and schedules varies greatly during the various times of the year. *Let's Go* helps steer you through the morass in the sections of the book on Seattle and the areas of BC and Alaska served by ferries. Be sure to consult each ferry company to clear up any questions and help you piece together your own itinerary.

By Motorcycle

Well, it's cheaper than driving a car—but the physical and emotional wear and tear of motorcycling may cancel any financial gain. Fatigue and the small gas tank conspire to force the motorcyclist to stop more often on long trips; experienced riders are seldom on the road more than six hours per day. Lack of luggage space can also be a serious limitation. If you must carry a load, keep it low and forward where it won't distort the cycle's center of gravity. Fasten it either to the seat or over the rear axle in saddle or tank bags.

Annoyances, though, are secondary to risks. Despite their superior maneuverability, motorcycles are incredibly vulnerable. Major enemies are crosswinds, drunk drivers, and the blind spots of cars and trucks. *Always ride defensively.* The dangers skyrocket at night; travel only in the daytime. Half of all cyclists have an accident within their first month of riding. Even if you've never met a person who's had an accident on a motorcycle, realize that serious mishaps are remarkably common and often fatal. Always wear the best helmet you can get your hands on. For information on motorcycle emergencies, ask your State Department of Motor Vehicles for a motorcycle operator's manual.

By Bicycle

Travel by bicycle brings you even closer to the countryside—and pavement. You move much more slowly for much more effort, but that doesn't mean you will be ill-rewarded. The leisurely pace gives you a chance to take in the view as well as the dust. Cycling is a popular activity for both residents and visitors in the Northwest.

Though you can carry much less than you could on a larger vehicle, assembling all the necessary equipment is, not surprisingly, the largest task you'll face as you prepare to tour by bike. Get in touch with a local biking club if you don't know a great deal about bicycle equipment and repair. When you shop around, compare knowledgeable local retailers to mail-order firms. If the disparity in price is modest, buy locally. Otherwise, order by phone or mail and make sure you have someone in town to consult with. Make your first investment in an issue of *Bicycling* magazine which advertises low sale prices. **Bike Nashbar** almost always has the lowest prices—if you can find a nationally advertised price that's lower, they will beat it by 5¢. Contact them at 4111 Simon Rd., Youngstown, OH 44513 (800-627-4227). Their own line of products, including complete bicycles, is an excellent value. Another exceptional mail-order firm which specializes in mountain bikes is **Bikecology,** P.O. Box 3900, Santa Monica, CA 90403 (800-326-2453).

Safe and secure bike use requires a quality helmet and a quality lock. A **Bell** or **Tourlite** helmet costs about $40—much cheaper than critical head surgery or a well-appointed funeral. **Kryptonite** locks begin at $20, with insurance against theft either for one or two years or up to a certain amount of money, depending on where you buy it.

Long distance cyclists should get in touch with **Bikecentennial,** P.O. Box 8308, Missoula, MT 59807 (406-721-1776). This national, nonprofit organization researches and maps long-distance bicycle routes and organizes bike tours for members. U.S. annual membership costs $22, $19 for students, and $25 for families; in Canada and Mexico, the charge is US$30 for individuals and $45 for families. Members receive maps and guidebooks (write or call for a free catalogue), route information, and nine issues of *BikeReport,* the organization's bicycle touring magazine. *Bicycling* magazine, noted above, is another good resource for bike travelers.

There are also a number of good books about bicycle touring and repair in general. Two which discuss how to equip oneself and plan a bicycle trip are *Bike Touring* (Sierra Club, $11) and *Bicycle Touring* ($5) from **Rodale Press,** 33 E. Minor St., Emmaus, PA 18908 (215-967-5171). *Bicycle Gearing: A Practical Guide* (The Mountaineers Books, $7) discusses in lay terms how bicycle gears work, covering everything you need to know in order to shift properly and get the maximum propulsion from the minimum exertion. Finally, 10-Speed Press publishes *The Bike Bag Book* ($4 plus $1 shipping), a bite-sized book of information with broad utility—just add creativity and stir. Write 10-Speed Press, Box 7123, Berkeley, CA 94707.

Information about cycling in the region is available from tourist bureaus, which often distribute free maps. You can obtain the *Oregon Bicycling Guide* and *Oregon Coast Bike Route Map* from the Bikeway Program Manager, Oregon Department of Transportation, State Highway Division, Salem, OR 97310 (503-378-3432). Mountaineers Books publishes a series about bicycling through Washington an Oregon. Another good guide is *Bicycle Touring in the Western United States,* by Karen and Gary Hawkins (Pantheon, $10). This book discusses planning and equipment as well as many things that seem obvious but never come to mind, such as road conditions and quality.

Bikers should remember that the Northwest possesses a sparser web of well-paved backroads than other regions of the U.S. Between the coast and the mountains, bikers should also be wary of strong, prevailing winds from the northwest. You can transport your bike with you as you travel by bus, train, or air—check with each carrier about weight limits, packing requirements, insurance, and fees.

Organized bicycle trips trade the burden of planning for hefty expenses. In Alberta and British Columbia, contact **Rocky Mountain Cycle Tours,** Box 1978, Canmore, AB T0L 0M0 (403-678-6770).

Let's Go urges you to consider the risks and disadvantages of hitchhiking before deciding whether to use your thumb as a means of transport. We do not recommend hitchhiking.

Accommodations

The Northwest has a pleasant variety of inexpensive alternatives to hotels and motels. Before you set out, try to locate places to stay along your route and make reservations, especially if you plan to travel during peak tourist seasons. If you are addicted to Hiltons and Marriotts beyond your means, consider joining **Discount Travel International,** 114 Forrest Ave., Ives Bldg., #205, Narberth, PA 19072 (215-668-2182). For an annual membership fee of $45, you and your household will have access to a clearing house of unsold hotel rooms (as well as airline tickets, cruises and the like), which can save you as much as 50%.

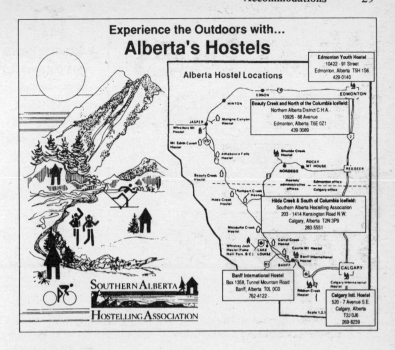

Experience the Outdoors with...
Alberta's Hostels

Youth Hostels

Youth hostels offer unbeatable deals on indoor lodging, and they are great places to meet other budget travelers from all over the world. Hostels as a rule are dorm-style accommodations where the sexes sleep apart, often in large rooms with bunk beds. (Some hostels allow families and couples to have private rooms.) Expenses and frills are kept to a minimum. You have to bring your own sleep sack (two sheets sewn together); sleeping bags are often not allowed. Hostels often have kitchens and utensils for your use, and some have storage areas and laundry facilities.

In the United States, **American Youth Hostels (AYH)** maintains 31 hostels in Washington, Oregon, and Alaska. Most of them are near the coast, and they cluster around the major cities. Basic AYH rules (with some local variation): check-in between 5 and 8pm, check-out by 9:30am, maximum stay 3 days, no pets or alcohol allowed on the premises. All ages are welcome. Hostels differ in size, and fees range from $7-12 per night. Hostels are graded according to the number of facilities they offer and the overall level of quality—consult *Let's Go* evaluations for each town. Reservations may be necessary or advisable at some hostels, so check ahead of time. AYH membership is annual: $25, $15 for ages over 54, $10 for ages under 18, $35 for a family. Nonmembers who wish to stay at an AYH hostel ususally pay $3 extra, which can be applied toward membership. IYHF memberships are recognized at all AYH hostels. For more information, contact AYH, 425 Divisadero St. #306, San Francisco, CA 94227 (415-863-9939). In Canada, the **Canadian Hostelling Association** is the counterpart to AYH. Most of the regulations are the same; fees range from CDN$4-15 per night. Annual membership costs CDN$21, CDN$12 for ages under 18, and CDN$42 for families. IYHF memberships are honored in Canada. For more information, contact Canadian Hostelling Association, National Office, 1600 James Naismith Dr., Gloucester, Ont. K1B 5N4 (613-748-5638).

Budget Chain Motels

Although many budget motels preserve single digits in their names (e.g. Motel 6), the cellar-level price of a single has matured to about $25. Nevertheless, budget chain motels still cost significantly less than the chains catering to the next-pricier market, such as Holiday Inn. Budget chains adhere more consistently to a level of cleanliness and comfort than their locally operated budget competitors; some budget motels even feature heated pools and pay-TVs. In bigger cities, budget motels are just off the highway, inconveniently far from the downtown area. If you don't have a car, you may well spend the difference between a budget motel and one downtown on transportation. Contact these chains for free directories:

Motel 6, 3391 S. Blvd, Rio Rancho, NM 87124 (505-891-6161).

Super 8 Motels, Inc., 910 8th Ave. NE, P.O. Box 4090, Aberdeen, SD 57402-4090 (800-843-1991).

Friendship Inns International, 2627 Paterson Plank Rd., North Bergen, NJ 07047 (800-453-4511).

Allstar Inns, LP, P.O. Box 3070, Santa Barbara, CA 93180-3070 (805-687-3383).

You may also want to consult an omnibus directory, like the *State by State Guide to Budget Motels* ($10) from **Marlor Press**, Contemporary Books, 180 N. Michigan Ave., Chicago, IL 60601 (312-782-9181), or the *National Directory of Budget Motels* ($5), from Pilot Books, 103 Cooper St., Babylon, NY 11702 (516-422-2225).

Bed and Breakfasts

As alternatives to impersonal hotel rooms, bed and breakfasts (private homes with spare rooms available to travelers) range from the acceptable to the sublime. B&Bs may provide an excellent way to explore with the help of a host who knows the region well, and some go out of their way to be accommodating—accepting travelers with pets or giving personalized tours. The best part of your stay will often

5,300 hostels in 68 countries on 6 continents.

One card.

With the American Youth Hostels Membership Card,

you can stay at 5,300 hostels around the world.

Hostels are great places to make new friends.

And the prices are incredibly low,

just 35¢ to $20 a night for a dorm-style room.

For an application, call 202-783-6161.

Or write: American Youth Hostels,

Dept. 801, P.O. Box 37613, Washington, DC 20013-7613.

INTERNATIONAL YOUTH HOSTEL FEDERATION
American Youth Hostels

be a home-cooked breakfast (and occasionally dinner). While many B&Bs do not provide phones, TVs, or showers with your room, they are usually delightful places.

Prices vary widely. B&Bs in major cities are usually more expensive than those in out-of-the-way places. Doubles, with complete or continental breakfast, can cost anywhere from $20 to $300 per night. Most are in the $30-50 range. Some homes give special discounts to families or senior citizens. Reservations are almost always necessary, although in the off-season you can frequently find a room on short notice. Many bed-and-breakfasts close down during the winter, though.

For information on Pacific Northwest B&Bs, contact **Bed and Breakfast International**, 1181-B Solano Ave., Albany, CA 94706 (415-525-4569). Various B&B guidebooks are available in bookstore travel sections. Since B&Bs often do not appear in any guidebook, however, check local phonebooks, visitors bureaus, and information at bus and train stations.

YMCAs and YWCAs

Young Men's Christian Associations offer lodging, showers (usually communal), and the use of their libraries, pools, and other facilities for a single composite fee. The price is usually lower than a hotel but perhaps higher than the local hostel. They are often located in urban downtowns, which can be convenient but a little gritty, depending on the city's age and nocturnal character. Many YMCAs accept women and families, but may set a minimum ages for unaccompanied youths.

Reservations are strongly recommended, and cost $3. Key deposits run about $5. For information and reservations for the U.S. or Canada, write the **Y's Way to Travel**, 356 W. 34th St., New York, NY 10001 (212-760-5856). Send a self-addressed envelope stamped with 45¢ postage for a free catalogue of services.

Most Young Women's Christian Associations accommodate only women. Non-members are usually required to join when lodging. For more information, write YWCA, 726 Broadway, New York, NY 10003 (212-614-2700).

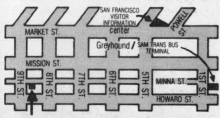

College Dormitories

Many colleges and universities fling open their residence halls to travelers when school is not in session (some do so even during term-time). No general policy covers all of these institutions, but rates tend to be low. *Let's Go* directs you to major educational institutions that offer accommodations. Since college dorms are popular with many travelers, you should write ahead for reservations if possible.

Students traveling through a college or university town while school is in session might try introducing themselves to friendly looking local students. At worst you'll receive a cold reception; at best, a good conversation might lead to an offer of a place to crash. Foreign visitors may have especially good luck here. In general, college campuses are some of the best sources for information on things to do, places to stay, and possible rides out of town. In addition, dining halls often serve reasonably priced, reasonably edible all-you-can-eat meals.

Camping and the Outdoors

In Northwest, mountains, forests, rivers, and glaciers are accessible not only to the expert adventurer and naturalist but to the average traveler. Books and other writings about the region and its natural attractions are easy to find. Three publishers in particular put out reading material that describes the parks and trails of the Northwest, as well as high quality books about camping, hiking, and biking in the area. Write or call to order or to receive a free catalogue:

> **Sierra Club Books**, 730 Polk St., San Francisco, CA 94109 (415-776-2211). Books about the national parks in the region, as well as *The Best About Backpacking* ($9), *Cooking for Camp and Trail* ($8), *Learning to Rock Climb* ($13), and *Wildwater* ($9). Shipping $3.

> **The Mountaineers Books**, 306 2nd Ave. W., Seattle, WA 98119 (800-553-4453 or 206-285-2665). Books too numerous to list individually include the *100 Hikes* series about trails in the region, as well as guides to bicycling in the Northwest and mountaineering medicine.

> **Wilderness Press**, 2440 Bancroft Way, Berkeley, CA 94704-1676 (415-843-8080). Specializes in hiking guides and maps for the Western U.S. Also publishes the excellent *Backpacking Basics* and *Backpackers' Sourcebook* ($8 each).

Take advantage of *Woodall's Campground Directory* (Western edition $9) and *Woodall's Tent Camping Guide* (Western edition $8). If you can't find a copy locally, contact **Woodall Publishing Company**, 28167 N. Keith Dr., Lake Forest, IL 60045-5000 (800-323-9076 or 708-362-6700). For **topographical maps**, write the **U.S. Geological Survery**, Map Distribution, Box 25286, Federal Center, Denver, CO 80225 (call 703-648-6892 or 202-343-8073 with questions) or the **Canada Map Office**, 615 Booth St., Ottawa, Ont. K1A 0E9 (613-952-7000), which distributes geographical and aeronautical maps as well.

Parks and Forests

At the turn of the century, it may have seemed unnecessary to set aside parts of the vast American and Canadian wilderness as reserves, but today that action is recognized as a stroke of genius. The Northwest's extensive system of government-protected parks are havens for plantlife, wildlife, and human-life in the region.

National parks protect some of America and Canada's most spectacular scenery. Alaska's dizzying Mt. McKinley, agate-still Crater Lake in Oregon, and the wilds of Jasper, Alberta, are treasures that will remain intact for generations. Though their official purpose is preservation, the parks make room for recreation as well. Many national parks have backcountry and developed tent camping; others welcome RVs, and a few offer opulent living in grand lodges. Internal road systems allow you to reach the interior and the major sights even if you are not a long-distance hiker. Ranger talks and guided hikes teach visitors about the parks. The larger and more popular national parks charge a $3-5 entry fee for vehicles, and

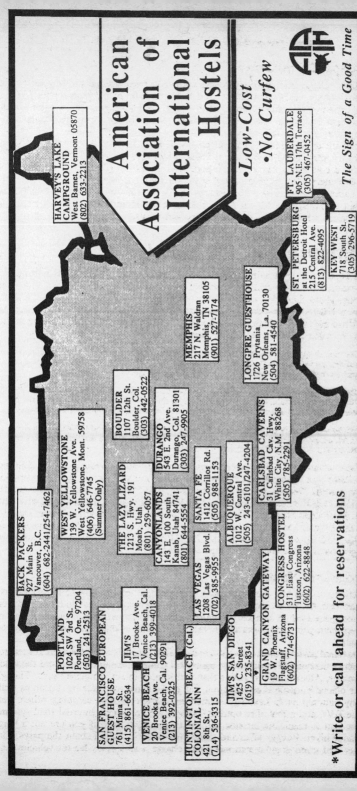

American Association of International Hostels

•Low-Cost
•No Curfew

The Sign of a Good Time

HARVEY'S LAKE CAMPGROUND
West Barnet, Vermont 05870
(802) 633-2213

FT. LAUDERDALE
905 N.E. 17th Terrace
(305) 467-0452

ST. PETERSBURG
at the Detroit Hotel
215 Central Ave.
(813) 822-4095

KEY WEST
718 South St.
(305) 296-5719

MEMPHIS
217 N. Waldran
Memphis, TN 38105
(901) 527-7174

LONGPRE GUESTHOUSE
1726 Prytania
New Orleans, La. 70130
(504) 581-4540

BOULDER
1107 12th St.
Boulder, Col.
(303) 442-0522

DURANGO
543 E. 2nd Ave.
Durango, Col. 81301
(303) 247-9905

BACK PACKERS
927 Main St.
Vancouver, B.C.
(604) 682-2441/254-7462

WEST YELLOWSTONE
139 W. Yellowstone Ave.
West Yellowstone, Mont. 59758
(406) 646-7745
(Summer Only)

THE LAZY LIZARD
1213 S. Hwy. 191
Moab, Utah
(801) 259-6057

CANYONLANDS
143 E. 100 South
Kanab, Utah 84741
(801) 644-5554

SANTA FE
1412 Corrillos Rd.
(505) 988-1153

ALBUQUERQUE
1012 W. Central Ave.
(505) 243-6101/247-4204

CARLSBAD CAVERNS
31 Carlsbad Cav. Hwy.
White City, N.M. 88268
(505) 785-2291

PORTLAND
1024 SW 3rd St.
Portland, Ore. 97204
(503) 241-2513

SAN FRANCISCO EUROPEAN GUEST HOUSE
761 Minna St.
(415) 861-6634

JIM'S
17 Brooks Ave.
Venice Beach, Cal.
(213) 399-4018

VENICE BEACH
20 Brooks Ave.
Venice Beach, Cal. 90291
(213) 392-0325

HUNTINGTON BEACH (Cal.)
COLONIAL INN
421 8th St.
(714) 536-3315

LAS VEGAS
1208 Las Vegas Blvd.
(702) 385-9955

JIM'S SAN DIEGO
1425 C. Street
(619) 235-8341

GRAND CANYON GATEWAY
19 W. Phoenix
Flagstaff, Arizona
(602) 774-6731

CONGRESS HOSTEL
311 East Congress
Tuscon, Arizona
(602) 622-8848

*Write or call ahead for reservations

sometimes a nominal one for pedestrians and cyclists as well. The $25 **Golden Eagle Passport** covers the fee at all U.S. parks (most parks sell the Passports as well). Seniors and disabled travelers are entitled to free passes (see Special Concerns under Planning, above). For information about camping, accommodations, and regulations at national parks, contact the following agencies. For Washington and Oregon: **Forest Service/National Park Service, Outdoor Recreation Information Center,** 915 2nd Ave., Seattle, WA 981074 (206-442-0181). For Alberta and British Columbia: **Canadian Parks Service,** 220 4th Ave. SE, #520, Calgary, AB T2P 3H8 (403-292-4440). For the Yukon Territory: **Canadian Parks Service,** 457 Main St., Winnipeg, Manitoba R3B 3E8 (204-983-2110). For Alaska: **Alaska Public Land Information Center,** 605 W. 4th Ave., #105, Anchorage, AK 99501 (907-271-2737). Visitor centers at parks offer excellent free literature and information, and the U.S. Government Printing Office publishes two useful pamphlets: *National Parks: Camping Guide* (S/N 024-005-01028-9; $3.50) and *National Parks: Lesser-Known Areas* (S/N 024-005-00911-6; $1.50). The Winnipeg office of the Canadian Parks Service distributes *Parks West,* a book about all the national parks of Western Canada.

State and provincial parks are, as one might expect, much like national parks, only they are operated by a lower level of government. Each of the states and provinces in the region is richly studded with parks of its own, smaller than the national parks but much more numerous. While they cannot always compete with the grandeur of Mt. Rainier or Banff, many state and provincial parks also offer some of the best camping around—handsome surroundings, elaborate facilities, and plenty of space. Prices for camping at public sites are almost always better than those at private campgrounds.

If you're really bothered by large crowds, stay away from the well-known parks during the peak tourist season, which is generally the summer. Many parks close for the winter, however, so you may not have this option. Don't let the swarming visitors dissuade you from visiting the large parks—these places are huge, and even at their most crowded they offer many chances for quiet and solitude. Reservations may be necessary for accommodations, especially those with solid walls (i.e., lodges). Even campsites are hard to come by at times; most campgrounds are first-come, first-pitched. Some parks limit the number of days you can stay in a campsite as well as the number of people you can have in your group (usually no more than 25 campers).

In the U.S., if you are a complete purist and even the national parks are too developed for your tastes, head for the **national forests.** Most are equipped only for primitive camping—pit toilets and no running water as a rule. Forests are less accessible than the parks, but less crowded as a consequence. They're also free. Backpackers can take advantage of specially designated **wilderness areas,** where regulations prohibit vehicles and there are no roads, making these areas even less trodden by the throngs. **Wilderness permits** are required for backcountry hiking and can usually be obtained (that often means purchased) at parks; check ahead to be on the safe side. One word of warning: Adventurers who plan to explore some real wilderness should always check in at a U.S. Forest Service field office for safety reasons before heading into the woods. Many of these wilderness areas are difficult to find and therefore under-utilized—so write ahead for accurate, detailed maps. For general information, contact the **Pacific Northwest Regional Office, U.S. Forest Service,** P.O. Box 3623, Portland, OR 97208 (503-326-2877), or the **Alaska Regional Office, U.S. Forest Service,** Federal Office Bldg., P.O. Box 21628, Public Affairs Office, Juneau, AK 99802 (907-568-8806).

The **Pacific Crest Trail,** which stretches from the Mexico-California border into Canada, is particularly attractive for one- or two-week hiking trips along its shorter segments. Heated cabins and some running tap water along the trails add convenience. Consult an area tourism bureau for maps of the trail. Another valuable source is *The Pacific Crest Trail,* Vol. 2 (Wilderness Press; $20), which covers Oregon and Washington.

Tent Camping, Hiking, and Climbing

As should be apparent from the preceding sections, to appreciate the beauty of the Northwest, to get a glimpse of the life that has been led in this region for centuries, to feel the grandeur of the landscape deep inside—you must go camping.

It's cheap, too.

Equipment

In the Northwest you and your equipment will be subject to weather conditions that may vary considerably even within a short time. The Climate section below has more detail about the weather, but prepare first for your nearly inevitable companions, the cold and rain, and remember that areas west of the mountains are rained upon much more than parts just east. Here is a primer on the basic equipment you'll need to be a safe and happy camper.

At the core of your equipment is the **sleeping bag.** Which one you buy will depend on the climate in which you will be camping. Sleeping bags are rated according to the lowest outdoor temperature at which they will still protect you. If a bag's rating is not a temperature but a seasonal description, keep in mind that "summer" translates to a rating of 30-40°F, "three-season" can be anywhere from 5-30°F, and "four-season" means below 0°F. When you check specific sleeping bags, get the most specific temperature rating you can. To choose a bag rating, figure out the lowest temperature you'll be sleeping in and subtract another few degrees. Sleeping bags are made either of down or of synthetic material. Down bags are warmer and lighter in weight, but they lose their insulating qualities while wet, and then dry out less quickly. Synthetic bags require more material to achieve the same level of warmth as down, and consequently weigh more, but they stay warmer even if soggy and dry out well. Lowest prices for acceptable sleeping bags: $45 for a summer synthetic, $110 for a three-season synthetic, $140 for a three-season down bag, and upwards of $200 for a down sleeping bag you can use in the winter. If you're using a sleeping bag for serious camping, you should also have either a foam pad or an air mattress to cushion your back and neck. Inch-thick foam pads start at $10 (high tech materials like Ensolite run a bit more), while air mattresses cost up to $50. Another good alternative is the **Therm-A-Rest,** which is part foam and part air-mattress and inflates to full padding when you unroll it (from $40).

When you select a **tent,** your major considerations should be shape and size. A-frame tents are the best all-around. When they are pitched, their internal space is almost entirely usable; this means little unnecessary bulk. Only one drawback: if you're caught in the rain and have to spend a day or two holed up inside your tent, A-frames can be cramped and claustrophobic. Dome and umbrella shapes offer more spacious living, but tend to be bulkier to carry. As for size, two people can fit in a two-person tent but will find life more pleasant in a four-person tent. If you're traveling by car, go for the bigger tent. If you're hiking, stick with a smaller tent that weighs no more than 3.5 lbs./1.5kg. Be sure your tent can protect you from the Northwestern damp by extending several inches above the ground and that it has a rain fly. Good two-person tents cost about $85, $115 for a four-person. You can, however, often find last year's version for half the price.

If you intend to do a lot of hiking or biking, you should have a **frame backpack.** Buy a backpack with an internal frame if you'll be hiking on difficult trails that require a lot of bending and maneuvering—internal-frame packs mould better to your back, keep a lower center of gravity, and have enough give to follow you through your contortions. An internal-frame backpack is also good as an all-around travel pack, something you can carry by hand when you return to civilization. External-frame packs are more comfortable for long hikes over even terrain; since they keep the weight higher, walking upright will not cost you additional exertion. The size of a backpack is measured in cubic inches. Any serious backpacking requires at least 3300 of them, while longer trips require around 4000. Add an additional 500 cubic inches for internal-frame packs, since you'll have to pack your sleeping bag inside, rather than strap it on the outside as you do with an external-frame pack. Backpacks with many compartments generally turn a large space into many unusable small spaces. Packs that load from the front rather than the top allow you access to your gear more easily (see Packing for more hints). Sturdy backpacks start anywhere from $85-125. Cheaper packs may be less comfortable, and the straps are more likely to fray or rip quickly. Test-drive a backpack for comfort before you buy it.

Other necessities include: **battery-operated lantern** (gas is inconvenient and riskier), **plastic groundcloth** for the floor of your tent, **nylon tarp** for general purposes, and a **"stuff sack"** or plastic bag to keep your sleeping bag dry. Don't go anywhere without a **canteen** or water bottle. Plastic models keep water cooler in the hot sun than metal ones do, although metal canteens are a bit sturdier and leak less. If you'll be away from parks with showers, bring **water sacks** and/or a **solar shower,** a small black sack with an attachable shower head. Although most campgrounds provide campfire sites, you may want to bring a small **metal grate** of your own, and even a grill. For those places that forbid fires or the gathering of firewood, you'll need a **camp stove** (Coleman is the classic, and they start at $25; a butane or white gas stove is an improvement, but more expensive). Make sure you have **waterproof matches.**

Shop around your area for the best deals on camping equipment. If you can, buy from a local retailer who can give you advice about using your equipment. Several mail-order firms offer lower prices, and they can also help you determine which item is the one you need. Call or write for a free catalogue:

Campmor, 810 Rte. 17N, P.O. Box 997-P, Paramus, NJ 07653-0997 (800-526-4784).

L.L. Bean, 1 Casco St., Freeport, ME 04033 (800-221-4221).

Recreational Equipment, Inc. (REI), Commercial Sales, P.O. Box C-88126, Seattle, WA 98188 (800-426-4840).

The mail-order firms are guides to the lowest prices; if the prices at your local dealer are reasonable in comparison, buy from there (you could try bargaining if you're so inclined). Look for end-of-season sales, too; often older but quite nice models go for about half their original price.

A good initial source of information on **recreational vehicles (RVs)** is the **Recreational Vehicle Industry Association,** 1986 Preston White Dr., P.O. Box 2999, Reston, VA 22090 (703-620-6003). For a free catalogue that lists RV camping publications and state campground associations, send a self-addressed, stamped envelope to **Go Camping America Committee,** P.O. Box 2669, Reston, VA 22090 (703-620-6003).

Wilderness Concerns

The first thing to preserve in the wilderness is you—health, safety, and food should be your primary concerns as you camp. See Health above for information about basic medical concerns and first-aid. A comprehensive guide to outdoor survival is *How to Stay Alive in the Woods,* by Bradford Angier (Macmillan, $6). Many rivers, streams, and lakes are contaminated with bacteria such as *giardia,* which causes gas, cramps, loss of appetite, and violent diarrhea. To protect yourself from the effects of this invisible trip-wrecker, always boil water before drinking or cooking with it, and bring water purification pills along. *Never go camping or hiking any significant time or distance alone.* If you're going into an area that is not well-traveled or well-marked, let someone know where you're hiking and how long you intend to be out. If something unexpected occurs while you're unreachable, searchers will at least know where to look for you.

The second thing to protect while you are outdoors is the wilderness. As thousands of outdoor enthusiasts traipse through the parks every year, the forests face being trampled to death. Be considerate of the environment. Because firewood is scarce in popular parks, campers are asked to make small fires using only dead branches or brush; the careful camper prefers a campstove. Check ahead to see if the park prohibits campfires altogether. To prevent long-term scarring of an area, make camp at least 100 feet from regularly used sites. Also, if there are no toilet facilities around, bury human waste 100 feet or more from any water supply to prevent contaminating lakes and streams. Keep soap or detergent away from bodies of water. Burn what garbage you can, being sure not to incinerate plastics (which cause poisonous fumes), and pack everything else out when you leave the campground. Never bury trash (see the next section on bears). And remember that hunting is strictly prohibited in all national, state, and provincial parks.

Bear Necessities

No matter how tame a bear appears, don't be fooled—they're wild and dangerous animals, and they're just not impressed or intimidated by humans. To avoid an unbearable experience, never feed a bear, or tempt it with such delectables as open trash cans. They will come back to demand seconds as a right. Keep your camp clean. Do not leave trash or food lying around camp. Burn waste to destroy its odors—never bury it. Store food in air-tight containers, then hang them in a tree 10 feet from the ground and 5 feet from the trunk. Avoid indulging in greasy foods, especially bacon and ham. Grease gets on everything, including your clothes and sleeping bag, and bears find it an alluring dressing for what or whomever is wearing it. Burn feminine hygiene materials as well—never throw these, or food, down a toilet. Park rangers can tell you how to identify bear trails (don't camp on them!). Bears are attracted to perfume smells; do without cologne, scented soap, and hairspray while camping. Stay away from dead animals and berry bushes—these are Le Ménu for bears. Always shine a flashlight when walking at night: the bears will clear out before you arrive given sufficient warning.

If you see a bear at a distance, calmly walk the other direction. If it seems interested, some suggest waving a long stick above your head; the general flailing creates the impression in the bear's eyes that you're much taller than a person, and it may decide that *you* are the menacing High Lord of the Forest. If you stumble upon a sweet-looking bear cub, leave immediately, lest its over-protective mother stumble upon *you.*

Organized Adventure

If you're a novice outdoorsman, don't lose heart—many organized adventure tours are designed especially for amateurs. The professionals will charge liberally for the guidance, however. Before you sign up for any organized trip, make sure you have done a substantial amount of bargain shopping. Begin by consulting tourism bureaus, which can suggest parks and trails as well as outfitters, and answer general questions. *Outside Magazine,* 1165 N. Clark St., Chicago, IL 60610, publishes an Expedition Services Directory in each issue.

The **Sierra Club,** 730 Polk St., San Francisco, CA 94109 (415-776-2211), plans a variety of outings. So does **TrekAmerica,** P.O. Box 1338, Gardena, CA 90249 (800-221-0596 or 213-321-0734); call or write for information on their Canada and Alaska trips. The **Pacific Crest Outward Bound School** (800-547-3312 or 503-243-1993) conducts programs in Oregon and Washington for adults and teenagers, emphasizing confidence building and communal cooperation. Among other trips, **Green Tortoise** organizes a 35-day expedition to Alaska and the Canadian Rockies (see By Bus above for more about Green Tortoise).

If the idea of Mt. Rainier piques your interest, take advantage of one of the many climbing schools in the Pacific Northwest. The **Lac Des Arcs Climbing School,** 1116 19 Ave. NW, Calgary, Alberta T2M 0Z9 (403-289-6795 or 403-240-6502), gives two- and four-day courses in rock climbing and mountaineering, which range in price from $100-250. Other trips and courses are offered by **Genet Expeditions, Inc.** (P.O. Box 230861, Anchorage, AK 99523; 800-334-3638 or 907-561-2123), and the Pacific Crest Outward Bound School. When you plan your climbing trips, remember that fatigue arrives faster at high altitudes. Let's be careful up there, and never go alone!

Outdoor Sports

Water Sports

The lattice-work of of fast-flowing rivers in the Pacific Northwest is ideal for canoeing, kayaking, and whitewater rafting. Throughout the book, boating opportunities are suggested in the Activities sections. Travel agents and tourism bureaus can recommend others.

The **River Travel Center,** Box 6, Pt. Arena, CA 95468 (800-882-7238), can place you in a whitewater raft, kayak, or sea-kayak though one of over 100 outfitters. Trips range in length from three to 18 days. British Columbia rafting trips (1-6 days, $25-155) are planned by **Clearwater Expeditions Ltd.,** R.R. 2, Box 2506, Clearwater, BC V0E 1N0. **Hells Canyon Adventures, Inc.,** Box 159, Oxbow, OR 97840 (800-422-3568; in OR, 503-785-3352), is the place to call for Snake River whitewater rafting, whitewater jet boat tours, and fishing charters. Rafting trips cost $90 per person for a one-day trip or $375 for three days; jet boat tour start at $20.

Sierra Club Books publishes a kayaking and whitewater rafting guide entitled *Wildwater* ($9). *Washington Whitewater* ($11 for each of two volumes) and *Canoe Routes: Northwest Oregon* ($9), published by The Mountaineers Books, might also interest you.

Snow Sports

Winter sports enjoy enormous popularity in the Northwest, where mountain peaks compete with skyscrapers for skyline prominence. You'll find every imaginable way to enjoy the winter wonderland: the fast-paced can rent snowmobiles, the laid-back can shuffle along on snowshoes, and the courageous can even steer a pack of sled dogs in Alaska or the Yukon.

Tourism bureaus can help you locate the best sports outfitters and ski areas. *Let's Go* suggests options in the Activities sections throughout the book. For Oregon and Washington skiing information, write the **Pacific Northwest Ski Association,** 640 NW Gilman Blvd., #104, Issaquah, WA 98027 (206-392-4220). The Sierra Club publishes *The Best Ski Touring in America* ($11), which includes Canada as well. The Mountaineers Books publishes good skiing guides for Oregon and Washington.

Pay attention to cold weather safety concerns. Know the symptoms of hypothermia and frostbite (see Health), and bring along warm clothes and quick energy snacks like candy bars and trail mix. Drinking alcohol in the cold can be particularly dangerous: even though you *feel* warm, alcohol slows your body's ability to adjust to the temperature and therefore makes you more vulnerable to hypothermia. Send for the U.S. Government Printing Office's *Winter Recreation Safety Guide* (S/N 001-000-03856-7, $2; see Planning Your Trip for address and phone).

Fishing and Hunting

Fish willingly flounder onto your boat throughout the Pacific Northwest, Western Canada, and Alaska. If you wish to encourage them, contact the appropriate department of fisheries for brochures that summarize regulations and make sport fishing predictions. Some fishing seasons are extremely short, so be sure to ask when the expected prime angling dates fall. Licenses are available from many tackle shops, or you can purchase them directly from the state or provincial department of fisheries. You need not reside in a state or province in order to hunt there, but steep license and tag fees will probably discourage you. If you must shoot, consult the appropriate departments of game to purchase licenses and receive regulations pamphlets.

Alaska: Fish and Game Licensing, 1111 W. 8th St., #108, Juneau, AK 99801 (907-465-2376). Nonresident fishing license $10 for 3 days, $20 for 14 days, $36 for a year. Nonresident hunting licenses $60, $96 for hunting and fishing. Big game tags, purchased before you hunt, range from $135 (deer) to $500 (musk ox).

Alberta: Fish and Wildlife Division, 9945 108th St., Edmonton T5K 2G6 (403-427-3590). Nonresident fishing license $15 for Canadians, $30 for non-Canadians. Nonresident hunting licenses: $15 wildlife certificate and resource development stamp, plus tags from $21 (wolf) to $276 (sheep).

British Columbia: Fish and Wildlife Information, Ministry of Environments, 780 Blanshard St., Victoria, BC V8V 1X5 (604-387-9737). Nonresident angling license $15 for 6 days, $27 for a year. Steelhead license $42. Kootenay Rainbow Trout permit $4.

Oregon: Department of Fish and Wildlife, 2501 S.W. 1st Ave., P.O. Box 59, Portland 97207 (503-229-5403). Fishing licenses $14.50 for residents, $35.50 for nonresidents. Hunting licenses $9.50 for residents, $100.50 for nonresidents. Combination licenses $21.50 (residents only). Salmon and sturgeon tags $5.50.

Washington: Department of Fisheries, General Administration Bldg. #115, Olympia 98504-0611 (206-753-6600). Licenses for food fish. Personal use license required (residents $3, nonresidents $10); nonresident salmon and sturgeon licenses an additional $3.

Department of Game, 600 N. Capitol Way, Olympia 98501-1091 (206-753-5700). Game fishing licenses $14 for residents, $40 for nonresidents. Hunting licenses $12 for residents, $125 for nonresidents. Combination licenses $24 (residents only).

Yukon Government, Department of Renewable Resources, 10 Burns Rd., Whitehorse Y1A 2C6 (403-667-5221). Nonresident fishing licenses $30 for Canadians, $35 for non-Canadians ($20 and $25 respectively for 3-day permits). Nonresident hunting licenses $25 for Canadians, $35 for non-Canadians (6-day licenses $15/20, 1-day $5 for anyone).

Many outfitters plan fly-in fishing trips or boating trips designed for fishers. These expeditions are expensive. If you are interested, consult a travel agent or tourism bureau for possibilities.

For International Visitors

Information Organizations

United States Tourist Offices, found in many foreign countries, offer enough free literature to paper a continent from sea to shining sea. If you can't find a U.S. Tourist Office in your area, write the **U.S. Travel and Tourism Administration,** Department of Commerce, 14th St. and Constitution Ave. NW, Washington, DC 20230 (202-377-4003 or 202-377-3811). USTTA has branches in Australia, Belgium, Canada, France, West Germany, Japan, Mexico, and the United Kingdom; contact the Washington office for information about the branch in your country. For general tourist information, you may also want to direct inquiries to the state, provincial and city tourist offices listed throughout the book and under Tourism Bureaus above. In Canada, contact **Travel CUTS,** 187 College St., Toronto, Ont. M5T 1P7 (416-979-2406).

The **Council on International Educational Exchange (CIEE)** has branches in Canada and overseas that sell charter airline tickets, International Student Identification Cards (ISICs), travel literature, and hostel cards. CIEE can arrange stays at private homes for up to four weeks. Branches can also help students to volunteer or paid positions through their work-exchange programs. If you can't locate an affiliated office in your country, contact their main office: 205 E. 42nd St., New York, NY 10017 (212-661-1414; 800-223-7402 for charter flight tickets only). For details about other CIEE programs, see Student Travel, Safety and Insurance, and Work above.

Another excellent information source is the **Institute of International Education (IIE),** 809 United Nations Plaza, New York, NY 10017 (212-883-8200). The IIE administers fellowships and educational exchange programs worldwide and distributes several excellent publications. Summer visitors should study *Summer Learning Options USA: A Guide to Foreign Nationals,* or write for their free pamphlet, "Basic Facts on Study Abroad". If you're interested in language and cultural programs, consult IIE's *English Language and Orientation Programs in the United States.*

The **Experiment in International Living** arranges homestays throughout the year for international visitors of all ages. Guests live with an American family for an extended time period. The Experiment also runs the International Student of English (ISE) Study Program, which offers language classes on select college campuses. Costs are fairly steep (about $1100 for a 4-week stay) but the experience is invaluable. For information on additional language training sessions, write to "Experiment" at Kipling Road, Brattleboro, VT 05301 (800-451-4465).

The **International Student Travel Conference (ISTC)** is extremely helpful for European students. ISTC arranges charter flights and discount air fares, provides travel insurance, publishes currency exchange rates weekly, issues the ISIC card, and sponsors the Student Air Travel Association for European students. Write for their *Student Travel Guide* at ISTC, Weinbergstrasse 31, CH-8006 Zurich, Switzerland (1-692769).

Founded to promote international peace and understanding, **Servas** matches hosts and travelers in about 100 countries. Stays are limited to two nights, unless your host invites you to stay longer; guests must complete their own arrangements with hosts in advance of their stay. Travelers pay a $45 fee per year to Servas, plus a $15 refundable fee. No money is exchanged between travelers and hosts—rather, they share conversation and ideas. Travelers must provide two letters of reference and arrange for an interview at least one month before the trip. Contact the U.S. Servas Committee, 11 John St., #706, New York, NY 10038 (212-267-0252).

See also Student Travel, Youth Hostels, Work, and Study above for other organizations that may help foreign travelers.

Documents and Formalities

If you are coming to the U.S. from overseas, obtaining the proper documents before you leave home will take time. Certain legal documents and identification cards will save you time and money. To find out about the International Student Identity Card (ISIC), see Student Travel.

Foreign visitors to the United States are required to have a **passport, visitor's visa,** and proof of plans to leave. That said, there are a number of exceptions. Canadian citizens who are adults may enter the U.S. freely, while those under 18 need the written consent of a parent or guardian. Mexican citizens may cross into the U.S. with an I-186 form. Mexican border crossing cards (non-immigrant visas) prohibit you from staying more than 72 hours in the U.S. or straying more than 25 miles from the border. In addition, visitors from the following nations need no visa to enter the U.S.: the U.K., Japan, Italy, West Germany, France, the Netherlands, Sweden, and Switzerland. Without a visa, however, these travelers must fly into the country on one of a specified list of carriers, have with them a ticket to leave the U.S., and stay not more than 90 days. For more information, contact the nearest U.S. consulate.

At the U.S.-Canadian border, people who are not citizens of either country will need a visa to cross in either direction, with the exception of citizens of Greenland, who can cross in either direction without a visa. (Other exceptions are nationals of the eight countries listed above.) Naturalized citizens should have their naturalization papers with them; occasionally officials will ask to see them. International visitors should have their papers handy and in good order, since customs officials on both sides of the border may be tough on anyone with a foreign accent.

Visas for the United States

To obtain a U.S. visa, contact the nearest **U.S. Embassy** or **Consulate.** Europeans can also write to the **Visa and Immigration Department,** 5 Upper Grosvenor St., London W1 (071-499-3443). **Visa Center, Inc.** secures visas to the United States and Canada for travelers from all countries. Cost varies with passport requirements. Contact Visa Center, Inc., 507 Fifth Ave., #904, New York, NY 10017 (212-986-0924) for information.

Most international visitors to the U.S. obtain a **B-2** or "pleasure tourist" visa, valid for six months. If you lose your visa once you reach the U.S., you must replace it through your country's embassy. If you lose your **I-94 form** (the arrival/departure certificate attached to your visa upon arrival), replace it at the nearest **U.S. Immigration and Naturalization Service** office. This office can also grant visa extensions up to six months for a fee of $35. For a list of offices, write the U.S. Immigration and Naturalization Service, Central Office Information Operations Unit, 425 I St. NW, #5044, Washington, DC 20536 (202-633-1900).

Working in the United States with only a B-2 visa is grounds for deportation. In addition, you need a **work visa** (the coveted "Green Card"). If you are considering working at any point during your visit to the U.S., see a consulate before you leave home to find out more. To **study** or engage in full-time **practical training** in the United States, you will need another separate visa. Requirements vary depending on the type of program you are pursuing.

Many colleges and universities in the U.S. and abroad have offices that give out specific advice and information on study and employment in the United States. Almost all American academic institutions accept applications from international students directly through their office of admission (for addresses and phones, see Study above). If English is not your first language, you will generally be required to take the **Test of English as a Foreign Language and Test of English as a Spoken Language (TOEFL/TSE),** which is administered in many countries. Each university determines its own minimum score for acceptance. For more information, contact the TOEFL/TSE Application Office, P.O. Box 6151, Princeton, NJ 08541 (609-921-9000). (See Study for additional information.)

Before leaving the United States, foreigners holding some work or student visas must obtain a **"Sailing Permit"** from the **Internal Revenue Service** within 30 days prior to departure. (This is to ensure that you do not owe taxes to the U.S. government.) If you have any questions, write to Director of International Operations, Internal Revenue Service, Washington, DC 20225.

Visas for Canada

Before embarking for Canada, call the Canadian Embassy, Consulate, or High Commission for a **visitor's visa.** Your time of stay will be fixed when you visa is issued. If you ask to remain in the country longer than 90 days, you must pay a non-refundable fee of $50, whether or not you request is granted. To get an extension once you are in Canada, apply at a **Canadian Immigration Centre (CIC)** *before* your current visa expires.

As in the U.S., you will need a different visa for working in Canada. An **employment authorization** must be obtained before you enter Canada; visitors are not ordinarily permited to change their status once they have arrived. Residents of the U.S., Greenland, St. Pierre, or Miquelon only may apply for employment authorization at a port of entry. To aquire an employment authorization, talk to a **Canadian Employment Centre (CEC)** or to a Canadian consulate.

To study in Canada, a **student authorization** in addition to your visitor's visa is necessary. A student authorization is good for one year. You must plan at least six months ahead to ensure that you collect all of the required paperwork (be sure to check the standards and requirements set by each school, especially those relating to health insurance and language testing). International students may, under some circumstances work in Canada, but in these cases, employment authorization must still be obtained from a CEC.

For specifics on official documentation, contact a CIC or consulate.

International Driver's License

If you are considering renting or buying a car during your visit, you will need a valid license. Foreign driver's licenses from nations under the 1949 Geneva Road Traffic Convention are vaild in the United States. An **International Driver's License,** while not required, is a good idea—it will help with local authorities, who may not realize that your foreign license is legal. Your national automobile association can help you obtain an International License.

Visitors from other nations must obtain a domestic license in order to drive in the U.S. To aquire one, you must go through a testing process; some states require you to enroll in a certified drivers' education course before you can be tested.

International Driver's Licenses are valid in Canada, but only in conjunction with a license from the visitor's home country.

Customs

All travelers may bring the following into the U.S. without paying duty: 200 cigarettes, $100 worth of gifts, and personal belongings such as clothes and jewelry. Travelers aged 21 and over may also bring in up to one liter of alcohol if they have been outside the U.S. for at least 48 hours; otherwise the limit is 4 oz. (150ml). You can also bring any amount of currency into the U.S., but if you are carrying over $10,000 you must fill out a reporting form.

Citizens of the U.S. returning from Canada may bring in up to $400 worth of items for personal or household use or as gifts, plus 200 cigarettes and one liter of alcohol. However, if you have been outside the U.S. for less than 48 hours, this exemption slips to $25, including 50 cigarettes and 4 oz. of alcohol. U.S. citizens may mail gifts to people in the U.S., provided no person receives more than $50 in value in a single day; gift packages should be labeled "Unsolicited gift," and marked with the nature and value of the package. Duty for goods beyond the exempt amount is about 10%. For comprehensive information about U.S. customs, obtain a copy of *Know Before You Go,* from the U.S. Customs Service, 1301 Constitution Ave., Washington, DC 20229 (202-566-8195).

Canadian citizens may bring back goods worth up to CDN$20 after a 24-hour absence, $100 after a 48-hour absence, or $300 after a seven-day absence. Travelers who leave for only a day cannot bring back any liquor or tobacco, while all others can bring 200 cigarettes and either one 40-oz. bottle or 24 12-oz. bottles or cans of liquor. If you exceed the duty-free limit, you must pay around 20% of the *entire* value. Canadians can use form Y-38 to mark valuables brought with them out of the country so that they can be returned duty-free. For more information, write for "I Declare/Je Declare" from Revenue Canada Customs and Excise Department, Communications Branch, Mackenzie Ave., Ottawa, Ont. K1A 0L5 (613-957-0275).

British citizens are allowed an exemption of £32, which includes 100 cigarettes, two liters of table wine, and one liter of alcohol over 22% by volume. Contact Her

Majesty's Customs and Excise Office, New King's Beam House, 22 Upper Ground, London SE1 9PJ (071-382-54-68).

Exemptions for Australian citizens are AUS$400 for those 18 and over, and AUS$200 for those under 18. Travelers ages 18 and over may bring back one liter of alcohol and 250 cigarettes. All goods must be carried back into the country with you and not mailed. Australians should note that they may not export more than AUS$5000 from the country without permission from the Reserve Bank of Australia. "Customs Information for All Travellers" is available from local offices of the Collector of Customs (Sydney, Melbourne, Brisbane, Port Adelaide, Fremantle, Hobart, Darwin) or from Australian consulates abroad.

New Zealand citizens under age 17 are exempt from duty on the first NZ$500 worth of goods they bring back—up to 250g tobacco, 4.5 liter of beer or wine, and 1125ml of liquor. New or expensive items should be registered with a Customs Office to avoid their being taxed upon your return. "Customs Guides for Travellers" is available from local Customs Offices or New Zealand consulates abroad.

Currency and Exchange

In both the United States and Canada, the main unit of currency is the **dollar** ($). Both dollars divide into 100 **cents** (¢). Paper money ("bills") comes primarily in six denominations, all of which are the same size and shape: $1, $5, $10, $20, $50, and $100. Occasionally you will encounter a $2 bill, more frequently in Canada than in the U.S. Coins vary in size and color, and each coin is worth a dollar or less. Pennies are worth 1¢ ($.01) and are made of copper. All other coins are silver: nickles, worth 5¢; dimes (smaller than pennies, strangely enough), worth 10¢; and quarters, 25¢. Half-dollar and dollar coins (known as silver dollars) exist but are rare.

In the United States, it is virtually impossible to pay for anything in foreign currency, and in some parts of the country you may even have trouble exchanging your currency for U.S. dollars. To avoid hassles, buy traveler's checks, and if you buy them in another currency, choose a widely known check. Some banks abroad offer their own traveler's checks, which may be difficult to cash here—see Money above for widely recognized traveler's checks. In addition, consider bringing along a credit card affiliated with an American company, such as **Interbank** (affiliated with MasterCard), **Barclay Card** (affiliated with Visa), and that old standby, **American Express**. These come in handy when paying for flights and car rentals, and sometimes can be used to pay for accommodations and food (although not at many places listed in *Let's Go*).

U.S. dollars are easier to use in Canada than vice versa, as the currency is generally stronger than its Canadian counterpart; see Money in the Planning section, above, for more information on currency exchange between the U.S. and Canada.

In both the U.S. and Canada, public telephones and most laundromats take coins and not tokens, and drivers of local buses generally do not give change for dollar bills. Keep this in mind and make sure to carry coins with you.

See Money above for more information.

Sending Money

Sending money is a complicated and expensive process—avoid it if at all possible. Advance planning can reduce both the cost and problems inherent in transferring money overseas. If you think you'll need money sent to you while you are in the U.S., visit your bank for a list of its corresponding banks here. Before you leave, you can also arrange for your bank to send money from your account to specific correspondent banks on specific dates.

If you're pressed for money and need it quickly, **cable transfer** is the fastest way to send money. Usually it takes 48 hours for your money to reach you in a major city and slightly longer if you are in an out-of-the-way location. You pay cabling costs plus whatever commission your home bank charges. If you do not have an account at the receiving bank, you may have to wait a little longer to receive your money. Less expensive than cabling, but slower, is the **bank draft**, or international money order. You pay a commission (around US$20) on the draft, plus the cost of sending it airmail (preferably registered mail). Through **American Express** (800-543-4080), you can be cabled up to $10,000 from France or Great Britain and receive the money within one to three days. Neither you nor the person who sends you the money needs to be an AmEx cardholder. The fee for this service is US$35 for a $500 money gram, and increases gradually for larger amour.ts.

Finally, if you are stranded in the U.S. with no money and no other recourse, your consulate can wire home for you and deduct the cost from the money you receive. Consulates are often less than gracious about performing this service, however, so turn to them only in desperation.

Communication

Mail

The **United States Post Office** is a government-run organization: draw your own conclusions. Individual offices are usually open Monday to Friday from 8am to 5pm and sometimes Saturday until noon. All post offices are closed on national holidays (see When to Go above for a list). Postcards mailed within the U.S. or to Mexico cost 15¢, letters 25¢. Postcards to Canada cost 22¢, letters 30¢. Postcards mailed overseas cost 36¢, letters 45¢. Aerograms are available at the post office for 36¢—these can be sent all over the world. Mail within the U.S. takes between a day and a week (less time to closer destinations and only a day or two within the same city); airmail to northern Europe, a week to 10 days; to southern Europe, North Africa, and the Middle East, two to three weeks; to South America, a week to 10 days. Service to other destinations may take even longer. Large city post offices offer **International Express Mail** service, in case you need to mail something to a major city overseas in less than 72 hours (and don't mind paying the steep rates).

The Canadian postal system is also publically operated. **Canada Post** requires a 39¢ Canadian postage stamp for all domestic first-class. Letters or postcards sent to the U.S. cost 44¢; items mailed to Europe weighing less than 20g cost 76¢.

Both the U.S. and Canada are divided into postal zones. Each American postal zone has a five-digit ZIP code, while Canadian postal codes are composed of six letters and numbers (e.g. A1B 2C3). Some American businesses and governmental offices have nine-digit codes, the last four numerals set off by a dash (e.g. 02138-0987).

The normal form of address in both the United States and Canada is as follows:

Miss Tess d'Uberville	(name)
D'Uberville Domestic Consultants, P.S.	(name of organization, optional)
1800 Languishing Lane, #2	(address)
Winslow, WA 98110	(city, state or province abbreviation, ZIP if U.S.)
USA	(country, if mailed from different country)
X0X 0X0	(postal code, if Canada)

When ordering books and materials from the U.S. and Canada, always include an **International Reply Coupon (IRC)** with your request. IRCs should be available from your home post office. Your coupon must have adequate postage to cover the cost of delivery.

See Keeping in Touch above for information about how others can write to you while you travel.

Telephone

Telephone numbers in the U.S. and Canada consist of a three-digit area code and a seven-digit number (divided into a group of 3 and a group of 4), written as 617-495-9659 or (617) 495-9659. Local calls require only the last seven digits. Within an area code, dial "1" before the seven-digit number to make a **non-local call**. To make a **long-distance call,** dial "1", then the area code, then the number. For example, to call Let's Go in Cambridge, MA from another state or from another area code within the state, you would dial 1-617-495-9659. To reach a telephone operator for assistance, you need only dial "0".

Pay phones are plentiful on street corners and in public areas such as restaurants, train stations, airports, and movie theaters. Most of them explain how to make both local and long-distance calls. To make a local call, deposit coins in the slot before dialing. Local calls cost 10-30¢, depending on the town, and in some places you will need additional coins if you speak longer than 3 minutes. If there is no answer or if you get a busy signal (a series of unpleasant beeps), your money will be returned when you hang up the receiver. Unlike pop machines, pay phones do not return excess change, so don't deposit more than you have to.

You can make a long-distance call to anywhere on the continent in any number of ways. The basic call is **station-to-station.** From a private phone, dial "1" plus the area code plus the number. From a pay phone, you usually do the same, and an operator will let you know how many coins to deposit and when. Otherwise, you can call **collect,** which means that the recipient of your call will be charged. Dial "0" plus the area code and number (you needn't deposit any coins), and tell the operator that you wish to make a collect call. The operator will ask for your name, and will ask whoever answers the phone if they will accept the call and the charges. Through the operator you can also make a **person-to-person** call—just specify to the operator the name of the person or people you wish to speak with, and if they are not home your call will be cancelled. Person-to-person calls can either be charged to you or made collect; either way, they cost more than station-to-station calls. Within North America, long-distance calls are discounted 35% between 5 and 11pm Sunday through Friday. This discount increases to 50% between 11pm and 8am during the week and from 11pm on Friday through 5pm Sunday.

International calls can be made from any phone. To call directly either from a private phone or with coins from a pay phone, dial 011, the country code, then the city code. From some phones you will need to dial "0" and give the number to the operator. To find out the cheapest time to call overseas, call the operator.

To find out the number of a person or a business, call **directory assistance.** Directory assistance is a free call from any pay phone, although sometimes you will have to deposit a coin, which will be returned to you at the end of your call. To reach local directory assistance anywhere, dial 411; within your area code but farther away, 1-555-1212; outside your area code, 1-area code-555-1212. To find out a toll-free number, call 1-800-555-1212.

Most of the information you will need in order to use the telephones, along with the numbers of just about every home and business in town, can be found in any local phone book. The **White Pages** gives private listings, while the **Yellow Pages** lists businesses by category. In larger cities, the White Pages and the Yellow Pages will be separate books, while in smaller towns, the two will be bound together in one book. Some pay phones have phone books nearby; otherwise, don't be afraid to call directory assistance or the operator, or to ask a local merchant if you can look at his phone book.

Telegrams

If a telephone call is impossible, cabling may be the only way to contact someone overseas quickly. A short message will usually reach its destination by the next day. **Western Union** (800-325-6000) charges about 25¢ per word, including name and address, for overseas telegrams. Call for general information and to check rates to specific countries.

Measurements

In the United States, the quaint British system of weights and measures lingers on, while Canada measures by the metric system. Here is a list of American units, their abbreviations, and their metric equivalents:

1 inch (in.) = 2.5 centimeters
1 foot (ft.; pl. "feet") = 0.3 meter
1 yard (yd.) = 0.9 meter
1 mile (mi.) = 1.6 kilometers
1 ounce (oz.) = 28 grams
1 pound (lb.) = 0.45 kilogram
1 quart (qt.), liquid = 0.9 liter

There are 12 inches in 1 foot, 3 feet in 1 yard, and 5280 feet in 1 mile. There are 16 ounces in 1 pound, 8 oz. (liquid) in 1 cup, 2 cups in 1 pint, 2 pints in 1 quart, and 4 quarts in 1 gallon.

To measure temperature, the U.S. resorts to the **Fahrenheit** (FARE-en-hite) scale, while Canada uses the **Celsius** scale. Those who are mathematically inclined can convert between them according to the following formulae: $°C = 5(°F - 32)/9$, $°F = 32 + 9°C/5$. Others should just remember that 32°F is the freezing point of water, 212°F its boiling point, and 98.6°F the normal human body temperature. "Room temperature" typically hovers around 68°F.

Electrical outlets throughout North American provide current at 117 volts, 60 cycles (Hertz). Appliances designed for a foreign electrical system will not operate without a converter or other adapter. Keep this in mind if you intend to use an electric razor, contact lens disinfectant system, hair dryer, or other small appliance. A department, hardware, or electrical supply store can equip you for US$18-30.

Time

The U.S. system of telling time is also slightly different from the European. America lives according to two 12-hour clocks, instead of one 24-hour clock. Hours between noon and midnight are *post meridiem* or **pm** (for example, 2pm); hours between midnight and noon are *ante meridiem* or **am.** Noon is 12pm and midnight is 12am; to avoid confusion, *Let's Go* says simply "noon" or "midnight."

The North American continent is divided into six **time zones.** Alberta is in the **Mountain time zone, while most of Oregon, Washington, British Columbia, and the Yukon are in the Pacific** time zone (one hour behind Mountain, two behind Central, and three behind Eastern). Alaska keeps **Alaska** time (one hour behind Pacific), except for some of the Aleutian Island towns, which go by **Aleutian-Hawaii** time, one hour behind Alaska time. Shortly after midnight the first Sunday in April, clocks are switched one hour forward to **daylight savings time**; on the last Sunday in October, again shortly after midnight, clocks are moved back one hour to **standard time.** When times are given with time-zone abbreviations, take this into account (e.g. PDT—Pacific Daylight Time, MST—Mountain Standard Time).

Getting There

Transportation to the Pacific Northwest from other parts of the world will be the major expense of your trip. The extent of the cost can be contained somewhat by thorough research and early planning. The simplest and surest way to choose from among the options is to find a travel agent who keeps abreast of the chaos in airfares and whom you can trust to save you money. In addition, check the travel section of any major newspaper for bargain fares, and consult CIEE or your national student travel organization—they sometimes have special deals that regular travel agents can't offer. For information on flying within the United States, see By Air above.

From Mexico

Finding bargains on travel in the States may not be easy from south of the border. Residents of North America are rarely eligible for the discounts that U.S. airlines, bus, and train companies offer visitors from overseas (see Getting Around: Discounts below). Most buses and trains from Mexico travel no farther than the U.S. border, but it is possible to arrange connections at San Diego, CA, Nogales, AZ, and El Paso, Eagle Pass, Laredo, or Brownsville, TX. **Amtrak, Greyhound** and their subsidiaries serve the towns along the U.S.-Mexico border. From Mexico there are numerous flights on American and Mexican carriers to New York, Houston, Dallas, and Los Angeles. Mexican residents who live more than 100 miles from the border may be eligible for "Visit USA" discount flight passes on some carriers; for information, see From Europe, below. Otherwise, because flying in the U.S. is expensive, it may be cheaper to fly on a Mexican airline to one of the border towns, and then to travel by train or bus from there. For more information, see Documents and Formalities and Getting Around above.

From Europe

Travelers from Europe will experience the least competition for inexpensive seats during the off-season. This need not mean the dead of winter. Peak season rates are generally set on either May 15 or June 1 and run until about September 15. You can take advantage of cheap off-season flights within Europe to reach an advantageous port of departure for North America. (London is an important connecting point for budget flights to the U.S.) Once in the States, you can catch a coast-to-coast flight to make your way out west; see By Air above for details.

Charter flights can save you a lot of money. You can book charters up to the last minute—some will not even sell tickets more than 30 days in advance. Many flights fill up well before their departure date, however. You must choose your departure and return dates when you book, and you will lose all or most of your money if you cancel your ticket. (Travel agents will cover your losses only in case of sudden illness, death, or natural disaster.) Charter companies themselves reserve the right to change the dates of your flight or even cancel the flight a mere 48 hours in advance. Delays are not uncommon. To be safe, get your ticket as early as possible, and arrive at the airport several hours before departure time. When making plans, try to investigate each charter company's reputation.

If you decide to fly with a scheduled airline, you'll be purchasing greater reliability, security, and flexibility. Major airlines do offer reduced-fare options. **APEX (Advanced Purchase Excursion Fare)** is one of the more sensible ways to go. It provides you with confirmed reservations, and you can make connections through different cities and travel on different airlines. Drawbacks include restrictions on the length of your stay (from 7-14 days minimum to 60-90 days maximum) and the requirement that you make reservations two weeks in advance (hence the name). APEX fares are generally not refundable, nor may you change your flight. You might also investigate unusual airlines that undercut the major carriers on regularly scheduled flights to an extremely limited number of cities. **Virgin Atlantic** and **Icelandair** have particularly low fares. Competition for seats on these small carriers is usually fierce, so book early.

Student discounts will appear with a magical ease if you look around for them. Many major carriers will sell off unbought APEX seats at a further discount to youth under age 24, beginning 72 hours before the flight. These fares allow an open return date, but restrict your stay to a maximum of two weeks—the last part of which you will have to spend trying to secure your ticket back. Such deals are never really a predictable way to travel, and are especially risky in high season. They can, however, save you a considerable amount of money if your schedule is flexible enough for you to take advantage of them.

From Asia, Australia, and New Zealand

Whereas European travelers may choose from a variety of regular reduced fares, their counterparts in Asia and Australia must rely on APEX. While fares may seem astronomical ($1500 one way from Australia to California is not unusual), the West Coast remains one of the world's more accessible areas for Asian and Australian travelers.

From Japan, U.S. airlines such as **Northwest** and **United Airlines** offer cheaper flights than Japan Airlines. **Qantas, Air New Zealand, United, Continental,** and **UTA French Airlines** fly between Australia or New Zealand and the United States. Prices are roughly equivalent among the six (American carriers tend to be a bit less), but the cities they serve differ. Super Saver fares from Australia have extremely tough restrictions. If you are uncertain about your plans, pay extra for a Super Saver that has only a 50% penalty for cancellation.

Getting Around: Discounts

Airlines and bus and train companies offer special discounts to foreign visitors traveling within the U.S. Other discounts (for children, families, senior citizens, and disabled travelers) are noted in Getting There and Getting Around above. International travelers should realize that given the long distances between points within the United States and Canada, North Americans rely on buses and trains for travel much less than everyone else in the world (a cross-country trip will take three or four days). Bus and train stations may seem a little unusual at first, and bus and train riders relatively uncommunicative. Expect, then, to rely on others less than you would at home.

Greyhound offers an **International Ameripass** for unlimited bus travel to foreign students and to faculty members and their families. Passes are valid in the U.S. only, not in Canada, and sold primarily overseas, although they can be purchased in New York, Los Angeles, San Francisco, or Miami for a slightly higher price. Prices are $125 for seven days ($135 if purchased in U.S.), $199 ($214 in the U.S.) for 15 days, and $279 ($299 in the U.S.) for 30 days. To obtain a pass, you need a valid passport and proof of your student or faculty status. Call Greyhound (800-237-8211) or stop in at one of Greyhound's overseas offices to inquire about special deals and tour programs for international travelers or to request the *Visit USA Vacation Guide,* which details services for foreign travelers in the U.S.

Amtrak's **USA Rail Pass,** similar to the Eurailpass, entitles foreign visitors to unlimited travel anywhere in the U.S. A 45-day pass costs $295. If you plan to travel by train only in the Northwest, purchase a Regional Rail Pass for the Far West ($179). All USA Rail Passes are 50% off for children ages 2-11. With a valid passport, you can purchase the pass at home or in New York, Boston, Miami, Los Angeles, or San Francisco. Check with a travel agent or Amtrak representative in Europe, or write to Amtrak International Sales, 400 N. Capital St. NW, Washington, DC 20001. If you're already in the U.S., call Amtrak for information (800-872-7245). Be smart about buying passes—they are not a bargain unless you plan to travel almost every day, and remember that not all towns in the Pacific Northwest are accessible by train.

Many major airlines offer special **"Visit USA"** passes and fares to foreign travelers. Purchase these tickets in your own country; one price pays for a certain number of "flight coupons," each good for one flight segment on a particular airline's domestic system within a certain time period. Often, the passes must be purchased when you buy a ticket to or from the States. Many different airlines offer these passes, but they come with innumerable restrictions and guidelines. Prices therefore vary a great deal. Consult a travel agent before you purchase any of these coupons to see whether you're really getting the best deal. Depending on the airline, the passes may be valid from 30 to 90 days. United Airlines offers special fares for travelers departing from many different regions of the world, including Asia, Europe, and Australia. When you purchase a pass, keep in mind the size of the airline. Eastern, United, American, and Northwest fly over the entire continent, while other airlines offer more limited or regional service. As always, a travel agent can help you work out the details.

Life in the Northwest

History

Most visitors to the Pacific Northwest, Western Canada, and Alaska expect to touch the Great Outdoors during their travels. Few seeking wilderness are disappointed. The wealth, beauty, and identity of the whole region well up in its natural resources. A brief tour through the history of the Northwest may end up in a Boeing assembly-line in Seattle, WA or in line for tea at the Empress Hotel in Victoria, BC, but it has to begin with the strictly physical outlines of the continent.

Whatever political chickenwire has been strung across the region in the last couple of centuries, the prehistorical customs of the Northwest recognized no such boundaries. About 20,000 years ago, at the end of the last Ice Age, adventurous Asian tribes trickled over the melting bridge to North America. Over the next 10,000 years, they stretched, looked around, and settled into their new continental home to create the Native American cultures from the northern California coast to the Alaskan tundra. These peoples built up two basic patterns along the geological divisions of the region, the Coastal and Plateau groups.

Along the coast, the ocean and the forests amply provided both the necessitities and luxuries of life. While each tribal group maintained its own lifestyle and allegiance, they shared salmon fishing and marine hunting, and the carpentry and wood-working that took its showiest form in the elaborately symbolic totem poles. These commemorated events with the animal signs of hereditary lineages through which the clans organized authority and social interaction. Property ownership underlay the ceremony of the potlatch ("gift" or "give"), a festival of passage in which the host handed down names and privileges along with huge amounts of wealth to the guests, proving power by a glorious excess of blankets and copper sheets (and, as demand has changed, even electric washers and dryers). The main communication between tribes was the trading language of the Chinook, who served as the prosperous middle men of the Northwest. After the advent of the European fur trade, this *lingua franca* incorporated about 300 Indian, French, English, and sign words, from "hiack" for "hurry up" to "Boston" for "American."

On the Plateau between the Cascades and Rockies, the tribes also hunted and gathered, but lived more on the move than their materialistic coastal neighbors. After about 1730, it was life on the hoof: horses made their way up the plains in advance of the white cavalry, and encouraged even wider nomadism. The inland tribes had a broadly level social system as well, with consensual government.

If the Native Americans have the main claim on the history of the Northwest through length of tenure, the Europeans have effected more change in a remarkably short period of time. Explorers brushed along the West Coast with the first waves of expansion, as the Elizabethan sea dog Sir Francis Drake harried the Spanish in the Pacific. Exploration was a dicey business, of course, and seldom was a voyage an unqualified success. The first mariners who navigated the Northwest Coast left little but names, and even those could be misleading—like the Spanish-employed captain who in 1592 ensured that the Europeans would be back by claiming to have located the "Northwest Passage" from Europe to Asia. The waterway between the U.S. and Canada now known as the Straits of Juan de Fuca did not cross the continent after all; Juan de Fuca's real name was Apostolos Valerianos. Vitrus Bering, sailing for Peter the Great of Russia in 1733, left both his name and his life in the straits between Asia and America. The real beginning of the white man's economy in the Northwest, though, followed Cook's voyage (still looking for the Northwest passage) in 1776. Shortly after the sophisticated Bostonian colonists threw their costumed tea-party in(to) the Boston Harbor, Cook's men took a few ragged otter pelts from Nootka Sound to Canton, where the furs fetched a small fortune.

The first gold rush in the Northwest was the surge of interest in "soft gold," and the next series of mapmakers finally began to pay more attention to the land than the water as they looked into the best routes to the "strip mines." The fur trade became the fur empire as it tied into the commercial bloodlines of the east though the Hudson Bay Company. Through fur, of course, the region also tied into the politics of empire: the Hudson Bay Co. was the outpost of Brittania. The first American expedition into the region under Lewis and Clark organized under President Jefferson's ambitions to divert some of the Northwestern pelts south and east, and they were followed in 1808 by Jacob Astor, who set up Fort Astoria on the Columbia. Politics proved stronger than profit shortly afterward: scared out of their skins, the Fort Astorians evacuated ingloriously at the start of the War of 1812.

The land of the Northwest had more to offer the swelling colony of Canada and the United States to the south. There were arable acres and convertable Native Americans. The transition from a primarily Indian to a primarily white population was partly a result of engineering, and partly a malevolent trick of nature: the strangers brought with them unfamiliar diseases, including small pox and influenza, which from the 1780s on decimated many of the tribal groups. Missionary fever followed in the 1830s; a wave of whites responded in horror to the Chinook custom of flattening babies' foreheads, and crusaders like the Whitmans rushed west to save souls and profiles. And the land itself called. Over the Oregon trail came settlers from the Midwest, bringing their ploughs and their political allegiance to the United States. Russia receded to above the 54th parallel; Polk won the 1844 presidential election with the slogan "54°40 or Fight," but did neither, splitting the Northwest with the English at the 49th parallel in 1846 instead. Dwindling and disputed territory became reservations for the Native American nations.

Oregon and Washington divided, Washington reluctantly giving up the name "Columbia" after the river which ran closer to western than congressional hearts. Oregon claimed statehood in 1859, and the territory to the north joined it 30 years later. In 1856 the land had once again offered riches for the grabbing, and this time miners swarmed up the coast to claim the real, metal kind of gold. Where revenue went, government followed: the Governor of Vancouver Island enlarged his jurisdiction to establish a real provincial administration over the mainland in Canada. The arrangement was official in 1866, and though Washington was "Washington," the coastal colony became *British* Columbia—"the citizens of the United States call their country also Columbia, at least in poetry," Victoria explained.

ǂ President Johnson, with unusual and accidental foresight, allowed his Secretary of State to buy Alaska from the Russians at about 2¢ an acre in 1867; more gold strikes in the 1880s and 90s made "Seward's Folly" look wise (especially in comparison to the behavior of the average prospector). Since the Yukon shared Alaska's mineral wealth, it clearly needed a guiding hand as well, and became a Canadian territory in 1898. Alberta, with its fertile agricultural plains, was created a province in 1905. Since then, of course, the golden wheat has shared the central economic glory with "black gold," the crude oil which currently reigns supreme among the valuable resources in the area.

And, of course, the land continued to fill with new people. The population of the Northwest boomed when the railroads finally roared to the coast (the race to build cross-continental tracks in the U.S. and Canada photo-finished in 1883). A journey of three to five months was suddenly a jaunt of five or six days, and the pace of life to and in the West never slowed down again. The composition of the populations was enlivened, too: the ties bound the coasts only with Chinese, Irish, and Eastern European immigrants helping to make tracks across the nation.

By the beginning of the twentieth century, Northwest history loses its distinct outlines and becomes national history. Not that its character has been swamped by entering the more mainstream: the 1930s and 40s, for example, saw a fierce attachment to populist politics in the U.S., and B.C.'s Social Credit Party, advocating a parity of producing and purchasing power for all, shook up Canadian politics in the same period. In 1989, the House of Representatives choose Tom Foley of Spokane as Speaker. His home district, of course, knows the nation's capital as "the other Washington;" keeping priorities and preferences straight, though, their state song is "Roll On, Columbia."

Arts

Costumed in fantastical cedar masks, the Kwakiutl tribe on the B.C. coast regularly enacted world-renewal ceremonies which included theatrical effects like tunnels, trapdoors, ventriloquism, and bloody sleight-of-hand beheadings. The performing arts have been dazzling audiences in the Northwest ever since. Those who prefer early theater (by European standards) won't want to miss the Oregon Shakespeare Festival in Ashland, where thousands spend a day or a week every summer enjoying the excellent in- and outdoor performances. Drama is also highly acclaimed at the Contemporary Theater of Lewis and Clark College in Portland; any time of year, Seattle offers a twinkling assortment of stage lights in its many fine theaters for new dramas. Seattle Opera puts on a show for the discriminating listener as well, with a classical and modern productions and a world-wide reputation for its Wagner. Chamber music afficianados can travel up to Sitka, Alaska for the Summer Music Festival, or down to the June and July Bach Festival in Eugene, OR, where Helmut Rilling waves his exquisite Baroque baton. If you're in the mood, you can stay south until August for the Mt. Hood Jazz Festival in Gresham, OR—the event has played host to such greats as Wynston Marsalis and Ella Fitzgerald. Or wander up to check out what's playing in Alberta's two Jubilee Auditoriums, stopping, of course, at Bumbershoot, Seattle's blow-out, four-day rain-or-shine festival of folk, street, classical, and rock music (over Memorial Day weekend).

You'll also want to take a look at the museums and exhibits while you're in the area. Some of the best art of the Northwest is still the Native American artifacts, from masks to totem poles. Two of the best places to see them are the Provincial Museum in Victoria, B.C. and the Thomas Burke Museum at the University of Washington in Seattle; the Portland Art Museum also houses an impressive fine collection. More modern Northwest residents, too, take pride in their own aesthetic contributions. Painter Emily Carr, from BC, blended Native elements with her work to create original Northwest images; in the 50s, the Northwest School comprising such abstract artists as Mark Tobey and Kenneth Callahan had considerable prominence. Visitors find imported art treasures in the Abanté Fine Arts Gallery in Portland, which houses works by French impressionist masters, or in the Seattle Art Museum, which displays a permanent Asian collection.

This is all just a survey—let *Let's Go* guide you to the arts, theater, and music in the Sights and Entertainment sections throughout the book.

Literature and Film

The Northwest has produced no major literary school of its own, but many writers who have lived or wandered there testify to the liberating effect of the frontier and the mountains. Travelers such as John Muir and John McPhee have celebrated the natural wonders of the region and written detailed descriptions of travelers' struggles to stay alive. Stories and novels by Raymond Carver and Alice Munro provide a glimpse of the people and society of the region. Other authors, such as Ursula K. Leguin and Jean M. Auel, have simply drawn from the surroundings as they write about other matters completely. Poet Theodore Roethke taught at the University of Washington in Seattle, bequeathing his lyric sensibility to a generation of Northwestern poets. Bernard Malamud taught for many years at Oregon State University as he wrote several of his best-known works.

What follows is a brief and idiosyncratic list of books by regional authors and about the region, from travel diaries to children's works. Check your local bookstore or library for other suggestions.

Cathedral by Raymond Carver

I Heard the Owl Call My Name by Margaret Craven

Instructions to the Double by Tess Gallager

Julie of the Wolves by Jean Craighead George

Sometimes a Great Notion by Ken Kesey

The Lathe of Heaven by Ursula K. Le Guin

Journals of Lewis and Clark by Merriwether Lewis and William Clark

Alaska by James Michener

Travels in Alaska by John Muir

Stories of Flo and Rose by Alice Munro

The Spell of the Yukon and Other Poems by Robert Service

Zen and the Art of Motorcycle Maintenance by Robert Pirsig

Traveling Through the Dark by William Stafford

Paul Bunyan by James Stevens

Poet in the Desert by Charles Erskine Scott Woods

In addition, the Northwest is a popular setting for movies and films. To get a visual sampling of the area before you go, take a look at one or two of the following, most widely available to be rented: *An Officer and a Gentleman; Immediate Family; Ice Station Zebra; Orca; Never Cry Wolf; Shoot to Kill.* And, of course, flip on the reruns of *Twin Peaks.*

Climate

Think of Alaska, and you may imagine igloos; think of Seattle, and chances are you'll be seeing umbrellas. The Pacific Northwest, Western Canada, and Alaska are considerably north of the Tropic of Cancer, but that doesn't mean they are always frozen, slushy, or even soggy. The climate you'll find in the Northwest depends hugely on what seaon and what part of the region you visit.

In Alaska the weather varies from the coast inland. In general, though, summer and early fall (i.e. June-Sept.) are the warmest and sunniest times of year. Wet, windy, and cold days even during the summer should be no real surprise, though. In Anchorage, the average temperature is around 20°F in January and 60°F in July. In Alaska's interior, the temperatures range from the 90s in the summers to the -70s in the wintertime. Remember also that as you progress farther north, summer days and winter nights become longer. The sun never sets over Barrow, Alaska—at least in summer. In the winter, it never rises. Elsewhere, in Alaska and the Yukon, summer days may last from 6am to 2am.

In Alberta, the north and south of the province differ in temperature, although the entire area tends to be dry and cool. In January, the average temperature is around 15°F in the south, closer to −20°F in the north; in the summer, both regions warm to around 70°F.

In British Columbia, Washington, and Oregon, the key weather-making factor is the mountains. The rule of thumb is that west of the mountains it *does* rain quite a bit, while to the east it is relatively dry. On the B.C. coast, the average temperature is about 35°F in January and a cool 65°F in the summer. Inland, winter temperatures hover around 0°F, while summer temperatures rise near 70°F. Temperatures in Washington range from an average of 35°F in January to 70°F in July—the west slightly colder, the east slightly warmer in the summer, and the other way around in the winter. Oregon is, on average, a little warmer than in Washington.

A Few Final Words

Those traveling to the Northwest from other parts of the U.S. or Canada will find it, by turns, charming, awe-inspiring, relaxing, and possibly even familiar. Visitors may, however, want to keep a handful of miscellaneous points in mind. Drivers do not like to honk very much. In general, lines form themselves and tend to procede just a little more strictly, and slowly, than in some other regions. Westerners call sweet, fizzy beverages "pop," long Italian sandwiches "subs," and the legumes that look and taste like chickpeas are "garbanzo beans." You'd be wrong to think that folks are friendly in or-a-GON, but residents of the Beaver State will be quick to welcome you to OR-i-gun.

OREGON

For decades, Oregon zealously protected its rocky shores and inland forests from interloping tourists and developers. The state today has adopted a more welcoming attitude toward the visitor. "Interpretive Centers" carry out their exegetical tasks almost everywhere, and excellent youth hostels operate in Ashland, Bandon, and Eugene. Scrambling for international renown, Oregon's Chambers of Commerce claim to guard the world's smallest park, tiniest navigable bay, and shortest river.

In recent years, Oregon's dusky forests have sparked considerable controversy. Environmentalists successfully halted logging in one-third of the state's timberland, arguing it would endanger, among other species, the rare spotted owl. At the same time, rising exports of unmilled logs deprived local mills of business. To protest their predicament, angry timber workers drove enormous trucks through the downtown streets of Portland. Though an uneasy truce was called, the "logging crisis" resumed in full fury after the June 1990 federal decision to protect the owl over the industry. Civil war may yet break out.

The intrepid duo of Lewis and Clark, Oregon's first *Let's Go* researchers, slipped quietly down the Columbia River when their transcontinental trek brought them to the area; later, waves of settlers thronged the Oregon Trail. Today, most travelers devolve to the Pacific, gaping at waves and cliffs rivaling California's Big Sur. Handsome as the coastal route is, you must venture inland to see some of Oregon's greatest attractions—the prehistoric fossils at John Day National Monument, the volcanic cinder-cones near Crater Lake, and the world-renowned Shakespeare festival in Ashland. To escape the anomie of the countryside, head for Portland, an easygoing metropolis known for its public art, fertile elephants, and bemused tolerance of off-beat lifestyles.

Practical Information

Postal Abbreviation: OR.

Capital: Salem.

Time Zone: Mostly Pacific (1 hr. behind Mountain, 2 behind Central, 3 behind Eastern). A small southeastern section is Mountain (1 hr. behind Central, 2 behind Eastern).

Drinking Age: 21.

Traffic Laws: Seatbelts required.

Visitor Information: State Tourist Office, 595 Cottage St. NE, Salem 97310 (800-547-7842). **Oregon State Parks,** 525 Trade St. SE, Salem 97310 (378-6305). **Department of Fish and Wildlife,** 506 SW Mill St., Portland 97208 (229-5403). **Oregon State Marine Board,** 3000 Market St. NE, #505, Salem 97310 (378-8587). **Statewide Road Conditions,** 976-7277.

Oregon Council American Youth Hostels: 99 W. 10th, #205, Eugene 97402 (683-3685).

Emergency: 911.

Area Code: 503.

Impractical Information

Nickname: Beaver State.

Motto: The Union.

State Song: Oregon, My Oregon.

State Flower: Oregon Grape.

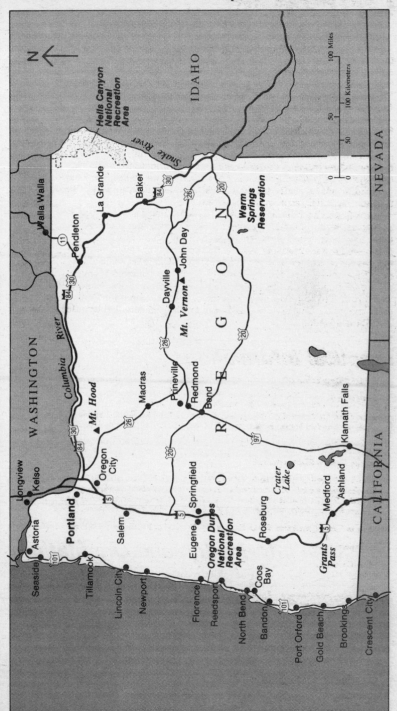

State Animal: Beaver.

State Fish: Chinook Salmon.

State Sports Team: Portland Trailblazers (Go Blazers!).

Portland

On the afternoon of May 18, 1980, Washington's Mt. St. Helens erupted violently in a jealous attempt to smother under a layer of volcanic ash the beauty of her southern neighbor, Portland. Fortunately for the largest city in Oregon, the frequent spring showers quickly restored the area's natural endowments to their pristine state.

Portlanders take full advantage of these endowments; drawn to a city which eschews urban existence, they are consummate hikers, bikers, runners, and grape-nuts kind of folk. Portland harbors the largest and smallest parks enclosed any United States city, as well as one of the two parks in the world located on a dormant volcano. The mighty Columbia River rolls majestically onward north of the city, while the Willamette River cuts through the city's heart, providing downtown denizens with a range of recreational possibilities. Five minutes west of this, dense forests hide miles and miles of well-maintained hiking trails winding through gentle hills.

Attractions in the immediate environs prove just as fantastic: on any *July* day you can schuss down the snow-covered slopes of Mt. Hood in the morning; watch the sun drop into the Pacific Ocean from the huge expanses of unpopulated sand; and then return to town in time to catch the outdoor jazz concerts which resonate from the midst of the municipal zoo (internationally renowned for its elephant-breeding success).

In the past five years, real-estate barons have discovered the last underdeveloped city on the west coast, summoning new superstructures from the ground while reincarnating old crumbling shells into art deco office spaces. Funded by a 1% tax on this new construction, Portland has cultured a prominent arts scene. The newly opened Center for the Performing Arts woos actors away from the world-renowned Shakespeare festival in Ashland. But in what some locals consider to be a more important offshoot of the recent growth, a flock of micro-breweries now pumps out vat after vat of the nations best ale.

Portland is a casual and idiosyncratic city—its name was decided upon by the toss of a coin (one more half-flip and Portland would have been called Boston, Oregon). Several years ago, a local tavern owner named "Bud" Clark posed for a poster entitled "Expose Yourself to Art," depicting a man in a trenchcoat flashing a public sculpture. Shortly thereafter, he was elected mayor.

Practical Information and Orientation

Visitor Information: Portland/Oregon Visitors Association, 26 SW Salmon St. (275-9750), at Front St. Distributes information. The free *Portland Book* contains maps, general information, and historical trivia. Open Mon.-Fri. 8:30am-5pm, Sat. 9am-3pm. Detailed city road maps are free at **Hertz,** 1009 SW 6th (249-5727), at Salmon.

Amtrak: 800 NW 6th Ave. (800-872-7245), at Hoyt St. To Seattle (3 per day, $27) and Eugene (1 per day, $23). Open daily 7:30am-9:45pm.

Greyhound-Trailways: 550 NW 6th Ave. (243-2323). Buses almost hourly to Seattle ($20-24 one way, 243-2313 for schedule) and to Eugene ($14.25 one way, 222-3361 for schedule). Ticket window open 5:30am-12:30am.

Green Tortoise: 205 S.E. Grand Ave. (225-0310), at Ash St. To Seattle (Tues. and Sat. at 4pm, $15) and San Francisco (Sun. and Thurs. at noon, $49).

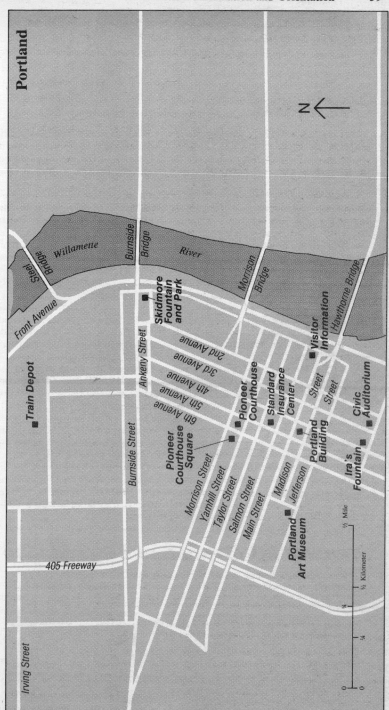

Portland

Willamette
River
Steel Bridge
Burnside Bridge
Morrison Bridge
Hawthorne Bridge

Front Avenue

N

Skidmore Fountain and Park

Ankeny Street

2nd Avenue
3rd Avenue
4th Avenue
5th Avenue
6th Avenue

Visitor Information

Street
Street

Train Depot

Burnside Street

Pioneer Courthouse

Standard Insurance Center

Civic Auditorium

Pioneer Courthouse Square

Portland Building

Ira's Fountain

Morrison Street
Yamhill Street
Taylor Street
Salmon Street
Main Street
Madison
Jefferson

Portland Art Museum

405 Freeway

Irving Street

½ Mile
½ Kilometer
¼
¼
0
0

City Buses: Tri-Met, Customer Service Center, #1 Pioneer Courthouse Sq., 701 SW 6th Ave. (233-3511). Open Mon.-Fri. 9am-5pm. Service generally 7am-midnight, reduced Sat.-Sun. 24-hr. recorded information numbers ("Call-A-Bus") for each bus: how to use the Call-A-Bus system (231-3199); fare information (231-3198); updates, changes, and weather-related problems (231-3197); special needs transportation (238-4952, Mon.-Fri. 8:30am-4:30pm); TDD information (238-5811); lost and found (238-4855, Mon.-Fri. 10am-5pm); bicycle commuter service (233-0564). Fare 85¢-$1.15 (see Getting Around). **MAX** is Tri-Met's "light rail," the above-ground equivalent of a subway. It only serves one line (from downtown east to the city of Gresham, near Mt. Hood) but uses the same fare system as the buses. Buses and MAX are free within *Fareless Square*, a 300-square-block region downtown bounded by the Willamette River, NW Hoyt, and the I-405 freeway.

Taxi: Broadway Cab (227-1234), **New Rose City Cab Co.** (282-7707). Both charge $1.30 for the first mi. plus $1.40 per additional mi. To airport from downtown Portland is $18-20.

Car Rental: Rent-A-Wreck, 2838 NE Sandy (231-1640). $15 per day with 50 free mi., 15¢ per additional mi. Must be 25 or older. **Thrifty Car Rental,** 632 SW Pine (227-6587). $34 per day, unlimited mileage. Must be 21 with credit card.

Metropolitan Arts Commission: 1120 SW 5th St., #1023 (796-5111).

Local Events Hotline: 233-3333.

Park Bureau/Public Recreation: 1120 SW 5th St. (796-5193 or 796-5100).

Laundromat: Springtime Cleaners and Laundry, 2942 SE Hawthorne Blvd. (235-5080), across from the hostel. Open daily 8am-10pm.

Ski Conditions: Timberline (222-2211); **Ski Bowl** (222-2695); **Mt. Hood Meadows** (227-7669).

Time/Weather: 778-6000.

Crisis Line: 223-6161. 24 hr.

Women's Crisis Lines: General/Rape Hotline (235-5333). Office at 3020 E. Burnside St. (232-9751). Open Mon.-Fri. 9am-4pm.

Women's Services: Women's Counseling of Portland, 19 SW Gibbs St. (242-0230). General counseling Mon.-Fri. 9am-5pm. **Women's Health Center,** 6510 SE Foster Rd. (777-7044). **West Women's Hotel Shelter,** 2010 NW Kearney St. (224-7718). **Women's Place Bookstore,** 1431 NE Broadway (284-1110). Local clearing house for area feminist events and services.

Men's Resource Center: 2036 SE Morrison (235-3433). Counseling. 24-hr. recording for appointments.

Gay and Lesbian Information: Phoenix Rising, 333 SW 5th (223-8299). Counseling and referral for gay men and women. Open Mon.-Fri. 1-4pm. **The Lavendar Network** (223-1150). General Information.

Abuse Hotline: 800-444-9999.

Senior Citizens' Services: County Committee on Aging (796-5269). **Senior Citizens' Crisis Line** (223-6161). **Oregon Retired Persons' Pharmacy,** 9800 SW Nimbus Ave., Beaverton (646-0591 for orders, 646-3500 for information). Open Mon.-Sat. 8:30am-5pm.

Child Care: Child Care Finders (244-1515).

24 Hour Nurse: 246-8773.

Fire: 248-0203

Police: 1111 SW 2nd (796-3097).

Post Office: 715 NW Hoyt St. (294-2300). General Delivery ZIP Code: 97208. Closer to the mall is the branch across the street from Pioneer Courthouse Square, 520 SW Morrison St. (221-0282). Both open Mon.-Fri. 7:30am-6:30pm, Sat. 8:30am-5pm.

Area Code: 503.

Getting Around

Portland sits just south of the Columbia River, about 75 mi. inland from the Oregon coast. The city is 637 mi. north of San Francisco; car travelers from the Bay Area should take Interstates 80, 505, and 5 north, or take the more scenic U.S. 101 north and cut inland via U.S. 26 from Cannon Beach. Portland lies 172 mi. south of Seattle, and is reached directly on I-5 north. East of the city, I-84 (U.S. 30) follows the route of the Oregon Trail through the Columbia River Gorge. West of Portland, U.S. 30 follows the Columbia downstream to Astoria. I-405 curves around the west side of the business district to link I-5 with U.S. 30.

Portland is on the major north-south routes of both Amtrak and Greyhound. Both stations are located within Tri-Met's Fareless Square (see City Buses). Greyhound also runs out to the coast and to Spokane, WA, for connections east.

The cheapest way to reach downtown from **Portland International Airport** is to take Tri-Met bus #12, which will arrive going south on SW 5th Ave. (Fare 85¢.) **Raz Tranz** (246-4676 for taped info) provides an airport shuttle ($5, under 12 $1) that leaves every 20 minutes and takes 35 minutes to reach major downtown hotels and the Greyhound station. The shuttle runs from 5am to midnight.

Portland can be divided into five districts. **Burnside Street** divides the city into north and south, while east and west are separated by the Willamette River. **Williams Avenue** cuts off a corner of the northeast sector, which is called simply "North." The Southwest district is the city's hub, encompassing the downtown area, the southern end of historic Old Town, and a slice of the wealthier West Hills. The heart of the hub is the downtown mall area between SW 5th and 6th Ave. Car traffic is prohibited here; this is the transit system's turf. Streets in the **Northwest district** are named alphabetically beginning with Burnside and continuing with Couch (pronounced KOOCH) through Yeon. The order is disrupted only where "X" and "Z" should be—you'll find Roosevelt and Reed St. instead. The Northwest district contains the northern end of Old Town. In the north this district is occupied by an industrial area bordering the river; to the west it is residential, culminating in the upper class Northwestern Hills area. Most students enrolled in Portland's several colleges and universities live in the Northwest. The **Southeast district** is a less well-to-do residential neighborhood; used-car dealers and the city's best ethnic restaurants line the main thoroughfares; older houses crowd the small side streets. Anomalous amidst its surroundings, Laurelhurst Park is a collection of posh houses around E. Burnside St. and SE 39th St. The **North** and **Northeast** districts are chiefly residential, punctuated by a few quiet, small parks. In the past few years, drug traffickers have based their operations in the Northeast.

The **Tri-Met bus system,** one of the nation's better systems of mass transit, weaves together Portland's districts. In the downtown mall, 31 covered passenger shelters serve as both stops and information centers. Southbound buses pick up passengers along SW 5th Ave.; northbound passengers board on SW 6th Ave. Bus routes fall into seven regional service areas, each with its own individual "Lucky Charm": orange deer, yellow rose, green leaf, brown beaver, blue snow, red salmon, and purple rain. Shelters and buses are color-coded for their region. A few buses with black numbers on white backgrounds cross town north-south or east-west transgressing color-coded boundaries.

Most of downtown, from NW Irving St. in the north to I-405 in the west and south and the Willamette River in the east, constitutes "Fareless Square." As the name suggests, the buses are free in this zone. The fare system comprises three zones defined by concentric circles around downtown. The center of the city on both sides of the river is Zone 1, a larger circle still within city limits is Zone 2, and outlying areas are Zone 3. Fare is 85¢ for one or two zones; $1.15 for three zones. Seniors and disabled riders pay 35¢ "Honored Citizen" fares; children under 7 are free when traveling with fare-paying adults. All-day tickets are $3. Pick up bus maps and schedules at the visitors center (see Practical Information), at Willamette Savings branches, or at the Tri-Met Customer Assistance Office along with **monthly passes.**

Libraries, universities, and a few participating businesses also have schedules. Buses generally run 7am to midnight, though Saturday and Sunday service is greatly reduced. Tri-Met also has special services for the disabled. Each of the 90 or so bus routes has its own 24 hr. recorded information line, which will tell you where each bus goes and how frequently it operates. (See City Buses in Practical Information.)

Accommodations and Camping

As Portland gentrifies itself, cheap lodgings dwindle. **Northwest Bed and Breakfast,** 610 SW Broadway (243-7616), has an extensive listing of member homes in the Portland area and throughout the Northwest. You must become a member ($10 per year) to use their lists and reservation services. They promise singles from $8 to $60 and doubles from $35 to $90. The houses are clean, and breakfast is included.

The remaining cheap hotels downtown are generally unsafe. The hostel is undoubtedly the best option. The motel strip on Barbur is also comely and accessible; N. Interstate Ave. and Motel 6 are generally better for people with wheels.

Portland International AYH Hostel, 3031 SE Hawthorne Blvd. (236-3380), at 31st Ave. Take bus #5 (brown beaver). Cheerful, clean, and crowded. Sleep inside or on the porch when it's warm. Kitchen facilities; laundromat across the street. Open daily 8-9:30am and 5-11pm. Members $8.75, nonmembers $11.75. Fills up early in the summer (particularly the women's rooms), so plan to arrive by 6pm or make reservations.

Aladdin Motor Inn, 8905 SW 30th St. (246-8241), at Barbur Blvd., an approximately 10 min. ride from downtown. Take bus #12 (yellow rose) from 5th Ave. Very nice rooms. A/C and kitchens available. Singles $29. Doubles $32.

Mel's Motor Inn, 5205 N. Interstate Ave. (285-2556). Take bus #5 (red salmon) from 6th Ave. No aspirations to elegance, but clean and comfortable with A/C and HBO. Singles $28. Doubles $32.

Motel 6, 3104 SE Powell Blvd. (233-8811). Take bus #9 (brown beaver) from 5th Ave. Another cardboard box motel. Small, clean rooms, pool. Singles $30. Doubles $36. *Always* full; call in advance.

Portland Rose Motel, 8920 SW Barbur Blvd. (244-0107). Take bus #12 (yellow rose) from 5th Ave. Dingy but seemingly safe. Singles $26. Doubles $30.

Youth Hostel Portland International, 1024 SW 3rd St. (241-2513). Accessible, but the neighborhood would make Mr. Rogers cringe. Washer and dryer in the lobby, laundromat a block away. Open 24 hr. AYH members $8.75 (*not* an AYH hostel), nonmembers $13-18; with private bath $18.

YWCA, 1111 SW 10th St. (223-6281). Women only. Situated on the park blocks, close to major sights. Clean and safe. Small rooms. Shared doubles $12. Singles $20, with bath $25.

Bel D'air Motel, 8355 N. Interstate Ave. (289-4800), just off I-5. Take bus #5 (red salmon) from 6th Ave. Its name is a bit pretentious; its decor is decidedly not. But hey, it has TVs. Call a week in advance. Singles $25. Doubles $30.

Ainsworth State Park, 37 mi. east of Portland on I-84, along the Columbia River Gorge. Hot showers, flush toilets, and hiking trails. Sites $9, with electrical $10, with full hookup $12.

Milo Molver State Park, 25 mi. southeast of Portland, off Hwy. 211, 5 mi. west of the town of Estacada. Fish, boat, and bicycle along the nearby Clackamas River. Hot showers, flush toilets. Sites $9, with electrical $10, with full hookup $12.

Food

Portland's restaurants reflect the health-conscious attitude of the people; it is easier to find a tofu burger on a whole wheat bun than a simple meat-and-potatoes dinner. Bear in mind that a restaurant's neighborhood is no indication of either its price or its quality; some of the city's finest affordable restaurants adjoin pornographic bookstores or sleazy used-car dealerships, while truly down-and-out cafés somehow continue to survive next to upscale luxury hotels.

The best produce in town is available at **Corno Foods,** 711 SE Union (232-3157), under the Morrison Bridge, a labyrinthine market skewed towards fruits and vegetables.

Southwest

The Original Pancake House, 8600 SW Barbur Blvd. (246-9007). Take bus #12, 41, or 43 (all are yellow rose) to Barbur Transit Center. One of the most popular restaurants in the Northwest with mammoth stacks of every pancake delicacy known. Pancakes ($3.50-5). Hr.-long lines on Sat. and Sun. morning. Open Wed.-Sun. 7am-3pm.

Macheesmo Mouse, 715 SW Salmon St. (228-3491). Fast and healthy Mexican food in a setting somewhere between a Hard Rock Café and the Pompidou Center. The $2.65 veggie burrito stands out. Open Mon.-Sat. 11am-10pm, Sun. noon-9pm. Locations also at 811 NW 23rd St. (274-0500) and 1200 NE Broadway (249-0002).

Foothill Broiler, 33 NW 23rd Pl. (223-0287), in the Uptown Shopping Center. Take bus #20 (deer) up Burnside. Fantastic food served by enterprising survivors of the 60s. Tasteful, revolving art and creative holiday decorations. Some of the best burgers in the Northwest ($3-5). Be prepared to wait in line. Open Mon.-Fri. 7:30am-7pm, Sat. 7:30am-4pm.

Hamburger Mary's, 840 SW Park St. (223-0900), at Taylor. Good food near the museums and theaters, with a relaxed atmosphere and eclectic decor: floor lamps dangle upside-down from the ceiling. Crowd is a mix of straight and gay clientele. Burgers with everything and fries $5, some excellent vegetarian fare. Often crowded; try to get a booth, the bar can be claustrophobic. Open daily 7am-midnight.

Escape from New York Pizza, 913 SW Alder St. (226-4129). Fred Astaire gazes down upon what is arguably the best pizza in town. Hefty cheese slice $1, with pepperoni $1.35. Large cheese pie $8. Try the Snake Pliskin special. Open Mon.-Thurs. 11:30am-9pm, Fri.-Sat. 11:30am-10pm. Second location at 622 NW 23rd St. (227-5423).

Jake's Famous Crawfish, 401 SW 12th St. (226-1419). At one time the best restaurant in Portland, it's now just the oldest. Jake's began in 1872 as a saloon, later metamorphosed into a soft-drink parlor during Prohibition, and then turned seaward for inspiration. The front dining room is plebeian, the rear two more formal. The power lunch reigns. Fresh salmon, shrimp creole, and fantastic steamed butter clams. Lunches around $6, dinners $10-15. Lunch Mon.-Fri. 11am-3pm. Dinner Mon.-Thurs. 5-11pm, Fri.-Sat. 5pm-midnight, Sun. 5-10pm. Call a week ahead for dinner reservations.

Dan and Louie's Oyster Bar, 208 SW Ankeny St. (227-5906). Legendary since 1907, Dan and Louie's has its own Oyster Bay in Newport, OR. Lunch specials are especially cheap, and the older waitresses keep you giggling. Try the Shrimp and Oyster Fry ($8.50), Hangtown Fry ($5), or 4 "shuck 'em yourself" oysters ($3). Open Sun.-Thurs. 11am-11pm, Fri.-Sat. 11am-midnight.

Yamhill Marketplace, 110 SW Yamhill (224-6705), at 1st St. Groceries, produce, baked treats and specialties on the 1st floor; international food stands amicably rub shoulders upstairs. Try the $3.50 shredded beef taco at **Carlos** or a large pastrami sandwich ($4) at **Shelley's Chicago Deli.** Marketplace open Mon.-Sat. 7am-6pm, Sun. 10am-6pm.

Metro on Broadway, 911 SW Broadway (227-2746). A chic place in which to gaze and be gazed upon; also a good place to come alone and read. The piano player and espresso seduce an artsy crowd. A circle of stands serves a wide variety of above-average foods. Try Mexican chocolate at **Ears to You** ($1.50) or yogurt milkshakes at **Split Decisions** ($2). Open Mon.-Thurs. 7am-11pm, Fri. 7am-midnight, Sat. 9am-midnight, Sun. 11am-6pm.

Maya's Tacqueria, 1000 SW Morrison St. (226-1946), at 10th. Genuinely Mexican, complete with wall-sized murals of Mayans doing Mayan things. Mongo Mayan burrito $4.50-5.50. Open Mon.-Sat. 10:30am-10pm, Sun. noon-8pm.

Northwest

Chang's Mongolian Grill, 1 SW 3rd St. (243-1991) at Burnside. Also at 2700 NW 185th (645-7718) and 1600 NE 122nd (253-3535). Ulan Bator's best cuisine in generous portions. All-you-can-eat lunches ($6) and dinners ($9). You select your meal from a buffet (fresh vegetables, meats, and fish), mix your own sauce to taste, and then watch your chef make a wild show of cooking it on a grill the size of a king-sized waterbed. Rice and hot-and-sour soup included. Neon Mongolian warriors decorate the walls. Open daily 11:30am-2:30pm and 5-10pm.

Alexis, 215 W. Burnside St. (224-8577). Genuine Hellenic food served by the friendly Bakouros family in an east Mediterranean atmosphere. Lamb souvlaki $10. Open Mon.-Thurs. 11:30am-2pm and 5-10pm, Fri. 11:30am-2pm and 5-11pm, Sat. 5-11pm, Sun. 4:30-9pm.

Rose's Deli, 315 NW 23rd Ave. (227-5181), at Everett St. Take bus #15 (red salmon). Rose has her own cookbook now, but fame hasn't corrupted her cooking. She still butters the city's best bagels in a bustling atmosphere. Great matzoh-ball soup ($2), cheese blintzes, and a pastry case that could fill you up by osmosis. Three other locations in the Portland area. Open Mon.-Thurs. 7am-11pm, Fri. 7am-midnight, Sat. 8am-midnight, Sun. 8am-11pm.

Fong Chong, 301 NW 4th (220-0235), in the heart of Chinatown. Portland's best *dim sum,* but be prepared to be aggressive. Harried waiters whiz by with their carts. Most dishes $1.50-3. Regular entrees $4-6. Open Mon.-Thurs. 10:30am-9pm, Fri.-Sun. 10:30am-10pm; *dim sum* daily 10:30am-3pm.

Saigon Express, 309 W. Burnside St. (227-7499). Exquisite Vietnamese food; not at all the cheesy place the name may suggest. Entrees $5-8, unusual combinations (such as shrimp and sugarcane) add that extra *je ne sais quoi.* Open Mon.-Sat. 11am-9pm.

Southeast and Northeast

Jarra's Ethiopian Restaurant, 607 SE Morrison St. (230-8990). Take bus #15 (brown beaver). Authentically hot cuisine served by a friendly staff. Scoop up the spicy morsels with spongy *injera* bread. Main dishes come with combinations of any 3 condiments: cottage cheese, mixed vegetables, or tomato salad with lettuce and collard greens. *Doro wat* (chicken in a very very very spicy sauce) $6.50. Open Mon.-Tues. 5-10pm, Wed. 11:30am-2pm and 5-10pm, Thurs.-Fri. 5-10pm, Sat. 4-10pm.

Bread and Ink Café, 3610 SE Hawthorne (224-5552). Somewhat overpriced but the food is good. Health conscious dinner entrees $7-15. Open Mon.-Sat. 7am-3pm, 5:30-10pm, Sun. 9am-2pm. Take bus #5 (brown beaver).

Yen Ha, 6820 NE Sandy Blvd. (287-3698). Eat the same wonderful Vietnamese food that wowed food critic Calvin Trillin a few years back. Entrees $4-7. Open daily 11am-10pm.

Ice Cream and Pastries

Roberto's, 405 NW 23rd St. (248-9040). Delicious dark chocolate ($22 per lb., $1 for a bite-sized morsel). Equally rich ice cream cones ($1.25). Also at 921 SW Morrison (224-4234), in the Galleria. Open Mon.-Thurs. 11am-10pm, Fri. 11am-11pm, Sat. noon-11pm, Sun. noon-10pm.

Papa Haydn's, 2 locations. 701 NW 23rd (228-7317). The composer of *Die Schöpfung* would have approved. Slightly overpriced lunch ($7) and desserts, but money was meant to be spent, right? Excellent variety of meringues. 5829 SE Milwaukee (232-9440). Take bus #19 (brown beaver). Reed College hangout. Great soups and desserts. Open Tues.-Thurs. 11:30am-11pm, Fri.-Sat. 11:30am-midnight, Sun. 10am-3pm.

Rose's Bakery, 35 NW 20th Place (227-4875). A wonderfully aromatic Viennese bakery. Monstrous pastries $1, ft.-wide raised donuts $1.50. **Rose's East,** 12329 NE Glissan (254-6545, take-out 254-6546). Open Mon.-Sat. 6:30am-6pm, Sun. 9am-5pm.

Sights and Activities

Generation spokesperson Kevin Young said of Portland's ubiquitous fountains, "The history of these erect water jets spurts as sordid as Jim Bakker's past." Indeed, all of Portland's fountains seem to have long, intricate histories. The 20 bronze drinking fountains located on strategic street corners throughout Portland were donated to the city by Simon Benson, a wealthy Prohibition-era Portlander, ostensibly to ease the thirst of loggers. Other *objets d'art* dot the downtown area—the product of a city law requiring that one percent of the costs of all construction and renovation work be devoted to public art projects.

Downtown

Portland's downtown area is centered on the **mall,** running north-south between 5th and 6th Ave., bounded on the north by W. Burnside St. and on the south by SW Madison St., and closed to all traffic except city buses. At 5th Ave. and Morrison St. sits the **Pioneer Courthouse,** the tribal elder of downtown landmarks. The monument now houses the U.S. Ninth Circuit Court of Appeals and is the centerpiece for **Pioneer Courthouse Square,** 701 SW 6th Ave. (223-1613), which opened in 1983. Forty-eight thousand citizens supported its construction by purchasing personalized bricks, and it seems as though all 48,000 make a daily pilgrimage to visit their gift to the city. Live jazz, folk, and ethnic music draws the rest of Portland to the square for the **Peanut Butter and Jam Sessions,** held every Tuesday and Thursday in summer from noon to 1pm.

Certainly the most controversial building in the downtown area is Michael Graves's postmodern **Portland Building,** located on the mall. This amazing confection of pastel tile and concrete has been praised to the stars and condemned as an overgrown jukebox. Opened with great fanfare in 1984, the city celebrated by perching a full-sized inflatable King Kong on the building's roof. Since the building is surrounded by narrow streets and tall buildings, it can be difficult to obtain a good view of the exterior. Make sure to visit the interior, which looks like something out of *Blade Runner.* On a niche outside the building's second floor, *Portlandia,* an immense bronze statue (second in size only to the Statue of Liberty) of the trident-bearing woman on the state seal (which to many looks like a man with breasts brandishing a large salad fork), reaches down to crowds below. The **Standard Insurance Center,** 900 SW 5th Ave., nearby, has also engendered controversy for the white marble sculpture out front, "The Quest." The sculpture is more commonly known to locals as "three groins in the fountain." Also notable is the glass **Equitable Building** at S.W. 6th and Alder designed by Pietro Belluschi.

West of the mall are the **South Park Blocks,** a series of cool, shady parks down the middle of Park Ave. Facing the parks, the **Portland Art Museum,** 1219 SW Park Ave. (226-2811), at Jefferson St., has an especially fine exhibit of Pacific Northwest Native American art, including masks, textiles, and sacred objects. The Asian galleries also deserve notice, particularly the Chinese furniture. International exhibits and local artists' works are interspersed. (Open Tues.-Sat. 11am-5pm, Sun. noon-4pm. Admission $3.50, seniors and students $1.50, under 12 50¢. Thurs. seniors get in free.) The **Northwest Film and Video Center** (221-1156), in the same building, screens classics and off-beat flicks.

Across the street, the **Oregon Historical Society Museum and Library,** 1230 SW Park Ave. (222-1741), stores photographs, artifacts, and records of Oregon's past 200 years. The maritime exhibit is especially good. The library is open to the public for research. (Open Mon.-Sat. 10am-4:45pm. Free.)

Four separate theaters make up the **Portland Center for the Performing Arts,** at 1111 SW Broadway (248-4496) on the eastern side of the Park Blocks. The **Arlene Schnitzer Concert Hall,** a recently refurbished marble and granite wonder, shares the corner of Broadway and Main with the brick and glass **Dolores Winningstad Theatre** and the **Intermediate Theater.** The **Civic Auditorium** is the Center's fourth component. At 222 SW Clay St., the modern, glass-fronted, 3000-seat auditorium plays host to opera, ballet, and the occasional jazz or folk concert.

The view from the Civic Auditorium includes Lawrence Halprin's **Forecourt Fountain** (better known as Ira's Fountain), Portland's most popular foot-soaking oasis. This terraced waterfall, at SW 3rd Ave. and Clay St., circulates 13,000 gallons of water every minute. Retreat to a secluded niche behind the waterfall and discover for yourself what the back side of water looks like.

Old Town, to the north of the mall, resounded a century ago with sailors who docked in the ports. The district has been revived with large-scale refurbishment of store fronts, new "old brick," polished iron and brass, and a bevy of recently opened shops and restaurants. A popular people-watching vantage point, the **Skidmore Fountain** at SW 1st Ave. and SW Ankeny St., marks the entrance to the quarter. Had the city accepted resident draftsman Henry Weinhard's offer to run draft beer through the fountain, it would have been a truly cordial watering hole indeed. Old Town also marks the start of **Waterfront Park.** This 20-block long swath of grass and flowers offers little shade, but provides great views of the Willamette River.

From March until Christmas, the area under the Burnside Bridge is given over to the **Saturday Market** (222-6072), 108 W. Burnside St. Saturdays from 10am to 5pm and Sundays from 11am to 4:30pm, street musicians, artists, craftspeople, chefs, and produce sellers clog the area. Many of these artists and craftspeople sell their work in the city's studios and galleries during the week.

Portland's finest galleries are centered downtown. The **Image Gallery,** 1026 SW Morrison St. (224-9629), shows an international potpourri of Canadian Eskimo sculpture and Mexican and Japanese folk art. (Open Mon.-Fri. 10:30am-6pm, Sat. 11am-5pm.)

The Portland Children's Museum, 3037 SW 2nd Ave. (248-4587), at Wood St. (take bus #41 or 43, both yellow rose), schedules organized games, races, arts activities, and hands-on exhibits. (Open Tues.-Sat. 9am-5pm, Sun. 11am-5pm. Suggested donation $3, children $2.) Sample some local lager at the **Blitz Weinhard Brewing Co.,** 1133 W. Burnside St. (222-4351), or take a stroll through all two ft. of **Mill Ends Park,** at SW Front and Taylor St. The tiniest park in the world is the product of a journalist's desire to put some token greenery outside his window. It is now protected from iconoclasts by a chain hanging lazily between two iron columns.

West Hills

Less than 2 miles west of downtown, these posh neighborhoods serve as a buffer zone between the soul-soothing parks and the turmoil of the anomic city below. Take the animated "zoo bus" (#63) or drive up SW Broadway to Clay St. and turn right onto Sunset Hwy. 26 (get off at zoo exit).

Washington Park and its nearby attractions are perhaps the handsomest sites in Portland. The park's looping trails are open daily 7am-9pm. "Bristlecone Pine" Trail is wheelchair accessible. Obtain maps at the information stand near the parking lot of the arboretum, or refer to those posted on the windows. **Hoyt Arboretum,** 4000 SW Fairview Blvd. (228-8732), at the crest of the hill above the other gardens, features many a conifer and "200 acres of trees and trails." (Free nature walks April-Oct. Sat.-Sun. at 2pm, and June-Aug. Tues 9:30am.) The walks take 60-90 minutes and cover 1-2 mi. The 3-mi. "Wildwood" Trail connects the arboretum to the zoo in the south. The **Japanese Gardens** (223-1321) arrange idyllic ponds and bridges into five contrasting formal patterns. Cherry blossoms ornament the park in summer, thanks to sister city Sapporo, Japan. (Open daily 10am-6pm; Sept. 16-April 14 daily 10am-4pm. Admission $3.50, ages over 60 and students with ID $2.) The **International Rose Test Garden,** 400 SW Kingston (248-4302), a few steps away, has bred prize-winning hybrids which include the "miniature roses" gathered around the information kiosk. The bushes bloom from June to November.

Below the Hoyt Arboretum lie many of Portland's most popular attractions. Although they can be crowded on hot summer days, each is worth seeing. The **Washington Park Zoo** (226-1561 for a person, 226-7627 for a tape) is renowned for its successful elephant-breeding and its scrupulous re-creations of natural habitats. Whimsical murals decorate the #63 "zoo" bus from the park to Morrison St. in the downtown mall. A miniature railway also connects the Washington Park gardens with the zoo (fare $2, seniors and children under 12 $1.50). The zoo features a number of interesting "animal talks" at various times on weekends and has a pet-the-animals children's zoo. The zoo's elephants are world famous—several are represented by Mike Ovitz—so watch it. (Open daily in summer 9:30am-7pm, gates close at 6pm. Call for winter hours. Admission $3.50, ages over 64 and under 12 $2. Tues. 3-7pm free.) If you're around in late June, grab your picnic basket and check out the zoo sponsored **Your Zoo and All That Jazz,** a nine-week series of open-air jazz concerts (Wed. 6:30-8:30pm), free with zoo admission. **Zoograss Con-**

certs features a 10-week series of bluegrass concerts (Thurs. 6:30-8:30pm), also free with admission.

Next to the zoo, the **Oregon Museum of Science and Industry (OMSI)**, 4015 SW Canyon Rd. (228-6674), will keep children and adults amused with do-it-yourself science, computer, and medical exhibits (including a walk-though heart). Don't miss the transparent woman. (Open Sat.-Thurs. 9am-7pm, Fr. 9am-8pm. Admission $5.25, ages over 64 $4.25, ages 3-17 $3.50.) The **Kendall Planetarium** within the museum gives daily shows for 75¢ extra (228-7827 for taped planetarium info). The planetarium also puts on laser shows Wed.-Sun. with painfully loud rock music and incredible laser special effects (admission $5, children $3.50); call 242-0723 for show times. Once overwhelmed by science, you can step outside into the small, immaculate garden of the Oregon Herb Society.

The **World Forestry Center**, 4033 SW Canyon Rd. (228-1367), specializes in exhibits on Northwestern forestry and logging, although it is now taking on the entire world. The eavesdropping trees in *The Wizard of Oz* would have grown extremely irritated if they had to listen to the Forestry Center's "talking tree" all day long; the 70-ft. plant never shuts up. (Open daily 9am-5pm. Admission $3, ages over 65 and under 12 $2.) The new and tastefully designed **Vietnam Memorial** is only a few steps up the hill. Also nearby is the quaint **Wisma Kaüel,** a residence designed by I.M. Pei and the Indonesian neo-existentialist architect Tidak Apa-Apa. Within an elephant's roar of the zoo, the **Maison de Galtonne** (still another creation of I.M. Pei, in collaboration with nationally renowned homeboy Michael Graves) stands as a shimmering reminder of the city's obscure contribution to the twisted yet sublime proto-Morehouseian movement so popular among the area's late 20th century quasi-intellectuals.

Northwest, North, and Northeast

From Washington Park, you have easy access to sprawling **Forest Park,** the largest park completely within the confines of an American city. The park is laced with hiking trails and garnished with scenic picnic areas. The **Pittock Mansion**, 3229 NW Pittock Dr. (248-4469), within Forest Park, was built by Henry L. Pittock, the founder of Oregon's largest (and now only) daily newspaper, the *Oregonian.* From downtown take crosstown bus #20 (orange deer) to NW Barnes and W. Burnside St., and walk ½ mi. up Pittock Ave. The 80-year-old structure, now owned by the city of Portland, will whisk you back to the French Renaissance. (Open daily 1-5pm. Admission $3, senior citizens $2.50, ages under 18 $1.)

Downtown on the edge of the Northwest district is **Powell's Book Store,** 1005 W. Burnside St. (228-4651), a cavernous establishment with an overwhelming collection of new and used books. Already informally considered the largest bookstore in the country, Powell's has recently added two more huge rooms. Any book that's not here probably hasn't been written. (Open Mon.-Sat. 9am-11pm, Sun. 9am-9pm.) Enter Portland's small **Chinatown** at W. Burnside St. and NW 4th Ave., through the gate adorned with guardian lions and ornate arches. Take bus #4 (red salmon) to the **John Palmer House,** 4314 N. Mississippi Ave. (284-5893), another Victorian mansion restored to its 1890 splendor. Debts are apparently being settled by the exorbitant prices exacted by the bed-and-breakfast establishment inside. (Open for tours Thurs.-Sun. noon-5pm. Admission $3, senior citizens and students $2.)

Farther out, geographically and spiritually, is the **Grotto,** at the Sanctuary of Our Sorrowful Mother, NE 85th Ave. and NE Sandy Blvd. (254-7371). Take bus #12 (purple rain). The splendid grounds are decorated with depictions of the Stations of the Cross and Mary's Seven Sorrows. You can behold the Columbia River gorge from the cliff. (Open daily 8am-sunset. Admission by donation.)

Some find shopping a religious experience in the **Nob Hill** district. Fashionable boutiques run from Burnside to Thurman St., between NW 21st and NW 24th Ave. Shopping Dorothy Hamill hopefuls make the pilgrimage to **Lloyd Center,** a shopping mall with an open-air ice-skating rink. (Admission $3, skate rental $1.) Also noteworthy here is the award-winning **Lloyd Cinema,** an ultramodern multiplex equipped with comfortable contour chairs and plenty of neon. Next door, sample the delectable offerings at **Holladay Market,** a collection of fresh fruit, dessert, spice, and vegetable stands.

Southeast

Southeast Portland is largely a residential district. **Reed College,** a small liberal arts school founded in 1909, sponsors numerous cultural events. In 1968 this radiant enclave of progressive politics became the first undergraduate college to open a nuclear reactor. The ivy-covered campus encompasses a lake and a state wildlife refuge. Tours (geared mainly to prospective students) leave Eliot Hall, 3203 Woodstock Blvd. at SE 28th, twice per day during the school year. (Mon.-Fri. at 10am and 2pm or 10:30am and 2:30pm. Individual tours by appointment in summer. Call 771-7511.) The **Chamber Music Northwest** festival (294-6400) holds concerts here every summer from late June to late July on Monday, Thursday, and Saturday at 8pm. Concerts sell out quickly; call ahead for tickets ($13, senior citizens and ages 7-14 $9). Across the street, in the lovely **Rhododendron Test Gardens,** SE 28th Ave. (796-5193), at Woodstock, 2500 rhododendrons surround a lake. The rhododendrons and azaleas are in full bloom April and May. (Open daily "in season" during daylight hours. Free, but $1 on Mother's Day. Sorry, Mom.)

Farther east in the southeast is **Mt. Tabor Park,** one of two city parks in the world on the site of an extinct volcano. More of a molehill than a mountain, the volcano is easily eclipsed by Mt. Tabor itself. Take bus #15 (brown beaver) from downtown, or drive down Hawthorne to SE 60th Ave. **Hawthorne Boulevard** has a high concentration of antique shops, used book stores, and second-hand clothing vendors. **Old Sellwood Antique Row,** at the east end of Sellwood Bridge, on SE 13th Ave. between Bybee and Clatsop St. has over 30 curiosity shops showcasing stained glass, rare books, and assorted "used" memorabilia at prices that may inspire you to hawk your own used items (face it, Mike, your bandana collection has got to go). (Hours vary, but all stores open Tues.-Sat.)

Sports

Contact the **Portland Park Bureau,** 1120 SW 5th Ave., #502 (796-5193), for a complete guide to Portland's many parks, which contain the usual hiking and cycling trails and lakes for swimming and sailing. Outdoor **tennis courts,** many of which are lighted for night play, are free and open to the public. The following parks have free **swimming pools:** Columbia, Creston, Dishman, Grant, Mt. Scott, Montavilla, Peninsula, Pier, and Sellwood. Special facilities and programs are provided for senior citizens and the disabled (call 248-4328).

The Oregon Road Runners Club (626-2348) sponsors several races each year. Most of the roads on the periphery of the city have ample bike lanes. The **Beavers** (223-2837) play Class AAA baseball and aspire to become Minnesota Twins at Civic Stadium, 1844 SW Morrison St. (248-4345; tickets $3-5). The Coliseum, 1401 N. Wheeler (238-4636) is home to the **Trail Blazers** (234-9291), crushed by the superb Detroit Pistons in 1990 but always #1 to enthusiastic fan Zanley. The **Winter Hawks** (238-6366) of the Western Hockey League, also play the Coliseum. Take bus #9 (brown beaver) or take MAX.

Entertainment

Portland is no longer the hard-drinking, carousing port town of yore; ships still unload their catch daily, but the sailors' favorite waterfront pubs have evolved into upscale bistros, french bakeries, and pulsating nightclubs. The best listings are in the Friday edition of the *Oregonian* and in a number of free handouts: *Willamette Week,* the *Main Event, Clinton St. Quarterly,* and the *Downtowner.* The first of these caters to students, the last to the upwardly mobile. Each is available in restaurants downtown and in boxes on street corners.

Music

Oregon Symphony Orchestra plays in Arlene Schnitzer Concert Hall (228-1353) Sept.-April. Tickets $10-28. "Symphony Sunday" afternoon concerts $5-8.

Portland Civic Auditorium, 222 SW Clay St. (248-4496). Attracts the usual hard rockin' arena acts, as well as a few jazz and opera stars. Ticket prices vary.

Sack Lunch Concerts, 1422 SW 11th Ave. and Clay St. (222-2031), at the Old Church. Free concert every Wed. at noon (except in the event of rain) during the summer.

Chamber Music Northwest performs summer concerts at Reed College Commons, 3203 SE Woodstock Ave. (223-3202). Classical music Mon., Thurs., Sat. 8pm. Admission $13, ages 7-14 $9.

Brown Bag Concerts, free public concerts given around the city in a summer 6-week series (at noon during the week and Tues. evenings). Check the *Oregonian* or call the Park Bureau at 796-5193.

Noon Lawn Concerts, at the Odell Manor Lawn, Lewis and Clark College (244-6161). Free classical concerts throughout June and July. Thurs. noon-1pm.

Peanut Butter and Jam Sessions at Pioneer Courthouse Square from noon to 1pm every Tues. and Thurs. during the summer months. A potpourri of rock, jazz, folk, and ethnic music.

Theater

While inferior to Seattle (both in variety and quality), Portland does benefit from a trickle-down-effect. College shows are inexpensive and often worthwhile.

Oregon Shakespeare Festival/Portland (248-6309), at the Intermediate Theater of PCPA, corner of SW Broadway and SW Main. Five-play series, focusing on those of the Bard, runs Nov.-Feb. World-class productions.

Portland Civic Theater, 1530 SW Yamhill (226-3048). The mainstage often presents musical comedy, the smaller theater-in-the-round less traditional shows. Tickets $6.50 or $9.50.

Oregon Contemporary Theater, 511 SW 10th St., Lewis and Clark College, Fir Acres Theater (241-3770). Considered one of Portland's most innovative companies.

New Rose Theater, 904 SW Main St. (222-2487), in the Park Blocks. Even mix of classic and contemporary productions. Tickets range from $9-14.

Artists Repertory Theater, SW 10th, on the 3rd floor of the YMCA. This small theater puts on excellent low-budget productions, many of them experimental. Tickets $10-15.

Portland State University Summer Festival Theater, at the Lincoln Hall Auditorium (229-4440). Schedules at the box office or the Portland Public Library. Performances mid-June to mid-July.

Portland Civic Auditorium, 222 SW Clay St. (248-4496). Occasional big splashy touring shows, now part of the Portland Center for the Performing Arts (PCPA).

Cinema

Most of Portland's countless movie theaters have half-price days or matinee shows. Consult the *Oregonian* and you will never have to pay the standard $6 ticket price for the average "major motion picture."

Movie House, 1220 SW Taylor (222-4595). Wine, cheese, and chess before art flicks. Tickets $6, ages over 62 and under 12 $3.

Cinema 21, 616 NW 21st (223-4515). Clean, attractive cinema showing mostly documentary, independent, and foreign films. Tickets $5, students and senior citizens $2.50; matinee seats $2.50.

Clinton Street Theater, 2522 SE Clinton St. (238-8899). Classic and foreign films $3, free popcorn Wed. nights. The execrable *Rocky Horror Picture Show* is shown every Fri.-Sat. at midnight.

Northwest Film and Video Center, 1219 SW Park Ave. (221-1156). Mostly documentary films on little-known places and peoples. Tickets $4, ages under 12 $2. Open Wed.-Sun.

Clubs and Bars

The best clubs in Portland are the hardest ones to find. Neighborhood taverns and pubs may be tucked away on back roads, but they are also those with the most character and best music.

Flyers advertising upcoming shows are always plastered on telephone poles around town. Those with dance fever should shake their thang down the length of 6th Ave. to find most of the dancing clubs. The under-21 crowd ought to head for the Confetti Club, 126 SW 2nd (274-0627; $6 cover, some $2 nights), for new-wave music, or try the Warehouse, 320 SE 2nd, for Top-40 tunes (232-9645).

Produce Row Café, 204 SE Oak St. (232-8355). Bus #6 (red salmon) to SE Oak and SE Grand, then walk west along Oak towards the river. 21 beers on tap ($1), 72 bottled domestic and imported beers (ranging in origin from China to Belgium), and a lovely outdoor beer garden. Ask one of the friendly bartenders to mix you the house special, a Black Velvet (Guinness Stout and champagne, $2.25). Open Mon.-Fri. 11am-1am, Sat. noon-1am, Sun. 2pm-midnight.

Mission Theater and Pub, 1624 NW Glisan (223-4031). Serves excellent home-brewed ales as well as delicious and unusual sandwiches ($4.50). Also offers free showings of double features (everything from Bogart to Allen) twice nightly. Relax in the balcony of this old movie-house with a pitcher of Ruby, a fragrant raspberry ale named after one of Mick Jagger's creations ($1.25 glass, $6.50 pitcher). Open daily 5pm-1am.

Goose Hollow Inn, 1927 SW Jefferson (228-7010). Bus #57 or 59 (orange deer). Mayor Bud Clark's place, always a popular neighborhood tavern, is now wall-to-wall with aspiring progressives. No music, however. Sandwiches $3-6.50. Open daily 11:30am-1am.

Brasserie Montmarte, 626 SW Park (224-5552). A high-class, expensive joint with live jazz every night. Open Mon.-Fri. 11:30am-2:30pm for lunch (around $6); Mon.-Sat. 5:30-10pm, Sun. 5:30-9:30pm for dinner (around $10).

East Avenue Tavern, 727 E. Burnside St. (236-6900). Bus #12, 19, or 20 (all brown beaver). Folk music. Open-mike nights make for unexpected variety: Irish, French, flamenco, bluegrass. Sometimes Apalacian clogging champ Stompin Geoff Chadsey makes a guest appearance. Cover $1-5, depending on the name and fame of the performer. Open Mon.-Sat. noon-midnight, Sun. 8pm-midnight.

Harrington's, 1001 SW 6th Ave. (243-2933), at Main St. A sight unto itself. Front door is a little gazebo and underground stairway in the middle of a downtown sidewalk. It's been listed as one of the nation's "top-10" bars by *Esquire,* which gives you an idea of the clientele (i.e. schmooz with people with names like Zanley Phränqué Galton the Third). Cover $1-5 Thurs.-Sat.; live music all week. Open Mon.-Fri. 11:30am-9pm. Take-out breakfast window opens at 7:30am.

Key Largo, 31 NW 1st Ave. (223-9919). Airy, tropical atmosphere. You can dance out on the patio when it's not raining. A variety of local and national bands. Rock, rhythm & blues, zydeco, and jazz. Cover $2-8. Open Mon.-Fri. 11am-2:30am, Sat.-Sun. noon-2:30am.

Seasonal Events

Rose Festival, first 3 weeks of June. The city decks itself in all its finery for Portland's premier summer event. Waterfront concerts, art festivals, parades, an air show, Navy ships, and Native American powwows. Unfortunately, with the influx of people comes an increase in crime (they never promised you a rose garden)—women walking alone at night should be careful. Call 248-7923 for taped info, 227-2681 for the offices.

Mt. Hood Festival of Jazz, Aug. 3-5, at Mt. Hood Community College in Gresham (666-3810). The premier jazz festival of the Pacific Northwest, with 20 hours of music over the course of a weekend; Stan Getz and Wynton Marsalis have been regulars in the past. Admission around $20 per day. Reserve well in advance. Write Mt. Hood Festival of Jazz, P.O. Box 696, Gresham 97030. To reach the festival, take I-84 to Wood Village-Gresham exit and follow the signs, or follow the crowd on MAX to the end of the line.

Artquake, Labor Day weekend. Music, mime, food, and neo-situationist hoopla in and around Pioneer Courthouse Square (227-2787). Rockin' good news.

Multnomah County Fair, late July-early Aug. Annual bash includes livestock fair, crafts, and country music at the Multnomah County Exposition Center in Portland. Admission $6. Call 285-7756.

Washington Park Festival, late July-early Aug. Pack a picnic supper and enjoy theater, music, and dance in the park's amphitheater. Check the *Oregonian* or call 796-5193 for information.

Magicazam, in early July. The largest traveling magic show in the U.S. appears at the Multnomah County Exposition Center (285-7756). Admission $4-5.

Near Portland

The bird's nest of highways that tangle around Portland also beckon you west to the coast, east through the regal Columbia River Gorge, and north into Washington for a series of daytrips. On the coast, Cannon Beach, Seaside, Astoria, and Tillamook are all just a scenic drive through the serene Tillamook State Forest. The burned-out shell of Mt. St. Helens is a short drive north into Washington State, or you can follow the footsteps of early pioneers along the Oregon Trail.

Sauvie Island and U.S. 30 West

Twenty minutes from downtown Portland nests Sauvie Island, a peaceful rural hideaway at the confluence of the Columbia and Willamette Rivers. On winter mornings, eagles and geese congregate along the roads, and in spring and summer, berries are everywhere. For many Portlanders, a trip to the island's **U-pick farms** (family operations announced by hand-lettered signs along the roads) is a seasonal tradition. Visit the **James Bybee House and Agricultural Museum,** on Howell Park Rd., built in 1859 on the eve of Oregon's statehood. (Open June 1-Labor Day Wed.-Sun. noon-4:45pm.) In the island's northwestern corner, beaches and a wildlife management area open nature to fishermen, hikers, and solitude seekers. (Open daily 4am-10pm.) To reach Sauvie Island, take U.S. 30 west out of downtown.

Farther north on U.S. 30, some 42 mi. from Portland, **Trojan Nuclear Power Plant** aims to convince tourists that nuclear power is "safe" and "efficient." The Trojan Visitors Center, 71760 Columbia River Hwy., Rainier (226-8510), has an exhibit on the mechanics of magnetism, electricity, and nuclear fission. Trojan is the only nuclear plant in the country that gives its visitors a look into the "Jane Fonda" room, so-named after the movie *The China Syndrome,* in which Jane Fonda witnessed the panic in the control room of a plant on the verge of a meltdown. (Visitors center open Mon.-Sat. 9am-5pm, Sun. noon-5pm; Labor Day-Memorial Day Wed.-Sat. 9am-5pm. Free.) Public tours of the plant itself are conducted several times per week; contact the visitors center for hours and reservations (which are usually necessary). If the visitors center or tour are not on your schedule, bring a picnic and dine with a view of the cooling tower; Trojan encourages recreational use of its 75-acre wooded area. U.S. 30 continues to follow the Columbia for about 35 mi. to the river's mouth at Astoria.

Columbia River Gorge

Fifteen million years ago, massive flows of lava poured out of rifts in the earth, covering northern Oregon with 25,000 cubic mi. of basalt. The Columbia River began carving its determined path through the rock, forming a narrow channel 3000 ft. deep and 55 mi. long. Walls of volcanic stone rise on either side of the grand river as it surges on its last lap to the sea. To follow the spectacular Columbia River Gorge, take I-84 east (old U.S. 30) to the Troutdale exit onto the **Columbia River Scenic Highway.** This highway, built in 1915, follows the crest of the gorge walls and affords legendary views. The famous **Vista House,** in Crown Point State Park, hangs on the edge of an outcropping cliff high above the river. A few meters past this house, a trail leaves the road to end in a solitary view of both the gorge and

Vista House. Reach Crown Point from the Scenic Hwy. or from the Corbett exit off I-84.

About two mi. farther east is one of the 20 waterfalls along this route, **Latourell Falls,** where you can clamber over jagged black rock to stand behind a plume of falling spray. Six miles farther, **Multnomah Falls** crashes 620 ft. into an astoundingly quiet pool at the bottom. The paved trail to the top of the falls is steep but rewarding. Hikers who would like to escape main-trail traffic can follow other paths into Mt. Hood National Forest. Get an inexpensive trail map from the Multnomah Falls gift shop. **Camping** is allowed at sites along the trails in **Ainsworth National Park** but accessibility varies seasonally. Check with posted regulations or with a Multnomah Falls park ranger for more information. For better prospects, try the Washington side of the river.

Exactly 44 mi. east of Portland is the oldest of the Columbia River hydroelectric projects, the **Bonneville Dam.** Pete Seeger was working for the Bonneville Power Co. when he wrote "Roll On Columbia," a salute to the river (and the BPC): "Your power is turning our darkness to dawn, so roll on Columbia, roll on." Across the river on the Washington side, a **visitors center** shows tourists a fish ladder and the dam's powerhouse and generator room. Follow the yellow arrows painted on the pavement to see the fish hatchery, where a little garden displays fishpools. (Visitors center and hatchery both open daily 8am-8pm. Free.) Also on this side of the river, don't miss dramatic **Beacon Rock,** the 848-ft.-high neck of an old volcano.

At the Cascade Locks, four mi. past Bonneville, take a **paddleboat ride** aboard the *Columbia Gorge* (374-8474 or 374-8619, in Portland 223-3928), a replica of the sternwheelers that used to ply the Columbia and Willamette Rivers. (Rides 1 hr. and longer. Lowest fare $12, children $6.)

Thirty-four miles east of Multnomah Falls is **Hood River,** a town known for tripendicular windsurfing and sailing. **The Dalles,** where Lewis and Clark camped in 1805 and which French explorers named "Le Dalle" (the trough) after the rapids around that section of the river, was the last stop on the agonizing Oregon Trail. **Fort Dalles,** a historical museum housed in the original 1856 surgeon's quarters, offers the memories of all this. For a free map including a walking tour, go to the **visitors center,** operating out of an 1859 county courthouse. The third week in July brings **Fort Dalles Days and Rodeo,** a wild-west extravaganza. In late April, when the region's cherry trees are at the height of blossoming glory, The Dalles presents George Washington's worst nightmare—a **Cherry Festival.**

Mount Hood

At the junction of U.S. 26 and Hwy. 35, 90 minutes from Portland and less than an hour from Hood River, is the glacier-topped volcano Mt. Hood. In early years Native Americans of the Willamette Valley—the Clackamas and Wasco—feared Mt. Hood's vile temper. Legend describes a brave warrior who tried to stop the devastating lava flows by hurling boulders into Mt. Hood's crater. The enraged mountain reportedly spit them back out, initiating a rock-throwing contest that lasted for four days. When the warrior realized that Hood's boulders were destroying his village below, he dropped to his knees in despair and was quickly swallowed up by lava. A huge rock outcropping called **Chief's Face** on Hood's northern side precisely marks this spot today.

The 11,235-ft. mountain has been behaving itself for some time now. Skiers can take advantage of the winter trails at three ski areas: **Timberline, Ski Bowl Multorpor,** and **Mt. Hood Meadows.** All three offer night skiing, and Timberline has summer skiing for the truly dedicated (you'll have to yield to the U.S. national team, however). Rental of skis, poles, and boots runs under $20 (under $10 for children) and lift tickets generally cost around $25. All three areas offer ski lessons (averaging a hefty $10 per hr.). Timberline's Magic Mile lift carries nonskiers up above the clouds for spectacular views of the mountain and surrounding environs ($4, children $2). Experienced hikers can tackle the mountain on foot (complete climbing equipment rental at Timberline $16.50).

Even if you decide to ski at Ski Bowl or Mt. Hood Meadows, turn up the 6-mi. road just off **Government Camp** to the W.P.A.-style **Timberline Lodge** (800-452-1335, 231-5400 from Portland), site of the outdoor filming of Stanley Kubrick's *The Shining*. The drive to the lodge allows spectacular views of the valley below. Next door is the **Day Lodge,** where skiers can store equipment without staying overnight, and the **Wy'east Kitchen,** a cafeteria alternative to the expensive dining at Timberline. Nonskiers can find non-stop fun on the mountain. Ski Bowl runs an alpine slide, a go-kart course, and groomed mountain-bicycle trails. In addition, hiking trails circle the mountain. The most popular is **Mirror Lake,** a 4-mi. loop open June through October. Start at a parking lot off U.S. 26, 1 mi. west of Government Camp. Ask at Timberline for all the hiking options.

From the Columbia River Gorge, you can also take Hwy. 35, south from Hood River, which wends through apple, pear, and cherry orchards. In April, when the trees are in bloom, the drive is particularly memorable. **Gray Line Tours,** 400 SW Broadway (226-6755), offers an eight-and-a-half-hour ride around Mt. Hood and through the Columbia River Gorge ($28, ages under 12 $14). Tours leave from the Imperial Hotel from mid-May to early October at 9am on Tuesdays, Thursdays, and Saturdays. This loop is very popular; on sunny weekends an endless stream of cars with Oregon license plate sind east from Portland around U.S. 26 and Hwy. 35.

Oregon City

Originally the capital of the Oregon Territory and the supposedly the first incorporated American city west of the Mississippi, this once-burgeoning community was settled around the tremendous 42-ft.-high Willamette Falls. Even before the settlers arrived, Native Americans had been fishing here for 3000 years. Oregon City built a thriving transportation industry carrying cargo and people around the falls to new northern settlements such as Portland. As these settlements grew, Oregon City declined into a suburb with a past. Take bus #32, 33, or 35 (all green leaf) to Oregon City from 5th Ave. in downtown Portland, or a 20 minute drive down Hwy. 43. The **"End of the Trail" Interpretive Center,** 500 Washington St. (657-8287), celebrates the end of the 2170-mi. Oregon Trail, which begins in Independence, MO. Pictures of covered wagons and tired, dusty-looking people inhabit this miniature museum. (Open Tues.-Sat. 10am-4pm, Sun. noon-4pm. Admission $3, seniors $1.50, children $1.) The **McLoughlin House,** 713 Center St. (656-5146), former home of beloved early Oregonian and fur trade baron Dr. John McLoughlin, has been restored with original furnishings. (Open Tues.-Sat. 10am-4pm. Admission $3, seniors $2, ages under 17 $1.)

The most distinctive structure in Oregon City is surely its **Municipal Elevator,** on Railroad St. at the end of 7th Ave. This dusty pink antique is built into a large hill and looks like it might have been picked up at George Jetson's garage sale. Nevertheless, rides are free and afford interesting views of the Smurfit paper mill. (Open Mon.-Sat. 7am-7pm.)

Come down from the dizzying heights to visit the less spectacular **Clackamas County Historical Society Museum,** 603 6th St. (655-2866). The generic exhibits feature pioneer and Native American relics. (Open Tues.-Sat. 10am-4pm. Admission $2.) If you sensibly decide to skip the museum, take the money you've saved and head for the **Sportcraft Marina,** 1701 Clackamette Dr. (656-6484), which rents boats and related equipment for reasonable prices; boats start at $20 per day. (Open daily 9am-6pm.) Oregon City's annual highlight is the **Riverfest** in mid-July, with a dunk tank, bingo games, and live bluegrass music.

What the city lacks in sights, it compensates for with a handful of down-to-earth restaurants that serve heavenly food. **Chris's Coffee Shop,** 210 7th St. (657-5111), grills imaginative burger specials ($2-4) and makes marvelous milkshakes ($1.50). City photos from the 40s adorn the walls. (Open Mon.-Fri. 6am-4pm, Sat. 7am-3pm.) **Main Street Eatery,** 716B Main St. (657-2865), serves sandwiches for $3-5. (Open Mon.-Fri. 6am-4pm, Sat. 8am-3pm.) Because of the easy access to Portland, there is absolutely no reason to spend the night in Oregon City. If trapped, stay at the **International Dunes Motor Inn,** 1900 Clackamette Dr. (655-7141); its luxurious rooms with VCR, cable, heated pool, and hot tub start at around $50 for a single.

The **Chamber of Commerce,** 500 Abernathy Rd. (656-1619), on the corner of Washington and 17th, offers the usual. (Open Mon.-Fri. 9am-noon and 1-5pm, Sat.-Sun. 11am-4pm.)

Oregon Coast

Oregon's western boundary deserves superlatives. The so-called "Pacific" hurls itself at the rocky shore with violent abandon. Only the most daring swim in its ice-cold surf; others are more than satisfied by the matchless views and huge stretches of unspoiled beach.

Possessively hugging the shore, **U.S. 101,** the renowned coastal highway, passes by a series of lofty viewpoints. From northernmost Astoria to Brookings in the south, the highway laces together the resorts and historic fishing villages that cluster around the mouths of rivers feeding into the Pacific. It is most breathtaking between the coastal towns, where hundreds of miles of state and national park allow direct access to the beach. Whenever the highway leaves the coast, look for a beach loop road. These are the "roads less traveled," which afford some of the finest scenery on the western seaboard.

Getting Around

Drive or bike for the most extensive and rewarding encounter with the coast. Remember that rain is frequent. The *Oregon Coast Bike Route Map* (available free from the Oregon Dept. of Transportation, Salem 97310, or at virtually any visitors center or Chamber of Commerce on the coast) provides invaluable information on campsites, hostels, bike repair facilities, temperatures, and wind speed.

For those without a car or bike, transportation becomes a bit tricky. **Greyhound's** coastal routes from Portland currently run only twice per day each way. Along the southern coast, the 10-hour Portland-Brookings route stops at Lincoln City, Newport, Florence, Reedsport, Coos Bay, Bandon, Port Orford, Gold Beach, and every suburb between Portland and the coast. In the north, the Portland-Tillamook-Astoria loop offers on-call service to Cannon Beach. Local public transportation goes from virtually all towns in between those points to Astoria, but no public transportation exists between Cannon Beach and Lincoln City.

Motorists may want to stock up and fill up before reaching the coast-bound highways as gasoline and grocery prices on the coast are about 20% higher than in inland cities.

Astoria

In 1805, Lewis and Clark forged their way across the not-yet won-west, proving that an overland passage across the continent was possible. At the end of their journey, they passed through an anonymous plot of land on the lower lip of the Columbia River mouth and spent the winter seven miles to the west. In 1811, this plot became the first American settlement on the West Coast when John Jacob Astor, on his way to to becoming the richest man in America, established on it a fur trading post. Thirty years later, the U.S. Postal Service introduced bureaucracy to the west when it opened up an office in downtown Astoria. Meanwhile, as traffic down the Columbia increased and immigrants began arriving, the town embarked upon a trajectory of rapid development. A beacon of expansion and prosperity, the frontier town signalled the future of the nation.

In 1911, Astoria held a centennial celebration and indeed it had much to celebrate—its canneries, fisheries, flouring mills, and sawmills were thriving. Between 1850 and 1920, its population had increased from 250 to 14,027.

The trajectory, however, was reaching its peak. On December 9, 1922, a massive fire struck at night. By noon the next day, the entire business district had been destroyed. The city began a reconstruction and fireproofing program, and by decade's end the area was better than new—just in time for the Great Depression.

The Depression hit the entire coast, and Astoria was not spared. The town entered into a decade-long economic coma. Miraculously, the U.S. Army decided to focus its western defense plan around the ailing city and brought it back to life. In a sudden turn of events, Astoria had inherited $15 million from its Uncle Sam.

With 34 canneries in operation, the post-war salmon industy boomed. But in the mid 50s, the salmon catch dwindled. And as the coastal waters became fished-out, canning companies migrated to Alaska. Astoria's dairy and manufacturing industries soon followed suit, taking most of the town's residents with them. In recent years, lumber—the only major industry left—was cut short when Congress voted to restrict logging to protect the infamous spotted owl and other endangered woodland creatures.

With no further natural resources to exploit, Astoria, like other towns along the coast, has resorted to tourism for its livelihood. Whereas it once boasted lumberyards, canneries, and warehouses, Astoria now claims museums, parks, and a lot of pretty old houses. As you stroll down the rows of empty hilly streets lined with resplendent (and fireproof) Victorian homes, contemplate whether Astoria still signals the future of America.

Practical Information and Orientation

Visitor Information: Greater Astoria Chamber of Commerce, 111 W. Marine Dr. (325-6311), just east of the U.S. 101 toll bridge to Washington. P.O. Box 176, Astoria 97103. Thoroughly stocked with information on Astoria, the coast, and southwest Washington. Open Mon.-Sat. 8am-6pm, Sun. 9am-5pm; Oct.-April Mon.-Fri. 8am-5pm, Sat.-Sun. 11am-4pm.

Greyhound (RAZ Transportation): 364 9th St. (325-5641), at Duane St. Leaves Astoria for Portland daily at 8:25am, 9:30am, and 7:15pm. Leaves Portland for Astoria daily at 6:30am and 4:30pm ($12, round-trip $22.80). Open Mon.-Sat. 8:45-noon and 4-7:30pm.

North Coast Transit: At the Greyhound station in Seaside (738-7083). Runs from Astoria to Seaside and back, serving towns in between. Leaves Astoria at 8:45am, 12:10pm, 3:20pm, and 5:40pm. To Seaside $2.25, round-trip $3.25.

Pacific Transit System: At the Greyhound terminal (206-642-4475, ext. 450). To Ilwaco and Chinook, WA. Fare 50¢. Buses leave Astoria daily at 7:30am, 11:40am, and 3pm.

TBR Transit: Also at the Greyhound terminal (325-3521 or 325-5189). Local bus service. One full city loop every 20 min. on the hr. Fare 45¢, students and under 12 35¢. Service Mon.-Sat. 6:30am-7:15pm.

Laundromat: 127 Bond St. (325-7815), behind the visitors center. Open daily 8am-10pm.

Clatsop County Women's Crisis Services: 1250 Duane St. (325-5735). 24 hr.

Senior Citizens Information Service: 818 Commercial St. (325-0123). Legal services. Open Mon.-Fri. 8:30am-12:30pm. Also community recreational center.

Children's Services: 325-4811. While primarily crisis-oriented, this county-run service also advises on child care and education in the Astoria area.

Ambulance: 642-2316.

Coast Guard: Clatsop Airport (861-2242), Warrenton. 24-hr. marine and air emergency service.

Clatsop County Sheriff: 325-2061.

Police: 642-4444.

Post Office: in the Federal Bldg. (325-2141), at 8th and Commercial. Open Mon.-Fri. 8:30am-5pm. General Delivery ZIP Code: 97103.

Area Code: 503.

Astoria is the only direct connection that the coast of Oregon has with Washington. Two bridges run from the city: the **Astoria Bridge,** which spans the Columbia River into Washington, and the **Youngs Bay Bridge,** to the southwest, over which Marina Drive becomes U.S. Hwy. 101. Warrenton lies a few miles west of the latter bridge. U.S. 30 ties Portland (100 mi. east) directly to Astoria. Astoria can also be reached from Portland via Hwy. 26 and U.S. 101 at Seaside.

Accommodations and Camping

For reasons unknown, motels in Astoria keep prices high; and bargains are difficult to find. The 10-mi. trek to Fort Stevens Park will let you pitch a tent in clean, albeit crowded, spaces.

Fort Columbia State Park Hostel (AYH), Fort Columbia, Chinook, WA (206-777-8755), within the park boundaries. Across the 4-mi. bridge into Washington, 2 mi. west on U.S. 101. Pacific Transit System will get you there for 50¢ (see Practical Information); otherwise you'll have to pay the $1.50 toll to cross the bridge. A practically deserted hostel located in the old army hospital of a turn-of-the-century fort. Glorious grounds, friendly staff, and a fire on chilly evenings. Kitchen and barbecue facilities. Lockout 9am-5pm, but hours not strictly enforced. Members $7.50, nonmembers $10.50.

Rivershore Motel, 59 W. Marine Dr. (325-2921), 1 mi. east of the bridge, on U.S. 30 along the Columbia. Pleasant motel with TV, phones, and kitchenettes. Singles $40. Doubles $45.

Astoria City Center Motel, 495 Marine Dr. (325-4211). Nothing fancy, but clean and comfortable. Singles $38. Doubles $44. In winter, prices drop $9.

Rosebrian Inn, 636 14th St. (325-7427), at Franklin. A cozy bed and breakfast in a restored Victorian home. Doubles $40, with private bath $55.

Fort Stevens State Park (861-2000), over Youngs Bay Bridge on U.S. 101 S., 10 mi. west of Astoria. A huge park with rugged, desolate beaches. 223 sites, facilities for the disabled, and hot showers. Sites $9. For reservations, write Fort Stevens, Hammond 97121.

Food

Meals in Astoria are generally wholesome, though not especially fancy. The **Safeway,** 11th St. and Duane, is open 24 hr. The **Community Store,** 14th and Duane (325-0027), sells natural and bulk foods. (Open Mon.-Fri. 9am-5:30pm.)

Pacific Rim, 229 W. Marine Dr. (325-4481), near Washington Bridge. Great food, no frills. Ignore the ugly, diner-like decor and try the Sicilian-style ravioli with basil and blue cheese for an unusual culinary experience. Italian dinner $5-7, burgers $2-3. Better-than-Pizza-Hut deep dish, square piaza $5. Open Sun.-Thurs. 11am-11pm, Fri.-Sat. 11am-midnight.

Columbian Café, 1114 Marine Dr. (325-2233). A gem for the vegetarian gourmet. Fresh pasta made daily, dishes around $8, salads $3. Special seafood dinners, depending on the catch of the day. Open Mon.-Fri. 8am-2pm. Dinners served Wed.-Thurs. 5-8pm, Fri. 5-9pm. At the adjacent **Bordertown Burrito Bar,** the Columbian Café's eccentric chefs cook up delicious vegetarian Mexican food. Most dinners $5-7. Open daily 11am-6pm.

Little Denmark, 125 9th St. (325-2409), downtown on the waterfront. Astoria's large Scandinavian contingent comes through with authentically bland Danish food and homemade pastries. Assortment of entrees and open-faced sandwiches $4.50. Open Mon.-Fri. 10am-4pm, Sat.-Sun. 9am-4pm.

Sights and Activities

Astoria is a city that should be viewed from above, so climb the 166 steps of the **Astor Column** on Coxcomb Hill Rd. Erected in 1922, the column's outside spirals with faded, storm-worn friezes depicting the history of the area—the discovery of the Columbia River by intrepid Robert Grey, the arrival of Lewis and Clark, and the settling of Astoria. Open from dawn to dusk, it is accessible by the TBR bus (see Practical Information). A hike up 8th St. followed by a left turn on Franklin Ave. is also rewarding.

Since the early 19th century, the elite of Astoria have hung their hats in the area surrounding **Franklin Avenue,** between 10th and 18th St. The houses, still in pristine condition, are a monument to the splendor of the city's past. It is easy to forget the somewhat seamier atmosphere of the dock while you enjoy the vast panorama of mountains and water. The indefatigable should proceed 1 block higher to **Grand Avenue,** parallel to Franklin, for more magnificent houses and an equally stunning view.

Fort Astoria, at 15th and Exchange St., is a replica of the straightforward square blockhouse built by John Jacob Astor's company in 1811. You can't go in, but you can gawk at the doorstep all day for free. Talks by buckskin-clad and rifle-toting guides are offered summer weekends at 11am, 12:30pm, 2pm, and 5:30pm. The **Flavel House,** 441 8th St. (325-2563), is a restored Victorian mansion owned by Astoria's first millionaire. Although the house's original furnishings are gone, the replacements are from the right period. Don't miss the basement, which houses such flotsam of history as a turn of-the-century switchboard and a horse carriage. The **Clatsop County Heritage Museum,** at 16th and Exchange St., houses photographic exhibitions, the usual assortment of old things, a fascinating exhibit on Oregon's first Chinese settlers, and, strangely enough, a collection of ancient Persian artwork. (House and museum admission $3, students $2, children $1. Open daily 10am-5pm; Nov.-April Tues.-Sun. noon-4pm.)

Across from the museum, the eccentric, talkative owner of the **Shallon Winery,** 1598 Duane St. (325-5978), will give you a tour of his small winemaking facilities along with his interpretation of the area's history. (Open daily noon-6pm.) Then he'll treat you to a taste of wines made from local berries and the only commercially-produced whey wines in town. (Usually open daily noon-6pm.) Nearby, the **Columbia River Maritime Museum,** 1793 Marine Dr. (325-2323), at the foot of 17th St., has, among a wide variety of nautical paraphernalia, sailing-ship models, early sea charts, and whaling exhibits. All displays are accompanied by well-written, detailed explanatory texts. Plan on spending over an hour here. Anchored outside is the *Columbia,* the last lightship to see active duty at the mouth of the Columbia River. (Museum open daily 9:30am-5pm. Admission $3, seniors $2, ages 6-18 $1.50.)

In the third week of June, Astoria holds its **Scandinavian Festival,** which is one of Clatsop County's biggest annual festivals. Begun as a fund-raiser and ethnic bonding event 20 years ago, the festival has burgeoned to attract blondes from all over the entire region. The celebration includes a parade, tug-of-war, folkdancing, and a profusion of ethnic foods (most Scandinavian).

The **Astoria Regatta,** held in early August, is one of the longest running community events in the Northwest, dating back to 1894. The regatta tradition remains strong—particularly in the afterglow of last year's celebration of the Coast Guard's 200th anniversary. It features food and craft booths, dance contests, softball and tennis events, and even a sailboat race or two.

Six miles west of Astoria, the **Fort Clatsop National Memorial** (861-2471) reconstructs the winter headquarters of the ragtag Lewis and Clark expedition, based on descriptions in their detailed journal. The crude fort housed Lewis and Clark, 24 enlisted men, three officers, a few interpreters and guides, Clark's slave York, and Lewis's dog Scannon. By the end, Scannon wasn't the only one with fleas. The **visitors center** shows a good slide presentation and a few exhibits. Park rangers give scheduled talks and demonstrations at 9:30am, 11am, 12:30pm, 2pm, 3:30pm, and 5pm. (Open daily 8:30am-6pm; Labor Day to mid- June 8am-5pm. Admission $1, ages over 63 and under 13 free, families $3.)

Fort Stevens State Park (800-452-5687 or 861-2000), off U.S. 101 on a tiny peninsula 10 mi. west of Astoria, has swimming, fishing, boating, beaches, and hiking trails. Fort Stevens was constructed in 1864 to guard against Confederate gun boats entering the Columbia, and the threat of its presence was seemingly enough to keep them at bay. Within the park lie the skeletal remains of the *Peter Iredale,* lost in 1906. The battered hulk of this 287-ft. British schooner makes a lonely and eerie sight at low tide. **Battery Russell,** (861-2471) also in the park, bears the dubious distinction of being the last mainland American fort to see active defensive duty since the war of 1812. At 10:30pm on June 22, 1942, a Japanese submarine offshore shelled the fort with 17 rounds. Today, in good sword-to-ploughshare fashion, the concrete gun emplacement has been taken out of service and converted to a playground.

Seaside

Seaside marked the end of the trail for Lewis and Clark, their last and most westward camp. Now the town flaunts cotton candy, arcades, and corn dogs as proof-positive of the manifest destiny of American culture, which makes of each new frontier the same old commercial strip.

Eccentric Portland railroad- and ship-builder Ben Holladay developed Seaside in the 1870s as a resort. A zoo and a racetrack were among Seaside's first structures, and Holladay's ships were ordered to fire cannon shots each time vessels sailed past the town. The years and the tourists have eroded much of Seaside's charm. Today the town is crowded with motels, fast food, and video arcades that clash uneasily with the brooding scenery of Oregon's coastline.

Practical Information and Orientation

Visitor Information: Chamber of Commerce, 7 N. Roosevelt St. (738-6391, in OR 800-444-6740), on U.S. 101 and Broadway. Well-versed staff armed and ready for every question about this town. The Chamber of Commerce doubles as a booking agency for most local motels. Open daily 8am-6pm; Oct.-May 8am-5pm.

Greyhound (RAZ Transportation): 622 12th Ave. (738-5121 for a recording, 739-8251 for information), in the relocated Prom Bike Shop. Leaves Portland at 6:30am for Seaside (2 hr., 15 min.) and Astoria (2 hr., 45 min.). The loop reverses itself after noon ($12, round-trip $22.80). **North Coast Transit** (738-7083) provides service between Astoria and Cannon Beach, with stops in-between at Warrenton, Gearhart, and Seaside. Buses leave Seaside both ways in front of Kerwin Rx Drugs at Holladay and Broadway. For Cannon Beach, buses leave at 9:45am and 4:20pm daily (20 min., $1.50, bikes 50¢); for Astoria, buses leave at 8:10am, 2:10pm, and 5:05pm (45 min., $2, bikes 50¢).

Car Rental: Advanced Auto (738-7278). $30 per day, 50 free mi., 15¢ each additional mi. Open Mon.-Fri. 8am-5pm.

Bike Rental: Prom Bike Shop, 622 12th Ave. (738-8251), in the Greyhound terminal. Bikes, bike carts, roller skates, and beach tricycles $4 per hr.; tandem bicycles $6 per hr. Unicycles by reservation only. ID required. Open Mon.-Fri. 10am-6pm, Sat.-Sun. 10am-dusk.

Laundromat: Holladay Coin Laundry, 57 N. Holladay St., at 1st Ave. (738-3458). Open daily 6am-11pm.

Senior Citizens Information Service: 1225 Ave. A (738-7393).

Children's Service Line: 325-4811 (Astoria).

Women's Crisis Service: 325-5735. 24hr.

Alcohol/Drug Help Line: 800-621-1646.

Police: 1000 S. Roosevelt Dr. (738-6311).

Post Office: 300 Ave. (738-5462). Open Mon.-Fri. 8:30am-5pm, Sat. for pickup 8-10am. General Delivery ZIP Code: 97138.

Area Code: 503.

Seaside lies 17 mi. south of Astoria and 8 mi. north of Cannon Beach along U.S. 101. Hwy. 26 ("The Sunset Highway") runs into U.S. 101 just south of Seaside along Saddle Mountain State Park; Hwy. 26 is the most direct route between here and Portland. The **Necanicum River** runs north-south through Seaside, approximately two blocks from the coastline, paralleled by U.S. 101 and Holladay Dr. to the east. All three are bisected by Broadway in the middle of town.

Accommodations

Motels' prices are directly proportional to their proximity to the beach. Though there are seemingly thousands of motels, the *cheapest* (i.e. the ones farthest from the beach) hover around $35 per night (cheaper during the off-season). The friendly neon "VACANCY" signs invariably flash "NO" by 5pm. To get ahead of the game, call the Chamber of Commerce for availability listings. They won't reserve a room for you, but they'll give you advice. Reservations should be made at least a couple of days in advance.

Holladay and Mariner Motels, 426 and 429 S. Holladay Dr. (738-3690). Holladay Dr. parallels U.S. 101, beside the Necanicum River, toward the ocean. The same people own both; the front office and pool are located at the Mariner. Small, quaint rooms with bathrooms on the hall. Singles $26. Doubles $31. Sept. 16-May 23 rooms $5 less.

Country Inn, 430 S. Holladay Dr. (738-8254), next to the Holladay. Real bedrooms, with bookshelves and raftered ceilings. The rooms aren't large, however, and there is some noise from the road. Singles $33. Doubles $39. Nov.-April singles $29, doubles $35.

Royale Motel, 521 Ave. A (738-9541), 1 block from the arcades of Broadway. Friendly management and clean rooms. Cable TV. Rooms $37-42; Sept. 16-May 15 $30-36.

Camping

Private campgrounds around town are for RVs only, and the closest state parks are Fort Stevens, 21 mi. north (see Astoria), and Saddle Mountain, 14 mi. southeast from the coast. Sleeping on the beach is illegal, and the police do patrol. Camping on the dunes around Gearhart, 2 mi. north of Seaside, is possible, but petty crime has been reported, so between winks keep an eye on your belongings.

Saddle Mountain State Park, at Necanicum Jct., 14 mi. southeast of Seaside off U.S. 26 on a winding 7½-mi. road. Nine primitive campsites. Flush toilets, no showers. Pretty forest setting near base of Saddle Mountain hiking trail. Sites $9.

Kloochy Creek, 7½ mi. southeast of Seaside, about 300 yds. off U.S. 26. Nine primitive sites clustered around the country's largest Sitka Spruce tree. (216 ft. tall, 52 ft. in circumference). Sites $6.

Food

Buck-fifty corn dogs, beachfront burgers, and fried starch are everywhere. Those who go "Hah!" to such low-brow cuisine should turn right around and march north to Gearhart or south to Cannon Beach.

Dooger's Seafood and Grill, 505 Broadway St. (738-3773). The best clam chowder in town, unadulterated by flour or cornstarch thickeners. Lunch special of fried oysters, shrimp salad, and garlic bread $6. Open daily 11am-10pm; Oct.-May daily 11am-9pm.

Chicago Pan Pizza Co., 111 Broadway St. (738-5217). All-you-can-eat pizza and salad deal ($5, after 5pm $6). Pizza baked to order, not congealed under a heat lamp. Open daily 11am-9pm.

Cannon Beach Bakery, (738-6140) at the Turnaround. A modest bakery a block from the beach. Despite the crowds that stream by, this place remains removed from the beachfront buzz, serving a variety of freshly baked goods. Humongous turnovers ($1), muffins (65¢). Open Wed.-Mon. 9am-5pm.

Sights and Seasonal Events

Seaside revolves around **Broadway,** a garish strip of arcades, shops, and salt water taffy joints running the ½ mi. or so from Roosevelt (U.S. 101) to the beach. The arcades offer some of the few remaining 10¢ games of skee ball in this country. The **Turnaround** at the end of Broadway signals an arbitrary end to the Lewis and Clark

Trail. In 1986, the Turnaround underwent a facelift to add to the $1.3 million spent on street improvements in 1982-3, and a statue of Lewis and Clark is planned for the end of the Trail. Eight blocks south of the Turnaround lies the **Saltworks,** a replica of the salt cairn used by the Lewis and Clark expedition to produce salt for preserving food. Over the memorial flies a 15-starred and striped U.S. flag—one of only three locations where it is legal to fly such a flag officially. More than 40 gallons of water are evaporated here daily.

A recent addition to the downtown beachfront culture is actually along the Necanicum River. **Quatat Marine Park** (from the Clatsop word meaning "village by the sea") spans four blocks between First Ave. and A Ave. and boasts peaceful dock walkways and benches removed from the teeming sidewalks of Broadway. Quatat Park also offers water sports of sorts: **Monkey Business** operates off a dock in the park, offering bumper boats (just inner tubes with motors) at $3 for 5 min., and paddle boats at $7 per ½ hr. for two people.

Travelers looking for Lewis and Clark in living color will get a kick out of the **Lewis and Clark Historical Drama**—a re-enactment of the last leg of their highly overrated journey. The drama does not relate Lewis and Clark's return east, where Lewis went on to a violent death three years later, and Clark to a series of undistinguished positions. Tickets are available at the Chamber of Commerce and at some stores. (Tickets $7.50, seniors $6.50, ages 6-15 $3. Performances mid-July to Aug. Thurs.-Sat. 8pm, Mon.-Tues. 2pm.) **Seaside Historical Museum,** 570 Necanicum Dr. (738-7065), houses a small piece of the largest Douglas fir tree ever found—225 ft. to the broken top, 15' 7" in diameter—and a remarkably good exhibit of Clatsop Native American artifacts. The museum, predictably, displays the pair's personal journals along with staged reenactment photos (enough, already). ($1 adults, 50¢ children. Open daily 10:30am-4pm; Oct.-April Wed.-Sun. 1-4pm.)

Seaside's beach is crowded but expansive. Three lifeguards are on duty from Memorial Day to Labor Day (daily 10am-6pm). The water, of course, is always too cold for swimming, but on "red flag" days the surf is also considered too rough. For a quieter beach, head to **Gearhart.** No lifeguard is on duty here, and since a drowning accident in 1983 town officials have advised against swimming. You can, however, explore the long stretch of sand and dunes safely.

Saddle Mountain State Park, 14 mi. southeast of Seaside on U.S. 26, is named for the highest peak in the coastal range. From Saddle Mountain's 3283-ft. summit, the views of the Cascades to the north are astounding. The 6-mi. trail, open March through December, is a good four-hour hike. Farther east on U.S. 26 lies the **Jewell Meadows Wildlife Area,** a wintering habitat for Roosevelt elk. Parking spaces throughout the refuge allow you to get out and wander about with the elk, present mostly in fall and winter. Black-tailed deer often show up in the spring and summer, and an occasional coyote may make a special guest appearance any time of year. Take U.S. 26 to Jewell Jct., then head north on the unmarked state road for 9 mi. to Jewell. Turn west and travel 1½ mi. on Hwy. 202 to the refuge area.

Seven miles south of Seaside on U.S. 101, **Ecola State Park** (436-2844) marks yet another end of the Lewis and Clark Trail. That elusive first glimpse of the Pacific could not have been more arresting. From the high ground, you can stare with wild surmise at **Haystack Rock** anchored just a little offshore. Beyond it, the tenacious old **Tillamook Lighthouse** clings like a barnacle to a wave-swept rock. Construction of the lighthouse, begun in 1879, continued for years while storms kept blowing the foundations away. Decommissioned in 1957 because of damage caused by storm-tossed rocks, the now privately owned lighthouse can be reached only by helicopter and only for the purpose of depositing ashes of the dead.

From Ecola State Park, you can take the 12-mi. round-trip hike to **Tillamook Head,** from which you can sometimes glimpse migrating whales. In the fall, ask a knowledgeable local to point out chanterelle mushrooms along the path. The trail is open year-round.

The **Seaside Beach Run** in mid-August carries on the tradition of the now-defunct Trail's End Marathon. The 8-mi. race on the beach leaves Seaside's Turnaround. Call the Chamber of Commerce for information.

Cannon Beach

A rusty cannon from the shipwrecked schooner *Shark* washed ashore at Ecola State Park, giving this town its name (good thing it wasn't a dead sailor). Distinguished from Seaside by its romance and subtlety, and from Astoria by its lack of any real history, Cannon Beach is tasteful and expensive. The town tries to blend inconspicuously with the grandeur of the northern Oregon coast, camouflaging its houses in thickets of trees and maintaining an unobtrusive beach front. Aesthetic sensibility runs amok in Cannon Beach: art galleries, pseudo-bohemian shops, and theater groups outnumber fast-food joints and neon signs. This is where wealthy Portlanders spend their weekends.

Practical Information and Orientation

Visitor Information: Cannon Beach Chamber of Commerce, 201 E. 2nd (436-2623), at Spruce St. P.O. Box 64, Cannon Beach 97110. Extremely helpful manager. Maps of the area. Open Mon.-Sat. 11am-5pm, Sun. 11am-4pm; sometimes closed on winter weekends.

Buses: Greyhound (RAZ). Transportation from Cannon Beach to anywhere is very limited. The town is included in the Portland bus loop, but only twice daily, and each time going different ways: northward to Portland via Tillamook leaves Cannon Beach at 9:07am, and the return trip comes in at 7:23pm. To: Portland $12, Tillamook and Astoria $5. Buses stop in front of the Chamber of Commerce. **North Coast Transit:** (738-7083). Buses leave downtown Cannon Beach at 10:10am and 4:40pm daily, servicing Seaside, Gearhart, Warrenton and Astoria.

Bike Rental: Mike's Bike Shop, 248 N. Spruce St. (436-1266), around the corner from the Chamber of Commerce. Maps of routes along old, untraveled logging roads. Mountain bikes and cruisers $3 per hr., beach tricycles(!) $5 per 75 min. Open in summer Mon., Wed.-Thurs., and Sat. 10am-6pm, Fri. 10am-7pm, Sun. noon-5pm.

Hospital: Seaside, 738-8463. **Cannon Beach:** walk in clinic (436-1142).

Lifeguard Service: 436-1581.

Weather: 861-2722 (national service).

Fire Dept.: 436-2280.

Police: 436-2811.

Post Office: 155 N. Hemlock St. (436-2822). Open Mon.-Fri. 9am-5pm. General Delivery ZIP Code: 97110.

Area Code: 503.

Cannon Beach lies 8 mi. south of Seaside and 42 mi. north of Tillamook on U.S. 101; it is 80 mi. from Portland via U.S. 26.

Accommodations and Food

Cannon Beach has a variety of pleasant motels, few of which are affordable. The budget-conscious might wish to camp out at **Oswald West** (see Cannon Beach to Tillamook), just south of town.

In keeping with Cannon Beach's character, the food here is served for the most part in trendy and pricy cafés. Be especially wary of the town's several overpriced bakeries. You will, however, find a few budget treasures.

McBee Court, S. Hemlock and Van Buren Rd. (436-2569), at old U.S. 101, ½ block from the ocean near Haystack Rock. A little south of the commercial center of town, but still on a noisy main street. Pleasant rooms 1 block from the beach. Singles $27, with hide-a-bed $36. Doubles $38. Separate 2-story townhouse with kitchen, fireplace, 1 double bed, 3 twins, and hide-a-bed $65. A few dollars less in winter.

Blue Gull Motel, 632 S. Hemlock St. (436-2714). Big clean rooms decorated with heavy-handed oil paintings of crashing surf. Set back from the street. TV with cable. Singles and doubles $36; in off-season $30, 2 for 1 special.

Hidden Villa, 188 E. Van Buren Rd. (436-2237), 2 blocks from beach. Singles $45. Doubles $49. In winter, rooms $10 less. Discounts for stays of longer than one night.

Lazy Susan Café, 126 N. Hemlock St. (436-2816). A gorgeous restaurant serving health food in sturdy crockery. Sandwiches $4-5, variety of omelettes $5. Make sure to order the waffles and fruit special ($5) when it's available. Open Thurs.-Mon. 7:30am-2:30pm, Sun. 8am-2pm for brunch only.

Osburn's Deli and Grocery, 240 N. Hemlock St. (436-2234). Hearty sandwiches to go ($4, available 11am-5pm). Open daily 8:30am-8:30pm; Labor Day-June 9am-7:30pm. **Osburn's Ice Creamery,** next door, scoops cones for $1.05. The fresh strawberry shake ($3), available in season, is nectar of the gods. Open daily 11am-6pm.

Dory's Launch Grill, at the corner of S. Hemlock and Gower St. on the south end of town. Ignore the fast food appearances of this place and dig into their hearty burgers ($2-3) and excellent clam chowder ($1.50).

Cannon Beach Seafood Co., 123 S. Hemlock St. (436-2272). Great prices for fresh seafood. Large shrimp cocktail $3. Fish and chips $3.37. Open daily Mon.-Thurs. 11am-6pm, Fri.-Sat. 11am-6:30pm, Sun. 11am-5:30pm.

Mariner Market, 139 N. Hemlock St. (436-2442). About the least expensive grocery store in town—which isn't saying much. Peanut butter ground while you wait ($2 per lb.). Open Mon.-Thurs. 9am-10pm, Fri.-Sat. 9am-11pm, Sun. 9am-9pm.

Sights and Activities

Rather than browse in the art galleries, you should spend a morning walking on the 7-mi. beach and admiring hulking **Haystack Rock.** The bay's 235-ft. centerpiece is spotted (and splattered) by gulls, puffins, barnacles, anemones, and the occasional sea lion. The tide pools below usually teem with colorful sea life. Tidal charts are avilable at the Chamber of Commerce, although digging for mussels and clams is now prohibited (enforced by the **Rock Police).** In an effort to educate the public on the rock's remarkably self-contained ecosystem, interpreters are present on weekends of especially low tides.

The **Coaster Theater** (436-1242), on Hemlock, stages three semi-professional productions from late June through August. (Box office hours July-Aug. Thurs.-Sat. noon-8pm. Or write Coaster Theater, P.O. Box 643, Cannon Beach 97110. Performances Thurs.-Sat. at 8pm. Admission $10.)

Try to schedule your itinerary around the **Sand Castle Competition.** Contestants pour in from hundreds of miles away and begin construction early in the morning, creating ornate sculptures from wet sand. In the evening, the high tide washes everything away, leaving photographs as the sole testimony to the staggering amount of creative energy expended during the day. The photos are prominently displayed in the Chamber of Commerce. Past creations have included Humpty Dumpty, King Tut, and Ozymandias, as well as a life-size sculpture of Ralph Kramden and Ed Norton which inexplicably bore a frightening resemblance to unconvicted felon Randy Nicolau and his sidekick, Michael "Evil" Flynn. Contact the Chamber of Commerce for the date of the 1990 competition.

In December, locals celebrate Christmas with a three-week festival, opening officially with a lamplighting ceremony on the first Friday of the month. A proclamation is read and the public ushers in the holiday season with songs and cider guzzling.

Cannon Beach to Tillamook

Tillamook County has been in various stages of convalescence since the summer of 1933, when a hellish fire raged for over a week, reducing 500 sq. mi. of the world's finest timber to charcoal. Fifty-six years later, Tillamook State Forest has been nursed back to health. The sedate beaches and trees of Tillamook County accommodate spillover from the more popular resorts to the north and south. Small towns strung out along the coastline—Manzanita, Nehalem, Rockaway, and Garibaldi—are generally uncrowded and peaceful. Tourist information for these towns is available at the visitors information bureau in Tillamook or the **Rockaway Beach Chamber of Commerce,** 216 N. U.S. 101 (355-8108).

Oswald West State Park, 10 mi. south of Cannon Beach, is a headland rain forest with huge spruce and cedar trees. The park is accessible only by foot on a ¼-mi. trail off U.S. 101. This doesn't quite qualify as "roughing it," for the State Parks Division is at hand to provide wheelbarrows for pushing gear from the U.S. 101 parking area to the 36 uncrowded, primitive campsites near the beach. The overnight camping season lasts from mid-May to October, and sites cost $7. From the park, take the 4-mi. **Cape Falcon** hiking trail farther out toward the water, or just follow the path from the campground down to one of Oregon's only surfing beaches.

Five miles south of Oswald, self-consciously quaint **Manzanita** sleeps on a long expanse of uncrowded beach. The **San Dune Motel,** 428 Dorcas Lane (368-5163), just off Laneda St., the main drag through town, has inexpensive, pleasant rooms 5 blocks from the shore. Suites cost $35-65 in summer, $30-45 in winter, and most rooms have fully equipped kitchens. Take advantage of these facilities, since the few restaurants in town are expensive.

Nehalem, a few miles south, is little more than a handful of "made in Oregon" shops marshalled along U.S. 101. Stop in at the **Bayway Eatery** (368-6495) for excellent $4 fish and chips. The slightly grubby diner is a favorite Nehalem hangout. (Open Mon.-Sat. 6am-9pm, Sun. 7am-4pm.) The **Nehalem Food Mart** stocks an impressive selection of imported beers. (Open Mon.-Tues. 9am-7pm, Wed.-Sat. 9am-9pm, Sun. 10am-6pm.) **Mystery Books,** next to the Food Mart, has a variety of mysterious books as well as hand-painted figures and stained glass (Open 10am-5pm daily, hours subject to small-town inconstancy). Three miles away, the **Nehalem Bay Winery,** 34965 Hwy. 53 (368-5300), hands out samples of local specialties ($11). (Open daily 10am-5pm.)

A few miles south of Nehalem, just north of Wheeler, **Nehalem Bay State Park** offers 292 sites ($10), including some hiker/biker sites ($2), and hot showers. If you prefer indoor accommodations, stop at the newly-renovated **Wheeler Fishing Lodge,** 580 Marine Dr. (368-FISH). This motel sports a variety of rooms ranging from $25-75; the premium one sits right on the water and has a jacuzzi. All the rooms have a refreshing, colonial antique feel to them, and the owner is a gracious host. The motel lies in the quiet town of **Wheeler,** whose quirky small-town levity has given way to a "down-to-business" attitude, as several of the shops downtown have recently been taken over and refurbished. The **Bayfront Bakery and Deli,** 468 Nehalon Blvd. (368-6599), serves baked goods right out of the oven, as well as $3.25 lunch sandwiches (Open Tues.-Sat. 8:30am-5:30pm.) A two-hour train ride might be the most relaxing—and slowest—way to get from Wheeler to Tillamook. Call **Coast Line Express** (842-2768) for times ($15, seniors $12, children $8).

Rockaway, about 8 mi. south of Wheeler, is a quiet retirement town with a long stretch of lonely beach and, mysteriously, about five penny arcades. The friendly, knowledgeable manager at the **Sand Dollar Motel,** on U.S. 101 (355-2301), rents clean rooms with showers from $25 (discount for seniors). This is one of the few affordable seaside motels in the state.

The larger town of **Garibaldi,** roughly 6 mi. south of Rockaway, is named after Guiseppi Garibaldi who it seems was a fisherman before he united Italy. A highly developed marina juts into the bay here, luring boaters but minimizing ocean and beach access for landlubbers. There are a few good places to eat in town. The **Bayfront Bakery and Deli,** 302 Garibaldi (322-3787), on U.S. 101, has a more extensive menu than its Wheeler branch, including barbecue ribs, pizza, and salads. The pies and baked goods still win out. (Open Tues.-Sat. 5:30am-5:30pm, Sun. 7am-4pm.) The **Old Mill Restaurant,** 3rd and Americana St. (322-0222), overlooks the boats and water from the Old Mill Marina. Turn west off U.S. 101 over the railroad tracks and follow the signs to the left. This faded wooden building contains an ordinary family-style restaurant. The daily lunch special costs $4, and they leave the skins on their french fries. A razor clam dinner is $12 and a bowl of clam chowder is $3.50. (Open daily 4:30am-10pm.)

Tillamook

Oregon's finest cheeses are cultured at the eastern shore of Tillamook Bay, where cow pastures predominate. Some visitors enjoy a brief jaunt through the surrounding bucolic countryside, but most just hanker for a hunk of cheese.

Practical Information and Orientation

Visitor Information: Tillamook County Chamber of Commerce, 3705 U.S. 101 N. (842-7525), next to the Tillamook Cheese Factory. Open Mon.-Sat. 9am-5pm; mid-June to Sept. also open Sun. 9:30am-2:30pm. Winters Mon.-Fri. 9am-5pm, Sat. noon-4pm.

Parks and Recreation: 322-3477.

Senior Citizen Information: 842-8748.

Children's Services: 842-2121.

Alcohol and Drug Abuse: 842-5571.

Tillamook Crisis and Resource Center: 842-9486.

Ambulance: 800-356-0460 or 842-4444.

Fire Dept.: 842-7587.

County Sheriff: 842-2561.

Police: 842-2522, in City Hall.

Post Office: 2200 1st St. Open Mon.-Fri. 8:30am-5pm. General Delivery ZIP Code: 97191.

Area Code: 503.

Tillamook lies 49 mi. south of Seaside and 44 mi. north of Lincoln City on U.S. 101. The most direct route from Portland is to take U.S. 26 to Hwy. 6 (74 mi.).

Accommodations, Camping, and Food

Tillamook's main occupation is to sate cheese-crazed tourists. Expect inflated seasonal lodging prices.

Tillamook Hostel (AYH), 408 Meadow Ave. (842-5683). More of a house than a hostel, located in a quiet residential neighborhood. Accommodates 4, so call or write for reservations. $6 per person.

El Rancho Motel, 1810 U.S. 101 N. (842-4413), between the center of town and the Tillamook Cheese Factory. Generic motel rooms; the highway noise will lull you to sleep. Free coffee. Guests pay $3 per ½-hr. to use tanning salon. Singles $32. Doubles $38. Rates may be lower off-season. Senior citizen discount.

Greenacres Motel, 3615 U.S. 101 N. (842-2731), next to the Cheese Factory. The Kraft American of Motels: small, yellowing and individually wrapped singles. Reserve at least two weeks in advance. Singles $24. Doubles $28.

Kilchis County Park, (842-8662). 8 mi. northeast of Tillamook, along Kilchis River Rd. 40 primitive sites near the river and the county ball field. Pets allowed. Tentsites $6.

Cape Lookout State Park, 13000 Whiskey Creek Rd. (842-4981). Hot showers, flush toilets. 53 full hookups, 193 tent sites. $8-11 in summer, $5-6 in winter. Hiker/biker sites $6. (See Tillamook to Lincoln City.)

La Casa Medello (842-5768), north of town on U.S. 101, down the street from El Rancho Motel. Tries hard to stay true to its motif, but what do you expect in Cheesetown, USA? Mild Mexican food prepared to order. Tacos $2, burritos $3.25. Dinners (about $7) come with rice, beans, and chips. Open Mon.-Fri. 11am-9pm, Sat.-Sun. 11am-10pm; in winter Mon.-Fri. 11am-8pm, Sat.-Sun. 11am-10pm.

Hadley House, 2203 3rd St. (842-2101), across from the courthouse. More-than-generous helpings of sea (and cheese) products, as well as American standbys. Teriyaki burger $4.25, sandwiches $4-6. Kitchen clatter competes with conversation, but the bread is always fresh from the oven and the colonial decor is refreshing. Full dinner $5.50.

Tillamook Cheese Factory, 4175 U.S. 101 N. (842-4481). Cheap breakfasts served 8-11am. Lunch specials $3.50. Homemade ice cream 95¢. Open daily 8am-8pm; Sept. to mid-June 8am-5pm.

Sights and Activities

In Native American parlance, Tillamook means "land of many waters." Whether these original inhabitants were referring to the frequent downpours or not remains a mystery. But in any case, the place can be very wet. That perhaps explains why so many of Tillamook's tourist attractions are indoors. The most visited of these is undoubtedly the **Tillamook Cheese Factory** at 4175 U.S. 101 N. (842-4481). The primary reason for the building's popularity seems not to lie in the self-guided tour, but rather in the adjacent ice cream parlor, where a cone of the local best goes for 95¢. The place is usually packed in summer. (Open daily 8am-8pm; Sept. to mid-June 9am-5pm.) Somewhat less crowded is the **Blue Heron French Cheese Factory,** 2001 Blue Heron Dr. (842-8281), 1 mi. south of the Tillamook factory on the east side of U.S. 101. The "factory" has stopped making cheese, but the sales room is more open to tasting than at Tillamook and features basket after basket of cheesy goodies to sample. Four bucks will buy you a wheel of their excellent brie. **Debbie D's Sausage Factory** 2110 N. Main (842-2622), is also defunct as a manufacturer of cheese, but sells a variety of treats and has wine tasting from 11am-7pm. Open daily 8am-7pm.

West of the highway, in downtown Tillamook, the **Tillamook County Pioneer Museum,** 2106 2nd St. (842-4553), features all manner of household and industrial goods from the pioneer era, labeled with yellowed donation cards. (Open Mon.-Sat. 8:30am-5pm, Sun. noon-5pm; Oct.-April Tues.-Sat. 8:30am-5pm, Sun. noon-5pm. Admission $1, ages 12-17 50¢, families $5, under 12 free.)

The first weekend in March, cheddar takes the back seat as Tillamook pays tribute to some of its earliest settlers in the **Swiss Festival** celebration. In addition to the "oompah" band, arts, crafts, and European foods are displayed and consumed.

Tillamook to Lincoln City

Between Tillamook and Lincoln City, U.S. 101 wanders eastward into forest land out of sight of the ocean. Consider taking instead the **Three Capes Loop,** a 35-mi. circle to the west that connects a trio of spectacular promontories—Cape Meares, Cape Lookout, and Cape Kiwanda State Parks. The beaches are secluded, and the scenery makes the uncrowded drive worthwhile. Cyclists should beware of the narrow twists and poor condition of the roads.

Cape Meares, at the tip of the promontory jutting out from Tillamook, is home to the **Octopus Tree,** a gnarled Sitka spruce with several trunks. Also at the park is the **Cape Meares Lighthouse,** built in 1890, which now operates as an on-site interpretive center. Climb to the top for sweeping views and a peek at the original lens of the big light. (Open May-Sept. Thurs.-Mon. 11am-6pm. Free.)

From here, continue 12 mi. southwest to **Cape Lookout** (842-4981), a reservation park with 193 tentsites and 53 full hookups for $8-11 ($5-7 in winter). The park is also equipped with showers, trails, and facilities for the disabled. For reservations, write Cape Lookout, 13000 Whiskey Creek Rd., Tillamook 97141.

Cape Kiwanda, the third promontory on the loop, is for day-use only. (Open 8am-dusk.) On sunny, windy days, hang gliders gather to test their skill at negotiating the wave-carved sandstone cliffs. The sheltered cape draws skin divers, and beach hikers come to sink their toes into the dunes. A state park trail overlooks the top of the cape before reaching the ocean. On the cape, just barely north of Pacific City, massive rock outcroppings in a small bay mark the launching pad of the flat-bottomed **Dory Fleet,** one of a few fleets in the world that launches beachside directly onto the surf. If you bring your own fishing gear down to the cape most mornings around 5am, you can probably convince someone to take you on board; the fee will nearly always be lower than those of commercial outfitters. If you want to guarantee a catch, or don't have your own gear, let **Pacific City Sporting Goods** (965-6466) take you salmon- or bottom-fishing ($60 per day). Make reservations, and be prepared to leave by 6am. The required one-day license can be purchased at the store for $5. There is a two-fish limit on salmon.

Pacific City is a delightful town unknown to most U.S. 101 travelers. Pacific City is home to the other Haystack Rock, equally as awesome as its brother to the north. This one has a handle jutting out from its northern edge, giving the impression that some prehistoric giant left it here when he got tired carrying it. The **Turnaround Motel**, 5985 Pacific Ave. (965-6496), has a few handsome suites with kitchens, living rooms, and excellent views (doubles $40). The undisputed king of nearby Gustation Hill is the **Riverhouse Restaurant**, 34450 Brooten Rd. (965-6722), overlooking the Nestucca River. Chowder and piled-high sandwiches cost $5-7. At dinner try the Oysters Kirkpatrick, oven-broiled with swiss cheese, bacon, and tomato ($12). (Open Tues.-Thurs. 11am-9pm, Fri.-Sat. 11am-10pm, Sun. 10am-9pm.) The **Chamber of Commerce** (965-6161) does not operate a regular office but does have a complete information sign and map posted at 34960 Brooten Rd., in the middle of nowhere.

Back on U.S. 101 about 8 mi. south, **Neskowin** appears to be little more than a motel by the side of the road. Squeezed into this parking lot complex, however, is the **Deli at Neskowin**, 4505 Salem Ave. (392-3838), a refuge for homesick New Yorkers. Pastrami sandwiches go for $4, and the pickled Oregon salmon combines the best of both coasts. (Open Sun.-Thurs. 8am-9pm, Fri.-Sat. 8am-10pm.) Driving south of Neskowin on U.S. 101, you should watch for signs of the **Siuslaw National Forest.** An 11-mi. road leaves U.S. 101 and passes by huge old trees dripping with moss (this is a northern rain forest). Five and a half mi. down the road from Neskowin is **Neskowin Creek Campground** (392-3131), where 12 primitive tentsites (outhouse only) are maintained for free camping.

U.S. 101 crosses Hwy. 18 at **Otis** (about two mi. east on Hwy. 18). The **Otis Café** (994-2813) serves some of the best home-style rhubarb pie around ($1.50). The place is often crowded; don't expect to get in and out quickly during peak hours. Your patience will be rewarded by $3 sandwiches on freshly baked bread and breakfast specials for $1.65. (Open Mon.-Wed. 7am-3pm, Thurs.-Sat. 7am-9pm, Sun. 8am-9pm.)

A dozen wineries lubricate Hwy. 18 on the way to Portland. A 9-mi. detour via Hwy. 99 W. and Hwy. 47 will take you to **Carlton,** home of the **Chateau Benoit Winery,** Mineral Springs Rd. (864-2991 or 864-3666). From Hwy. 47 in Carlton, take Rd. 204 1.3 mi. east, then go 2½ mi. south on Mineral Springs (Whew!). The winery specializes in Pinot Noir, Chardonnay, and Riesling. (Tasting hours Mon.-Fri. 11am-5pm, Sat.-Sun. noon-5pm.)

Lincoln City

Lincoln City is actually five towns incorporated into one, all conspiring to make you drive at 30 mi. per hour past 7 mi. of motels, gas stations, and tourist traps. Bicyclists will find it hellish, and hikers might do better to cut 3 blocks west to the shore. There is little reason for drivers to stop in what is perhaps the crassest city on the Oregon coast except to fill their gas tanks and stomachs, or maybe spend the night in a cheap motel.

Practical Information

Visitor Information: Lincoln City Chamber of Commerce, 3939 NW U.S. 101 (800-452-2151 or 994-3070). Brochures covering everything in Lincoln City. Open Mon.-Fri. 9am-5pm, Sat. 9am-4pm, Sun. 10am-3pm.

Greyhound: 316 SE U.S. 101 (994-8418), behind the bowling alley. To Portland ($12) and Newport ($5). Each route twice a day. Open Mon.-Sat. 9:30am-5:30pm.

Taxi: 996-2772 or 994-8070.

Car Rental: Robben-Rent-A-Car, 3232 NE U.S. 101 (867-3615, 954-6435 after hours). Additional location at airport (994-5530). $25 per day plus 25¢ per mi. Must be 21 with major credit card.

Community Swimming Pool: 994-5208 or 994-2131. Nonresidents $1.50, showers 75¢.

Senior Citizen Center: 994-2722.

Children's Services: 265-8537.

Alcoholics Anonymous: 994-4045.

Hospital: N. Lincoln Hospital, 3043 NE Park Dr. (994-3661).

Coast Guard: In Depoe Bay (765-2123).

Police: 1503 E. Devils Lake Rd. (996-3636).

Post Office: E. Devil's Lake Rd. (994-2148), 2 blocks east of U.S. 101. Open Mon.-Fri. 8:30am-5pm. General Delivery ZIP Code: 97367.

Area Code: 503.

Accommodations and Camping

The cheaper motels cozy up to noisy U.S. 101. Camping is available within walking distance of Lincoln City, but arrive as early as possible—the sites fill by mid-afternoon almost every day during the summer.

City Center Motel, 1014 NE U.S. 101 (994-2612). Rooms are clean with thin walls. Cable TV. Some rooms with kitchens. Singles $26. Doubles $28. Late Oct.-Memorial Day prices $5 lower.

Bel-Aire Motel, 2945 NW U.S. 101 (994-2984), at the north end of town. Singles $27. Doubles $29. Rates $2 less in winter.

Southshore Motel, 1070 SE 1st (994-7559), on the fabulous D River, a little off the highway. Pleasant rooms. Cable TV, spa, sauna. Singles $29. Doubles $32.

Budget Inn, 1713 NW 21st St. (994-5281). Still on the highway. First-floor rooms are protected from the noise by a bank of earth; 3rd-floor rooms have balconies with sea views. Singles $30. Doubles $38.

Captain Cook's Motel, 2626 NE U.S. 101 (994-2522), 3 blocks from the ocean. Big rooms with big TVs. Bring your earplugs: the highway runs through the lobby. One bed $28. Two beds $32.

Devil's Lake State Park, 1452 NE 6th St., Lincoln City 97367 (994-2002). Clearly marked turn east off U.S. 101. 100 closely spaced sites that fill up quickly in summer. Call before 4pm. Sites $9, RVs $11, hiker/biker camp $1. Reservations recommended. Open April-Oct.

Food

Head down to Depoe Bay or Newport for good seafood. The **Safeway** and **Thriftway** markets, both on U.S. 101 are open 24 hr.

Foon Hing Yuen, Inc., 3138 SE U.S. 101 (996-3831). Generous portions of good Chinese food. Despite the name, the *pork chow yuk* ($5.25) is a delicious dish. The only restaurant in town that doesn't close before 10pm. Take-out available. Open Mon.-Fri. noon-midnight, Sat.-Sun. noon-2am.

René's Place, 660 SE U.S. 101 (996-4161). René, a former Czechoslovakian maitre d', cooks, while his wife and daughter serve the varied continental menu. Complete dinners ($9-13) and full lunches ($5). A local favorite and critically acclaimed eatery. Daily specials $7-10. Open Wed.-Sun. noon-8pm.

Williams' Colonial Bakery, 1734 NE U.S. 101 (994-5919). This could be any bakery anywhere in the United States. Still, it's hard to go wrong with the three S's: sugar, starch, and satisfaction. Coffee 35¢, apple fritters 45¢, glazed doughnuts 35¢. Open daily 6:30am-7pm.

A Lil' Cheesecake Restaurant and Bakery, 2156 NE U.S. 101 (994-7323). Dumb name but good food. Sauteed shrimp in eggs with croissant and home fries $5.50. Spaghetti or tortellini with homemade bread $5. Open daily 7am-2pm.

Lighthouse Brew Pub, 4157 N. Highway (994-7238), in Lighthouse Sq. at the north end of town. Six in-house beers at $2.10 a pint. Sandwiches and burgers $3-5. Ask about tours of the brewery ("Capt. Neon's Fermentation Chamber"). Open Mon.-Thurs. 11am-11pm, Fri.-Sat. 11am-1am.

Sights and Activities

Lincoln City's focal point and rather dubious claim to fame is the **D.** All public routes to the beach cross the D, and streets in Lincoln City are numbered from it. Marketed as "the world's shortest river," the D is a 100- to 300-yd. overflow from Devil's Lake. Thousands of tourists each year pull over, snap a picture, and zoom off faster than you can say "who gives a flying ...."

A pleasant detour on **East Devil's Lake Road** leads around the lake to quiet, clearly marked fishing and picnic sites. **Road's End Park,** a couple of miles past the Lighhouse Square turn-off at the north end of town features a beautiful beach.

Film buffs should know that *Sometimes a Great Notion* (based on the Ken Kesey novel) was shot in Lincoln City. The fake old house that was used as the set can be seen by turning east off U.S. 101 onto the Siletz River Hwy. Continuing the cinematographic motif, a Hitchcockesque assortment of more than 4000 dolls stares glassy-eyed from dusty cases at **Lacey's Doll and Antique Museum,** 3400 NE U.S. 101 (994-2392). (Open daily 8am-5pm; during the school year 9am-4pm. Admission $2, ages under 10 25¢.)

Two Oregon wineries maintain tasting rooms in Lincoln City. **Honeywood Gift Shop and Winery,** 30 SE U.S. 101 (994-2755), across from the D, offers complementary tasting and is open daily from 10am to 6pm. The **Oak Knoll Winery,** 3521 SW U.S. 101 (996-3221), with $1 tastings, is open Monday through Saturday from 11am-5pm, Sunday from 11am-5pm.

Lincoln City is the self-inflicted "Kite Capital of the World." The last week of September sees the D River beach overrun with kite flyers. Everyone is welcome to participate. Call the Chamber of Commerce for information (see Practical Information).

Lincoln City to Newport

Between Lincoln City and Newport the state park system gets down to business. There are rest stops every few miles and one overnight state park. Off County Rte. 229 to Forest Service Rte. 19 is the free **North Creek Campground,** a small area within the Siuslaw National Forest (drinking water not available). Just south on U.S. 101 and around the corner from the Salishan Lodge, the **Alder House Glassblowing Factory** is open for public viewing. The artisans explain the process as they blow and shape all conceivable glass objects. Of course, they also encourage you to buy their artwork, in the "low, low price range" of $5-103. (Open Tues.-Sun. 10am-5pm.) A few hundred yards up the road, **Mossy Creek Pottery** hawks imaginative clay creations (mugs $5) with similar creativity. (Open daily 10am-5:30pm.)

Boiler Bay Wayside, 5 mi. south of Salishan, takes its name from the remnant of a locally famous disaster. In 1910, the wooden schooner *J.J. Marhoffer* burst into flames and burned at sea. The captain, his wife, and 21 crew members watched from safety as the hulk washed up on shore. Only the charred remains of the *Marhoffer's* boiler—still visible at low tide—survived.

A few mi. south on U.S. 101, diminutive **Depoe Bay,** undercut Portland's "smallest park" and Lincoln City's "smallest river," by claiming the smallest navigable harbor in the world. The motels charge hefty rates (in the $35-50 range for singles). Stop for lunch at the **Chowder Bowl,** on U.S. 101 (765-2300), an off-shoot of the famous Newport restaurant. The excellent chowder ($2.50) is a meal in itself. While you eat, watch the choo-choo train circle the room—and if you want to act like a tourist, ask your waitress to blow the whistle. (Open daily 11:30am-9pm.)

Watching the life of the sea, rather than just eating it, is also popular in Depoe Bay. The best gray whale viewing points in this important "whale watching capital of the Oregon coast" are along the seawall in town, at the Depoe Bay State Park Wayside, and at the **Observatory Lookout,** 4½ mi. south of town. Go out early in the morning on a cloudy, calm day between December and May for the best chance of spotting the huge grays. Gray whales have the longest known migration of any mammal: 12,000 mi. round-trip each year from the Arctic waters of the north to the coastal waters of Baja California in Mexico, where the females let the little Whalensloose.

Several outfitters charter fishing trips from Depoe Bay. **Deep Sea Trollers,** in the Spouting Horn Restaurant (765-2248), provides five-hour trips for $38 per person. Trips leave at 6 and 11am. Reserve ahead by calling or writing to P.O. Box 513, Depoe Bay 97341. **Depoe Bay Sportfishing and Charters,** on U.S. 101 (765-2222), at the south end of the Depoe Bay Bridge, also heads out for five-hour trips for the same price. Reservations are always necessary for charter trips. Depoe Bay holds a popular **Salmon Bake** at Fogarty Creek State Park on the third Saturday of September. (Admission $9, children $4.) Call the Chamber of Commerce at 765-2361 for more information.

Just south of Depoe Bay, take the famous **Otter Crest Loop,** a twisting 4-mi. drive high above the shore, which allows spectacular vistas at every bend. At **Cape Foulweather,** Captain James Cook first struck the North American mainland in 1778. When he named the cape (he was greeted with a gale), Cook wasn't kidding; winds at this 500-ft. elevation often reach 100 mi. per hour. A lookout at the wayside has telescopes for spotting sea lions on the rocks below—weather permitting, of course. Also on the loop, the incredible **Devil's Punchbowl** demonstrates the brutal force of the waves. The roof of a cave here has collapsed, leaving arched walls standing to create a voluminous cauldron. The waters churn in and out of this huge double boiler at your feet.

Just south of Satan's Punchbowl, the road returns to U.S. 101 and brings the eager camper to **Beverly Beach State Park,** a year-round reservation campground in gorgeous, rugged terrain. Swimming in the crashing surf here is forbidden even to the lunatics who might try it; the views from the hiking trails will satisfy most visitors anyway. Hot showers and facilities for the disabled are available, as well as a few hiker/biker spots. (Sites $9, hookups $11.) For reservations during the summer, call 265-9278 or write 198 NE 123rd St., Newport 97365.

New Age sportsmen shouldn't miss **Agate Beach Wayside,** an excellent place (as is the entire Newport Area) to hunt for semi-precious stones. The Newport Chamber of Commerce (see Newport Practical Information) puts out a free pamphlet entitled *Agates: Their Formation and How to Hunt for Them.* The brochure recommends October through May as the prime months, although the stones are, of course, here year-round.

Just north of Agate Beach is the **Yaquina Head Lighthouse,** a photogenic coastal landmark, said to be the brightest on the coast of Oregon. (Open daily noon-5pm; Labor Day-Memorial Day Mon.-Fri. noon-5pm. Admission 50¢.) A nature station has recently been opened in the area for seal- and whale-watching.

Newport

Part tourist mill, part fishing village, part logging town, Newport offers an escape from U.S. 101's malls and gas stations. Recently refurbished, the town's waterfront is aflutter with quaint tourist traps. Originally a turn-of-the-century sea town where wealthy Portlanders could go to escape the mosquitoes, Newport has matured into a late 20th-century sea town where wealthy Portlanders can go to escape the mosquitoes.

Practical Information

Visitor Information: Chamber of Commerce, 555 SW Coast Hwy. (265-8801). Friendly office with a free, thorough guide and map to Newport. On the weekends, the volunteers may know less about Newport than you do. Open daily 8:30am-5pm; Nov.-Jan. Mon.-Fri. 8:30am-5pm.

Newport Parks and Recreation Office: 169 SW Coast Hwy. (265-7783).

Greyhound: 956 SW 10th St. (265-2253). To Portland ($15) and San Francisco ($81).

Newport Area Transit (NAT): 265-8088. Runs a 1-hr. route around Newport daily 7am-7pm. Fare 50¢; 3 rides for $1.25. Map available at the Chamber of Commerce.

Taxi: Yaquina Cab Company, 265-9552. 24 hrs.

Car Rental: Surfside Motors, 27 S. Coast Hwy. (265-6686).

Newport Public Library: 35 NW Nye St. (265-2153). Open Mon. and Wed. 1-8pm, Tues. and Thurs. 10am-8pm, Fri.-Sat. 1-6pm.

Weather: 265-5511.

Children's Serivce: 265-8557.

Adult and Family Services: 265-2248.

Hospital and Ambulance: 265-3175.

Fire Dept.: 265-9461.

Police: 265-5331.

Post Office: 310 SW 2nd St. (265-5542). Open Mon.-Fri. 8:30am-5pm. General Delivery ZIP Code: 97365.

Area Code: 503.

Accommodations and Camping

God is in His heaven, but the motel situation in Newport is dismal. The cheapest ones are on U.S. 101, with predictable consequences. **Bed and breakfasts** are a tempting alternative, but the prices (about $50) may be prohibitive.

Sands Motor Lodge, 206 N. Coast Hwy. (265-5321). Less noise than at Penny Saver, and lower prices. Cable TV and telephone. Doubles and singles $30 in summer. 10% discount for seniors.

Willers Motel, 754 SW Coast Hwy. (800-433-2639 or 265-2241). Free HBO. Singles and doubles $22-36; Nov. to mid-June $22. Rooms for groups available at lower rates per person.

Money Saver Motel, 861 SW U.S. 101 (265-2277). Pleasant rooms, cable TV, some kitchens. Singles $36. Doubles $38.

Penny Saver Motel, 710 N. Coast Hwy. (265-6631). The name speaks volumes. Kitchens, telephones, and queen-sized beds. No view, of course. Color TV. Free coffee and fruit. Singles $38. Doubles $42. In winter prices $4 lower.

Finding a place to pitch your tent near Newport can prove tricky. The few private campgrounds are overrun by RVs, and campground owners have established facilities geared exclusively toward these monstrosities. Campers should escape to the many state campgrounds along U.S. 101, where sites average $9 and hookups go for $11. **South Beach State Park,** P.O. Box 1350, Newport 97366 (867-4715), 2 mi. south of town, has 254 full-hookup sites and showers ($11). Just north of town, **Beverly Beach State Park,** HC 63, Box 684, Newport (265-9278), has 279 sites, 152 specifically for tents ($9). Both campgrounds are usually full by noon.

Food

The eating is excellent and expensive in Newport, both at Nye Beach and on the bay.

The Chowder Bowl, 728 NW Beach Dr. (265-7477), at Nye Beach. Renowned bowls of chowder $2.75. Huge shrimp basket with fries and garlic bread $9.50. Their pies are also famous ($1.50 per slice). Open Mon.-Thurs. 11am-8pm, Fri.-Sat. 11am-9pm, Sun. noon-8pm. Also at 434 SW Bay Blvd. (265-5575), on the same block as the Whale's Tale, where *gelato* is the specialty (95¢ per cone).

Don Petrie's Italian Food Company, 613 NW 3rd (265-3663), across the street from the Chowder Bowl. Incredible vegetarian manicotti ($7) includes cheesy garlic bread. Spinach fettuccine ($5.75) is equally good. The lasagna ($7) is fit for Don Desai. Open Mon.-Thurs. and Sun. 4:30-9pm, Fri.-Sat. 4:30-9:30pm; in winter daily 4:30-8pm.

The Whale's Tale, 452 SW Bay Blvd. (265-8660), on the bayfront at the corner of Fall St. This famous place is great fun—decorated with local art and mismatched old wooden chairs and tables. For breakfast, try the internationally celebrated Eggs Newport: Oregon shrimp and 2 poached eggs on an English muffin, topped with Bearnaise sauce, plus home fries ($7). Or how about the oft-praised poppy seed pancakes for $3.75? Dinners can be expensive (*cioppino* $12), but good sandwiches start at $4.25. Live local music Sat. night and during Sun. brunch. Open Mon.-Fri. 7am-9pm, Sat.-Sun. 9am-9pm; Nov.-May Thurs.-Tues. only.

Canyon Way Bookstore and Restaurant, 1216 SW Canyon Way (265-8319), up the hill from the bayfront. 60¢ espresso whimsically cheaper than 70¢ regular coffee. Extensive wine and beer list (imported beer $1.50-2). Lunch $3-8. Open Mon.-Sat. 11am-3pm and 5-9pm; Sun. brunch 10am-3pm. Deli open all day. Reservations suggested.

Oceana Food Coop, 415 NW Coast St., Nye Beach (265-8285). Health food store with gourmet tendencies. The fresh cream cheese puts the brand names to shame. You pay for the quality, however, and nonmembers must add 10% to the listed prices. Open daily 10am-7pm.

Sights and Activities

Among the many West Coast pioneer museums (my goodness, Alex, is there one in *every* seaside town?), Newport's **Lincoln County Historical Society's Burrows House and Log Cabin,** 545 SW 9th (265-7509), stands apart. For once, the exhibits *are* unusual, especially the room devoted to Newport Bay's shipwrecks. (Open Tues.-Sun. 10am-5pm; Sept.-May Tues.-Sun. 11am-4pm. Free.)

Another budget-minded and worthwhile stop is in Yaquna Bay State Park. At the southwest end of town, on the north side of the bay, the **Yaquna Bay Lighthouse** watches over the fleets of fishing boats that cruise in and out of the bay daily. The short-lit lighthouse (in operation from 1871 to 1874) has become an attraction in Newport due to the fact that it is haunted. The legend is verified in a 20-minute video in the lighthouse itself. The video also has footage of the Coast Guard's dramatic rescue of the crew of the Blue Magpie in 1983. The crew was salvaged, but not the ship—on clear days, a portion of it can be seen from the lighthouse. (Open daily noon-5pm, 50¢ a person.)

On the other side of the bridge, beside the bay, three tourist traps lie within 100 yd. of one another at 250 SW Bay Blvd. The **Wax Works Museum** crams as many lifelike figures as it can into cramped spaces. The scenes, however, are not quite as lifelike: Michael Jackson, Liza Minnelli, George Burns, and Kenny Rogers manage to find themselves in the same nightclub—and, in another exhibit, Yoda and the Hobbit midget-wrestle. Next door, **Ripley's Believe It or Not** exhibits bizarre displays and freaky facts which do not warrant the price of admission, and *that* you can believe. The **Undersea Gardens,** in the shade across the street, is home to 5000 marine specimens, including Armstrong the Giant Octopus. (Each museum $5 adults, $4 seniors, $3 children. All open daily 9am-8pm; in winter, 10am-5pm).

The **Mark O. Hatfield Marine Science Center** (867-0100), across the bridge to the south on Marine Science Dr., is the hub of Oregon State University's coastal research. The Center's aquarium and museum explain current work and display Pacific Northwest marine animals in their natural environment. Beginning the third week of June, the center (named after Oregon's eminent U.S. senator) offers a free educational program called Seataugua, in which marine biologists give talks, show films, and lead nature walks. Call the center (ext. 226) for a complete schedule. (Open daily 10am-6pm; Nov.-April 10am-4pm. Free.)

If you have the time and money, try **salmon-** or **bottom-fishing** with one of Newport's charter companies. **Newport Tradewinds,** 653 SW Bay Blvd. (265-2101, 24 hr.), offers a variety of trips year-round. (A 5-hr. crabbing run costs $45, a 12-hr. run $125.) Fishing runs last five or eight hours. Whale-watching trips last only two and a half hours, and cost $24. These leave daily at 6am, 11:30am, 2:30pm, and 3:30pm. **Cape Perpetua Charters,** 839 SW Bay Blvd. (265-7777, 24 hr.), is another good company, and clearly the better catch. (5-hr. trip $37; 8-hr. trip $75. 10% discount for seniors and ages 11-17.) The local bird watchers club, **Yaquina Birders and Naturalists,** leads free field trips, and welcomes guests. (Usually 1 trip per month.) Call 265-2965 for more information. For those who'd like to put a little zest into their day, **Alpine Vineyards** has constructed a tasting room at 818 SW Bay Blvd. in Newport. (Open daily noon-5:30pm; Sept. 16-June 14 call 265-6843 to check hours.)

Some of the sheltered coves in the area, especially those to the north around Depoe Bay, are excellent for scuba diving. Rent equipment and get tips from **Newport Water Sports,** S. Jetty Rd., South Beach (867-3742), at the south end of the bridge. (Open daily 6am-6pm. Full top-of-the-line gear rental about $25, $35 on the weekend.)

Popular festivals in Newport include the **Newport Seafood and Wine Festival** in mid-February, showcasing Oregon wines, food, music, and crafts (with a focus on the wine and food) and **Newport Loyalty Days and Sea Fair Festival,** in early May, with rides, parades, fried chicken, and sailboat races. Contact the Newport Chamber of Commerce (see Practical Information) for more information on both events.

Newport to Florence

In the 50 mi. between Newport and Florence, the vistas remain vast as the towns dwindle in size. The **Siuslaw National Forest,** on the coast nearby, provides even more camping than usual, some of it free. Take the time to drive inland on the forest service roads for gorgeous, wooded scenery. As you leave the stoplights of Newport behind, you will come upon **South Beach State Park,** two mi. south, off U.S. 101. South Beach has 254 crowded sites (including a few for the hiker/biker set), hot showers, hiking trails, and facilities for the disabled. Reservations can be made by writing P.O. Box 1350, Newport 97365. (Sites $9.)

Farther south is the town of **Waldport** on Alsea Bay. In Waldport, the tiny **Pine Beach Motel,** 8090 U.S. 101 (563-2155), has a cozy atmosphere and color TV. Removed from the hustle and bustle of Waldport the motel is only a short walk downhill to the town and an even shorter walk to the beach. (Singles $25. Doubles $35.) The **Waldport Motel** (563-3035) on U.S. 101 sits right in the middle of town luring visitors with its seashell collages and HBO. (Singles $30. Doubles $40.) The selection at **The City Bakery,** U.S. 101 (563-3621) could be more extensive but at least they're cheap. Loaf of bread 99¢. Poppy seed muffin 40¢. (Open Mon.-Sat. 4am-5pm). **Leroy's Blue Whale,** next door (563-2050) is your classic local dive with decent food. Squid and fries $3.75. (Open daily 6am-9pm.) **The Continental Deli,** is neither; large sandwiches are $2.60. In mid-June, Waldport hosts the **Beachcomber Days and Speed Boat Races** (563-2198), featuring parades and children's events, all topped with a 5-mi. beach run from Patterson State Park. The **Chamber of Commerce** (563-2133) operates a visitors information booth here that offers one of the best views of the ocean and the river. (Open daily 9am-4pm.) Pick up general information on camping in the Siuslaw National Forest, or stop by the **Waldport Ranger Station** (563-3211).

Four miles south of Waldport, camp at **Beachside State Park,** which has 60 sites and hot showers (no hiker/biker spots). Beachside is a reservation park; write P.O. Box 1350, Newport 97365. Less than 1 mi. south, the forest service operates **Tillicum Beach,** with 58 sites and drinking water. Sites $7.

The name of **Yachats** (pronounced YAH-hots) is derived from a Chinook word meaning "dark waters at the foot of the mountain." This tiny town gains a measure of renown from its position at the mouth of the Yachats River. The original **Leroy's**

Blue Whale (547-3399), right on the highway in the center of town, is a cafeteria-style restaurant with tasty fish and chips ($4.25). (Open daily 7am-10pm.) **On the Rise Bakery**, next to the Chamber of Commerce, is a pleasant place to have a cup of coffee. Jumbo cinnamon rolls 75¢. Head west two blocks to reach **Rock Park Cottages** (547-3214 or 343-4782). The five delightful cabins are well-equipped with kitchens and dishes, bookshelves, board games, and lovely wood paneling. Right on the beach, the cottages are quiet and available at weekly rates. (Doubles $28-38; in winter $22-32. Extra double bed $4 per night.) Three miles south of Yachats, on U.S. 101, there are several hiker/biker campsites in **Neptune State Park.** The second weekend of July, the town indulges in the **Yachats Smelt Fry,** during which 700 pounds of delicate smelt are served on the grounds of the Yachats School. For information, contact the Chamber of Commerce. In early November, the **Yachats Kite Festival** fills the skies with colorful kites. Competitions are held on the beach. Contact Robert Oxley, P.O. Box 346, Yachats 97498. The **Chamber of Commerce,** P.O. Box 174, Yachats 97498 (547-3530), in the center of town, has information on the village, the national forest, and local beaches (open daily 9am-5pm).

The **Cape Perpetua Visitors Center,** P.O. Box 274, Yachats 97498 (547-3289), is located midway down the Siuslaw National Forest's shoreline. High on a basalt cliff, the center grants mesmeric views of the capes and surf below. A number of hiking trails lead to other viewing points, or down to coves and tidal pools. The forest service offers free lectures and hikes throughout the summer, and the center itself features dioramas and displays explaining the geology and biology of the area. Unless the weather is really lousy, don't bother with the free 15-minute film, *Forces of Nature.* The visuals are all right, but you can walk down to the water to see the crashing waves for yourself. (Center open daily 9am-5pm; Labor Day-Memorial Day Fri.-Sun. 10am-4pm. Sites $6.) Especially impressive is **Devil's Churn,** where lava flows have formed a basin for the waves to roar in at high tide. From the center, take the **Cape Perpetua Auto Tour,** a 22-mi. loop through the forest on forest service roads; signs along the way describe the local flora. The equally enchanting **Cummins Ridge Trail** leaves just south of the visitors center and winds 2½ mi. down to the beach.

Two miles south of Cape Perpetua, the **Gull Haven Lodge,** 94770 U.S. 101 (547-3583), clings to the cliff high above the gorgeous sea. When reserving a room, ask for "the nest," a tastefully decorated cabin perched alone right over the beach. The bathroom is in the main house, but otherwise the cabin is idyllic—kitchenette, Native American woven bedspreads, butcher block tables, hanging plants, and large plate-glass windows, all for only $40. Equally nice units in the main building start at $30. Reservations essential. Nearby **Ocean Beach State Park** forbids camping, but its silky sands make for an excellent daytrip. Campers can instead try **Rock Creek Campground,** run by the forest service (16 sites, $8). But the real winner is **Carl G. Washburne State Park,** 12 mi. south of Yachats. The park has excellent hiking, fishing, and swimming, as well as campsites with hot showers. (Tents $9, RVs $12. Open Memorial Day-Labor Day.) To tour the **Haceta Head Lighthouse** in the park, you must first call the Coast Guard (997-3631). Between here and Florence, the forest service operates three more campgrounds: Alder Lake Dune, Sutton Lake, and Sutton Creek. Nearly all state parks provide drinking water for parched throats, but no showers for parched souls.

C & M Stables, 90241 U.S. 101 N. (997-7540), 8 mi. north of Florence, keeps horses for beach or trail rides. The rate is $20 for 90 minutes or $25 for two hours. A two-hour sunset ride is $23. (Stables open daily 9am-sunset. Hours vary; call ahead for specifics and reservations.)

From Newport to Coos Bay, U.S. 101 is studded with signs pointing the way to the enormous **Sea Lion Caves** (547-3415 or 547-3111), 12 mi. north of Florence. To get to this sea lion riviera, ride down one of the elevators. The ride costs $6, but the caves are spectacular. Stop at the overlook a few hundred yards north on U.S. 101, just before the tunnel, for a free view of the slippery seals below.

Florence

If all you did was pass through Florence on U.S. 101 to the dunes, you'd think
it was just like any other strip clinging to the highway. But if you go two blocks
off the highway to Bay St., you'll discover the tiny, reconstructed Old Town on
the Siuslaw River, lair of health stores, charming craft shops, and superb seafood.

Practical Information

Visitor Information: Chamber of Commerce, 270 U.S. 101 (997-3128), 3 blocks north of the
Siuslaw River Bridge. Open daily 9am-5pm.

Greyhound: 478 U.S. 101 (997-8782), just north of the Florence city center. Open Mon.-Fri.
9am-5pm, Sat. 9am-1pm. To Portland ($15) and San Francisco ($80).

Taxi: Florence Taxi, 1250 Upas St. (997-8520).

Car Rental: Berg Chevrolet Olds Buick, Inc., 2630 U.S. 101 (997-7101). $26 per day plus
10¢ per mi. Must be 19 with a credit card.

Hospital: Peace Harbor Hospital, 1525 12th St. (997-8412).

Police/Fire: 989 Spruce (997-3515).

Post Office: 770 Maple St. (997-2533). Open Mon.-Fri. 8am-5pm. General Delivery ZIP
Code: 97439.

Area Code: 503.

Like most sizable towns on the Oregon Coast, Florence is the meeting point for
two highways and two bodies of water. Hwy. 126 and the Siuslaw River travel east
out of Florence into the Siuslaw National Forest; 61 mi. later U.S. 126 links with
Eugene. Unlike most coastal towns, Florence's waterside **(Bay St.)** fronts the river,
not the Pacific Ocean. U.S. 101 runs perpendicular to Bay and brackets the Floren-
tine motel strip.

Accommodations

Florence offers few really cheap rooms, but at least you get what you pay for.
Stiff competition has led to high quality, not low prices. Inexplicably, every motel
below save one is decorated in blue.

Villa West Motel, 901 U.S. 101 (977-3457), at 9th St. Huge elegant rooms. A classy joint,
through and through. Singles $34. Doubles $36.

Florence Coast Motel, 155 U.S. 101 (997-3221), just north of the bridge. The exterior looks
like a huge country home and the lobby would fit in a small Hilton, but don't be fooled: the
rooms are standard motel-style. Rooms from $34.

Ocean Breeze Motel, 85165 U.S. 101 (997-2642), 1 mi. south of the bridge. Big blue rooms
in a small blue motel. Singles $34. Doubles (which include a second bedroom) $46.

Silver Sands Motel, 1499 U.S. 101 (977-3459). The blue decor is mercifully not tacky. Quiet
rooms. Singles from $36. Doubles from $48.

Money Saver Motel, 170 U.S. 101 (997-7131), adjacent to Old Town. One of the only non-
blue motels in town but other than that similar to a Motel 6. Singles $40. Doubles $46.

Food

Almost all of the restaurants in Florence line Bay St. along the waterfront.

Mo's, 1436 Bay St. (997-2185), in the heart of Old Town. One of the Oregon chain that offers
consistently great seafood. Waterfront view. Expect a short wait for a table and use the time
to scour the menu for alternatives to the usual (Slumgullion ($5) and Oyster Stew ($5) for
example). Full dinners of salmon or oysters are around $7. Open daily 11am-9pm.

Bridgewater Seafood Restaurant and Oyster Bay, 1297 Bay St. (997-9405), at Laurel St. This gorgeous restaurant is in the 1901 Kyle Building, which was used until 1961 as the general store. The current owners intended to re-create "Rick's" from Casablanca. They didn't quite succeed but its spacious light atmosphere is a relief from the crowded comraderie of most of the Florence seafood places. Oyster burgers ($5), seafood omelette ($5). Dinners are pricey ($10-17). Open Sun.-Thurs. 11am-9pm, Fri.-Sat. 11am-10pm.

Weber's Fish Market and Restaurant, 802 U.S. 101 (997-8886), at the junction with Hwy. 126. Simple but tasty menu. Crab for $4 per lb. and smoked samon for $12 per lb. Grilled oysters and garlic bread ($6.50). Open 7am-9pm daily.

Old Town Coffee Co., 1269 Bay St. A local hangout with a view of the river and the 1926 Siuslaw bridge. The usual coffee drinks plus some more exotic ones (Irish Mocha Mint $1.85). Great homemade cookies for only 30¢. Chess buffs should check out the foot-high pieces on the large wood set in the back. Open daily 7am-6pm.

Pizza Express, 1285 Bay St. (997-8073). Follow your nose to the only homemade pizza in Florence—and deep dish at that. You'll think you're in Italy. Interesting toppings include smoked oyster. 10" deep dish starts at $6.25. Free delivery within a 4-mi. radius, 25¢ per mi. thereafter. Open Sun.-Thurs. 11am-11pm, Fri.-Sat. 11am-midnight.

Sights and Activities

Florence's major attraction is its **Old Town;** wander around the restored buildings and the tacky tourist shops, and then stop at **The Renowned Unknown Gallery** (next to the coffeehouse), where a display of local artists (kindergarten and up) is "open weekends and sunny afternoons." Or climb the stairs from Bay St. for a closer look at Florence's bridge. Built in 1936 by a WPA crew, the bridge is one of the many along the coast with intriguing art-deco detail work. The bridge spans the harbor and lifeline of the city, Siuslaw River, named for the Natives who once populated this area. In 1855, the Siuslaw signed a treaty to sell a million acres of land to the U.S. government; when the money never came, the Siuslaw took the government to court—and lost. In 1860, they were granted homesteading tracts of 160 acres each. Only three tracts and seven Siuslaws survive today. Some artifacts from this vanished people, as well as from the white settlers who usurped their home, are on display at the **Siuslaw Pioneer Museum,** 85290 U.S. 101, 1 mi. south of the bridge (997-7889). Once a barn, then a church this museum displays centuries-old clothes and other niceties. Open Tues.-Sun. 10am-4pm.

Cross the bridge and head west on South Jetty Rd. for easy access to the beach and dunes; waterfowl and deer frequent the marshlands along this road. At the last parking lot on the road is the **Beached Whale Memorial,** a tragic tribute to the 41 cetaceans who were cast ashore in 1979.

Crabbing, clamming, and fishing equipment can be rented at **Port of Siuslaw Marina** harbor at 1st St. (997-3040), where salmon charters leave daily. During the third week in May, Florence holds its annual **Rhododendron Festival.** Begun in 1908 to celebrate the blooming of the flowers, the festival includes a parade, a carnival, boat races, a popular road race, and of course, a rhododendron show.

Reedsport and the Dunes

For 42 mi. between Florence and Coos Bay, the beach widens to form the **Oregon Dunes National Recreation Area.** Shifting hills of sand rise to 500 ft. and extend inland up to 3 mi. (often to the brink of U.S. 101), clogging mountain streams and forming numerous small lakes. The dunes were created by glaciation 15,000 years ago and reached their maximum development 9000 years later. A constant, unidirectional wind maintains their shape. Hiking trails wind around the lakes, through the coastal forests, and up to the dunes themselves. In many places, no grasses or shrubs grow, and you can see only bare sand and sky. Other places, however, feel more like the Gator Bowl parking lot than the Gobi Desert. Campgrounds fill up early with dune buggy and motorcycle junkies, especially on summer weekends. The blaring radios, thrumming engines, and staggering swarms of tipsy tourists might drive you into the sands seeking eternal truth—or at least a quiet place to crash.

Practical Information

Visitor Information: Oregon Dunes National Recreation Area Information Center, 855 U.S. 101, Reedsport (271-3611), just south of the Umpqua River Bridge. The U.S. Forest Service runs this center with typical aplomb. Don't bother the staff—the free guide can answer most of your questions anyway. Ask to see the scintillating movie on Mt. St. Helens. Open Mon.-Fri. 8am-4:30pm, Sat.-Sun. 9am-5pm; Labor Day-Memorial Day Mon.-Fri. 8am-4:30pm. Reedsport Chamber of Commerce, U.S. 101 and Hwy. 38 (271-3495), a cute little shack across the street from the NRA office. Open Mon.-Fri. 9am-5pm, Sat.-Sun. 10am-5pm.

Greyhound: 1625 U.S. 101, Reedsport (271-5423), at the 1-Stop Market. The bus drops people off here but will only pick up by prior arrangement.

Coast Guard: near the end of the harbor, at the foot of the mountain in Winchester Bay (271-2137).

Taxi: Reedsport Taxi (271-5112). About $6 to the dunes.

Laundromat: Mid-Coast Linen and Cleaners, 117 N. 3rd, Reedsport (271-2679).

Fire: 124 N. 4th, Reedsport (271-2423).

Police: 136 N. 4th, Reedsport (271-2109).

Post Office: 301 Fir St. (271-2521). Open Mon.-Fri. 9am-5pm. General Delivery ZIP Code: 97467.

Area Code: 503.

The dunes firm control of the coastline is broken only once along the expanse when the Umpqua and Smith Rivers empty into Winchester Bay, about 20 mi. south of Florence. Reedsport, with almost 5000 people, is a typical highway town, with its motels, banks, and fast food places neatly subdivided by U.S. 101 and Hwy. 38, which connects with I-5 60 mi. to the east. Avoid Reedsport and stay in Winchester Bay, the small fishing village at the mouth of the bay of the same name. Just 4 mi. south of Reedsport, Winchester Bay is easily passed by on U.S. 101, exposing only about three blocks to the highway and saving the rest of its charm for those knowledgeable enough to make the turn-off.

Accommodations

The motels in Winchester Bay are not any more expensive than those in Reedsport and all are within a few blocks of the water. Reservations are necessary to ensure one of the cheaper rooms, and on a weekend during fishing season you may have to pay slightly more to stay in Winchester Bay. All motels (even those in Reedsport) fill up at night; arrive in the afternoon to prevent a forced long drive to the next town.

Salmon Harbor Motel, on U.S. 101 (271-2732), at the farthest north point of Winchester Bay. Ironically, the farthest of the 3 Winchester Bay motels from the harbor (but by only a few blocks). Pleasant rooms that retain charm despite being on the highway. Singles from $20.50. Doubles from $28.50, with kitchens $33.50.

Winchester Bay Motel, at the end of Broadway (271-4871), on 4th St. past dock A in Winchester Bay. This clean, quiet 50-room motel is a good place to catch up after weeks of camping out. Color TV and free coffee. Singles $30. Doubles $35. Prices go up $5-10 on weekends. Kitchens $10 extra. Labor Day-Memorial Day singles $25, doubles $30.

Harbor View Motel, Beach Blvd. (271-3352), spitting distance from the boats. Shabby, but clean. Color TV and some kitchenettes. Singles $21. Doubles $30. Mid-Sept. to April singles $18.50, doubles $23.

Fir Grove Motel, 2178 Winchester Ave., Reedsport (271-4848). Winchester Ave. runs to the east diagonal to U.S. 101, intersecting the highway just before the Scholfield Creek Bridge; the motel is at the intersection. The rooms are rather small. Color TV, free coffee, outdoor pool. Singles $32. Doubles $42. In winter singles $25, doubles $28.

Camping

This national recreation area is subsumed under the Siuslaw National Forest, so the forest service's pamphlet *Campgrounds in the Siuslaw National Forest* covers those in the dunes. The sites closest to Reedsport are in Winchester Bay. The campgrounds that allow dune buggy access—South Jetty, Lagoon, Waxmyrtle, Driftwood II, Horsfall, and Bluebill—are generally loud and rowdy in the summer. Call 800-283-CAMP for more information.

Surfwood Campground, ½ mi. north of Winchester Bay off U.S. 101 on the beach side (271-4020). Luxury! All the luxuries of (some people's) home: laundromat, heated pool, grocery store, sauna, tennis court, and hot showers. Sites $9, full hookups $11. Call at least a week in advance during the summer.

Windy Cove Campground (271-5634), adjacent to Salmon Harbor in Winchester Bay. A county park with rather steep rates for tent camping. A foghorn will keep you company all night long. 75 sites with drinking water, hot showers, flush toilets, and beach access. Sites $7.

Umpqua Lighthouse (271-3546) and **William H. Tugman,** 5 and 8 mi. south of Reedsport, respectively. Hot showers, boat launches, hiker/biker sites. The Umpqua site is on **Lake Marie,** a cold but swimmable lake with a beach. Tugman has facilities for the disabled. Sites $9.

Tahkenitch Landing, 7 mi. north of Reedsport, has 27 sites with pit toilets and drinking water. Swimming, boating, and fishing on nearby Tahkenitch Lake. Sites $7.

Food

Winchester Bay again wins the contest with Reedsport for charm and originality. Restauranteurs pride themselves on their seafood, especially salmon.

Seven Seas Café, Dock A, Winchester Bay (271-4381), at the end of Broadway at 4th St. A small diner crowded with marine memorabilia and navigational charts. The local fishing crowd gathers at this self-proclaimed "haunt of the liars" to trade big fish stories. The seafood comes in huge helpings—don't order the Captain's seafood platter ($6) unless you plan to stay put for quite some time. Fish and chips $4-5, deep-fried prawns $6, coffee 40¢. Open Fri.-Tues. 8am-2pm.

Pizza Rays, 705 Beach Blvd., Winchester Bay (271-2431), near Dock F. The good food and video games attract families and fishermen alike. Pick up a personal pizza for a picnic ($5). Open daily 4:30am-9pm.

Seafood Grotto and Restaurant, 8th St. and Broadway, Winchester Bay (271-4250). An unexpectedly excellent seafood restaurant showcasing a large Victorian doll house. Lunches $5-7. Large salmon steak $10. Dinners include clam chowder or salad, and a baked potato or rice. Even if you don't eat here, stop by to pick up a free postcard of the dollhouse. Open Sun.-Thurs. 8am-9pm.

Sugar Shack Bakery and Restaurant, 145 N. 3rd, Reedsport (271-3514). Won't win any Mr. Clean certificates of merit, but has delicious sweets and fast meals. Try the large apple fritters (65¢). Sandwiches $3. Open daily 5am-around dusk, depending on the weather.

Maddie's Fish'n Chips, 4 Lynn Dr. (568-3968). Monotone blue decor with stenciled pigs on the walls. A ceramic (blue) moose guards the cash register. Enormous portions suggest renaming this restaurant Whale'n Chips. Open daily 6am-10pm.

Activities

Romp in the dunes—why else are you here?

Those with little time or low sand-tolerance should stop at the **Oregon Dunes Overlook,** off of U.S. 101 about halfway between Reedsport and Florence. Steep wooden ramps lead to the gold and blue swells of the dunes and the Pacific. Trails wander off from the overlook, as they do at several other points on U.S. 101. The *Sand Tracks* brochure (available at the Information Center) has a detailed map of the dunes and its trails inside. For dune encounters of a closer kind, venture out in wheels. **Sand Dunes Frontier,** 83960 U.S. 101 S. (997-3544), 4 mi. south of Florence, gives 25-minute **dune buggy rides** ($6, under 11 $3, under 5 free). The Frontier also has mini-golf for $3 and men's bathroom stalls decorated with endearing slogans. The rides are more fun than the schticky base camp would suggest and the drivers have lots of good stories to tell. One mile south of Sand Dunes Frontier, is **Lawrence of Florence,** cleverly named after the British bedouin, the 20s film star Florence Lawrence, *and* the housekeeper from *The Jeffersons.* Camel rides in a pen cost $3 for adults, $2 for children. (Open daily in summer from 10am.) If you really want to tear up the dunes, shell out $25 for the first hour and $15 per additional hour on your own dune buggy. **Dunes Odyssey,** on U.S. 101 in Winchester Bay (271-4011), and **Spinreel Park,** Wildwood Dr., 8 mi. south on U.S. 101 (759-3313; open daily 8am-6pm), both offer rentals at the same prices.

Inside **Umpqua Lighthouse State Park,** 6 mi. south of Reedsport, the Douglas County Park Department operates the **coastal visitor center** (440-4500), in the old Coast Guard administration building. The center has small exhibits on the shipping and timber industries of the turn-of-the-century. (Open May-Sept. Wed.-Sat. 10am-5pm, Sun. 1-5pm. Free.)

When you tire of dune doodling and museum dawdling, go deep-sea fishing with one of the many charter companies that operate out of Salmon Harbor, Winchester Bay. **Main Charters,** 4th and Beach St. (271-3800), is one of the cheapest. Four-hour salmon trips cost $32 per person, five-hour bottom-fishing expeditions $35 per person. **Gee Gee Charters, Inc.** offers four-hour fishing trips for $35, ages over 59 and under 16 $30. The required one-day license for salmon fishing ($5) may be purchased at any of the charter offices. Trips leave at 6am, 10am, and 2pm. Call the day before for reservations.

At the **Dean Creek Elk Viewing Area,** two mi. east of Reedsport on Hwy. 38, you can observe the Roosevelt Elk, Oregon's largest land mammal, which was named after animal-killer/President Teddy Roosevelt.

Coos Bay/North Bend

Largest city on the Oregon Coast, the industrial lumber town of Coos Bay has suffered greatly from recent closings of local plants and Spotted Owls are shot on site. Staggering under an unemployment rate near 20%, the town has faced an exodus of local workers. Its downtown shopping mall seems almost deserted. Nevertheless, Coos Bay has managed to retain the character of its seafront, with rattling traps, rolling logs, and smelly fish. The town also offers the best places to stay while you inch farther down the coast toward Bandon.

Practical Information and Orientation

Visitor Information: Chamber of Commerce, 50 E. Central (800-824-8486 or 269-0215; in OR 800-762-6278), 5 blocks west from U.S. 101, off Commercial Ave. in Coos Bay. Not as well-stocked as the Chamber of Commerce in Bandon. Good county map $1. Open Mon.-Tues., Thurs. 8:30am-6:30pm, Wed., Fri. 9am-5pm, Sat. 10am-4pm, Sun. noon-3pm; Sept.-May Mon.-Fri. 9am-5pm, Sat. 10am-4pm. **North Bend Information Center,** 138 Sherman Ave. (756-4613), on U.S. 101, just south of the harbor bridge in North Bend. Open Mon.-Fri. 8:30am-5:30pm, Sat. 10am-3pm; Labor Day-Memorial Day Mon.-Fri. 8:30am-5pm.

Oregon State Parks Information: 1155 S. 5th St. (269-9410).

Coos County Parks Department: 267-7009, toll-free from Coos Bay. Open Mon.-Fri. 8am-noon, 1-5pm.

Greyhound: 275 N. Broadway (267-6517), at the Tioga Hotel, in a somewhat seedy neighborhood. To Portland ($20.50) and San Francisco ($63). Open Mon.-Fri. 7-11am, noon-4pm, Sat. 8-11am, noon-4pm. In North Bend, flag down buses at the corner of Virginia and Sherman.

The Shuttle: 267-4521. Low-cost transportation within Coos Bay/North Bend and environs. Scenic and historical tours. Any round-trip within city limits (i.e. Coos Bay or North Bend) $5. To Shore Acres State Park one way $7. No set schedual. On call 24 hr.

Taxi: Yellow Cab, 267-3111. 24 hr. Senior citizen and student discount.

Coos Bay Public Library: 525 W. Anderson (267-1101). Open Mon.-Wed. 10am-9pm, Thurs.-Sat. 10am-5pm.

Help Line: 269-5910. 24 hr.

Coast Guard: 888-3266 (in Charleston).

Medical Emergency: Bay Area Hospital (269-2313).

Police: 269-1151.

Post Office: 4th and Golden (267-4514). Open Mon.-Fri. 8:30am-5pm. General Delivery ZIP Code: 97420.

Area Code: 503.

After faithfully hugging the coastline for many miles, U.S. 101 slants east to Coos Bay/North Bend. Hwy. 42 heads 85 mi. from Coos Bay (the town) to I-5 and U.S. 101 continues north into dune territory. Coos Bay and North Bend make up the northeast tip of the southern peninsula in Coos Bay (the bay). U.S. 101 skirts the east side of both cities and the Cape Arago Hwy. continues west to Charleston, at the mouth of the bay.

Accommodations

Timber Lodge Motel, 1001 Bayshore Dr., Coos Bay (267-7066), on U.S. 101. Close to downtown. Big rooms with nice finishing touches. Not the usual roadside dump. Singles $26. Doubles $36.

City Center Motel, 750 Connecticut St., North Bend (756-5118), off U.S. 101; convenient to the Greyhound station. Pleasant rooms for low rates. Phones, HBO in every room. Singles $28. Doubles $34.

Parkside Motel, 1490 Sherman Ave. (756-4124), on U.S. 101 on the north edge of town. Cute blue motif, nice rooms. Some kitchens. Singles $28. Doubles $35.

Captain John's Motel, 8061 Kingfisher Dr., Charleston (888-4041). Next to the small boat basin in Charleston, 9 mi. from the maddening crowd of Coos Bay, closer to state parks and beaches. Within walking distance of the docks. Singles and doubles $30.

Tradewinds Motel, 1504 Sherman Ave., North Bend (756-6398), on U.S. 101. Tiny (but comfortable) rooms with color TV. Not as nice as the Parkside next door. Singles $30. Doubles $33. In winter, about $4 less. Reservations recommended.

Camping

The state-run and private campgrounds make full use of the breathtaking coast. Always obtain reservations for summer.

Bluebill Forest Service Campground, off U.S. 101, 4 mi. northwest of North Bend, in the Horsfall Beach area. 19 sites. Trails lead to the ocean and dunes. Sites $7.

Sunset Bay State Park 13030 Cape Arago Hwy., Coos Bay 97420 (888-4902), 12 mi. south of Coos Bay and 3½ mi. west of Charleston on the Coos Bay/Bandon loop. Akin to camping in a parking lot, but the cove looks like Club Med. 108 sites with hot showers and facilities for the disabled. Sites $9, with hookups $11, RVs $11. Reservations accepted by mail. Open mid-April to Oct.

Bastendorff Beach Park (888-5353). A county park 10 mi. southwest of Coos Bay. Highly developed sites include hot showers (25¢), flush toilets, and hiking trails. Sites $7, with hookups $9. No reservations, but fills early. Open year-round.

Food

The Blue Heron, 100 Commercial St., Coos Bay (267-3933), at the corner of U.S. 101, Charleston turn-off. Friendly atmosphere and a well-stocked magazine rack. Famous for its wholesome homemade foods. Gigantic muffins $1.50. Lunches are in the $5-7 range. Go for the German sausage plate ($5.75). Dinners a bit more, but sublime: oysters on a bed of spinach fettucini, $9.50. Open daily 9am-10pm.

Sea Basket, in Charleston Boat Basin (888-5711), 9 mi. west of Coos Bay. Head south on Cape Arago Hwy. Baskets of local oysters, prawns, or scallops ($4.50)—not to mention steaks and an amazing salad bar—attract an enthusiastic marina crowd. Open daily 6am-8pm.

Carolyn's Breakfast Barn, in Charlestown Boat Basin just across the bridge (888-4512). Where the local fishermen like to hang out. Inexpensive egg dishes in a diner setting. Open daily 6am-2pm.

Woodie's Quik Wok, 3385 Broadway, North Bend (756-7275). Chinese food alá McDonald's. Stick to the old reliables, such as Moo Shu Pork and Kung Pow Chicken. Lunches $3.75. Dinners $5.50. Open Jan. 1-March 31 Mon.-Thurs. 11:30am-8pm, Fri. 11:30am-9pm, Sat. noon-9pm, Sun. noon-8pm.

Sights and Activities

One of the most dramatic spots in the central coast is also probably one of the most overlooked. The **South Slough Sanctuary** (888-5558) protects 4400 acres of estuaries, where salt and fresh water mix. The Slough area teems with wildlife, from sand shrimp to deer to *homo photographis.* Numerous hiking trails weave through the sanctuary; take a lunch and a friend and commune with the blue heron. South Slough is virtually inaccessible without a car but many Bandon hostlers make the Slough a daytrip expedition and you can often round up a shared ride. Take the exit off U.S. 101 or turn south off Cape Arago Hwy. onto Seven Devils Rd. and travel 4 mi. to the new visitors center and headquarters which explains the ecology of the estuarine environment. (Open daily 8:30am-4:30pm; Sept.-May Mon.-Fri. 8:30am-4:30pm. Free.) The trails are always open.

Coos Bay is one of the few places in western Oregon where life slows down as you near the ocean shore. Escape the industrial chaos by following Cape Arago Hwy. from Coos Bay to **Charleston.** (The signs alternately say Charleston and Ocean Beaches.) A town where crusty old sea salts seem at home, Charleston is a more pleasant place to stay for an extended period than its two big brothers. It's also a convenient stop on the way to **Shore Acres State Park.** Once the estate of local lumber landlord Louis J. Simpson, the park contains botanical gardens which survived the razing of the mansion. The beautiful flowers are a refreshing change of scenery from endless seashell-strewn beaches. The egret sculptures are a more recent addition, courtesy of some artistically-inclined convicts from the state penitentiary. (Open 9am-dusk, $1 per car. Disabled access.) Farther down the same highway is **Cape Arago,** notable mainly for its wonderful tide pools. Large sand bars rise and fade for some distance from the actual shore, giving a misleading impression of water depth. But what keeps ctenaphores and other invertebrates happy caused endless trouble for early sailors. Some believe the cape to be Sir Francis Drake's "bad bay," his mysterious temporary port of anchor in 1579.

Back in Charleston, make arrangements to tour the **Coast Guard Lifeboat Station** (888-3266) in the Charleston Marina (tours available anytime by prior reservation) or hop on board one of the many charters nearby. **Charleston Charters,** P.O. Box 5457 (888-4846) is one of the largest outfits. five-hour fishing trips leave at 5 and 10:30am ($40); less energetic baycruises are only $20. Freshwater fanatics should drive northeast from Eastside on the Coos River Rd. past the town of Allegany to **Golden and Silver Falls State Park.** There, ¾ mi. in from the road, twin falls (about 1 mi. apart) crash 200 ft. into a grove of red alder and Douglas fir.

Coos County suffers from a surfeit of museums, and unfortunately, none are particularily enthralling. North Bend is home to the **Coos County Historical Museum,** in Simpson Park (756-6320), just off U.S. 101 south of McCullough Bridge. The museum focuses on local Native and pioneer history, with a special emphasis on the logging and fishing industries and on pioneer children. A 1922 logging train engine stands at the entrance, and inside is a collection of spinning wheels that would have made Rumplestiltskin green with envy. (Open Tues.-Sat. 10am-4pm, Sun. 1-4pm; Oct.-Memorial Day Tues.-Sat. 10am-4pm. Admission 50¢, under 13 25¢.)

South of Coos Bay here is the **Marshfield Sun Printing Museum,** 1049 N. Front St. (269-1363), at the corner of Front and U.S. 101, across from the Timber Inn.

The first floor remains in its early 20th-century configuration. Some of the equipment dates to the paper's beginning in 1891. Upstairs are exhibits on the history of printing, American newspapers, and early Coos Bay neé Marshfield. (Open June-Aug. Tues.-Sat. 1-4pm. Free.)

In North Bend, the **Little Theatre on the Bay,** (756-4336) corner of Sherman and Washington St., presents musical cabaret with a regional flavor on Saturday nights. Their 1990-91 season includes *Annie* and *Blithe Spirit.*.

The **Pacific Power and Light Company Wind Turbine**, a cockamamy attempt to find an alternative source of power during the oil panic in the 70s, is now the world's largest and most expensive "wind farm." This plant at Whiskey Run on Cape Arago Hwy. is no threat to OPEC yet. and provides only limited electricity to a few hundred nearby homes. The theory is noble, and you can have it explained to you in exhaustive detail at the interpretive center. Although the doomsayers of the 70s who predicted immediate enslavement by the Arab oil mongers may have been hinting at windmills, it took an Oregonian to build one.

Seasonal Events

The annual **North Bend Air Show,** held the second weekend after the 4th of July, takes off each day at 8am with a pancake feed and continues until 5pm. The air shows occur between noon and 3pm. For further information, write to the North Bend Air Show, Inc., 1321-D Airport Way, North Bend 97459, or call 756-1723 (days) or 267-7330 (evenings). Tickets are $6, ages 6-12 $3, and can be obtained from the office at Safeway, or at the door ($2 extra). At the **Coos Bay Speedway,** south of Coos Bay near Coquille, each Sunday afternoon (1-5:30pm), sports enthusiasts cheer local heroes in open competition, street-stock, and jalopy-style racing. (Admission $8, seniors and ages 7-12 $6, under 7 free. Call 267-7045 for more information.)

The **Oregon Coast Music Festival** (269-4150), in mid-July, includes a series of classical, jazz, and folk performances around town and in Bandon and Reedsport. (Tickets $8-10, seniors and ages 6-18 $6-7.) For ticket information, write the Music Enrichment Association, P.O. Box 663, Coos Bay 97420 (267-0938). In late August, Coos Bay touts a native fruit with the **Blackberry Arts Festival.** Downtown crowds with square dancing, wine tasting, concerts, and crafts. In early September, Oregon memorializes its favorite son in the **Steve Prefontaine 10K Road Race,** named after the great Olympic athlete who died in an automobile accident in the bell lap of his career. The race attracts dozens of world-class runners to the area. For information on both these events, contact the Chamber of Commerce.

Bandon

"No one really lives in Bandon. Everyone's just apassing through. Some just pass through longer than others." Coming from one such rolling stone at rest, that's a fairly accurate description of this laid-back artists' colony. Graced with spectacular coastal scenery, Bandon somehow manages to avoid the tacky trinket trade. Filled with fresh-fish stores and charming boutiques, the Old Town achieves what every coastal village aspires to: the essence of quaintness.

Practical Information and Orientation

Visitor Information: Chamber of Commerce, 2nd and Chicago St. (347-9616). Well-equipped with useful maps of the town and surrounding area. Ask about touring the Myrtlewood shops and about wood-carving classes. Arranges tours to Glen Flora Cranberry Bogs, Magness Woods, and Seagull Myrtlewood. The guide to the town is inexplicably 63 pages long. Open daily 10am-5pm, 10am-4pm in the winter.

Greyhound: 610 2nd St. (347-3324). Bus stop is 1½ blocks from the hostel. To Portland ($24) and San Francisco ($70). Open Mon.-Sat. 9am-5:30pm.

Laundromat: Lila's Dry Cleaning and Landromat, Woodland Heights Shopping Center, just south of the Old Town. Open daily 8am-8pm.

Library: at City Hall. The Bandon library has a paperback swap rack, perfect for replenishing your reading stockpile if you haven't already picked up the visitors guide.

Coast Guard Summer Patrol: 347-3122 or 888-3266.

Police/Fire: 347-2241. City Hall at Oregon (U.S. 101) and S.W. 4th St.

Post Office: 105 12th St. (347-3406), 1 block east of U.S. 101. Open Mon.-Fri. 9am-5pm. General Delivery ZIP Code: 97411.

Area Code: 503.

Bandon lies at the mouth of the Coquille river, 24 mi. south of Coos Bay on U.S. 101 and 85 twisting mi. west of I-5 on Hwy. 42. Most of the restaurants are in **Old Town,** roughly 2nd St. to the water between Deleware and Edison St. Motels cast up on Beachloop Drive and S. Jetty Rd. as well as U.S. 101.

Accommodations and Camping

Staying at the hostel is the best (and cheapest) way to remain in the middle of things. Reservations strongly advised in the summer.

Sea Star Hostel (AYH), 375 2nd St. (347-9533) in Old Town. A fine wooden building with a quiet courtyard, a clean, well-equipped kitchen, and a common area flooded with sunshine from the skylight. Three "couple rooms" (private lodgings with loft-beds for 2) available at no extra charge. It's not uncommon for the whole hostel to light an impromptu beach bonfire. People come for a night and end up staying the week. No lockout and no curfew. Members $7, nonmembers $10. Reservations recommended.

Sunset Motel, 1755 Beach Loop Dr. (347-2453). By far the nicest motel in Bandon. Spectacular ocean vistas, easy beach access, lovely wood-paneled rooms. Some cottages hang right over the beach. Singles from $35. Doubles from $40.

Lamplighter, at junction of Hwy. 425 and U.S. 101. Small attractive motel on the outskirts of town. Singles $30. Doubles $36.

Bandon Wayside Motel, Hwy. 42 S. (347-3421), 3 blocks east of U.S. 101. Plain but cheap motel. Away from the action. Singles $20. Doubles $36.

Sea Star Guest House, 370 1st St. (347-9632). Although new ownership hasn't changed the hostel much, rooms at the guest house have almost doubled in price. Lovely rooms with river view starting at $40.

Bullards Beach (347-2209), 1 block and a bridge north of town on U.S. 101. Approximately 100 sites, a few of which are hiker/biker. Wheelchair-accessible, with hot showers. Reserve well in advance. Sites $9, hookups $10.

Blue Jay Campground (347-3258), 3 mi. south of town on Beach Loop Dr. Quiet sites for both tents and RVs. Hot showers. Sites $8. Open summers only.

Food

Bandon food is overpriced without being expensive. Consider hoarding free samples at the Cheese and Cranberry factories or buying your own crab trap (see Sights).

Chicago St. Eatery, 130 Chicago St. (347-4215), in Old Town. Mexican and Italian food in a place that looks like it was built from driftwood. Surprisingly upscale atmosphere. All lunch specials are $3.49, dinner $7. Open Mon.-Sat. 11am-9pm.

Bandon Fish Market, 1st St. (347-4282). From the sea to the frying pan to your mouth—fresh, delicious seafood prepared at a snail's pace. Clam chowder $1.50, fish and chips $3.35. Crab bait to-go, 50¢ per head. Picnic tables outside. Open daily 11am-8pm.

Minute Café, 145 N. 2nd St. (347-2707). Diner-style food at the local hangout. Soup and salad $3.50. Popular breakfast spot. Open daily 5:30am-3:30pm.

Andrea's Old Town Café, 160 Baltimore Ave. (347-3022), between 1st and 2nd St., 1½ blocks west of the hostel. Gourmet food in a far-out atmosphere—a huge mural à la Maurice Sendak covers half a wall (there are also outdoor tables). Favorites are raspberry blintzes ($5 in season) and curried lamb crepes ($6). Dinner menus always include at least 1 vegetarian dish, and average $12. Sat. night and Sun. brunch occasionally accompanied by classical guitar, folk music, or jazz. Open Mon.-Sat. 9am-9pm, Sun. 10am-2:30pm. Reservations recommended.

Ragtime Pizza, 490 Hwy. 101 (347-3911), 2 blocks north of Old Town. Nothing special, but the all-you-can-eat pizza and salad bar is a great deal (Mon.-Fri. 11:30am-1:30pm $4.75, ages under 12 $3). Open Mon.-Sat. 11am-10pm, Sun. noon-10pm.

Sea Star Bistro, 375 2nd St. (347-9632). This former coffeehouse in the front of the hostel building has been transformed by the new owners into a pricey eatery. The food is tasty, but entrees are in the $8-10 range.

Bandon Boatworks, South Jetty Rd. (347-2111). Seafood overlooking the Coquille River. Dinner is expensive but at lunch, sauteed fish with slaw and garlic bread is $4.25. Open Tues.-Sat. 11:30am-2:30pm and 5-9pm, Sun. noon-8:30pm.

University of Bandon Coffeehouse, on S. Jetty Road. There is no university in Bandon and this art gallery is only a coffeehouse two nights a week, but the locals pack the place anyway.

Sights and Activities

Bandon's **Old Town** is home to two highly touted food factories: the **Cheddar Cheese Factory** (recently reopened after a 2-year hiatus) and **Cranberry Sweets.** The Cheese Factory on 2nd St. distributes an enormous range of free samples. Come in the morning if you want to see the cheese made. Picnickers can pick up a pound of flavored cheddar for $3.50. (Open Mon.-Sat. 8:30am-6pm, Sun. 9am-5pm.) Don't leave town without filling up on the free samples at Cranberry Sweets, at the corner of 1st and Chicago; especially delicious are the mocha fudge and lemon-meringue-pie candies. (Open daily 9am-6pm.)

Only one mi. downstream from the Old Town, the surf leaps up against islands scattered in typical Oregon-coast fashion. Low tide reveals neon-orange starfish and bright green sea anemones clinging to the lower surfaces of gigantic rocks. Mussels grow in grotesquely large colonies and can be harvested at low tide (6 dozen max. per person per day).

Pick up clamming brochures and information at the youth hostel. To catch crabs, buy bait and purchase or rent a crab net for $5 a day at the **Bandon Bait Shop,** 1st and Alabama St. (347-3905), on the waterfront. (Open April-Nov. daily, depending on weather, 8am-7pm. $30 deposit required.) Observe the laws regulating the crabs and fish you can keep; carry a ruler, and keep only male crabs over four inches. If you're unsure, ask anyone at the bait shop or on the docks.

It's not *Life on the Mississippi,* but the **Sternwheeler Rose** will take you from the docks on a riverboat tour of the Coquille (pronounced ko-KEEL) River and estuary, past a series of historic sites—Native American burial grounds, an old barge ruin, and fish weirs among them. The daily cruises leave at 11am, 1pm and 3pm. (Fare $7, ages 5-11 $5, under 5 $3.) The boat can accommodate 90 passengers; call ahead on warm, sunny days. The ticket office (347-3942) is on the waterfront in Old Town, 1 block north of U.S. 101. (Open daily 11am-3pm.) Two blocks west of Old Town on 1st St., the Bandon Historical Society operates the **Coquille River Museum** (347-2164), in the old Coast Guard building. Photographs of the 1936 fire that leveled Bandon stand out among the usual relics from previous settlements. (Open Tues.-Sun. 1-4pm; in winter Fri.-Sun. 1-4pm. Free.) **Harbor Hall,** 210 E. 2nd St. (347-9712), in Old Town, is a recent addition to Bandon's nightlife. On occasional weekend nights, the Hall hosts concerts at 8pm. (Tickets $3-15, depending on the performer.) During the day, the hall is used for workshops, meetings, ceremonies, and community events. The Bandon community theater group also uses the theater.

West Coast Game Park, seven mi. south on U.S. 101, is a better-than-average "walk-thru safari." All creatures great and small from elk to bison roam over 21 acres. (Admission $5.50, ages over 60 $4.75, children 7-12 $4.25, 2-6 $3. Open daily 9am-dusk.) Bandon's most striking geographical feature is **Bullard's Beach State Park,** one mi. north of town on U.S. 101. Bullard's plunges the visitor into miles of gorgeous walking and beachcombing territory. Fishing and boating are also good here, and there is a fully developed campground. The 1896 **Coquille Lighthouse,**

on a spit inside the park, is 10 mi. away from Old Town by land, but only two to three mi. by water. (Open in summer only.) Four mi. north of town on U.S. 101 are the **cranberry bogs,** on Randolph Rd.

Beach Loop Drive leaves the town heading south, clings to the coast, and traverses a series of state parks (day use only) and beaches. **Bandon Beach Loop Stables** (347-9181), four mi. from Old Town just past Crooked Creek, rents horses by the hour, day, or week for beach trail rides ($15 per hour; they give lessons as well). **Crooked Creek** is one of several state parks along the coast. Just north are **Bandon** and **Bandon Ocean State Parks,** both staging dramatic views of off-shore rocks.

Beach access roads lead from Beach Loop Dr. to several rocky promontories just north of the state parks, including **Face Rock.** North of Coquille Point are more rock stacks with names like Garden of Gods Rocks and Cat and Hatton's Rocks. **Free Flight,** the Betty Ford Center of our fine feathered friends, is southwest Oregon's bird rehabilitation home (347-3886). Bird sanctuaries exist at Elephant and Table Rock and the Coquille River Estuary. North of the Sisters, where the river mouth opens to the sea, is the site of the 1915 wreck of the *S.S. Fifield.* North of the mouth, near the lighthouse, the *Oliver Olsen* sank decades later. Part of the wreck is still visible on clear days at low tide.

1991 will mark the 45th Anniversary of Bandon's zany **Cranberry Festival** (347-2257), held every year in September. The very red berry is celebrated with a fantastic food fair, spellbinding exhibits on "cranberries through history," parades, square dances, "jam" sessions, and a seven-mi. run from Bullard's Beach.

Port Orford

The people of Port Orford, the westernmost city in the Lower 48, boast that their town is the earliest pioneer settlement on Oregon's southern coast. In 1851, nine early settlers lost a skirmish at the over-grandly named Battle Rock to 400 Native Americans. The city gave up military aspirations, but after a short heyday lost its allure as a seaport as well. Today it is too tiny to deserve even the appellation "small town." With Bandon so close, it is best to make Port Orford a day trip and marvel at the surrounding cliff-cropped beaches.

Practical Information

Visitor Information: Information Center (332-8055), at Battle Rock, the southernmost point of "town" on the west side of U.S. 101. More brochures than one would expect a town this size could produce.

Greyhound: (332-1685). Buses stop at the K store, across from the Port Orford Motel. To Portland ($24) and San Francisco ($70).

Post Office: Jackson and 7th St. (332-4251). General Delivery ZIP Code: 97465.

Area Code: 503.

U.S. 101 nips through Port Orford so quickly that unless you know where Battle Rock is, you'll never catch a glimpse of it. The town is about 45 mi. south of Bandon and 30 mi. north of Gold Beach.

Accommodations and Camping

As with all the coastal towns, prices rise with the temperature.

Battle Rock Motel, P.O. Box 288 (332-7331), across from the Rock itself. Large, pleasant rooms. Each guest receives an enameled oyster. Great waterfront view. Singles $25. Doubles from $40.

Shoreline Motel, P.O. Box 426 (332-2901), next door to the Battle Rock Motel. Outstanding view. Clean rooms. A/C, TV with cable. Singles $34. Doubles $40. Prices lower in winter.

Port Orford Motel, 1034 Oregon St. (332-1685). Cheaper than the two waterfront motels and closer to the bus line. The landscaping—all roses and calla lilies—is lovely. The buildings are currently being renovated. About 10 min. from the beach. Any size room for 1-2 people, $29.

Humbug Mountain State Park (332-6774), 7 mi. south of Port Orford. 80 tentsites. Stunning scenery, good showers, flush toilets. Mosquitoes will keep you company at the hiker/biker sites ($2 per person); grassy $9 sites are a 10-min. walk down the road. No reservations accepted. Hookups $12.

Cape Blanco State Park (332-6774), 9 mi. north of Port Orford, off U.S. 101. Showers, flush toilets. Sites $10, hiker/biker sites $2.

Elk River Campground (332-2255), on Elk River Rd. off U.S. 101. Off the beaten path but excellent, clean sites with hot showers. Sites $6, with full hookups $9.

Food

Though some fry their food better than others Port Orford's restaurants serve the same seafood and burgers you can get anywhere else along the coast.

The Truculent Oyster, 236 6th St. (332-9461). Woodsy seafood. A bit overrated, and the name is by far the high point. Entrees are expensive ($5-10). Chowder and bread $3.50. Open daily 11am-9pm.

The Wheelhouse Restaurant, 521 Jefferson St. (332-1605). Locals flock here. Burgers, homemade soups, and pies. Clamfritter sandwich $3.50. Open Mon.-Fri. 6am-8pm, Sat.-Sun. 7am-8pm.

Sights

The view of the ocean from **Battle Rock** ranks among the most melodramatic on the entire Oregon coast. Be prepared to turn at the visitors center or else you will speed by and have to make a dangerous U-turn. Head down to the beach and take the short, well-worn path to the top of the mammoth rock outcropping. Look for the plaque honoring one of the original survivors of Battle Rock. Port Orford's beach is quite windy, so bring a jacket. Turn your back to the wind and watch the sand blow in huge, feathery plumes straight into the crashing waves. For other magnificent views, take a walk through **Humbug Mountain State Park,** seven mi. south of town. Modern survivors of the three-mi. hike up the mountain win a tremendous panorama of the entire area. **Fishing** in the two nearby rivers (the Sixes and the Elk) is fantastic. Ask at the information center for details. **Scuba divers** come for Port Orford's protected coves, where the water temperature rises to a mild 50°F and water clarity ranges from 10 to 50 ft. in summer.

The town itself is small and pleasant. The brochure *Port Orford's History in its Architecture* is an enlightening companion to a relaxed 10-minute stroll through the (entire) town. Several houses date back to the end of the 19th century. The most impressive building in the area, nine mi. north of town, is the restored **Hughes House** built by Per Johan Lindberg, a locally famed Swedish carpenter. (Open in summer daily 9am-5:30pm.)

Halfway down the road to Gold Beach, 13 mi. south on U.S. 101, the frontispiece of the **Prehistoric Gardens,** 36848 U.S. 101 (332-4463), arrests visitors unprepared for a full-sized Tyrannosaurus Rex with a yellow underbelly. The Rex is one of over 20 life-sized prehistoric animals carved by sculptor E.V. Nelson. Despite earnest attempts to recall the golden days of dinosaurs, the effect is like seeing all the parade floats lined up at the start. Your six-year-old will never forgive you if you don't spend the $2 to visit.

Stone Butte Stables (8¼ mi. north on U.S. 101) offer trail rides for $12 for one hour or $20 for two hours. The Sunset Barbecue ride is $25 per person.

Gold Beach

Gold Beach is Kodak Picture Perfect Moment country. From Port Orford south to the California border, the green hills shade to a golden brown, mingled with the yellow and lavender of wildflowers. The jagged coastline in this area is perhaps the most sublime on the coast. Through the middle of this splendor cuts the wild Rogue River, slow and peaceful by the time it reaches Gold Beach. Just inland, the Siskiyou National Forest smiles upon hikers and photographers with scenery lifted from a coffee-table book.

Practical Information and Orientation

Visitor Information: Chamber of Commerce, 510 S. Ellensburg (247-7526; 800-452-2334 outside OR). Tiny office with little information. Open Mon.-Sat. 9am-5pm.

Gold Beach Ranger District Office: 1225 S. Ellensburg (247-6651), on U.S. 101. Free packet details camping and recreation in the district. Open daily 7:30am-5pm.

Greyhound: 310 Colvin St. (247-7710). Tiny smoke-filled box. Better to wait across the street in the public library. Two per day to Portland ($29) and San Francisco ($82). Open Mon.-Sat. 10:40am-5pm.

Taxi: Gold Beach Cab (247-2205).

Laundromat: Stansell's Coin-op Laundry, 811 S. Ellensburg (247-2532), U.S. 101 S., near 8th St.

Police: 510 S. Ellensburg (247-6671).

Fire: 510 S. Ellensburg (247-7029).

Post Office: Moore St. (247-7610). Open Mon.-Fri. 8:30am-5pm. General Delivery ZIP Code: 97444.

Area Code: 503.

Gold Beach lies at the mouth of the Rogue River on U.S. 101, equidistant (approximately 30 mi.) from Port Orford to the north and Brookings to the south. The main drag is **S. Ellensburg (U.S. 101),** where almost all restaurants and motels are located.

Accommodations and Camping

Rates increase by about $6-10 every month in the summer. Beware arriving late without a reservation: your options may quickly dwindle to a $40 (or more) bed.

Oregon Trail Lodge, 550 N. Ellensburg, Box 721 (247-6030). Wonderful rooms, on a par with more expensive motels. Best value in the area. Singles $23. Doubles $29.

River Bridge Inn, U.S. 101 and Jerry's Flat Rd. (247-4533 or 800-453-4511). Handsome rooms with river views (some with kitchenettes). Extremely friendly management. Singles $36. Doubles $42. Rooms with views $4 more.

Western Village Motel, 9755 S. Ellensburg (247-6611). Largish rooms with a professional flair. HBO, A/C. Singles $38. Doubles $44, but prices may be negotiable.

City Center Motel, 150 Harlow St. (247-6675), just off Ellensburg. Cheap prices. Cheap product. Singles $28. Doubles $40.

Indian Creek Campground, 94680 Jerry's Flat Rd. (247-7704). Take a right turn just south of the bridge. All the friendly amenities of a KOA, and the prices, too. Showers could pass inspection in the Banff Springs Hotel. A recreation room and laundromat, emblazoned with "spiritually uplifting" poetry. Tent sites (isolated from the roar of RV engines) $8. Full hookups $10.

Arizona Beach Campground (332-6491), 2 mi. north of Gold Beach on U.S. 101. The smell of the seaspray, the roar of the waves. Tent sites $10.

Food

If eating well means anything to you, you've come to the wrong town. The restaurants by the water are very pricey and the remaining options serve food that is simply *jejune.*

Grant's Pancake and Omelette House, Jerry's Flat Rd. (247-7208), next to Indian Creek Camp. A good 20-min. walk from the port. This local hot(cake) spot flips piles of pecan-packed pancakes ($4). Open daily 6am-2pm.

Ethel's Fine Foods, 347 N. Ellensburg (247-7713), next to the movie theater. Another fave rave of the natives, this small café serves up the usual conglomerate of seafood and burgers ($3-5) but express yourself instead with the daily specials like the deep-fried mushroom basket ($3.50). Open Mon.-Sun. 6:30am-8pm.

The Golden Egg, 710 S. Ellensburg (247-7528). Only a Nietzchean superhen could lay an omelette selection this varied, (27 kinds; $4-7). Try the avocado and cheese ($4.50). Typical burger lunches $4-5, steak-and-seafood dinners under $10. Open daily 6am-9pm.

Spada's, 1020 S. Ellensburg (247-7732). A huge menu in a family-style restaurant. Dinners are expensive, but lunch deli specials are in the $4 realm. Try to drop in for the Sun. champagne brunch, an all-you-can-eat arrangement ranging from standard breakfast to standard beef teriyaki ($8, children $6). Open daily 6am-10pm.

Activities

Gold Beach's main appeal lies in the Rogue River and its spectacular approach through rugged canyonlands to the sea. A free pamphlet at the ranger station outlines a self-guided **driving tour** through the Siskiyou. The tour begins on Hunter Creek Rd. just south of Gold Beach and loops north through the forest, eventually following the course of the Rogue back into town. Allot about three hours for the drive.

You can leave your car behind to hike the famed **Rogue River Trail,** which follows the 65-mi. river through the canyon past threatening rapids, massive rock outcroppings, and dense forests. Reach the trail by crossing the Lobster Creek Bridge, across from the Quosatana campground (4¼ mi. northeast on U.S. 595, then 10 mi. northeast on U.S. 33), and starting east on Silver Creek Rd. The trail dies at Grave Creek, 27 mi. northwest of Grants Pass.

The best way to see all this rugged glory without much exertion is to take a jet boat up the river. **Jerry's Rogue River Jet Boats,** just across the bridge to the west of U.S. 101 (800-458-3511 or 247-4571), runs trips from May through October in large motorboats. A 64-mi. round-trip excursion goes all the way to the town of Agness and surveys much of the wildlife and scenery en route. (Fare $25, ages 4-11 $10.) The 104-mi. round-trip runs up the river to the base of the infamous "Blossom Bar" rapid, crashing through other white water on the way up. (Fare $50, ages 4-11 $25.) Both trips stop for lunch (not included in the fare). Jerry's staff is friendly and informative. Reservations are recommended. Send a 25% deposit to P.O. Box 1011, Gold Beach 97444. (Office open May-Oct. daily 7am-9pm.)

Daily from April through October, **Courts River Running White Water Trips** (800-367-5687 or 247-6676) runs the same routes, leaving from Jots' Resort at the north end of the Rogue River Bridge, west of U.S. 101. The 64-mi., six-hour trip includes lunch or dinner in Agness. (Fare $25, ages 5-12 $10, under 5 free.) The 104-mi., eight-hour trip stops briefly in Agness and longer at the Paradise Bar Lodge. (Fare $50, ages 6-12 $25, under 5 free.) You may stay the night and resume the trip the next day. (Singles at the lodge are $65 May-June and Oct., $75 July-Sept. 4 meals included.)

If you are not up to the rigors of "runnin' the Rogue," **Indian Creek Trail Rides,** Jerry's Flat Rd. (247-7704), guides sturdy horses over the river and through the woods. (Rides cost $12 per hr., $25 for the 2½-hr. lunch ride.) Before you leave Gold Beach, stop at the **Curry County Museum,** 950 S. Ellensburg (247-6113), which illustrates the history of the area. Excellent old photographs and Native American petroglyphs give a brief but fascinating picture of days gone by. (Open June-Sept. Wed.-Sun. 1-5pm; Oct.-May Fri.-Sat. noon-4pm. Free.) Seven mi. south of Gold Beach on U.S. 101, **Cape Sebastian State Park** has a good trail down to a remarkable ocean overlook. Water, water everywhere, but no rest rooms or drinking facilities at the park.

From late June to late August, visitors can enjoy **Gold Beach Summer Theatre** at the Curry County Campgrounds. The theater presents serious drama and light comedy, usually modern. (Admission $6.50, senior citizens and students $5, and ages 4-12 $2.50.) Contact Gold Beach Summer Theatre Inc., P.O. Box 1324, Gold Beach 97444 (800-542-2334; in OR, 800-452-2334).

Other seasonal events of interest are the **Clam Chowder Cook-off** on the first weekend in May, and the Annual Rogue River **Jet Boat Marathon** on the first weekend in June.

Brookings

Brookings is one of the few Oregon coastal towns that has remained relatively tourist-free. Although gorgeous beaches and parks surround Brookings, it is accessible only by U.S. 101 and tends to be more of a stopover than a destination. So while good restaurants and lodgings are not abundant, the beaches are among the most unspoiled on the Oregon coast.

In **Azalea State Park,** downtown, lawns are encircled by large native azaleas, some of which are over 300 years old. Two rare weeping spruce trees also grace the park's grounds. Picnic areas and facilities for the disabled are provided. The pride of Brookings is its annual **Azalea Festival,** held in the park during Memorial Day weekend. The Chetco Valley Historical Society Museum, 15461 Museum Rd. (469-6651), 2½ mi. south of the Chetco River, occupies the oldest building in Brookings. Exhibits include the patchwork quilts and wedding dresses of white settlers and Native American basketwork. (Open Wed.-Sun. noon-5pm, Thurs. noon-4pm. Free.)

Stay at the **Chetco Inn Hotel,** 417 Fern Ave. (469-9984), a hotel on a hill (behind the Shell station overlooking the town). A clean and gracious interior is disguised by the soon-to-be-resurrected facade. (Singles $30. Doubles $36.) **Harris Beach State Park,** two mi. north of Brookings, has 66 tentsites in the midst of a grand natural setting. The park is equipped with showers, hiker/biker sites, and facilities for the disabled. (469-2021; open year-round. Sites $9.) **Loeb State Park,** eight mi. east of Brookings, has good swimming, fishing, tent, and hiker/biker sites (also $9). A one mi. trail leads to a soothing redwood grove. For more unspoiled campsites off the beaten path, continue east seven more mi. past Loeb to the charming **Little Redwood** campground (sites $4).

Mama's Authentic Italian Food, 703 Chetco Ave. (469-7611), in the Central Mall, is worth the ½ hr. trip from either Gold Beach or Crescent City. "Mama" Antonia Lucarini delights in stuffing her clientele with fresh bread and pasta. Entrees bring a choice of soup or salad, and (mmm) garlic bread. Try the delicious ravioli ($6.25). Seniors get a 10% discount and all orders are available without meat. (Open daily 11am-9pm.) **Lyn's Country Tea Room,** 1240 Chetco Ave. (469-7020), is noteworthy for its home-baked pastries and bread. Try the plum pudding. (Open Tues.-Sat. 8am-2:30pm.)

The **Oregon State Department of Economic Development Information Center,** 1650 U.S. 101 (469-4117), maintains an exceptionally well-stocked office just north of Brookings and answers questions regarding the Oregon coast. (Open May-Nov. Mon.-Sat. 9am-6pm, Sun. 9am-5pm.) The town's **Chamber of Commerce,** 97949 Shopping Center Rd. (469-3818), is across the bridge to the south, just off the highway. (Open Mon.-Fri. 9am-5pm; call for weekend hours.) The **Chetco Ranger Station,** 555 5th St. (469-2196), distributes information on this area of the Siskiyou National Forest. (Open Mon.-Fri. 7:30am-4:30pm.) The **Greyhound** station is at Tanburk and Railroad (469-3326). The **Laundromat** (469-3975), open 24 hr., is known to locals by its sobriquet "The Old Wash House"; you'll find it near the Chamber of Commerce booth, at the Brookings Harbor Shopping Center. The **post office,** 711 Spruce St. (469-2318), is open Mon.-Fri. 9am-5pm (General Delivery ZIP Code: 97415).

Inland Valleys

While the jagged cliffs and coastal surf seduce tourists and nature lovers to the Oregon coast, the lush inland valleys are the state's breadbaskets. The bulk of Oregonians live in the Willamette, Rogue, and Umpqua river valleys, where vast tracts of fertile land and huge forests support a large agricultural industry and (until the spotted owl legislation) immense lumber mills.

Interstate 5, which runs north and south through the three West Coast states, traverses rolling agricultural land that is punctuated by comparatively barren urban centers. Farthest south, the **Rogue River Valley,** from Ashland to Grants Pass, is generally hot and dry in the summer—the temperature climbs a sweltering 100°F on many days. Whitewater rafting, fishing, and spelunking offer refuge from the heat. Eugene, Oregon's second largest city and bawdiest college town, rests at the southern extreme of the temperate **Willamette Valley.** This carpet of agricultural land extends about 20 mi. on either side of the highway and runs 80 mi. or so north until it bumps into the suburban hills that house Portland's bedroom communities.

It is possible to travel the 250-mi. stretch of I-5 from tip to toe in less than six hours, but lead-foot out-of-staters should be wary—Oregonians obey speed limits, and the highways are of poor quality. To make matters worse, the snowy winters make road construction possible only in summer; you may well find yourself behind the wheel in traffic jams in 100° weather. But don't despair; the Oregon Parks and Recreation Department maintains rest areas every 30 to 40 mi. along the interstate. Public rest rooms, phones, picnic tables, and "animal exercise areas" are available. Rest areas are shaded, grassy, and generally well-kept, but travelers should bring their own toilet paper. Tents may not be pitched in public rest areas, but those motorists who have developed the talent for slumbering on a back seat may park for up to 18 hours.

Salem

Salem is a small town trying to dress up for its job as the state capital. While the downtown area is brand new, much of Salem retains the look and flavor of the missionary settlement it was in 1851, when it beat Oregon City in the competition to be capital.

Practical Information and Orientation

Visitor Information: Visitors Center, 1313 Mill St. SE (581-4325), part of the Mission Mill Village complex (see Sights). Brochures on Salem and other parts of the state. Open Mon.-Fri. 8:30am-5pm, Sat. 10am-4pm, Sun. 1-4pm; in fall and winter Mon.-Fri. 8:30am-5pm. **Chamber of Commerce,** 220 Cottage St. NE (581-1466). Open Mon.-Fri. 8:30am-5pm.

Amtrak: 13th St. and Oak St. SE (588-1551), across from Willamette University. One train per day to Portland ($11).

Greyhound: 450 Church St. NE (362-2428), at Center St. To Portland $6. Open daily 6:30am-9pm.

Local Transportation: Cherriots (Salem Area Transit) (588-2877). 18 buses originate from High St.; terminals are in front of the courthouse. Fares 25-50¢, depending on distance. Service Mon.-Fri. 6am-6:15pm (buses every ½-hr. during rush hours), Sat. 7:45am-6:15pm (every hr.).

Taxi: Salem Yellow Cab Co., 362-2411.

Car Rental: National, 695 Liberty St. NE (800-227-7368 or 585-4226). Open Mon.-Fri. 8am-6pm.

Laundromat: Suds City Depot, 1785 Lancaster Dr. NE (362-9845). Open daily 7:30am-9pm.

Women's Crisis Center: 399-7722.

Emergency: 911.

Police: 555 Liberty St. SE (588-6123), in City Hall.

Post Office: 1050 25th St. (370-4700). Open Mon.-Fri. 9am-5:30pm. General Delivery ZIP Code: 97301-9999.

Area Code: 503.

Halfway between the equator and the North Pole, bordered on the west by the Willamette River and on the east by I-5, Salem is 47 mi. south of Portland.

Accommodations and Camping

Lady luck wins out in Salem: the only good deal downtown is the women-only Y. Other inexpensive lodgings are a long hike from the center of town and the closest camping is 26 mi. north.

YWCA, 768 State St. (581-9922), next to Willamette U. and Capital Park. Women only. A scenic and safe location. Rooms $13. Key¯deposit $3.

Friendship City Center Motel, 510 Liberty St. SE (364-0121), about ½ mi. from the Capitol, the budget lodgings closest to downtown. Singles $35. Doubles $40.

Motel 6, 2250 Mission St. SE (588-7191), 1 mi. east of town. Singles $30. Doubles $36.

Super 8 Motel, 1288 Hawthorne NE (370-8888), 1 mi. northeast of city center, exit 256 off I-5. More luxurious than most. Singles $40. Doubles $45.

All-Star Inn, 1401 Hawthorne NE (371-8024), a standard motel chain with the cheapest rooms in Salem. Singles $24. Doubles $32.

Silver Falls State Park, 20024 Silver Falls SE (Hwy. 214), Sublimity (873-8681), 26 mi. from Salem. Oregon's largest state park offers swimming, hiking trails, and views of multitudinous waterfalls, the tallest (spectacular Double Falls) crashing 178 ft. Campsites $8, with electricity and water use $10.

Food

Restaurants in Salem are generally overpriced and not particularly good, though there are a few exceptions. At least you'll be able to eat well (and cheaply) for a day or two. Better options send up smoke signals near **Willamette University. Commercial Street SE** is neon America's version of Main St., lined on both sides with chain supermarkets, franchise restaurants, and "Drive-up Divorce" booths.

Off-Center Café, 1742 Center NE (363-9245). A paper sign on the window reading "Yes, this is the Off-Center Café" welcomes you to this dingy local favorite. This café is definitely left of center and serves great health food. Bean breakfast $4. Open Tues.-Sat. 6am-3pm, Thurs.-Sat. 5-9pm, Sun. 8am-2pm.

Pilar's, in the Reed Opera House. Elegant but not expensive, dining in purple palatial splendor. Try the tapas for 2 ($10) or *panzanitas* (large raviolis) $6. Open Mon.-Sat. 11am-9pm.

La Casa Réal, 698 12th St. SE (588-0700). Healthy Mexican food such as Taco de Halibut ($4.25) and Santa Fe Burrito ($5). Open Mon.-Thurs. 11am-10pm, Fri.-Sat. 11am-11pm.

Sights

The **State Capitol** (378-4423), on Court St. between W. Summer and E. Summer St., is capped by a 24-ft. gold-leaf statue of the quintessential "Oregon Pioneer." The combination of this statue with big blocks of white Vermont marble and large murals gives the capitol an imposing, temple-like appearance; the whole structure is vaguely reminiscent of government buildings found in foreign dictatorships. Fortunately, the Capitol's interior is much more personable. Despite persistent conflicts between loggers and environmentalists, the legislative chambers are designed for laid-back lawmaking. The carpet on the Senate floor is checkered with salmon and sheaves of wheat, while the House's carpet depicts a forest of Christmas trees. There are temporary art exhibits on the main floor. Although the tower is closed until the summer of 1993 due to the not-at-all-exaggerated perils of asbestos, the gold-plated pioneer atop the tower remains steadfast. The capitol is open for roaming Sat. 9am-4pm, Sun. noon-4pm. Free 30-minute tours are offered Mon.-Fri. from 9am-4pm.

Across the street is **Willamette University**, 900 State St. (370-ö300). Founded by Methodist missionaries in 1842, it is billed as "the oldest university of the West."

The **Reed Opera House Shopping Mall,** on Liberty St. between Court and State, symbolizes the fate of the Old West. The building's brick facade and long windows remain intact, but its insides have been gutted and remodeled with clothing stores and specialty shops that wear the structure's history like a period costume. Those who can't bear to see this elegant old building tarted up in neon should head for **Mission Mill Village**, 1313 Mill St. SE (585-7012), a group of historic houses where employees in pioneer garb demonstrate forest cooking, carving, and hunting. The village includes a reasonably interesting woolen mill/museum and several stores more closely tied to the contemporary consumer economy. Tours of the houses and mill leave hourly. (Admission $2 for either the house or the mill, $3 for both. Seniors and students $1.50 and $2.50.) The **Marion Museum of History** (364-2128) is part of the village but charges a separate admission fee. Inside rare relics of the Kalpuy-ans survive, although the tribe was destroyed by 19th-century settlers. (Open daily 1-4:30pm. Admission $1, seniors and children 50¢.)

The **Enchanted Forest** (363-3060), a Liliputian Disneyland, is 7 mi. south of Salem on I-5. The park's displays bring nursery rhymes to life. (Open March 15-Sept. 30 daily 9:30am-5:30pm. Admission $3.50, children $3, plus 50¢ for the haunted house and 75¢ for the bobsled.)

Bush's Pasture Park, 600 Mission St. SE, is an 80-acre park with rose gardens, tennis courts, and lots of shade. The park—perhaps emblematic of America in 1990—is an ideal picnic spot. The **Bush House** (363-4714) is a well-restored Victo-rian mansion built in 1877 by a banker and newspaper publisher. Hourly tours Tues.-Sun. noon-5pm ($1.50, seniors $1, students 75¢). Taste Oregon's fruit and wines at the **Honeywood Winery** (362-4111), founded in 1934, it's the oldest winery in the state. Tasting room open Mon.-Fri. 9am-5pm, Sat. 10am-5pm. Call in advance for tours.

Eugene and Springfield

Nestled between the Siuslaw (pronounced see-YOU-slaw) and the Willamette National Forests, Oregon's second largest city sits astride the Willamette River, touching tiny Springfield to the east. Not small or quaint enough to be a town, not big or (despite its efforts) sophisticated enough to be a metropolis, Eugene is a city open to interpretation. City slickers can shop and dine in downtown's Pedestrian Mall and 5th Street Market. Outdoor types can raft the river, bike and run on its banks, or hike in one of the large parks near the city. And as home to the University of Oregon, Eugene crawls with art museums, ice cream parlors, and all the other trappings of a college town in the age of mass academia.

The footloose and fancy-free have dubbed Eugene "the running capital of the universe." Only in this city could the annual Bach Festival (in late June) be accompanied by the "Bach Run," a 1 to 5km dash through the city's downtown area. Nike, which started in Eugene (and, incidentally, was Johann Sebastian's preferred brand of footwear), sponsors the event which culminates in a performance of the so-called "Sports Cantata" (BWV 12 "Weinen, Klagen, Laufen," or "Weeping, La-menting, Running").

Practical Information and Orientation

Visitor Information: Eugene-Springfield Convention and Visitors Bureau, 305 W. 7th (800-452-3670 or 484-5307; outside OR 800-547-5445), between Lincoln and Lawrence St. downtown. Maps, brochures, listings, and guides to everything you might want to do in the 2 cities. Open Mon.-Fri. 8:30am-5pm, Sat. 10am-4pm.

Park Information: Willamette National Forest Service, 211 E. 7th Ave. (687-6521). **Eugene Parks and Recreation Dept.,** 858 Pearl St. (687-5333 for general information, 687-5360 for athletics, 342-5746 for arts, 687-5311 for specialized recreation for the disabled), in City Hall. Open Mon.-Fri. 8am-5pm. Also at 777 High St. (687-5333).

University of Oregon Switchboard: 795 Willamette St. (346-3111). Referral for just about everything—rides, housing, emergency services. Open Mon.-Fri. 8am-5pm.

Amtrak: 4th and Willamette St. (800-872-7245). To: Seattle ($48), San Francisco ($99), and Portland ($23).

Greyhound: 9th and Pearl St. (344-6265). Nine buses north, 6 south per day. Open daily 6am-10:30pm. Storage lockers $1 per day.

Green Tortoise: 937-3603. Three buses per week head south from Seattle to San Francisco, and 3 head north on the same route. Half the price of Greyhound. Call for details. Open daily 9am-3pm.

Lane Transit District (LTD): 10th and Willamette St. (687-5555). Provides public transportation throughout the towns of Eugene and Springfield. Pick up a map and timetables at the Convention and Visitors Bureau, the LTD Service Center, or 7-Eleven stores. Many routes are wheelchair-accessible—look for the international accessibility symbol. Fares Mon.-Fri. 65¢, Sat.-Sun. 30¢; seniors and children ½-price.

Ride Board: Erb Memorial Union (EMU) basement (345-4600), University of Oregon. Open during the school year daily 7am-11:30pm; mid-June to mid-Sept. 7am-7pm.

Taxi: Yellow Cab (746-1234).

Bike Rental: Pedal Power, 6th and High St. (687-1775), downtown. 6-speeds $2.50 per hr., $12 per day, $30 per week. Tandems $5 per hr., $20 per day. Children's bikes available. Baby seats provided for 3-speeds at no extra cost. Credit card or Oregon driver's license required. Open Mon.-Sat. 9am-6pm, Sun. 10am-5pm.

University Events and Activities Line: 346-4636. 24 hr.

Laundromat: Club Wash 595 E. 13th St. (342-1727). Open daily 7am-1am.

Rape Crisis Network: 650 W. 12th St. (485-6700). Crisis intervention for rape, abuse, and sexual harassment. Open Mon.-Thurs. 9am-5pm. Answering service 24 hr.

Women's Referral and Resource Service: EMU, #336 (346-3327), University of Oregon. Open during the school year Mon.-Fri. 9am-5pm; erratic summer hours.

Gay Hotline: 683-CHAT. Confidential crisis intervention and referral. Open Thurs.-Sun. 8pm-midnight.

Police/Fire: 777 Pearl St. (687-5111) at City Hall.

Post Office: In **Eugene,** 5th and Willamette St. (341-3611), or in the EMU Bldg. at the university. Open Mon.-Fri. 8:30am-5:30pm, Sat. 10am-2pm. General Delivery ZIP Code: 97401. In **Springfield,** 760 A St. (747-3383). Open Mon.-Fri. 8am-5pm. General Delivery ZIP Code: 97477.

Area Code: 503.

Eugene sleeps 100 mi. south of Portland on the I-5 corridor. The University of Oregon campus lies in the southeastern corner of town, bordered on the north by Franklin Boulevard, which runs from the city center to I-5 and Springfield. First Avenue mostly parallels the winding Willamette River, and Willamette Avenue intersects the river, dividing the city into east and west.

Accommodations

Eugene has the usual assortment of motels; the cheapest are on E. Broadway and W. 7th St. The hostel, though far from downtown, is the least expensive and most interesting place to stay. The closest legal camping is 12 mi. away, although it is said that people camp by the river (especially in the wild and woolly northeastern side near Springfield). Most park hours are officially 6am to midnight. Lone women should avoid the university campus vicinity at night.

The Green House Home Hostel, 1117 W. 11th St. (344-5296). This newly opened 5-bed hostel serves also as a private residence, a community meeting place, and headquarters for the Green Party. It is on its way to becoming a self-sufficient, alternative-energy, global-village eco-home. Always a hive of activity, so much so that hostelers might feel lost in the shuffle. Never boring. Check-in before 11pm. Kitchen open 4:30-6:30pm. Flexible curfew and kitchen hours. Members and nonmembers $7. Reservations essential.

66 Motel, 755 E. Broadway (342-5041). Very professional, very cheap and, not surprisingly, very crowded. Singles $23. Doubles $32.

Executive House Inn, 1040 W. 6th (683-4000). No A/C but huge rooms with refrigerator and sink. Singles $20.50.

Downtown Motel, 361 W. 7th Ave. (345-8739). Where traveling music groups stay. Flowers in every room. Coffee shop next door. Cable TV, A/C. Singles $26. Doubles $38.

Eugene Motor Lodge Motel, 476 E. Broadway (344-5233). Comfortable rooms with firm beds. A/C, some with kitchenettes. Pool and adjacent café open 24 hr. Singles $24. Doubles $34.

Broadway Motel, 659 E. Broadway (344-3761). Cheap and clean, but not for arachnophobiacs. TV, A/C. Singles $18. Doubles $22.

Fantasyland, 568 W. 7th Ave. (687-0531). Most rooms here are generic and comfortable, but a few more dollars will buy a trip to fantasyland—suites with leather waterbeds, heart-shaped tubs, and velvet wallpaper. VCR rentals for $9 include unlimited free films (adult or otherwise). Singles $26. Doubles $28.

Timbers Motel, 1015 Pearl St. (343-3345), ½-block from Greyhound. 24-hr. desk, so these clean and small rooms are perfect for late-night bus arrivals. Cable TV, A/C. Singles $28. Doubles $38.

Camping

Campers with cars should drive the 20 mi. down Hwy. 58 into the Willamette National Forest, where lovely marshland sites with water are available along the river for $3. The swamp gives the tree bark and ferns an eerie phosphorescence in some seasons, especially in the **Black Canyon** campground.

Fern Ridge Lake, 12 mi. west of Eugene on Hwy. 126. Campgrounds on the southwest spit of land that projects into the lake at Fern Ridge Shores. Sites $7.

Fall Creek Lake, Lookout Point Lake, and **Hills Creek Lake,** 20 mi. southeast of Eugene on Hwy. 58. Overnight camping allowed on all 3 lakes. Sites $7.

Dorena Lake and **Cottage Grove,** 20 mi. south of Eugene on I-5. Park manager's office 942-5631. Equipped for camping. **Schwarz Park,** at the west end of Dorena Lake, is one of the few free campgrounds. No piped-in water.

Food

The monotony of pizza joints in this university town is broken by a smattering of ethnic restaurants. Taverns and snack-shops make "all-nighters" possible until 3am. Some of the best food downtown is in the enormous open-air **City Center Mall,** centered on E. 11th and Willamette St. For the less hungry or less affluent, street vendors in this area provide cheap sustenance.

Downtown

Keystone Café, 395 W. 5th St. (342-2075). An eclectic local granola co-op which serves up incredible food made from homegrown ingredients. Burgers $2-5. Tofu enchilada $2.25. Huge slices of fresh pie $1.50. Open daily 7am-9pm.

de Frisco's, 99 W. 10th St. (484-2263). Upscale eartery with offerings like Alligator Pear Burger ($5.25). Open Mon.-Thurs. 11am-midnight, Fri.-Sat. 11am-2am.

Kestrel Café, 454 Willamette St. (344-4794). Lots of excellent vegetarian and Mexican food. Smallish portion of chicken rancheros ($5). Open daily 7am-3pm and Tues.-Sat. 5-9pm.

Allann Bros. Bakery, 152 W. 5th Ave. (342-3378). Delicious baked goods and salads in a bright, airy atmosphere. Fill a thermos with coffee for $1.95. Lunch specials $3-4. Open daily 6am-midnight.

Ambrosia, 1174 E. Broadway. Yuppies come here for the red fringed lamps and amazing Italian food. *Calzone Modo Nostra* ($8). Sit outside or beneath huge tapestries indoors. Open Sun.-Thurs. 11am-10pm, Fri.-Sat. 11am-midnight.

Prince Pücker's Ice Cream Parlor, 861 Willamette St. (343-2621). Homemade ice cream from all-natural ingredients. Best ice cream in Eugene—try the raspberry truffle. "Baby" size (1 scoop) 50¢. Experience the Euphoria Ultra Chocolate Sundae ($1.99). Open Mon.-Thurs. 11:30am-11pm, Fri. 11:30am-midnight, Sat. noon-midnight, Sun. noon-11pm.

University Area

Taylor's Bayou Kitchen (Louisiana Cookin'), 894 E. 13th St. (344-1212), right across from the university. Low-key, low-priced; friendly waiters, plenty of beer. Spare ribs smothered in spicy cajun sauce at 85¢ per bone are probably the best deal. On Mondays, try the *Jambalaya* with slaw and French bread ($4.25). At 8pm nightly, this mild-mannered restaurant rocks with live music that echoes throughout the campus. Restaurant open Mon.-Sat. 11am-8pm. Nightclub open 8pm-3am.

Guido's, 801 E. 13th St. (343-0681). Good Italian dinners that average $6. Pastrami sandwich $4. Open daily 11am-11pm and 5-10pm. Move around vacantly to top-40 tunes Wed. and Fri.-Sat. 11pm-2:30am. On dance nights from 10-11pm well-drinks are only $1.50.

Sights and Activities

Mad dogs and Eugeneans go out in the midday sun. Despite the roasting temperatures of a Willamette Valley summer, noon is when recreational centers and museums open. Even the Saturday market drags its feet until the sun reaches the magical meridian.

Set off south on Willamette St. The 3½-mi. **South Hills Ridgeline Hiking Trail,** with views of the Cascades starts at the intersection of 52nd Ave. and Willamette St., and extends east to Dillard Rd.

Closer to and north of downtown is **Skinner's Butte Park,** on the southwest side of the river. Named for the city's founder, it gazes on his lifework: the development of Eugene and the river valley. Just to the east is **Alton Baker Park,** the main drag for runners. Ride or jog east along the bank of the Willamette River to the point where N. Adams St. intersects the bike path. Here the **River House** contains the offices for the city's outdoor program and is a meeting place for outdoor activities. The nearby **Owen Memorial Rose Garden,** just under the I-5 overpass, is perfect for a picnic, despite the rattle of mid-afternoon traffic.

The **Lane County Historical Museum,** 740 W. 13th Ave. (687-4239), arranges a more formal, historical, exalting look at the city than old Skinner's. (Open Tues.-Sat. 10am-5pm. Admission $1, seniors 75¢, children 50¢.)

Reception centers for the University of Oregon handle tours and distribute campus maps at **Oregon Hall,** E. 13th Ave. and Agate St., and at the visitors parking and information booth, just left of the main entrance on Franklin Blvd. The spacious lawns of the campus befit picnics. The **University Museum of Art** (686-3027), on 13th St. between Kincaid and University St., houses contemporary Northwest and American art, as well as an extensive collection from the Pacific Basin. (Open Sept.-June Wed.-Sun. noon-5pm. Free. Call the museum office for tours.) A few blocks away, the **Museum of Natural History,** 1680 E. 15th Ave. (686-3024), at Agate, shows a collection of relics from the peoples of the Pacific Rim that includes a 7000-year-old pair of running shoes—a primitive "swoosh" is still visible. (Open Wed.-Sun. noon-5pm. Free.)

Museum Park, a large tract of land across the river, was originally intended to house all of the city's museums. Plans for this mammoth complex, however, have apparently been shelved. The **Willamette Science and Technology Center,** 2300 Centennial Blvd. (687-3619), is the lone survivor of this bureaucratic tangle. Planetarium shows are given Tues.-Fri. at 3pm and Sat.-Sun. at 1pm and 3pm. (Open

Tues.-Sun. noon-5pm. Admission $2.50, seniors and students $2, children $1. Plane-tarium shows $1.50, seniors and students $1.)

Downtown, store browsers mill around the mall between 8th and 10th St., at the north end of Willamette; punks gather at the central fountain. Nearby, the $26 million **Hult Performing Arts Center,** the city's crown jewel, resides at One Eugene Center (687-5000), 6th and Willamette St., and features a spectrum of music from the blues to Bartók. (Free tours in summer Fri.-Sat. at noon; in winter Sat. at noon. Call 687-5087 for information and reservations.) The Community Center for the Performing Arts, better known as **WOW Hall,** 291 W. 8th St. (687-2746), is an old Wobblie (International Workers of the World) meeting hall that for years has sponsored concerts by lesser-known artists. Brochures announcing these off-beat acts are plastered everywhere. When Emma Goldman asserted, "If I can't dance, I don't want your revolution," little did she know that one day her era's most radical organization would leave behind only a dance hall.

Only a beat away from the heart of tourist country lurks the highly acclaimed **Fifth Street Market** (484-0383), at 5th and High St. This collection of overpriced boutiques and eateries attracts both those who consider "foreign" food superior, no matter how hastily prepared, and those who are under the impression that British cuisine is "gourmet." The leafy central courtyard is a pleasant place to linger over an au lait. Instead of falling victim to this labyrinth of pseudo-sophistication, head to the **Saturday Market** at 8th and Oak, held weekly between March 30 and Christ-mas (call 686-8885 for more information). The food here (ranging from blintzes to berries to burritos) is tastier, healthier and cheaper than that at Fifth. Far from the chains of wage-slavery, this crafts market has survived since 1969.

In and around the two cities are a bevy of tours for the industrial-minded. One of the more popular is of the **Weyerhaeuser Pulp and Paper Mill,** 785 N. 42nd St., Springfield (746-2511). Tours start at the plant entrance in summer Mon.-Fri. at 9am; winter hours vary and require advance notice. The **Hinman Vineyards,** 27012 Briggs Hill Rd., Eugene (345-1945), organizes tours by appointment only; speak to Doyle Hinman. (Tastings and tours Feb.-Dec. noon-5pm. The tasting area is oc-casionally closed on weekends in the summer when classical concerts are held.) **For-geron Vineyards,** 89697 Sheffler Rd., Elmira (935-1117), has daily visiting hours (June-Sept. noon-5pm; Oct.-Dec. and Feb.-May Sat.-Sun. noon-5pm). The **Williams Bakery,** 1760 E. 13th St., Eugene (485-8211), offers tours during the school year (Sun.-Mon., and Wed.-Fri. 9am-3pm). Call in advance for reservations. **Oregon Aqua Foods,** 88700 Marcola Rd., Springfield (746-4484), a salmon hatchery, gives tours from late May to mid-September. Call ahead for dates, times, and reservations.

Ouzel Outfitters, P.O. Box 11217, Eugene 97440 (947-2236), leads trips down the Willamette. In Springfield, **McKenzie River Rafts** (726-6078) gives tours start-ing at 9:30am near the lower river and ending at around 5pm (from $30 per person). The visitor information center can supply a list of several other companies. Reserva-tions are recommended on weekends. Check local river conditions and maps, since there are some dangerous areas on the Willamette near Eugene.

If you just have an afternoon hour to spare, canoe or kayak the **Millrace Canal,** which parallels the Willamette for three or four mi. This shallow waterway passes under many small foot bridges and through several pipes. While not clean enough for swimming, the river is perfect for lazing in the sun. Rent canoes or kayaks (life vests and paddles but no spray skirts) from **EMU Waterworks Company,** 1395 Franklin Blvd. (686-4386, 686-3705, or 686-3711), run by University of Oregon stu-dents. (Open in summer daily noon-dusk.)

University sports facilities are open to the public from mid-June to mid-August ($1 per day). The pool, indoor tennis courts, and outdoor racquetball courts are open daily 8am-5pm. Gyms, weight rooms, and indoor racquetball courts are open Monday through Friday only. Pick up a list of exact times from the information desk or from the recreation office at 103 Gerlinger Hall (686-4113). You can rent miscellaneous sports equipment (bats, balls) from various community centers. (Duf-fle bags of equipment, called "picnic kits," are available for $5 per day with deposit. Contact the Department of Parks. See Practical Information.)

Seasonal Events

There are several annual festivals: the **Irish Festival** around St. Patrick's Day, the unseasonal **Springfield Springfest** during the second week of May, and the two-week **Bach Festival** beginning the last week of June. Featuring frivolity like the Bach Run and an appearance by P.D.Q. Bach, it sobers up for some serious music as well. Helmuth Rilling, world-renowned authority on baroque music, travels here each year from his native West Germany to lead some of the country's finest musicians in performances of Bach's cantatas and concerti. (Write to the Hult Center Ticket Office, One Eugene Center 97401; or call 687-5000 for reservations or further information. Tickets run from $5-25.) The enormous **Oregon Country Fair** takes place in the middle of June and lasts three days. (Admission $6 per day; $5 for the 1st day only.) To alleviate the yearly traffic jams, Lane County Transit provides bus service (25¢) to and from the fairgrounds in Veneta. Buses leave every ½ hour in the morning from the LTD Customer Service Center, and take off again before the fairgrounds close at 7pm. The fair is a huge crafts-and-music happening, characterized by some as the entire 1960s squashed into one weekend. For information, exact dates, and other festivals, especially in the summer and fall, call the Eugene Visitors Center or the Springfield Chamber of Commerce (746-1651).

Near Eugene and Springfield

Eugene and Springfield lie at the southern end of the Willamette Valley, whose fertile floor and richly forested hills attracted Oregon's waves of pioneer settlers. Relics of pioneer days and dollops of the wilderness await those who venture off I-5. One of the favored drives in the area runs from Hwy. 126 to U.S. 20 and then back to 126. The 50-mi. loop surveys the McKenzie Valley and the McKenzie Pass, where lava outcroppings served as a training site for astronauts preparing to walk on the moon.

Fifty miles south of Eugene is the **Willamette National Forest** and the start of the 13-mi. McKenzie River Trail. The trailhead is 55 mi. northeast of Eugene on Hwy. 126, 1.2 mi. past McKenzie Bridge. Five **campgrounds** serve the area. Contact the Parks Department or the Willamette National Forest Service (see Eugene and Springfield Practical Information).

The small-town scenes in National Lampoon's *Animal House* were filmed in **Cottage Grove**, 20 mi. south of Eugene off I-5, and the town couldn't have needed more than a spit-polish for its big-screen debut. Maps for self-guided car tours of a nearby **ghost town** and its **Bohemian Mines** are available at the **Chamber of Commerce**, 710 Row River Rd. (942-2411). The trip is best made between May and October, as snow clogs the rough road to Bohemia during other months. **The Goose,** a 1914 steam engine, departs for a two-hour sweep through the Cascade Mountains on summer weekends, leaving Cottage Grove at 10am and 2pm. (Rides $7.50, ages 2-11 $3.75.) The Oregon Pacific and Eastern Railroad depot (942-3368), which runs The Goose, is impossible to miss—it's the noisiest spot in town.

Twenty miles north of Eugene by exit 216, the small town of **Brownsville's** met a sad fate when I-5 made obsolete the iron horse that had once been the town's lifeblood. Today it keeps its false storefronts polished in hopes of wooing lost motorists.

Overnight camping along the shady creek banks is allowed at Brownsville's **Pioneer Park,** one block west of Main on Park. Sites are $5, trailer and RV sites $10. Clean public toilets are maintained by the city, and campfires are permitted in designated areas. Serving the tiny community with a common kitchen, a performance stage, a Little League baseball diamond, and a dirt-bike track, the main park closes its gates at dusk. Call for reservations at 466-5666. From Brownsville, Main Street meanders idyllically northward into a backroad that eventually reaches I-5. When the road forks, keep to the left, and when in doubt, follow the signs directing you to Albany or Lebanon. A left onto Hwy. 34 leads straight to I-5. Go at sunset—hum a tune, pick a wildflower, watch a tractor plow, or say "moo" to a cow.

Grants Pass

Workers building a road through the Oregon mountains in 1863 were so excited by the news of General Ulysses Grant's victory at Vicksburg that they up and named the town after the burly alcoholic and president-to-be. Today both tourists and locals find the town an excellent base camp from which to attack the mountains. Grants Pass is a bazaar of outfitters, river runners, and adventure travel companies—as well as its share of cheap motels and fast food joints. Despite this, all is relatively still and what lettle human hubbub exists is found at the water's edge where marinas and raft docks sandwich the Rogue River.

Practical Information and Orientation

Visitor Information: Visitor and Convention Bureau (476-7717 in OR, or 800-547-5927) at 6th and Midland. Brochures about all of Josephine County. Eager and pleasant volunteer staff. Open Mon.-Fri. 8am-5pm, Sat.-Sun. 9am-5pm.

Greyhound: 460 Agness Ave. (476-4513), at the east end of town. To Portland ($55) and San Francisco ($39). A limited number of storage lockers (75¢ per 24 hr.) lurk next to the station. Open Mon.-Fri. 7am-6:30pm, Sat. 7am-2pm.

Taxi: Grants Pass Taxi (476-6444).

Car Rental: Select Auto Rental, from $15 daily, 50 free mi. plus 15¢ per additional mi. Must be 25 with deposit of insurance deductible.

Laundromat: MayBelle's Washtub, 333 S.E. 8th St. (431-1317). Open daily 7am-10pm.

Women's Crisis Support Team: 479-9349. 24 hr.

Hospital: Josephine Memorial Hospital (476-6831).

Police: Justice Building (479-6370).

Post Office: 132 NW 6th St. (479-7526). Open Mon.-Fri. 9am-5pm. General Delivery ZIP Code: 97526.

Area Code: 503.

I-5 curves around Grants Pass to the northeast, heading north to Portland; south of the city, U.S. 199 runs along the infamous Rogue River before making the trip 30 mi. down to Cave Junction. The two main north-south arterials are 6th St. (one-way south) and 7th St. (one-way north). 6th St. is the east and west divider and the railroad tracks (between G and F St.) divide north and south addresses.

Accommodations and Camping

Grants Pass has a stupefying number of ugly jello-molded motels, most along 6th St. As Grants Pass is a favorite highway rest stop, rooms fill up quickly, especially on weekends.

As with the rest of the Inland Valleys, Grants Pass suffers from a shortage of nearby campgrounds. There are free campsites at **Rogue State Park,** 16 mi. east on I-5, and grassy, quiet sites at **Les Clare RV Park,** 2956 U.S. 99 (479-0046; sites $9.50, hookups $13.50). Another option is **Schroeder Campgrounds,** four mi. south of town; take Hwy. 199 to Willow Lane; then follow the signs one mi. to the campground. Call 474-5285 for information on this and other Josephine County parks. Sites and showers are excellent, and the campground is often full by the mid-afternoon. (Sites $9, with hookups $12.)

Fordson Home Hostel (AYH), 250 Robinson Rd., Cave Junction 97523 (592-3203). 37 mi. southwest on U.S. 199. Inaccessible except by car. Only 3 beds. Bunks $4, in winter $5. Reservations necessary.

The Flamingo Motel, 728 NW 6th St. (476-6601). Wonderfully tacky landscaping. Clean but tiny rooms. Interesting clientele, but safe. Small pool. HBO. Singles $25, with 2 beds $29.

Motel 6, 1800 NE 7th St. (474-1331). Low prices without having to worry whether you have been properly vaccinated. Cable TV, swimming pool, and A/C. Singles $28. Doubles $34.

Regal Lodge, 1400 NW 6th St. (479-3305). A polished affair but the rooms themselves are only average. Singles $28. Doubles $34.

Food

Amazingly enough, Grants Pass offers a surprising number of alternatives for the numbed palate.

Pongsri's, 1571 N.E. 6th St. (479-1345). Somehow combines down-home atmosphere with spicy Thai food. Thai afficianados will love it, the meat-and-potatoes crowd should think again. Lunch special $3. (Served Tues.-Fri.) Open Tues.-Sun. 11am-9pm.

Joy's Kitchen, 428 S.W. 6th St. (479-1814). Good healthy food. Try the Tofu Scrambled ($3.10) for breakfast or Joy's Nut Loaf ($4.55) anytime. Daily lunch specials $4.25, Mon.-Fri. from 11am. Open Mon.-Fri. 6:30am-2:30pm, Sat. 8am-2:30pm.

J.J. North's Grand Buffet, 1150 NE E St. (479-5331), in Grants Pass Shopping Center. Huge buffet lunch and dinner $6.49. Where locals go to pig out. Seniors get discounts. Open Mon.-Sat. 11am-3:30pm; Mon.-Thurs. 3:30-8:30pm, Fri-Sat. 3:30-9pm, Sun. noon-8pm.

Black Forest, 820 N.E. E St. (474-2353), on the other side of the shopping center. An upscale Denny's (complete with revolving pies). Popular with families and seniors. Although they sell the usual multi-meal menus, they're famous for their Belgian Waffles ($3.50) and ice cream sundaes (from $2.50). Open daily 6am-10pm.

Matsukaze, 1675 N.E. 7th St. (479-2961). Standard Japanese food in a pleasant setting. Daily lunch specials ($3.50-4). Try the *Makunouchi Bentu,* a combination lunch to go served in an ornate box ($5.45).

Near Grants Pass

A few miles east of Grants Pass in the town of **Rogue River** is the **Valley of the Rogue State Park** (see Accommodations and Camping). You can savor the Rogue (one of the few rivers in the United States to be protected by the government as a "Wild and Scenic River") by raft, jetboat, mail boat, fishing poles, or a walk along the banks. Possible excursions range from two-hour scenic tours (**Hellgate Excursions, Inc.,** 479-7204; $12, ages 4-11 $6) to four-day fishing outings (**Rogue Excursions Unlimited,** 773-5983).

When you're so sated with rafting that a Class IV rapid draws no more than a yawn, you can hike in the Rogue State Park or head south if you have a car. While Gold Hill (20 mi. east on I-5) may be famous for the large cave of bat guano that police keep a 24-hour watch on, it also houses the **Oregon Vortex/House of Mystery** (855-1543). Here, balls roll uphill, pendulums hang at an angle, and people seem to vary in height depending on where they stand. The bizarre phenomena are supposedly due to a local perturbation of the earth's magnetic field. (Open June-Aug. daily 9am-4:45pm; March-Oct. 14 Fri.-Tues. 9am-4:45pm. Admission $3.)

For a more spectacular geocuriosity, see the **Oregon Caves National Monument** by taking U.S. 199 south 30 mi. to Cave Junction, then following Hwy. 46 east for 20 mi. Here in the belly of the ancient Siskiyous, limestone compressed to marble was carved out by acidic waters. Dissolved and redeposited, the limestone filled huge open chambers with exotic formations, whose slow growth is nurtured by the constant climate of 39-43°F. (This place is *cold.*) (75-minute tours are conducted as groups of 16 form. Tours mid-June to Aug. daily 8am-7pm; May to mid-June and Sept. daily 9am-5pm; Oct.-April daily at 10:30am, 12:30pm, 2pm, and 3:30pm. Admission $6, ages under 12 $3, under 6 not admitted but onsite child care is available. Call 592-3400 for more information.) **Noah's Ark,** 27893 Redwood Hwy. (592-3882) is a tame petting zoo in Cave Junction that older siblings will probably groan at but that young children will love. Open 9am-6pm daily. Admission $4.50, ages over 60 and 7-12 $3.25, 3-6 $2.25.

Jacksonville

The biggest of Oregon's gold boomtowns, Jacksonville played the role of rich and lawless frontier outpost with appropriate debauchery and zest. But the town's salad days were brief. Gold dwindled, the railroad and stagecoach lines took Jacksonville off their routes, and the city lost the county seat to Medford. On the brink of oblivion, Jacksonville was rescued by nostalgia. During the 50s, the town was rehabilitated; today, it is a national historic landmark. A stroll down Main Street will unveil views of several balustraded, century-old buildings: the United States Hotel, the Methodist-Episcopal Church and the old courthouse, among others.

The town's greatest attractions are the costumed guided tours that are given daily from 1 to 5pm at the **Beekman House** and the informative lecture on 19th-century banking at the **Beekman Bank** on California St., four blocks south. Visit the **Jacksonville Museum** in the County Courthouse on 5th St. (899-1847; open daily 9am-5pm; Labor Day-May Tues.-Sun. 9am-5pm; free), and leave the kids locked up next door in the jail (now the **Children's Museum**), complete with organ and a wagon the Ingalls would be proud of. (Same hours as the museum.) Exploring the past is parching work, and sampling free wine is the perfect remedy. The **Tasting Room,** at 690 N. 5th St., offers vintages from the nearby Valley View Vineyard. (Open daily 11am-5pm.)

For an excellent overview of the town's sights, catch the 30-minute trolley tour at the Beekman Bank, 3rd and California St. (Runs daily 10am-5:30pm on the hour. Fare $2.50, under 12 $1.) Those who don't want to hike into the hills can make a trip to **Siskiyou Llama Expeditions,** P.O. Box 1330 (899-1696), which rents and sells these beasts of burden for wilderness treks.

Jacksonville becomes schizophrenic every summer with the **Peter Britt Music Festivals.** Artists as diverse as Gladys Knight, the Butch Thompson Trio, and Sha-Na-Na make up the "jazz" festival, Mozart and Beethoven take a bow for the classical team, and everyone else is lumped together as Folk/Country. (Tickets for single events run from $8-$22, youth 12 and under about half-price; package deals in all sizes also available.) For information, write Peter Britt Festival, P.O. Box 1124, Medford 97501 (773-6077 in OR, or 800-882-7488).

Try to avoid spending the night in town. There are no campgrounds, and rooms at the **Jacksonville Inn,** 175 E. California St. (899-1900), for all its charm and free Belgian-waffle breakfasts, start at $50. You can savor pasta or salads ($5-6) in the inn's elegant dining room, or grab some chow at the **Mustard Seed,** 5th and C St., which broils thick burgers for $2-4. For a more varied menu at subterranean prices, grab a cup of chili ($1.50) at **The Claim Jumper's,** an outdoor café at 115 W. California St. (Open daily 10:30am-5pm.)

Drop by the **visitors center** in the old railway station on Oregon St., where the eager staff will supply you with directions and pamphlets. The **post office** is right next door at 175 Oregon St. (Open Mon.-Fri. 8:30am-5pm; ZIP Code: 97530.)

To reach Jacksonville (or "J-ville" as residents affectionately call it), take Hwy. 238 southwest from Medford. Or catch the #30 bus at 6th and Bartlett in Medford (buses Mon.-Sat.; see Medford Practical Information). Jacksonville can be reached by bus from Ashland only via Medford. In a state with so many former boom towns that now contain little more than post offices and a token dilapidated tavern, it would be a shame to miss a ghost town as spirited as Jacksonville.

Medford

A long time ago, Jacksonville was the center of the Rogue River Valley and nearby Medford was just a bend in the river. Then came the railroads, promising jobs, trade, and growth. Jacksonville refused to pay the $25,000 kickback demanded by the self-confident leaders of the new industry and so, to spite the county seat, the lines were laid in Medford instead. Within 20 years, Medford's community of log cabins and trappers had seized power (and the county government) from Jacksonville. Today, Medford, a heavily industrialized city of 40,000, makes the money while Jacksonville, small and rustic, withers away.

Practical Information

Visitor Information: Medford Visitors and Convention Bureau, 304 S. Central Ave. (772-6293), at 10th St. Enthusiastic, with stacks of maps and directories. Open Mon.-Fri. 9am-5pm. A small packet of information, including a city map and sealed with teddy bear and heart stickers, is left by the door after they close. Aw.

Medford-Jackson County Airport: 770-5314. Off Biddle Rd., north of town. Served by United Airlines and a variety of regional carriers.

Greyhound: 212 Bartlett St. (779-2103), at 5th St. Five per day to Portland ($58) and San Francisco ($86). Open daily 6am-midnight.

Rogue Valley Transportation: 3200 Crater Lake Ave. (799-2988). Connects Medford with: Jacksonville, Phoenix, White City, Talent, and Ashland. Buses leave 6th and Bartlett Mon.-Fri. 8am-5pm. Limited service Sat. 9am-5pm. Fare 60¢ plus 10¢ each zone crossed, seniors and students in grades 1-12 pay ½-price.

Cascade Bus Lines: 664-4801. Service to Eagle Point and White City.

Taxi: Medford Cab Co. 773-6665.

Car Rental: Budget, 773-7023. **National,** 779-4863. Both are at the airport.

Public Library: 413 W. Main St. (776-7281), at Holly St. Open Mon.-Thurs. 9:30am-8pm, Fri.-Sat. 9:30am-5pm.

Hospital: Providence, Crater Lake Ave. and Woodrow St. (773-6611). Emergency care 24 hr.

Fire: City Hall, at 8th and Oakdale (770-4460).

Police: City Hall (770-4783).

Post Office: 333 W. 8th (776-3604), at Holly St. Open Mon.-Fri. 8:30am-5:30pm. General Delivery ZIP Code: 97501.

Area Code: 503.

Orientation

Medford lies on I-5 in southern Oregon, at the intersection of Hwy. 238. Grant's Pass is 30 mi. to the northwest, Ashland 12 mi. to the southeast. Central Ave. (Hwy. 99) has a number of cheap motels and retaurants. Main Street (Hwy. 238) intersects Central in the heart of the city and then proceeds west to Jacksonville.

Accommodations

Central Ave.'s small, clean motels are depressingly similar, though many are cheaper than Motel 6 (hard to believe, but true). These are good places to take a break and shower after camping. There are no campgrounds within 15 mi. of town, just several grassy areas styled "day-use parks" with wooden picnic tables.

Valli Hai Motel, 1034 Court St. (772-6183). A nice place run by a friendly couple but a bit out of the way. Pleasant, well-scrubbed rooms with dark wood ceilings. Singles $22. Doubles $26.

Sierra Inn Motel, 345 S. Central Ave. (773-7727). Better-than-average rooms. Laundry and kitchen facilities available. Singles $25. Doubles $30.

City Center Motel, 324 S. Central Ave. (773-6248). Next door to the information center. Dukes it out with Motel 6 in Medford's lodgings cellar—slightly larger and more interesting rooms, with free HBO (a retort to the Motel 6 swimming pool). Singles $22. Doubles $25.

Motel 6, 950 Alba Dr. (773-4290), on the northwest edge of town. On the other side of the freeway, it is inconvenient for those without cars. Swimming pool. Often full. Singles $25. Doubles $31.

Food

If you've been contemplateing a fast, this is the place to start it. You're better off dining in Ashland (12 mi. away).

Bobbio's, 317 E. Main St. (773-7173). A day-glow pizzeria, with roller-skating waitresses and a pink '57 Chevy de rigeur. Square pan pizzas are all named after popular songs from the 50s. Try the *Locomotion* for $6.75. Yummy shakes ($1.50). Open Mon.-Thurs. 11am-11pm, Fri.-Sat. 11am-midnight, Sun. 11am-10pm. Mon.-Fri., the bakery opens at 5:30am.

Yellow Submarine Sandwich Shop, 137 S. Central Ave. (779-7589), at 9th St. Tables inside and out; also emminently picnic-able. Subs range from 4" ($2) to 24" ($9). Open Mon.-Sat. 10am-5pm.

Kim's, 2321 Hwy. 99 (773-3653), 1 mile south of Medford. Chinese food of McDonald's quality (think McMooshee). Lunch specials $4. Open Sun.-Thurs. 11am-11pm, Fri.-Sat. 11am-midnight.

"Sights"

You're in for a treat, boys and girls! Slightly north of the city limits, the **Medford Corporation,** on North Pacific Hwy. (773-7491), allows free self-guided tours of its sawmill operations. The tours reveal the strange secrets of plywood production. (Tours Mon.-Fri. 7am-3pm.) On Hwy. 62, in the nearby town of **Trail,** the **Cole Rivers Fish Hatchery** (878-2335) has self-guided tours Mon.-Fri. 8:30am-4pm. The hatchery is an important part of the ongoing effort to stock the Rogue. The **Valley View Vineyard,** 1000 Applegate Rd. (899-8468), just south of the town of **Ruch,** gives wine tastings. (Open daily 11am-5pm, Jan.-April 14 Sat.-Sun. 1-5pm; vineyard tours by appointment.)

　　Harry and David's Original Country Store, one mi. south of Medford on 99 (776-2277) is the L.L. Bean of the fruit world. The factory complex also includes a 43,000-ft. show garden for **Jackson & Perkins,** the world's largest rose growers. (Open daily 9am-5pm.)

　　Crater Lake is as accessible from Medford as it is from Klamath Falls. Follow Hwy. 62 east. On the way, you should stop at **Beckie's Café** (560-3563), at the Union Creek Resort. This friendly, wood-paneled restaurant has lunches ($3-5) and luscious homemade pies ($1.50).

　　For a sensationalist alternative to the nearby Shakespeare Festival, check out the old-fashioned **melodrama** in **Talent,** between Medford and Ashland. Hiss at the villain ("You *must* pay the rent!"), sigh for the damsel in distress ("I *can't* pay the rent!") and cheer for the hero ("*I'll* pay the rent"). The festivities take place from June through Labor Day on Fridays and Saturdays at 8pm in the **Minshall Theatre,** 101 Talent Ave., P.O. Box 353, Talent 97540 (535-5250). (Admission $6, children under 12 $3.50.)

　　The April **Pear Blossom Festival** is a favorite for runners who come for the 10K. Other activities include a street fair, a band festival, a golf tournament and, of course, a parade. A more recent addition to the social calendar is the **Dixieland Jazz Jubilee,** held in October. Ten bands gather from across the country to blow their chops in Medford.

Ashland

Before their expropriation by the guardians of gentility, Shakespeare's plays were common entertainment for 19th-century Americans. Ashland's informal, rural setting on the California border returns the plays to this forgotten context each summer with its world-famous Shakespeare festival. Over 55-years, the festival has sired delightful shops, lodgings, and restaurants. Although more expensive than its neighbors, Ashland is very reasonable when compared with other towns in the U.S. of equivalent charm and elegance. From February to October, the festival puts on an astonishing number of plays with an accomplished roster of performers. While the repertory is by no means limited to the 16th century, Shakespeare's works dominate the three stages. Ashland's balmy climate allows for nightly performances in the outdoor Elizabethan theater, with a money-back guarantee in case of rain.

All of Ashland is a stage, but the men and women are merely players on it for only half the year. October's rains see the last of the Shakespeare buffs, and bring in the Southern Oregon State College students. Come Thanksgiving, the nearby Siskiyou Mountains are blanketed with snow and sprinkled with cross-country skiers. Vertical-minded skiers swarm to Mt. Ashland. Spring thaw brings in the hikers, bikers, and rafters, even as the skiers leave. And yea, the cycle beginneth anew when Shakespeare wakes to walk again.

Practical Information

Visitor Information: Chamber of Commerce, 110 E. Main St. (482-3486). A harried, busy staff. Play schedules and brochures, several of which contain small but adequate maps. *The Portable Ashland* outlines a good walking tour of the city. Does *not* sell tickets to performances. Open Mon.-Fri. 9am-5pm. **Information Kiosk,** center of Lithia Park Plaza, open June to mid-Sept. 9am-8pm.

Oregon Shakespearean Festival Box Office: P.O. Box 158, Ashland 97520 (482-4331), next to the Elizabethan Theater. Rush tickets (½-price) occasionally available ½-hr. before performances that aren't sold out. A better bet might be standing room tickets ($7), available only for sold out shows at the Elizabethan Theater.

Greyhound: 91 Oak St. (482-2516), between Lithia Way and E. Main St. Three departures north and 4 south per day. To Portland ($49) and San Francisco ($51). Open Mon.-Sat. 8am-5pm.

Rogue Valley Transportation: 779-2877, in Medford. Schedules available at the Chamber of Commerce. Fare 60¢, plus 10¢ for each zone change. Ages over 65 and 6-11 ½-price. The #10 bus serving Ashland runs every ½ hr. 5:03am-8:03pm. Service Mon.-Sat. to Medford, and from there to Jacksonville (on bus #30).

Taxi: Ashland Taxi 482-3065. 24 hr.

Laundromat: B.J.'s Homestyle Laundromat, 1712 W. Main (773-4803). Open daily 8am-9pm.

Road Conditions: 1-976-7277.

Helpline: 779-HELP.

Police: 1155 E. Main St. (482-5211).

Fire: 488-5336.

Post Office: 120 N. 1st St. at Lithia Way (482-3986). General Delivery ZIP Code: 97520.

Area Code: 503.

Ashland is 15 mi. north of the California border, the last Oregon town on I-5. Hwy. 66 traverses 64 stunning miles from Klamath Falls to Ashland but goes no farther west. Downtown Ashland centers around E. Main St., stocking restaurants just past the bridge on N. Main.

Accommodations and Camping

Definitely shoot for the hostel during festival time. In winter Ashland bursts with inexpensive hotels. In summer, rates double in virtually every hotel and the hostel is impenetrable. This is one town where you must make a reservation if you want a room. Summer nights see vacancy signs only in Medford. Ashland is not rich in campgrounds.

Ashland Hostel (AYH), 150 N. Main St. (482-9217), a few blocks west of Greyhound. In May and June this well-kept hostel swarms with school groups in town for a little culture. The wonderful owner-managers will help you any way they can, from tracking down theater tix to suggesting activities on days when the play's not the thing. Laundry facilities. Members $7.50, nonmembers $10.50. Reservations advised, the earlier the better.

Manor Motel, 476 N. Main St. (482-2246), at Hwy. 99, 6 blocks northwest of the theaters. Lovely and quiet with A/C and TV. Family suites available. Singles $30. Doubles $35. Nov. to mid-June singles $24, doubles $26.

Vista 6 Motel, 535 Clover Lane (482-4423), on I-5 at exit 14. Small rooms. Not center-stage for the main attractions. Friendly management. A/C, small pool. Singles $26. Doubles $30. Winter and spring discounts.

Columbia Hotel, 262½ E. Main St. (482-3726). A cozy little European inn 1½ blocks from the theaters. Splendid decor is straight from the 1940s, with magnificent sitting room lifted from the pages of an Agatha Christie novel. Bathroom down the hall. No singles. Doubles from $38; Nov. to mid-June $30. Children under 12 free.

Jackson Hot Springs, 2253 Hwy. 99 N (482-3776), off exit 19 from I-5, down Valley View Rd. to Hwy. 99 N. The campground nearest downtown. Separate tent area; tent rentals available. Hot showers. Sites $8, with hookups $9.

Glenyan KOA, 5310 Hwy. 66 (482-4138), 5 mi. out of town southeast on Hwy. 66, exit 14 from I-5. Typical high quality and price of a KOA. Showers, laundromat, and a petite grocery store. Sites $12.75, with hookups $14.75.

Emigrant Lake (776-7001), 6 mi. southeast on Hwy. 66, exit 14 off I-5. Hot showers and laundromat. Sites $8. Open April 15-Oct. 15.

Food

Ashland cooks up an impressive spread for its festival guests. Unfortunately, the steep prices are also aimed at the moneyed theater patrons. Many restaurants stay open past their posted time on show nights. The hostel has kitchen facilities; **Sentry Market,** 310 Oak St. (482-3521), is open until 9pm.

Thai Pepper, 84 N. Main (482-8058). Curries and seafood prepared exquisitely (if not entirely traditionally) in an elegant environment. Dinners $8-12. Open Mon.-Thurs. 5-9pm, Fri. 11:30am-2pm and 5-10pm, Sat. 5-10pm, Sun. 5-8:30pm.

Teresa's Cantina, 76 N. Pioneer St. (482-1107), at Main. Wholesome Mexican food in a busy congenial atmosphere. Spread the salsa-smothered, 1-lb. plus *cantina burrito* ($7) with some of the best homemade guacamole north of the border. Intriguing appetizers include the *ceviche tostaditos* (tostadas covered with white fish, $5.25). Excellent place to bring children: the management *looooves* them. 10% discount for seniors. Open Tues.-Sat. 11am-9pm.

Brothers Restaurant and Delicatessan, 95 N. Main. A tratitional New York deli and café (homemade potato pancakes, $5) with some off-beat selections, such as a tofu burrito for $6.50. Open Tues.-Sun. 7am-8pm.

Backporch BBQ, 92½ N. Main St. (482-4131), north of The Plaza, above the creek. Smashing in the summer. Texas-style barbecue ($7-9) and margaritas ($2.50) consumed outside to the tune of the bubbling creek. Live music until 2am on summer weekends. Restaurant open June-Aug. daily 11:30am-2pm, 5-9pm. Bar open until 2am. In winter, open 5-9pm.

The Bakery Café, 38 E. Main St. (482-2117). *The* breakfast place. A menu as schitzophrenic as Ashland itself. Blueberry cheese blintzes ($6.25) share the stage with Szechuan Sesame Noodles ($4.50). Always crowded, always delicious. Open daily 7am-9pm.

Key of C Coffee House, 116 Lithia Way (488-5012). A nice, if stark, espresso house. The caffeine is cheap (75¢-$1.25) and the service good. Homemade bagels are 75¢; homesick New Yorkers (if they exist) should go for "The Ultimate" (lox, cream cheese, tomato and onions, $3.50). Open daily 7am-4pm.

Geppetto's, 345 E. Main St. (482-1138). A local favorite, with chef from the "Yuppie" school. Dinners average $10, but you can get a pesto omelette for $5.75 at breakfast. Lunches in the $4-6 range. Open daily 8am-midnight.

Sights and Entertainment

The **Shakespeare Festival,** the brainchild of local teacher Angus Bowmer, began with two plays performed by schoolchildren during a boxing match intermission. Today, professional actors perform four Shakespeare plays and a host of other classic and modern dramas February through October on the three Ashland stages. The **Agnus Bowmer** is a large (600-seat) traditional indoor theater that stages both Shakespeare and more recent plays and any boxing is over the hotter tickets. The

Elizabethan Stage is the exclusive province of outdoor Shakespeare. Modeled after a London theater of 1600, the Elizabeth is open only June to September. The newest of the three theaters is the intimate **Black Swan,** home to small-scale productions, often of alternative works. Plays that open in the fall of one season often continue in the spring of the next year. The House is dark on Mondays.

Due to the tremendous popularity of the productions, reservations are recommended one to two months in advance. (Admission $8.40-20. For complete ticket information, write Oregon Shakespeare Festival, Ashland 97520, or call 482-2111.) From March to May, half-price rush tickets are often available an hour before every performance that is not sold out. Some half-price student-senior matinees are offered. In the summer, almost everything is sold out and obtaining tickets can be very difficult; arrive at the box office by 9:30am on the day of any show. Locals occasionally leave their shoes to hold their place in line, and you should respect this tradition. At 9:30am, the box office releases any unsold tickets for the day's performances. If no tickets are available, you will be given a priority number, entitling you to a place in line when the precious few tickets that members have returned are released (1pm for matinees, 6pm for evening performances). The box office sells a limited number of standing-room tickets for sold-out shows at the Elizabethan Theater ($7).

The **Backstage Tours** ($6, children under 12 $3) provides a wonderful glimpse at the festival from the other side of the curtain. Tour guides (usually actors or technicians) tell about everything from bird songs during an outdoor Hamlet to just what ghastly events take place every time they do "that Scottish play." Tours last two hours and leave from the Black Swan at 10am. Admission fee includes a trip to the **Exhibit Center** (482-2111) ($1, children under 12 50¢) for a close-up look at sets and costumes. Bring a camera to record your own role in the dress-up room. (Open Tues.-Sun. 10am-4pm, fall and spring, 10:30am-1:30pm.)

"Give me excess of it, that surfeiting the appetite may sicken and so die." Still haven't had enough theater? The **Cabaret Theater** (488-2902), at 1st and Hagarcline, stages light musicals in a "sophisticated" setting with drinks and hors d'oeuvres. (Tickets $8-14.) Small groups, such as **Actor's Theater of Ashland, Studio X,** and the theater department at **Southern Oregon State College,** also raise the curtains sporadically throughout the summer. The **Schneider Museum of Art,** on the Southern Oregon State campus (482-6245), displays college-sponsored contemporary art exhibits that change every two weeks. (Open Tues.-Fri. 11am-5pm, Sat.-Sun. 1-5pm. Free.) For less-renowned art at reasonable prices, try the **Saturday Marketplace** on Guanajuato Way behind the plaza. (Open May-Sept. Sat. 10am-6pm.)

Before it had Shakespeare, Ashland had **lithia water,** which was reputed to have miraculous healing powers. The mineral springs have given their name to the well-tended **Lithia Park,** west of the plaza off Main St. To taste the vaunted water itself, head for the circle of fountains in the center of the plaza, under the statue of horse and rider—the water is as delicious as sulphur. Guided historical tours leave from the fountain at 10am, 2pm, and 8pm every day in the summer. (Tickets $5, seniors $4, children under 16 $2, families $12.) The daily events taking place in Lithia Park are tabulated in brochures and described at the Plaza Kiosk. The park itself has hiking trails, picnic grounds, a Japanese garden, duck and swan ponds, and a creek that trips over itself in ecstatic little waterfalls.

If the park and its infamous waters fail to refresh you, find your way to the **Valley View Tasting Room,** 52 E. Main St. (482-8964), where 14 different wines are uncorked for your sampling. As a mere sip is never enough, the wines also come by the glass ($1). (Open daily 10am-6pm.)

If your muscles are calling for a little abuse after all this R&R, you can join the **Pacific Crest Trail** from here. Or take advantage of the variety of **raft** companies that offer daytrips on local rivers. **Noah's** offers full- and half-day trips for both beginners and experts. Prices range from $40-100 (write P.O. Box 11, 97520, or call 488-2811). For a tamer experience, try the double-flumed, 280-ft. waterslide at **Emigrant Lake Park** (10 slides for $3.50), or just practice your freestyle in the lake. The park also offers sailing lessons through the **Hobie House Marina** (488-

0595). (Open in summer 10am-6pm; sailboard $10, Hobie Cat $25, lessons $15 per hr., full-day rental $50-80 with a $25-50 deposit.) There is also swimming in the town pool (50¢).

Equipment for most outdoor activities can be bought or rented from **Ashland Mountain Supply,** 31 N. Main St. (488-2749), at The Plaza. You will pay top dollar here, but the equipment is new, and the location central. Tents $10 for 2 days; Farmer John wetsuits $7 per day; mountain bikes $9 for 2 hr., $20 per day. Deposit required. Ice axes and crampons also for rent. (Open daily 10am-5:30pm.) **Headwaters River Adventures** (488-0583) operates out of the store and runs daily river trips for $55 and up.

Mount Ashland has 22 ski trails of varying intensity (from moguls to bunny hills), with two chair lifts and three surface lifts. (Open Thanksgiving-April. Day skiing daily 9am-4pm, night skiing Thurs.-Sat. 4-10pm. Full-day ticket $11 weekdays, $22 weekends. Full rental $12.) Daily buses run to Ashland and Medford. Contact **Ski Ashland,** P.O. Box 220, Ashland 97520 (482-2897; snow conditions 482-2754). **Jackson Hot Springs,** two mi. north of Ashland on Hwy. 99 (482-3776), runs year-round private mineral baths.

One of the first highlights of the festival comes with the **Feast of Will** on June 15, breaking into dinner in Lithia Park and more merrie madness. **Fourth of July** celebrations in Ashland include a parade, food and game booths in Lithia Park, music, and, oddly enough, fireworks. **Halloween** is a trick-or-treating excuse for very high spirits; the Chamber of Commerce may purse its lips, but other town officials have been known to sponsor a free shuttle that transfers ghosts and goblins from one bar to another. In summer, the **Ashland City Band** sets up every Thursday at 7:30pm in Lithia Park (information 482-9215).

Bars and Dancing

Jazmin's, 180 C St. (488-0883). Locals set the tone. Sidewalk café, dance floor, and live music Thurs.-Sat. 9:30pm. Cover from $1. Dinners $6-13. Restaurant open daily 4-10pm. Bar open Thurs.-Sat. 4pm-2:30am.

Cook's, 66 E. Main St. (482-5145). Pool table, small dance floor. Sandwiches $2.50. The bar in the front becomes a gay scene on weekends after 9pm. Open daily noon-2:30am.

Log Cabin Tavern, 41 N. Main St. (482-9701). The cheapest brew around: $1.50 per pitcher, 35¢ per glass. An older crowd sits beneath older photographs. Open daily 10am-2:30am.

Eastern Oregon

The triangle of land between Portland, Bend, and John Day was once one of the great centers of volcanic activity on the North American continent. The nearby Cascades, which run just west of center through Oregon, were spat forth hundreds of millions of years ago by volcanic eruptions, and later shaped by glaciers to their present form. In more recent history, the jagged mountain range was the last obstacle between pioneers on the Oregon Trail and the coast. Since then, the Cascades have become a vast wilderness recreation area, with high peaks, ancient Evergreen forests, mountain streams, and caves that attract hikers, fishermen, and spelunkers year-round.

East of the Cascades, most of Oregon's principal sights are in the upper half of the state. The desert area is sliced by several rivers, including the John Day, much of which rakes alongside U.S. 26 through Malheur National Forest. In the state's northeast corner, beyond the Blue Mountains, the area's population is concentrated in the city of Pendleton. The beautiful rolling hills and mountains make this area is one of the prettiest in Oregon. The dramatic gorges of Hells Canyon National Recreation Area hem the Idaho border. In this region a car is a boon—distances are great and buses take roundabout routes.

Klamath Falls and Crater Lake

Mirror-blue Crater Lake, Oregon's only National Park, was regarded as sacred by Indian shamans, who forbade their people to view it. Iceless in winter and flawlessly circular, from an elevation of over 6000 ft. it plunges to a depth of 2000 ft., making it the nation's deepest lake (and second deepest in the hemisphere).

Practical Information and Orientation

Visitor Information: Crater Lake National Park Visitors Center (524-2211), on the lake shore at **Rim Village**. Get pamphlets and advice regarding trails and campsites. Open daily 8am-7pm. The **Klamath County Chamber of Commerce**, at 125 N. 8th (884-5193), isn't equipped to answer more than simple questions; instead, try their booth at **Veterans Park** on Lake Ewauna. Open Mon.-Sat. 8am-8pm, Sun. 10am-6pm.

Greyhound: 1200 Klamath Ave. (882-4616). Two buses daily, one north to Bend, one south to Redding. Open Mon.-Fri. 6am-6pm and 11:30pm-12:30am, Sat. 6am-3:15pm.

Taxi: Klamath Cab Co. 882-7875.

Limousine Service: W.W. Enterprises (884-7433) runs charters from Klamath Falls to Crater Lake, which cannot easily be reached except by car. $45 for 2 is a bit excessive but larger groups (up to 9, $55-60) even out the fee.

Police: Klamath Falls (883-5333).

Highway 62 through Crater Lake National Park is open year-round, but its services and accommodations are available only during the summer. After skirting the southwestern side of the lake, Hwy. 62 heads southwest to Medford and southeast to Klamath Falls. To reach the park from Portland, take I-5 to Eugene, then Hwy. 58 east to U.S. 97 south. Many roads leading to the park are closed or dangerous during the winter (depending on the weather, this could be as late as June); call ahead for road conditions (1-238-8400). Hwy. 138 heads west from U.S. 97 and approaches the lake from the north, but this route can only be used during the summer. Admission to the park (charged only in summer) is $5 for cars, $3 for hikers and bikers.

Klamath Falls lies 24 mi. south of the Hwy. 62/U.S. 97 intersection, at the southern tip of Upper Klamath Lake. Many roads lead to this small town: historic Hwy. 66 heads west to Ashland, Hwy. 39 goes south to Redding, Hwy. 140 runs east to Nevada, and U.S. 97 continues south to Weed. Main St. is just that, with most of the restaurants and motels on or a few blocks from it. Very little happens in the winter. The lake is effectively, if not officially, closed then, and Klamath Falls motels have lots of room.

Accommodations and Camping

The only hotel in the park is **Crater Lake Lodge,** Rim Village (594-2511), open from June to September. Ordinarily, you should call far in advance for reservations; but at the moment there's no rush as the lodge is closed indefinitely for major renovations. Staying here will put a crater in your wallet: cottages start at $36, and $47 is the minimum for a room with a view of the lakes.

Inexpensive campsites dot U.S. 97 to the north. Klamath Falls has several affordable hotels; you may be wise to sack out in the town and base your visits to Crater Lake from there.

Pony Pass Motel, 75 Main St. (884-7735), in Klamath Falls. Large, comfortable rooms at the edge of town with A/C and HBO. The second floor rooms overlooks Lake Ewauna. Free coffee. Singles $25. Doubles $35.

Maverick Motel, 1220 Main St. (882-6688), down the street from Greyhound in Klamath Falls. A bit north of the action but only a short walk. Small but elegant rooms. TV, A/C, and a handkerchief-sized pool. Singles $26. Doubles $34.

Molatore's Motel, 100 Main St. (882-4666), across the street from the Pony Pass. A cut above budget both in price and quality. This well-maintained, 104-unit motel caters mostly to business travelers. Large pool, immense rooms with A/C, TV and coffee. Singles from $32. Doubles from $40.

Mazama Campground (594-2211), in Crater Lake National Park. The 200 sites in this monster facility are usually tyrannized in summer by mammoth RVs, creating the ambience of a parking lot. Sites $7.

Lost Creek Campground (594-2211), in Crater Lake National Park. Hidden at the southwest corner of the park, this campground has only 12 sites. Try to secure a spot in the morning.

Food

Eating inexpensively in Crater Lake is difficult. Crater Lake Lodge has a small dining room, and Rim Village has several groceries that charge high prices for a skimpy array of foodstuffs. As in most national parks, the best plan is to buy supplies in nearby towns and cook your own meals once inside. (Check with the rangers about the forest fire risk before building a campfire, however. If it has been very dry and hot lately, succumb to Colman technology.) If you're coming from the south, **Fort Klamath** is the final food frontier before your trek through the park. Stock up here at the **Old Fort Store** (381-2345; open daily 8am-8pm). There are several affordable restaurants in Klamath Falls.

McPherson's Old Town Pizza Co., 722 Main St. (884-8858), between 7th and 8th. Set in typical Romano-Western style with Roman architecture and reliefs of cows' skulls, this local favorite has some of the cheapest and tastiest food in the area. The lunch buffet ($4.75) includes a salad bar and is a great buy. Personal pizzas from $3. Try the Downtown Delight (Italian sausage and mushroom). Open daily 11am-11pm. Lunch buffet Mon.-Fri. 11:30am-1:30pm, Sat.-Sun. noon-2:30pm.

Hobo Junction, 636 Main St. (882-8013) at 7th St. The perfect place to stock up for a picnic or simply to relax with *Critical Inquiry* among the potted plants. Good deli fare, with hearty $1 bowls of chili and 22 varieties of hot dogs. Try #8, the Hobo Dog (cheddar and Swiss cheese, bacon, and salsa, $2.60). Open Mon.-Thurs. 11am-4:30pm, Fri. 11am-7pm.

The Blue Ox, 535 Main St. (884-5308). Slow service but portions of Bunyanic proportions. $4 buys a mammoth Oxburger and just $1.25 gets you 2 eggs, hashbrowns, and toast. Breakfast served all all day. Open daily 7am-8pm.

Sights

As you approach Crater Lake, you won't see anything remarkable. It's just a lake; it could be any lake; the sky and mountains steal the show. As you ascend, however, the lake's reflected blue becomes almost unreal in its placidity. In 4850 BC, Mt. Mazama ironically created this serenity with one of the Earth's most destructive cataclysms. This massive eruption buried thousands of square miles in the western U.S. under a deep layer of ash.

Rim Drive, open only in summer, is a 33-mi. route high above the lake. Points along the drive offer views and trailheads for hiking. Among the most spectacular are **Discovery Point Trail** (from which the first pioneer saw the lake in 1853), **Garfield Peak Trail,** and **Watchman Lookout.**

The hike up **Scott Peak,** the park's highest (just a tad under 9000 ft.), begins from the drive near the lake's eastern edge. Although steep, the 7½-mi. trail to the top gives the persevering hiker a unique view of the lake that validates the sweat spent getting there. Steep **Cleetwood Trail,** a 1-mi. switchback, is the only one that leads down to the water's edge. From here a boat tours the lake (fare $10, ages 12 and under $5.50. Tours run hourly from 10am-4pm, July-Sept.). Both **Wizard Island,** a cinder cone 760 ft. above lake level, and **Phantom Ship Rock** are fragile and tiny specks when viewed from above, yet they appear surprisingly large from the surface of the water. Picnics and fishing are allowed, as is swimming—if you can withstand the frigid 50°F temperature. All the fish in the lake were introduced artificially, but because the lake is a closed system with no streams feeding it, the water is too pure to support life and only three species remain. Park rangers lead free walking tours daily in the summer and periodically during the winter (on snowshoes). Call the visitors center at Rim Village for schedules.

If pressed for time, walk the easy 100 yd. from the visitors center down to the **Sinnott Memorial Overlook**—the view is the area's best and most accessible. For a short lecture on the area's history, attend one of the nightly ranger talks (8pm) or catch a 15-min. film at Rim Village.

Make the effort to spend some time in charming Klamath Falls. The free 45-min. historical and architectural tour of the city in a restored 1906 trolley is fun. Bounce along happily as the driver tips his period bowler hat to passing locals and points out local exotica, including the first replica of an Egyptian temple built on the West Coast (which is also a former Ford showroom). Those on a tight schedule can make do with the Historic Walking Tour Guide. Catch the trolley at either the **Baldwin Hotel Museum**, 31 Main St. (883-4207; open Tues.-Sat. 10am-5pm) or at the larger, more exciting **Klamath County Museum**, 1451 Main St. (883-4208; open Tues.-Sat. 9am-5pm, 11am-5pm in the winter). Both museums are free and mix local history with archeology in a fascinating jumble. Also worth a drive is the **Weyerhauser Sawmill** (884-2241), which offers a chance to follow the transformation of trees from their natural state into plywood. Take a free tour of the world's largest producer of pine lumber. Although interesting, the tour takes a whopping 2½ hours. (Tours June-Sept. Mon.-Fri. 10am.) The **Favell Museum**, 125 W. Main St. just past Hwy. 97 (882-9996) displays Native American artifacts as well as paintings by premier Western artists. (Open Mon.-Sat. 9:30am-5:30pm. Admission $4, seniors $3, ages 6-16 $1.)

Bend

Bend has always been in the middle of things. Originally at the juncture of Native American trails, Bend is now a hub of central Oregon's highway system where U.S. 97 and U.S. 20 intersect. In Bend you will find what the rest of eastern Oregon is missing: fast-food restaurants, traffic jams, and *people*. With 19,000 inhabitants, the city has the state's largest concentrated population east of the Cascades, and more cultural, athletic, and culinary options than many of its neighbors.

Bordered by Mt. Bachelor, the Deschutes River, and a national forest, Bend makes an ideal way station for hikers and bicyclists. The lofty peaks of the Cascades, snow-capped even in August, will lure you out of town to the west. The town itself offers many restaurants that are both good *and* cheap, an elusive combination in eastern central Oregon.

Practical Information

Visitor Information: Chamber of Commerce, 63085 N. Hwy. 97 (382-3221). Open Mon.-Thurs. 9am-5pm, Fri. 9am-6pm.

Greyhound: 2045 E. Highway 20 (382-2151), a few miles east of town. Buses spiral out from Bend to: Portland, Yakima, Salem, and Redding. Open daily 8am-5pm, 9-10pm.

Transcentral: 1289 N.E. 2nd St. (382-0800). Provides van service to the Portland Airport. Leaves from the Touch of Class Motor Inn every day at 6:15am. $35 one-way, $60 round-trip.

Taxi: Owl Taxi, 1917 NE 2nd St. (382-3311). 24 hr.

AAA: 20360 Anderson Rd. (382-1303). Open Mon.-Fri. 8am-5pm.

Camping Equipment: Bend Rental Helps, 353 SE 3rd St. (382-2792). Tents $15.75 per day, $40 per week. Open Mon.-Sat. 7:30am-6pm.

Laundromat: Nelson's, 407 SE 3rd St. (388-2140). One block from Royal Gateway. Open daily 5:30am-10:30pm.

COBRA (Central Oregon Battering and Rape Alliance): 800-356-2369.

Hospital: St. Charles Medical Center, 2500 N.E. Neff Rd. (382-4320).

Police: 388-5555.

Post Office: 2300 NE 4th St. (388-1971), at Webster. Open Mon.-Fri. 9am-5pm. General Delivery ZIP Code: 97709.

Area Code: 503.

U.S. 97 bisects Bend—the downtown area lies to the west along the Deschutes River; Wall and Bond St. are the two main arteries.

Accommodations and Camping

Bend's flock of cheap motels trail down 3rd St. (U.S. 97). Last year's price war left the survivors bruised and battered, so this year prices are a bit inflated, especially during July and August. You can stay free at the campgrounds in the **Deschutes National Forest** (pronounced duh-SHOOTS), but you must tote your own water. Contact the **National Forest Office,** 1645 E. Hwy. 20 (388-2715), for details.

Royal Gateway Motel, 475 SE 3rd St. (382-5631). Big rooms that fill up fast, often with families. A winner in the aforementioned war. Singles $26. Doubles $34. Make reservations.

Holiday Motel, 880 SE 3rd St. (382-4620). Small rooms with thin walls but the folks are real friendly and the beds real comfortable. Really. Singles $26. Doubles $31.

Edelweiss Motel, 2346 NE Division (382-6222), at Xerxes St. near the northern intersection with 3rd St. Far from the madding crowd of 3rd St.—and everything else, too. Small rooms with no telephones. Singles $22.54. Doubles $33.10.

Chalet Motel, 510 SE 3rd (382-6124). Newly spruced up with bigger rooms (some with kitchens). Singles $28. Doubles $34.

Tumalo State Park, 5 mi. northwest of town on U.S. 20. 88 sites along the Deschutes River, 20 with water and electricity. Facilities include hot showers and flush toilets. Open April 15-Oct.; reservations recommended. Sites $6.

Elk Lake Recreation Area, on Forest Service Road 46, 30 mi. from Bend in the national forest. 53 sites with pit toilets; no drinking water. Open June-Sept.

Bend KOA Kampground, 63615 N. U.S. 97 (382-7728), 2 mi. north of Bend. Typical KOA. Sites $4, with full hookup $16-18.

Food

Restaurants in Bend generally maintain high standards. While downtown offers a host of pleasant cafés, 3rd St. also has a surprising number of decent eateries.

Deschutes Brewery and Public House, 1044 NW Bond St. (382-4242). Delicious food and beer. Daily specials $4-5, daily homemade sausage special $4.50. Pint of ale, bitters, or stout brewed on the premises $2. Homemade rootbeer $1.25. Open Mon.-Thurs. 11am-11:30pm, Fri.-Sat. 11am-12:30am, Sun. noon-10pm. Minors not allowed after 8:30pm.

The Hong Kong, 480 SE 3rd St., across from the Royal Gateway. Healthful and tasty Chinese (mostly Mandarin and Cantonese) and American food. Certified by the American Heart Association. Combination plate $6. Open Mon.-Thurs. 11am-10pm, Fri. 11am-11pm, Sat. noon-11pm, Sun. noon-10pm.

D&D Bar and Grill, 927 NW Bond (382-4592), downtown. For the *really* hungry. The specials really are. Try the Mexican Omelette Dinner ($5). Breakfasts are cheap (hashbrowns and sausage $1.50). The soothing clink of pool balls above rock anthems and the chatter of sated locals give this find some character. Open daily 6am-9pm.

Sargent's Café, 719 SE 3rd St. (382-3916). A crowded, friendly diner. All-you-can-eat spaghetti $5. Open daily 5:30am-9:30pm.

De Nicola's Pizza, 811 NW Wall (389-7364). Unpretentious pizza for the younger set. Try the 10" Mt. Bachelor Special ($7.75). Open Mon.-Fri. 11am-9pm, Sat. 11:30am-9pm.

Rolaine's Cantina, 785 SE 3rd St. (382-4944), across from Albertson's. Mexican specials of almost frightening proportions. Try the vegetarian *burrito rolaine* ($5.20), and garnish it with gobs of "killer" salsa (available upon request). Open Mon.-Fri. 11:30am-10pm, Sat.-Sun. noon-10pm.

Sights and Events

Just east of the intersection of U.S. 97 and 20, **Pilot Butte State Park** spreads 101 acres around Pilot Butte, a 511-ft. cinder cone. Climb to the top for an excellent view of the Cascade Range. Six mi. south of Bend on U.S. 97, the **High Desert Museum** (382-4754) shines as one of central Oregon's feature attractions, maintaining live exhibits on the fragile ecosystem of the Oregon plateau. The museum presents useful facts (bet you never would have guessed that a horned owl's eyeball is bigger than its brain) and explanations of the geological history of the area. The main building is solar-heated and contains an auditorium in which park rangers lecture on Oregon's ecology. Especially fascinating are the otter feedings (10:30am, 1pm, 3:30pm), although young children may be distressed to see the otters hunt down and shred live fish. The museum also features a 15-min. desert slide show, offered every hour on the half-hour. (Open daily 9am-5pm, Oct. 1-March 31 9am-4pm. Admission $2, senior citizens $1.50, ages 6-12 $1.) Five mi. farther south on U.S. 97 is **Lava Butte**, which resembles Pilot Butte in height and geology, and the view of the Cascades from the top is, likewise, extraordinary. The **Lava Lands Visitor Center** (593-2421), at the base of the butte, offers interpretive dioramas and information. The **Lava River Caves**, three mi. farther on U.S. 97, were formed by age-old lava flow from the nearby volcanoes. In the midst of endless juniper bushes, the caves are a welcome change of scenery (and temperature—carry a sweater). A self-guided 1.2-mi. tour allows you to explore on your own. (Open May 15-late Sept. daily 8:30am-5pm. Admission $1, under 13 free.)

West of Bend, **Century Drive** (Cascade Lakes Hwy.) makes its dramatic 89-mi. loop over Mt. Bachelor, through the forest, and past the Crane Prairie Reservoir before rejoining U.S. 97. Thirty campgrounds, fishing areas, and hiking trails pock-mark the countryside. Allow a full day for the spectacular drive, and pack a picnic lunch. You can ski the 9075 ft. (3100 ft. vertical drop) **Mt. Bachelor**, 22 mi. down this highway, where the U.S. Ski Team trains. (Daily lift passes $23, ages over 65 $11.50, ages 7-12 $14. Many nearby lodges offer 5-night ski packages. Prices include lift tickets and range from $150-$290. Call 382-8334.)

The **Bend Bucks** Class A baseball team slides into Bend from June to September as future Wade Boggses slug their way to the majors in Vince Genna Stadium, 401 SE Roosevelt, just off 3rd St. (Admission $2.50.) Would-be Supermen and Wonder-women ski, bike, canoe, and run in the **Pole, Pedal, Paddle Race** each May (389-0399). June brings the **Cascade Festival of Music** with a wide variety of concerts. Write 842 NW Wall St., #6, for tickets and info. On the third weekend of July, local visual and performing artists aestheticize at the **Festival of the Arts** in Drake Park.

U.S. 20 and 26

One of the two main routes across the Cascades, U.S. 26 winds southeast from Portland to Prineville. The other route, U.S. 20, makes more of a straight line from coastal Newport to Bend and avoids U.S. 26's soporific traversal of the Warm Springs Indian Reservation. U.S. 26 runs east of the Bend area and is the more visually pleasing of your two options: while U.S. 20 blazes through eastern Oregon's high desert, U.S. 26 winds through the foothills of the scenic **Blue Mountains** en route to the two roads' final junction in Vale, some 250 mi. east of Bend.

U.S. 20

Moving inland from Newport on the Oregon Coast, U.S. 20 crosses I-5 just east of Corvallis, tackling the Cascade Range along the South Santiam River. Just past Cascadia, U.S. 20 cuts through the towering Douglas firs of **Willamette National Forest,** whose well-marked fishing and hiking areas extend roughly south to Hwy. 126 and north to Hwy. 22 and Detroit Lake. **Detroit Lake State Park** (854-3346), 3½ mi. west of Detroit on Hwy. 22, has 300 sites with flush toilets and hot showers for $7 (with electrical hookup $8, with full hookup $10). East and south of Detroit

Lake is the **Mount Jefferson Wilderness,** in the southernmost corner of Mount Hood National Forest. The 10,495-ft. Mount Jefferson actually lies within the Warm Springs Indian Reservation. Take Hwy. 22 to the wilderness area trailheads.

East of U.S. 20's junction with Hwy. 22, the heavily forested **Santiam Pass** rises 4817 ft., clearing the way between the **Mount Jefferson Wilderness** and the **Mount Washington Wilderness.** The McKenzie Pass Highway (Hwy. 126) meets U.S. 20 on its way to Bend at **Sisters,** a charming (albeit self-consciously quaint) village that is an important supply station for backpackers on the Pacific Crest Trail. Sisters hosts one of the better rodeos in the area during the second weekend of June. Reserve tickets ($7-10) with the **Sisters Rodeo Association,** P.O. Box 1018, Sisters 97759 (549-0121). For wilderness information, stop at the **Ranger Station,** on the highway at the west end of town, and pick up directions to **Lava Lake Camp,** a magnificently isolated, free campsite located among lava fields about 20 mi. out of Sisters.

For 40 mi., Hwy. 126 follows the McKenzie River, paralleling U.S. 20 to the south. Chinook salmon lure anglers here from all over. For more information visit the **Sisters Chamber of Commerce** (549-0251; open Mon.-Fri. 9am-5pm).

Below Sisters, U.S. 20 continues along the edge of the Deschutes National Forest, which grows southward almost to Crater Lake. The forest features five wilderness areas, a string of fishing lakes, a handful of canoeing rivers, and a top-notch ski resort on Mt. Bachelor. (Prices vary; call 382-8334.) Camp anywhere in the forest. The Deschutes National Forest Office, 1645 E. U.S. 20, Bend (388-2715), administers the area. (Open Mon.-Fri. 7:45am-4:30pm.)

U.S. 26

From Portland, U.S. 26 runs through the forested Cascades and then north of U.S. 20 over the deserts of central and eastern Oregon. After threading through the Mount Hood Wilderness Area, the highway enters **Warm Springs Indian Reservation,** a transition region from national forest to eastern desert, located about 100 mi. east of Portland. The nearest vacation draw is the **Kan-Nee-Ta Resort,** about 15 mi. north. Originally intended to offer the "life of another culture," the resort has deteriorated into an commercialized lodge with a golf course and the works. Rooms start at $40 per person (call 553-1112 or 800-831-0100 if you are so moved).

Every Sunday at 1pm, a Don Ho-like emcee leads a group of Native American dancers through a performance in the main plaza of **Warm Springs.** Imagine Englebert Humperdinck hosting an Indian cabaret—don't kick yourself for missing it. Instead, head for the weekly **salmon bake,** held every Saturday night from 5 to 7pm. The price is a bit steep ($18, children $2), but you can gorge yourself while you watch Native Americans in full regalia. Particularly compared to the reservations in Washington State, the Warm Springs Reservation is not the richest experience in Native American culture.

Another expensive way to amuse yourself in Warm Springs is to raft down the Deschutes River ($35 per day). Call **Rainbow Rafting** (553-1663).

Madras lies on U.S. 26 about 10 mi. past Warm Springs and 40 mi. short of Bend. Famous for its shirts and the "Rockhounds," people who excavate for rocks and fossils, who dominate the area. You can dig alongside them at the **Richardson Recreational Ranch,** Gateway Rd. (475-2680), 11 mi. north of town on U.S. 97. Ten mi. south of town in **Cove Palisades State Park,** a man-made lake sits alongside slabs of frozen lava 80 ft. thick. The **Madras Chamber of Commerce,** 4th and D St. (475-2350), seems about as big as the town itself. (Open Mon.-Fri. 9am-5pm, Sat. 10am-2pm; off-season Mon.-Fri. 9am-5pm.)

John Day Fossil Beds National Monument

On its way east from Prineville, U.S. 26 passes by two of the three "units" (that's what the Park Service calls them) that comprise the beautifully vast and barren **John Day Fossil Beds National Monument.** The **Painted Hills** lie three torturously curvy miles northwest of Mitchell off U.S. 26. Erosion has exposed the palette of 30 million years of lava flows in layers of red, pink, gold, bronze, black, and clay. Climb the ½ mi. trail to get a spectacular view of this area, particularly at dawn. **Clarno** is the most inaccessible of the three, 20 mi. west of Fossil on Hwy. 218. Fossil lies on Hwy. 19, about 70 mi. northwest of Dayville, or take Hwy. 207 from Mitchell until it intersects with Hwy. 19. Trails of various lengths lead from the base of the palisades by mudslides riddled by weather to reveal 40-million year old plant fossils buried inside. Watch out for snakes. The closest unit to the highway, **Sheep Rock,** is a mere babe in the woods; remains found here are only 25 million years old. The **Sheep Rock Outlook,** 5 mi. west of Dayville, just off U.S. 26 on Hwy. 19, looks out over the massive rock formation and the fossil-thick valley below. The main **Visitors Center** is a restored ranch house just down the hill from the overlook. Fossil exhibits attempt to explain all to the geologically inept. Open daily 8:30am-6pm. Fossil preparation demonstrations Sat.-Sun. 1-4pm.

The monument headquarters is in the **Parks Department,** a large pink building at 420 W. Main St., John Day (575-0721; open Mon.-Fri. 8am-4:30pm). The staff will tell you everything you always wanted to know about fossils (but were too afraid to ask). The **Grant County Visitors Information Center,** on Main St., just east of town, overflows with information on Oregon in general (575-0547; open Mon.-Fri. 9am-5pm). For more area-specific facts, try the **Malheur National Forest** ranger station on the eastern edge of town at 139 NE Dayton (575-1731; open Mon.-Fri. 7:15am-5pm), or the Parks Department. If you stay overnight in John Day, try **Little Mac's Motel,** 250 E. Main (575-1751). Large, attractive rooms have Disney, HBO on the tube. (Singles $25. Doubles from $31.) Eat at the **Mother Lode Restaurant,** 241 W. Main (575-2714) for hearty but uninspiring food. Sandwiches $3-5. A special menu offers selections for seniors. (Open Mon.-Fri. 5am-9pm, Sat.-Sun. 6am-9pm.)

In John Day itself, the **Kam Wah Chung and Co. Museum,** on Canton St. near City Park, showcases personal possessions that Chinese immigrants brought to Grant County during the 1862 gold rush. The highlight is a large collection of herbal medicines. The building itself, once the center of the Chinese mining community in eastern Oregon, dates back to the 1860s. (Open May 1-Oct. 31 Mon.-Thurs. 9am-noon and 1-5pm, Sat.-Sun. 1-5pm. Admission $1.50, children 50¢.)

"Nobody here likes it indoors," quips one resident of the sleepy timber, ranching, and mining town of John Day (pop. 1200). During hunting season (Sept.-Nov.), the town heads for the hills in the **Malheur National Forest** (pronounced mal-HERE). Ask at the ranger station about licenses to kill black bears, bighorn sheep, mule deer, salmon, steelhead, and trout. Camp wherever you please in the forest—except, of course, near "No Trespassing" signs. Some areas in the forest even have vault toilets and drinkable water. The more adventurous might penetrate the two government-regulated wilderness areas, **Strawberry Mountain** and **Monument Rock.** Get maps and guidance from the ranger station before venturing out.

Prineville

With clean and friendly streets, a historical museum, red meat restaurants, a yearly rodeo, and proximity to outdoor activities, the only remotely distinguishing feature about Prineville is the profusion of churches—23 for a population of 5000. All things considered, the oldest city in central Oregon, has got all the charm and character of the quintessential central Oregon town. Despite this, it's worth a visit anyway.

Practical Information and Orientation

Visitor Information: Prineville Crook County Chamber of Commerce, 390 N. Fairview (447-6304), off 3rd. The usual pamphlets and a very friendly staff. Open Mon.-Fri. 9am-noon, 1-5pm.

Greyhound: 1825 E. 3rd (447-5516), about 1 mi. east of town.

Laundromat: The Laundry, 250 E. 4th (447-3126).

Dial-A-Ride: 447-6429.

Rape Crisis Line: 389-7021.

Hospital: Pioneer Memorial, 1201 N. Elm (447-6254).

Fire: 400 E. 3rd (447-4168).

Police: 400 E. 3rd (447-4168).

Post Office: Federal Building (447-5652). Open Mon.-Fri. 9am-5pm. General Delivery ZIP Code: 97754.

Prineville is at the junction of U.S. 26 and Hwy. 126, just west of the **Ochoco National Forest** (pronounced OH-chuh-coe), 36 mi. northeast of Bend and 148 mi. southeast of Portland. Hwy. 126 runs west from Prineville, hooking up with U.S. 97 at Redmond.

Accommodations and Camping

Almost all motels are along 3rd St. Rooms fill up quickly, particularly on the weekends, and rates increase correspondingly. You can camp anywhere in the forest for free as long as you leave no trace of your stay. Many campgrounds dot the area, with fees from $3-5. Contact the Forest Supervisor at Ochoco National Forest, P.O. Box 490, Prineville 97754-0490, for details.

Carolina Motel, 1050 E. 3rd (447-4152). Small rooms, nice bathrooms. Laundry, movies available. Singles $24. Doubles $30.

City Center Motel, 509 E. 3rd (447-5522). Filled with charm, this place is small, but harmless. Free coffee. Singles $24. Doubles $30.

Ochoco Inn, 123 E. 3rd (447-6231). Caters to convention trade. Rates are, of course, higher during the rodeo. Singles $32. Doubles $40.

Food

Prinville's restaurants give food a bad name. There is, however, a Dairy Queen on 3rd St. (it's a sorry day, indeed, when *Let's Go* recommends a Dairy Queen).

Makin' Bacon, 323 N. Main (447-7679). Design your own sandwiches ($3.50 and up, based on weight) in syrupy sweetshop surroundings. Large homemade soup $2. Open Mon.-Fri. 9:30am-5:30pm, Sat. 9am-5pm.

The Coffee Pot, 386 W. Main (447-1043). Burgers "from A to Z": 26 varieties served with fries or tater tots ($2-4). Tasty and filling. Try the jalapeño burger. Small bakery in back sells fresh twists for 50¢. Open Mon.-Fri. 5am-9pm, Sat.-Sun. 5am-10pm.

Arnold's Drive-In, 36 E. 3rd (447-9920). Have the "all-u-can eat" ribs ($6) delivered to your window by a roller-skate-demon.

"Sights" and Events

Prineville's star attraction (and what an attraction) is the **Bowman Museum**, 246 N. Main (447-3715), at the corner of 3rd St. Its collection of tobacco cans, bank books, and Bibles once belonged to 19th-century Prineville folk. Artfully arranged to affect your sense of nostalgia, the Bowman also includes a 1908 Sears Roebuck catalog and a portion of the first Japanese plane shot down in WWII (over Hawaii, not Prineville). (Open April-Dec. Mon.-Fri. 10am-5pm, Sat. noon-5pm. Donations only.) Rockhounds really do come from all over, seeking agates, jasper, petrified wood and other unusual stones. Both free and commercial diggings abound; the Chamber of Commerce has some suggestions.

Things get a little crazy during the second weekend in July as the **Crooked River Roundup** moseys into Prineville. The usual rodeo business follows the diminutive heels of the "Little Britches Parade," and the town plays cops-and-robbers in the staged bank robbery. Write for tickets ($6-8) at P.O. Box 536, Prineville 97754, or call 447-6535 for info. You can hunt, fish, and ski in the Ochocos; contact the ranger for details.

Baker City

When gold was discovered in them thar' hills south of the Powder River Valley in 1861, a settlement sprang up where the river intersected the Oregon Trail. Today, Baker is a rest stop for truckers, a base for hikers and wilderness lovers, and a fine spot for an afternoon stroll.

Practical Information and Orientation

Visitor Information: Baker County Chamber of Commerce, 490 Campbell St. (523-5855, 800-523-1235 from outside OR). Everything a visitors center should be and more. Housed in a wonderful wooden house, the lower level contains enough brochures for 3 states and the upper level is a small museum of delightful antique furniture and photos. The friendly volunteers seem to know everyone in town by their first name. Open Mon.-Sat. 8am-6pm.

Greyhound: 512 Campbell St. (523-5011), in the Truck Corral Café. Buses east to Boise (2 per day) and west to Portland (2 per day). Open daily 7-9am, 5-7pm.

Taxi: Baker Cab Co., 515 Campbell St. (523-6070). Up to $3.25 within Baker City, $1 per mi. outside city limits.

Laundromat: Williams Cleaners and Laundry, 1935 Valley (523-3651).

Help Inc. Senior Services: 523-6591.

Hospital: St. Elizabeth, 3325 Pocahontas Rd. (523-6461). 24 hr.

Police: 1655 1st St. (523-3644).

Post Office: 1550 Dewey Ave. (523-4237). Open Mon.-Fri. 8:30am-5pm, Sat. 10am-noon. General Delivery ZIP Code: 97814.

Area Code: 503.

Baker City lies 44 mi. south of La Grande on I-84 in northeast Oregon. Hwy. 86 leads east from the city to Hells Canyon and Hwy. 7 leads west, hooking up with U.S. 26 to John Day and Prineville. Campbell and Main St. are the principal thoroughfares, Main runs parallel to I-84 and Campbell intersects the latter just east of the city. Other important streets are Broadway Ave., which intersects Main St. in the busiest section downtown, and Bridge St., an offshoot of Main St. to the southeast.

Accommodations and Camping

Baker City has several motels, most of which are a little above budget range. Most places will knock off a few dollars if you nudge. Camping is easy and free—just find a comfortable spot by the Powder River. For information about where you can and can't camp, call the U.S. Forest Service at 523-6391.

Hereford Motor Inn, 134 Bridge St. (523-6571), just off Main St. Big rooms with ugly (but matching!) furniture and "interesting" lamps. Cable TV, A/C, phone. Singles $21. Doubles $27.

El Dorado Motel, 695 Campbell St. (523-6494), right next to Greyhound. Polished motel, with neo-Conquistador architecture. Big rooms with matador paintings. Indoor pool and jacuzzi, TV, A/C. Singles $29. Doubles $32. Family (2 adjoining rooms) $40.

Oregon Trail Motel, 211 Bridge St. (523-5844), right across from Hereford. Smallish rooms. Pool, cable TV, A/C. Senior citizens get a discount. Singles $26. Doubles $34.

Mt. View Campground, 9th and Hughes Lane (523-4824), exit 302 off I-84. A clean, spacious campground and trailer park in the hub of things. Showers, heated pool, water, and electric hookups available. Sites $10 plus $2 for each kid.

Union Creek Campground, Box 54, Baker (894-2210), at Phillips Lake. Follow signs to Sumpter, and go 20 mi. down Hwy. 7 to this lovely park. Beach, but no shower. Sites $7. Full hookup, $10. Heater or A/C $1 per day. Senior citizen discount.

Food

The Brass Parrot, 2190 Main at Church St. (523-4266). Polly wanna taco? Try the Mexican food for a refreshing change from eastern Oregon's slimy hamburgers. Relax in a cool dining room with a delicious frozen peach-wine margarita ($1.50) and a monstrous burrito ($3.65). Open Mon.-Sat. 10am-9pm.

Klondike's Pizza, 1726 Campbell St. (523-7105). Good pizza in what looks like a reclaimed bordello. Cutely named pizzas (depending, of course, on your definition of cute), including Pyrite Pete's Pleaser. Pies come in 4 sizes and range in price from $2.85-14.60. Try the Mother Lode Deli pizza topped with "everything but the ovens." Open Sun.-Thurs. 11am-midnight, Fri.-Sat. 11am-1am.

Oregon Trail Restaurant, 211 Bridge St. (523-5844, ext. 179). Plain food, caters to older folks. Big, cheap portions—try the 5-oz. steak ($6). Cosmopolitan clocks mark the time in Baker, Boise, Anchorage, Omaha, and New York. A slice of pie $1.35. Open daily 7am-9pm.

Sights and Seasonal Events

Baker City's greatest attraction is the surrounding hill area, which turns an almost supernatural green in the summer months. Pack a picnic lunch and hike in almost any direction. Twenty minutes east or west should take you far enough. Within Baker City itself, the five-year-old **Oregon Trail Regional Museum,** 2490 Grove St. (523-9308), off Campbell St., is the center of attention. Century-old artifacts from the area seem out of place alongside a semi-precious stone collection which rivals the Smithsonian's: Isophere Cochrane's hand-made wedding dress hangs next to the world's largest cluster of fluorite and quartz. Tucked away at the back of the museum is a room illuminated only by its shelf of phosphorescent rocks. (Open May-Sept. daily 9am-4pm. Suggested donation $1, children 50¢.) The Chamber of Commerce sells a guide to several walking tours of the city ($3), which indicates all the "century" houses.

If the kids get bored, take them to **Geiser Pollman Park** on Campbell St., a big field with a playground, two blocks from Main St. along the river. Next to the park, the **Public Library** (523-6419), on Resort St., has a huge selection of children's books. (Open Mon.-Thurs. 10am-9pm, Fri. 10am-5pm, Sat. 10am-4pm, Sun. 1-4pm.)

The **Miners' Jubilee,** the third weekend of July, stages a hot-air balloon race, a triathlon, and the world championship porcupine sprints. Porcupines train all year for this Olympic Exhibition Event (1992).

The largest flea market in eastern Oregon buzzes in nearby **Sumpter** three times per year: Memorial Day weekend, Independence Day weekend, and Labor Day weekend. Sumpter, originally named "Fort Sumpter" by zealous Southwesterners in 1862 (but abbreviated after the North won the Civil War), operates a 100-year-old train from Baker City to this quasi-ghost town (summer weekends and holidays, 10am, noon, 2pm, 4pm. $4, 16 and under $3, family $10).

Hells Canyon National Recreation Area

Spectacular, wild, and well-nigh inaccessible, Hells Canyon is truly rewarding for those willing to make the effort. Bighorn sheep, the tempestuous **Snake River,** spectacular "Grand Canyonic" vistas, and unspoiled archeological sites all harmonically converge in an area thankfully untouched by the tourist steamroller. Hells Canyon is the deepest gorge on the continent; it's an 8000-ft. drop from the summit of Idaho's **Seven Devils** mountains to the frothing river below. The Snake River

Canyon's gorge gained dubious renown when Evel Knievel attempted to jump it on a motorcycle in the late 70s. (Kids, ask your parents first.)

Although Chief Joseph and his band of Nez Perce lived in the canyon, nobody has since attempted to blaze a trail though the region, which straddles the borders of Idaho, Washington, and Oregon and encompasses the Snake, Imnaha, and Rapid Rivers. Consequently, getting to Hells Canyon remains, well, hell. From the Oregon side, take either Hwy. 82 to **Enterprise** or Hwy. 86 through Halfway to Hells Canyon Dam. Several U.S. Forest Service roads descend from U.S. 95 on the Idaho side, near Riggins. Public transportation to the area is practically nonexistent. If there is absolutely no way for you to obtain a car, contact the **Wallowa Valley Stage** (503-569-2284). Wallowa runs one van per day from La Grande to Enterprise, and conducts occasional group tours to the lookouts on the Oregon side.

If you come to Enterprise or to U.S. 95 with a car, make sure your vehicle is solid and safe, since the roads to the viewpoints are bad when not horrid. Many are impassable during the winter. Even in the summer, some roads are advised only for Jeeps. For a view of the Canyon (and the Imnaha River), take the gravel-paved Zumwalt Road (County Rd. 697) out of Enterprise some 40 mi. to the **Buckhorn Lookout.** Glimpses of the legendary Snake River are harder to find. From Enterprise, drive through **Joseph** to **Imnaha.** From Imnaha, it's an extremely rough, 24-mi., two-hour drive to the 90-ft. observation tower at **Hat Point Lookout,** but the view of the canyon, the river, and the Seven Devils beyond makes it worth shattering your nerves. Hwy. 86 and the roads leading from Halfway are less challenging. Past Halfway on I-82 is a series of dams at the southern tip of the canyon. The **Oxbow Dam** is the closet to Halfway; the road continues to Hells Canyon Dam across the Idaho border. There is actually a road that crosses the Wallowa Mountains, the only route connecting the towns along 82 and 86 without having to return to I-84. It's not on any map and even the locals don't know what its called but this paved ghost-road (used mostly by loggers) provides mind-boggling scenery. Ask in Joseph for directions; while the road is clearly marked in Halfway, there is nothing so conventional as a signpost on the other side.

From Idaho, Forest Service Rd. 517 departs U.S. 95 just south of Riggins and leads to **Heavens Gate Lookout,** in the heart of the Seven Devils. Heavens Gate provides a rare angle: the Snake *without* the Seven Devils in the background. Before setting out on any of the roads listed above, visit or contact the **U.S. Forest Service** stations in Enterprise, right on Hwy. 82 (503-426-3151), or in Riggins, on Hwy. 95 (208-628-3916). The helpful rangers will tell you which roads are passable and which are vacationing as waterslides. Primitive, cheap ($3 or free) **campsites** abound along all of the area's roads. Pick up a full listing of campsites at either of the Forest Service stations, or call the ranger station to reserve roomy cabins ($20 per couple, $5 per additional person). **Wallowa Llamas** offers several different trips through the Wallowa mountains and into Hells Canyon. They range from easy to strenuous, and from three to seven days. Tents, meals, and llamas are supplied; you provide sleeping bags, stamina, and $225-$600. Write Rt. 1, Box 84, Halfway 97834 or call 742-2961 or 742-4930.

A view is nice, but there's nothing like plunging into the canyon or slithering down the Snake. The Forest Service maintains only some of the 900 mi. of trail running through the canyon; the others are hard to use (let alone find). As with the local roads, inquire about trail conditions at the Forest Service offices. This is an area prone to forest fires, so be careful. It's easier, and perhaps more exciting, to view the canyon from the water itself. A wide range of both **jet boat** and **raft trips** are available for the adventurer willing to shell out $45-90 per day. **Hells Canyon Adventures** offers the most varied options and a toll-free number (800-422-3568). For a complete list of boat runners and rafting groups, contact the **Hells Canyon Chamber of Commerce,** P.O. Box 841, Halfway 97834 (503-785-3393).

La Grande

In the mid 1800s, La Grande served as a pit stop for pioneers on the Oregon Trail; today it serves a similar function for West Coast truckers. In 1864, La Grande inherited the newly-created seat of Union County. Ten years later, the first vote was taken and according to the stately processes of democracy the nearby town of Union won over the seat. A Union posse immediately descended into La Grande and forcibly seized the records, stamps, and paraphenalia, and carted them home. It took another ten years, but when the ballot box granted La Grande the seat back, La Grandians returned the favor by storming into Union and wresting control from its rival. Thes towns have since discontinued this practice.

La Grande claims the Blue Mountains and the Grande Ronde River as its backyard, though neither of these is particularly visible from the town itself. Despite a few good restaurants, La Grande has less small-town charm than some of its neighbors. And beware: if you mispronounce "La Grande" with even the slightest hint of a French accent, you might as well have the word "tourist" stamped on your forehead.

Practical Information and Orientation

Visitor Information: La Grande-Union County Chamber of Commerce, 1502 N. Pine Ave. (963-8588), off Spruce. The pamphlet selection will assuage your fears—there is much more to do in the surrounding area than in La Grande itself. Open Mon.-Fri. 9am-noon, 1-5 pm.

Greyhound: 2108 Cove Ave. (963-5165), off U.S. 82 in the northeast corner of town. Buses east to Boise (2 per day) and west to Portland (2 per day). Open Mon.-Fri. 8am-noon and 2-6pm, Sat. 8am-noon and 4-5pm.

Taxi: Rainbow Cab Co., 1609 Albany (936-6960). Anywhere within the city $3.

Laundromat: Stein's Wash Haus, Island City Strip (963-9629). Open Mon.-Fri. 7am-5:30pm.

Senior Citizen Services: Union County Senior Center, 1504 Albany Ave. (963-7532).

Hospital: Grande Ronde Hospital, 900 Sunset Dr. (963-8421).

Police: 963-9110.

Post Office: 1202 Washington (963-2041). Open Mon.-Fri. 9am-5pm. General Delivery ZIP Code: 97850.

Area Code: 503.

La Grande is on I-84, halfway between Pendleton and Baker. The two main roads are Adams Ave., which runs into U.S. 30, and Highway 82, which leads to Hell's Canyon. Though the Chamber of Commerce's pamphlet *Where to Stay* has a good city map on the back, there's not enough town in this town to get seriously lost.

Accommodations and Camping

Almost every motel is along Adams Ave. In summer, square dancers and other conventioneers book the motels solidly; call a day in advance to ensure a room. Camping is free and generally unrestricted—pitch a tent anywhere in the mountains. Closer to town, try **Morgan Lake,** 2 mi. outside La Grande on B Ave., or **Hillgard Park,** at the edge of the Umatilla Forest, 8 mi. west on U.S. 30. Camping along the Grande Ronde River is permitted.

Broken Arrow Lodge, 2215 Adams Ave. (963-7116). Definitely the nicest in the budget range. Clean, comfy rooms with cable TV, A/C and free coffee. Courtesy car to bus station. Singles $26. Doubles $30. Senior citizen discount.

Stardust Lodge, 402 Adams Ave. (963-4166), on the western edge of town. Huge rooms, HBO, A/C, heated pool, and courtesy car from station. Singles $24.15. Doubles $31.50. Senior citizen discount.

Orchard Motel, 2206 Adams Ave. (963-6160). Small but comfortable wood-paneled rooms, some with kitchenettes. HBO, A/C, free continental breakfast. Singles $23. Doubles from $27. Senior citizen discount.

Moon Motel, 2116 Adams Ave. (963-2724). Cheaper, but not quite as clean or accommodating as the more expensive motels. Tiny rooms. Cable TV, A/C, and free coffee. Singles $19. Doubles $28. Senior citizen discount.

Food

There are a few good restaurants around Adams Ave. to save you from the fast food strip along the highway.

Mamacita's, 110 Depot St. (936-6223), just off Adams Ave. Mexi-funk at its finest. Try the Veggie Burrito ($4.50). Open Tues.-Thurs. 11am-2pm and 5:30-9pm, Fri. 11am-2pm and 5:30-10pm, Sat. 5:30-10pm, Sun. 5:30-9pm.

Golden Crown, 1116 Adams Ave. (963-5907). Surprisingly good Chinese food considering the tacky sign of monumental size announcing its presence miles away. Open daily 11am-10pm.

Farm House Restaurant, 401 Adams Ave. (963-9318). Popular with the over-60 crowd. Savor the terrific spicy apple pie ($1), a perfect dish in a setting straight out of Frank Capra. Sandwiches $3, dinners $6. Open daily 6am-9pm.

DeBorde's Café, 1414 Adams Ave. (963-6439), in Pat's Alley, a mini-mall. Looks like a coffeeshop, tastes like a coffeeshop . . . , this place is singular in its unsingularity. Breakfast and lunch $2-3, dinner $7. Open Mon.-Fri. 6am-10pm, Sat. 6am-8pm.

Sights and Activities

Let your imagination run free, and the **Oregon Trail** will be loads of fun. If you squint, the beat-up Fords along I-84 might become hyperkinetic horse-drawn wagons, hell-bent from Missouri to the Pacific. To hike along more than a few steps of the trail, you must contact the Chamber of Commerce (963-8588) for a special tour, because much of the trail now crosses private property.

The **Hot Lake** (963-5587), about 10 mi. southeast of town on Hwy. 203, is a 185° steambath that has been ministering to panacea-seekers since 1812. Associated with turn-of-the-century quackery, the mineral bathing here now offers to releive the pains of cancer, arthritis, and other diseases. (Write Hot Lake Co., Box 1601, La Grande 97850 for details on Hot Lake's miracle cure. Open Wed.-Sun. 1-9pm. Admission $6.)

Hunters stalk the area from October through February, targeting mule deer and Rocky Mountain elk. Also during this time, skiers drive the 41 mi. to **Anthony Lakes** on I-84, where they can ski all day for $14. (Write P.O. Box 3040, La Grande 97850 or call 963-8282.) Those who seek more exotic thrills can traverse the Wallowa-Whitman National Forest atop a llama. The 4-hour ride is $15 complete with riding lesson. (Contact **Hurricane Creek Llamas,** Rte. 1, Box 123, Enterprise 97828, 432-4455.)

The **Timber Festival,** held in the third week of June, showcases the town's three world-champion lumberjacks in tree topping, axe throwing, speed climbing, and straight chopping competitions. Fun even for the casual observer, it's more so if you hang out with locals and cheer on their favorites. For three weeks beginning in mid-August, the **Oregon Trail Pageant** summons forth the past with dramatic reenactments and dancing performances.

Pendleton

Ordinarily, Pendleton saddles up at its own pace, offering few reasons to come down. But when the **Pendleton Round-Up** goes down in mid-September, 45,000 fans ride up. In Downtown, men gussied up in Stetson hats down shots and talk up horses—these men and wouldn't be caught with their pants down in a Marlboro ad. When the rodeo hits Pendleton, everything turns upside down.

Practical Information and Orientation

Visitor Information: Pendleton Chamber of Commerce, 25 SE Dorion Ave. (276-7411). A brusque staff flings out pamphlets galore. Open Mon.-Fri. 9am-5pm.

Greyhound: 320 SW Court Ave. (276-1551), a few blocks west of the city center. Buses leave 4 times daily: 2 to Portland ($25) and 2 to Boise ($32). Open Mon.-Fri. 8am-5pm, Sat. 8-11am, 2:30-4pm.

Taxi: Elite Taxi (276-8294).

Car Rental: Ugly Duckling Rent-A-Car, 309 SW Emigrant Ave. (276-1498). The only way to enjoy the Blue or Wallowa Mts. without your own car. $20 per day plus 20¢ per mi. $50 deposit or credit card required to rent for more than 1 day. Must be over 21. Open Mon.-Fri. 8am-5pm, Sat. 8am-noon.

Rape Crisis Line: 278-0241.

Hospital: St. Anthony's, 1601 SE Court Ave. (276-5121).

Police: 34 SE Dorian Ave., in the basement of City Hall (276-4411).

Post Office: Federal Building, 104 SW Dorion Ave. (278-0203), at SW 1st. Open Mon.-Fri. 9am-5pm, Sat. 10am-1pm. Speedy Delivery ZIP Code: 97801.

Area Code: 503.

Pendleton is on I-84, just under the Washington border, about the same distance (200-230 mi.) from Portland, Spokane, and Boise. **Raley Park,** home of the Round-Up Grounds, is the spiritual center of town, while Main Street is the geographic one.

Pendleton's street design has its peculiarities. The city has many streets (running east to west) which are named with startling originality—1st St., 2nd St., and so on. Unfortunately they were so tickled with their creativity they decided to use the names again. Consequently, there are *two* 1st Streets, one SE and one SW, *two* 2nd Streets, etc., which are parallel to each other.

Accommodations and Camping

During most of the year, lodging in Pendleton is inexpensive. To stay here during the Round-Up, however, you must reserve rooms six months in advance. Rates double, and prices on everything from hamburgers to commemorative cowboy hats become celestial. Pendleton has no camping areas nearby. For more information on camping around here, contact the **State Highway Division,** 104 SE 12th St. (276-1241).

Pioneer Motel, just off Hwy. 11 on SE Court Pl. Large pleasant rooms. A bit removed from downtown but close to the hospital and wool mill. Singles $19. Doubles $23.

Longhorn Motel, 411 SW Dorion Ave. (276-7531), around the corner from the bus station. Don't let the scruffy exterior deter you. These are the nicest cheap rooms in downtown Pendleton. Singles $20. Doubles $26.

Seven Inn (276-4711), 5 mi. west of town at exit 202 off I-84 (outside the reach of the city's motel tax). Horribly inconvenient for travelers without a car, but it offers unparalleled rolling farmlands. Across from a huge truck weighstation, this quiet motel is popular with families (only $2 extra for kids) and those who appreciate the big rooms.

Motel 6, 325 SE Nye Ave. (276-3160), on the south side of town. Not in the middle of things, but easy access to I-84. Cable TV, A/C, and heated pool. Singles $24.60. Doubles $30.50.

Emigrant Springs State Park, 26 mi. southeast of Pendleton on I-84. The best campground within 50 mi. Numerous sites (and hot showers) in a shady grove of ponderosa pines (see Sights and Activities).

Food

Vegetarians, head for the grocery store. This is steak country and Pendleton restaurants offer little else. Menus are depressingly similar.

Bread Board, 141 S. Main St. (276-4520). No 72-oz. steaks here. Great $2 sandwiches and 75¢ cinnamon rolls in a friendly atmosphere, with national newspapers strewn about. Try Mirka's French Fantasy for breakfast—croissant, eggs, ham, and cheese ($2.25). Open Mon.-Fri. 8am-3:30pm.

The Circle S, 210 SE 5th St. (276-9637). Don't let the 3-ft. axe door handle scare you away from a great Western barbecue restaurant. Drink beverages from Mason jars while you enjoy a Teriyaki Burger and fries ($4) and a creme de menthe sundae ($1.75). If you can eat the 72-oz. sirloin ($45) in an hour, like John Candy in *The Great Outdoors,* it's free. Smaller portions also available. Open Tues.-Sat. 7am-10pm, Sun. 7am-3pm.

Rainbow Café, 209 S. Main St. (276-4120). Where the cowboys chow down. Classic American bar-cum-diner with rodeo decor. Good, hearty food. Burger and beer $3-4. Open daily 6am-2:30am.

The Club Café, 138 Main St. (276-9825), next to the Curio Shop. The food isn't great, but the regulars don't seem to mind. Sit at the counter and watch TV. Filling breakfasts $3-4. Open Mon.-Sat. 6am-6pm.

Sights and Activities

The Pendleton Round-Up (276-2553), a premier event on the nation's rodeo circuit, draws ranchers from all over the U.S. For "four glorious days and nights," yahoo at steer roping, saddle-bronc riding, bulldogging, and bareback riding, not to mention non-equine attractions such as lying contests, buffalo-chip tosses, quick draws, and greased pig chases—and, of course, the infamous "Let-'er-buck" room. For more information or tickets ($5-10), write to the Pendleton Round-Up Association, P.O. Box 609, Pendleton 97801. The **Round-Up Hall of Fame,** SW Court Ave. (276-2553), at SW 13th St., gives tours by appointment during the week. The hall has captured some of the rodeo's action for all eternity, including Pendleton's best preserved Round-Up hero, a stuffed horse named "War Paint."

Unless you have some special interest in wool you may want to bag the hyper-hyped tour of the **Pendleton Woolen Mills,** 1307 SE Court Ave. (276-6911). You will be entrusted with the world-famous, top-secret blanket-making process and then admitted to the gift shop, where you can spend twice your motel fee on a genuine Pendleton scarf. (Tours given Mon.-Fri. at 9am, 11am, 1:30pm, and 3pm. Free.) A newer tourist attraction is the **Pendleton Underground Tours,** 370 S.W. 1st (276-0730). A hokey but fun look at wild yesteryear, the tour walks through the tunnels used by the Chinese railroad workers and features stops at the Shamrock Cardrooms and the Cozy Rooms Bordello. Tour times vary widely so call ahead. Office hours Mon.-Sat. 8am-5pm.

The second floor of **Hamley's Western Store,** 30 SE Court Ave. (276-2321), is an art gallery. On display are bronze sculptures of men, bronze sculptures of horses, and bronze sculptures of men on horses; there is also a small collection of contemporary Native Art. Ask in front for someone to show you part (surely not all) of the 80-hour saddlemaking process that goes on at the back of the store. (Open Mon.-Sat. 8:30am-5:30pm. Free.) The eclectic **Curio Shop,** 142 S. Main (276-4434), sells everything from Native jewelry and sports pennants to hunting knives and sex aids (open Mon.-Sat. 8:30am-5:30pm).

Pendleton was once an important stop on the ol' **Oregon Trail.** Thousands of weary westward-bound pioneers pulled up their wagons at what is now **Emigrant Springs State Park,** 25 mi. southeast of town on I-84. Exhausted from thousands of miles of prairie and desert, caravans could rest here before the final push to the Promised Land in Portland. The wagon trains are gone now, but big game hunting remains popular in the Blue Mountains; mule deer and Rocky Mountain elk are favorite victims.

WASHINGTON

Washington has two personalities, clearly split by the Cascade Range. While Western Washington is saturated by high rainfall, a concentrated population and a liberal frame of mind, the eastern half is characterized by hot, dry summers, wide-open spaces, and more conservative politics.

Washington natives, whether of Bellingham or Walla Walla, tend to be an independent breed. In 1988, twenty years after a Republican governor founded (and later became president of) the first "alternative" state university (Evergreen), Pat Robertson captured the state's delegates to the Republican convention. State voters do not register political affiliation, but make active use of the initiative and referendum, participate in blanket primaries and gather in caucuses every four years.

Most of Washington's population is clustered around Puget Sound, an area that bustles with international ports and aerospace activity. Seattle life is intimately tied to its arts community and the *New York Times* laments that there is more good theater in Seattle than on Broadway (a backhanded compliment, perhaps). The east is far less congested; residents and tourists can enjoy its rolling countryside without jostling for space. Native American reservations dot the area and rodeos and wineries share the land with equanimity.

The wet portion of Washington ignores the raindrops which keep falling on its head and munches happily on the abundant seafood. Salmon and shellfish are available at the Pike Place Market in Seattle or closer to the source at spots like Dungeness (as in the crab) on the Olympic Peninsula. But pity not the residents of eastern Washington. Time that might otherwise be devoted to cracking geoduck shells can be spent savoring fruit fresh from the orchards of Wenatchee and Yakima.

Washington runs the gamut of terrain; deserts, volcanoes, untouched Pacific Ocean beaches, and the world's only non-tropical rain forest await exploration. There's rafting on the Skagit, Suiattle, Sauk, Yakima, and Wenatchee Rivers; sea kayaking in the San Juan Islands; and sand castle building on the Strait of Juan de Fuca. Beach bums can sleep on the banks of the Columbia or the shores of the Pacific. Mount Rainier has fantastic hiking, while the Cascades boast perfect conditions for nearly every winter activity. Seattle and Spokane drape themselves over equally handsome green landscapes, showing that botany and bottom line can still intersect. Fortunately, Washington is a compact state by Western standards—most places are within a day-trip away.

Practical Information

Capital: Olympia.

Visitor Information: State Tourist Office, Tourism Development Division, 101 General Administration Bldg., Mailstop AX 13, Olympia 98504 (206-753-5600). Open Mon.-Fri. 8am-5pm, phone information 9am-4pm. **Washington State Parks and Recreation Commission,** 7150 Cleanwater Lane, Olympia 98504 (206-753-2027, during summer in WA 800-562-0990). **Forest Service/National Park Service Outdoor Recreation Information Office,** 915 2nd Ave. #442, Seattle 98174 (206-442-0170). Open Mon.-Fri. 8am-5pm.

Emergency: 911.

Time Zone: Pacific (3 hr. behind Eastern).

Postal Abbreviation: WA.

Drinking Age: 21.

Traffic Laws: Mandatory seatbelt law.

Area: 68,192 square miles.

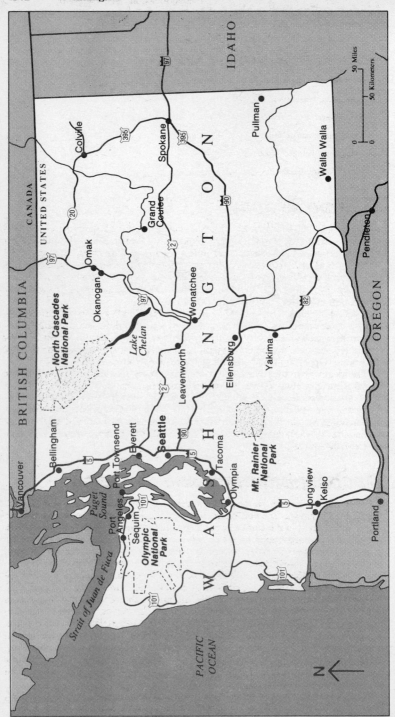

Area Codes: 206 in western Washington, 509 in eastern Washington.

Impractical Information

Nickname: Evergreen State.

State Song: Washington, My Home.

State Flower: Coast Rhododendron.

State Dance: Square Dance.

State Rock: Petrified Wood.

State Mollusk: Geoduck.

Getting Around

Bus remains the cheapest way to travel long distance in Washington. Greyhound serves the two transportation centers, Spokane and Seattle, along with other major cities in between. Local buses cover most of the remaining cities, although a few areas (such as the northwestern Olympic Peninsula) have no bus service. There is one Amtrak **train** line from Los Angeles to Vancouver with many stops in western Washington; another line extends from Seattle to Spokane and on to Chicago. Amtrak serves most large cities along these two lines.

Hitchhiking in the San Juans and on the southern half of Whidbey Island is locally accepted if not legal. Hitching on the Olympic Peninsula is less speedy; hitching in other parts of western Washington is neither speedy nor safe. No Hitchhiking Permitted signs are posted on all highways except those surrounding the town of Raymond. Opportunities for thumbing decrease as you go east.

The ideal way to tour Washington is by **car.** Many startling drives, such as the North Cascades Hwy. (Hwy. 20) and the back entrance into Mt. Rainier (Hwy. 410), are accessible only by automobile. As a rule, roads in Washington are well-maintained and suitable for travel in any kind of vehicle. Gas prices jump 10% over national averages in the San Juan Islands. Two-lane undivided highways are the norm in rural Washington, and parts of western Washington are overrun with massive logging trucks.

Accommodations and Camping

Washington's **hostels** are generally uncrowded, even during July and August. Motel 6 still ranks as the best budget motel, though it's often the most crowded. Cheap hotels exist in downtown areas of most large cities, but safety is not assured.

State park campgrounds have less expensive, more secluded sites than private campgrounds; they give better access to trails, rivers, and lakes. Drivers alike will find state park campgrounds (standard sites $7.50) more accessible than Department of Natural Resources (DNR) and national forest campgrounds. Most campgrounds have sites for hikers and bikers for $3. The state park system charges $10.50 for full hookups and $3 for extra vehicles. Six-minute showers cost 25¢. Some parks allow self-registration; others have rangers register campers at their sites in the evening. Expect long, slow lines if the campground requires registration at the office. Campers who arrive after dusk needn't register until a ranger checks the sites in the morning. The gates open at 6:30am in the summer (8am from October 16 to March 31) and close at 10pm. Most parks stay open year-round, although some close between October and March. Pets must be on an 8-ft. leash and accompanied by owners at all times.

Be aware that several state parks—including Belfair, Birch Bay, Fort Flagler, Steamboat Rock, Fort Canby, Twin Harbors/Grayland Beach, Lake Chelan, Pearrygin Lake, and Moran—accept reservations for Memorial Day through Labor Day and may be filled up weeks in advance, especially during July and August. Reservations can be made in January, and must be done two weeks in advance. Fort Worden, near Port Townsend, also accepts reservations, but only for full-hookup sites.

Drivers can enjoy the solitude of the many National Forest and DNR sites. While some national forest campgrounds cost $5, most cost $2-4, and many others are free. National park campgrounds accessible by road cost $6 on average and are generally in the best settings. Olympic National Park has some free campgrounds accessible by car. Campgrounds that can be reached only by trail are usually free.

Seattle

A city in the shadow of a mountain, Seattle is an odd fusion of big city pretention and small town pace. Here octogenarian architects tote backpacks, university professors row to work, thirtysomething lawyers wear Birkenstocks, and everyone paws through the fresh greens and sea creatures at the Pike Place Market. No one culture dominates the city. Like other major cities in the West, Seattle has long welcomed immigrants from Asia and the city looks increasingly to the Pacific Rim for trade. Recent years have seen countless new buildings go up downtown and the skyline continues to grow denser and higher. In 1990 Seattle presented the Goodwill Games to an international audience, furthering its reputation as a cosmopolitan city.

Surrounded by water on three sides, with mountain ranges to the east and west, every hilltop in the city offers an impressive view. Unfortunately, Seattle spends nearly three quarters of the year blanketed by clouds. Undaunted, residents spend as much time as possible in the great outdoors, bike-riding around the many parks or skiing in the nearby Cascades.

In 1851 pioneers named their new city New York Alki, meaning "New York By and By." These days the mere mention of New York or California is enough to make a native skittish. Prompted by a hometown organization called Lesser Seattle, many inhabitants ballyhoo their city's reputation as the rain capital of the U.S. in an effort to keep the city to themselves. (Actually, Seattle catches less precipitation each year than quite a few other major cities.)

Seattle has spawned musicians such as Jimi Hendrix, Heart, and Mud Honey, and is known nationally for its excellent cultural offerings. The theater community supports Broadway shows and alternative vaudeville while the opera consistently sells out. You can wander among large-scale museums and parks, small galleries, and personable bistros. In other words, there's a lot more to Seattle than is visible from the top of the Space Needle.

Practical Information

Visitor Information: Seattle-King County Visitors Bureau, 666 Stewart St. (461-5840), on the Galleria level of the Convention Center. Enter at Union and 7th. Well-stocked with maps, brochures, newspapers, and transit schedules. Information on the rest of WA. Staff is helpful, though somewhat harried during the summer. Open Mon.-Fri. 8:30am-5pm, Sat. 10am-4pm. From 5-7:30pm, call the airport branch at 433-5218. **Tourism BC,** 720 Olive Way, Seattle 98101 (623-5937). Information on travel to British Columbia. Open Mon.-Fri. 9am-1pm and 2-5pm.

Seattle Parks and Recreation Department: 5201 Green Lake Way N., Seattle 98103 (684-4075). Open Mon.-Fri. 8am-6pm. **National Park Service, Pacific Northwest Region,** 83 S. King St., 3rd floor (442-4830).

Currency Exchange: Deak International, 906 3rd Ave. (623-6203). Open Mon.-Fri. 9am-5pm. **Mutual of Omaha,** behind the American Airlines ticket counter at Sea-Tac Airport (243-1231). Open daily 6am-9pm.

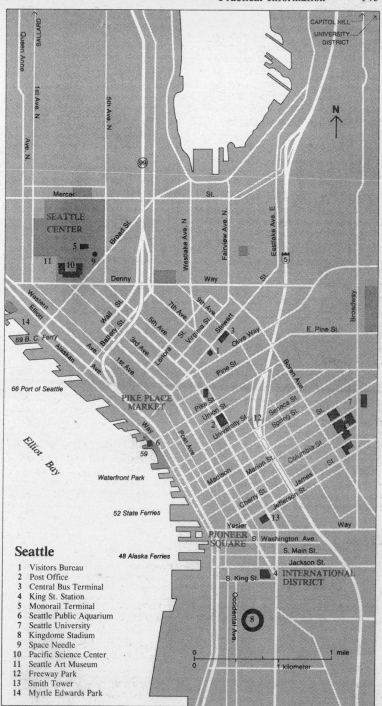

Seattle

1 Visitors Bureau
2 Post Office
3 Central Bus Terminal
4 King St. Station
5 Monorail Terminal
6 Seattle Public Aquarium
7 Seattle University
8 Kingdome Stadium
9 Space Needle
10 Pacific Science Center
11 Seattle Art Museum
12 Freeway Park
13 Smith Tower
14 Myrtle Edwards Park

Airport: Seattle-Tacoma International (Sea-Tac), on Federal Way, south of Seattle proper. General information 433-5217. **Sea-Tac Visitors Information Center** (433-5218), in the central baggage claim area across from carousel 10. Helps with initial transportation questions. Open daily 9:30am-7:30pm. Foreign visitors should contact **Operation Welcome** (433-5367), at the Information Center, where staff members answer questions on customs, immigration, and foreign language services in just about every possible language.

Amtrak: King Street Station, 3rd and Jackson St. (800-872-7245). Trains to: Portland (3 per day, $27), Tacoma ($9), Spokane ($60), San Francisco ($146), and Chicago ($196). Station open daily 6am-10pm; ticket office 5:10am-5:30pm.

Greyhound: 8th Ave. and Stewart St. (624-3456). To: Sea-Tac Airport (4 per day, $2.50), Spokane ($33), Vancouver, BC ($29.95), and Portland (2 per day, $24.95). Open daily 5:30am-9:30pm, midnight-2am.

Green Tortoise Alternative Travel: 324-7433 or 800-227-4766. "Buses" leave from 9th Ave. and Stewart. Trips leave Thurs. and Sun. at 8am for Portland (5 hr., $15), Eugene, OR (7½ hr., $25), Berkeley, CA (26 hr., $49), San Francisco (27 hr., $59), and Los Angeles ($79, Thursday trip only). Reservations are required and should be made 3-4 days in advance. See Getting Around By Bus in the General Introduction for more information.

Metro Transit: Customer Assistance Office, 821 2nd Ave., in the Exchange Building downtown. Open Mon.-Fri. 8am-5pm. 24-hr. information 447-4800. TTY service 684-1739. Fare 55¢; during weekday peak hours 75¢. Buy an All-Day Pass ($2.50; includes 2 monorail tickets) and *really* explore the city. Weekend all-day passes are $1 and do not include monorail tickets. Ride free in the area bordered by Jackson St. on the south, 6th Ave. and I-5 on the east, Battery St. on the north, and the waterfront on the west. Transfers valid for 2 hr. and for Waterfront Streetcars as well.

Ferries: Washington State Ferries, Colman Dock, Pier 52 (464-6400; in WA 800-542-0810 or 800-542-7052). Service to Bremerton on Kitsap Peninsula, Winslow on Bainbridge Island, and passenger-only to Vashon Island. Ferries leave frequently daily 6am-2am. Fares from $3.30; car driver $5.55. **BC Stena Line,** Pier 48, 2700 Alaskan Way (624-6986). Daily cruises on the *Crown Princess* to Victoria, BC. ($30, round-trip $40; ages over 65 $25, round-trip $35; ages 5-11 $15, round-trip $20. Bikes $4, motorcycles $9. Car and driver $40.)

Car Rental: Five & Ten, 14120 Pacific Hwy. S. (246-4434). $17 per day with 100 free miles plus 5¢ per additional mile. Must be 21 with credit card or $120 deposit. Airport pickup. Open Mon.-Sat. 8am-6pm, Sun. 12:30-6pm. **A-19.95-Rent-A-Car,** 804 N. 145th St. (365-1995). $20 per day ($25 under 21) with 100 free miles plus 20¢ per additional mile. Free delivery. Drivers under 21 welcome, must have verifiable auto insurance. Credit card required. **BEST Rent-a-Car,** 6501 Aurora Ave. N (784-2378). $18 per day with 100 free miles plus 10¢ per additional mile. AYH members, $20 per day with 150 free miles. Must be 21 with credit card.

Automobile Club of Washington (AAA): 330 6th Ave. N. (448-5353). Provides maps, tourbooks, and Triptycks to AAA members. Open Mon.-Fri. 8:30am-5pm, Wed. 8:30am-6:30pm.

Ride Board: 1st floor of the Husky Union Building (the HUB), behind Suzallo Library on the UW main campus. Matches cars and riders for destinations across the country. Check the bulletin board at the hostel as well.

Bike Rentals: Gregg's, 7007 Woodlawn Ave. NE (523-1822). 10-speeds and mountain bikes $25 per day; other bikes $3.50 per hr. Must have credit card. Open Mon.-Sat. 9:30am-9pm, Sun. 9:30am-6pm. **The Bicycle Center,** 4529 Sand Point Way (523-8300). 10-speeds only. $4 per hr., $13 per 24 hr. Credit card or license required as deposit. Open Mon.-Thurs. 10am-8pm, Fri.-Sat. 10am-6pm, Sun. noon-5pm. **Alki Bikes,** 2722 Alki Ave. SW (938-3322). Mountain bikes $7 per hr., $17 per day; 10-speeds $4 per hr., $13 per day. Credit card or license required as deposit. Open Mon.-Thurs. 10am-7pm, Fri. 10am-8pm, Sat. 10am-6pm, Sun. noon-5pm.

Bookstores: University Book Store, 4326 University Way NE (634-3400). The second largest college bookstore in the country. Textbooks are in the basement. Good collection of children's books on the 2nd floor. Open Mon.-Wed. and Fri-Sat. 9am-9pm, Thurs. 9am-9pm. **Left Bank Books,** 92 Pike St. (622-0195), in the Pike Place Market. A large leftist bookstore lazily awaiting the revolution. Good prices on new and used books. Open Mon.-Sat. 10am-9pm, Sun. noon-5pm. **Shorey's Book Store,** 110 Union St. (624-0221), downtown. One of the oldest and largest bookstores in the Northwest, Shorey's sells new, used, and rare books. Open Mon.-Sat. 9am-6pm, Sun. noon-6pm. **Elliott Bay Books,** 101 S. Main St. (624-6600) in Pioneer Sq. Vast collection. The store sponsors reading and lecture series. Open Mon.-Sat. 10am-11pm, Sun. noon-6pm. Beauty and the Books, 4213 University Way NE (623-8510). Large collection of used books. Check out the sales in the basement and don't forget to pet the cats. Open daily 10am-10pm.

Seattle Public Library: 1000 4th Ave. (386-4636). Quiet and relaxed modern facility. Pick up a copy of the SPL *Events* newsletter for listings of free lectures, films, and programs. Tours leave the information desk Wed. and Sat. at 2pm. **Quick Information** (386-4636) answers questions about everything from a Plautus quote to the phone number of a Vietnamese deli. Open Mon.-Thurs. 9am-9pm, Fri.-Sat. 9am-6pm, Sun. 1-5pm; June-Aug. Mon.-Sat. only.

Ticket Agencies: Ticket Master, 201 S. King St. #38, Seattle 98104 (628-0888). Open Mon.-Sat. 10am-10pm, Sun. 10am-6pm. **Ticket/Ticket,** 401 Broadway E (324-2744) on the 2nd floor on the Broadway Market. Half-price day-of-show tickets to local theater, music, and dance performances. Cash only. Open Tues.-Sun. 10am-7pm.

Jazz Hotline: 102 S. Jackson (624-5277). Recorded information on area happenings.

Laundromat: Downtown-St. Regis, 116 Stewart St., attached to the St. Regis Hotel (see Accommodations). A somewhat suspicious area, so bring a friend and watch your laundry. Open 24 hr. **Queen Anne Maytag Center,** Queen Anne N. and W. Boston (282-6645). On the top of Queen Anne hill, north of downtown. Attended facility. Take bus #3, 4, or 13. Open daily 7:30am-10:30pm.

Crisis Clinics: 461-3222.

Suicide Prevention: 447-3222. 24 hr.

Seattle Rape Relief: 1825 S. Jackson St., #102 (632-RAPE; 632-7273). 24 hr. Crisis counseling, advocacy and prevention training.

University of Washington Women's Information Center: Cunningham Hall, in the main campus (545-1090). Monthly calendar, networking, and referral for women's groups throughout the Seattle area. Open Mon.-Wed. and Fri. 9am-5pm, Thurs. 9am-9pm.

Senior Citizen Information and Assistance: 1601 2nd, #800 (448-3110). Open Mon.-Fri. 9am-5pm.

Travelers Aid: 909 4th Ave., #630 (461-3888), at Marion, in the YMCA. Free services for stranded travelers who have lost wallets, grandmothers, or their marbles. Open Mon.-Fri. 8:30am-9pm, Sat.-Sun. and holidays 1-5pm.

Operation Nightwatch: 1315½ 1st Ave. (448-8804). Emergency aid in the downtown area. Street ministry operates nightly 9:30pm-2am. Answering machine 24 hr.

International District Emergency Center: 623-3321. Multilingual counselors available. 24 hr.

Fremont Public Association: 3601 Fremont N. (632-1285). Food bank and free legal clinic. Open Mon.-Fri. 8am-5pm.

Poison Information: 526-2121.

AIDS Hotline: 587-4999.

Gay Counseling Service: 329-8707. Open Mon.-Fri. noon-9pm.

Gay/Lesbian Visitors' Guide: 322-0903. Recorded information about entertainment, clubs, and stores that cater to the homosexual community.

Lesbian Resource Center: 1208 E. Pine (322-3953). Support groups, drop-in center, lending library, workshops, and job referrals. Open Mon.-Fri. 2-7pm, Sat. 11am-2pm.

Health Care: Aradia Women's Health Center, 112 Boylston St. E. (323-9388). Appointments are necessary and should be made one week in advance; urgent cases given priority. Staff will refer you elsewhere when booked. Open Mon.-Fri. 10am-6pm. **Country Doctor Community Clinic,** 500 19th Ave. E. (461-4503). Family care. Open Mon.-Tues., Thurs.-Fri. 9am-1pm and 2-5pm, Wed. 6-9pm. Appointments necessary. **Harborview V.D. Clinic,** 325 9th Ave. (223-3590), south wing, 3rd floor in the Harborview Medical Complex. Walk-in only. Open Mon.-Wed., Fri. 7:30am-5pm.; Thurs. 7:30am-7pm; Sat. 7:30am-3pm.

Police Department: 610 3rd Ave. (386-1234).

Fire Department: 301 2nd Ave. S (386-1400).

Post Office: Union St. and 3rd Ave. (442-6255), downtown. Open Mon.-Fri. 8am-5:30pm. General Delivery ZIP Code: 98101.

Area Code: 206.

Getting There and Getting Around

Seattle is a long, skinny city stretched out north to south between long, skinny **Puget Sound** on the west and long, skinny **Lake Washington** on the east. The head of the city is cut from its torso by Lake Union and a string of locks, canals, and bays. These link the saltwater of Puget Sound with the freshwater of Lake Washington. In the downtown area, avenues run northwest to southeast and streets southwest to northeast. After Western Ave. the avenues run numerically up the hill to 6th Ave. Downtown streets run south to north in pairs: Jefferson, James, Cherry, Columbia, Marion, Madison, Spring, Seneca, University, Union, Pike, Pine. To remember the order of the pairs keep repeating "Jesus Christ Made Seattle Under Protest."

Outside the downtown area everything is vastly simplified: avenues run north to south and streets east to west, with only a few exceptions. The city is split into quadrants: 1000 1st Ave. NW is a far cry (and hike) from 1000 1st Ave. S. All city maps and telephone books include grids that impart spatial significance to this alphanumeric cipher.

The city is easily accessible by **car** via I-5, which runs north-south on the eastern side of the downtown area, and by I-90 from the east, which ends its path from Boston just south of the city center. From I-5, take any of the exits from James to Stewart St. to downtown (including Pioneer Square, Pike Place Market, and the waterfront). Take the Mercer St./Fairview Ave. exit to the Seattle Center. The Denny Way exit leads to Capitol Hill, and farther north, the 45th St. exit will take you to the University District. Getting back on the freeway from the downtown area is a challenge, even for long-time residents. The freeway is always visible; just drive around until you spot a blue I-5 sign. I-99 skirts the western side of downtown, offering some of the best views from the Alaskan Way Viaduct. I-99 is less crowded than I-5 and is often the better choice when driving to the northwestern part of the city.

Transportation options from the mammoth **Seattle-Tacoma International Airport (Sea-Tac)** are numerous. **Gray Line coaches** and **limousines** both will whisk you to and from downtown ($6 each way, $11 round-trip). **Greyhound** makes the trip four times daily ($2.50 one-way). Metro buses #174 and 194 are cheaper and run daily every half-hour from 6am-1am. (Fare $1.25 during peak hours, 85¢ off-peak; ages under 18 75¢ during peak hours, 55¢ off-peak.) A taxi ride from the airport to downtown Seattle costs about $22.

Seattle's **Metro Transit** system provides extensive, reliable, and inexpensive service by bus and electric trolley throughout the city and major suburbs. The monorail operates from Westlake Center to the Seattle Center only. The newly-opened bus tunnel should reduce the downtown congestion. The hassles of downtown traffic jams and expensive parking can be avoided by taking the bus. However, making connections all across the city often entails long waits, especially in the evening.

Buses operate daily from 6am to 1 or 2am and a few buses offer "night owl service" from 1:30-4:30am. Express buses do not run on weekends. Fares are based on a two-zone system. Zone 1 includes everything within the city limits (65¢ during peak hours, 55¢ off-peak); Zone 2 comprises anything outside the city limits ($1.25 peak, 85¢ off-peak). Ages 5-17 pay 75¢ peak and 55¢ off-peak in either zone. Ages over 64 and disabled people with reduced fare permits pay 25¢ anywhere at all times. Peak hours in both zones are generally weekdays 6-9am and 3-6pm. Everyone rides free in the **Magic Carpet Zone** downtown (known to everyone but Metro as simply the "ride free zone"), from Jackson St. to Battery St. and between 6th Ave. and the waterfront. The free zone does not apply at night. Drivers usually announce when the bus passes out of the free zone. Transfers are free and valid for two hours anywhere in Zone 1 if you board in that zone, or in either Zone 1 or 2 if you board in Zone 2.

A number of pass options are available. The **All-Day Pass** provides unlimited travel on weekdays (available from the driver, $2.50). But the real steal comes on the weekends when an all-day pass is only $1. On Sundays and holidays two children ages 5-15 ride free with an adult. For long-term visitors, the **Monthly Pass Plus** is a godsend. Two-zone unlimited travel for one month costs $42, one-zone just $26. The pass is valid at all times and comes with a wealth of discounts on theater tickets, restaurants, museums, shops, and travel agencies. Senior citizens and disabled riders can obtain a $2 monthly sticker to go on their reduced fare permit, allowing them to travel anywhere in the system for free. All passes, as well as timetables and a free, comprehensive map, are available from the Metro Customer Assistance Office (see Practical Information). **Timetables** and **maps** are also available at public libraries, 7-11 stores, Wendy's, Albertson's, the visitors bureau, and on buses.

Routes and buses equipped with lifts are marked by blue **wheelchair accessibility** signs. **Bike racks** for two bicycles are also placed on the front of the buses that run from downtown Seattle to Bellevue and Kirkland. Not all buses are equipped with racks and bikes can be loaded only at designated stops; check out Metro's "Bike & Ride" pamphlet for the particulars.

Metro extends into Seattle's outskirts, covering the whole of King County as far east as North Bend and Carnation, south to Enumclaw, and north to Snohomish County, where Metro bus #6 hooks up with Community Transit. This line runs to Everett, Stanwood, and well into the Cascades. Metro bus #174 connects in Federal Way to Tacoma's Pierce County System. (See Tacoma and Near Seattle for more information.)

Accommodations

The Seattle International Hostel is undoubtedly the best option for the budget traveler staying downtown. For those tired of the urban scene, the Vashon Island Hostel is ideal. (From downtown take bus #54 to the Fautleroy dock. See Tacoma Accommodations.) **Pacific Bed and Breakfast,** 701 NW 60th St., Seattle 98107 (784-0539), can set you up with an interesting B&B in the $40-85 range for a single. (Open Mon.-Fri. 9am-5pm.)

Downtown

Seattle International Hostel (AYH), 84 Union St. (622-5443), at Western Ave. 125 beds in sterile rooms, immaculate facilities, plenty of modern amenities, and a friendly, knowledgeable staff. Check-in may be tedious and security tight, but the location is convenient and the crowd alluring. Loads of information about Seattle in the library and on the brochure racks. The view of the bay will mollify your temper when the traffic gets too loud. Sleep sacks required. Open daily 7-10am and 5pm-midnight. Members $10, nonmembers $13.

YMCA, 909 4th Ave. (382-5000), near the Madison St. intersection. Men and women welcome; must be over 17. Small but well-kept rooms. The dorm bunks available for AYH members are far inferior to the hostel's. Good location, tight security. Free local calls from in-room phone, TV lounge on each floor (color TVs in some rooms), laundry facilities, and use of swimming pool and fitness facilities. Clean and pleasant. No curfew. Singles from $37.51. Doubles from $44. Weekly: singles from $157.76, doubles from $180. AYH members pay $16.97 for a dorm bunk. Weekly rates may be applied after three days.

YWCA, 1118 5th Ave. (461-4888), near the YMCA. Take any 4th Ave. bus to Seneca St. Women only, ages under 18 require advance arrangement. Great security and location, but an older and less elegant facility than the YMCA. Housing desk open 24 hr. No curfew. Singles $24, with bath $29. Doubles $35, with bath $39. Weekly: singles $143, with bath $173. Additional charge for health center use. Key deposit $2.

St. Regis Hotel, 116 Stewart St. (448-6366), 2 blocks from the Pike Place Market. Pleasant management and excellent security. The neighborhood is a little squalid, though. No visitors after 10pm. Laundromat on the first floor. Singles $25, with bath $31. Doubles $31, with bath $37.

Moore Motel, 2nd and Virginia (448-4852). Next to the historic Moore Theater. Big rooms include 2 beds, bath and TV. $39, single or double occupancy.

Pacific Hotel, 317 Marion St. (622-3985), between 3rd and 4th Ave. Recently renovated and upgraded and the prices reflect it. Quiet location, not as safe as it could be. Nice rooms, rickety old elevator. Singles $45, doubles $55.

Commodore Hotel, 2013 2nd Ave. (448-8868), at Virginia. Not as well-kept as the other hotels but clean and seemingly safe. AYH members can get a dorm bed for $11. If you're willing to sacrifice color TV and private bath the rates are a real bargain. Singles $19.50, with color TV and bath, $35. Doubles $24, with 2 beds and bath $42.

Other Neighborhoods

Park Plaza Hotel, 4401 Aurora Ave. N. (632-2101). Just north of the Aurora bridge. Surprisingly quiet. The orange external decor is unfortunately repeated inside as well. Singles $28. Doubles from $30.

Nites Inn, 11746 Aurora Ave. N. (365-3216). One of the many motels that line Aurora north of 85th St. (Take bus #6.) This one rises above the usual sleaze with professional service. Singles $32. Doubles $34.

Hillside Motel, 2451 Aurora Ave. N. (285-7860). Just south of the bridge. 11 small units with hot plates. Very noisy. Singles $30. doubles $35.

Motel 6, 18900 47th Ave. S. (241-1648), exit 152 off I-5. Take bus #194. Near Sea-Tac but very inconvenient to downtown. Crowded, make reservations. Singles $29.78. Doubles $36.41.

The College Inn, 4000 University Way NE (633-4441). European-style B&B in the University District. Breakfast served in a lovely refinished attic. Antiques and individual wash basins in every room. The rooms facing 40th are the quietest. Singles from $37. Doubles from $45.41.

Food

By a Sound full of fish and in a state tacked in place by orchards, Seattle rivals San Francisco in culinary excitement and eclecticism. City center eateries range from ritzy shops along 5th Ave. to skid-row coffee houses along 1st. Avoid the many boring diners and pseudo-health-food rip-offs. Fresh seafood and produce are always in season. If you want to eat in, buy fish right off the boats at **Fisherman's Wharf,** at NW 54th St. and 30th Ave. NW in Ballard, along bus route #43. The wharf is usually open from 8am to 3 or 4pm. Or visit one of Seattle's active **food coops,** such as those located at 6518 Fremont N. in Greenlake and at 6504 20th NE in the Ravenna District north of the university. Also in Ravenna is a fine produce stand, **Rising Sun Farms and Produce,** 6505 15th Ave. NE (524-9741).

Seattlites are serious about coffee. When civic leaders visited Philadelphia last year, they brought their own beans. Espresso stands dot almost every corner of downtown (a local favorite is the one in front of Nordstrom's on 5th Ave.) and every restaurant and café serves espresso drinks. The two major local roasters are **Starbuck's** and **SBC.** Both have many shops downtown.

Pike Place Market

Farmers have been selling their own produce here since 1907, when angry Seattle citizens demanded an alternative to the middle merchant. A nasty fire in 1941, the draft, and the internment of Japanese-Americans during World War II almost did away with the market, but in the last 15 years, a rehabilitation drive has restored it. Lunatic fishmongers and produce sellers bellow at customers and at each other while street performers do their thing and, all the while, unsuspecting tourists wonder what they've walked into. Seattlites accept the whole affair with equanimity and elbow their way through at day's end in search of something special for dinner. The market's interesting conglomeration of self- and full-service restaurants allows you to duck the crowds. Chic shops and restaurants proliferate, but the farmers and fishmongers are the mainstays of the market. Hunt around for end-of-the-day specials on produce, and don't forget to put some quarters into Rachel, the life-sized brass piggy underneath the clock. The monthly *Pike Place Market News,* available free throughout the market, has a map of the market, and the low-down on the latest events, new merchants, and old-timers. An information table in front of the bakery in the main market can answer your questions. (Table and market open Mon.-Sat. 9am-6pm; many stands also open Sun.)

El Puerco Lloron, 1501 Western Ave. (624-0541), at the 2nd level of the Hillclimb overlooking the waterfront. Some of the best Mexican food in Seattle—no nachos here. The entire place has been transplanted from Tijuana, down to the wooden masks, bird cages, *piñatas,* card tables, and folding chairs. Two tamales $3.75. Open Mon.-Sat. 11:30am-9pm, Sun. noon-7pm.

The Market Café, 1523 1st Ave. (624-2598). Good food, tremendous portions. Breakfasts are especially overwhelming—the $4.50 *huevos rancheros* keep you going until the next morning. Try the black beans with rice ($3.25) at lunch. Open Mon.-Sat. 7:30am-5pm.

Soundview Café (623-5700), on the mezzanine level in the Main Arcade. This wholesome self-serve sandwich-and-salad bar offers fresh food, a spectacular view of the Sound, and occasional poetry readings. Get a View Special (eggs and potatoes) for $2.60, try the West African nut stew ($2), or bring a brown-bag lunch—the café provides public seating. Open Mon.-Sat. 7am-5pm.

World Class Chili, 1411 1st Ave. (623-3678), in the South Arcade. And you thought real chili didn't exist this far north. Do penance while eating a Texas-sized portion of Seattle's best ($3.50). Four different kinds to choose from; California-style contains chicken instead of beef. Open Mon.-Sat. 11am-6pm.

Copacabana, 1520½ Pike Pl. (622-6359). Music and passion are always in fashion. The outdoor tables are probably the best place in the market to watch the harried crowds go by. Try the Bolivian *salteñas,* the house specialty (meat and raisin pastries, $3). Open Mon.-Thurs. 11:30am-4pm, Fri.-Sat. 11:30am-9pm.

Three Girls Bakery, corner of Pike and Pike Pl. (622-1045). Order to go or sit in the café. The display alone will make you drool. Mammoth apple fritters for 85¢. Open market hours.

Emmett Watson's Oyster Bar, 1916 Pike Pl. (488-7721). Watson is the local columnist and California-basher who founded Lesser Seattle (motto: Keep the Bastards Out). The restaurant isn't as interesting as the crusty old legend himself but the patio is pretty and the oysters plentiful. You haven't really experienced oysters until you've tried the Oyster Bar Special ($5.25). Open Mon-Fri. 6:30-10:30am, Sat.-Sun. 8-11am; daily 11:15am-6pm.

Athenian Inn, 1517 Pike Pl. (624-7166), in the main market. A Seattle tradition, but mostly because of its age (over 80) and location. Dinners are expensive but the breakfast options are cheap and intriguing. Philadelphia Scrapple and Bacon is $5.25. Sit at the bar and ponder why all old restaurants have dark wood paneling. 16 varieties of beer on tap. Open daily 7am-7pm.

International District

Along King and Jackson St., between 5th and 8th Ave., Seattle's International District crowds together immigrants—and chefs—from China, Japan, the Philippines, and Southeast Asia. Fierce competition keeps prices low and quality high. Don't shy away from a shabby exterior—the quality of the facade is often inversely proportional to the quality of the food. **Uwajimaya,** the largest Asian retail store in the Pacific Northwest, is at 519 6th Ave. S. (624-6248). A huge selection of Japanese staples, fresh (often still swimming) seafood, wide variety of dried and/or instant foods (great for camping), a sushi bar, and a bakery make this Seattle institution a must. Don't overlook the gift shop and bookstore upstairs. (Open daily 9am-6pm.) Take bus #7.

A Little Bit of Saigon, 12th and S. Jackson (325-3663). Large Vietnamese restaurant. A favorite with immigrants and the more trendy restaurant-hopping crowd fed up with Thai food.

Chau's Chinese Restaurant, 4th and Jackson (621-0006). The best in late night seafood if not in decor. Try the geoduck with ginger sauce ($5.75). Open Mon.-Thurs. 11am-12:30am, Fri. 11am-1am, Sat. 4pm-1am, Sun. 4pm-11:30pm.

Ho Ho Seafood Restaurant, 653 S. Weller St. (382-9671). Elegant yet laid-back. Generous portions. Great seafood. Check the blackboard for daily specials. Santa's favorite. Entrees $4.50-10. Open Sun.-Thurs. 11am-1am, Fri.-Sat. 11am-3am.

House of Hong Restaurant, 409 8th Ave. S. (622-7997), at Jackson. May not look like much from the outside, but serves up the most popular *dim sum* in town ($10, 11am-3pm). Open Sun.-Thurs. 11am-10pm, Fri.-Sat. 11am-midnight. Reservations recommended.

Lao Chorearn Restaurant, 121 Prefontaine Pl. S. (223-9456). Exquisite Laotian cuisine. Slightly pricier (albeit slightly snazzier) than the Viet My next door. Experience *soom tun* (green papaya salad with peanuts, shrimp, chili, and lime) for $3. One-block-long Prefontaine Pl. is impossible to find by name; look for Washington and 4th. Open Mon.-Fri. 11am-3pm and 5-9pm, Sat. 1-9pm.

Phnom Penh Noodle Soup House, 414 Maynard Ave. S. (682-5690). Excellent Cambodian cuisine. Head to the upstairs dining room for a good view of the park and a large bowl of noodles. Try the #1, the Phnom Penh Noodle Special ($3.50). Some people come here every week and never order anything else. Open Mon.-Tues, Thurs. 8:30am-6pm, Fri.-Sat. 8:30am-7pm, Sun. 8:30am-6pm.

Viet My Restaurant, 129 Prefontaine Pl. S. (464-8681). Not the place for a first date, but consistently delicious Vietnamese food at great prices. Try *bo la lot* (beef in rice pancakes, $3.50), or shrimp curry ($4.25). Avoid the lunch rush. Open Mon.-Sat. 11am-8pm.

Pioneer Square

Historic Pioneer Square is an area of *haute couture* and *haute* prices. The best strategy is to pack a lunch and picnic in Occidental Park or Waterfall Park, along with the myriad street people.

Trattoria Mitchelli, 84 Yesler Way (623-3883), toward the waterfront. A warm, cozy place to eat breakfast and an elegant late night café. Lunch on a large antipasto ($5) or the pasta of the week ($4-5). Dinners from $9. Open Mon.-Fri. 7am-4am, Sat. 8am-4am, Sun. 8am-10pm.

Ivar's Fish Bar, Pier 54 (624-6852), on the waterfront. One of a string of seafood restaurants founded by and named for the late Seattle celebrity Ivar Haglund. This locals' favorite charges $2.89 for fish and chips, and serves the definitive Seattle clam chowder. Dine with the gulls and pigeons in covered booths ouside. Open daily 11am-2am.

The Bakery, 214 1st Ave. S. (622-3644). Walk-up cafe and deli in the Grand Central Arcade. Buy a loaf of bread for $2.85 or Irish soda bread for 85¢. Come early—these famous pastries sell out fast. Eat at outdoor tables in the attractive antique arcade or in Occidental Park. Open Mon.-Fri. 7am-6pm, Sat.-Sun. 9am-5pm. Espresso ($1.50) bar open daily 11am-5pm.

Elliott Bay Book Company and Café, 101 S. Main St. (682-6664). Free coffee refill to get you through the duller patches of *Middlemarch.* Sandwiches $3.50-4.50. Café open Mon.-Fri. 7am-10:30pm, Sat. 10am-10:30pm, Sun. 11am-5pm. See bookstore listing under Practical Information.

Fran-Glor's Creole Café, 547 1st Ave. S (682-1578) near the Viaduct. Genuine gumbo with crabmeat, sausage, and who knows what else. The bric-a-brac and the jazz are vintage New Orleans. Eclectic poster collection. Lunches from $4.50. Open Tues.-Sat. noon-9pm.

Capitol Hill

Climb the low hill northeast of downtown and scout the blocks along Broadway between Seattle University and Volunteer Park for Fellini-esque frolics. The Broadway Theatre is now a Pay 'n Save and Trattoria Paslincci has been replaced by a copy store, but Dick's is still going strong—they haven't paved over the dance steps yet. **15th Street** is more sedate, a pleasant yuppie lane with a twist. The imaginative shops, elegant clubs, and espresso houses which drape Capitol Hill are particularly popular among Seattle's gay community. Bus #7 goes along Broadway, #10 along 15th St.

Dick's, 115 Broadway Ave. E (323-1300). A Broadway institution, recently made famous in Sir Mix-A-Lot's rap "Broadway." The first place homesick Seattlites go when they return after a long trip, this local drive-in burger chain also has locations in Wallingford, Queen Anne and Lake City. Dick's Deluxe Burger ($1.50). Good shakes (90¢). Open 10:30am-2am.

Gravity Bar, 415 Broadway E (325-7186) in the Broadway Market. Blast off from a table or kneel at the bar. Infamous fruit and vegetarian drinks. Try the DennisHopper (carrot, beet, and garlic) for $3.50. Open Mon.-Fri. 8am-11:30pm, Sat.-Sun. 8am-12:30am.

Deluxe Bar and Grill, 625 Broadway E. (324-9697). A jazzy indoor/outdoor joint where you can enjoy great breakfasts for under $4. Sampler of any 3 beers $3.25. Open Mon.-Thurs. 10am-11pm, Fri. 10am-1am, Sat.-Sun. 9am-1am. Bar open Mon.-Wed. 10am-1am, Thurs.-Fri. 10am-2am, Sat.-Sun. 9am-2am.

Matzoh Mamma's, 15th and Republican (324-MAMA). Kosher-style (not *glatt* kosher) deli and restaurant. Try the chicken soup ($2.75) or the *Nudnik* sandwich ($6.95). Eat eat eat. Open daily 7:30am-9pm.

Giorgina's Pizza, 131 15th Ave. E (329-8118). Great New York-style pizza, across the street from Group Health. The adventurous should try the Ardriana pizza (ham, artichoke hearts, and zucchini). Half pizzas $6-10. Slices also available upon request. Open Mon.-Thurs. 11am-10pm, Fri. 11am-11pm, Sat. noon-11pm, Sun 4-10pm.

The Cause Celebre, 524 E. 15th Ave. (323-1888), at Mercer St. The special province of Seattle's well-fed left. Stay away if you don't like feminist music or neighboring discussions on Bob Avakian and the struggle for Chinese succession. Alfresco dining on the spacious porch. The homemade ice cream and baked goods are sublime. Free evening entertainment. Great Sun. brunch. Lunch sandwiches $3-6. Open Mon., Wed.-Sat 9am-9pm; Tues., Sun. 9am-5:30pm.

Kidd Valley, 135 15th Ave. E (328-8133). Next to Giorgino's. Local upscale burger chain known for their extremely messy, extremely yummy burgers ($2-3) and fantastic shakes ($1). Open Mon.-Fri. 7am-9pm, Sat.-Sun. 8am-9pm.

Kokeb Restaurant, 926 12th Ave. (322-0485). Behind Seattle University at the far south end of Capitol Hill, near the First Hill neighborhood. An intriguing Ethiopian restaurant that serves hot and spicy meat stews on spongy *injera* bread. Very purple. Entrees $8-9. Open Mon.-Fri. 5-10pm, Sat.-Sun. 5pm-2am.

Piecora's Pizzeria, 1401 E. Madison St. (322-9411), a few blocks southeast of most of the action. Your basic New York-style pizza parlor, replete with olive oil and Brooklyn accents served in what looks like a converted firehouse. Interesting crowd. Half-pizza $5. Lunch special $3.75. Open Mon.-Thurs. 11:30am-11pm, Fri. 11:30am-midnight, Sat. noon-midnight, Sun. noon-10pm.

University District

The titanic **University of Washington,** between Union and Portage Bays (north of downtown), supports a colorful neighborhood of funky shops, ethnic restaurants, and coffeehouses—lots of coffeehouses. Most of the good restaurants, jazz clubs, cinemas, and cafés are within a few blocks of **University Way.** Ask for University Way, however, and prepare for puzzled looks. It's know as "the Ave." (one syllable) to locals. To reach the university, take buses #70-74 from downtown. Buses #7 and 43 get there via Capitol Hill.

Last Exit on Brooklyn, 3930 Brooklyn Ave. NE (545-9873), 1 block west of University Way at NE 40th St. The Exit never quite left the 60s and aging hippies watch aspiring chessmasters (Yasser Seirawan got his start here) battle it out in a large smoky room. Dirt-cheap espresso (60¢). Try the espresso float ($1.45) or the honey bran loaf (75¢). Open mike Mon. at 9pm. Open Mon.-Thurs. 7am-midnight, Fri. 7am-2am, Sat. 11am-2am, Sun. 11am-midnight.

Ezell's, 4216 University Wy. NE (548-1455). Possibly the best fried chicken west of the Mississippi. Order the spicy version of the snack pack (leg or thigh, fries and a roll) for $2.39. Their rolls are good enough to be dessert themselves, but Ezell's poundcake and other scrumptious desserts are impossible to pass up (Oprah Winfrey broke her famous diet here when she couldn't pass them up). The original Ezell's (501 23rd, across from Garfield High School) is in the Central District. Open Mon.-Sat. 10am-11pm, Sun. 11am-10pm.

Unique Café, 4228 University Wy. NE (623-2181). A recent and welcomed addition to the plethora of area coffeehouses. This quiet, spacious café offers cheap espresso drinks (75¢-$1.50) and excellent desserts. Try the carrot bread ($1). Open Mon.-Fri. 8am-11pm, Sat.-Sun. 9am-10pm.

Macheesmo Mouse, 4129 University Wy. NE. Healthy Mexican fast food in a neon setting. This West Coast chain has other Seattle locations, including one on Broadway. Try the chicken majita for only $4.95 and 860 calories. Open Mon.-Sat. 11am-9pm, Sun. noon-9pm.

Silence-Heart Nest, 55th and University Wy. NE (524-4008). Vegetarian and Indian food served up by followers of Sri Chimnoy. Try *calananda* (described as East Indian calzone) or the Bliss-Burger ($4 each). Open Mon.-Tues., Thurs. 11am-8pm; Wed. 11am-3pm; Fri.-Sat. 11am-9pm.

Asia Deli, 4235 University Way NE (632-2364). No corned beef here—this atypical deli offers quick service and generous portions of delicious Vietnamese and Thai food (mostly of the noodle persuasion). Try the sauté chicken and onions ($3.45), and don't forget the banana with tapioca in coconut milk (90¢), a superb palate cleanser. Open Mon.-Sat. 11am-9pm, Sun. noon-8pm.

The Unicorn Restaurant, 4550 University Way (634-1115). Renowned for its large collection of obscure English ales ($2.50-3), the Unicorn also cooks up a mean steak-and-kidney pie ($6). Try their afternoon special of tea and scones ($2.50). Open Mon.-Sat. 11:30am-10pm, Sun. 5-9pm.

Grand Illusion Cinema and Espresso, 1405 50th St. NE (525-9573), at University Way. Relaxing coffeehouse with an overstuffed green couch in front of the working fireplace. Small wooden terrace and in-house theater (see Entertainment). Hot and cold coffees and other drinks 60¢-$2. Try the whole wheat cream scone (70¢). Open Mon.-Sat. 8:30am-11:30pm, Sun. 8:30am-10:30pm.

Dankens, 45th and University Way NE. Good ice cream made in the store. Known nationally for their Chocolate Decadence. One scoop $1.30. Open Mon.-Thurs. noon-11:30pm, Fri.-Sat. noon-12:30am, Sun. noon-11pm.

Arnold's Fun Food and Games, 3947 University Way NE (633-2181). An updated version of its *Happy Days* namesake, this cheap hamburger joint has become a hangout for local Joanies and Chachies. Doughnut and coffee 50¢. Huskyburger and fries $3. Save your quarters to use on the jungle of video games. Open Sun.-Thurs. 7am-midnight, Fri.-Sat. 7am-2am.

Espresso Roma Café, 4201 University Way NE (633-2534). The best thing about it is its location in the heart of the Ave.—sit at outdoor tables and watch the crowds. But the cement basement decor and the higher prices make this café otherwise inferior to the other Ave. coffeehouses. Muffins ($1.30). Open Mon.-Fri. 7am-midnight, Sat.-Sun. 8am-midnight.

Other Neighborhoods

Burk's Cafe-Creole and Cajun, 5411 Ballard Ave. (782-0091). A relaxed Creole cafe. Lunch sandwiches reasonably priced at $5, dinners $7-11. Try the crawfish with remoulade sauce ($4.95). A bowl of pickled okra sits at every table. Open Mon.-Sat. 11am-10pm.

Zesto's Burger and Fish House, 6416 15th NW (783-3350). This Ballard High hangout has been serving students and frying fish since 1952, and even local fishermen rave about Zesto's "oriental-style" batter. Filling fish and chips dinners run $4, and distinctive "snowshoe" fries make the deal a good one. Good burgers ($1.70-4.85), too. Open Mon.-Fri. 9am-11pm, Sat.-Sun. 11am-11pm.

Greenlake Jake's, 7918 E. Greenlake Dr. N. (523-4747), on the north shore of Green Lake. A favorite drive-in (or roll-in) for the lake's runners, skateboarders, and roller skaters. Great breakfasts. 2 blueberry muffins $1.50. Large lunches. Open daily 7am-9pm.

Spud, 6860 E. Greenlake Way N., across the lake from Greenlake Jake's. Serving the Seattle staple of fish and chips ($2) for 51 years. Clams and chips $2.10. Open daily 11am-10pm.

The Dog House, 2230 7th Ave. (624-2741), 3 blocks north of Greyhound between Bell and Blanchard St. This 24 hr. Seattle favorite is perfect for the night you arrive at Greyhound with no place to go. The waitresses will call you "honey" and Dick Dickerson will serenade you on the electric organ Wed.-Sun. 9pm-1:30am. Although the diner caters almost exclusively to locals, the prices run high. Try the Mutt Burger ($3.50). Full bar open daily 6am-2am.

Julia's 14 Carrot Café, 2305 Eastlake E. (324-1442), between Lake Union and I-5 at Lynn St. Only Julia's could make edible nut burgers which don't crumble, dry up, or stick in the back of your throat ($3.50). Great baked goods, too. Open Mon. 7am-2pm, Tues.-Sat. 7am-10pm, Sun. 8am-3pm.

Sights and Activities

If you are a latter-day Phineas Fogg with only a day to spare in Seattle, despair not. In one day of dedicated sightseeing you can cover a good deal of the city. Many sights are within walking distance of each other, or are within Metro's free zone. You can easily explore the market, waterfront, Pioneer Square, and International District in one excursion. But don't ignore the more relaxing natural sights. Take a rowboat out on Lake Union, bicycle along Lake Washington or hike through the wilds of Discovery Park.

The Downtown, Waterfront, and Seattle Center

Westlake Park, with its art deco brick patterns and "Wall of Water" is a good place to take a break and listen to the steel drums. This small triangular park, on Pike St. between 5th and 4th Ave., is bordered by the original Nordstrom's and the gleaming new Westlake Center. Take a quick jaunt to the southeast to the new green glass **Convention Center,** which houses great artwork as well as tourists. Next to the Convention Center is **Freeway Park,** a delightful oasis of greenery and waterfalls on Seneca St. at 7th Ave. Both the Convention Center and the part were built right over I-5. Many of the business district high rises warrant a closer look. **The Pacific First Centre** at 5th and Pike diplays a breathtaking collection of glass art commissioned from the prestigious Pilchuk School. Other notable buildings include the **Washington Mutual Tower** on 3rd Ave. and the complex of buildings around 6th and Union.

A short walk down Pike St. is the **Pike Place Market,** a public market frequented by tourists and natives in equal proportions. Local farmers, fish vendors, bakeries, craft sellers, restaurants and boutiques layer into a three-block indoor/outdoor area. An information table at the corner of Pike St. and Pike Pl. (across from the newsstand) provides information about market history as well as shop (and restroom) locations. (Market open Mon.-Sat. 9am-6pm. Information booth open Mon.-Sat. 10am-5pm.)

The **Pike Place Hillclimb** descends from the south end of the market down a set of staircases leading past more chic shops and ethnic restaurants to Alaskan Way and the **waterfront.** (An elevator is also available.) The **Seattle Aquarium** (625-4357) sits at the base of the Hillclimb at Pier 59. Outdoor tanks re-create the ecosystems of salt marshes and tidal pools, employing marine birds and mammals as well as members of the finny tribe. The aquarium's star attraction is the 360° Puget Sound tank, alone worth the price of admission. Don't miss the daily 11:30am feeding. (Open daily 10am-7pm; Labor Day-Memorial Day 10am-5pm. Admission $4.50, senior citizens and ages 13-18 $2.50, ages 6-12 $1.75.)

Next to the Aquarium is **Omnidome** (622-1868). The only good thing about this large wrap-around movie screen is that you get two movies for the price of one. The theater and the screen are of marginal quality and neither film uses the Omnidome format particularly well. *The Eruption of Mt. St. Helens* offers some striking photography but little else. It alternates every half-hour with *Nomads of the Deep,* a preachy film about frolicking humpback whales. On the whole, save your money and see the infinitely better IMAX at the Pacific Science Center. (Films shown daily 10am-8pm. Tickets to 2 movies $5, senior citizens and students $4, ages 6-12 $3; with admission to aquarium $8, senior citizens and ages 13-18 $5.50, ages 6-12 $3.75.)

Pier 59 and the aquarium are geographically in the middle of the waterfront district. Explore north or south by foot or by **streetcar.** The circa-1927 cars were imported from Melbourne, Australia in 1982; Seattle sold its original streetcars to San Francisco, where they now enjoy international fame. (Streetcars run every 20 min. Mon.-Sat. 7am-11pm, Sun. 10:15am-9:45pm; in winter every ½-hr. until 6pm. 60¢ for 1½ hour of unlimited travel. Metro passes are good on the streetcar. On Sun., under 16 ride free with 1 paying passenger.)

North of Pier 70's tourist-priced shopping arcade, **Myrtle Edwards Park** stretches along the water to the granaries on Piers 90 and 91. Despite lovely grassy areas and equally good views, Myrtle Edwards is frequented less than other downtown parks (perhaps it's the name).

South of the aquarium two companies offer tours of the Elliott Bay harbor. Both tours sail past the Coast Guard outposts around Harbor Island and Alki Point, the site of the first European settlement in Seattle. **Harbor Tours** (623-1445) leaves from Pier 56 (June-Sept. 5 per day; May and Oct. 3 per day. Fare $7.50, senior citizens $6.50, teens $5, and children $3). A recent entrant into the historic harbor tour racket, **Major Marine Tours** (783-8873) includes a barbeque chicken dinner with their tour. Tours noon to 6pm daily departing on the hour from Pier 54. (June-Sept. fare $6.50, senior citizens $5.50, children $4.) Also from Pier 56, ferries leave for **Blake Island Marine State Park** twice per day during the summer. After a narrated tour of the harbor, the ferry docks at **Tillicum Village,** where you'll eat "Indian-style" salmon in a long house, visit a wood carver, and watch a "rare presentation" of Native dance and other Native activities. The package (with dinner) lasts 4 hours and costs $32 (senior citizens $29, youths $21, children $12). Call 443-1244 for more details.

Among the many tourist shops along the waterfront **Ye Olde Curiosity Shop** on Pier 54 deserves note. Founded in 1899 this locally famous part-museum/part-store displays such items as the dehydrated body of "Sylvester" and Siamese twin calves.

Colman Dock, Pier 52, is now the departure point for the Washington State Ferries to Bremerton and Bainbridge Island (see Getting There). Taking a ferry to Bremerton or Winslow (on Bainbridge Island) is a glorious way to see Seattle, even if you just turn around and come back. Round-trip fare is $3.30 for a pedestrian, $6.15 for a car and driver. The dock has gone through a number of incarnations and was at one time the home base of the Mosquito Fleet. Pick up a free copy of the *Historic Old Colman Dock* pamphlet inside the terminal for stories of the dock's—and Seattle's—past. Today, Colman Dock pales in comparison to its past; in fact, it's pretty boring.

Take the monorail from the third floor of the Westlake Center to **Seattle Center.** The 74-acre, pedestrians-only park was originally constructed for the 1962 World's Fair and still attracts thousands of sightseers daily. Located between Denny Way and W. Mercer St., and 1st and 5th Ave., the Center has eight gates, each equipped with a model of the Center and a key to its facilities. The **Pacific Science Center** (443-2001), within the park, houses a **laserium** (443-2850) and an IMAX theater (443-4629) in addition to other interesting displays. The laser and IMAX shows are among the finest entertainment in the city. (Science Center open daily 10am-6pm; Labor Day-June Mon.-Fri. 10am-5pm, Sat.-Sun. 10am-6pm. Admission $5, senior citizens and ages 6-13 $4, ages 2-5 $3.) Laser and IMAX shows are $1 extra apiece. Evening IMAX shows run Thurs.-Sun. $4, senior citizens and ages 6-13 $3, ages 2-5 $2. The evening laser shows rock to music by groups such as U2 and Led Zeppelin. Tues.-Sun., $5.50. The **Space Needle** (443-2100), sometimes known as "the world's tackiest monument," has an observation tower and restaurant. On clear days, the view from atop is without peer; on cloudy days, forget it. (Admission $4.75, ages 5-12 $2.75.) After working up an appetite in the Center's amusement park, head next door to the **Center House,** home to dozens of shops and restaurants. Food offerings range from Mongolian to Mexican. (Open in summer daily 11am-9pm; in spring 11am-7pm; in fall and winter Sun.-Thurs. 11am-6pm, Fri.-Sat. 11am-9pm.)

Although Seattlites generally disdain the Center (leaving it to tourists and suburbanites), they do turn out for the frequently held performances, special exhibits, and festivals. For recorded information regarding special events and permanent attractions at the Center, call 684-7165. The Center has an **information desk** (625-4234) on the court level in the Center House. (Open daily 1-4pm.) The visitors bureau (447-4244) also runs an **information booth** next to the monorail terminal. (Open Memorial Day-Labor Day daily 10am-6pm.) See Seasonal Events for information on the ever-popular Folklife Festival, the Bite of Seattle, and Bumbershoot, all held annually at the Center.

Pioneer Square and International District

From the waterfront, it's just 2 blocks to historic Pioneer Square, where 19th-century warehouses and office buildings were restored in a tantrum of prosperity during the 70s. The *Compleat Browser's Guide to Pioneer Square,* available in area bookstores, provides a short history and walking tour, in addition to listings of all the shops, galleries, restaurants, and museums in the square. After an aborted attempt by pioneers to claim the land on Alki Beach (now West Seattle) in 1851, the settlers settled instead on the site which is today Pioneer Square; this area quickly became Seattle's first city center. "Doc" Maynard, a notorious early resident, gave a plot of land here to one Henry Yesler on the condition that he build a steam-powered lumber mill. No sooner said than done, the mill was fed with logs dragged down the steep grade of Yesler Way, earning that street the epithet "Skid Row." Years later, the center of activity moved north, sending Pioneer Square into decline, thereby coining "skid row" as the term for a neighborhood of utter poverty and despair.

When Seattle nearly burned to the ground in 1889, an ordinance was passed to raise the city 35 ft. At first, shops below the elevated streets remained open for business and were moored to the upper city by an elaborate network of stairs. In 1907 the city moved upstairs permanently, and the underground city was sealed off. Tours of the vast underworld are now given by **Bill Speidel's Underground Tours** (682-4646). Speidel spearheaded the movement to save Pioneer Square from the anathema of renewal. The tours are informative and irreverent glimpses at Seattle's beginnings; just ignore the rats that infest the tunnels. Tours (1½ hr.) leave from Doc Maynard's Pub at 610 1st Ave. (6-8 per day, 10am-6pm). Reservations strongly recommended at least one day in advance. (Admission $4, senior citizens $2, students $3.25; ages 6-12 $2.75)

Once back above ground, learn about the next major event in the city's history at the **Klondike Gold Rush National Historic Park,** 117 S. Main St. (442-7220). Not really a park, this "interpretive center" (as the Park Service would have it) depicts the lives and fortunes of the miners. A slide show weaves together seven photographers' recordings of the mostly unsuccessful ventures of the miners. The first Saturday of each month at 3pm, the park screens Charlie Chaplin's 1925 classic, *The Gold Rush.* (Open daily 9am-5pm. Free.)

While in Pioneer Square, browse through the 31 local art galleries, distributors for many of the Northwest's prominent artists. The first Thursday evening of each month, the art community sponsors the "First Thursday," a well-dressed and well-attended gallery walk. A few of the square's notable galleries are **Flury and Co. Gallery,** 322 1st Ave. S. (587-0260), which features vintage photographic portraits of Native American life (open Mon.-Sat. 10am-6pm, Sun. noon-5pm); **Linda Farris Gallery,** 320 2nd Ave. S. (623-1110), which promotes innovative Seattle artists (open Tues.-Sat. 11:30am-5pm, Sun. 1-5pm); **Native Design Gallery,** 108 Jackson St. (624-9985), housing imported art from Africa, South America, and India (open Tues.-Sat. 11am-5pm); and **Sacred Circle Gallery,** 607 1st Ave. (285-4425), guardian of a loudly applauded collection of contemporary Native American art (open Tues.-Sat. 9am-5pm). Stop in also at the **Seattle Indian Arts and Crafts Shop,** 113 Cherry St. (621-0655), run by the American Indian Women's Service League. A nonprofit business, the shop features Native American art of the Pacific Northwest. Proceeds go toward scholarships for Native American students and food and shelter for needy Native Americans. (Open Mon.-Fri. 10am-5pm, Sat. 11am-4pm.) Another important landmark of the Pioneer Square area is the **Smith Tower,** for years the tallest building west of the Mississippi. The 21-story tower was commissioned in 1911 by L. C. Smith at a cost of $1,500,000. The building was later owned by local celebrity and fish-and-ships mogul Ivar Haglund.

Many Seattlites consider the **Kingdome**, down 1st Ave. (340-2100 or 340-2128), the only serious challenger to the Boeing field as the city's ugliest building. Tours of the stadium include a stop at the **Royal Brougham Sports Museum.** (Tours leave daily from Gate D on the north side of the dome at 11am, 1pm, and 3pm; Nov.-April at 1 and 3pm. Otherwise, stadium only open during sporting events. Admission $2.50, senior citizens and children $1.25.)

Three blocks east of Pioneer Square, up Jackson on King St., is Seattle's **International District.** Though sometimes still called Chinatown by Seattlites, this area is now home to peoples from all over Asia. The 45-minute slideshow *Seattle's Other History*, presented at the **Nippon Kan Theater**, 628 Washington St. (624-8801), explores the years of discrimination endured by Seattle's Asian community. (Presentation given whenever large enough groups accumulate; call ahead. Admission $2.) Whether or not you see the show, pick up the brochure *Chinatown Tour: Seattle's Other History*, which is available for free at the Nippon Kan Theater, itself a good place to start your tour of the district. The theater was built in 1909 to house weddings and cultural events. An advertising screen dating from the same period is painted with the symbols and names of various Japanese merchants, some of whom are still doing business in the district today. The Nippon Kan fell into disrepair during World War II and was only restored and reopened in 1981.

Behold also the **Tsutakawa Sculpture** at the corner of S. Jackson and Maynard St. and the gigantic dragon mural in **Hing Hay Park** at S. King and Maynard St. Stop in at the **Wing Luke Memorial Museum**, 414 8th St. (623-5124). This tiny museum houses a permanent exhibit on the different Asian groups that have settled in Seattle as well as temporary exhibits by local Asian artists, such as sculptor George Tsutakawa. Occasional free demonstrations of traditional crafts are also scheduled. (Open Tues.-Fri. 11am-4:30pm, Sat.-Sun. noon-4pm. Admission $1.50, students and children 50¢.)

Capitol Hill

Capitol Hill inspires extreme reactions from both its residents and its neighbors. The former wouldn't live anywhere else, while the latter never go near the place. The district's leftist and gay communities set the tone for its nightspots (see Entertainment), while the retail outlets include a large number of collectives and radical bookstores. Saunter down Broadway or its cross streets to window-shop, or walk a few blocks east and north for a stroll down the hill's pretty residential streets, lined with well-maintained Victorian homes. Bus #10 runs along 15th St. and #7 cruises along Broadway.

Volunteer Park, between 11th and 17th Ave. at E. Ward St., north of the main Broadway activity, beckons tourists to travel east of the city center. Named for the "brave volunteers who gave their lives to liberate the oppressed people of Cuba and the Philippines," the park boasts lovely lawns and an outdoor running track. Climb the water tower at the 14th Ave. entrance for stunning 360° views of the city and the Olympic Range. The views rival those from the Space Needle, and what's more, they're free. On rainy days, languish amid the orchids inside the glass conservatory (free). The **Seattle Art Museum**, 14th St. E. and Prospect (625-8901), houses an excellent collection of Asian art. Pick up a program listing or call 443-4670 for information about special exhibits, lectures, demonstrations, and films at the museum. (Open Tues.-Wed. and Fri.-Sat. 10am-5pm, Thurs. 10am-9pm, Sun. noon-5pm. Admission $2, students, ages over 64 and under 12 $1; free Thurs.)

The **University of Washington Arboretum** (325-4510), 10 blocks east of Volunteer Park, has superb cycling and running trails, including Lake Washington Blvd., a smooth bicycling road which runs the arboretum's length north to south and then continues along the western shore of Lake Washington as far south as Seward Park. A tranquil **Japanese Garden** (684-4725) is located in the southern end of the arboretum at E. Helen St. Take bus #43 from downtown. The nine acres of sculpted gardens include fruit trees, a reflecting pool, and a traditional tea house. (Open March-Nov. daily 10am-8pm. Admission $1.50, senior citizens, disabled people, and ages under 19 75¢. Arboretum open daily dawn to dusk; greenhouse open Mon.-Fri. 10am-4pm.)

North of the arboretum near Husky Stadium sits the **Museum of History and Industry,** 2161 E. Hamlin St. (324-1125). The museum includes exhibits on Seattle's and King County's earliest pioneer settlers and relates amusing anecdotes of the city's slow beginnings. (Open daily 10am-5pm. Admission $3; senior citizens, disabled, ages 6-12 $1.50. Tues. by donation.)

University District

With 35,000 students, the **University of Washington** is the state's cultural and educational center of gravity. The "U District" swarms with students year-round, and other Seattlites also take advantage of the many bookstores, shops, taverns, and restaurants. Stop by the friendly and helpful **visitors information center,** 4014 University Way NE (543-9198), to pick up a map of the campus and to obtain information on the university. (Open Mon.-Fri. 8am-5pm.)

On the campus, visit the **Thomas Burke Memorial Washington State Museum,** NE 45th St. and 17th Ave. NE (543-5590), in the northwest corner of the campus. The museum houses artifacts of the Pacific Northwest's Native American tribes. Especially good are the scrimshaw displays. The museum will be closed for renovation until March 1991. (Open daily 10am-5pm, Thurs. until 8pm.) The Astronomy Department's **observatory** is open to the public for viewings on clear nights (543-0126). The **UW Arts Ticket Office,** 4001 University Way NE (543-4880), has information and tickets for all events. (Open Mon.-Fri. 10:30am-4:30pm.) To reach the U-District, take buses #71-74 from downtown, #7, 43, or 48 from Capitol Hill.

Waterways and Parks

A string of attractions festoon the waterways linking Lake Washington and Puget Sound. Houseboats and sailboats fill **Lake Union.** Here, the **Center for Wooden Boats,** 1010 Valley St. (382-2628), maintains a moored flotilla of new and restored small craft for rental. (Rowboats $7 per hr., sailboats $8-25 per hr. Open Wed.-Sun. noon-6pm.) **Kelly's Landing,** 1401 NE Boat St. (547-9909), below the UW campus, rents canoes for outings on Lake Union. (Sailboats $10-34 per hr., also day rates. Hours determined by weather. Ususally Mon.-Fri. 10am-dusk, Sat.-Sun. 9am-dusk.) **Gasworks Park,** a much-bruited kite-flying spot at the north end of the lake, was reopened a few years ago by the EPA after being shut down due to an excess of toxins. Don't be daunted by the large hill. At the top is a gorgeous view and an interactive sundial in which your body acts as the pointer. **Gasworks Kite Shop,** 1915 N. 34th St. (633-4780), is 1 block north of the park. To reach the park, take bus #26 from downtown to N. 35th St. and Wallingford Ave. N. The popular **Burke-Gilman Trail** runs from Latona St. at NE Northlake, just next to the Washington Ship Canal Bridge and I-5, through the university, past Sand Point and Magnuson Park, north to NE 145th. Since the trail prohibits motorized traffic, it is ruled by cyclists, runners, and walkers.

Farther west, the **Hiram M. Chittenden Locks** are movers and shakers of ships. On fine summer days, good-sized crowds turn out to watch their boat-loving neighbors jockeying for position in the locks. A circus atmosphere develops at peak hours, as all the boats traveling between Puget Sound and Lake Washington try to cross over. (Viewing hours daily 7am-9pm.) If listening to the cries of frustrated skippers doesn't amuse you, proceed to the **Fish Ladder** on the south side of the locks to watch trout and salmon hurl themselves over 21 concrete steps on their journey from the sea. Take bus #43 from the U District or #17 from downtown. The busiest salmon runs occur from June to November; steelhead trout run in the winter, cutthroat trout run in the fall. Afterwards, you can listen to lectures held in the visitors center (783-7059) during the summer Tuesdays at 7:30pm. The U.S. Army Corps of Engineers gives talks with frivolous names like "The Corps Cares About

Fish" and "A Beaver in Your Backyard?" (Visitors center open daily 11am-8pm; Sept. 16-June 14 Thurs.-Mon. 11am-5pm.)

Farther north, on the northwestern shore of the city, lies the **Golden Gardens Park,** in the Loyal Heights neighborhood, between NW 80th and NW 95th. A small boat ramp is at the southern end of the park. All will enjoy a picnic supper eaten as the sun sets over Shilshole Bay. Several expensive restaurants are located on the piers to the south, and the unobstructed views of the Olympics make their uniformly excellent seafood almost worth the price (see Food).

Ethnic historians passing through the Scandinavian neighborhood of **Ballard** may want to stop at the **Nordic Heritage Museum,** 3014 NW 67th St. (789-5707). Take bus #17. (Open Tues.-Sat. 10am-4pm, Sun. noon-4pm. Admission $2.50, senior citizens and students $1.50, ages 6-16 $1.)

Directly north of Lake Union, the beautiful people run, roller skate, and skate-board around **Green Lake.** Take bus #16 from downtown Seattle to Green Lake. The lake is also given high marks by windsurfers, but woe to those who lose their balance. Whoever named Green Lake wasn't kidding; even a quick dunk results in gobs of green algae clinging to your body and hair. A more pleasant way to view the lake is by renting a boat from **Greenlake Rentals** on the eastern side of the lake (sailboards $10 per hr., pedalboats $6, canoes and rowboats $5). But watch out, on sunny afternoons the boat renters, the windsurfers, and the local crew teams make the lake very crowded. Next to the lake is Woodland Park and the **Woodland Park Zoo,** 5500 Phinney Ave. N. (789-7919), best reached from Hwy. 99 or N. 50th St. Take bus #5 from downtown. The park itself is shaggy, but this makes the ani-mals' habitats seem all the more realistic. The African Savannah and Gorilla Houses reproduce the wilds, while the Nocturnal House reveals what really goes on when the lights go out. The newly opened elephant habitat has furthered the zoo's interna-tional reputation for creating natural settings. It's one of only three zoos in the U.S. to get Humane Society Grade 1 approval. (Open daily 10am-6pm; in winter closing time depends on day length. Admission $4, ages 6-17 $2, senior citizens, disabled people 50¢.)

A number of other worthwhile parks and attractions are spattered across the city. **Discovery Park,** on a lonely point west of the Magnolia district and south of Golden Gardens Park, at 36th Ave. W. and Government Way W., is comprised of acres of minimally tended grassy fields and steep bluffs atop Puget Sound. At its northern end is the **Indian Cultural Center** (285-4425), operated by the United Indians of All Tribes Foundation. (Open Wed.-Fri. 8:30am-5pm, Sat.-Sun. 10am-5pm. Free.)

Seward Park is the southern endpoint of a string of beaches and park land along the western shore of Lake Washington. Take bus #39 during peak hours; bus #31 Mon.-Fri. 9am-3pm and Sat. 6am-7pm. The park has a number of beaches, wooded areas, and walking and biking trails, as well as a fishing pier, picnic shelters, tennis courts, and an arts center (723-5780). After exercising in the park, refresh yourself with a tour of the **Rainier Brewery Co.,** 3100 Airport Way S. (622-2600), off I-5 at the West Seattle Bridge. Take bus #123. Attentiveness is rewarded with free beer (root beer for those under 21) and cheese and crackers. (Tours Mon.-Fri. 1-6pm. Free.)

Directly to the west is **Alki Beach Park,** a thin strip of beach wrapped around residential West Seattle. The water is cold, but the view of downtown Seattle in one direction and of the Olympics in the other is scrumptious. The Coast Guard's **Alki Point Lighthouse,** 3201 Alki Ave. SW (932-5800), is open for tours Sat.-Sun. noon-4pm, Mon.-Thurs. by appointment only (call one day in advance). The first white settlers of Seattle set up camp here in 1851, naming their new home New York Alki (Alki is a Native American word meaning "by and by"). By the time the settlement moved to Pioneer Square, new arrival Doc Maynard suggested that perhaps "New York by and by" was too deferential a name and that the city should be named for his friend Chief Sealth, whose name was eventually mangled into Seat-tle. A monument to the city's birthplace is located along Alki Beach at 63rd Ave. SW. South of Alki, **Lincoln Park,** along Fauntleroy Way, is the departure point for ferries to Vashon Island (see Near Tacoma). Take bus #18 to Lincoln Park.

The park has a number of playing fields, tennis courts, picnic tables, swimming beaches, bicycling trails, and the Colman Pool, open only during the summer.

Sports and Recreation

Seattle parks are a relentless carnival of running and cycling trails, tennis courts, and playing fields. There are more than 200 road races each summer in the Northwest. Pick up a copy of the pamphlet *Your Seattle Parks and Recreation Guide,* available at the visitors bureau or the Parks Department. Zan Galton wanna-bes will also want to get their hands on a free copy of the monthly *Sports Northwest,* available from area sports outfitters. The paper includes calendars of competitive events in the Northwest, as well as book reviews and recreation suggestions.

Distance bicyclists should note the 192-mile **Seattle to Portland Race,** in which 1600 people compete annually. Call the **bike hotline** (522-2453) for more information. The Seattle Parks Department also holds a monthly **Bicycle Sunday** from May to September, when Lake Washington Blvd. is open only to cyclists from 10am-5pm. Contact the Parks Department's Citywide Sports Office (684-7092) for more information. Dear to the heart of many Seattle cyclists is **Marymoor Velodrome** (282-8356), in Redmond off Hwy. 520 at the Hwy. 901 exit. The velodrome is open to the public when not in use for competition, and offers classes on the ways of the track. Watch the sweaty races sponsored by the Washington State Bicycling Association from May through August on Friday nights at 7:30pm. Pack a picnic supper and sit on the lawn. All the buses that cross Lake Washington have bike racks—call Metro (447-4800) for more information.

White water rafting has become extremely popular in Washington in the last decade. While the navigable rivers all lie at least two hours from Seattle by car, many outfitters are based in the Seattle area. River running is currently unregulated, and over 50 companies compete for a growing market. The best way to secure an inexpensive trip is to call some outfitters and compare competitors' prices; they are often willing to undercut one another. Look under "Guides" in the Yellow Pages. In recent years rafting companies have attempted to subject themselves to a regulatory bureaucracy of their own making, **River Outfitters of Washington (ROW)** (485-1427), which sets safety guidelines for its members. Even if your outfitter does not belong to ROW, be sure it lives up to ROW's basic safety standards. Under no circumstances should a single raft navigate a river unaccompanied; guides should possess basic water and safety skills and should have been trained at least twice on each river that they run commercially; all guides should have Standard First Aid and CPR certification; and all rafts should be rigged with bail buckets, throw lines, and extra paddles. Some of the larger companies have on-shore support staff at all times. Spend the extra dollars to ensure the highest level of safety. Private boaters should remember that whitewater is unpredictable and potentially dangerous. And even if you are schooled in the ways of wild water, *always* scout out new rivers before running them. ROW has a list of tips for private boaters, and outfitters can give you an idea of the navigable Washington rivers.

The **Northwest Outdoor Center,** 1009 NE Boat St. (632-1984), on Lake Union, holds a number of instructional programs in whitewater and sea kayaking during the spring, summer, and fall. (3-day introduction to sea touring $25 if you have your own boat. Equipment rentals available.) The center also leads a number of excursions—sea kayaking through the San Juan Islands or backpacking and paddling through the North Cascades. (Open Mon.-Fri. 10am-8pm, Sat.-Sun. 10am-6pm.)

South of Seattle, the 30-year-old **Longacres** track (226-3131) still has classic thoroughbred racing (April-Oct. Wed.-Sun.). Washington State does not allow off-track betting but the smiling tellers at Longacres will be happy to take your money. From Seattle, take I-5 south to exit 157 Empire Way. Or take Metro's Longacres Special direct service from 2nd and Pine downtown. (One way $3, round-trip $3.50; no passes or transfers accepted. Departure times vary, so pick up a schedule.) Once per month, Saturday morning workouts are free to the public. Talk to jockeys, watch a film, and receive free souvenirs of your visit. Meet at 8am at the north end of the grandstand. Every Saturday and Sunday, free tours of Longacres are conducted by an ex-jockey. Reservations are required. (Grandstand admission $3, clubhouse $5, children under 10 free.)

Since the days of the Klondike rush, Seattle has been one of the foremost cities in the world for supplying expeditions into the wilds. Besides a host of ordinary army-navy surplus stores and campers' supply shops, Seattle is home to many world-class outfitters. **Recreational Equipment Inc. Coop (REI Coop),** 1525 11th Ave. (323-8333), is the favored place to buy high-quality mountaineering and water recreation gear. Take bus #10. For a few dollars you can join the coop and receive a year-end rebate on your purchases. REI also offers its own backpacking and climbing trips and clinics, and presents free slide shows and lectures on topics such as trekking through Nepal, bicycling in Ireland, improving your fly-fishing techniques, etc. Call or stop by the store for a full schedule. (Open Mon.-Tues. 10am-6pm, Sat. 9:30am-6pm, Wed.-Fri. 10am-9pm, Sun. noon-5pm.) **Second Wind,** 300 Queen Anne N. (329-5921), sells much cheaper second-hand equipment, and **North Face,** 4560 University Way NE (574-6276), also has its headquarters in Seattle (open Mon.-Fri. 9am-8pm, Sat. 10am-7pm, Sun. noon-5pm).

Seattlites do take some time out from their own activities to watch others play. By far the most popular of Seattle's three professional teams is the **Seahawks** (827-9766; tickets $7-24), the perennial almost-ran. They play football in the same Kingdome that the **Mariners** (628-0888, tickets $4.50-10.50) play baseball in, but the stadium is far more suited to football than baseball. With a new owner and a new image, the Mariners have recently seen more hometown support but the Kingdome remains one of the worst places in the country to watch baseball. The Seattle **Supersonics** (281-5800) (known more casually as the "Sonics") are the only Seattle team to ever win a national title and their basketball games in the Coliseum in Seattle Center are well-attended. The University of Washington Huskies lap up local popularity as well. While the football team plays to full crowds in Husky Stadium, where some (mostly Seattlites) say the "wave" was invented, it's been ten years since they won the Rose Bowl. The really hot team on campus is the top-10 Women's Basketball team. Call the Athletic Ticket Office (543-2200) for schedules and price information.

Entertainment

Obtain a copy of *The Weekly,* 75¢ at newsstands and in boxes on the street, for a complete calendar of music, theater, and special events. The Friday inserts of the *Seattle Times* and *Seattle Post-Intelligencer* ("Tempo" and "What's Happening," respectively) have similar listings. The free *Rocket,* available in music stores throughout the city, is a monthly off-beat guide to the popular music scene around the Puget Sound area. *Seattle Gay News,* 25¢ in boxes on the street, lists events and musical happenings relevant to the gay community.

During summertime lunch hours downtown, the city-sponsored free **"Out to Lunch"** series (623-0340) brings everything from reggae to folk dancing to the parks and squares of Seattle. The **Seattle Public Library** (625-2665) shows free films as part of the program and has a daily schedule of other free events, such as poetry readings and children's book-reading competitions. *Events,* published every two months, is a calendar of the library's offerings (available at libraries throughout the city).

Music and Dance

The **Seattle Opera** (443-4700) performs in the Opera House in the Seattle Center throughout the winter. In 1991, this imaginative and expert company will put on *Don Giovanni* and *Ariadne of Naxos,* among other works. The popularity of the program requires that you order tickets well in advance, although rush tickets are sometimes available 15 minutes before curtain-time ($8 and up). Write to the Seattle Opera, P.O. Box 9248, Seattle 98109. The **Seattle Symphony Orchestra** (447-4747), also in Seattle Center's Opera House, performs a regular subscription series from September through June (rush tickets $4 and up) under the talented baton of Gerard Schwarz, as well as special pops and children's series. More recently, the symphony has been playing summer series in the gorgeous, renovated Fifth Avenue Theater. The **Pacific Northwest Ballet** (547-5900) starts its season at the Opera House in December with the spectacular Maurice Sendak-designed version of the "Nut-cracker." The season continues through May with four or five slated productions. The University of Washington offers its own program of student recitals and con-certs by visiting artists. Call the Meany Hall box office at 543-4880.

Theater

Devotees of the stage could argue that the best thing about Seattle is its theater, and with good reason. Boasting the third-largest number of professional companies in the U.S., Seattle supports an exciting array of first-run plays (many eventually move on to New York) and alternative works, particularly in the many excellent semi-professional groups. Although touring companies do pass through, they are nowhere near as interesting as the local scene.

Seattle Repertory Theater, 225 Mercer (443-2222), in the wonderful Bagley Wright Theater in Seattle Center. Artistic director Daniel Sullivan and the Rep. won the 1990 Tony award for Regional Excellence. Their winter season combines classic (usually including one Shake-speare), contemporary, and original productions. Recent plays that got their start at the Rep. include *The Heidi Chronicles, Fences,* and *I'm not Rappaport.* Tickets $9-23.50.

A Contemporary Theater (ACT), 100 W. Roy (285-5110), at the base of Queen Anne Hill. A summer season of modern plays, often off-beat premieres. Tickets $10-19.50.

The Empty Space Theatre, 107 Occidental Ave. S (467-6000) near the Market. It almost folded last year but the space is not empty yet and the zany comedies continue. Winter season tickets $13-18.

Intiman Theater at the Playhouse in Seattle Center (626-0782). Their summer season usually snags the best local actors for a classical repertoire. Tickets $13-19.50.

Bathhouse Theater, 7312 Greenlake Dr. N (524-9108). This small company is known for its popular restaging of radio skits and transplanting Shakespeare (e.g., a Wild West *Macbeth*, Kabuki *King Lear*, and *Midsummer Night's Dream* set in the 50s). Tickets $10-15.

Seattle Group Theatre, 3940 Brooklyn NE (543-4327), next to the Last Exit, in the U District. Home to **The Group,** one of Seattle's most innovative small theater ensembles, performing original and avant-garde works. Tickets $8-14.50.

Alice B. Theater (32-ALICE). Theater locations change. This gay/lesbian theater company keeps getting hotter. Their witty musicals are particularly sparkling. Tickets $10-12.

New City Theater, 1634 11th Ave. (323-6800), on Capitol Hill. The most alternative of the alternative theaters, the size and type of their offerings swings wildly. Ticket prices change accordingly.

University of Washington School of Drama Theaters (543-4880). The 3 UW theaters—the Penthouse, Meany Hall, and Glenn Hughes Playhouse—offer a wide variety of works, from children's shows to classical and contemporary theater. Of particular interest is the free open-air Shakespeare in the summer. Call for information on the wide variety of UW cultural activ-ities.

Paul Robeson Community Theater, 500 30th S. (322-7080). Performs works by Black artists, often at the Langston Hughes Cultural Center on Capitol Hill.

Taverns and Clubs

One of the joys of living in Seattle is the abundance of community taverns dedi-cated not to inebriating or scoping, but rather to providing a relaxed environment for dancing and spending time with friends. In Washington a tavern serves only beer and wine; a fully licensed bar or cocktail lounge must adjoin a restaurant. You must be 21 to enter bars and taverns. The Northwest produces a variety of local beers, some sold in area stores, but mostly just on tap in bars, including **Grant's, Imperial Russian Stout, India Pale Ale, Red Hook, Ballard Bitter,** and **Black Hook.**

For $5 or so, catch an evening of live stand-up comedy in one of Seattle's comedy clubs, such as Pioneer Square's **Swannie's Comedy Underground,** 222 S. Main St. (628-0303; acts daily 9 and 11pm).

The University Bistro, 4315 University Way NE (547-8010). Live music (everything from blues to reggae) nightly. Happy hours (4-7pm) feature pints of Bud for $1.25, pitchers $4. Cover Tues. $2, Wed.-Sat. $3-5, no cover Sun.-Mon. Open Mon.-Fri. 11am-2am, Sat. 6pm-2am.

Murphy's Pub, 2110 N. 45th St. (634-2110), in Wallingford, west of the U District. Take bus #43. A classic Irish pub with a mile-long beer list. Popular with young folks, Murphy's has live Irish and folk music nightly. Cover charge $1-2. Open daily 1pm-2am.

Central Tavern, 207 1st Ave. S. (622-0209). One of several good live rock 'n' roll taverns in Pioneer Sq. On weekends, walk around the square to find a tavern to your liking; many participate in a $6 joint cover. Open Mon.-Thurs. 11:30am-midnight, Fri.-Sat. 2pm-2am, Sun. 2-10pm.

Squid Row Tavern, 518 E. Pine (322-2031). Bizarre paintings, black booths, a bar, and earfuls of melodious punk rock. Cover $4. Pint of Bud $1.50. Open Mon.-Fri. noon-2am, Sat. 4pm-2am, Sun. 6pm-2am.

The Borderline, 608 1st Ave. (624-3316), in the heart of Pioneer Sq. Under-25 crowd dances to a mix of music from Motown to new-wave. Occasional live bands. Happy hour (8-10pm) features 50¢ pints of Bud and Bud Lite and free snacks. Fri.-Sat. cover $2 for men, $1 for women. Open Thurs.-Sat. 8pm-2am.

The Double Header, 407 2nd Ave. in Pioneer Sq. (464-9918). Claims to be the oldest gay bar in the country. An oom-pah band plays nightly to a mostly middle-aged crowd of gay men and women. Open daily 10am-2am. No cover.

The Frontier, 2203 1st Ave. (441-3377). Free dancing nightly to a live DJ. The new sound system in this go-go club attracts both gay and straight crowds. Bar open daily 10am-2am. Dancing Wed.-Sat. 10pm-2am. Restaurant open Mon.-Fri. 6am-10pm, Sat. 10am-10pm, Sun. 10am-6pm. No cover.

New Melody Tavern and Dance Hall, 5213 Ballard Ave. NW (782-3480), in Ballard. Along with beer and well drinks, this out-of-the-way dance bar delivers some of Seattle's best jazz and bluegrass. Open Mon.-Fri. 5pm-2am, Sat. 6pm-2am. Cover $3-9.

Cinema

Most of the theaters that screen non-Hollywood films are on Capitol Hill and in the University District. Expect to pay $6. Seven Gables has recently bought up the Metro, the Neptune, and others. $17.50 buys admission to any five films at any of their theaters.

The Egyptian, 801 E. Pine St. (323-4978), at Harvard, on Capitol Hill. This handsome art-deco theater shows artsy films and is best known for the Seattle Film Festival, held here throughout May. The festival includes a retrospective of one director's work and a personal appearance by the featured director. Festival series tickets are available at a discount. Tickets $6, 1st matinee $3.50.

The Harvard Exit, 807 E. Roy (323-8986), on Capitol Hill. Quality classic and foreign films. Half the fun of seeing a movie here is the theater itself, a converted old house—the lobby was once the living room. Arrive early for complimentary cheese and crackers over a game of chess, checkers, or backgammon. Admission $6, senior citizens and children $3.50, 1st matinee $3.50.

Neptune, 1303 NE 45th St. (633-5545), just off University Way. A repertory theater, with double features that change daily. Admission $6, senior citizens and children $3.50. *The Rocky Horror Picture Show* has been playing at midnight for as many Saturdays as anyone can remember.

Seven Gables Theater, 911 NE 50th St. (632-8820), in the U District, just off Roosevelt, a short walk west from University Way. Another cinema in an old house. Shows independent and classic films. Admission $6, senior citizens and children $3.50, 1st matinee $3.50.

Market Theater, 1428 Post Alley (382-1171), downstairs from the Pike Place Market. Shows good foreign flicks and those like *Airfeet of Desire* and *Attack of the Killer Ice Cream Sandwiches.* Admission $5.50, senior citizens $4.50, children $2.75.

Grand Illusion Cinema, 1403 NE 50th St. (523-3935), in the U District at University Way. A tiny theater attached to an espresso bar, showing low-budget films. Admission $5, senior citizens and students $3, matinees $4.

Metro Cinemas, 45th St. and Roosevelt Way NE (633-0055), in the U District. A large, generic 10-theater complex. Half the screens show mainstream movies, the other half are reserved for contemporary art films. Admission $6, senior citizens and children $3.50, 1st matinee $3.50.

Seasonal Events

Seattlites never let the rain dampen their spirits. Pick up a copy of the Seattle-King County visitors center brochure *Coming Events,* published every season, for an exact listing of innumerable area happenings. One of the most notable events is the **Northwest Folklife Festival,** held on Memorial Day weekend at the Seattle Center. Artists, musicians, and dancers congregate to celebrate the heritage of the area. The Japanese community celebrates with the traditional **Bon Odori** festival in the International District the third week of July when temples are opened to the public and there are dances in the street. **Street fairs** throughout the city are popular conglomerations of crafts and food stands, street music, and theater. Especially of note are those in the University District during mid- to late-May, the Pike Place Market over Memorial Day weekend, and the Fremont District (633-4409) in mid-June. The **Bite of Seattle** is an extremely popular celebration of food, held in mid-July in the Seattle Center. The summer is capped off with the massive **Bumbershoot** (683-7337), held in the Seattle Center over Labor Day weekend. This fantastic arts festival attracts big-name rock bands, street musicians, and an exuberant crowd. (Fri. free, Sat.-Sun. $4 at the door, $3 in advance.)

The first three letters in Seattle mean a great deal to this city. Head up to Puget Sound to take in the **yachting season,** which falls off in May. **Maritime Week** (467-6340 or 329-5700), during the third week of May, should buoy your spirits, and the **Seattle Boats Afloat Show** (634-0911) in mid-August gives area boaters a chance to show off their craft. At the beginning of July, the Center for Wooden Boats sponsors the free **Wooden Boat Show** (382-2628) on Lake Union. Don't go without your blue blazer and skipper's cap. Size up the entrants (over 100 traditional wooden boats) and then watch a demonstration of boat-building skills. The year-end blowout is the **Quick and Daring Boatbuilding Contest,** in which Dennis O'Conner (or Chris O'Connor) look-alikes go overboard trying to build and sail wooden boats of their own design using a limited kit of tools and materials. The telltale signs of this fest—plenty of music, food, and alcohol—make the sailing smooth.

The biggest and zaniest festival of them all is the **Seattle Seafair** (623-7100, hotline 421-5012), spread out over three weeks from mid-July to early August. The whole city contributes with street fairs, big, little, and ethnic parades, balloon races, musical entertainment, and a seafood fest. The festival ends with the totally insane **Emerald City Unlimited Hydroplane Races,** in which everybody grabs anything that will float and heads to Lake Washington for front row seats. As the sun shines more often than not during these weeks, half the city seems to turn out in inner tubes.

The year ends with the annual **Christmas Cruise** in early December. Every vessel in town sparkles with lights. Boats promenade along Lake Washington and Elliott Bay, with local choirs belting it out nightly.

Near Seattle

Fatigued? Exhausted? Hectic big city life got you down? Well come on over to Lake Washington! Simply cross on the the two floating bridges and you'll be in a biker's and picnicker's dream come true. In general, these towns are of no interest to the sightseer, but the spacious parklands and miles of country roads delight those who have an affinity for the outdoors. Seattle's outskirts are astonishingly rural; only **Bellevue** across Lake Washington has developed anything akin to urban flair. Although bowling and movie-going draw the big evening crowds in this affluent suburb, Bellevue is beginning to show the early signs of a nightlife in its downtown restaurants and clubs. The July **Bellevue Jazz Festival** (455-6885), in particular, attracts both the local jazz cats and national acts.

If nothing else, a jaunt to suburbia grants a fine view of Seattle against a mountainous backdrop. The hills due east of the city, known affectionately as the "**Issaquah Alps**," are filled with good hiking trails.

Head farther out for lovely country excursions. Take I-90 to **Lake Sammamish State Park,** off exit 15, for excellent swimming and waterskiing. The park also has volleyball courts and playing fields. You might want to continue onward to the towns of **Snoqualmie** and **North Bend,** 29 mi. east of Seattle. In Snoqualmie, the **Puget Sound Railroad Museum,** 109 King St. (746-4025), on Hwy. 202, features a collection of functional early steam and electric trains. The impressive equipment is housed in the classic old Snoqualmie Depot. Train rides on these old beasts run to North Bend, offering views of Snoqualmie Falls. (Open April-Sept. Sat.-Sun. 11am-5pm. Round-trip rides $7, senior citizens $5, children $3.) In North Bend, the **Snoqualmie Valley Museum,** 320 North Bend Blvd. S. (888-0062), resurrects a *fin-de-siècle* parlor and kitchen, and displays locally-retrieved Native American artifacts. (Open Sat.-Sun. 1-5pm. Sometimes open during the week; call for information.) North Bend operates a **visitor information booth** in summer at the corner of North Bend Blvd. and Park Ave. (888-1678).

Twenty-four miles east, I-90 climbs to Snoqualmie Pass and some of the most popular **skiing** in the state. Four resorts share the slopes, often offering interchangeable lift tickets and free shuttles, during the November to April season. Restaurants, ski schools, night skiing, and a ski shop complete the facilities. Three of the resorts, **Snoqualmie** (434-6161), **Alpental** (434-6112), and **Ski Acres** (434-6671), are run by the same company. In the off-season call their business office (262-8182). **Pacific West** (462-7669) is independent.

Back in North Bend, take bus #210 or Hwy. 202 north to view the astounding **Snoqualmie Falls** (featured in the TV show, *Twin Peaks*). Washington State residents are quick to mention that they are 100 ft. higher than Niagara. The falls were formerly a sacred place for coastal Native Americans, who called them *Sdokwalbu.* Now Puget Power has the capacity to turn the falls on and off depending on the secular needs of the hydroelectric plant (founded in 1898). Puget Power maintains public picnic facilities at the falls.

In the spring and summer, a number of **U-Pick berry farms** lining Hwy. 202 north along the Snoqualmie River open for the season. In Woodinville is the **Ste. Michelle Vintners,** 14111 NE 145th St. (488-7733), the leaders in the recent move to popularize Washington wines. From downtown Seattle take bus #310 during peak hours only. The 45-minute tours of the facility, which resembles a French château, finish with wine tasting for those 21 and over. (Tours Mon.-Thurs. 10am-4:30pm, Fri.-Sun. 10am-6pm.)

The Seattle area is heavily garnished by the many facilities of the **Boeing Aircraft Industry,** Seattle's most prominent employer. When last seen in the 1950s, Thomas Pynchon was working for this glittering jewel of the military-industrial complex, writing technical manuals. Free tours of one Boeing plant are given 25 mi. north of Seattle in **Everett.** Take I-5 to exit 189, then Hwy. 526 west. Tickets for the twice-daily tour are available first-come, first served at 8:30am at the plant—they go fast. Call the Everett Tour Center at 342-4801 for more information. At Boeing Field to the south of Seattle is the **Museum of Flight,** 9404 E. Marginal Way S. (767-7373). Take I-5 south to exit 158 and turn north onto E. Marginal Way S., or take bus #123. The museum is in the restored Red Barn where William E. Boeing founded the company in 1916. Inside, photographs and artifacts trace the history of flight from its beginnings through the 30s. Included is an operating replica of the Wright Brothers' wind tunnel. Rare aircraft sometimes participate in special events on the grounds nearby. The July 14-15 Airshow is always a hit. (Open daily 10am-5pm. Admission $4, senior citizens and ages 12-18 $3, ages 6-12 $2.)

Just south of Des Moines on Hwy. 509 off Hwy. 99 is **Saltwater State Park.** Take bus #130. The park has extensive foot trails through the Kent Smith Canyon, a beach for swimming and clamming, and 53 campsites with pay showers and flush toilets. (Sites $7.)

From Colman Dock (Pier 52) on Seattle's waterfront, ferries run to the town of **Bremerton,** on the Kitsap Peninsula, which serves as the Puget Sound Naval Shipyard (see Kitsap Peninsula).

Ferries also depart from Colman Dock for the town of **Winslow** on **Bainbridge Island,** a charmingly rural spot homesteaded by late-19th century Swedish and late-20th century Californian immigrants. In Winslow, follow the photographic record of these settlements at the **Bainbridge Island Historical Museum** on High School Rd. (open Sat. 10am-4pm; free) or pick up your spirits with a bottle of Ferry Boat White from the **Bainbridge Island Vineyards & Winery** (842-9463). Here you can sample the local grape, or tour the fields where it is grown; just turn right at the first white trellis on Hwy. 305 as you come from the ferry (open Wed.-Sun. noon-5pm, tours Sun. 2pm; free). To satisfy more substantial hunger, stop at the firecracker- and flower-festooned **Streamliner Diner,** 397 Winslow Way (842-8595), where the amazing, eccentric natural food and rich pie (slice $2.50) tempt the Northwest traveler. (Open Mon.-Fri. 7am-3pm, Sat.-Sun. 8am-2pm.)

For less decadent fun, head for one of the island's state parks. **Fort Ward,** southwest of Winslow, offers boat launches, picnic facilities, and an underwater scuba diving area (day-use only). **Fay-Bainbridge,** on the northern tip of the island just 1½ mi. from **Cliffhaven,** has good fishing and 36 **campsites** with pay showers and flush toilets. (Sites $6.) Ferries to the island run daily two hours to 45 minutes apart 5am-2am.

Puget Sound

According to Native American legend, Puget Sound was created when Ocean, wishing to keep his children Cloud and Rain close to home, gouged out a trough in western Washington and molded the dirt into a wall of mountains. Ever since then, Cloud and Rain have kept near the sea, rarely venturing across the Cascade Range to the interior tablelands. Most of Washington's residents also stick close by the water, making their homes in the Sound's labyrinth of inlets, bays, and harbors.

From Bellingham in the north through Seattle to industrial Tacoma, cities and towns form an almost continuous East Coast-style megalopolis along I-5. The bay's southern shore curves around past Lacey to Olympia, the state capital, and beyond that to the Olympic Peninsula. A few dozen islands speckle the Sound, providing tranquil retreats to harried city dwellers. The San Juan Islands, off Anacortes, catch the brunt of the tourist traffic. Vashon Island, between Seattle and Tacoma, remains quiet.

Puget Sound attracts as many water breathers as city dwellers. **Greenpeace Northwest,** 4649 Sunnyside Ave. N., Seattle 98103 (633-6020), runs a dozen weekend daytrips throughout the summer to view killer whales, porpoises, puffins, seals, sea lions, and eagles ($40-45). Although pods of orcas can be sighted anywhere in the Sound, the southwest coast of San Juan Island is the favorite haunt of the highly intelligent, black-and-white cetaceans.

An extensive web of roads and ferries ensnares the cities and islands of Puget Sound. Information on ferries to specific destinations is given in the Getting There and Practical Information sections of each city or area. If you're driving, you should arrive at the ferry terminal early and get in the line that matches your destination (cars are boarded according to their exit points). Cyclists and pedestrians travel cheaply and never have to wait in line. Try to avoid ferries across the Sound during commuter rush hours and the San Juan ferry on Friday afternoons. Larger cars and RVs may have to wait for a place; RVs pay an extra fee.

Olympia

Olympia was once a peaceful, easy-going fishing and oystering port at the southernmost end of Puget Sound. While still peaceful and easygoing, has made the gradual transition from small seaport to small capital city quite smoothly. The sprawling Capitol Campus reigns over downtown, with whitewashed buildings and perfectly manicured lawns. Downtown Olympia, somewhat eclipsed by its legislative neighbor, has a character all its own—home to a host of turn of the century buildings and tiny specialty shops. And, as capital of the Evergreen State, it is only fitting that Olympia draws on its natural setting. The shimmering waters of Puget Sound assure that it remains a seaport in appearance if not at heart.

Practical Information and Orientation

Visitor Information: Greater Olympia Visitors Convention Bureau, 316 Schmidt Pl. (357-3370). Bureaus of brochures, information, and sound advice. Open Mon.-Fri. 9am-5pm, Sat. 10am-4pm. **Department of Trade and Economic Development, Tourism Division,** General Administration Bldg., #G-3 (800-541-9274, in WA 800-562-4570). Choose your brochure with care. **City of Olympia Parks and Recreation Department,** 222 N. Columbia Ave. (753-8380). Open Mon.-Fri. 8am-9pm.

Washington State Parks and Recreation Commission: 7150 Clearwater Lane (753-5755; in summer 800-562-0990 Mon.-Fri. 8am-5pm). All the latest on the state parks. Immensely helpful staff.

Department of Natural Resources (DNR): John Cherbert Bldg. (800-527-3305 or 753-5327), in the Capitol Group on Water St. between 15th and 16th St. The *Guide to Camp and Picnic Sites* describes all the free DNR sites throughout the state. Ask for *Your Public Beaches,* about waterfront areas in the Puget Sound area. Open Mon.-Fri. 8am-5pm.

Department of Fisheries: 115 General Administration Bldg. (753-6600), just outside the Capitol Group at Columbia and 11th St. Information on saltwater fishing and shellfish, including season and limit designations. Open Mon.-Fri. 8am-5pm.

Department of Wildlife: 600 N. Capitol Way (753-5700). Information and licensing for freshwater fishing and game hunting. Open Mon.-Fri. 8am-5pm.

Greyhound: 107 E. 7th St. (357-5541). To Seattle (9 per day, $8.70); Portland (7 per day, $5); and Spokane (4 per day, $31). Open daily 7am-8:45pm.

Buses: Intercity Transit, 526 S. Pattison (786-1881). Office open Mon.-Fri. 9am-5pm; phone staffed Mon.-Fri. 7am-7pm, Sat. 8am-5pm. Buses run Mon.-Sat. 5:50am-8pm. Fare 35¢, ages 6-17 25¢; seniors and disabled people 10¢ with IT reduced-fare cards ($2) available from the IT office. Day passes are 75¢, youths 50¢, seniors and the disabled 20¢. Everyone rides free 11am-2pm in the downtown zone (bounded by the Capitol Group and the port). All buses begin and end their routes at 4th and Columbia. The **Capitol Shuttle,** set up to give Capitol employees transportation, is free to the public. Buses run between the campus and downtown every 10 min. Call Intercity Transit for information. Custom buses run where normal fixed routes stop—buses run Mon.-Fri. Call 943-7777 for information.

Taxi: Red Top Taxi, 357-3700. **South Sound Taxi,** 357-5757.

Car Rental: Rent-A-Dent, Olympia Airport (786-8333). $18 per day with 100 free mi. plus 15¢ per additional mi. Must be 21 with credit card. Open daily 8am-5pm.

Bike Rental: Olympic Outfitters, 407 E. 4th Ave. (943-1997). Mountain bikes $15 per day, 10-speeds $12.50 per day. Deposit $50, or leave a credit card number. This enormous sports shop also rents tents, skis, mountain climbing gear, and sailboards. Open Mon.-Fri. 10am-7pm, Sat. 10am-6pm, Sun. 10am-5pm.

Public Library: E. 8th and S. Franklin St. (352-0595). Open Mon.-Thurs. 10am-9pm, Fri.-Sat. 10am-5pm.

Lesbian Resource Center: Evergreen State College, CAB 305 (866-6000, ext. 6544). For the gay and lesbian community. Open during the school year Tues.-Thurs. 10am-4pm.

Women's Shelter: Safeplace, 754-6300. 24-hr. counseling and housing referral.

Women's Health Clinic: Evergreen State College CAB 305 (866-6000, ext. 6200). 24 hr.

Post Office: 900 S. Jefferson St. (753-9474). Open Mon.-Fri. 7:30am-6pm. General Delivery ZIP Code: 98501.

Area Code: 206.

Greyhound stops in downtown Olympia on its way up and down I-5. The Amtrak depot is almost 8 mi. southeast of the city, and there is no bus service to downtown, with the exception of the Custom Bus system (35¢) for which you must call ahead (see Practical Information). Intercity Transit provides limited service to the three "capital cities": Olympia, Tumwater, and Lacey (see listing above). Supplementary transport is provided for seniors and the disabled by **Special Mobility Services** at 825 Legion Way SE (754-9393).

Accommodations and Camping

The hotels and motels in Olympia generally cater to lobbyists and lawyers, not to budget tourists. Since the nearest hostel is all the way out in Tacoma, and the two local universities save all their rooms for their own students, your choices here are limited. Camping is the most financially appealing option in the area.

Holly Motel, 2816 Martin Way (943-3000), on a main east-west drag, east of town. Take exit 109 off I-5, or bus #61 or 62. The beds are a little narrow, but the rooms are comfortably roach-free. Small pool that occasionally has water in it. Singles $22, with TV $29. Doubles with TV $31.

Bailey Motor Inn, 3333 Martin Way (491-7515), just off exit 107. Clean, comfy rooms, and a full, indoor heated pool to boot. Singles from $34. Doubles from $44.

Super 8 Motel, 4615 Martin Way (459-8888), just outside Olympia in Lacey; take exit 109 off I-5. More upscale than Motel 6 (by at least 2 points), but essentially a bland representative of the national chain. Singles $37. Doubles $40.

Motel 6, 400 W. Lee St. (754-7320), in Tumwater. Take exit 102 off I-5 and head east on Trosper Rd., then south one block on Capitol Blvd. and west again on W. Lee St. Or take bus #13 from downtown. Comfortable rooms right next to the freeway. Color TV and swimming pool. Singles $29. Doubles $32. Each additional person $6.

Millersylvania State Park, 12245 Tilly Rd. S. (753-1519), 10 mi. south of Olympia, off I-5. The park's old-growth forest will outlive the swimmers and campers who use it. 216 crowded sites for camping, with pay showers and flush toilets. Facilities for the disabled. Primitive hiker/biker sites available. Standard sites $7, RV hookups $9.

Capital Forest Multiple Use Area, 15 mi. west of Olympia. Administered by the DNR. 50 campsites scattered among 6 campgrounds. Camping is free and requires no notification or permit. Pick up a forest map at the visitors bureau or at the state Department of Natural Resources office (see Practical Information).

Food

There is eating potential along bohemian 4th Ave., east of Columbia, especially when the pace picks up during the school year. The **farmer's market** (866-6835), at Capital Way and Thurston Ave., allows the farmer and the consumer to be friends. (Open May-Oct. Thurs.-Sun. 10am-3pm.)

Barb's BBQ Soul Cuisine, 203 W. 4th Ave. (786-9835). Enjoy pictures of Black political and musical figures on the wall while Barb whips up her fabulous soul food. The dinners ($7) overflow with beans, rice, veggies, and incredible cornbread. Try the ribs or the catfish. Live jazz Wed.-Sun. at 8pm. Open Mon.-Thurs. 6-8:30pm, Fri. 6-11pm, Sat. 6pm-midnight.

The Sub Shop, 915 Capitol Way S (786-6742). A tiny sandwich shop that barely has enough room for a cash register. Footlong subs with nuclear-powered flavor ($3.50-4.75). Open Mon.-Fri. 10am-5pm, Sat. 11am-3pm.

Smithfield Café, 212 W. 4th Ave. (786-1725). This cozy café with mellow jazz and modern art serves coffee (65¢), cappuccino ($1.20), and espresso (90¢). The relaxed and eclectic crowd also digs the fresh pastries, especially the blueberry bran muffins (90¢) and cherry turnovers ($1). Open Mon.-Fri. 7am-10pm, Sat. 8am-10pm, Sun. 8am-8pm.

Jo Mama's Restaurant, 120 N. Pear St. (943-9849), in an old house on the corner of State and Pear. Homemade pizza served in an all-wood, "old-tavern" atmosphere. The food is somewhat overpriced (8-inch vegetarian pizza $14—feeds 2 hungry people), but the ambience compensates. You'll feel like your're in the galley of a ship. Open Mon.-Thurs. 11am-11pm, Fri. 11am-midnight, Sat. 4pm-midnight.

The Falls Terrace Restaurant, 106 S. Deschutes Way (943-7830). Take exit 103 off I-5. Very elegant, but not fancy-schmancy. Dinner prices are out of sight, but you can enjoy the great view of Tumwater Falls over a $6 lunch. Open Mon.-Fri. 11am-9pm, Sat. 11am-10:30pm, Sun. 11:30am-9pm. Make reservations.

Sights

Begin your exploration of the capitol area at the **State Capitol Information Center,** on Capitol Way between 12th and 14th Ave. (586-3460). The staff here can provide you with information on the Capitol Group and save you a trip to the Chamber of Commerce. (Open Mon.-Fri. 8am-5pm.) Take a free tour of the **Legislative Building** (586-8687) to get a peek at the public realm. The building's spectacular dome (the fifth tallest dome in the world, 19 stories high) is scaled by a spiralling staircase of some 200-odd steps. The panorama of Olympia from the top more than offsets the sweat. An enormous wool, velvet, and velour carpet covers over 1200 square feet of the State Reception Room's teakwood floor; when the handpainted rug was completed, the original pattern was destroyed so it could never be used elsewhere. Even those who don't relish carpets will enjoy the informative tours given by a knowledgeable corps of tour guides (45-min., daily 10am-3pm). Committed sightseers should arrive on Wednesday afternoon to complete the double feature with a short tour of the nearby **Governor's mansion** (586-8687; 15-min. tours Wed. 1-2:30pm, otherwise by appointment only).

Capitol Lake Park, next to the Legislative Building, is a favorite retreat for runners, sailors, and swimmers. Spawning salmon head for Tumwater Falls late August through October; you can spot the lox leaping through the air as they cross the lake. The **State Capitol Museum,** 211 W. 21st Ave. (753-2580), exhibits local artwork and historical fragments. (Open Tues.-Fri. 10am-4pm, Sat.-Sun. noon-4pm. Free.)

The city offers a number of budget deals after dark. The **State Theater,** 204 E. 4th Ave. (357-4010), shows modern movies for $1.50. During the summer, the city schedules free jazz, ensemble, and symphony concerts (Wed. at 7:30pm and Fri. at noon; call 753-8183).

Near Olympia

The **Mima Mounds** (753-2400), an unusual geologic formation, have been preserved in a Department of Natural Resources prairie park 10 mi. south of Olympia. The self-guided interpretive trails are wheelchair-accessible. (Open daily 8am-dusk.) Take I-5 south to exit 95; 1 mi. west of Littlerock, follow Wadell Creek Rd. west.

The **Nisqually National Wildlife Refuge** (753-9467), located off I-5 between Olympia and Tacoma (exit 114), has recently set neighbor against neighbor in the quiet Nisqually delta. While environmentalists treasure the delta as the home of diverse marsh and marine life, developers hope to cast some of their bread upon the water and its environs. For the time being you can watch the protected wildlife from blinds or walk the trails through the preserve. (Open Mon.-Fri. 7:30am-4pm. Free.)

Olympia Beer (754-5177), actually brewed south of the capital city in **Tumwater**, has recently been taken over by the Pabst Company, which now produces a number of different beers on the premises. Tour the facility and have a brewski on the house. (Open daily 8am-4:30pm. Free.) The brewery, visible from I-5, can be reached from exit 103 in Tumwater. Nearby, **Tumwater Falls Park** practically begs for picnickers.

Ten miles south of the city is **Wolfhaven** (264-4695). Established in 1982 to save 20 wolves, the haven now preserves 40 wolves of six different species. Tour the grounds ($3 adults, $2 children) or take part in the Howl-in every Fri. and Sat. from 7-10pm (adults $4, children $2.50). Groups cower around a campfire and tell stories to the accompaniment of the howling residents. (Open May-Sept. daily 10am-5pm, Oct.-April Wed.-Sun. 10am-4pm.)

Elma, a small town 26 mi. west of Olympia on Hwy. 12, proudly sponsors a **Slug Festival** the first weekend in August. The festival features a parade, a street fair, and, for the *grande finale,* slug races. It's a champion slug indeed which can slime the full -furlong before the five-minute time limit is called.

Tacoma

Boston has its Worcester, New England has its Midwest, St. Paul has its Minneapolis, Manhattan has New Jersey, LA has itself, and Seattle has its Tacoma. Yet though it may be only a Triple-A town compared to its glamorous major league sibling on the Sound, and Seattlites will advise the traveler to avoid this industrial port city, Tacoma is hardly shabby. Brightest of its gems is Point Defiance Park at the northern tip of the city. Even people from you-know-where will occasionally make the half-hour trip down I-5 to see musical and sporting events at the Tacoma Dome. With two major universities (Universty of Puget Sound (UPS) and Pacific Lutheran University (PLU)) and a growing arts scene, Tacoma is beginning to get a reputation for things other than its infamous pulpy aroma.

Practical Information and Orientation

Visitor Information: Tacoma/Pierce County Visitor Information Center, 950 Pacific Ave., #450 (627-2836), on the 4th floor of the Seafirst Center. Volunteers interpret local bus schedules, calendars of events, and city maps. Open daily 8:30am-5pm. For more detailed information, take the elevator down to the 3rd floor, where the staff of the **Tacoma/Pierce County Chamber of Commerce** (627-2175) will be glad to assist. Open Mon.-Fri. 8am-5pm.

Amtrak: 1001 Puyallup (627-8141 or 800-872-7245). Take bus #400 or 401. To Seattle (3 per day) and Portland (3 per day). Two trains per day persevere south to San Francisco and Los Angeles. Open daily 6am-9:30pm.

Greyhound: 1319 Pacific Ave. (383-4621), in Tacoma's least gem-like area. Buses leave almost every hour to Seattle (one way $6) and Portland (one way $16.75). Open daily 7am-8:30pm.

Pierce County Transit: 3701 96th St. SW (581-8000). Economical transportation throughout the city and county. Buses run daily 5am-1am, depending on route number (fare 65¢; weekdays after 6pm and weekends 50¢). Pick up map and schedule at the Chamber of Commerce or at the bus stop at 904 Broadway, downtown across from the Pantages theater. Bus service for the disabled also available (call 581-8100). The #601X Olympia Express will take you to Olympia for $1.25. Office open Mon.-Fri. 8am-5pm.

Taxi: Yellow Cab, 472-3303. **United Taxi Co.,** 531-7489.

Car Rental: Budget Rent-A-Car, 1305 Pacific Ave. (383-4944). From $20 per day with 100 free miles plus 30¢ per additional mile. Must be 21 with credit card.

Laundromat: One Stop Laundromat and Video, 232 St. Helens (between 2nd and 4th) (572-6909). Open daily 10am-8pm.

Time and Weather: 922-8282.

Pierce County Park and Recreation: 9112 Lakewood Dr. SW (593-4176).

Help Lines: Coast Guard, 800-592-9911. 24 hours. **Rape Relief,** 474-7273. 24 hr. **Tacoma Area Coalition Task Force for the Disabled,** 565-9000. Open Mon.-Fri. 8:30am-5pm. **Crisis Line,** 759-6700. **Poison Center,** 594-1414. **Safeplace,** 627-4050. **Sexual Assault Crisis Center,** 597-6424.

YWCA Support Shelter for Battered Women: 383-2593.

Post Office: 11th and A St. Open Mon.-Fri. 8am-5:30pm. General Delivery ZIP Code: 98402.

Area Code: 206.

Tacoma lies on everyone's north-south route through Washington. Both Amtrak and Greyhound pass through, and I-5 skirts the downtown area. From Seattle, take **local transit** and save some money. Hop on Metro bus #174 during off-peak hours (#171 or 175-7 during peak hours) from 2nd and Pike St. to the Federal Way Park and Ride. Transfer here to Pierce Transit bus #500, which will take you downtown. Federal Way is within Metro's two-zone area. ($1.25 peak, 85¢ off-peak.)

The city center is accessible from exit 133 off I-5. **Pacific Avenue** is the main drag, passing by the Greyhound and Trailways depots, the post office, and the landmark Old City Hall. Downtown streets run east-west, avenues north-south up to **Division Avenue.** The deep water harbor is at the southeast end of **Commencement Bay,** Tacoma's *raison d'être.* The port waterfront extends along **Ruston Way** to **Point Defiance,** then turns sharply south along **The Narrows,** which is less built up. To navigate these twisted streets, pick up a map from the Chamber of Commerce. The area near the Greyhound station is dingy, especially after business hours. But it, along with the infamous "hill" beyond Division St. has improved significantly over the last few years. Feel free to eat dinner in the area, but don't hang around outside at night.

Accommodations and Camping

Camping on Mt. Rainier, reveling in Seattle, or relaxing in a small town somewhere on Puget Sound are all more appealing options than spending your money on the expensive hotels and sleazy motels of Tacoma. The two hostels near Tacoma are undoubtedly your best option; hop the ferry to Vashon Island to escape the brouhaha of the metropolises on the Sound.

Vashon Island Hostel (AYH), Cove Rd. (463-2592), at 121st Ave. SW, in nearby Vashon Island. Take the ferry from Point Defiance and then bus #118 (which leaves only at 4:15 and 6:30pm, so timing is important). After waking up in a comfortable log cabin or teepee, fix breakfast with the complimentary pancake mix and have a chat with the friendly owner. Don't forget to explore Vashon (see Near Tacoma). Bikes can be rented from the hostel. Seldom crowded. Check-in 5-10pm. Members $7, nonmembers $10. Open May-Sept.

Clara's Home Hostel (AYH), 5535 Frances (952-4640), 7 mi. north of the city. Clara will take great care of you; just be sure to write or call ahead for reservations. Kitchen facilities, washer and dryer, a gorgeous view of Puget Sound. Families with children welcome. Members $5.

Portage Inn, 3021 Pacific Hwy. E. (922-3500), exit 136B off I-5 and **Travellers Inn,** across the street. These motels have the same prices, and essentially the same rooms. They're a bit inconvenient to get to without a car, but they're closer (and more confortable) than the Motel 6. Travellers Inn has a tiny pool. Singles $30. Doubles $35.

Valley Motel, 1220 Puyallup Ave. (272-7720). No glamour, but clean and safe. Closer and cheaper than anything but the Olympus. Small rooms. Singles $25. Doubles $29. Large rooms are $1 more and include kitchenettes. $2 key deposit.

Motel 6, 1811 S. 76th (473-7100). Your basic comfortable sterility. Pool and a hot tub are a bonus, but it's a few miles south of the main action and the prices are certainly not $6. Singles $28. Doubles $34.

Olympus Hotel, 815 Pacific Ave. (272-7895), in the city center. An impressive lobby serves as a false front for an otherwise third-rate hotel. Dining room attached. Inspect a room before putting your money down. Singles $22. Doubles $35. Key deposit $5.

Dash Point State Park (593-2206), on Hwy. 509 across Commencement Bay, in the northeast corner of the city. Take bus #63. Thick forest, wide beach, and a terrific view. Tent sites $7.25, full hook-up $9.50.

Kopachuck State Park (265-3606), on Henderson Bay across the Narrows, about 12 mi. northwest of the city center, west of Hwy. 16 on local roads. Take bus #100. Specializes in water recreation, including clamming. Tent sites $7.25, full hookup $9.50.

Food

Lessie's Southern Kitchen, 1416 6th Ave. (627-4282). Beckoning aroma from a mile away. Alabama cooking in a friendly Tacoma café. Cheat on your diet with crawfish ($6) or ribs ($7) or as much of the menu as you can eat at one sitting. Open Mon.-Sat. 7am-7pm.

Bimbo's, 1516 Pacific Ave. (383-5800). Ignore the construction work that makes it impossible to see the restaurant from the street. Tuscan food in a restaurant straight from Little Italy. Enjoy the ravioli ($5.40) or the bolder rabbit sauté ($6.20). Daily specials as well. Open Mon.-Thurs. 11am-10pm, Fri.-Sat. 11am-11pm. Sun. noon-10pm.

Bob's Java Jive, 2102 S. Tacoma Way (475-9843), south of downtown and directly below the I-5 skyway. Take bus #300 from Jefferson and Broadway downtown. A cabaret-café shaped like a teapot. Two monkeys (Java and Jive) live in a cage in the back room. A locals-only affair until 8pm, when the cabaret starts. Hamburgers and sandwiches around $2. Open Mon. 11:30am-midnight, Tues.-Thurs. 3pm-midnight, Fri. 11:30am-2am, Sat. 6pm-2am.

Antique Sandwich Company, 5102 N. Pearl St. (752-4069), near Point Defiance. A gathering place for local folk musicians, aimless recent college graduates, and families with small children. Good natural food. Homemade soups as well as whole-wheat honey desserts. Espresso shakes $2.50. For a richer meal, try the "poor boy sandwich" ($5). Fri. and Sat. concerts 8pm, Sunday classical concerts 3pm. Open mike Tues. at 7pm. The restaurant's bulletin board chronicles local happenings. Open Mon., Wed.-Thurs., and Sat. 7am-8pm, Tues. 7am-10pm, Fri. 7am-9pm, Sun. 8:30am-7pm.

Ya Shu Yuen, 757 S. 38th St. (473-1180). A small Chinese restaurant in the midst of Tacoma's tiny Asian district. (Take bus #54.) Eat the egg rolls and admire the artistic placemats. Open Tues.-Thurs. 1-9pm, Fri. 11am-10pm, Sat. 12:30-10pm, Sun. 4-9pm.

O'Shea's, 786 Commerce St. (383-8855), downtown. The café is good, but the bakery is the place to binge. Try the incredibly sinful 7-layer bars ($1). Interesting lunch menu changes daily ($5). Breakfasts of waffles or pancakes with fresh fruit ($3). Without a doubt the best eatery in the downtown area. Open Mon.-Fri. 7am-3pm, Sat. 8am-2pm.

Mrs. Frisbee's Bakery Deli and Coffee Shop, 710 S. 38th St., (475-8450 or 472-7591), just down the street from Ya Shu Yen. Get a ham-and-cheese sandwich for $1.75, and save some change for dessert—sublime neopolitans cost 99¢, enormous apple cinnamon muffins only 89¢. Look for the daily bakery specials. Open Mon.-Sat. 6am-6pm, Sun. 10am-4pm.

Tacoma Salmon House, 2611 Pacific (627-0141), near I-5. Good seafood in a woodsy atmosphere. The abundance of totems can be scary. Lunch specials from $5. Mon.-Fri. 11am-3pm. Open Mon.-Thurs. 11am-10pm, Fri. 11am-11pm, Sat. 4-11pm, Sun. noon-9pm.

Moctezuma's Restaurant, corner of 56th and Tyler (474-5593), 1063 mi. north of the border. Above-par burritos, tostadas, and enchiladas ($3.50-4). Try the Langostino Enchilada—that's right, baby lobster, Mexican style ($3.75). Open Mon.-Thurs. 11am-10pm, Fri.-Sat. 11am-11pm.

Sights and Activities

Predictably, the most attractive sights in Tacoma line up along the waterfront. Huge freighters steam out of the sprawling port to bring the lumber and paper products of the central Cascades to the world. Survey the activity from a vantage point in **Commencement Park** or **Marine Park,** both on **Ruston Way** just north of downtown. The city has developed much of Ruston Way's two-mi. waterfront along Commencement Bay as a recreational area for biking, hiking, scuba diving, and boating. On a clear day, this road offers a great view of Mt. Rainier as it looms over Tacoma's skyline.

But for tourist and weekending native alike, Tacoma's most interesting waterfront real estate is the 700-acre **Point Defiance Park.** The five-mi. loop drive passes by all of the park's attractions and offers postcard visions of the Puget Sound and miles of woodland trails as well. **Owen Beach** looks across at Vashon Island and is a good launching point for rambles down the beach. The loop then brushes the spot where, in 1841, U.S. Navy Captain Wilkes proclaimed that if he had guns on this and the opposite shore (Gig Harbor) he could defy the world (hence the name). The meticulously restored **Fort Nisqually** (591-5339), in the park, is definitely worth a visit. The British Hudson's Bay Company built the fort in 1832 to offset growing commercial competition from Americans. The indoor **museum** dips the fort into the Sound's history. (Fort open Wed.-Fri. 9am-4:30pm, Sat.-Sun. 12:30-4:30pm. Museum open Tues.-Sun. 1-4pm.) **Camp Six Logging Museum** (752-0047) retrieves an entire 19th-century logging camp from the dustbin of history. The camp includes buildings and equipment, and offers a 1-mi. ride on an original steam logging engine. (Open Memorial Day-Labor Day Sat.-Sun. 11am-6pm. Admission $1.50, senior citizens and children 75¢.) The park's prize possession is the **Point Defiance Zoo and Aquarium** (591-5335). Penguins, polar bears and sharks populate the aquarium and the zoo features a reproduction of Southeast Asia (scaled down, of course). Open daily 10am-7pm; Labor Day-Memorial Day 10am-4pm. Admission $5.50, seniors $5; ages 5-17 $3.75, ages 3-4 $1.75, under 3 free.

Tacoma's excellent **Washington State Historical Museum,** 315 N. Stadium (593-2830), has comprehensive exhibits on Washington's natural and man-made history. Currently undergoing major renovation, the museum will reopen in the spring of 1991. The **Pantages Centre** (591-5890), on the Broadway Mall downtown, is a recently rejuvenated cultural center in the historic theater of the same name. It embraces both local repertory companies and national touring shows. Tours of the theater are offered at any time between Mon.-Fri. 11am-6pm, Sat. 10am-4pm, but arrangements must be made two weeks ahead of time. If you're just passing through, it's probably worth a call to see if you can join a prearranged tour. Until they manage to acquire his birthplace on "J" St., the basement of the Pantages will probably remain the home of the **Bing Crosby Historical Society** (627-2947). Bing spent his first three years in Tacoma, and this display casts a retrospective glance on those auspicious times. (Real fans should shuffle east to the Crosby Library in Spokane to see a piece of Bing's right index finger bone.) Society open Mon.-Fri. 11am-3pm. The city sponsors free outdoor concerts in summer, including a regular schedule of noon and evening performances by the **Tacoma Symphony,** and jazz and classical artists. Contact the Chamber of Commerce for more information. Aesthetes should make a quick stop at the convenient **Tacoma Art Museum** (272-4258), at 12th and Pacific Ave. downtown. This eclectic collection brings a needed dose of local artwork to Tacoma's depressed downtown area. (Open Mon.-Sat. 10am-5pm, Sun. noon-5pm. Admission $2, senior citizens and students $1. Tues. free.)

Near Tacoma: Vashon Island

Only a short ferry ride from Seattle or Tacoma, lush Vashon Island is, for the moment anyway, spared the scourge of tourism. Of the many ways a day might be spent on Vashon, most are free. **Biking** is rapturous throughout the island—the Westside Highway is particularly flat and sunny. The **Wax Orchards,** 204th and 131st St. (463-9735), processes all-natural preserves and other fruity items. For safety reasons, they discourage large groups from descending en masse, but they will graciously let smaller numbers wander through the plant; they even offer free tastings. Open daily 9am-3:30 or 4pm.

Skiing buffs should examine the famed **K2 Ski Factory,** located just outside the town of Vashon (463-3631; tours given by appointment Tues. and Thurs. at 10am or 1pm). With one out of every 10 residents of the island a professional artist, aesthetic praxis is common. **Blue Heron Arts** coordinates most activities. Call 463-5131 for a tour or details on upcoming classes and events. The small gallery is open Tue.-Sat. noon-5pm.

The whole island gets in on the action of the **Strawberry Festival,** held in mid-July. Enjoy miles of food and craft booths, day-long musical performance and every known way of using strawberries (well, almost every way). The wacky parade through the town of Vashon traditionally features camels, the Rototiller Drill Team, and mobs of five-year-olds impersonating strawberries.

The best budget accommodation on Vashon Island is unquestionably the hostel (see Tacoma Accommodations). There are no campgrounds on the island, but you can put up a tent on the hostel's lawn and use its facilities for $5 per night.

In an **emergency,** call the Coast Guard at 463-2951. In a **medical emergency,** call 463-3696 Tues.-Sat. 9am-5pm; otherwise phone Seattle. The **post office** is in downtown Vashon (463-9390) and is open Mon.-Fri. 9am-5pm. The General Delivery ZIP Code is 98070.

Bellingham

Founded by Whatcom loggers and coal miners in the 1850s, this town's flighty name rested briefly on Sehome before finally landing on Bellingham. Local poet Ella Higginson once bragged that she had lived in three different cities without ever having moved a block.

Together with Fairhaven, its southern neighbor, Bellingham set its sights on becoming the terminus of the transcontinental railroad. So hell-bent were the residents on capturing that ultimate spike that when the famed feminist-anarchist Emma Goldman blew into town, they trooped en masse to jeer her, fearful that her intent was to smear Bellingham's all-American image as the promised land of free enterprise. The townspeople's splenetic efforts went for naught, however—the railroad line ended 90 mi. to the south.

During the late 60s, the well-meaning Bellinghamites took another blow to their collective self-esteem when an army of hippies descended upon the railroad-less town. With people sleeping on the side of freeways and squatting in abandoned warehouses, Bellingham had inexplicably become the Mecca for those seeking an alternate lifestyle. Before they could catch their collective breath, the aggrieved townsfolk had a conniption fit when they learned that Western Washington University's Fairhaven College was offering a philosophy/physical education course entitled "Self Love."

Practical Information and Orientation

Visitor Information: 904 Potter St. (671-3990). Take the Lakeway exit from I-5. Prepare yourself for a flood of Whatcom County trivia and non-trivial information. Extremely helpful staff. Open daily 9am-6pm; in winter 8:30am-5:30pm. **Bellingham Parks and Recreation Department,** 3424 Meridian St. (676-6985).

Greyhound: 1329 N. State St. (733-5251). To: Seattle (7 per day, $10); Vancouver (5 per day, $8); Mt. Vernon (6 per day, $4). Open Mon.-Fri. 6am-6pm, Sat.-Sun. 8am-5pm.

Whatcom County Transit: 676-7433. All buses originate at the terminal in the Railroad Ave. mall on Magnolia St., where maps and schedules are available. Fare 25¢, seniors 10¢; no free transfers. Buses run every 15-30 min. Mon.-Fri. 7am-6pm, reduced service Sat. 9am-5pm.

Lummi Island Ferry: 676-6730, at Gooseberry Pt. off Hackston Wy. 26 trips back and forth each day. The first leaves the island at 6:50am; the last departs the mainland at 12:10am. Fare $1, driver and car $2.

Taxi: Superior Cabs, 734-3478. **Bellingham Taxi,** 676-0445. Both 24 hr.

Car Rental: U-Save Auto Rental, 1100 Iowa (671-3687). Cars from $18 per day with 100 free mi., 20¢ per additional mi. Must be 21, with credit card or $250 deposit. Open Mon.-Fri. 9am-6pm, Sat. 9am-5pm.

Laundromat: Bellingham Cleaning Center, 1010 Lakeway Dr. (734-3755). Open daily 7am-10pm.

Ski Report: 671-0211 or 733-8180 (second number also gives windsurfing conditions in summer).

Mountain Pass Conditions: 1-976-7623. Nov.-March 24 hr. Toll call.

Ride Board: Viking Union at Western Washington University. Rides most often to Seattle and eastern Washington, but also to diverse regions of the continent.

Senior Services: Information and assistance 733-4033 (city), on the corner of Ohio and Cornwall St. on bus 10B; 398-1995 (county).

Crisis Centers: Bellingham, 734-7271. Whatcom County, 384-1485. Both open 24 hr.

Pharmacy: Fountain Super Drug Store, 2416 Meridian (733-6200). Open Mon.-Sat. 9am-10pm, Sun. 10am-7pm.

Hospital: St. Luke's General, 809 E. Chestnut (734-8300). Open 24 hrs.

Post Office: 315 Prospect (676-8303). Open Mon.-Fri. 8am-5pm. General Delivery ZIP Code: 98225.

Area Code: 206.

Bellingham lies along I-5, 90 mi. north of Seattle and 57 mi. south of Vancouver. Bellingham's downtown is a small shopping and business area centered on Holly St. and Cornwall Ave., perfumed by the Georgia Pacific paper plant. Western Washington University climbs a hill to the south along Indian St., and Old Fairhaven Village (the "South Side" to the locals) fronts the south end of the bay along South State St. Suburbs and 130 acres of city parks circle the city. **Whatcom County Transit** provides service throughout the area.

Reach **Fairhaven** either by heading south along State St. from downtown or by taking the Fairhaven exit (#250) off I-5. From the south, consider taking the bayside **Chuckanut Drive** (Hwy. 11) instead of I-5. Chuckanut leaves I-5 at exit 231 in Skagit County and follows the water and mountains into Fairhaven Village. Larrabee State Park is along this drive. Startling views of the San Juan Islands and sparkling Puget Sound appear through the trees. This route is not recommended for cyclists; the road is extremely narrow and seems to be a favorite spot for hotrodders. Cyclists should stick to Hwy. 9, a more manageable stretch that pops up on the east side of I-5. Fairhaven is also on Bellingham bus lines 1A, 1B, 2B, 5A, and 7B.

Accommodations and Camping

Most of Bellingham's motels serve traveling salespeople and other itinerants, and the rooms lack both tranquility and a bay view. One alternative is the local bed-and-breakfast association **Babs,** P.O. Box 5025, Bellingham 98227 (733-8642), which offers doubles averaging $50.

YWCA, 1026 N. Forest St. (734-4820), up the hill, 1 block east of State St., about 4 blocks from Greyhound. Only women over 18 allowed. A pleasant, older building. Some rooms have views. Large rooms with sink; bathroom down the hall. Check-in Mon.-Fri. 8am-9pm, Sat. 9am-5pm. No curfew. Private singles $15, adjoining singles $10.

Mac's Motel, 1215 E. Maple St. (734-7570), at Samish Way. Large clean rooms. Pleasant management, cats—lots of cats (all over the place). Cats. Cats. Cats. Singles $22. Doubles $30.

Motel 6, 3701 Byron Ave. (671-4494), Samish Way exit off I-5, between Denny's and the Calico Inn Pancake House. Noisy location on freeway. Singles $25. Doubles $31. Reservations sometimes necessary in summer.

Bell Motel, 208 N. Samish Way (733-2520), on the strip. Hard beds and plain decor. Free local calls. Refrigerator in most rooms. Singles $38. Doubles $45. Kitchens $5.

Larrabee State Park, Chuckanut Dr. (676-2093), 7 mi. south of Bellingham. 100 sites on Samish Bay. Check out the nearby tidal pools or hike to alpine lakes. For your listening pleasure, trains thunder by nightly; tracks separate the campground from the bay. The 3 walk-in tentsites are the most appealing option. Sites $7.50. Hookups $10.50.

Food

The **Community Food Co-op,** 1059 N. State St. (734-8158), at Maple, has all the essentials plus a wide selection of dried and fresh fruits. Non-members pay 6½% above ticketed price. (Open Mon.-Sat. 9am-8pm, Sun. 11am-6pm.)

The Bagelry, 1319 Railroad Ave. (676-5288), 1 block south of the City Transit terminal. Order a veggie-laden bagel sandwich for $3, or just have a bagel (8 kinds) with cream cheese (12 flavors) for $1.60. The pumpernickel-pineapple combination is not recommended. Open Mon.-Fri. 7am-5pm, Sat. 8am-5pm, Sun. 9am-4pm.

Bullie's Restaurant, 1200 Harris (734-2855), in the Fairhaven Marketplace. Decor is enhanced by an old gas pump converted into a cylindrical fish bowl. Burgers $5, Tex-Mex, and Potato Skin Dinners ($6). The Aloha pineapple burger is Charo's favorite. Massive beer selection. Open Mon.-Sat. 6am-10pm, Sun. 6am-9pm.

Tony's Coffees and Tea Shop, 1101 Harris Ave., Fairhaven Village (733-6319), just down the hill from S. State St. This Fairhaven institution is at once café and coffee market. Some tables are inlaid with hand-painted tiles, and local artists display their work on the walls. Coffee, bagels, and pastries in a free floating atmosphere of sitar music, paisley, and a pierced nose or two. "Toxic milkshake" $1.65. Free live music Fri. and Sat. nights. Open daily 7:30am-11pm. Same cinnamon rolls for ½-price at the Great Harvest Bakery in the Bellingham Mall (671-0873), on Samish Way. Bakery open Tues.-Sat. 9:30am-6pm.

GJK Greek Cafe, 1219 Cornwall Ave. (676-5554). Plaster of Paris and accents of Athens. Gyros $4, *souvlaki, baklava,* and more esoteric dishes. Open Mon.-Sat. 11am-9pm.

Mexican Village Café, 2010 N. State St. (676-8033), 8 blocks northeast of downtown. Full meals $5-7, tacos $1.50. Open Tues.-Sun. 4:30-8:30pm.

The High Country, 119 N. Commercial St. (733-3443), at the top of the Bellingham Towers downtown. Elevated dining at elevated prices; go up for a drink and the fabulous views. Open Mon.-Fri. 11:30am-2pm and 5:30-9:30pm, Sat.-Sun. 5:30-10:30pm.

Sights and Activities

When the trans-continental railroad by passed Bellingham and nearby Fairhaven, construction of many buildings stopped short. In Fairhaven especially, buildings were left to rot. It was not until after a developer caught sight of Fairhaven's decaying buildings about 10 years ago that the area (now called the South Side) began to revitalize.

Though odd for any town (and especially one which was spat on by the railroads), old railway cars frequently serve as restaurants and shops, particularly in the fully restored **Marketplace,** at Harris Ave. and 12th St. This is also the setting for the annual **Christmas Arts and Crafts Fair** (Sat.-Sun. for 3 weeks before Christmas). The fair imports live music and other forms of entertainment. *Fairhaven,* a free brochure available from the visitors center, describes a short walking tour through the area.

The **Whatcom Museum of History and Art,** 121 Prospect St. (676-6981), between Holly, Prospect, and Central St. downtown, dates from the same boom era as the South Side buildings. The towering red Victorian, once the city hall, is visible from most of downtown. It now displays first-rate exhibitions of modern art and local history. The exhibits are impeccably presented, a rare achievement for a county museum. There is absolutely no reason to miss a free museum of this caliber. (Unless it's closed—hours only Tues.-Sun. noon-5pm.)

Like every other city in Northwest Washington, Bellingham isn't far from tranquil hiking trails and scenery that will make you glad you brought along your camera. Hike up **Chuckanut Mountain** through a quiet forest to overlook the islands that fill the bay. You can occasionally spot Mt. Rainier to the south. A 2½-mi. hike uphill leaves from Old Samish Hwy. about 1 mi. south of the city limits. The beach at **Lake Padden Park,** 4882 Samish Way (676-6989), delights those who find Puget Sound a little chilly. Take bus #5B or 10A 1 mi. south of downtown. A lifeguard stands guard Memorial Day through Labor Day. The park also has miles of hiking trails, a boat launch (no motors allowed), tennis courts, and playing fields. The park is wheelchair-accessible. (Open daily 6am-10pm.)

Whatcom Falls Park, 1401 Electric Ave., due east of town, also has fantastic hiking trails, picnic facilities, and tennis courts. Upper Whatcom Falls trail (1.6 mi.) leads to the falls themselves, converted into an unofficial waterslide by the locals. Take bus #4A or 11A. (Open daily 6am-10pm.) Fishing is good in both these lakes and also in **Lake Samish** and **Silver Lake,** north of the town of Maple Falls off the Mt. Baker Hwy. (See Near Bellingham for information on Silver Lake County Park.) The lake trout season opens the third Sunday in April. **Fishing licenses** ($3) are available from the Department of Fisheries (586-1425), at any sporting goods store, and at some hardware stores.

Popular with South Side residents, **Interurban trail** runs 6.6 mi. from Fairhaven Park to Larrabee State Park along the route of the old Interurban Electric Railway. The trail is less developed than those at Padden and Whatcom Lakes and follows a creek through the forest. Occasional breaks in the trees permit a glimpse of the San Juan Islands. More information on these and other city parks is available from the Parks and Recreation Department (see Practical Information).

Western Washington University (676-3424) is the nexus of much of the activity in and around the Bellingham area. The campus ornaments a sylvan setting with 16 pieces of outdoor sculpture, commissioned from local and nationally known artists. A free brochure, available at the Visitor Information Center, guides the visiting critic around campus from piece to piece. Friday nights, a program of concerts called **Mama Sundays** heats up the Viking Union on campus. Top-notch folk and bluegrass are the norm ($1-5). The **Western Visitors Center** is at the entrance to the college on South College Dr., and information is also available at the Whatcom County Visitors Center in Blaine. Here you can pick up a schedule for the Faculty of Dramatic Arts **Summer Stock Theater** which runs from July 17 to August 25 (676-3873). Take bus #3B, 7B, or 8A to reach the campus.

The Alaska Marine Highway

Since the days of the Alaska Gold Rush, Seattle served as the most important link for trade and transportation to Alaska. But no longer. Competitive bidding has resulted in the Alaska ferry being moved up the Sound to Bellingham. The ferry stops at **Prince Rupert, BC, Ketchikan, Wrangell, Petersburg, Juneau,** and **Haines** before arriving in **Skagway** on Monday afternoon; you can make stopovers at any port along the way. This well-equipped vessel offers a spectacular trip to the north for travelers with some time and money to spare. Reservations for all passenger tickets out of Bellingham are recommended, as well as reservations for berths. Summer passages are booked six months in advance, but you may be able to find space on a standby basis. (Standby fare identical to regular fare.) The wait list for standby passengers opens at 8:30am on the Monday before Friday's departure. Walk-ons have a decent chance for a ride if they sign up before Thursday, though space for vehicles is less certain. Reserved vehicles must check in at the Bellingham terminal three hours prior to departure or at the Prince Rupert terminal two hours prior to departure. Cabins are very remote possibilities for those on standby; sleeping bags in the lounges is a pleasant, and free, alternative. (Departures Fri. at 6:15pm from the Fairhaven Terminal. To Skagway $218 and Haines $214. To Skagway cars up to 10 ft. $244, 10-15 ft. $512. Senior citizens travel free from Ketchikan to Skagway from October to April with a pass, available with proof of age at port of embarkation; those taking advantage of this new deal must book 30 days in advance and are confined to standby status. Pets $10 extra, health certificate required.) For reservations, write to the Alaska Marine Highway, P.O. Box R, Juneau, AK 99811-2505 (800-642-0066 or 907-465-3941). For general information, write the **Alaska State Division of Tourism,** P.O. Box E, Juneau, AK 99811 (907-465-2010).

The weekend-long ride is a fantastic voyage past glaciers, wooded islands, and snow-capped peaks and whales, seals, and eagles often escort the ship. The **Tongass**

National Forest even trots out an interpretive program when ferries sail by its holdings.

Alaska Motorcoaches makes regular connections between Seattle and Prince Rupert, and those who can reach Prince Rupert by land will save $106 on the Seattle-Skagway passage.

Near Bellingham

The *pièce de résistance* of Whatcom County is certainly **Mount Baker,** which dominates the landscape and the recreational economy of the area. Exit 255 off I-5, just north of Bellingham, leads to Hwy. 542, the Mt. Baker Highway. Fifty-six mi. of roadway traverse the foothills, endowed with spectacular views of Baker and the other peaks in the range. Crowning the Mt. Baker-Snoqualmie National Forest, Mt. Baker contains excellent downhill and cross-country facilities, usually open from late October through mid-May. The peak reaches 10,778 ft. and the longest downhill run plummets 6500 of these. Call 734-6771 in Bellingham for more information on the operation and resort. On your way to the mountain, stop at the **Mount Bakery,** 3706 Mt. Baker Hwy. (592-5703), for gigantic apple fritters and other muffins, donuts, and pastries (under 50¢). (Open Mon.-Sat. 6am-6pm.)

Mount Baker Vineyards, 4298 Mt. Baker Hwy. (592-2300), fewer than 10 mi. outside the city limits, is one of a number of successful vineyards in Washington. The processing and storage areas are open to the public and guided tours are conducted daily. (Open Wed.-Sun. 11am-5pm; Jan.-March Sat.-Sun. 11am-5pm.)

Silver Lake Park, 9006 Silver Lake Rd. (599-2776), 28 mi. east of Bellingham on the Mt. Baker Hwy. and 3 mi. north of Maple Falls, is operated by the Whatcom County Parks and Recreation Department. The park tends 113 campsites near the lake along with facilities for swimming, hiking, and fishing. (Tentsites $6. Hookups $7.50.)

The *cogniscenţi* flee the town of **Lynden,** which gained local notoriety when it outlawed public dancing wherever liquor is served. Blue suede shoes may have gone by the wayside, but clogging is still esteemed by the town's Dutch community, which also keeps a steady supply of tulips and miniature windmills on display. **Holland Days,** in early May, features a wooden shoe race. The **Lynden Pioneer Museum,** 217 Front St. (354-3675), owns a fine collection of over 100 buggies, tractors, and old cars, dating from the 1850s and donated entirely by town residents. (Open Mon.-Sat. 10am-5pm; Oct.-May Thurs.-Sat. noon-4pm. $1 donation requested.) Just down the street, **Dutch Mother's Restaurant and Bakery,** 405 Front St. (354-2174), celebrates Lynden's gastronomic heritage with Dutch baked goods, served by waiters in full Netherlandish costume. (Breakfast under $5, lunch and dinner $11-15.) Reach Lynden via I-5: going south, turn east off exit 270; going north, head north off exit 256. Call or visit the **Tourist Information Center,** 1775 Front. St. on the southern end of town (354-5995) for more information.

Lummi Island, off the coast of Bellingham, was for centuries the fishing and hunting ground of the Lummi nation of Native Americans. Now the Lummis are confined to a reservation on the northwestern side of Bellingham Bay, and the island has been overrun by hermits. The island is distinctly rural, with paved roads only on the northern half. Old logging roads chessboarding the rest of the island are perfect for hiking up to Lummi Mountain or down to the island's various bays and tidal pools. Bicyclists will find the island roads peaceful; traffic is unbearably light and fairly slow. The Department of Natural Resources (DNR) operates a five-site campground on the southeast tip of the island, accessible only by boat.

Lummi Island can be reached by **ferry** from Gooseberry Point on the Lummi Indian Reservation, 15 mi. from Bellingham. Take I-5 north to exit 260; left on Hwy. 540 will lead you west about 3½ mi. to Haxton Way. Turn south and follow signs to the ferry terminal. For 10 days in June each year, the ferry is sent to Seattle for maintenance. During this interlude a walk-on ferry is substituted, so call before taking your car (ferry information 676-6730).

Twenty miles north of Bellingham is the border town of **Blaine,** the busiest port of entry between Canada and the U.S. (And judging by the number of BC and Alberta license plates at the town's gas stations, a good percentage of that traffic is Canucks filling up on cheap U.S. gas.) If you plan to promenade in Blaine in less than formal attire, be prepared with some friendly small talk for U.S. border patrol agents. Those who get turned away from the Canadian border for lack of sufficient funds (you need CDN$500 if you're headed for Alaska) or identification often head for Blaine, and border patrol prides itself on catching these undesirables with blanket stop-checks.

The main attraction in Blaine is the **Peace Arch Park Heritage Site** (332-8221; open for day use only). Uncharacteristically gracious in defeat, the U.S., after losing the war of 1812, figured that it was better to trade with Canada than to war with her and pushed for a rapid rapproachment and built this arch as a token of goodwill in 1814. With two gates, one hinged on the U.S. side, the other on the Canadian, the gate can be closed only by mutual consent. Though it has never been closed, a recent poll found that while Americans most commonly describe Canadians as "friendly," Canadians most commonly describe Americans as "snobs." (Open daily 6:30am-10pm; Oct. 16-March 8am-5pm. Toilets, kitchen facilities.)

The spit of land encompassing **Semiahmoo Park** (371-5513), one mi. south of Blaine, was first inhabited by the coastal Salish people, who harvested shellfish when the tide was low. Clam digging is still a popular activity. Buckets and shovels may be rented from the park, and a $3 license is required. Three buildings from the former Alaska Packers Association cannery, which operated on the spit for 74 years, are now used by the park as an **interpretive center,** preserving the history of both the local canning industries and the natural environment. Take Drayton Harbor Rd. around to the southwestern side of Drayton Harbor. (Open mid-Feb. to Dec. Wed.-Sun. 1-5pm. Admission $3.) The park also hosts such events as wool-spinning and weaving shows and traditional salmon bakes. For information on all Whatcom County Parks, contact the Parks and Recreation Board Headquarters and Information Center, 3373 Mt. Baker Hwy. (733-2900). The **Blaine Visitors Center,** 900 Peace Portal Dr. (332-4544) is a storehouse of information on these parks as well as all points of interest in the area, both American and Canadian. (Open daily 8am-7pm.)

The **Birch Bay Hostel (AYH),** on the former Blaine Air Force Base (371-2180), is one of the best hostels in the Pacific Northwest and has a spacious common area with a cable TV and extensive cooking facilities. The rooms are spotless, and the manager helpful. Take either the Birch Bay-Lynden Rd. exit or the Grandview Rd. exit off I-5 and head west. Blaine Rd. will take you to the Alderson Rd. entrance to the Air Force base. The hostel is building #630. (Open June-Sept. AYH members only, $7.50.) The **Westview Motel,** 1300 Peace Portal Dr. (332-5501), also offers excellent lodgings (singles $23, doubles $27).

The best seafood in town is at the **Harbor Cafe,** on Marine Dr. (332-5176), halfway down the pier. The $6 fish and chips, salad bar and roll included, is hard to resist. And why would you want to?

For camping, **Birch Bay State Park,** 5105 Helwig Rd. (371-2800), 10 mi. south of Blaine, operates 156 sites near the water. The Semiahmoo Native Americans used this area and the marshland at the southern end of the park to harvest shellfish and hunt waterfowl. Three hundred species of birds live in the **Terrell Creek Estuary.** The park is also a good area for crabbing, scuba diving, waterskiing, and swimming. To reach the park, take the Birch Bay-Lynden exit off I-5 and turn south onto Blaine Rd. When you run out of road, turn east onto Bay Rd. Turn south on Jackson Rd. and take it to Helwig Rd. The way is well-marked from the freeway. (Open year-round. Sites $7.50.)

The Blaine **Greyhound Station** (733-5251) is located on Martin St. between 3rd and 4th St. (Open Mon.-Fri. 9am-5pm, Sat 9am-2pm).

Seasonal Events

Whatcom County has a number of annual fairs and festivals that celebrate its modestly colorful past. Held on Gooseberry Point ⸱ the Lummi Island Reservation, the **Lummi Stommish Indian Water Carnival** (75⸜ '221) is entering its 44th year. The three-day carnival at the end of June stages traditional dances, war-canoe races, arts and crafts sales, and a salmon barbecue.

Loggers succeeded Natives in Whatcom County, but fête themselves earlier in June at the 27-year old **Deming Logging Show** (592-2423). Logging stuntpeople converge here from throughout the region to compete in axe-throwing, log-rolling, and speed climbing. To reach the Showgrounds, take Mt. Baker Hwy. 12 mi. east to Cedarville Rd. and head north. Signs beckon you to the grounds.

The crowning event of the two-week **Ski to Sea Festival** (734-1330) is an 85-mi. relay race from Mt. Baker to Bellingham Bay over Memorial Day weekend. Team members ski, run, bicycle, canoe, and sail to the finish line. Parades precede the event.

The **Northwest Washington Fairgrounds** (354-4111), in Lynden, hosts a number of wing-dings throughout the summer, including the **Lynden Spring Fair,** at the end of June (with its old-fashioned draft-horse-plowing competition) and the **Northwest Washington Fair,** in mid-August.

San Juan Islands

The San Juan Islands are an uncorrupted treasure. Bald eagles spiral above haggard hillsides and family farms, pods of killer whales spout offshore, and despite the lush vegetation it never seems to rain. To travelers approaching from summer resorts teeming with vacationers, the islands will seem blissfully quiet. Even in midsummer, it is possible to drive the back roads and pass another car just once every hour. For this reason, islanders don't begrudge admission to their towns and campsites. Although tension is starting to build between the locals and visitors from Seattle and California who are buying up huge chunks of the islands at exorbitant prices, quiet, well-behaved tourists and their dollars are still very welcome on the San Juans.

An excellent guide to the area is *The San Juan Islands Afoot and Afloat* by Marge Mueller ($10), available at bookstores and outfitting stores on the islands and in Seattle. *The San Juans Beckon* is published annually by the *Islands Sounder,* the local paper, to provide up-to-date information on island recreation. You can pick it up free on the ferries and in island stores. The *San Juanderer* also has a fari amount of useful information, including tide charts and ferry schedules (free on ferries or at the tourist centers).

Getting There

Washington State Ferries serve the islands daily from **Anacortes** on the mainland. To reach Anacortes, take I-5 north from Seattle to Mt. Vernon. From there, Hwy. 20 heads west; the way to the ferry is well-marked. **Evergreen Trailways** buses to Anacortes depart Seattle from the Greyhound depot at 8th Ave. and Stewart St. twice per day. Call 728-5955 for exact times.

Of the 172 islands in the San Juan archipelago, only four are accessible by ferry. Ferries leave about every other hour for Lopez, Shaw, Orcas, and San Juan Island. In summer, two additional ferries per day travel directly to San Juan Island. One ferry per day continues year-round from San Juan Island to the town of Sidney, BC, just north of Victoria on Vancouver Island. The ferry system publishes its schedule every season.

In Anacortes, you can purchase a ticket to Lopez, Shaw, Orcas, or San Juan Island. You pay only on westbound trips to or between the islands; no charge is levied on eastbound traffic. (In effect, any ticket to the islands is a round-trip ticket.) You can thus save money by traveling directly to the westernmost island on your itinerary and then making your way back island by island. The ferry unloads first at Lopez Island, then at Shaw, Orcas, and finally San Juan. It is possible to purchase one-way tickets to Sidney, or from Sidney to the islands. Foot passengers travel in either direction between the islands free of charge. Fares from Anacortes to San Juan Island are $4.65 ($2.35 for seniors and ages 5-11), $6.25 for bikes, $9.50 for motorcycles, and $19 for cars. Fares to the other islands en route are generally a few dollars cheaper. Inter-island fares average $2.25 for bikes and motorcycles, $7.75 for cars. The one-way fare to Sidney is $6.05, $8.55 for bikes, $13.15 for motorcycles, and $31.25 for cars in summer ($26.05 in winter). Some car spaces are available from the islands to Sidney. Reservations are recommended: call before noon the day before your trip to ensure a space. For specific departure times and rates, call Washington State Ferries (206-464-6400; in WA 800-542-0810). The ferry authorities only accept cash or in-state checks as payment. You may park your vehicle for free in Anacortes at the parking lot on the corner of 30th and T St. A free, reliable shuttle then whisks you four mi. to the terminal.

San Juan Island

Although San Juan is the last stop on the ferry's route, it is the most frequently visited island and home to the largest town in the group, **Friday Harbor.** Since the ferry docks right in town, the island is also the easiest to explore. San Juan was the site of the Pig War, which pitted the U.S. against England in a phony war for control of the islands. The 1846 Treaty of Oregon did not assign the San Juans to either Canada or the U.S., and when the Canadian Hudson's Bay Company established a salmon-curing station and a sheep farm on the island, the Company assumed its ownership would go undisputed. The Territorial Congress of Oregon, oblivious to British intentions, declared the islands its own in 1853. By 1859, 25 Americans lived on San Juan Island. When an American farmer shot a British pig found rooting one morning in his garden, the situation became intolerable and both countries had no choice but to send in troops, thus initiating perhaps the least-known international dispute in U.S. history. For 12 years, two thoroughly bored garrisons stared across the island at each other, occasionally rousing to join in horse races and Christmas dances. Their descendants now sublimate their energies into more peaceful pursuits, primarily the bustling tourist industry on this island.

Practical Information

Visitor Information: National Park Service Information Center and **Chamber of Commerce Information Center,** northeast corner of 1st and Spring (378-2240). Answers *any* question about San Juan or Friday Harbor. Open Mon.-Fri. 8am-4:30pm, Sat.-Sun. 10:30am-3:30pm.

U.S. Customs: 271 Front St. (378-2080; or 800-562-5943 for 24-hr. service).

Ferry Terminal: 378-4777. Open 24 hr.

Taxi: Island Taxi, 378-5545. **Primo Taxi,** 378-3550.

Car Rental: Friday Harbor Rentals, 410 Spring St. (378-4351), in the Friday Harbor Motor Inn. $45 per day. 50 mi. free, 25¢ per additional mi. Major credit card required.

Bike Rental: Island Bicycles, 380 Argyle St., Friday Harbor (378-2442). 1-speeds $2 per hr., $8 per day; 5-speeds $3 per hr., $12 per day; 10-speeds $4 per hr., $16 per day; mountain bikes $5 per hr., $20 per day. Also rents child carriers, trailers, and panniers. Provides maps of the island and suggests bike routes. Open Mon.-Sat. 10am-5:30pm, Sun. noon-5:30pm; Labor Day-Memorial Day Thurs.-Sat. 10am-5:30pm.

Moped Rental: Susie's Mopeds (378-5244), in Churchill Sq. above the ferry lanes on Dixon St. between A and B St. Mopeds $10 per hr., $40 per day. Credit card required. Open March-Oct. daily 10am-6pm.

Tours: Friday Harbor Motor Inn, 410 Spring St. (378-4351), sends a double-decker bus ($10) around the island via English Camp and Lime Kiln Park (for whalewatching) daily at 1:30pm.

Senior Citizens' Center: 145 Rhone St. (378-2677).

Laundromat: Up a wooden alley on Spring St. between 1st and Front. Open daily 7:30am-9pm.

Pharmacy: Friday Harbor Drug, 210 Spring (378-4421). Open Mon.-Sat. 9am-7pm.

Sheriff: 135 Rhone St., at Reed St. (911 emergency, 378-4151 nonemergency. You be the judge.)

Medical Services: Inter-Island Medical Center, 550 Spring St. (378-2141). Open Mon.-Fri. 9am-5pm. 24-hr. emergency service; call 911 in emergencies.

Post Office: Blair and Reed St. (378-4511). Open Mon.-Fri. 8:30am-4:30pm. General Delivery ZIP Code: 98250.

Area Code: 206.

With a hostel and bicycle, car, and boat rentals all just one block from the ferry terminal, Friday Harbor makes an ideal starting point for exploration of all the islands. Miles of road traverse all corners of the island from Friday Harbor's eastern hub. Unfortunately, the roads aren't well-marked, so plot your course carefully on one of the maps available free at the information center in Friday Harbor (see Practical Information). **Hitching** is fairly common, and it's a relatively safe means of travel on the island.

Accommodations and Camping

San Juan's campgrounds have become wildly popular of late; show up early in the afternoon.

Friday Harbor Youth Hostel (AYH), 35 1st St. (378-5555), in the Elite Hotel. No kitchen facilities or common areas, but café downstairs. The women's dorm is airy, well-lit and clean. The men's dorm is cramped and dirty by comparison, but still tolerable. Both have lockers, but you have to supply your own lock. Check in on the 3rd floor 8-11pm. High-season prices $8, nonmembers $14; private room (1 or 2 people) $35.

San Juan County Park, 380 Westside Rd. (378-2992), 10 mi. west of Friday Harbor on Smallpox and Andrews Bays. Public campgrounds. Sit on the bay where Native Americans with smallpox fever swam to cool themselves (thereby catching pneumonia). Cold water and flush toilets. Bikers and hikers $3; cars, campers, and trailers $12.50.

Lakedale Campgrounds, 2627 Roche Harbor Rd. (378-2350), 4 mi. from Friday Harbor. San Juan Tours and Transit provides service. Pay showers, fishing, and swimming in freshwater lakes. Bikers and hikers $3.50, vehicles $8 plus $1.50 per person. Canoe rentals $16 per day, plus $10 refundable deposit. Swimming available to noncampers for $1.50 per day, ages under 6 75¢.

Food

If you listen very closely, you can actually hear the parks and shoreline drives begging you to pack a picnic lunch and explore. Stock up on bread and cheese at **King's Market,** 160 Spring St. (378-4505; open daily 8am-10pm).

Driftwood Drive-In, corner of 2nd and Court. Amiable management with great burgers for $2.45 and shakes as thick as Michael Raynor's Canadian accent for $1.30. Open daily 7am-7pm.

San Juan Donut Shop, 209 Spring St. (378-2271). Another local hangout. Breakfast under $5, with oodles of bagels and croissants. Cheeseburger $2. Open Mon.-Sat. 5am-5pm, Sun. 6am-noon.

The Hungry Clam, on 1st St. near Spring. The unmistakable spout of the fast-food leviathan. Clam basket $5, burger $3.25. Open Mon.-Fri. 11am-8pm, Sat. 11am-9pm, Sun. noon-6pm.

Funk 'n' Junk Bakery, 65 Nickel St., behind the antique store. The truly bold opt for the jalapeño jack cheese croissant ($1.75); the rest settle for nutty chocolate chip cookies. Hours vary.

Sights and Activities

Friday Harbor is less than charming when the tourists are out in full force, but quite appealing other times, especially in winter. Take the time to poke around the galleries, craft shops, and bookstores. The **Whale Museum**, 62 1st St. (378-4710), will teach you more than you ever wanted to know about the giant cetaceans, starring skeletons, sculptures, and information on new research. The museum even has a toll-free **whale hotline** (800-562-8832) to report sightings and strandings. (Open daily in summer 10am-5pm, in winter 11am-4pm. Admission $2.50, seniors and students $2, ages under 12 $1.) The free **San Juan Historical Museum**, in the old King House at 405 Price St. (378-4587), across from the St. Francis Catholic church, explodes with exhibits, furnishings, and photographs from the late 1800s. (Open June-Labor Day Wed.-Sat. 1-4:30pm.)

A drive around the perimeter of the island takes about 90 minutes, and the route is flat enough to keep cyclists happy. The **West Side Road** traverses gorgeous scenery and allows your best chance of sighting orcas (killer whales) offshore. For those without private transportation, **San Juan Tours and Transit Co.** (378-5545) runs two sight-seeing tours of the island every afternoon. The two-hour tours circle the island, stopping at Roche Harbor, English and American Camps, and Lime Kiln Lighthouse (see Practical Information).

To begin a loop of the island, head south out of Friday Harbor on Mullis Rd., which merges into Cattle Point Rd. on the way to **American Camp** (378-2240), five mi. south of Friday Harbor. The camp dates to the Pig War of 1859, when the U.S. and England were at befuddled loggerheads over possession of the islands. Two of the camp's buildings still stand. An interpretive shelter near the entrance to the park explains the history of the conflict; there is also a self-guided trail from the shelter through the buildings and past the site of the English sheep farm. Every weekend from June to September volunteers in period costume re-enact daily life at the camp. Watch your footing; it would seem that gigantic rabbits have rampaged across this terrain recently. (Free.) A ½-mi. jaunt farther down the road to **Cattle Point** rewards you with blissful, clear-weather views of the distant Olympic Mountains.

Returning north on Cattle Point Rd., consider taking the gravel False Bay Rd. to the west. The road will guide you to **False Bay**, a true bay that is home to a large number of nesting bald eagles. A University of Washington biology preserve, the bay is the site of many student projects, each indicated by markers. False Bay is almost a guaranteed spot for eagle watching. During the spring and summer at low tide, walk quietly along the northwestern shore (to your right as you face the water) to see the nesting national emblems.

Whale-watching at **Lime Kiln Point State Park**, a few miles north, is best during salmon runs in the summer. Check the whale museum for day-to-day information on your chances of sighting the orcas and minkes looming off-shore.

Farther north on False Bay Rd., you'll run into **Bailer Hill Road**, which turns into West Side Rd. when it reaches Haro Straight. (You can also reach Bailer Hill Rd. by taking Cattle Point Rd. to Little Rd.) Slopes softened with wildflowers rise to one side, and rocky shores fall to the other.

The Pig War casts its comic pallor over **English Camp**, the second half of San Juan National Historical Park. The camp lies on West Valley Rd. on the sheltered Garrison Bay. From West Side Rd., take Mitchell Bay Rd. east to West Valley Rd. Here, four original buildings have been preserved, including the barracks, now used as an **interpretive center.** The center chronicles the "war" and sells guides to the island. It also shows a relatively interesting 10-minute slide show on the struggle. (Park open year-round; buildings open Memorial Day-Labor Day daily 9am-6pm. Free.)

Roche Harbor Resort, Roche Harbor Rd. (378-2155), on the northern side of the island, began as a lime mine and kiln which the British built (probably to pass the time) during their occupation. Bought up by magnanimous industrialist John S. McMillan in 1886, Roche Harbor became a full-fledged company town. McMillan paid his workers in scrip, redeemable only at the company store (still standing today), and, when a strike broke out, sanguinely sacked his whole crew. In 1956, the entire town was delivered from the company to be turned into a resort. The **Hotel de Haro,** built by McMillan in 1887 to accommodate clients, is the center of the resort. Stop by the information kiosk in front for a copy of the $1 brochure, *A Walking Tour of Historic Roche Harbor,* which tosses a little history of the "town" in with architectural and social commentary. Much of the grounds is open to the public. Don't miss the bizarre **mausoleum** that McMillan had built for himself and his family. The Masonic symbolism that garnishes the structure is explained in the *Walking Tour.* (Grounds open 24 hr. Tennis courts and swimming pool open only to those staying at the resort.)

Those eager to fish or clam ought to pick up a copy of the Department of Fisheries pamphlet, *Salmon, Shellfish, Marine Fish Sport Fishing Guide,* for details on regulations and limits. The guide is available free at Friday Harbor **Hardware and Marine,** 270 Spring St. (378-4622). Free hunting and fishing licenses are required on the islands, and can be obtained from the hardware store. (Open Mon.-Sat. 8am-6pm, Sun. 10am-4pm.) Check with the **red tide hotline** (800-562-5632) if you'll be gathering shellfish; the nasty bacteria can wreak satanic horrors on your intestines.

Several small-scale entrepreneurs rent out or charter boats to visitors for expeditions on the water or to neighboring small islands. **San Juan Kayak Expeditions** (378-4436) leads two- to four-day trips in stable two-person sea kayaks. These excursions (given June-Sept.) offer a peaceful and personal way to see the hidden niches of the archipelago. They supply equipment and camping gear. ($125 for a 2-day trip, $175 for a 3-day trip, and $225 for a 4-day trip, including 2 hot meals per day.) Make reservations early by contacting the company at 3090-B Roche Harbor Rd., Friday Harbor 98250.

The annual **San Juan Island Traditional Jazz Festival** brings several swing bands to Friday and Roche Harbors on the last weekend in July. A $35 badge ($40 if purchased after July 1) will gain you admission to all performances, but you'll have just as much fun for free by joining the festive crowd of revelers in the streets outside the clubs. Single performance tickets range in price from $5-15. For more information, contact San Juan Island Goodtime Classic Jazz Association, P.O. Box 1666, Friday Harbor 98250 (378-5509).

Orcas Island

Mount Constitution overlooks much of Puget Sound from its 2409-ft. peak atop Orcas Island, the largest of the San Juan chain. In the mountain's shadow dwells a small population of retirees, artists, and farmers tending to understated homes and surprisingly few tourists. Surprising, because with its state park and youth hostel, Orcas has perhaps the best tourist facilities of all the islands.

Practical Information and Orientation

Visitor Information: Chamber of Commerce, North Beach Rd. next to the museum (see Sights), ½ block north of Horseshoe Hwy. An unstaffed shack with racks of pamphlets.

Ferries: Washington State Ferry (376-4389 or 376-2134). 24 hr. The only way onto the island from Anacortes. **Island Shuttle Express** (671-1137). Service to Bellingham and Friday Harbor (1 per day, $12 one way, $22 round-trip). Walk-on or bicycle passengers only.

Bike Rental: Wildlife Cycle A St. and North Beach Rd. in Eastsound (376-4708). 18-speeds for $5 per hr., $20 per day. Open Mon.-Sat. 10:30am-5:30pm.

Moped Rental: Key Moped Rentals (376-2474), at the Sears Bldg. on Prune St. in Eastsound; also at ferry landing and on Rosario Rd. in the Rosario Resort. $10 per hr., $40 per 8-hr. day. Driver's license and $10 deposit required. Helmets included. Open May-Sept. daily 10am-6pm.

Senior Services Center: across from the museum on North Beach Rd. in Eastsound (376-2677).

Library: On Horseshoe Hwy., across from Emmanuel Church in Eastsound (376-4985). Open Tues.-Wed. 10am-7pm, Thurs. 10am-9pm, Sat. 10am-4pm.

Pharmacy: Ray's, next to Templin's in Eastsound (376-2230). Open Mon.-Sat. 9am-6pm, Sun. 11am-2pm.

Emergency: 911.

Post Office: A St., in Eastsound Market Place (376-4121), ½ block north of the Chamber of Commerce. Open Mon.-Fri. 9am-4:30pm. General Delivery ZIP Code: 98245.

Area Code: 206.

Because Orcas is shaped like a horseshoe, getting around is a bit of a chore. The ferry lands on the southwest tip. Travel nine mi. northeast up the horseshoe to reach Eastsound, the island's main town. Olga and Doe Bay are yet another eight and 11 mi. from Eastsound, respectively, down the eastern side of the horseshoe. Stop in one of the shops at the landing to get a free map. (Most shops open daily 8:30am-6:30pm.)

Gas prices on Orcas often run 40¢ more per gallon than on the mainland. Tank up in Anacortes, if not sooner. The only gas stations on the island are located at Deer Harbor, Eastsound, and the ferry landing.

Accommodations and Camping

Avoid the bed and breakfasts (upwards of $60 per day) of the "Healing Island" and stay at the hostel. If the hostel is full, try a campground.

Doe Bay Village Resort, Star Rte. 86, Olga 98279 (376-2291 or 376-4755), off Horseshoe Hwy., on Doe Bay Rd. 8 mi. out of Moran State Park. On a secluded bay. No single-sex dorms. The resort comes with kitchen facilities, a health food store, and plenty of grounds to wander. The crowning attraction is the steam sauna and mineral bath, available to hostelers at $3 per day. (Nonlodgers $5. Bathing suits optional.) Members $9.50, nonmembers $12.50. Camping $8.50. Cottages from $32.50. Imaginative and flexible work-trade program. Guided kayak trips $25 per half-day (see Sights). Reservations recommended. Open year-round.

Outlook Inn (376-2200), on the north side of Horseshoe Hwy. in the center of Eastsound. Consider draining your wallet into this renovated Victorian inn; all rooms are enhanced by period antiques. Singles from $55. Doubles $60. Reservations required in summer. Write P.O. Box 210, Eastsound 98245.

Moran State Park, Star Rte. Box 22, Eastsound 98245 (376-2326). Follow Horseshoe Hwy. straight into the park. Four different campgrounds with a total of 151 sites. About 12 sites remain open year-round, as do the restrooms. Backcountry camping not permitted. All the best of San Juan fun—swimming, fishing, and hiking. Arresting grounds, amiable staff. Rowboats $6 per hr., paddleboats $7 per hr. Standard sites, hot showers $7; hiker/biker sites $3. **Information booth** at park entrance open Memorial Day-Labor Day daily 8am-10pm. Park open daily 6:30am-dusk; Sept.-March 8am-dusk. Reservations strongly recommended May-Labor Day. Send $11 ($7 site plus $4 reservation fee).

Obstruction Pass: DNR maintains 9 primitive sites, accessible only by boat or foot. Just past Olga, turn off Horseshoe Hwy. and hang a right to head south on Obstruction Pass Rd. Soon you'll come to a dirt road marked "Obstruction Pass Trailhead." Follow the road for about one mi. The sites are a ½-mi. hike from the end of the road. No drinking water, so bring plenty. Sites free.

Food

All the essentials can be found at **Templin's General Store** in the middle of Eastsound (376-2101; open Mon.-Sat. 8am-8pm, Sun. 10am-6pm). Also try the **Farmers' Market** in front of the museum (see Sights), every Saturday at 10am.

Sonnie's Café (376-2008), on A St. beside the Post Office off North Beach Rd. Decent, run-of-the-mill fare for under $6 (not too *Cher*) with an extensive vegetarian selection. Open Mon.-Sat. 8am-4pm, Sun. 10am-2pm.

Sunny Side Espresso (376-2828), in Eastsound Sq. Upbeat, offbeat staff serve up croissants ($1.15) and sandwiches ($4.25). Buy bags of day-old pastry at half price. Open Mon.-Sat. 8am-6pm, Sun. 10am-3pm.

La Famiglia, Prune Alley, Eastsound (376-2335). Relaxed Italian cooking and seafood in a family atmosphere. Sunny veranda with flower boxes everywhere. Great cheesecake. Seafood special changes daily. Lunches $5.50, dinners $7.50. Open Mon.-Sat. 11:30am-2:30pm and 5-9pm, Sun. 5-9pm. Reduced hours in winter.

Doty's A-1 Drive-In and Bakery (376-2593), across from the Chamber of Commerce. Pure diner atmosphere, pure diner food. Breakfast $4. Freshly baked breads and pastry. Open Mon.-Sat. 6:30am-8pm, Sun. 7am-4pm.

The Shoals, behind the Old Orcas Hotel at the ferry landing. Mediocrity is everywhere here. The Salieri Burger $3.15, deli sandwiches $4. Watch the ferries dock. Open daily 6:30am-7:30pm.

The Lower Tavern, Horseshoe Hwy., Eastsound (376-4848). Keep an eye on the trophies mounted precariously overhead as you try to eat the full "catastrophe" meal ($5.75). Chili $3.25. Open Mon.-Sat. 11am-midnight, Sun. noon-8pm.

Café Olga (376-4408), in the Orcas Island Artworks Bldg. at the Olga crossing, a few miles beyond Moran State Park. A cooperative gallery converted into an artsy and overpriced coffeehouse. Chicken cashew sandwich $5.65, blackberry pie $2.50. Open March-Dec. daily 10am-6pm.

Sights and Activities

Moran State Park is unquestionably Orcas's greatest attraction. Over 21 mi. of hiking trails cover the park, ranging in difficulty from a one-hour jaunt around Mountain Lake to a day-long constitutional up the south face of Mt. Constitution. Pick up a copy of the trail guide from the rangers. However you do it, be sure to reach the top of **Mount Constitution,** the highest peak in the islands. From here you can see other islands in the group, as well as the Olympic and Cascade Ranges, Vancouver Island, and Mt. Rainier. The stone tower at the top was built in 1936 by the Civilian Conservation Corps as a fire lookout and tourist observation tower. It's a torturous climb to the the top; if you haven't got a car, consider hitching. And be warned: rental mopeds can't make the ascent. Down below, you can swim in either of two freshwater lakes easily accessible from the highway, or rent rowboats ($6 per hr.) and paddleboats ($7 per hr.) from the park.

Olga is a miniscule collection of buildings that strains the definition of "town." At the Olga crossing stands an old strawberry-packing plant, now converted by an artists' cooperative into **Orcas Island Artworks** (376-4408), a shop carrying high-quality, high-priced local crafts and clothing. (Open March-Dec. daily 10am-6pm.) Continue along Horseshoe Hwy. to **Doe Bay Village Resorts** (376-2291), where you can soak in the natural mineral waters, sweat in the sauna, and see prophetic visions as you jump into the cold bath (bathing suits are the exception). (See Accommodations and Camping.) The **Sea Kayak Tour** of the surrounding islands is a fascinating, albeit expensive, "water-hike" of the north end of Puget Sound. ($25 per 4-hr. tour. Tours leave at 9am, 2:30pm and 6pm daily June-Sept. and include a ½ hr. of dry-land training.) The resort grounds are secluded and make for good wandering. Check first with the manager to learn the perimeters and parameters of the resort.

Eastsound, smack at the top of the horseshoe, offers great views from the highway and from the adjacent beach. Stop into the picturesque and peaceful **Emmanuel Church** (1885) on Main St. (376-2352), just across from the library. Islanders transcend sectarian differences and worship in the same building. The Episcopalians, who own the church, hold their services at 8 and 10am on Sundays; Lutherans push in at 2pm and Roman Catholics make their move at 4:30pm. Around the corner, two doors from the Chamber of Commerce on North Beach Rd., is the delightfully anachronistic **Orcas Island Historical Society Museum** (376-4849). A number of log cabins have been moved from their original sites and fitted together to make this museum. Information on the history of the cabins is available and accurate; displays, however, are jumbled, and many items unmarked. What labels there are seem somewhat lacking in scholarly precision (i.e., "very old fishing rod"). Don't miss the well-preserved foot-powered dental drill—one of the finest of its kind in a Washington museum. The staff is rich with information on the island. (Open Memorial Day-Labor Day Mon.-Fri. 1-4pm, Sat. 10am-4pm. Admission $1, children 50¢, families $3.)

Lopez Island

Smaller than either Orcas or San Juan, Lopez (or Slow-pez, as it's called) is an island of 1200 fishermen and farmers. Lopez lacks some of the tourist facilities of the other islands and some of the tourists as well; you know, therefore, that the amiability of the locals is genuine. Hitching on the island is widespread and rapid; it's also the only way to get from the ferry terminal (376-2326) into Lopez Village without your own car or bicycle.

Lopez Island is best for those who seek solitary beach walking or tranquil bicycling. Since Lopez Village (with all of 8 buildings, the largest town on the island) is 3½ mi. from the ferry, it's best to BYOB (bring your own bicycle). If you need to rent a bike, head to **Lopez Bicycle Works** (468-2847), south of the village, next to the island's Marine Center. The cheerful staff will give you a detailed map of island roads, complete with distances, even if you don't rent. Ten-speeds cost $3.50 per hour or $16 per day; mountain bikes cost $5 per hour or $20 per day. (Open daily 10am-6pm; May and Sept. Thurs.-Mon. 10am-5pm; April Thurs.-Sun. 10am-5pm.)

Small, day-use parks on the south end of the island, **Agate Beach Park** and **Mud Bay Park** offer a change from mainland campgrounds. The only other "sight" is the **Lopez Island Historical Society Museum** in Lopez Village (468-2049), 1½ blocks from the New Bay, across from the San Juan County Bank. Besides exhibits on island history, this new facility boasts an open shed filled with old canoes and obsolete farm equipment. (Open Fri-Sun. noon-4pm and by appointment. Free.)

The **Post Office** telephone number is 468-2282; the **Senior Citizens' Helpline** is 468-2421; the **emergency number,** the same on all the San Juans, is 911.

Accommodations, Camping, and Food

Lopez supports two bed and breakfasts: **MacKaye Harbor Inn** (468-2253), and **Inn at Swift's Bay** (468-3636). Reservations are generally required at least six weeks in advance for the summer season, and $65-75 per night is the rule. Bring your tent instead. Rediscover canned asparagus and croissant pizza at **Lopez Village Market** in the village (open Mon.-Sat. 9am-7pm, Sun. 10am-6pm).

Islander Lopez Marine Resort (468-2233) on Fisherman Bay Rd. about ½ mi. south of Lopez village. Barren cabins (no phone, no showers or bath, 1 single bed) $40 per night. Office open daily 6am-1am.

Odlin Park (468-2496), just off the road, a little over a mile from the ferry terminal. 30 sites. Short on privacy, but long on facilities with a kitchen with a wood stove and cold running water, boat launch, volleyball net, and softball diamond. Day-use daily 6am-9pm. Sites $8 per vehicle up to 4 people, each additional person $2. A grassy lawn provides some hiker/biker sites at $1.50.

Spencer Spit State Park (468-2251), on the northeast corner of the island, about 3½ mi. from the ferry terminal. 45 sites, with a mile of beachfront that provides good clamming year-round. No hookups. Flush toilets, but no showers. Standard sites $7.50. 8-bunk covered shelters $10.50.

Hummel Haven Bicycle Camp, on Center Rd. just south of Hummel Lake (468-2217), 4¼ mi. from the ferry landing. This quiet bike camp prohibits motorized vehicles, though you can park outside the grounds. Swim or fish in the lake. Boat rental $3.50 per hr.; bike rental $10 per day. Make reservations at least 2 weeks in advance for July and Aug. Contact the camp at Rte. 2, Box 3940, Lopez 98261. Sites $2.50 per person. No deposit needed.

Bay Café, Fisherman Bay Rd. (468-2204), across from the post office in Lopez Village. Enjoy the creative omelettes while you listen to soft music—with whale songs dubbed over it, for heaven's sake. Open Wed.-Sat. 11:30am-2pm and 6-8pm, Sun. 8am-noon and 6-8pm.

Holly B's, Lopez Plaza (468-2133). Nothin' says lovin' like Holly B's oven. Pastries and bread 55¢ and up. Starbuck's coffee 60¢, refills 25¢. Open Thurs.-Mon. 8am-6pm.

Gail's Restaurant and Delicatessen, across the road from Lopez Plaza (468-2150). Young urban professionals will find familiar food, atmosphere, and prices. Deli sandwiches $4.50, seafood dinners $12.50. Open in summer Sun.-Fri. 8am-3pm and 6-8pm, Sat. 8am-4pm and 6-9pm; reduced hours in winter.

The Fogged Inn (468-2281), at the ferry landing. A burger shack disguised as an RV. Standard burgers $3. Open Mon.-Sat. 6:30am-7pm, Sun. 7:30am-7:30pm.

Whidbey Island

The second largest island in the contiguous U.S., telephone-receiver-shaped Whidbey Island sits in the rain shadow of the Olympic Mountains. The clouds, wrung dry by the time they finally pass over Whidbey, release a scant 25" of non-shovelable precipitation on Whidbey per year, leaving the island with one of America's highest sunshine slugging averages. Rocky beaches are bounded by bluffs blooming with wild roses and crawling with blackberry brambles.

The island was originally inhabited by the Skagit nation of Native Americans, whose peaceful ways and gradual obliteration few recall today. The history of European settlement and development, on the other hand, is prominently displayed. The island was named in 1792 for Captain Joseph Whidbey, who sailed through Deception Pass, north of the island, on *H.M.S. Discovery.* Pioneer homesteaders followed in the mid-19th century. The town of Coupeville has been designated a national historic reserve, maintaining nearly 100 original homes and commercial buildings.

In 1941, the U.S. Navy placed a massive air station outside Oak Harbor, irrevocably transforming that community of 600 on the island's northern tip. Of the 10,000 current residents, 7200 are Navy affiliates. Since then, the inhabitants of the lower two-thirds of the island have become quick to assert that they live on *South* Whidbey Island.

Practical Information

Chamber of Commerce: Oak Harbor, 5506 Hwy. 20, about 1½ mi. north of the town center (675-3535). Open Mon.-Fri. 9am-5pm, Sat. 9am-6pm, Sun. 10am-4pm; Sept.-May open Mon.-Fri. 9am-5pm. **Coupeville,** 504 N. Main St. (678-5434). Open Mon.-Fri. 9am-noon, 2-5pm. **Langley,** P.O. Box 403 (321-6765), behind the Star Bistro Café (see Food), fronting the alley between 1st and 2nd St. Open Mon.-Fri. 10am-3pm.

Library: Oak Harbor Public Library, 3075 300th W. (675-5115), in City Hall, lower level. Open Mon.-Thurs. noon-9pm, Fri.-Sat. 9am-5pm.

Laundromat: Coupeville, 11 Front St. Well-stocked with a curiously diverse selection of in-flight magazines (Air Canada, Quantas, Cathay Pacific). Open daily 8am-8pm.

Crisis Center: 678-5555 or 321-4868. 24 hr.

Pharmacy: Penn Cove, 402 N. Main (678-2200), across from Whidbey Island Bank. Open Mon.-Sat. 9am-7pm, Sun. 10am-4pm. For emergency prescriptions, call 679-4418.

Hospital: Whidbey General, 101 Main St. (678-5151), in Coupeville.

Police/Fire: 911.

Post Offices: Oak Harbor, 7035 70th St. NW (675-6621). Open Mon.-Fri. 8:30am-5pm. General Delivery ZIP Code: 98277. **Coupeville,** 201 N.W. Coveland (678-5353). Open Mon.-Fri.

9:30am-4:30pm, Sat. 11am-1pm. General Delivery ZIP Code: 98239. **Langley,** 115 2nd St. (321-4113). Open Mon.-Fri. 8:30am-5pm. General Delivery ZIP Code: 98260.

Area Code: 206.

Getting There and Getting Around

The southern tip of Whidbey Island lies 40 mi. north of Seattle as the African swallow flies. The 20-minute **ferry** to Clinton, at the southern end of the island, leaves from Mukilteo (pronounced mu-kul-TEE-o), a small community just south of Everett. Take I-5 north from Seattle and follow the large signs to the ferry. Avoid commuter traffic eastbound in the morning and westbound at night. Ferries leave Mukilteo every half-hour from 6am to 11pm, and leave Clinton every half-hour from 5:30am to 11:30pm. The exact schedule changes with the seasons; call Washington State Ferries at 800-542-7052 for detailed information. (Car and driver $3.75, each additional passenger $1; bicycle and rider $3. Walk-on $1.65; ages over 65, 5-12, and disabled travelers 50¢; under 5 free.) Small surcharges are added in summer.

You can also reach Whidbey Island from Port Townsend on the Olympic Peninsula. Ferries leave the terminal in downtown Port Townsend for Keystone, on the west side of the island, eight times per day between 7am and 5:45pm. Ferries return from Keystone to Port Townsend eight times per day between 7:45am and 6:30pm. Throughout the summer, ferries run later at night and more frequently on weekends, and extra daily ferries shuttle extra crowds in August. (35 min. Car and driver $5.55; bicycle riders $3.50. Walk-on $1.65; ages over 64, 5-12, and disabled travelers 80¢; under 5 free.) For more information, call Washington State Ferries.

To reach Whidbey from the north, take exit 189 off I-5 and go west toward Anacortes. Be sure to stay on Hwy. 20 when it heads south through stunning Deception Pass State Park (signs will direct you); otherwise you will get to Anacortes. **Evergreen Trailways** runs a bus to Whidbey from Seattle. The bus leaves Seattle at 4:30pm and arrives in Anacortes at 8pm (Mon., Wed., and Fri.). It returns to Seattle from the Anacortes ferry dock at 8:25am, leaving downtown Anacortes at 8:35am and arriving in Seattle at 11:55am (Mon., Wed., Fri.).

Unfortunately, **Island Transit** (678-7771 or 321-6688) runs only one intra-island bus line—King Automobile still reigns. There is, however, only one main road: Hwy. 525 on the southern half of the island, which transmutes itself into Hwy. 20 around Coupeville. **The Pedaler,** 1504 E. Hwy. 525, Freeland (321-5040), seven mi. from Clinton, rents bicycles by the hour ($3), by the day ($14.50), and by the week ($43.50). Bicycle helmets come at no extra cost. Transporting bikes on the ferry is also easy and inexpensive (see above). On the north end of the island, **Dean's Sports Plus,** 8118 Hwy. 20 (679-6145), rents you mountain bikes for the day for $14 (no hourly rental). Open Mon.-Fri. 9am-6pm, Sat. 9am-5pm, Sun. noon-4pm. Bicyclists will have safer and more scenic rides away from Hwy. 525/20 (where motorists are often unmindful of speed limits and shoulders are narrow).

Stop at one of the real estate offices in Clinton, or in any one of the state parks, to pick up a free detailed **map** of the island. None of the roads is well-marked, and it's easy to become hopelessly lost.

Accommodations

Inexpensive motels are few and far between on Whidbey, and those that do exist are often a little run-down. Still, reservations are always sensible, especially in rain-free July and August. A number of bed and breakfasts offer pleasant, homey rooms for a few more dollars. Contact **Whidbey Island Bed and Breakfast Association,** P.O. Box 259, Langley 98260 (321-6272), for a full listing; reservations are necessary.

Tyee Motel and Café, 405 S. Main St., Coupeville (678-6616), across Hwy. 20 from the town proper, toward the Keystone ferry. Clean, standard motel rooms, with showers, but no tubs. The setting is bleak—you can forget you're on an island—but it's within walking distance of Coupeville center and the water. Café open Mon.-Fri. 6:30am-8:30pm, Sat. 6:30am-9pm. Singles $30, each additional person $4.

Crossroads Motel, 5622 Hwy. 20 (675-3145), on northern edge of Oak Harbor. Cinderblock construction suggests a past as cheap military housing, but the rooms are immaculately kept and comfortable. Fully equipped kitchens available. Singles $32. Doubles $39. $5 each additional person. Rooms with kitchens $43.

Acorn Motor Inn, 8066 Hwy. 20 (675-6646), in Oak Harbor, across the street from Safeway. A well-maintained motel run by pleasant managment. Well-furnished, the elegant Acorn is a step up from most. Singles $44. Doubles $46. Continental breakfast included.

Camping

Four state parks on a 50-mi.-long island can hardly be passed up. They are listed here south to north.

Fort Ebey State Park, 395 N. Fort Ebey Rd. (678-4636). North of Fort Casey and just west of Coupeville. Take Libbey Rd. turn-off from Hwy. 20. Miles of hiking trails and easy access to a pebbly beach make this, the island's newest campground, also the island's best. 50 sites for cars and RVs ($7.50), 3 sites for hikers and bikers ($3). Open year-round.

South Whidbey State Park, 4128 S. Smuggler's Cove Rd. (321-4559), 7 mi. northwest of Freeland via Bush Point Rd. and Smuggler's Cove Rd. On a cliff in a virgin stand of Douglas fir. Steep ¼-mi. trail leads down to a broad but rocky beach. 46 sites, deer browse by RVs. Sites $7.50. Open year-round.

Fort Casey State Park, 1280 S. Fort Casey Rd. (678-4519), right next to the Keystone ferry terminal, 3 mi. south of Coupeville on Fort Casey Rd. 35 sites interspersed with *fin-de-siècle* military memorabilia. Sites aren't too pretty, but fill up early in summer because of their proximity to the ferry. Sites $7.50. Open year-round.

Deception Pass State Park, 5175 N. Hwy. 525 (675-2417), 8 mi. north of Oak Harbor. The highway passes right through the park on Deception Pass Bridge. The park has 8½ mi. of hiking trails and freshwater fishing and swimming. Jets flying overhead from Oak Harbor Naval Air Station will lull you to sleep. 250 standard sites ($7.50), 4 rustic sites for hikers and bikers ($3). Open year-round.

Food

Smoked salmon is the dish of choice on Whidbey; every town (and every highway milepost) has its share of salmon shacks. The restaurants below are listed from south to north.

Mike's Place, 215 1st St. (321-6575), in Langley, right across the street from the Doghouse. Although Mike's only opened in 1985, its $2.25 clam chowder is already considered the best on the island. The nightly all-you-can-eat specials are also highly recommended. Monstrous but mediocre cheese blintzes $4.55, lunches $4-6, dinners under $10. Open Mon.-Fri. 7am-10pm, Sat.-Sun. 8am-10pm.

Doghouse Tavern, 230 1st St. (321-9996), in Langley, on the main drag of a 1-block town. A local hangout that serves 10¢ 6-oz. beers with lunch (limit 2). Eat $4 sandwiches and $4.55 corn soup out of an edible bread bowl, either in the tavern or around the back in the "family restaurant." Open Mon.-Sat. 11am-1am, Sun. noon-1am.

Star Bistro Café, 201½ 1st St. in Langley (221-2627). Expensive food, but the view is incredible; to economize, eat at Mike's, then come here to enjoy the light Reggae and a cranorange fizz ($1.75). Open Mon. 11:30am-3pm, Tues.-Thurs. 11:30am-9pm, Fri.-Sat. 11:30am-10pm, Sun. 10am-8pm.

Toby's Tavern, 8 Front St. (678-4222), Coupeville, in the 1890 Whidbey Mercantile Company Bldg. Like everything else in Coupeville, the building is a historical landmark. Inside, the tavern (a favorite with locals) serves $3.50 burgers, $4.50 sandwiches, and beer. Open daily 11am-11pm.

Miss Emmy Lou's, 180 Coveland St. in Coupeville (678-6248). A quaint eatery with moderate-sized lunches for $5. Emmy Lou's got no views. Open Wed.-Mon. 9am-2pm.

Jason's (679-3535), Hwy. 20 at Goldie Rd. in Oak Harbor, across from the Crossroads Motel. Regulation chain-restaurant fare: burgers, steaks, and spaghetti. Locals swear by the mushroom burger ($4.50). Breakfast under $5, lunch $3-4, dinner $5-8. Perhaps named after Jason Mazzone as it is open 24 hr.

Sights and Activities

You could spend days exploring Whidbey Island, or only a few hours as you wait for transport connections. Whichever interval you choose, spend no more time in **Clinton** than it requires to get off the ferry, scratch those mosquito bites, and get up the hill. In general, the island's interior regions are uninspiring; the island's real beauty lies along its circle of beaches.

Less than three mi. from the center of Clinton, Langley Rd. heads north to the little town of **Langley.** Located just to the west of a small shopping plaza, the road is not well marked. If you find it, poke around the various arts and crafts shops on 1st St. Langley has decorated on the Old West motif—wooden sidewalks connect false fronts of antique shops and taverns. The ensemble is not overdone, however, and the metamorphosis from run-down small town to *Gunsmoke* set isn't nearly as bad as it could be.

During the first weekend in July, the townspeople close down 1st St. for the **Choockokam Arts Festival,** displaying jewelry, pottery, and other local artworks. Call the Childer's Proctor Gallery (221-2978) for more information. The stairs at 2 Front St. lead down to **Seawall Park,** which has several picnic tables scattered along a grassy stretch by the water.

On the west side of **Useless Bay,** uninterrupted beach stretches from Bayview Beach along **Double Bluff Park** to the tip of the Double Bluff Peninsula. Comb the 1½-mi. beach, explore the bluffs, or just soak up the sun. Perhaps the single most impressive vista on the island is the view of Seattle and Mt. Rainier from the parking lot at the end of Double Bluff Rd. The bay can be reached by Double Bluff Rd., about five mi. west of Langley Rd. and one mi. east of Freeland.

A more ideal spot for the blithe spirit is **South Whidbey State Park,** 4128 S. Smuggler's Cove Rd. (321-4559), about seven mi. north of Freeland. The park wraps around the west coast of the island, covering 87 acres of virgin forest. Park by the tiny outdoor amphitheater and walk down the bluff to the beach (10 min.). Wander along the pebbly beach approximately 1½ mi. in either direction—to Lagoon Point in the north or to a lighthouse on Bush Point in the south. (See Camping for the park's overnight facilities.)

Around the bend to the north, Fort Casey and Fort Ebey State Parks sustain the Park Service's domination of Whidbey's western shore. **Fort Casey State Park,** 1280 S. Fort Casey Rd. (678-4519), is right next to the Keystone ferry terminal, three mi. south of Coupeville. The park is situated on the site of a late 1890s fort designed, along with Fort Worden and Fort Flagler on the mainland, to defend against a long-anticipated attack from the west. The fort was updated and reactivated with the onset of each major war until the military lost patience and, in 1956, sold the property to the Park Service. The **Admiralty Head Lighthouse,** also dating from the turn of the century, now functions as an **interpretive center,** expounding on the fort's history. (Open Wed.-Sun. 10am-6pm.) Tours of what remains of the fort are given on weekends at 2pm and start at the main gun sites. For the less militarily inclined, Fort Casey also operates recreational facilities, including an underwater reserve, boat launch, camping facilities, and shower rooms for scuba divers. (Interpretive center open in winter only for large groups by appointment. The park is open year-round.)

Public beach lands extend north of the ferry landing all the way to Partridge Point, north of Fort Ebey State Park. This is perfect territory for an all-day beach expedition. Access to the beach is also permitted at **Ebey's Landing,** halfway between the two state parks and the site of the original 1852 pioneer settlement. Well-remembered Isaac Ebey, who led the small group of settlers to Whidbey Island, was decapitated by members of the Haida nation (of coastal Vancouver Island) to avenge one of their leaders.

Fort Ebey State Park, 395 N. Fort Ebey Rd. (678-4636), is accessible from Libbey Rd. off Hwy. 20 north of Coupeville, by Valley Drive's park entrance. The way from the highway to the park is well marked, but the way back to the highway from the park is not—take breadcrumbs or remember your route. The park is also the driest spot on the island; prickly pear cacti grow on the parched bluffs. The park facilities are well-maintained. Signs explaining the causes of erosion (and probably contributing to the process) crop up on dunes which shrink daily.

Both parks and the town of Coupeville are contained within **Ebey's Landing National Historical Reserve,** established by the Federal Government for the "preservation and protection of a rural community." Many of Coupeville's homes and commercial establishments date from the 19th century. The town extends along East Front St. between two blockhouses. Constructed in 1855, the blockhouses were meant to withstand a predicted Skagit uprising that never occurred. Two of the fortified buildings remain standing: the **John Alexander Blockhouse,** at the west end of town, and the **Davis Blockhouse,** at the edge of the town's cemetery in the west end.

Two miles southeast of Coupeville, on Hwy. 20, DNR's Rhododendron Park has picnic areas and six free campsites, which almost always fill early during summer months. Coupeville's **City Park,** one block west of the wharf, also operates picnic areas and a reservable community kitchen. During the second weekend in August, Coupeville hosts a popular **Arts and Crafts Festival** (678-6636), drawing artists from all over the Northwest. For information on other Coupevilliana, contact the **Central Whidbey Chamber of Commerce,** P.O. Box 152, Coupeville 98239 (678-5434).

The Navy's EA-6B Prowler jets, designed for tactical electronic warfare, keep the peace near the town of **Oak Harbor,** on Oak Harbor Bay at the northern end of the island. The town was named for the Garry oaks that once dominated the landscape. The Chamber of Commerce insists that the influence of early Dutch settlers can still be felt, but fast-food restaurants generally make more of an impact. **City Beach Park,** downtown, maintains a free swimming pool, kitchens, and tennis courts. (Buildings and facilities open April-Nov.; park open year-round.) During the last weekend in April, Oak Harbor plants tulips and puts on wooden shoes for the annual **Holland Happenings.** In mid-July the city sponsors **Whidbey Island Race Week,** a colorful yacht regatta.

A few miles north on Hwy. 20, the sword and plough share the field at the U-Pick Strawberry Farms, where the roar from low-flying Navy jets virtually rattles the fruit from the plants.

When the Skagit tribe lived and fished around Deception Pass, it was often raided by the Haida tribe from the north. A bear totem of the Haidas now occupies the north end of West Beach in **Deception Pass State Park,** 5175 N. Hwy. 20 (675-2417). Make sure to visit the WPA bridge on Hwy. 20 E. for the view of the crashing waves. The pass itself was named by Captain George Vancouver, who found the tangled geography of Puget Sound as confusing as most visitors do today. The trails and shelters were developed during the Depression by the Civilian Conservation Corps. A brand-new **interpretive center** in the Bowman area, just north of the bridge, gives a good overview of the environmental army that built so many of the park facilities in the Pacific Northwest. This is the most heavily used of Whidbey's four state parks, and its views are achingly beautiful. There are camping facilities, a saltwater boat launch, and a freshwater lake for swimming, fishing, and boating. Eight-and-a-half mi. of trails allow a closer look at the tidal pools, beaches, and beasts of the area. (A fishing license, available at most hardware stores, is required for fishing in the lake; the season runs from mid-April to Oct. Park open year-round.)

Near Whidbey Island

La Conner, once a fishing village on the Swinomish Channel, is now a lure for shoppers, with posh galleries, stylish boutiques, and gelato emporiums. La Conner lies four mi. south of Hwy. 20 on La Conner-Whitney Rd. Take Hwy. 20 east from Whidbey Island to the mainland.

The **Skagit County Historical Museum,** 501 4th St. (466-3365), at the top of the hill in La Conner, shows exhibits of settler life in Skagit county. Behind the ugly concrete exterior stand full-scale replicas of an old-time general store, a blacksmith's shop, a bedroom, and a kitchen. (Open Wed.-Sun. 1-5pm. Admission $1; ages under 13 50¢.) **Gaches Mansion,** 2nd and Calhoun St. (466-4288), a restored Victorian mansion built in 1891, also houses the **Valley Museum of Northwest Art.** (Open April-Oct. Fri.-Sun. 1-5pm; Nov.-March 1-4pm. Free.) The **La Conner Volunteer Firefighter Museum,** 615 1st St., sets the sirens of small-town Americana a-wailing. The displays, visible through a street-level window (there's no entry to the one-room building), include a horse-drawn pumper "used in the 1906 San Fransisco [sic] fire."

The few places to stay in La Conner are expensive, but if you can afford it, try **Katy's Inn Bed and Breakfast,** 3rd and Washington (466-3366). The elegantly furnished rooms ($55; up to 2 people) place a jar of candy at every bedside. Budgetarians should head for the campgrounds on Whidbey Island, less than 10 mi. away.

The **Calico Cupboard,** 720 S. 1st St. (466-4451), emphasizes baked goods and vegetarian delights. The interior looks like an oversized dollhouse with its quaint country decor. Breakfast and sandwiches average $5. (Open Sun.-Thurs. 8am-11pm, Fri.-Sat. 8am-11:30pm. Tea served 2:30-5pm.) **At's A Pizza,** 201 E. Morris (466-4406), serves less flowery fare, such as cold sandwiches and mediocre pizza, in a tavern-like atmosphere. (Open Sun.-Thurs. 11am-10pm, Fri.-Sat. 11am-midnight.)

The **Rhododendron Cafe,** 553 Chuckanut Dr. in Bow (766-6667), at the crossroads of Hwy. 11 and 237, north of La Conner, serves superb food in a subdued setting. A refurbished gas station, the restaurant provides a break from the old hamburger-and-fries routine, generally under $10. Vegetarian specials are served nightly, and the pan-fried oysters ($9) are recommended. (Open Wed.-Thurs. 4-9pm, Fri.-Sat. 11am-3pm and 4-9pm, Sun. 10am-3pm and 4-9pm.)

A few miles inland on I-5, the city of **Mt. Vernon** hosts the two-day Mt. Vernon/Skagit Valley Tulip Festival in early April. Fertile Skagit Valley is best known for its tulips, which bloom in April (daffodils bloom in March and irises in late May). **West Shore Acres,** 956 Downey Rd. (466-3158), one mi. west of La Conner-Whitney Rd. on Downey Rd., tends display gardens and sells flowers and bulbs. (Open March 23-April daily 10am-6pm.) **Westwinds Motel,** 2020 Riverside Dr., Mt. Vernon (424-4224), peddles spacious rooms past their prime. (Singles $30.)

The La Conner **post office** (General Delivery ZIP Code: 98257) is at 1st and Washington St. The **area code** is 206.

Other Islands

With one store and 100 residents, **Shaw Island** was not designed with tourists in mind. Only one building serves island visitors: a combination ferry terminal/general store/post office/dock/gas station, run by Franciscan nuns. The island's 11 mi. of public roads, however, endear it to hikers and bikers. The library and museum, near the center of the island, at the intersection of Blind Bay and Hoffman Cove Rd., open only on Mondays and Saturdays. A little red schoolhouse stands on the other side of the untraveled road. **Shaw Island County Park,** on the south side of the island, has eight campsites ($6), which fill quickly. There are no other accommodations on the island.

Washington State Parks operates over 15 **marine parks** on some of the smaller islands in the archipelago. These islands, accessible by private craft only, have anywhere from one to 51 mainly primitive campsites. The park system publishes a pamphlet on its marine facilities, available at other island parks or hardware and supply stores. One of the most popular is **Sucia Island,** site of gorgeous scenery and torturous geology. Canoes and kayaks can easily navigate the archipelago when the water is calm, but when the wind whips up the surf, only larger boats (at least 16 ft.) are safe. Navigational maps are essential to avoid the reefs and nasty hidden rocks that surround the islands.

The Department of Natural Resources operates three parks; each has three to six free campsites with toilets but no drinking water. Cypress Head on **Cypress Island** has wheelchair-accessible facilities.

Olympic Peninsula

In the fishing villages and logging towns of the Olympic Peninsula, locals jest about having webbed feet and using Rustoleum instead of suntan oil. The area's heavy rainfall (up to 200" per year on Mt. Olympus) is wrung out of the moist Pacific air by the Olympic Mountains. While this torrent supports bona fide rain forests in the peninsula's western river valleys, towns such as Sequim in the range's rain shadow are the driest in all of Washington, with as little as 17 inches of rain a year.

Extremes of climate are matched by extremes of geography. The beaches along the Pacific strip are a hiker's paradise—isolated, windy, and wildly sublime. The glaciated peaks of the Olympic range exhibit spectacular alpine scenery; the network of trails covers an area the size of Rhode Island (but don't let that discourage you). These wild, woody mountains resisted exploration well into the 20th century.

Because it compresses such variety into a relatively small area, the Olympic Peninsula is one of Washington's best destinations for those seeking accessible wilderness and outdoor recreation. U.S. 101 loops around the peninsula, stringing together scattered towns and attractions on the nape of the mountains. The numerous secondary roads departing from U.S. 101 were designed with exploration in mind, although many are gravel-covered, making biking into the heart of the park difficult. Heart o' the Hills Road to Hurricane Ridge makes a particularly good detour, providing an unbeatable panorama of the mountains. Hwy. 112 follows the Strait of Juan de Fuca out to Neah Bay, the driftwood-laden coastal town near Cape Flattery. Greyhound runs only as far as Port Angeles to the north and Aberdeen/Hoquiam to the south. Although local transit systems extend public transportation a little farther, the western portion of the peninsula and the southern portion of Hood Canal are not on any regular routes.

Hitchhiking is illegal on U.S. 101 southwest of Olympia. Elsewhere, thumbing can often be slow, and you may well be stranded in the rain for hours. On one of summer's many sunny days, you can often catch a ride with a forester or fisherman. Bicycling is dangerous in some spots, particularly along Crescent Lake just west of Port Angeles—the shoulders are narrow or nonexistent, the curves are sharp, and the roads serve as race tracks for any number of speeding logging trucks. Motoring suits the peninsula best, although some of the beaches and mountain wilds can be reached only on foot. Extended backpacking trips are particularly rewarding.

Camping

Although many towns on the peninsula cater to tourists with motels and resorts, camping will put you closer to the natural splendor which you came to see (and will be cheaper). The Olympic National Forest, the state of Washington, and Olympic National Park all maintain a number of free campgrounds. In addition, the national park has many standard campgrounds (sites $5). The numerous **state parks** along Hood Canal and the eastern rim charge $4 per night, with an occasional site for tenters at only $1-3 per night. The national forest and the park services welcome **backcountry camping** (free everywhere), but a permit, available at any ranger station, is required within the park. Camping on the beaches is especially easy, although you should be sure to bring a supply of water. The beaches in the westernmost corner of Neah Bay and from the town of Queets to Moclips farther south fall within Native American reserve land. Visitors should be aware that reservation land is private property—travelers are welcome, but local regulations prohibiting alcohol, fishing without a tribal permit, and beachcombing should be obeyed. The Quinault Indian Reservation gained acclaim 20 years ago by forcibly ousting vandals trespassing on their beaches.

Washington's **Department of Natural Resources (DNR)** manages the huge tracts of land on the Kitsap Peninsula and along the Hoh and Clearwater Rivers near the western shore, as well as smaller, individual campsites sprinkled around the peninsula. Except for the high summer, DNR camping is generally free and uncrowded and no reservations are required. Some of these sites allow RVs, some do not have drinking water, and most have good fishing. Unfortunately, many sites cannot be found without a map. The DNR publishes a guide to all its Washington sites, and additional maps of its Multiple Use Areas (MUAs). Maps of Hoh-Clearwater MUA and Tahuya MUA (on the Kitsap Peninsula) are available from DNR, Olympic Area, Rte. 1, P.O. Box 1375, Forks 98331 (206-374-6131), and at most DNR campgrounds.

Keep an eye out for other camping possibilities, such as county and city parks and ITT Rayonier's **Tumbling Rapids Park** off U.S. 101 in Sappho, 55 mi. west of Port Angeles. This campground with rest rooms, picnic area, and community kitchen is maintained by the giant company for public use.

Be warned: in the summer, competition for campground space can be fierce. From late June on, most sites are taken by 2 or 3pm, so start hunting early; in the more popular areas of the national parks (such as the Hoh River), find a site before noon, or plan on sleeping elsewhere.

Kitsap Peninsula

The amorphous Kitsap Peninsula resembles a half-completed landfill project jutting into Puget Sound. Especially on the section encircled by the Hood Canal, a plethora of backroads and campgrounds lays out the blueprints for a cyclist's paradise.

Getting to the Kitsap Peninsula from Seattle is easy: ferry service to either Bremerton or Winslow (see Near Seattle), on adjacent Bainbridge Island, starts at 6am daily (call 464-6400 Monday to Friday 9am to 5pm for precise information). North of Seattle, Edmonds is connected to Kingston on the top end of the peninsula, and service is equally frequent. Coming from the northwest, the **Hood Canal Bridge** crosses the northern end of Hood Canal and links the peninsula with the towns along the Strait of Juan de Fuca.

Once there, getting around is also easy. **Kitsap Transit** Route #90 runs between Bremerton and Winslow from Monday to Friday (call 479-3588 for times) with frequent flag stops.

The area is reasonably compact, and can be covered by bike in a day. Kitsap Way (the road which Bus #90 follows) is peppered with $30-and-up hotel chains, but for cheaper lodgings, consider spending the night in Seattle.

If you're intent on spending the night here, one possibility is **Scenic Beach State Park,** near the village of Seabeck on the west coast of the peninsula. The park has 50 campsites with water and bathrooms (sites $7, walk-in sites $3). From Silverdale, take Anderson Hill Rd. or Newberry Hill Rd. west to Seabeck Hwy., then follow the highway seven mi. south to the Scenic Beach turnoff. Cyclists beware of the staggering hills along this route.

The Bremerton Kitsap County Visitor and Convention Bureau, 120 Washington St. (479-3588), is just up the hill from the ferry terminal. The office supports a flotilla of pamphlets on Bremerton and nearby towns, and the lively staff tries hard to cover up the city's fundamental drabness. (Open Mon.-Fri. 9am-5pm., Sat. 10am-4pm; Mon.-Fri. 9am-5pm Labor Day to Memorial Day.) The **post office** is stationed at 602 Pacific Ave. (373-1456; General Delivery ZIP Code: 98310).

Bremerton has a sizeable US Navy repair yard, with everything but a full-blown dry-dock. You'll swear you have stepped into a Tom Clancy novel; every third person has a Navy security pass swinging from his or her neck. As you climb the small hill leading up from the ferry docks, turn right at 130 Washington St. and you'll find the **Bremerton-Naval Museum** (479-7447). Thrill to the sight of large action photos from WWII and transparent models of destroyers and aircraft carriers measuring up to 3m. The museum's most prized possession is also its most recently acquired one: the destroyer *C. Turner Joy* (of Tonkin Bay infamy). (Free, though donations are requested. Open Tues.-Sat. 10am-5pm, Sun. 1-5 pm.)

When the dinner bell rings in Bremerton, locals head for the slightly upscale **Boat Shed,** 101 Shore Dr. (377-2600), on the water immediately below the northeast side of the Manette Bridge. Terrific seafood and sandwiches ($5) and super nachos ($5). Open Mon.-Thurs. 11am-midnight, Fri.-Sat. 11am-1am, Sun. 3-10pm.

Near Bremerton, at the **Forest Theater,** to the west off Seabeck Rd., the Mountaineer Players have been putting on foot stompin' musicals on their outdoor stage, rain or shine, for the last 68 years. Performances begin Memorial Day weekend and continue for the next three weekends. Tickets $7. Call 284-6310 for current info.

If you ask nicely, the driver of Bus #90 will let you off at the Longhouse Convenience Store. Follow the road one mi. to the fascinating **Suquamish Museum** (sue-QUAH-mish, 598-3311). If you're driving or hitching, you'll find the museum 7 mi. north of Winslow, on the north side of the Agate Pass Bridge on Hwy. 305. Run by the tribe on the Port Madison Indian Reservation, the small museum is devoted entirely to the history and culture of the Puget Sound Salish Native Americans. Arrestingly displayed photographs, artifacts, and quotations from tribal elders piece together the lives of those who inhabited the peninsula before the arrival of the white man. (Open daily 10am-5pm. Admission $2.50, senior citizens $2, children under 12 $1.) Chief Sealth, for whom Seattle was named, belonged to the Salish nation, and his grave is located up the hill, about a 15 min. walk away. The chief's memorial of cedar war canoes over a Christian headstone is an excellent example of the Catholic-Native North American religion that rose briefly in the 19th century. Next to the gravesite is a Suquamish city park that was once the site of **Old Man House,** a cedar loghouse burned by federal agents in 1870 as part of an attempt to eliminate communal living by Native Americans.

The **Kitsap County Historical Museum** (692-1949), on NW Byron and Washington in Silverdale, is your typical small town museum. The displays dilate on boats, logging, and daily life on the peninsula. (Open Tues.-Sat. 10am-5pm. Admission $1, families $2.)

Hood Canal

No one is quite sure how the ribbon of water that separates the Kitsap and Olympic peninsulas came to be called "Hood Canal" instead of its original "Lord Hood's Channel," but carelessness on the part of cartographers is as good a guess as any.

U.S. 101 parallels the west bank of the canal, from **Potlatch State Park** in the south to **Quilcene** (Quil-SEEN) in the north. This flat, scenic road, highlighted by a challengingly steep pass just outside Quilcene, is well-suited for cycling. Without a bike or a car, abandon any hopes of seeing this area: there are no buses and hitching is both illegal and foolhardy, as cars move too fast and the roads have no shoulders.

West of the canal, the **Olympic National Forest** rims the eastern edge of the national park. Much of the forest is more developed and more accessible than the park and gives those with little time or small appetites for the outdoors a "taste" of the peninsula's wildlife. Stop by one of the forest's **ranger stations** along the canal to pick up information on camping and trails in the forest. The two stations are in **Hoodsport,** P.O. Box 68, ZIP 98548 (877-5254; open daily 8am-4:30pm from the first Sunday in May to the last Saturday in September and other times Mon.-Fri. 7am-4:30pm) and **Quilcene,** U.S. 101 S. (765-3368; open Mon.-Fri. 8am-5pm, Sat.-Sun. 8:30am-5pm). Both are marked clearly with signs on the highway. Many of the forest service **campgrounds** cost only $4, including **Hamma Hamma,** on Forest Service Rd. 25, 7 mi. northwest of Eldon; **Lena Creek,** 2 mi. beyond Hamma Hamma; **Elkhorn,** on Forest Service Rd. 2610, 11 mi. northwest of Brinnon; and **Collins,** on Forest Service Rd. 2515, 8 mi. west of Brinnon. All are marked on U.S. 101 and have drinking water, as well as good fishing, hiking, and gorgeous scenery.

Unfortunately, many of these are accessible only by gravel roads, which are difficult, if not impossible, to navigate by bicycle. Adjacent to the Hoodsport Ranger Station is a **post office** (877-5552; open Mon.-Fri. 8am-12:30pm and 1:30-5pm, Sat. 8:30am-11:30pm; General Delivery ZIP Code: 98548).

Lake Cushman State Park (877-5491), 7 mi. west of Hoodsport on Lake Cushman Rd., stretches by a comely lake with good swimming beaches. The park is also popular as a base camp for extended backpacking trips into the national forest and park. Lake Cushman has 70 tent sites at $7.50 and 30 more with full hook-up for $10.50 in addition to flush toilets and pay showers (25¢ for 6 min.) for all patrons. Clinging to a quiet cove is **Mike's Beach Resort and Hostel**, N. 38470 U.S. 101 (877-5324), two mi. north of Eldon. The hostel, which is not AYH affiliated, lacks a kitchen but contains a small grocery store. (AYH Members $5, nonmembers $7.50. Check-in 7am-10pm, open April 15-Nov. 1.) The **Hungry Bear Café** (877-5527), in Eldon, serves the Hood Canal specialty—geoduck (GOO-ey-duck) steak ($8). Adventurous eaters will find that the geoduck, a giant clam that lives 2½ to 7 ft. below the surface of Hood Canal's beaches, has a taste somewhere between that of a razor clam and a scallop. Those feeling less daring might want to stick with a hamburger ($1.50-5). This small café is inhabited by scores of taxidermied bears (but please don't feed the animals . . . they're already stuffed). (Open Mon.-Fri. 9am-7pm, Sat.-Sun. 8am-8pm).

Strait of Juan de Fuca

From Port Townsend to Cape Flattery, the northern rim of the Olympic Peninsula defines the U.S. side of the Strait of Juan de Fuca. This sapphire passage, from the Pacific Ocean to Puget Sound, was named for the legendary explorer, alledgedly the first European to enter the ocean inlet. The shores are dotted with small towns, many of them old salmon fishing ports still sighing after bounties of the past.

Port Townsend

Port Townsend's buildings have been fabulously restored to their original Victorian splendor. The lace and upright charm are intact; not a cracked window or loose shingle is to be found. The entire business district of this "peninsula off a peninsula" has been declared a national landmark. Seen from a ferry boat in the strait, Port Townsend's Victorian houses on the overhanging bluff obscure the highway behind, creating the illusion of a town that time forgot.

With their beards, fisherman's caps, and scruffed denim jackets, the town's sailors and amateur boat-builders seem like incarnations of a Hemingway novel. But if you keep a close eye on these old salts, you may see them stop in at bars only to forego the traditional beer and crackers in favor of cappuccino and breadsticks.

Practical Information and Orientation

Visitor Information: Chamber of Commerce, 2437 Sims Way, Port Townsend 98368 (385-2722), about 10 blocks from the center of town on Hwy. 20. The free map and visitors guide, enthusiastically distributed, fulfill all your needs. Open Mon.-Fri. 9am-5pm, Sat. 10am-4pm, Sun. 11am-4pm.

Jefferson County Transit: 425 Washington St. (385-4777). Also the number to call for **Greyhound** information. Jefferson County Transit's Greyhound connection bus stops in Port Ludlow several times daily.

Ferries: Washington State Ferry (800-542-0810). Runs from the dock at Water St., west of downtown. **Northcat Transportation Inc.**, 1322 Washington St. (385-3590). 2-hr. trips to Edmonds via Kingston (5am, 10:15am, and 3:30pm). $6.65 one way. No cars. Runs year-round.

Taxi: Key City Transport, 385-5972. 24 hr.

Bike Rental: Barnacle Bill's Bike Rental, 215 Tayler St. at Water St. (385-6470). Top-quality mountain bikes for $5 per hr., $20 per day.

Boat Rental: Field Dock, Port Ludlow Marina (437-2222), in Port Ludlow, south of Port Townsend. Sailboats $6 per hr., $18 per 4 hr.

Public Library: 1220 Lawrence (385-3181), uptown. Open Tues.-Thurs. 11am-9pm, Fri.-Sat. 11am-5pm.

Jefferson County Crisis Line: 385-0321. 24 hours.

Senior Services: Olympic Area Agency on Aging, 385-2564. **Senior Assistance,** 385-2552.

Pharmacy: Don's, 1151 Water St. (385-2622). Open Mon.-Fri. 9am-7pm, Sat. 9am-6pm, Sun. 11am-5pm.

Hospital: Jefferson General, 385-2200. **Emergency Medical Care,** 385-4622. On the corner of Sheridan and 9th St. in the west end of town.

Police: 607 Water St. (385-2322).

Post Office: 1322 Washington St. (385-1600). Open Mon.-Fri. 9am-5pm. General Delivery ZIP Code: 98368.

Area Code: 206.

Port Townsend can be reached by ferry from the town of Keystone on Whidbey Island, or by car either from U.S. 101 along Hood Canal or from the Kitsap Peninsula across the Hood Canal Bridge. **Greyhound's** daily Seattle-to-Port Angeles run connects with **Jefferson County Transit** in the town of Port Ludlow for the last leg to Port Townsend. Jefferson County Transit serves the Port Townsend area Monday through Friday from 8am to 6pm, weekends for the link with Greyhound only. A Port Townsend shuttle bus loops around the town itself, and other service extends west along the strait to Sequim. (Fare 50¢, seniors and students 25¢, under 6 free. Daily passes $1.50.)

From Victoria, BC, two ferries per day run to Port Angeles (4 in summer), a mere $1 bus ride from Port Townsend. To reach Port Angeles from Port Townsend, hop on Jefferson County Transit bus #8 (at Water and Quincy St.) to Sequim (30 min.), where you can catch Clallam Transit System bus #30 to Port Angeles (30 min.).

Accommodations and Camping

Port Townsend's hostel and campground rest near the town. So many cheap beds in such a small town doesn't make sense, but who's complaining?

Fort Worden Youth Hostel (AYH), Fort Worden State Park (385-0655), 2 mi. from downtown. The bulletin boards and trekkers' log are good, if somewhat dated sources of information on budget travel around the Olympics and elsewhere. Kitchen facilities. Check-in 4:30-9pm. Check-out 9:30am. Curfew 11pm. Members $7.50, nonmembers $10.50. Family rates available. Open Jan. 4-Dec. 14.

Fort Flagler Youth Hostel (AYH), Fort Flagler State Park (385-1288), on handsome Marrowstone Island, 20 mi. from Port Townsend. Fantastic for cyclists—miles of pastoral bike routes weave through Marrowstone. Hostel virtually unoccupied, even in summer. Members $7, nonmembers $8.50. Call ahead during off-season to ensure that the hostel will be open.

Point Hudson Resort, Point Hudson Harbor (385-2828), at the end of Jefferson St. Fading wooden structures tell of a past when Point Hudson was the major resort in the area. Today, recreational-boat builders hammer away outside your window, and a bratty buoy clangs incessantly. Very well-kept rooms. Singles and doubles start at $43, $50 w/bath.

Camping: You can camp at **Fort Worden State Park** (385-4730) for $9.50 per night, or at **Old Fort Townsend State Park** (385-4730) for $7 per night. The latter is 5 mi. south of Port Townsend just off Hwy. 20. Fort Worden is open year-round; Old Fort Townsend mid-May to mid-Sept. You can also camp on the beach at **Fort Flagler State Park** (753-2027) for $7.50.

Food and Entertainment

Strap on your Birkenstocks and grab your organic essentials while you can at **The Food Co-op,** 1033 Lawrence (385-2883), at Polk. National co-op members pay the marked price, others pay 10% more. A **Safeway** serves those reluctant to co-op-erate.

Burrito Depot, 609 Washington St. at Madison (385-5856). Their monster Veggie Burrito ($4.40) is a meal and a half. Open Mon.-Sat. 8am-8pm.

Linda's Country Kitchen(385-5645), in Victoria Square on the corner of Tyler and Water St. Satisfying breakfast, including thickly-sliced Canadian bacon $3.50. Open daily 8am-5pm.

Bread and Roses Bakery and Deli, 230 Quincy St. (385-1044). Gargantuan raspberry croissant $1.50, turkey and swiss croissant $1.75. Open Mon.-Sat. 7am-5pm, Sun. 7am-4pm.

Landfall, 412 Water St. (385-5814), on Point Hudson. Seafood, salads, and Mexican food. Expensive dinners, but reasonable for lunch and breakfast. A huge bowl of homemade fish and chips rings in at a salty $4.95. Tasty sourdough French toast $2.75. The boat-making crowd hangs out here, seasoning their food with shoptalk about lamination and wind resistance. Open Mon.-Tues. 7am-3pm, Wed.-Sun. 7am-9pm.

Elevated Ice Cream Co., 627 Water St. (385-1156). Friendly owners receptive to the scruffy traveler. Delicious homemade ice cream and decent espresso (75¢). One scoop of ice cream or 2 mini-scoops of Italian ice $1.05. Open daily 9:30am-10pm; in winter 11am-10pm.

Town Tavern, 939 Water St. Mellow pool players and live entertainment on weekends: Irish, folk, and rock. $2-3 cover. Open daily 10am-2am.

The Back Alley Tavern, 923 Washington St. (385-6536). Reggae and rock. Cover $2.50-4. Jam sessions Sun. evenings.

Sights and Seasonal Events

Port Townsend's early pioneer settlers built sturdy maritime-style houses, but their wealthier successors preferred huge Queen Anne and Victorian mansions. Of the over 200 restored homes in the area, some have been converted into cozy, but costly bed and breakfasts; others are open to tours. The 1868 **Rothschild House,** at Franklin and Taylor St., has period furnishings and herbal and flower gardens. (Open daily 10am-5pm; Sept. 16-May 14 Sat.-Sun. 11am-4pm. Admission $1.) Or peek into the **Heritage House** at Pierce and Washington (open daily 12:30-3:30pm; admission $1.50) or the **James House** at Harrison and Washington (open daily 11am-4pm; free).

Take the steps on Taylor St. down to **Water Street,** the town's quaint main artery. Here, the brick buildings of the 1890s are interspersed with newer shops and cafés in the old-style motif. The **Jefferson County Museum,** at Madison and Water St. (385-1003), holds vestiges of the town's wild past. Highlights include a dazzling kayak parka made of seal intestines and the inexplicably ubiquitous, pedal-powered dentist's drill. A definite must-see. (Open Mon.-Sat. 11am-4pm, Sun. 1-4pm. Donations $1.)

The red **bell tower** on Jefferson St. alerted firefighters in Port Townsend for 80 years. No one goes up to ring the bell these days, but the base of the tower grandly overlooks the town. An old Romanesque clock tower hovers over the **County Courthouse,** at Jefferson and Walker St. Farther southwest is the **Manresa Castle** on Sheridan St. (385-5750), built in 1892 and used as a Jesuit school for 42 years. Now a hotel, it is open for wandering.

Point Hudson, the hub of the small shipbuilding area, forms the corner of Port Townsend, where Admiralty Inlet and Port Townsend Bay meet. North of Point Hudson are several miles of beach, Chetzemolka Park, and the larger Fort Worden State Park. As you walk along the pretty coastline, don't let the tide sneak up on you; you could easily find yourself on your own private island with no escape. **Fort Worden** (385-4730), a strategic military post dating from the turn of the century, guards the mouth of Puget Sound, commanding fine views of the sound and the Cascades. The fort was pressed into service in 1981 as a set for the movie *An Officer and a Gentleman.* The **Marine Science Center** on the Fort Worden Dock (385-5582) keeps live sea critters to touch and observe; this is your big chance to see a live sand dollar. (Open Tues.-Sun. noon-6pm. $1.)

Eighteen miles south of town on Marrowstone Island, **Fort Flagler State Park,** another retired military post, has slightly more run-down barracks than Fort Worden, but only a fraction of the tourists. Explore the gun emplacements, watch the sailboats on Puget Sound from the outpost high above the water, or stroll along the almost deserted beach down below.

From mid-June to early September, the **Centrum Foundation** sponsors a series of festivals in Fort Worden Park. The foundation supports bluegrass, jazz, folk, and classical music along with poetry readings, dance performances, and painting displays. Two of the most popular events are the **Fiddle Tunes Festival** in early July and **Jazz Port Townsend** in late July. Tickets are $6 for most single events; combination tickets can be purchased to cover the whole of each festival. For a schedule, write the Centrum Foundation, P.O. Box 1158, Port Townsend 98368 (385-3102). The **Rhododendron Festival,** held in mid-May, hosts arts and crafts displays, a clambake, bathtub race, parade, and fireworks. Contact the Chamber of Commerce for more information.

Port Angeles

Port Angeles, the last major town on the peninsula before Aberdeen, has a lingering reputation as a cheerless industrial complex dominated by paper and plywood mills. Though the Port Angelites are working to eradicate this unflattering image, the town's greatest asset will always be an unparalleled view of the gorgeous blue bay below. Stop here for information, transportation connections, or before driving up to the stupendous Hurricane Ridge, but don't stay around long—the rest of the peninsula awaits.

Practical Information and Orientation

Visitor Information: Chamber of Commerce, 121 E. Railroad (452-2363), next to the ferry terminal. Has an arsenal of literature and schedules. In addition to lists of lodgings, the center provides a free telephone for calling motels. Open daily 8am-10pm; in winter 10am-4pm. **Clallam County Parks and Recreation Department,** Courthouse Bldg. (452-7831, ext. 291), at Lincoln and 4th St. Open Mon.-Fri. 8:30am-4:30pm.

Buses: Greyhound, 215 N. Laurel (452-7611), near the ferry dock. To Seattle (2 per weekday, $15). **Clallam Transit System,** 694 Monroe Rd. (800-858-3747 or 452-4511). Open Mon.-Sat. 5am-9pm.

Ferries: Black Ball Transport (457-4491), foot of Laurel St. (Service to Victoria: May 11-Sept. 30, 4 per day; Oct.-May, 2 per day. $5.75 on foot, $23 with car.)

Taxis: Blue Top Cab Company, 452-2223. 24 hr.

Car Rental: All-Star, 602 E. Front St. (452-8001), in Aggie's Motel complex. $20 per day. Must be 21 and pay rental in advance. Credit card or $100 deposit required. The office is never manned; you must call ahead for someone to meet you. 24 hr. **Budget,** 111 E. Front St. (452-4774), has rentals with unlimited mileage for $10 per hr. Open daily 7am-6pm; Oct.-May Mon.-Fri. 8am-5pm.

Camping Supplies: Browns, 112 W. Front St. (457-4150), between Laurel and Oak. Well-stocked, with friendly service from knowledgeable salespeople. Bargains here, however, are getting increasingly hard to find. Open Mon.-Sat. 9am-5:30pm.

Public Library: 207 S. Lincoln St. (452-9253). Open Mon.-Wed. 10am-8pm, Thurs.-Sat. 10am-5pm.

Senior Citizen's Center: 215 Lincoln St. (452-3221).

Laundromat: Peabody Street Coin Laundry, 212 Peabody St. Wash 75¢, dry $1. Open 24 hr.

Weather: 457-6533. 24 hr.

Pharmacy: Jim's, 221 Peabody St. (452-4200). Open Mon.-Fri. 8:30am-7pm, Sat. 8:30am-5pm.

Crisis Line: Rape Relief/Safehome, 603 E. 8th St. (683-1101). 24 hr.

Coast Guard: 457-4404 in emergencies. 24 hr.

Post Office: 424 E. 1st St. (452-9275), at Vine. General Delivery ZIP Code: 98362. (Open Mon.-Fri. 8:30am-5pm, Sat. 9am-noon.)

Area Code: 206.

Clallam Transit System ("The Bus") serves the Port Angeles area and connects with Jefferson Transit in Sequim. (Buses run Mon.-Fri. 6am-7:30pm, Sat. 9am-5pm. Fare 50¢.)

Accommodations and Camping

Port Angeles' seedy hotels are a reminder of the town's long-standing tradition as a rough-and-tumble port town. Fortunately, there is a hostel and cheap camping abounds in the scenic environs.

House of Health Hostel, 511 E. 1st St. (452-7494). With a large kitchen, plenty of showers, comfortable beds, and a genuine Finnish steam bath downstairs, why stay anywhere else? (Members $9.50, non-members $11). Reception 7-10am and 5-10pm. $2 linen rental. Open April-Oct. 31. Be sure to call ahead, as House of Health is currently for sale.

All-View Motel, 214 E. Lauridsen Blvd. (457-7779), on U.S. 101 at Lincoln St. Take bus #22 from Oak and Railroad to Lincoln and Lauridsen. Quiet, residential neighborhood. Well-equipped rooms: cable TV, laundry facilities, some kitchens. $2 discount for senior citizens. Singles from $35 (phones $1 extra), doubles from $45.

Dan Dee Motel, 132 E. Lauridsen Blvd. (457-5404), on U.S. 101. Take bus #22 from Oak and Railroad to Lincoln and Lauridsen. Relatively clean rooms with fuzzy color TVs. Some kitchenettes. Singles $28. Doubles $32.

Heart o' the Hills Campground (452-2713), 5½ mi. from Port Angeles inside Olympic National Park. Go up Race Rd. past the park's visitors center and toward Hurricane Ridge. 105 idyllic campsites. Drinking water and toilets, but no showers. Sites $5. Open year-round.

Elwha Campground (452-9191), 3 mi. up Elwha River Rd., which leaves U.S. 101 9 mi. west of Port Angeles. Not as lovely as Heart o' the Hills, but not as crowded either. Sites $5. Open year-round.

Altaire Campground, another 2 mi. up Elwha River Rd. Virtually identical to Elwha Campground, only higher on the hill. Sites $5. Open year-round.

Boulder Creek Campground, at the end of Elwha River Rd., 8 miles past Altaire. The closest free campground to Port Angeles. Park at the end of the road, and hike 2 mi. along an abandoned road. You'll need a free backcountry permit (available at the trailhead). 50 sites.

Food

In a town that makes its living off the sea, the absence of reasonably priced seafood is inexplicable. In fact, there is a severe shortage of any cheap food at all. If you're low on money and feel that you must eat, you can always fall back on the fast-food chains that line the eastern half of Front and 1st St.

Joshua's at 136 E. 1st St. (457-7473) is the best cash-for-calories exchange you can find. $6.25 will get you The Kitchen Stove (a 4-egg omelette) that would leave Andre the Giant bloated. Try the monstrous homemade cinnamon buns ($1.75) if you dare.

First Street Haven, 107 E. 1st St. (457-0352). The First Street Haven's strawberry Belgian waffles ($4) will transport you to Brussels. Not as cost-efficient as Joshua's, however. Open Mon.-Fri. 7am-4pm, Sat. 8am-4pm, Sun. 8am-2pm.

Steve's Bakery, 110 E. 1st St. (457-4003). Foot-long maple bars (65¢), cake donuts (15¢), and healthy-looking loaves of bread ($1). Open Tues.-Fri. 7am-5pm, Sat. 7am-4pm.

Sights and Activities

The most compelling aspect of Port Angeles is the surrounding countryside. Unfortunately, without a vehicle, your only chance of seeing it is by paying $10.75 to **Olympic Van Tours** for a three-hour tour (check out the kiosk on the sidewalk by the ferry docks, or call 452-7949). Far more accessible by foot is the **Arthur D. Feiro Marine Laboratory** (452-9277). The lab offers touch tanks and excellent displays of local marine life. (Open daily 10am-8pm; in winter Sat.-Sun. noon-4pm. Admission $1, ages under 12 50¢.) Also on the pier is an observation tower with great views of the port and the Olympic Mountains that overlook the town. (Open daily 6am-10pm.) The **Clallam County Courthouse Museum,** 319 Lincoln St. (452-7831, ext. 364), on the second floor of the old Clallam Courthouse, lets you get up close to a lighthouse light, a stereopticon (with shelves full of picture-cards), and a fully preserved turn-of-the-century courtroom. (Open Mon.-Sat. 10am-4pm; in winter Mon.-Fri. 10am-4pm. Free.)

No visit to Port Angeles is complete without a trip up Hurricane Ridge Rd. to (you guessed it) **Hurricane Ridge.** Thick populations of bear and deer roam the woods, as alpine meadows leap straight out of *The Sound of Music.* The often-crowded ridge is the easiest point from which to grab a hiker's view of the range. However, on the many trails that begin here (including some for senior citizens and the disabled), the crowds quickly dissipate. Be alert while in the tourist-ridden parking area: deer, grown brazen, often graze in the parking lot. Hitching to the top is not an ordeal; you might stop in at the visitors center, at the base of the road, and ask around for a ride. Although the snow is too heavy and wet to be much good for winter sports, the park service nonetheless runs cross-country and downhill skiing on Hurricane Ridge during the winter (lift ticket $12). Sledding is discouraged because of past mishaps.

The **visitors center,** 3200 Mt. Angeles Rd. (452-4501, ext. 230), at Race St., dispenses free wilderness permits for backcountry camping. (Open daily 8am-6pm, shorter hours in winter.) The **Pioneer Memorial Museum,** near the visitors center, strips bare the life of the early logger and displays pressed specimens of park flora. (Open same hours as visitors center. Free.)

Near Port Angeles

Jutting into the Strait of Juan de Fuca, some 15 mi. east of Port Angeles and 6 mi. from the tiny town of Sequim (pronounced SKWIM), the **Dungeness Spit National Wildlife Refuge** protects seals, waterfowl, shellfish, and the occasional human on its 7-mi. stretch of beach. Unfortunately, the refuge is so isolated that it is virtually inaccessible to travelers without vehicles of their own. Although you can reach Sequim from Seattle via Greyhound ($11), from Port Townsend via Jefferson County Transit, or from Port Angeles via the Clallam Transit System, you still must walk the remaining 6 mi. to the refuge; Sequim does not include a bicycle rental shop among its resources. Cars are not allowed on the spit itself, and the entrance fee is $2. Spitting is prohibited.

Sequim, an oasis of dry weather in a soggy region, has seen rapid growth in the last few years as a retirement center. The **Sequim-Dungeness Museum,** 175 W. Cedar (683-8110), in the old post office, exhibits local historical artifacts, including handiwork by the Klallam and Lummi nations. (Open Wed.-Sun. 9am-4pm.) Drink your fill at the **Neuharth Winery,** 148 Still Rd. (683-9652 or 683-3706), which opens its cellars for tasting and tours. (Open daily 9:30am-5:30pm; in winter Wed.-Sun. 9:30am-5:30pm.) English pastries run $2-5 at **Scarborough Fayre,** 126 E. Washington St. (683-7861). Open Mon.-Sat. 10am-5pm. Seafood, including deep fried geoduck ($7) is available at **Vern's Seafood** (683-1055) on Hwy. 101 (the eastern extension of Washington St. at S. Brown Rd.; open daily 11am-pm, Oct.-April Mon.-Sat 11am-9pm). West of Sequim, on the way to Port Angeles, is the **Olympic Game Farm,** 383 Ward Rd. (683-4295), home to several retired Disney stars, including Bozo, the female brown bear who played Ben in *Grizzly Adams.* (Open daily 9am-6pm; Labor Day-Memorial Day 9am-5pm. Walking and driving tours $4). S~
Chamber of Commerce (683-6197), ½-mi. east of town on the cor~, running
and Rhodofer Rd., is swimming in pamphlets, including *Pep~*~
newspaper covering the local arts scene and seasonal eve~
is one block south of U.S. 101 on Sunnyside. G~
The local **area code** is 206.

Camping sites are plentiful. **Seq~**
of Sequim on U.S. 101, has ~
with full hookups.) F~
Dungeness Fork~

water, and hiking trails. The most popular spot in the area, however, is the **Dungeness Recreation Area** (683-5847), a Clallam County Park. Turn north on Kitchen-Dick Rd. off 101 to reach the home of the famous Dungeness crab. Clamming, crabbing, and beachcombing are major activities. Before collecting any shellfish, however, be sure to call the Washington State Red Tide Hotline at 800-562-5632 to make sure these nasty little algae haven't poisoned your catch. (Sites $5 resident, $7 non-resident. Open Jan. 15-Oct. 9.)

Five miles west of Port Angeles along U.S. 101 is the cut-off for Hwy. 112. Eight mi. up Hwy. 112 is the turn-off for the **Salt Creek Reservation Area** (928-3441, open year-round, sites $7). Salt Creek is the site of WWII coastal defense batteries and once boasted a 16" gun. It now boasts showers, kitchen facilities, pit toilets and interesting tidal pools.

For some inspiring hiking, instead of taking Hwy. 112, stay on U.S. 101 for another 25 mi. to **Soleduck Road,** and head south for another 14 mi. to the **Trail Head.** From there wonderfully scenic trails run along the **Soleduck River; Soleduck Falls** and **Lovers' Lane** trails offer particularly good views of the river. But take note: these are among the most heavily trafficked trails in the park. For more secluded hiking, try **Aurora Ridge** instead. For further information and free overnight camping permits, get in touch with the **Ranger Station** on Soleduck Rd. (open daily 9am-5pm, 327-3583). The **Sol Duc Hot Springs** (327-3583), two mi. up from the Trail Head, is where diehard hot-tubbers can soak all day for $3.95. The cement decks, chlorine smell, and shower-before-you-enter signs detract from the pristine source of the naturally hot water (open May 21-Oct.1 9am-9pm).

Back on U.S. 101, another 23 mi. west is the town of **Forks,** a supply center for the region's logging industry. Pick up maps and information at the **Tourist Information Center,** in the south end of town. (374-2531; open May 1-Oct. 31, 4am-5pm daily.) Before taking off into the wilderness, however, sample the scrumptious pies at **Pacific Pizza,** on U.S. 101 in Forks (374-2626). Seafood lovers should try the shrimp pizza, fruit lovers the apple pizza, and purists the 8" cheese pizza (each $4.55). A small pitcher of soda pop costs $1. (Open Sun.-Thurs. 11am-10pm, Fri.-Sat. 11am-11pm.)

Stay at the **Rainforest Home Hostel (AYH)** between mileposts 169 and 170 on U.S. 101 (20 mi. south of town). Check-in 5-10pm daily. (Members $6, $7.50 in winter (after Oct. 1), add $3 for non-members. Full kitchen facilities and showers.)

At the westernmost point on the strait within Washington State is **Neah Bay,** the only town in the Makah Indian Reservation. On the pier, the **Windsong Café** offers burgers for $2.25-4.75 and clam chowder for $2. The Clallam Transit System reaches Neah Bay via Sappho. Take bus #14 from Oak St. in Port Angeles to Sappho (60 min.). Then take bus #16 to Neah Bay (60 min.). Check schedules at the Port Angeles Greyhound Station to avoid excessive layovers. In case of **emergency** in Neah Bay, call 645-2701 (645-2236 in a **marine emergency**). Neah Bay's **ZIP code** is 98357. The local **area code** is 206.

Cape Flattery, the northwesternmost point in the contiguous U.S., sits in the corner of Neah Bay's backyard, but the dirt road out is hard to follow. Watch for signs "cape trails" at the west end of town. Follow the signs (and the dirt road) to a dead end, where a well-marked trailhead sends you toward Cape art work hour hike rewards those willing to risk twisted ankles with fantashouses artifacts island just off the coast and Vancouver Island across the strait. 500 years ago buried and preserved Flattery is **Hobuck Beach,** where camping and picnicking a slope-roofed shelter ideally suited to south lie the more secluded beaches, which can be a private property; visitors are welcome, but eah Bay for reservation regulations. Washington, the Makah nation (whose this fishes, and produces magnificent d **Research Center** (645-2711) where a huge mudslide foot-long house, with been replicated at the museum. (Open daily 10am-5pm; in winter Wed.-Sun. 10am-5pm. Admission $3, senior citizens and students $2.)

During the last weekend of August, Native Americans from throughout the northwest come to participate in the **Makah Days.** Packed full of sporting events, canoe races, traditional dances and bone games (a form of gambling), the festival attracts tribes from as far away as Canada and La Push. Don't miss the delicious Salmon Bake. Contact the cultural center for more information.

Olympic National Park

Lodged among the august Olympic mountains, Olympic National Park unites 900,000 acres of velvet-green rainforest, jagged snow-covered peaks, and ominously dense evergreen forest. This enormous region at the center of the peninsula allows limited access to four-wheeled traffic. No scenic loops or roads cross the park, and only a handful of secondary roads attempt to penetrate the interior. The roads that do exist serve as trailheads for over 600 mi. of hiking trails. The only people who seem not to enjoy this wildly diverse, wet wilderness are those who come unprepared: a parka, good boots, and a waterproof tent are essential in this area.

Practical Information and Orientation

Visitor Information: Park Service Visitors Center, 3002 Mt. Angeles Rd., Port Angeles (452-4501, ext. 230), off Race St. Main information center; fields questions about the whole park—camping, backcountry hiking, and fishing. Wilderness permits and map of the locations of other park ranger stations. Also houses the **Pioneer Memorial Museum** (see Port Angeles Sights). Open daily 8am-6pm, reduced hours in winter.

Park Superintendent: 600 E. Park Ave., Port Angeles (452-4501, ext. 311). Open Mon.-Fri. 8am-4:30pm.

Park Weather: 452-9235. 24 hr.

Park Radio: 1610 AM for road closures and general weather conditions.

Park Emergency: 452-4501. Operates 8am-5pm, other times 911.

The perimeters of the park are well developed. The park service runs **interpretive programs** such as guided forest walks, tidal pool walks, and campfire programs out of its various ranger stations (all free). For a full schedule of events throughout the park, obtain a copy of the park newspaper from ranger stations or the visitors center. A $3 entrance fee per car is charged at the more built-up entrances, such as the Hoh, Heart o' the Hills, and Elwha—all of which have paved roads, showers and toilet facilities. The fee buys an entrance permit good for 7 days. A similar pass for hiker/bikers costs $1.

July, August, and September are the best months for visiting Olympic National Park, since much of the backcountry often remains snowed-in until late June, and only the summer has a good number of rainless days. **Backpackers** should come prepared for a potpourri of weather conditions at any time. Always wear a wool hat in winter; hypothermia is a leading cause of death in the backcountry (see Health in the General Introduction for more details). Backcountry camping requires a free wilderness permit, available at ranger stations and trailheads. The park service's backcountry shelters are for emergencies only; large concentrations of people attract bears.

Never, ever drink even one mouthful of untreated water in the park. *Giardia,* a very nasty microscopic parasite, lives in all these waters and causes severe diarrhea, gas, and abdominal cramps. Symptoms, which often don't appear for weeks after ingestion, can put a serious damper on your travels. Carry your own water supply, or boil local water for five minutes before drinking it. Dogs are not allowed in the backcountry and must be leashed at all times within the park.

Mountain climbing is tricky business in the Olympic Range. Although the peaks are not high in absolute terms (Mt. Olympus is only 7915 ft. above sea level), they are steep and their proximity to the sea makes them prone to nasty weather. The quality of rock is poor, and most ascents require sophisticated equipment. Climbers are required to check in at a ranger station before any summit attempt. The rangers urge novices to buddy up with experienced climbers who are "wise in the ways of Northwest mountaineering."

Berry picking ranks high on the list of summer activities, and is easy as pie on the peninsula. Newly cleared regions and roadside areas have the best pickings; raspberries, strawberries, blueberries, and huckleberries are all common. Bears are also fond of this fruit; if one stumbles onto your favorite berry patch, share.

Fishing within park boundaries requires no permit, but you must obtain a state game department punch card for salmon and steelhead trout at outfitting and hardware stores locally, or at the game department in Olympia. The **Elwha River** is best for trout.

Eastern Rim

The eastern section of the park is accessible through the Olympic National Forest from U.S. 101 along Hood Canal. (See Hood Canal for information on camping in the forest.) The auto campgrounds are popular with hikers, who use them as trailheads to the interior of the park. **Staircase Campground** (877-5569), 19 mi. northwest of Hoodsport at the head of Lake Cushman, has a ranger station that offers interpretive programs on weekends. (59 sites open year-round, $5.) **Dosewallips**, (pronounced doh-see-WALL-ups) on a road that leaves U.S. 101 3 mi. north of Brinnon (27 mi. north of Hoodsport), has 32 free but less well-developed sites. The ranger station, open from June through September only, has no electricity or telephones. A spectacular trail leads from here across the park to Hurricane Ridge.

Northern Rim

Both **Heart o' the Hills** (452-2713; 105 sites) and **Elwha Valley** (452-9191; 41 sites) campgrounds have interpretive programs and ranger stations (see Port Angeles), as does **Fairholm Campground** (928-3380, 87 sites), 30 mi. west of Port Angeles at the western tip of Lake Crescent. (Sites $5. Open year-round.) The **Lake Crescent** station (928-3380) has an extensive interpretive program but no camping. The **information booth** here is open Memorial Day to Labor Day daily from 11:30am-4:30pm. **Soleduck Hotsprings Campground** (327-3534), to the southeast of Lake Crescent, 13 mi. off U.S. 101, is adjacent to the commercial hot springs resort (see Port Angeles Sights and Activities). A roving naturalist is on duty in the afternoon, and there are scheduled programs in the evening. (Sites $5.) The grounds are shut down when it snows.

The main attraction of the northern area, especially for those not planning back-country trips, is **Hurricane Ridge,** with its splendid views of Mt. Olympus, the Bailey Range, and Canada on clear days. (See Port Angeles Sights and Activities.)

Rain Forests

Washington is home to the only temperate rain forests in the United States. The rain forests along the Hoh and Queets rivers are canopied by particularly lush growths of gigantic trees, ferns, and mosses. Although the forest floor is thickly carpeted with unusual foliage and fallen trees, the Park Service keeps the many walking trails clear and well-marked. The first campgrounds along the Hoh River Rd., which leaves U.S. 101 13 mi. south of the town of Forks, are administered by the Department of Natural Resources (DNR) and accept no reservations. Drinking water is available at the **Cottonwood** and **Minnie Patterson** sites only. They are usually much less crowded than the Hoh, and the sites are about twice as roomy. You can obtain a separate map of the Hoh-Clearwater Multiple Use Area (MUA) from the DNR main office in Forks or at Minnie Patterson (see Olympic Peninsula Camping).

The **Hoh Rain Forest Campground and Visitors Center** (374-6925) is located 19 mi. down the Hoh River Road from the junction with Hwy. 101. Think twice about cycling down or hitching if you don't have a car: there are no shoulders, the road has a lot of blind corners, and the damn-the-torpedoes-logging-truck-drivers are scary.

If you succeed in making it down, there are several worthwhile hikes into the rainforest. The **Hoh River Trail** is for pros, but the **Hall of Mosses** and **Spruce** trails require only an hour and are wheelchair-accessible. Camping is available year-round and costs $5. (Visitors center open in summer daily 9am-5pm.) Try to camp near the riverbed in loop A. Deer stroll casually through your campsite here, and herds of elk can often be spotted in the riverbed early in the morning.

Throughout this region, even the air seems fertile, and touring the area, even if you've only got an afternoon, is rewarding. As you drive back up to Hwy. 101 you'll notice that the countryside looks like it's been shaved for surgery; these are actually clear-cuts, the after-effects of logging.

Farther south, after U.S. 101 rejoins the coast (see Ocean Beaches below), the park's boundaries extend southwest to edge the banks of the **Queets River.** The road here is unpaved and the campground at the top is free. (26 sites; open June-Sept.) The park and forest services share the land surrounding **Quinault Lake and River.** The park service land is accessible only by foot. The forest service operates a day-use beach and an information center in the **Quinault Ranger Station,** South Shore Rd. (288-2444; open daily 7:30am-5pm; in winter Mon.-Fri. 7:30am-5pm).

Ocean Beaches

The rugged and deserted beaches along the peninsula's western edge are especially magnificent during winter storms. Hike miles out of civilization's reach (with the exception of a few shelters around Mora). Beware, though, of incoming tides that can trap you against steep cliffs—clip and carry a tide chart from a local newspaper. Bald eagles rise to greet windy days in this area and whales and seals tear through the magnificent sea.

Mora (374-5460), near the Quillayute Indian fishing village of **La Push,** and **Kalaloch** (962-2283), have campgrounds (sites $5) and ranger stations. The Kalaloch (pronounce KLAY-lok) Center, including lodge, general store, and gas station, is the more scenic of the two, with 195 sites near the ocean.

Southwest Washington

At the climax of its Washington odyssey, the Columbia River makes a breathless descent into the Columbia River Gorge. As it moves seaward, the river becomes a border between Oregon and Washington for several hundred miles before ending in the Pacific. Resort towns conspire at the mouth of the river and around the bays and fishing ports to the north. The towns are small and rarely dovetail smoothly—wild marshlands and grasslands intercept, harboring coastal fauna in several good state parks and wildlife refuges. For **information** about the area, contact the Tourist Regional Information Program, SW Washington, P.O. Box 128, Longview 98632. In an **emergency,** call the state police (206-577-2050). From Memorial Day to Labor Day, call 800-562-0990 for Washington Park information.

Longview/Kelso

The twin towns of Kelso and Longview hold hands over the Cowlitz River near its confluence with the Columbia, just across from Rainier, OR. Longview was the first planned city west of the Rockies, and Kelso was founded by Highland Scots. Today, neither urban planning nor bagpipes define the sister cities as definitively as do their convention centers. Although there are several sights worth seeing, Kelso and Longview together warrant no more than a day's visit.

Practical Information

Visitor Information: **Longview Chamber of Commerce,** 1563 Olympia Way (423-8400). Open Mon.-Fri. 9am-5pm. **Kelso Chamber of Commerce,** 105 Miner Rd. (577-8058), exit 39 off I-5, near Kelso Rd. With its diagrams and dioramas, it's a good source of Mt. St. Helens information. Open daily 9am-5pm.

Greyhound: 1109 Broadway, in Broadway Hotel, Longview (423-7380). Buses to: Portland (6 per day, $7); Olympia (7 per day, $10); Seattle (7 per day, $15); and Vancouver, BC (4 per day, $50).

Community Urban Bus: 577-3399. Runs Mon.-Fri. 7am-6pm, Sat. 9am-6pm. Buses leave "Triangle Center" on the west bank of the Cowlitz in Longview every hr. on the hr. Fare 50¢, day pass $1. Free transfers.

Pacific Ferry: 800-542-7042 or 800-542-0810. Puget Island to Oregon (8 min., $2 per car).

Police: In Longview, 577-3157. In Kelso, 423-1270.

General Delivery ZIP Code: Longview: 98632. Kelso: 98626.

Area Code: 206.

Accommodations, Camping, and Food

Motel 6, 1505 Allen St., Kelso (636-3660), across from the Chamber of Commerce. So immaculate it is used as a convention center by soap salespeople. Cable, pool, and A/C. Singles $28. Doubles $34.

Electra Motel, 1744 10th Ave., Longview (423-5040). Color TV, kitchen, and living room in singles make up for peeling paint. No reservations. Singles $22. Doubles $28.

Oaks Trailer and RV Park, 636 California Way, Longview (425-2708), exit 36 off I-5. Deluxe accoutrements include, of all things, free cable TV. Sites $10.50.

Commerce Café, Commerce Plaza, 1338 Commerce Ave. (577-0115). Average prices (breakfast $2-3). Open Mon.-Thurs. 7am-9pm, Fri. 7am-10pm, Sat. 9am-10pm.

Hilander Restaurant, 1509 Allen St., Kelso (423-1500), near Motel 6 across from Volcano Center. Breakfast $2-5. Burgers $3-5. An adjacent bowling alley provides striking accompaniment to your meal. Open Sun.-Thurs. 7am-10pm, Fri.-Sat. 7am-11pm.

Sights

Famous for its January and February **smelt run,** when thousands of the tiny fish take the kamikaze trip from the ocean to the river, Kelso has earned the title of "Smelt Capital of the World." Local civic groups herald the impending downfall of civil society with the annual "smelt eating contest" the first Sunday in March. For a few dollars, watch the local heroes compete for prizes by stuffing themselves silly with phenomenal numbers of smelt. Contestants are said to fast for days in advance.

See a display of reconstructed pioneer-era buildings, Cowlitz and Chinook Indian artifacts, and a new exhibit on the role of transportation in the history of Washington at the **Cowlitz County Historical Museum,** 405 Allen St. (577-3119). (Open Tues.-Sat. 9am-5pm, Sun. 1-5pm. Free.) At the museum, a pamphlet details a walking tour of Kelso's century houses. The **Volcano Information Center,** in the same building as the Chamber of Commerce, features detailed accounts of the eruption of nearby Mt. St. Helens and dramatic pictures of rescue attempts. (Open daily 9am-5pm; Nov.-April Wed.-Sun. 9am-5pm.)

Take an inside look at Washington's second largest company (after Boeing) at the **Weyerhauser Company Mill Site,** Industrial Way (425-2150). Hour-long tours depart from the gatehouse just inside the main gate. (Tours given Mon.-Fri. 9:30am and 1:30pm; Labor Day to mid-June only on Fri. by appointment. Under 10 not allowed.)

The **Highlander Festival,** held during the third week of September, celebrates Kelso's Scottish heritage. Kelso residents cap off a day of bagpiping with an exciting round of canine weight-pulling. From featherweights to heavyweights, dogs see how much they can drag by their teeth.

Longview was named after its wealthy founder, R.A. Long, who fancied himself a visionary when he sent for Kansas City planners to build a city for his workers. Now a logging town and major deep-water port of declining population, Longview is decidedly not the stuff of visions. There is, however, a pleasant wooded park surrounding mile-long **Lake Sacajawea** in the center of town. Relax here or tour Longview port. (1-hr. tours daily 10am-1pm. Call 425-3305.) The innocuous **Monticello Convention Site,** at 18th, Maple, and Olympic Ave., commemorates the 1852 political gathering that made Washington a state (though it took the federal government 37 years to ratify the compact).

Longview/Kelso to the Pacific

Access to the beaches on the coast from Longview and Kelso is smooth. From Naselle, **Highway 401** rambles south past the mouth of the Columbia, a more scenic road than either Hwy. 4 or U.S. 101. By car, take exit 39 off I-5 and follow Hwy. 4 (Ocean Beach Highway) west. The latter allows good bicycling along the scenic Columbia River. Those hitching avoid Hwy. 4 and cross the bridge to Rainier, OR, where U.S. 30 continues to Astoria.

Although much of the **Willapa Hills** area, along Hwy. 4, is owned by timber companies, it still explodes with bears, deer, geefels and gonks. The **Columbian White-Tailed Deer National Wildlife Refuge** covers 9800 acres of island and mainland around **Cathlamet.** From headquarters (795-3915), two mi. off Hwy. 4, a walk or drive on the local roads yields close-up sightings of park deer. Connected to Cathlamet (see below) by Hwy. 409, rural **Puget Island** is prime bicycling country in the middle of the Columbia. The **Wahkiakum County Historical Museum,** a folksy, crowded collection of local memorabilia, beckons just one block from Hwy. 4 on River St. The delightfully unpretentious museum shows old photos of Scandinavian immigrants and local logging operations. (Open Tues.-Sun. 1-6pm; Dec.-March Thurs.-Sun. 1-4pm.) There are numerous little parks along the Columbia River. Watch for huge ocean-bound vessels navigating the currents.

Just west of Cathlamet on Hwy. 4, **Skamokawa** (pronounced ska-MOCK-away) is a riverside village that has changed little since the turn of the century. Across the creek from town, **Skamokawa Vista Park** (789-8605) permits picnics, camping with tents or RVs, and enjoyment of the playgrounds and tennis park next to the Columbia River.

Columbia River Mouth and Long Beach Peninsula

In 1788, British fur trader and poor loser Captain John Meares, chagrined after his repeated failure to cross the treacherous Columbia River Bar, named the water now known as Baker Bay, **Deception Bay,** and the large promontory guarding the river's mouth **Cape Disappointment.** Since then over 230 vessels have been wrecked, stranded, or sunk where the Columbia meets the ocean—a region aptly named "the graveyard of the Pacific."

Fort Columbia State Park (777-8221) is on U.S. 101 northwest of the Astoria Megler Bridge and 1 mi. east of Chinook. An interesting complex of buildings and historical sites, the fort was built in 1895 and armed with huge guns to protect the mouth of the river from enemies who never arrived. The park's **interpretive center** entertainingly re-creates life at the fort. A mile-long woodland trail takes you past several historical sites, including an abandoned observation station. (Park open daily 6:30am-dusk; Oct. 16-March Wed.-Sun. 8am-dusk.) What was once the hospital is now the **Fort Columbia Youth Hostel**, P.O. Box 224, Chinook (777-8755). The hostel is rarely full. There are some rooms available for couples and families. (Members $5, nonmembers $7. Open June 6-Sept. 15.) The only drawbacks are a military atmosphere, including a 9am check-out time. The park locks up at dusk, even though the hostel is only open for registration from 5:30-10pm. You can get to Fort Columbia from Astoria on bus #14.

In nearby Ilwaco, **Fort Canby State Park** offers camping and more Lewis-and-Clarkiana. The U.S. Coast Guard maintains a **Lifeboat Station and Surf School** in the park, where arduous training in rough winter surf pays off in summer; the students often have to abandon their maneuvers and attend to a real rescue of swimmers or vessels. Given the treacherous river entrance, it is not surprising that two lighthouses were built here. This is one of the busiest search-and-rescue stations in the United States.

You can watch the Coast Guard's brave training exercises or photograph the distant lighthouses from many angles. The Cape Disappointment Lighthouse (built in 1856, the oldest in the Northwest), and the North Head Lighthouse, built in 1898, are both in the park and accessible by 4-mi. forest trails. **Waikiki Beach,** in a sheltered area near the park's center, is (though not quite like Honolulu!) ideal for swimming in summer, beachcombing after storms in winter, and ship-watching day in and day out. It is near the park's main attraction, the **Lewis and Clark Interpretive Center** (642-3029 or 642-3078). Here the legendary expedition is described ad nauseam with journal entries, photos, and equipment. The center also delves into Native American lore and probes Cape Disappointment's recent role as a strategic military stronghold. (Open daily 9am-6pm; Oct.-May Wed.-Sun. 9am-5pm.) The park has 190 tentsites ($7.50-10.50), which fill up on summer weekends. To reserve a site, write Fort Canby State Park, P.O. Box 488, Ilwaco 98624, or call the park office (642-3078). To reach the park, exit U.S. 101 at Ilwaco and head 2 mi. southwest. Ignore the many signs pointing right—*that* road is a mile longer. **Pacific Transit** buses (642-4475) connect Ilwaco with the north Washington coast and with Astoria, OR (fare 35-50¢). From Ilwaco you can walk the 2 mi. to the park.

In Ilwaco, the **Heritage Museum**, 115 SE Lake St., lines up the usual suspects: Native crafts, pioneer memorabilia, and a rotating display of local artwork. (Open Mon.-Sat. 9am-5pm, Sun. 1-4pm. Admission $1.25, senior citizens and children 50¢.) And for something completely different, the restored railway depot behind the museum runs a miniature train through a scale model of the peninsula as it looked in the 20s. For a better view of Ilwaco's modern-day lifeline, try charter fishing. The best deal is **Reel 'Em In Charters and Café** at the Port of Ilwaco. Eight-hour salmon tours including coffee, lunch, and tackle start at $48. (Sun.-Thurs. at 5am.) Write P.O. Box 489, Ilwaco 98624 for reservations, or call either 642-8511 or 642-3511. **Heidi's Inn**, 126 Spruce (642-2837), has cable TV and kitchen and laundry facilities. (Singles $26. Doubles $34.)

Long Beach Peninsula, with its 28 mi. of unbroken beach, is the next best thing to a private Riviera. Fishing, swimming, boating, and kite-flying fill in the seasons between pounding winter storms on this uncrowded stretch. You can **beachcomb** for peculiar pieces of driftwood and glass balls from Japanese fishing nets. (Permit required for gathering driftwood in state parks.) Driving on the beach is common and legal on the hard, wet sand above the lower clam beds. From October to mid-March, look for people chasing the limit of 15 meaty razor clams. Even Mikey K. could outsmart the tasty, fast-digging bivalves if he knew the standard techniques (look for dimples or bubbles in the sand). If you're willing to shell out $10.50 for an annual nonresident license (Washington residents $3.50) and spend a few days learning the ropes, you may harvest a seafood feast. The *Chinook Observer's* Long Beach Peninsula Guide and the **state fisheries** (Ocean Park, 753-6600) advise clammers. Consult fisheries' regulations before digging in. Free tide tables are available at information centers and many places of business. These are useful both for clamming and to avoid being marooned.

Berry picking keeps many travelers well-fed in late summer; look for wild varieties in the weeds along the peninsula's roadsides. The peninsula contains nearly 500 acres of cranberry bogs. Just be careful about picking on private property and watch out for bears and automobiles.

Pacific Transit (in Raymond 642-4475, in Naselle 484-7136, farther north 875-6541) provides local transportation. For 85¢ and a transfer, you can take a bus as far north as Aberdeen. Schedules are available in post offices and visitors centers. (Service Mon.-Fri. 2-3 times per day.)

In **Seaview,** about 10 mi. north on the peninsula, the **visitors information center** (642-2400), at the intersection of U.S. 101 and Hwy. 103, welcomes tourists Mon.-Sat. 10am-5pm and Sun. 10am-4pm.

Farther north, the city of Long Beach draws the serious traveler to its strip of video arcades, bumper cars, kiddie rides, and junk food. Right in the middle of things lurks **Marsh's Free Museum,** 409 S. Pacific Ave. (642-2188), really a large store selling myriad geegaws and *tchatchkes.* The promised "exhibits" in the back are mostly old coin-operated peepshows or player pianos. Don't miss "Jake," however—this mummified half-man, half-crocodile is a local cult favorite. (Open daily 9am-10pm.) Two blocks west of Pacific Ave. you'll find the beach. Here you can ride bumper boats or rent a horse at **Double D Ranch**—it costs $10-11 per hour and a wrangler goes with you to make sure you don't gallop into the ocean. Late July brings the **Sand Castle Festival** to Long Beach. In 1989, a world record trembled when participants built a three mile long fortress of sand. The cheapest place to sleep is the **Sand-Lo-Motel,** 1906 Pacific Hwy. (642-2600). The rooms are clean and large. (Singles $26. Doubles $32.)

Continuing up the peninsula, the quiet residential community of **Ocean Park** is home to **Jack's Country Store,** at Bay and Veron (665-4988), *the* place for groceries, hardware, and just about everything else. Prices are reasonable. (Open daily 8am-8pm.) You can refuel at the **Bay St. Café,** Bay St. (665-4224), a block from the beach, with cheap and tasty burgers on fresh buns ($2.75-3.45).

Oysterville is a preserved 1854 town and was put on the National Register of Historic Places in 1976. For a walking tour of this peaceful hamlet, pick up a free guide at the church. Don't wander *into* the houses, though—people still live in them. For once, the past has not been tainted by commercialism—there's no way to spend money in Oysterville.

Nearby **Nahcotta** relies on the oyster for both entertainment and financial solvency. Nahcotta's claim to fame is **The Ark,** easily the finest restaurant in the area. Dinner might cost over $15 but it will overwhelm you with fresh seafood, homemade baked goods and pastries, and Northwest specialties—all elegantly prepared and served. (Open Tues.-Sun. for dinner and Sun. for brunch.) Make reservations a couple of days in advance (665-4133).

Leadbetter Point State Park, on the Long Beach peninsula's northernmost tip, is a favorite with photographers, nature lovers, and mosquitoes. Bring bug repellent to make sure that you don't lose kids and small pets to carniverous insects. The park is a gris-gris of grass, a flimflam of fleas and a mishmash of marsh. Farther down the peninsula, **Pacific Pines** and **Loomis Lake State Parks** are also perfect spots for hiking, picnicking, and surf fishing.

Willapa Bay and Grays Harbor

Willapa Bay, just north of Long Beach, is known for its wildlife but not its wild life. A drive up U.S. 101 and west on Hwy. 105 at Raymond is a feast for the eyes, compensating for the protected bay's deficiencies as a swimming and sunning spot. The small towns along the peninsula take aim at tourists and bristle with the usual array of souvenir shops and overpriced seafood restaurants. The state parks that clutter the region are all for day use only. (All parks open daily 6:30am-dusk; Nov.-March 8am-dusk. Call 665-5557 for information.)

Your first stop heading north on U.S. 101 should be the **Willapa National Wildlife Refuge,** a sanctuary for seabirds and waterfowl. You'll need a car to get there, but once you've arrived, plan to spend two or three hours of soggy hiking in the swamplands. For **South Bend** (accessible by Pacific Transit) the oyster is its world; Willapa Bay reputedly occupies 25,000 acres of oyster beds. You can tour the fully automated **Coast Oyster Company** (875-5557); the shellfish are great but they cost as much as pearls. **Bob's Pizza and Seafood,** on the other shell, is an average family-type place with average family-type place prices. The **Pacific County Museum and Visitors' Center** (875-5224) reveals this area's fixation with its history and its ancestors, housing various trinkets donated by Pacific County residents. They also have reference materials on everybody who's ever lived and died in South Bend, in addition to a fascinating collection of historical books for sale. While walking through the streets at night, try not to look too closely at the benches dedicated to the local dead; they are waiting to be included in a new Stephen King novel.

Raymond, 4 mi. from South Bend, is another quiet roadside logging town. The town relives its heyday during the annual **Loggers Fest,** held the first weekend of August. **Pizza Loft,** 226 Duryea St. (942-5109), is where local lumberjacks go for pizza and sandwiches. (Lunch special Mon.-Fri. $3. All-you-can-eat spaghetti Mon. nights $5. Open Mon.-Sat. 11am-10pm, Sun. noon-9pm.) **Maunu's Mountcastle Motel,** 524 3rd St., is just about the only lodging in the area; its clean rooms include color TV and A/C. (Singles $30. Doubles $40.) The **Raymond Visitor Information Center** is not particularly helpful and is located in the Century 21 building at 625 Heath St., just off U.S. 101. (942-5419; open daily 9am-5pm).

If you still have gas or gumption, drive west to **Tokeland** for good beaches and beachcombing. **Frances,** a ghost town on Hwy. 6, 15 mi. east of Raymond, suddenly comes alive with tourists twice a year during its Swiss-American celebrations. The first week in July is time for the **Schwingfest** ("schwinging" is Swiss wrestling optionally set to German Jazz), where you can watch the competitions, eat bratwurst, and polka down.

North of Willapa Bay at the far southwest corner of the Olympic Peninsula, the restless waters of Grays Harbor make a sizable dent in Washington's coastline. Long sandbars protect the harbor, itself undistinguished. The spits also extend north and south of the bay, forming wide, fine-grained beaches that stretch for miles. The inevitable resort area creeps north to Moclips near the **Quinault Indian Reservation.** Mobs of vacationers invaded the turf of the Quinault nation until August of 1969, when the Quinault people booted the littering and vandalizing visitors off their tribal beaches. This bold move brought a flood of supportive letters to the Quinault's mailboxes. A small museum (276-8211) up the coast in **Taholah,** in the office of the Quinault Historical Foundation, exhibits these political memoranda alongside more ethnological displays. (Open Mon.-Fri. 10am-4pm.) You'll see more if the staff is on hand, so call ahead to arrange a guided tour (as well as to get directions—it's a little tough to find). Grays Harbor Transit's Rte. 50 stops in Taholah.

Westport and **Grayland,** on Grays Harbor's Southern Spit, are known for salmon and cranberries, respectively. Focus your attention on Westport. At least every other storefront by the waterside Westhaven Dr. is devoted to charter fishing. Besides salmon fishing, most companies have also branched into bottom fishing, tuna fishing, and whale watching tours. **Deep Sea Charters,** across from float six (800-562-0151), is one of the cheapest, with full day trips at $55, plus $6 for tackle. But prices vary; get a list from the Chamber of Commerce and call around.

Generic clam strips and chowder joints are almost as common as charters. For a more serious dining experience, try **Arthur's,** 2681 Westhaven Dr. (268-9292). Lunches start at around $5. Dinners are costlier: a plate of salmon costs $13. The dining room is cozy and tastefully appointed. (Open Tues.-Sun. 11:30am-2pm and 5-9pm.)

The **Maritime Museum,** 2201 Westhaven Dr. (268-0078), is a fun mix of old seafaring equipment and other mundane objects. The museum is run by an ensemble

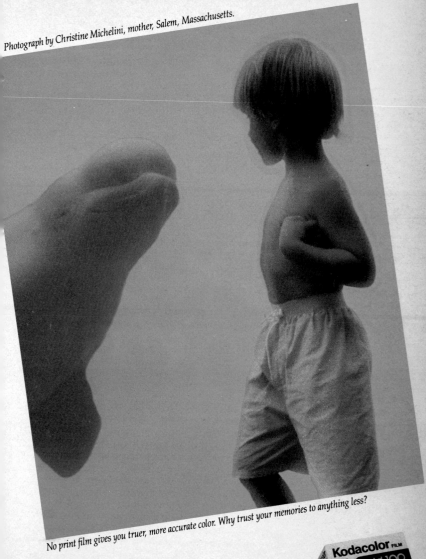

Photograph by Christine Michelini, mother, Salem, Massachusetts.

No print film gives you truer, more accurate color. Why trust your memories to anything less?

Show Your True Colors.™

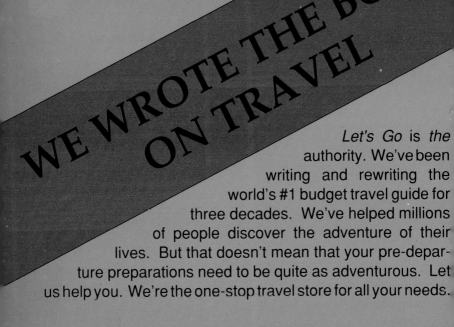

CARRY-ON RELIEF.

Look for the 1991 Let's Go® Travel Catalogue in this Book

LET'S G☺ Travel
one source for all your needs

of elderly women, one of whose 3rd grade report card is on display. (Open Wed.-Sun. noon-4pm; Sept.-May Sat.-Sun. noon-4pm.) Several notches on up the tacky-meter is the **Westport Aquarium and Giftshop,** (emphasis on the latter) 321 Harbor St. (268-0471). A wayward shark and a tired old octopus more or less comprise the entire aquarium. (Open daily 9am-9pm. Admission $2.50, children $1.50.)

Dozens of cheap motels line Hwy. 105 in Westport; the motels along the water-front are slightly pricier. The **Chamber of Commerce,** 1200 N. Montesano St. (268-9422), is only too eager to help you out. (Open daily 9am-5pm.)

Buses for Taholah, Westport, even Raymond and Olympia, originate from the **Aberdeen Station,** Wishkah and G St. (800-562-9730). The fare is only 25¢ ($1 to Olympia). Surrounding the station is the heavily industrialized city of **Aberdeen,** which, along with its sister city **Hoquiam,** suffers from a bad reputation. The residents of the rest of Washington call these port towns the mud puddles of the North-west—not just a reference to the torrents of rain. In the drier summer, however, their strategic location and low prices make them fine places to rest and refuel, if not necessarily linger, between the Olympic beaches and the more expensive inland mountains and cities.

The main point of interest in these vilified villages is **Hoquiam's Castle,** 515 Chenault Ave. (533-2005), a large Victorian home that stores trinkets and antiques from the area. (Open daily 11am-5pm; in winter by appointment only. Admission $3, seniors $2, under 16 $1.) The **Aberdeen Museum of History,** 111 E. 3rd St. (533-1976), discovers slide shows and antique firefighting equipment. (Open Wed.-Sun. 11am-4pm; Sept.-May Sat.-Sun. noon-4pm. Free.) If you haven't been camping long enough to yearn for the comforts of a cheap motel, make a stop in **Montesano,** a small town about 20 minutes east of Aberdeen on Hwy. 12. From Montesano, you can waltz into the hills for an overnight stay and a swim at **Lake Sylvia.** (Sites $6. Park closes to noncampers at 8pm.)

A string of inexpensive motels assures cheap rooms to those stopping overnight. In Aberdeen, the best option is undoubtedly the **Towne Motel,** 712 E. Wishkah (533-2340), a few blocks east of the bus station. Ignore the slightly dilapidated exte-rior—these small, tidy rooms have it all: cable TV with HBO, A/C, in-room coffee, minifridges, and potted plants. (Singles $25. Doubles $27.) The **TraveLure Motel,** 532-3280 623 W. Wishkah, has larger rooms and movies available, but no potted plants to speak of. (Singles $30. Doubles $38.) For more information on this area, pay a visit to the nice folks at the **Grays Harbor Chamber of Commerce,** 2704 Sum-ner Ave., Aberdeen 98520 (532-1924).

Cascade Range

As the 1980 eruption of Mt. St. Helens powerfully attested, the relatively young Cascade Range is still evolving. While a handful of white-domed beauties attract the most interest, the bulk of the range consists of smaller systems that together form a natural barrier from the Columbia Gorge to Canada. The mountain wall intercepts moist Pacific air, and is responsible both for Seattle's cloudy weather and the 300 rainless days per year in the plains of eastern Washington.

Although much of the heavily-forested range is accessible only to hikers and horseback riders, four major roads cut through the mountains along river valleys, each offering good trailheads and impressive scenery. **Highway 12** through White Pass goes nearest Mt. Rainier National Park; **Interstate 90** sends four lanes past the major ski resorts of Snoqualmie Pass; scenic **Highway 2** leaves Everett for Ste-vens Pass and descends along the Wenatchee River, a favorite of whitewater rafters; **Highway 20,** the **North Cascades Highway,** provides access to North Cascades Na-tional Park from spring to fall. These last two roads are often traveled in sequence as the **Cascade Loop.**

Greyhound covers the routes over Stevens and Snoqualmie Passes to and from Seattle, while **Amtrak** cuts between Ellensburg and Puget Sound. Rainstorms and evening traffic can slow **hitchhiking** down; locals warn against thumbing across Hwy. 20—a few hitchers have apparently vanished over the last decade. The mountains are most accessible in the clear months of July, August, and September; many high mountain passes can be snowed-in the rest of the year. The best source of general information on the Cascades is the joint **National Park/National Forest Information Service,** 915 2nd Ave., Seattle 98174 (442-0181 or 442-0170).

North Cascades

The North Cascades, an aggregation of dramatic peaks north of Stevens Pass on Hwy. 2, is subject to a number of different agencies. Pasayten and Glacier Peak are designated wilderness areas, each attracting hefty numbers of large backpackers and mountain climbers. Ross Lake Recreation Area surrounds the Hwy. 20 corridor, and North Cascades National Park extends north and south of Hwy. 20. The Mt. Baker/Snoqualmie National Forest borders the park on the west, the Okanogan National Forest to the east, and Wenatchee National Forest to the south. Highway 20, the North Cascades Highway (open April-Nov., weather permitting), provides the major access to the area, as well as jaw-dropping views past each new curve in the road. A favorite stomping ground for deer, mountain goats, black bears (and even a few grizzlies), the North Cascades remain one of the last great expanses of relatively untouched land in the continental states.

A wide selection of books can help plan a hike in the North Cascades. Ira Springs's *101 Hikes in the North Cascades* (The Mountaineers Press) ranks among the most readable for recreational hikers, while Fred Beckley's *Cascade Alpine Guide* (The Mountaineers Press) interests the more serious high-country traveler and mountain climber.

Practical Information and Orientation

North Cascades National Park: 2105 Hwy. 20, Sedro Woolley 98284 (206-856-5700). Open Sun.-Thurs. 8am-4:30pm, Fri.-Sat. 8am-6pm.

Mt. Baker/Snoqualmie National Forest: Outdoor Recreation Information Office, Jackson Federal Building, 915 2nd Avenue, Seattle 98174 (206-442-0170).

Okanogan National Forest: 1240 2nd Ave. S., P.O. Box 950, Okanogan 98840 (509-422-2704).

Wenatchee National Forest: 301 Yakima St., P.O. Box 811, Wenatchee 98801 (509-662-4335).

Snow Avalanche Information: 206-526-6677.

Area Code: 206 west of the Cascades, 509 to the east.

Highway 20 (exit 230 on I-5) gives the best first impression of the North Cascades. A feat of modern engineering, Hwy. 20 follows the Skagit River to the Skagit Dams and lakes, whose hydroelectric energy powers Seattle; then it crosses the Cascade Crest at Rainy Pass (4860 ft.) and Washington Pass (5477 ft.), finally descending to the Methow River and the dry Okanogan rangeland of eastern Washington.

Greyhound stops in Burlington once per day on the Seattle-Portland route, and **Empire Lines** (affiliated with Greyhound) serves Okanogan, Pateros, and Chelan on the eastern slope. Hitching can be frustrating, since nervous RV owners generally blow exhaust in your face. Local traffic, your only hope, vanishes at night.

Skagit Valley

Sedro Woolley, though situated in the rich farmland of the lower Skagit Valley, is primarily a logging town. Locals turn out in droves for the annual **Sedro Woolley**

Loggerodeo, which begins the Friday before the Fourth of July. Axe-throwing, pole-climbing, and sawing competitions vie with rodeo events such as bronco-busting and calf-roping, and free-flowing beer for center stage. For information write the Sedro Woolley Chamber of Commerce, 714 Metcalf, Sedro Woolley 98284 (855-1841). (Open Mon.-Thurs. 9:30am-5pm, Fri. 9:30am-6pm, Sat. 9am-1pm.) North Cascades National Park Headquarters (856-5700) is on Hwy. 20 (open Sun.-Thurs. 8am-4:30pm, Fri.-Sat. 8am-6pm).

Highway 9 leads north of town through inspiring forested countryside, providing somewhat indirect access to **Mount Baker** via the forks at the Nooksack River and Hwy. 542. Mt. Baker (10,778 ft.) has been belching since 1975, and in winter, jets of steam often snort from its dome. The snow tarries long enough here to extend the ski season to the Fourth of July, when the zany **Slush Cup** challenges skiers of both alpine and water persuasions (the run begins in snow, and finishes 2000 ft. below in a giant slushie).

As you continue west, Hwy. 20 forks at **Baker Lake Road** which dead-ends 25 mi. later at **Baker Lake.** There are several campgrounds along the way, but only **Horseshoe Cove** and **Panorama Point** offer toilets and potable water (sites $7.50). All other grounds are free.

Back on Hwy. 20, you'll cross streams like **Coal Creek** which are marked as salmon runs. Fishing is tantalizingly prohibited, and in spring and fall, you can't see the water for the fish.

You would only have to sneeze four times in succession to miss the town of **Concrete** and its three neighbors—and perhaps you may want to do so. If you do feel compelled to investigate, you will certainly be welcomed; the ratio of Welcome to Concrete signs to inhabitants is comically high. If you drive through at lunchtime, stop at the **Mount Baker Café,** 119 E. Main (853-8200; open daily 6am-8pm). The road from Concrete to Mt. Baker runs past the lakes created by the Upper and Lower Baker Dams. Concrete information and solid help are available from the **Chamber of Commerce** (853-8400), tucked away in the old depot between Main St. and Hwy. 20 (follow the railroad tracks east upon entering town. Open Sat.-Sun. 9am-4pm). The **Senior Center** is also at this address and number. The information center can tell you if the **Puget Power Fish Facility's** salmon taxi service is in operation. After all, salmon don't have wheels of their own. Spawning salmon are taken from the water east of town and transported to the top of Lower Baker Dam. If you come to Concrete in late August, you'll be just in time for the **Good Olde Days Celebration,** whose ordinarily feverish pitch of excitement peaks during the scarecrow-judging contest and bed race.

Neighboring **Rockport** borders **Rockport State Park,** a park blessed by magnificent Douglas firs, a trail that accommodates wheelchairs, and 50 campsites ($7, with full hookup $9.50). The sites are fully developed, densely wooded, and among the nicest in the state. The surrounding **Mount Baker National Forest** permits free camping closer to the high peaks. From Rockport, Hwy. 530 stems south to **Darrington,** for some unknown reason home to a large population of displaced North Carolinians and therefore to a well-attended **Bluegrass Festival** on the third weekend of July. Darrington's **ranger station** (436-1155) is on Hwy. 530 at the north end of town. (Open Mon.-Fri. 6:45am-4:30pm; in winter also open Sat.-Sun. 8am-5pm.) If Rockport is full, continue one mi. east to Skagit County's **Howard Miller Steelhead Park** and its 20 $7 sites (with toilets and water) on the fast-flowing Skagit River.

Stop in **Marblemont** to dine at the **Mountain Song Restaurant,** 5860 Hwy. 20 (873-2461). The Mountain Song serves hearty and healthy meals—try the trout dinner ($8.50) or the BLT ($4.25, emphasis on L and T). Open daily 8am-9pm.

Pitch your tent at the free sites in the **Cascade Islands Campground,** on the south side of the Cascade River (ask for directions in town). Bring heavy-duty repellant to ward off the swarms of mosquitoes.

From Marblemount, it's 22 mi. up Cascade Rd. to the trailhead for a nine mi. hike to **Cascade Pass.** From the pass, the **Park Service shuttle** (3 trips daily June-Sept., 2 hr., one way $4) runs the 26 mi. between **Cottonwood** and the extremely isolated town of Stehekin (pronounced steh-HEE-kun), which can only be reached by boat, sea-plane or foot. (The shuttle was ferried in some years ago.) Check at the **Marblemount Ranger Station** (873-4590), one mi. north of Marblemount on a well-marked road from the west end of town, to see if the shuttle is running. (Open daily 8am-4:30pm.)

Skagit Dams to Washington Pass

Newhalem is the first town in the **Ross Lake National Recreation Area,** a buffer zone between Hwy. 20 and North Cascades National Park. The town is owned and operated by Seattle City Light Power Company, but feels like it was designed by a used-car salesman. Everywhere you go, City Light lets you know what a wonderful job they've done in flooding thousands of acres of virgin forest. A small grocery store and hiking trails to the dams and lakes nearby are the highlights of Newhalem. Information is available at the **visitors center,** on Hwy. 20. (Open late June-early Sept. Thurs.-Mon. 8am-4pm. At other times, stop by the general store; open daily 8am-8pm. Call 206-386-4489.)

The artificial expanse of **Ross Lake** (plugged up by Ross Dam on the west) extends back into the mountains as far as the Canadian border and is ringed by 15 campgrounds—some accessible only by boat, others by trail. The trail along Big Beaver Creek, a few miles north of Hwy. 20, leads from Ross Lake into the Picket Range and eventually to Mt. Baker and the **Northern Unit** of North Cascades National Park. The **Sourdough Mountain** and **Desolation Peak** lookout towers near Ross Lake offer eagle's-eye views of the range.

The National Park's **Goodell Creek Campground,** just south of Newhalem, has 22 sites suitable for tents and trailers and a launch site for whitewater rafting on the Skagit River. (Drinking water and pit toilets. Sites $3. Open year-round.) **Colonial Creek Campground,** 10 miles to the east, is a fully developed, vehicle-accessible campground with flush toilets, a dump station, and campfire programs every evening. (Open mid-May to Nov.; 164 sites, $5.) **Newhalem Creek Campground,** another National Park facility, keeps 50 developed sites ($5).

Diablo Lake lies directly to the west of Ross Lake. The foot of Ross Dam acts as its eastern shore. The town of **Diablo Lake,** on the lake's northeast shore, is the main trailhead for hikes into the southern unit of North Cascades National Park. The Thunder Creek Trail traverses Park Creek Pass to Stehekin River Rd., in Lake Chelan National Recreation Area. Diablo Lake supports a boathouse and a lodge that sells groceries and gas.

The **Pacific Crest Trail** crosses **Rainy Pass,** 30 mi. farther on the North Cascades Hwy., on one of the most scenic and perilous legs of its 2500-mi. Canada-to-Mexico span. The trail leads up to **Pasayten Wilderness** in the north and down to **Glacier Peak** (10,541 ft.), which commands the central portion of the range. (Glacier Peak can also be approached from the secondary roads extending northward from the Lake Wenatchee area near Coles Corner on U.S. 2, or from Hwy. 530 to Darrington.) There are groomed **scenic trails** of one to three mi. that you can hike in tennis shoes, provided the snow has melted (which doesn't occur until mid-July, if ever). An overlook at Washington Pass rewards a very short hike with a flabbergasting view of the red rocks of upper Early Winters Creek's Copper Basin. According to a descendant of Henry Cowell, the vista is the single most dramatic in the state, if not the entire Pacific Northwest. It's only a five minute walk on a paved trail, which is wheelchair-accessible. Look for rock climbers on Liberty Bell Mountain across the pass to the south, but don't distract them—it's a long way down. (For information on the eastern slopes of the North Cascades, see Okanogan.)

Farther west is the town of **Winthrop,** child of an unholy marriage between Bonanza and Long Island Yuppies who think a rusty horseshoe counts as an antique. Founded by Harvard alumnus Guy Waring in 1891, this town's name is borrowed from John Winthrop, the first govenor of Massachusetts (and also a Harvard graduate).

The great billows of hickory-scented smoke draw customers to the **Riverside Rib Co. Bar B-Q,** 207 Riverside (996-2001), which serves fantastic ribs in a "converted" prairie schooner (a covered wagon); it also has filling vegetarian dinners for $6.25. (Open daily 11am-9pm.) If it's breakfast you need, try **The Palace,** at 149 Riverside (996-2245). Open daily 7am-10pm. Across the street is the **Winthrop Information Station** (996-2125), on the corner of Hwy. 20 and Riverside. (Open Memorial Day-Labor Day 9am-5pm.)

The summer season is sandwiched by rodeos on Memorial and Labor Day weekends. If you're not there for either you can always mark time at the **Shafer Museum,** 285 Castle Ave. (996-2712), up the hill overlooking the town, 1 block west of Riverside Ave. The museum deploys all sorts of pioneer paraphernalia in a log cabin built in 1897. (Open daily 10am-5pm. Free.) You can rent horses at the **Rocking Horse Ranch** (996-2768), nine mi. north of Winthrop on the North Cascade Hwy. ($10 per hr.) Mountain bikes are available at the **Virginian Hotel,** just east of town on Hwy. 20 ($4.50 1st hr., $3 per additional hr., $20 full day). The **Winthrop Ranger Station,** P.O. Box 158 (996-2266), up a marked dirt road at the west end of town, dispenses information on camping in the National Forest. (Open Mon.-Fri. 7:45am-5pm, Sat. 8:30am-5pm.) North of Winthrop, the **Early Winters Visitor Center** (996-2534), outside Mazama, is aflutter with information about the Pasayten Wilderness, an area whose relatively gentle terrain and mild climate endear it to hikers and equestrians. (Open in summer Sun.-Thurs. 9am-5pm, Fri.-Sat. 9am-6pm; in winter, weekends only.)

Fourteen miles west of Winthrop on Hwy. 2, **Early Winters** has 15 campsites ($5). **Klipchuk,** one mi. farther west, tends 39 developed sites ($5). Cool off at **Pearrygin Lake State Park** beach. From Riverside west of town, take Pearrygin Lake Rd. for four miles. Sites ($6) by the lake have flush toilets and pay showers. Arrive early, since the campground fills up in the early afternoon.

Flee Winthrop's prohibitively expensive hotel world and sleep in **Twisp,** the town that should have been a breakfast cereal. Nine miles south of Winthrop on Hwy. 20, this peaceful hamlet offers low prices and far fewer tourists. Stay at **The Sportsman Motel,** 1010 E. Hwy. 20 (997-2911), whose barracks-like exterior masks tastefully decorated rooms and kitchens. (Singles $25. Doubles $30. Oct. 31-June 15 singles $18, doubles $23.) The **Blue Spruce Motel** (997-8852) offers barely tolerable accommodations just a ½-block away. (Singles $24. Doubles $36.) The **Twisp Ranger Station,** 502 Glover St. (997-2131), employs an extremely helpful staff ready to strafe you with trail and campground guides. (Open Mon.-Fri. 7:45am-4:30pm, Sat. 10am-2pm.) The **Methow Valley Tourist Information Office,** in the community center-cum-karate school at the corner of Hwy. 20 and 3rd, dispenses area brochures with more civility. (Open Mon.-Fri. 8am-noon and 1-5pm.)

The **Methow Valley Farmer's Market** sells produce from 9am to noon on Saturdays (April-Oct.) in front of the community center. Join local workers and their families at **Rosey's Branding Iron,** 123 Glover St. (997-3576), in the center of town. The Iron offers special menus for dieters, senior citizens, and children. All-you-can-eat soup and salad $6. (Open daily 5am-9pm.)

Five miles east of Twisp, the Forest Service operates an advanced training station for **Smoke Jumpers,** hell-bent hotshots like Dave Stires, who parachute voluntarily into the middle of blazing forest fires. Occasionally the service gives tours and runs training sessions that the public can watch. Call the station at 997-2031 for details.

Leavenworth

"Willkommen zu Leavenworth" proclaims the decorous wooden sign at the entrance to this curious resort. Once a dying mill town, Leavenworth "went Bavarian" in the mid-60s at the suggestion of solicitous German emigrés. A meager resemblance to Oberammergau (the sibling city in the old country) notwithstanding, merchants have been raking in the proceeds from beer steins and dinners served by a phalanx of waiters dressed in Lederhosen or Dirndl. The town's establishments frequently sport names that are freakish fusions of German and English. Have your hair cut at Das Klip und Kurl, and shop at a crenelated Safeway market. The German gimmick lures skiers during the peak season from November to March; in the slow summer months, this *kleines Dorf* survives on profits from functionless wooden knick-knacks and taste-tests between local Mt. Rainier beer and German brew. Today, an estimated one million people visit this Swiss Miss-commercial each year, with massive influxes coming during the city's three annual festivals. The sidewalks are filled with quaint (read: expensive) stores and loudspeakers pump the theme from the wedding scene of the *Deer Hunter.* Never mind that no one knows any German; this town is an experience in bizarre American vacation fun.

Practical Information and Orientation

Visitor Information: Chamber of Commerce, 703 U.S. 2 (548-5807), in the Innsbrucker Bldg. Very helpful and knowledgeable staff, many of whom see nothing amusing in their town's ridiculous gimmick. Open Mon.-Sat. 9am-noon and 1-5pm; Labor Day-Feb. 15 and April 15-Memorial Day Mon.-Sat. 9am-5pm; Feb. 16-April 14 Mon.-Fri. 9am-5pm.

Ranger Station: 600 Sherbourne (782-1413), just off U.S. 2. Pick up a well-organized guide to trails in Wenatchee National Forest and a list of the 8 developed campgrounds within 20 mi. of Leavenworth. Families should consult the 1-page "list of relatively easy, short hikes." The Enchantment Lakes trail is the most popular, but be sure to apply for a permit before tackling this treacherous route. Open daily 7:45am-4:30pm; in winter Mon.-Fri. 7:45am-4:30pm.

Greyhound: on U.S. 2 (548-7414), at the Kountry Kitchen Drive-In. Three buses per day to Spokane ($25.15) and Seattle ($18.80). Open daily 10am-9pm.

Bike Rental: Icicle Bicycle Rentals (548-7864), on U.S. 2 west of town. Tandems and mountain bikes at reasonable rates.

Laundromat: Die Wäscherei (548-9942), intersection of Front St. and U.S. 2, at the east end of town. Open daily 7am-10pm.

Hospital: Cascade Medical Center, 817 Commercial Ave. (548-5815). Formerly named "General Hospital."

Emergency: 911.

Post Office: 960 U.S. 2 (548-7212). Open Mon.-Fri. 9am-5pm, Sat. 9:30-11am. General Delivery ZIP Code: 98826.

Area Code: 509.

Leavenworth is located in Chelan County, on the eastern slope of the Cascades, near the geographical center of Washington. U.S. Hwy. 2 bisects Leavenworth within 200 ft. of the main business district. the main north-south route is U.S. 97, which intersects Hwy. 2 six mi. southeast of town. Leavenworth is approximately 121 mi. east of Seattle, 190 mi. west of Spokane.

Accommodations and Camping

If you can't get a room at the Hotel Edelweiss or the Bavarian Inn, consider leaving town; most hotels start at $40 for a single. Call ahead for reservations on weekends.

Camping is plentiful in Wenatchee National Forest. **Icicle Creek Road,** the last left in town on U.S. 2 heading toward Seattle, climbs the mountainside, following the creek. Ten miles from town, a series of Forest Service campgrounds squeeze between the creek and the road. The first five all have drinking water and cost $5 per site, while the last two cost only $4. You will find more isolated spots by pulling off the road and hauling your gear down the banks of the Icicle. Even this area is popular, however; if you seek solitude, avoid weekends after Memorial Day. In any case, come early, or you may not find a spot.

Hotel Edelweiss, 843 Front St. (548-7015), downtown. Bless Mike Krivan's hotel forever. Plain but clean rooms; bar and cocktail lounge downstairs. "Room" 14 has no TV, bath, or windows, but it's only $15 (be sure to set an alarm). Room 10 is graced with a TV and a window, but no bath or sink ($16). Other singles with bath and TV from $24.

Bavarian Inn, 100 U.S. 2 (548-4760). All 5 rooms in this immaculate inn have TV, bath, A/C, and an elegant glass table. Four rooms have 2 large beds; one has 3. Rooms start at $45. Try bargaining with the out-going manager, especially on weekdays. Reservations recommended.

Chalet Park, Duncan Rd. (548-4578), off U.S. 2, next to Duncan's Orchards fruit market. This small campground is close to the highway but otherwise quiet. Sites $10 for 1 or 2 people, full hookups $15. Baths and showers included. Open April 15-Oct. 15.

KOA Kampground, 11401 Riverbend Dr. (548-7709), ¼ mi. east of town on U.S. 2. A vacationland in itself, with laundry, basketball, volleyball, playground, swimming pool, pool table, video games, and a well-stocked convenience store. Quiet hours 11pm-8am. Two people $16, each additional adult $4. Electrical hookup $4, sewer $5. Kamping Kabin (a wooden shack) $25. Klean bath, showers inkluded. Open March-Dec.

Food

Predictably, Leavenworth's food mimics German cuisine; surprisingly, it often succeeds. Those who wish to avoid burgers and hot dogs and swallow some *schnitzel,* however, should prepare to pay $8-12 for a full dinner. But don't fret—if you get bored of bratwurst and the entire German leitmotif, you can always opt for pizza or Mexican.

Winzig's Burger Haus, 701 U.S. 2 (548-5397). The *kinder* eat here, cramming down $1.89 burgers with a *wunderschön* spicy house sauce and 45¢ soft ice cream cones. Thick milkshakes $1.25. Open Sun.-Thurs. 11am-7pm, Fri.-Sat. 11am-8pm.

Oberland Bakery and Café, 703 Front St. (548-7216). The pop music and modern decor are a refreshing change. $3.75 buys the rights to a generous sub. All-you-can-eat brunch on Sun. 10am-2pm ($7). Open in summer daily 9am-5:30pm.

Hansel und Gretel Delicatessen, 819 Front St. (548-7721). Tasty bratwurst and "knackwurst" ($2.75). The sandwiches are the wurst. Mingle with the Americans who stop by on their lunch break. Open daily 7am-9pm.

Wolfe's, 220 8th St. (548-7580). American fast-food with German efficiency. Try the beer-battered onion rings for $2, hot dog "a la American" (why not *auf Amerika?*) for $1.25, or super-deluxe cheeseburger for $3. Sit outside or carry your grub and grog to the gazebo downtown. Open Mon.-Fri. 11am-4pm, Sat.-Sun. 11am-6pm.

Leavenworth Pizza Company, in the Clock Tower Building on Hwy. 2 (548-7766). Boasts "the finest pizza East of the Cascades"—and the only pizza in Leavenworth. Build your own 10" pizza for $5.75 (50¢ additional toppings) and dig into the most un-Alpine food in the city. Open daily 11am-10pm.

Mini-Market, 285 U.S. 2 (548-5027). An otherwise run-of-the-mill convenience store merits mention for 10¢ coffee and 50¢ hot cider or hot egg nog. Open daily 6am-midnight.

Sights and Entertainment

Whitewater **raft trips** on the Wenatchee River are expensive thrills—the cheapest one-day trips are $39. Individuals can sign up at short notice; groups must call in advance. (Try **Wenatchee Whitewater,** P.O. Box 12, Cashmere 98815; 800-423-8639 ext. 162 or 782-2254.) Downhill or cross-country skiing during the winter can be found 58 mi. away at **Stevens Pass** (206-973-2441).

For slower joy rides, try the **Eagle Creek Ranch** (north on Hwy. 209, right on Eagle Creek Rd. for 5½ mi.; 548-7798) or the **Red Tail Canyon Farm** (11780 Freund Canyon Rd., 2½ mi. up Hwy. 209; 548-4512). The former takes kids under 9 on sleigh rides ($4) and hay rides ($10). Parents tag along for $10 each. The latter also runs hay rides ($6; ages under 12 $4).

On your way up Icicle Rd., stop at the **Leavenworth National Fish Hatchery** (548-7641) to see exhibits on local river life. In the summer, adult salmon (sometimes reaching 30 lbs.) fill the holding ponds. (Open daily 7:30am-4pm.)

On your way south to the U.S. 97 junction, stop in **Cashmere** at the **Aplets and Cotlets Factory,** 117 Mission St. (782-2191), for free tours of the plant and ample samples of the gooey candies. (Open Mon.-Fri. 8am-6pm, Sat.-Sun. 10am-4pm; Nov.-May Mon.-Sat. 8-11:45am and 1-4:45pm.) On U.S. 2 in Cashmere, the **Chelan County Museum** (782-3230) displays artifacts of the Native Americans whose land this used to be.

In Leavenworth, the **Historic Movie and Photo Gallery** at 801 Front St. continuously shows a 30-minute history of the Bavarian village. The film appears to have been recorded on a VHS camcorder, but the content is fascinating. The **Washington State Leaf Festival,** a celebration of autumn, runs for nine days from the last week in September until the first week in October. It includes a "Grand Parade," as well as art shows, flea markets, and street dances. "Smooshing," a four-person race run on wooden two-by-fours, is the highlight of the **Great Bavarian Ice Fest,** held on Martin Luther King Day weekend. (Right.) **Maifest,** held during the second weekend in May, celebrates the spring with appropriate German bombast. Featured events include a *Volksmarch,* street dances, a Maypole dance, and too much (i.e., some) polka music. Leavenworth summons holiday spirit and seas of tourists for the **Christmas Lighting,** the first two weekends in December; people from "all over the world" come to revel in the strings of light on Front St. amidst yuletide snow and "O, Tannenbaum."

Mount Rainier National Park

At 14,410 ft., Mt. Rainier rises elegantly over the other mountains in the Cascade range, two mi. taller than many of the surrounding foothills. Residents of Washington refer to it simply as "The Mountain," while Pete Seeger called it "that great strawberry ice cream cone in the sky."

Be prepared for rain on the western side. Warm ocean air condenses when it reaches Rainier and falls on the mountain at least 200 days of the year. When the sun does shine, you will understand why Native Americans called Mt. Rainier "Tahoma" (Mountain of God).

Although each year 2500 determined climbers find an expedition to the summit exhilarating, you can remain at slightly lower elevations and still enjoy midnight views of the mountain silhouetted against the moon. Fun-loving locals ride innertubes down the slick sides in winter, and romp in alpine meadows full of unparalleled wildflower displays during the summer. If you join them, you'll lessen cost and personal risk—without diminishing epiphanies.

Practical Information and Orientation

Visitor Information: Longmire Museum and Hikers' Center. Lodging, food, exhibits, and souvenirs. Open daily 8am-5:30pm; mid-Sept. to mid-June 9am-5pm. **Paradise Visitor Center.** Lodging, food, souvenirs. Open daily 9am-6pm; mid-Sept. to mid-June hours depend on funding. **Sunrise Visitors Center.** Snacks and gift shop. Open same hours as Paradise. **Ohanapecosh Visitors Center.** Information only. Open same hours as Paradise. All centers can be contacted ℅ Superintendent, Mt. Rainier National Park, Ashford 98304, or telephoned through the park's central operator (569-2211).

Park Headquarters: Tahoma Woods, Star Rte., Ashford 98304 (569-2211). Open Mon.-Fri. 8am-4:30pm.

Gray Line Bus Service, 2411 4th Ave., Seattle (343-2000). Excursions from Seattle to Rainier daily May 15-Oct. 15 ($25 single-day round-trip, under 13 $15; $5 surcharge to reserve a return on a later bus). Buses leave from the Space Needle in Seattle Center at 9:15am and return around 7pm, leaving you 2 hr. at the mountain, ample time to tromp through the trails leaving from Paradise.

Recorded Weather Information: 569-2343. Weather forecasts and mountain conditions are also posted once per day at all ranger stations.

Park Emergency: 569-2211 (Mon.-Fri. 8am-4:30pm), 569-2662 (Mon.-Fri. 4:30pm-8am, Sat.-Sun. 24 hr.).

Post Office: In the National Park Inn, Longmire. Open Mon.-Sat. 9am-5pm. General Delivery ZIP Code: 98397.

Area Code: 206.

To reach Mt. Rainier from the west, drive south from Seattle on I-5 to Tacoma, then go east on Hwy. 512, south on Hwy. 7, and east on Hwy. 706. This scenic road meanders through the town of Ashford and into the park by the Nisqually entrance. Hwy. 706 is the only access road open throughout the year; snow usually closes all other park roads from November through May. The total distance from Tacoma is 65 mi. You can also take I-90 from Seattle east to Bellevue, then Hwy. 405 south to Renton, and Hwy. 169 south through Maple Valley and the town of Black Diamond. At Enumclaw, head east on Hwy. 410 through the Wenatchee National Forest and into Mt. Rainier National Park by the White River entrance. The distance from Seattle is approximately 60 mi.

The cities of Yakima and Leavenworth guard the eastern gateway to the park. Take I-82 from the center of town to U.S. 12 heading west. At the junction of the Naches and Tieton Rivers, go either left on U.S. 12 or continue straight up Hwy. 410. U.S. 12 runs past Rimrock Lake, over White Pass to Hwy. 123, where a right turn leads to the Stevens Canyon entrance to Rainier. Hwy. 410 ascends Chinook Pass and ultimately runs north-south inside Rainier Park. The change in vegetation and terrain on the eastern ascent to the park is remarkable: dry plains around Yakima are followed by canyons lined with ponderosa pine, then stands of Douglas fir take center stage. Hwy. 410 offers more scenic views, but Hwy. 123 is 10 mi. closer to Yakima.

Hitchhiking along the mountain roads is exceptionally good. Park Service employees will often give lifts to stranded hikers. However, the main reason it's so good is that passersby realize how far away civilization is: be careful and avoid getting marooned in the middle of nowhere. Don't hesitate to ask a person in uniform for assistance; personnel here are as helpful and friendly as they come, especially when the peak is visible and spirits are high.

Summer temperatures stay warm during the day, but become chilly at night. You should be prepared for rapid changes in weather. (See Camping in the General Introduction.) The park is staffed with emergency medical technicians and owns a number of emergency vans. Rangers can provide first-aid. The nearest medical facilities are in Morton (40 mi. from Longmire) and Enumclaw (50 mi. from Sunrise).

Admission to the park is $5 per car or $2 per hiker. Gates are open 24 hour, with free admission in the evenings. The park has four **visitors centers** (see Practical Information). Guest Services headquarters are three mi. west of the Nisqually entrance toward Ashford, off Hwy. 7 on Kernahan Rd.

The **Gifford Pinchot National Forest** is headquartered at 500 W. 12th St., Vancouver 98660 (696-7500). The section of the Mt. Baker-Snoqualmie National Forest that adjoins Mt. Rainier is administered by the **Wenatchee National Forest**, P.O. Box 811, Wenatchee 98801 (509-662-4335). Closer ranger stations are at 16680 Hwy. 410, Naches 98937 (509-658-2435 or 658-2436) and at Star Rte., P.O. Box 189, Naches 98937 (509-672-4101 or 672-4111).

Accommodations, Camping, and Food

The towns of **Packwood** and **Ashford** have a few motels near the park. For general lodging information and reservations within the park, call 569-2275.

Paradise Inn, Paradise (569-2291). This rustic inn, built in 1917 from Alaskan cedar, offers paradisiacal views of the mountain. Wake up early to hike the heavenly Skyline Trail, which starts in the heavenly parking lot. Small singles and doubles with shared bath $45 plus 9% tax, each additional person $8. Open late May-early Oct. Reservations required in summer; call at least a month ahead.

National Park Inn, Longmire (569-2706). Less dramatic view than in Paradise, but convenient for cross-country skiing. Singles and doubles with shared bath $40, each additional person $8. Reservations required for weekends and recommended for weekdays.

Camping at the auto campsites between mid-June and late Sept. requires a do-it-yourself permit ($6), available at the campsites. **Alpine** and **cross-country camping** require free permits year-round and are subject to certain restrictions. Be sure to pick up a copy of the *Backcountry Trip Planner* at any ranger station or hikers' center before you set off. Alpine and cross-country permits are strictly controlled to prevent environmental damage, but auto camping permits are easy to get. The best developed auto campgrounds are at **Sunshine Point** near the Nisqually entrance, at **Cougar Rock** near Longmire, at **Ohanapecosh,** at **White River** in the northeast corner, and at **Carbon River.** Open on a first-come, first-camped basis, they fill up only on the busiest summer weekends. Sunshine Point is the only auto campground open throughout the year. With a permit, cross-country hikers can use any of the free, well-established **trailside camps** scattered throughout the park's backcountry. Most camps have toilet facilities and a nearby water source; some have shelters as well. Most of these sites are in the low forests, although some are found high up the mountain on the glaciers and snow fields. More adventurous cross-country hikers can test their survival skills in the vast cross-country zones in any of the low forests, and in the sub-alpine zone. In both areas, fires are prohibited and there are limits on the number of members in a party. Talk to a ranger for details. Mountain- and glacier-climbers must always register in person at ranger stations in order to be granted permits.

The **national forests** outside Rainier Park provide both developed sites (free to $5) and thousands of acres of free campable countryside. Avoid eroded lakesides and riverbanks. Minimum-impact camping fire permits, which allow hikers to use small fires that don't sterilize the soil, are available at national forest ranger stations (see Practical Information). Don't count on receiving one, however, since the small number of backcountry sites limits the supply of permits. Try calling ahead to reserve one.

There is no middle ground for food prices. Edible items within the park are either very expensive (at the Longmire, Paradise, and Sunrise concession stands) or free (no fishing permits are required for any of the park's lakes or streams, but contact a ranger about seasons and catch limits). The towns in the immediate vicinity of Rainier are equally overpriced; stock up on supplies in Seattle, Tacoma, or Yakima before entering the park.

Sights and Activities

Much of the activity in Rainier occurs at the park's four visitors centers (see Practical Information). Each has displays, a wealth of literature on everything from hiking to natural history, postings on trail and road conditions, and a ranger to fill in the gaps. Guided trips and talks, campfire programs, and slide presentations are given at the visitors centers and vehicle campgrounds throughout the park. Check at a visitors center or pick up a copy of the free annual newsletter, *Tahoma,* for details.

A car tour provides a good introduction to the park. All major roads offer scenic views of the mountain and have numerous roadside sites for camera-clicking and general gawking. The roads to Paradise and Sunrise are especially picturesque. **Stevens Canyon Road** connects the southeast corner of the national park with Paradise, Longmire, and the Nisqually entrance, unfolding truly spectacular vistas of Rainier and the rugged Tatoosh Range. Mt. Adams and Mt. St. Helens, not visible from the road, can be seen clearly from the mountain trails.

Several less developed roads provide access to more isolated regions, often meeting trailheads that crisscross the park or lead to the summit. Cross-country hiking and camping outside designated campsites is permissible through most regions of the park, but a permit is always required for overnight backpacking trips. The **Hik-**

ers Center at Longmire has information on day and backcountry hikes through the park and dispenses camping permits. (Open June 15-Sept. 30 daily 7am-7pm.)

A segment of the **Pacific Crest Trail (PCT),** running between the Columbia River and the Canadian border, crosses through the southeast corner of the park. Geared for both hikers and horse riders, the PCT is maintained by the U.S. Forest Service. Primitive campsites and shelters line the trail; no permit is required for camping, although you should contact the nearest ranger station for information on site and trail conditions. The trail, sometimes overlooking the snow-covered peaks of the Cascades, snakes through delightful wildlife areas.

A trip to the summit of Mt. Rainier requires a fair amount of special preparation and expense. The ascent involves a vertical rise of 9000 ft., usually taking two days, with an overnight stay at Camp Muir on the south side (10,000 ft.) or Camp Schurman on the north side (9500 ft.). Shelters are provided, but climbers should be prepared to camp if these are full. Tribute was recently paid to an intrepid young climber who made head turns in 1890 when, decked out in her skirt and corset, she became the 1st woman to conquer the peak.

Experienced climbers may form their own expeditions if they complete a fairly detailed application; consult a climbing ranger at Paradise, Carbon River, or White River stations. Solo climbing requires the consent of the superintendent. Novices can sign up for a **summit climb. Rainier Mountaineering, Inc. (RMI)** offers a one-day basic climbing course followed by a two-day guided climb; the package costs $250 and requires good physical fitness. Headquartered in their Guide House in Paradise (569-2227), RMI is also the only organization in the park that rents equipment: ice axes, crampons, boots, packs, and helmets at about $6.50 per day per item. You must bring your own sleeping bag, headlamp, and rain jacket, corset, and pants, and carry four meals in addition to hiking gear. For more information, contact park headquarters or RMI at (Oct.-May) 535 Dock St, #209, Tacoma 98402 (206-627-6242 or 206-569-2227); (June-Sept.) RMI, Paradise 98398 (206-569-2227).

Less ambitious, ranger-led **interpretive hikes** interpret everything from local wildflowers to area history. Each visitors center (see Practical Information) conducts its own hikes and each has a different schedule. The hikes, lasting anywhere from 20 minutes to all day, are ideal outings for families with young children. These free hikes complement evening campfire programs, also conducted by each visitors center.

Longmire

Longmire's **museum** dwells modestly on Rainier's past. The rooms are filled with exhibits on local natural history and the history of human encounters with the mountain. One interesting display reveals the disappointing secret of the mountain's name: "Rainier" has nothing to do with either a weather report or Monaco's monarch, but rather derives from a forgotten Tory politician who never even saw the peak. (See Practical Information for hours.)

Longmire-area walks and programs run by the visitors center typically include night meadow walks and hikes into the surrounding dense forest. The **Hikers Center** is an excellent source of information and guidance for all backcountry trips except summit attempts. Free information sheets are available for specific day and overnight hikes throughout the park. Look closely at the relief model of the mountain before plunging into the woods. Remember that a permit is required for backcountry camping.

Longmire remains open during the winter, as a base for snowshoeing, cross-country skiing, and other alpine activities. **Guest Services, Inc.,** runs a **cross-country ski center;** a typical package costs $8. The trails are difficult, but you can snowshoe eight months out of the year. Some diehards even enjoy winter hiking and climbing out of Longmire.

Paradise

Contrary to what Joni Mitchell might say, Paradise is not a parking lot but rather a town in southern Washington. The area was introduced to the world by the Longmire family, who thought the vast meadows of wildflowers were the Northwest's Elysian Fields. Those who visit Paradise on a clear, sunny day will probably agree. It sits well above the timberline, and even in mid-June the sparkling snowfields blind visitors staring down at the forest canyons thousands of feet below. The road from the Nisqually entrance to Paradise is open year-round, but the road east through Stevens Canyon is open only from mid-June through October, weather permitting. The **Paradise Visitors Center** offers radiant choirs, audiovisual programs, and an observation deck. Nearby inner-tubing runs bring hosts of suffering parents with their 10-year-olds. From January to mid-April, park naturalists lead **snowshoe hikes** to explore winter ecology around Paradise. (Sat.-Sun. at 10:30am, 12:30pm, and 2:30pm. Snowshoe rental $1.) You'll need snowshoes: the world record for snowfall in one season (93 ft.!) was set here in the winter of 1971-1972.

Paradise serves as the starting point for a number of trails heading through the meadows to the nearby Nisqually Glacier, or up the mountain to the summit. Many trails allow up-close views of Mt. Rainier's glaciers. The 4½-mi. **Skyline Trail** is the longest of the loop trails out of Paradise (3-hr. walk). The marked trail starts at the Paradise Inn, climbing above the treeline. Skyline is probably the closest a casual hiker will come to climbing the mountain. The first leg of the trail is often hiked by climbing parties headed for Camp Muir (the base camp for most ascents to the summit). The trail turns off before reaching Camp Muir, rising to its highest elevation at **Panorama Point.** Although only halfway up the mountain, the point is within view of the glaciers, and the summit appears deceptively close. Turn around to witness rows and rows of blue-gray mountaintops, with Mt. St. Helens and Mt. Adams presiding over the horizon. Heading back down the trail, you will cross a few snow fields and do some boulder-hopping. Since route conditions vary a great deal, contact a ranger station at Paradise, White River, Sunrise, or Longmire for information on crevice and rockfall conditions.

The mildly strenuous, half-day hike up to **Pinnacle Peak,** which begins across the road from Reflection Lakes (just east of Paradise), presents a clear view of Rainier.

Ohanapecosh and Carbon River

The **Ohanapecosh Visitor Center** and campground are located in a lush forest along a river valley in the park's southeast corner. The **Grove of the Patriarchs** here is one of the oldest stands of original trees in Washington. These 500- to 1000-year-old Douglas firs, cedars, and hemlocks create a serene spot for easy hiking. The visitors center has displays on the forest and naturalist programs that include walks to the grove, Silver Falls, and Ohanapecosh Hot Springs.

Carbon River Valley, in the northwest corner of the park, is one of the only true rain forests in the continental U.S. The Carbon River Rd. entrance is accessible from Hwy. 165. Several good hiking trails beginning on Carbon River Rd. offer the solitude missing from the Longmire and Paradise areas in summer.

Sunrise

The winding road to Sunrise, the highest of the four visitor centers, alternates vistas of the Pacific Ocean, Mt. Baker, and the heavily glaciated eastern side of Mt. Rainier. Nine out of ten experts agree that the mountain views from Sunrise are among the best in the park.

Wonderland Trail passes through Sunrise on its way around the mountain. A popular 95-mi. trek circumscribing Rainier, the trail traverses ridges and valleys; the lakes and streams near the path are trout-ridden. The entire circuit takes 10-14 days, involving several brutal ascents and descents. Be careful of early snow storms in September, snow-blocked passes in June, and muddy trails in July. Rangers can provide information on weather and trail conditions; they also can store food caches for you at ranger stations along the trail.

The hike from Fryingpan Creek Bridge (3 mi. from the White River entrance) to Summerland is popular for its views of Mt. Rainier and the Little Tahoma Crag; behold elk and mountain goats grazing on the surrounding slopes. The circuit runs

4.2 mi. from the road along Fryingpan Creek to the Sunrise campground, ranger station, and meadows.

Cowlitz Valley

The Cowlitz River winds through miles of unspoiled territory on its journey west and south to the Columbia River. Fed by streams tumbling out of the Cascade Crest, the river forms part of the waterbed for both the **Mount Adams** and **Goat Rocks Wilderness Areas** (to the west and northwest of Mt. St. Helens, respectively). Both areas are superlative hiking country (accessible only on foot or horseback) and count the **Pacific Crest Trail** among their excellent trail networks. The rugged Goat Rocks area is famed for its herd of mountain goats, while Mt. Adams seduces hundreds of climbers each year to its sensuous snowcapped summit (12,307 ft.). Contact the U.S. Forest Service for trail guides and other information on these wilderness areas.

The Cowlitz passes closest to Mt. St. Helens near the town of **Morton.** This logging town is served by U.S. 12 from the east and west (I-15 exit 68), Hwy. 508 from the west (I-5 exit 71), and Hwy. 7 from the north. Hitching on U.S. 12 is generally good; try asking a logging truck for a ride when it stops at a weigh station.

Morton hosts an annual **Logger's Jubilee** in the second weekend of August. Admission ($5) entitles you to join the crowds cheering sawyers, climbers, and choppers on their way to glory; parades, a carnival, and a barbecue contribute to the festive atmosphere.

Morton and other towns near Mt. St. Helens have capitalized on the public interest in the now *passé* 1980 eruption. All the stores sell containers of ash and other St. Helens *dreck* (ash glass paperweights, pens, thermometers, and Christmas-tree ornaments). The Morton airfield is one of several that offer $40-50 flights to view Mt. St. Helens. Good places to gawk at the mountain along the Cowlitz include the Hopkins Hill/Short Road viewpoint off U.S. 12, two mi. west of Morton. Look for the turn-off on the northern side of the road. Revive yourself in Morton at the **Cody Café,** on Main St. (496-5787). This classic hometown diner serves a whopping stack of pancakes for $2.50. Lunches run $3-5. (Open daily 6am-8pm.) The **Morton Chamber of Commerce,** P.O. Box 10, can be reached at 496-3260. The **post office** is on Hwy. 7. (General Delivery ZIP Code: 98356.)

The Cowlitz River, once wild and treacherous, has been tamed considerably by the Tacoma City Light hydroelectric project. The Mayfield and Mossyrock Dams back water up into the river gorge to create two lakes, **Mayfield** and **Riffe,** both major recreation areas. **Ike Kinswa State Park** and **Mayfield Lake County Park,** on Mayfield Lake off U.S. 12, each offer camping and excellent rainbow- and silver-trout fishing year-round. Public boat launches provide access to Mayfield, the lower of the two lakes.

Riffe Lake, much larger than Mayfield, was named in memory of Riffe, a town flooded by the creation of the enormous Mossyrock Dam. Scuba divers come here to explore the remains of this and another town, Kosmos, which was also washed out so the city of Tacoma could read at night. Hang gliders come from all over to hurl themselves off the ridge behind the lake near the town of **Glenoma,** riding near-ideal wind currents for phenomenal distances. Mossyrock Park campers on the south shore can drop by the display at Hydro Vista next to the dam. Tacoma City Light offers free guided tours of the whole Cowlitz River Development complex by reservation (383-2471 in Tacoma).

One of the more interesting features of the complex is the **Cowlitz Salmon Hatchery,** south of the town of Salkum just off U.S. 12. The free self-guided tours of the facility include views of fish ladders, the spawning center, and the tanks where the salmon are kept. This facility releases 17.5 million chinooks (young salmon) each year. Displays show the tragic life cycle of the salmon—born in the rivers, fattened in the ocean, and finally propelled upstream to spawn and die. Such hatcheries have been installed all over the Northwest, both to encourage salmon fishing and to compensate for changes in the environment wrought by hydroelectric projects. A small **trout hatchery,** on U.S. 12 just south of Ethel, has a similar set-up. For more information, contact the Department of Public Utilities Light Division, P.O. Box 11007, Tacoma 98411.

Below the dams, the Cowlitz River courses through farmland, flowers, and blueberries. Hosts of local farms dot the hillside along the road, many offering U-pick berry bargains during the summer harvest season (late June-Aug.).

Mount St. Helens

On May 18, 1980, sixty-nine years to the day after the death of Gustáv Mahler, Mt. St. Helens exploded into space. In the aftermath of the largest natural disaster in recorded American history, a hole two miles long and a mile wide opened in the formerly perfect cone. Ash from the crater blackened the sky for hundreds of miles and blanketed the streets of towns as far as Yakima, 80 mi. away. Debris spewed from the volcano-flooded Spirit Lake, choked rivers with mud, and descended to the towns via river and glacier. Entire forests were leveled by the blast, leaving a stubble of trunks on the hills and millions of trees pointing like arrows away from the crater. Because the blast was lateral, not vertical, it was more destructive as no energy was dissipated fighting gravity.

Once the jewel of the Cascades, today the Mt. St. Helens National Monument (now administered by the National Forest Service) looks like a disaster area. The vast expanses of downed timber look like nothing more than an immense graveyard, a memorial to a blast many times stronger than any man-made detonation to date. The spectacle of disaster is dotted with signs of returning life: saplings push their way up past their fallen brethren, insects flourish near newly formed waterfalls, and a beaver has been spotted in Spirit Lake. Nature's power of destruction, it seems, is matched only by her power of regeneration.

The surrounding area is now the **Gifford Pinchot National Forest.** Much of the monument area, which is shaded on Forest Service maps, is off-limits to the public because of the unpredictability of the volcanic crater and the delicate geological experiments conducted by scientists. Roads inside the restricted zones are undergoing construction, so expect delays or minor mixups.

Practical Information and Orientation

Visitor Information: Mount St. Helens National Volcanic Monument Visitor Center (247-5473), on Hwy. 504, west of Toutle. Take exit 49 off I-5, and follow the signs. The best place to start a trip to the mountain—information on camping and access to the mountain, as well as displays on the eruption and the mountain's regeneration. Interpretive naturalist activities mid-June to Aug. The free 20-min. film *The Eruption of Mt. St. Helens* has fine footage of monstrous steam clouds, muddy ash, and debris choking the Toutle River. Interpretive programs explain the eruption and the state of the mountain. Open daily 9am-5pm. Other visitors centers—Castle Rock, Yale, Iron Creek, and Pine Creek—provide information on the social, economic, and botanic aspects of the eruption.

Gifford Pinchot National Forest Headquarters: 500 W. 12th St., Vancouver, WA (696-7500). Camping and hiking information within the forest. Additional **ranger stations** are located at Randle (497-7565), north of the mountain on U.S. 12, east of the visitors center; Packwood (494-5515), farther east on U.S. 12; Wind River (427-5645), south of the mountain on Forest Service Rd. 30, north of the town of Carson in the Columbia River Gorge; and Mt. Adams (395-2501), at Trout Lake, southeast of the mountain on Hwy. 141, above White Salmon in the Columbia River Gorge.

Buses: Gray Line, 400 NW Broadway, Portland, OR (503-226-6755). Buses from Portland to Mt. St. Helens (round-trip $26, ages under 13 $14).

Current Volcanic Activity: 696-7848. 24-hr. recorded information. Another major eruption is unlikely (but, then again, everyone though the mountain was dormant in 1979).

Emergency: On the south and east sides of the monument, report emergencies directly to the Pine Creek Information Center or the Iron Creek Information Center, both on Forest Service Rd. 25. 24 hr. On the west side, dial 911.

Area Code: 206.

If you can only spend a short time in the area, visit the **Mt. St. Helens National Volcanic Monument Visitor Center,** on Hwy. 504 near Toutle (take exit 49 off I-5). But if you want a closer view of the volcano, plan to spend the whole day in the monument and visit either the southerly Pine Creek Information Center or the northerly Woods Creek Information Center. While not as large as the center near Toutle, the latter two are each within a mile of excellent viewpoints. From the north, get onto U.S. 12 and turn south on Forest Service Rd. 25 at the town of Randle toward the Woods Creek center. From the south, take Hwy. 503, which turns into Forest Service Rd. 90 in Yale; follow 90 to the Pine Creek center. Those wishing to climb the mountain (see Sights) must enter the monument via Hwy. 503, because all climbers must check in at Yale. Extensive rebuilding efforts have made such a mess of things that only the rangers in each visitors center know exactly what's going on.

Camping

Campsites are scattered throughout the national forest; some are free, some exact a $4-6 fee. For those who want an early start touring the mountain, there are two primitive campgrounds relatively near the scene of the explosion. The closest is the **Iron Creek Campground,** on Forest Service Rd. 25, near the junction with Rd. 76. The other is **Swift Campground,** on Forest Service Rd. 90, just west of the Pine Creek Information Station. Both charge $5 per site and are scenic and uncrowded. **Seaquest State Park** (274-8633), on Hwy. 504, east of the town of Castle Rock at exit 49 off I-5, has 70 sites ($7), some of which are primitive and reserved for the hiker/biker set. The campground is on Silver Lake, excellent for bass fishing.

Sights

From Road 25, turn east on Road 26, whose one lane (with turn-offs) follows the side of a ridge. This devastated valley did not even receive the brunt of the blow; the explosion vented its principal energy north. Viewpoints along the road are listed on handouts at the visitors center.

Road 26 ends at one viewpoint, but you can continue toward the crater over 6 mi. of the newly paved, two-lane Road 99. Curves, clouds of ash, and precipices make this stretch a 20- to 30-minute excursion without stops. **Windy Ridge,** at the end of the stretch, is worth the obstacle course. From here you can climb an ash hill that gives a tremendous view of the crater from 3½ mi. away. The Forest Service staff conducts nature programs around Road 99.

Road 25 ends to the south at Road 90. Go west here and then north on Road 83 to reach **Ape Cave,** a broken 2½-mi.-long lava tube formed in an ancient eruption. Rent a lamp, bring your own flashlight, or shadow a well-lit group. There are fine interpretive tours at noon, 1pm, and 2pm.

On very clear days, you might hire a plane to fly over the crater. **Sunrise Aviation** (496-5510) in Morton, on U.S. 12 east of the visitors center, flies for $40 per person (2-person min.). The ride is thrilling and takes in more than would ever be visible from the ground. The highlight is the close-up look inside the crater, where you can snap Kodaks of the hissing ash dome (just don't fall out).

In the last few years, several hiking trails have been reopened. One of these leads to a unique lava canyon exposed by the Muddy River mud flow. Hwy. 504 to Coldwater Lake will be reconstructed, opening up western views of the dome, crater, and newly formed lake. A shuttle bus from there to Johnson Ridge will allow a view directly into the crater, including the spectacle of scientists on the job.

Those with a sense of adventure, the proper equipment, and the foresight to have made reservations (required May 15-Oct. 31) can scale the new, stunted version of the mountain to glimpse the lava dome from the crater's rim. Although not a technically difficult climb, the route up the mountain is steep and often unstable (especially at the rim). Sir Edmund Hillary wanna-bes are encouraged to bring the whole package: ice axe, hard hat, sunglasses, sunscreen, crampons, rope, climbing boots, and foul-weather clothing. Between May 14 and November 1, the Forest Service allows only 100 people to hike to the crater each day. Reservations can be made in person at the Mt. St. Helens National Volcanic Monument Visitor Center (see Practical Information), or by writing to the center at 3029 Spirit Lake Hwy., Castle Rock 98611. The **Yale Climbing Center**, a one-room building on Hwy. 503 south of Cougar, reserves 30 of each day's permits for standbys who show up as early as 6pm the day before they plan to climb.

Eastern Washington

In the rainshadow of the Cascades, the hills and vales of the Columbia River Basin once grew little more than sagebrush and tumbleweed. Thanks to irrigation and several strategically placed dams, the basin now yields bumper crops of nearly every imaginable variety of fruit. The same sun that toasts the region's orchards ripens flocks of pale, sun-starved visitors from western Washington who crowd the banks of Lake Chelan and Moses Lake. Farther east, ranching, wheat farming, and mining dominate the economy. Spokane, the largest city east of the Cascades, poses no real threat to the cultural preeminence of the Puget Sound area. Out by the Idaho border, the pickup truck rules life and motion, and many citizens still carry the guns that "won the West."

U.S. 97, stretching north to south on the eastern edge of the Cascades, strings together the main fruit centers and mountain resorts along the Columbia River Basin. **Interstate 90** emerges from the Cascades to cut a route through Ellensburg, Moses Lake, and Spokane, while **Interstate 82** dips south through Yakima and Toppenish.

Greyhound runs on I-90 and makes passes into the Tri-Cities and Yakima. **Empire Lines** runs from Spokane (624-5163) to Grand Coulee (633-2771) and Brewster (689-5541), and along U.S. 97 from Oroville on the Canadian border to Ellensburg (925-1177), with stops in Chelan (682-5541) and Wenatchee (662-2183), among other towns. **Amtrak's "Empire Builder"** serves Spokane, the Tri-Cities, the Columbia River up to Yakima, Ellensburg, and Tacoma.

Lake Chelan

The serpentine body of Lake Chelan (pronounced shuh-LAN) slithers northwest from the Columbia River into the eastern Cascades. Although the dry, brown lakeshore around the faded resort town of Chelan isn't impressive, the shores farther north are handsome indeed. The lake, at points 1500 ft. deep (the third deepest in the U.S.), extends far into Wenatchee National Forest and pokes its northwesternmost tip into the Lake Chelan Recreation Area, a part of North Cascades National Park. The town of Stehekin caps the lake, accessible only by foot, boat, or plane.

Practical Information

Visitor Information: Lake Chelan Chamber of Commerce, 102 E. Johnson (682-3503 or 800-4CHELAN). This modern facility offers plenty of information on the town of Chelan and nearby Manson, but not much on the surrounding wilds (head for the ranger station for that). Open daily 8am-5pm.

Chelan Ranger Station: 428 W. Woodin Ave. (682-2576 or 682-2549), just south of Chelan on the lakeshore. Joint station for the Forest and Park Services. Staff will explain the byzantine regulations for parks, forests, and recreation areas. Open Mon.-Sat. 7:45am-4:30pm; Oct.-May Mon.-Fri. 7:45am-4:30pm.

Greyhound: 113 N. Sanders (682-2332), at Circle 5 Deli and Groceries.

Laundromat: Chelan Cleaners, 127 E. Johnson (682-2816). Open daily 7am-10pm, winter 7am-8pm.

Pharmacy: Green's Drugs, 212 E. Woodin Ave. (682-2566). Open Mon.-Sat. 9am-6pm, Sun. 9am-4pm.

Hospital: Lake Chelan Community, 682-2531. Open 24 hr.

Emergency: 911.

Post Office: 144 E. Johnson (682-2625), at Johnson and Emerson. Open Mon.-Fri. 9am-4:30pm. General Delivery ZIP Code: 98816.

Area Code: 509. When dialing within Chelan, you need only dial the last 5 digits.

Accommodations, Camping, and Food

Exploiting the sun-starved citizens of western Washington, Chelan has jacked up the prices on just about everything from scuba gear to Silly-Putty. Most motels and resorts in town are unaffordable during the summer. You can sleep for free on the banks of the Columbia River in Pateros, 21 mi. north of Chelan on I-97, although you will be joining a questionable crowd of vagrants in a city park. The cheapest food can be bought at local fruit stands, the farmers' market, or the **Safeway** on 106 Manson Rd. (682-2615; open daily 6am-midnight).

Mom's Montlake Motel, 823 Wapato (682-5715), at Clifford. Mom takes good care of you with well-kept rooms, half with kitchens. Make yourself presentable before checking in, because she turns away "the rowdy-looking elements." Singles $38. Doubles $40.

Travelers Motel, 204 E. Wapato Ave. (682-4215). Kitchens, A/C, cable TV, and barbecues. Singles $35, with bath $40. Doubles $45, with bath $55.

Lakeview Motel, 102 Woodin Ave. (682-5657). An ordinary over-the-tavern type hotel. Call ahead to reserve a room with a view of the lake. Shared bathrooms, no TVs. Singles $40. Doubles $45. $5 per additional person.

Lake Chelan State Park (687-3710), 9 mi. from Chelan up the south shore of the lake. Highly developed. Hot showers and facilities for the disabled. Lifeguard on duty at the beach. The 144 sites fill up quickly in summer. Sites $7, with hookup $9.50. Reservations are necessary; write Lake Chelan State Park, Rte. 1, P.O. Box 90, Chelan 98816. Open April-Sept.

Twenty-Five Mile Creek State Park (687-3610), 18 mi. up the lake's shore, beyond Lake Chelan State Park. A smaller, concession-operated park with a swimming pool. Sites $9.50. Open Memorial Day to Labor Day.

Lakeshore RV Park (682-5031), in town. Tents prohibited Memorial Day to Labor Day but permitted the rest of the year. This is a good place for late evening arrivals in the off-season, especially if you're heading up the lake first thing in the morning. Sites $10-18.

Golden Florin's Bear Foods, 125 E. Woodin Ave. (682-5535). Natural foods in industrial quantities. All the latest self-help manuals. Open Mon.-Sat. 9am-7pm, Sun. noon-5pm.

Judy Lane Bakery, 216 Manson Rd. (682-2151). Delicious baked goods. Chili dog $2.59. Open Sun.-Thurs. 7am-9pm, Fri.-Sat. 7am-10pm.

Sights and Activities

Pull over in Chelan only long enough to see the huge collection of antique apple-labels in the **Lake Chelan Historical Museum** at the corner of Woodin Ave. and Emerson St. (682-2138; open June-Oct. Mon.-Sat. 1-4pm; free).

There are no day hikes out of Chelan itself. Head up to Twenty-Five Mile Creek, or better yet, find your way to **Stehekin,** a town inaccessible by road. The **Lake Chelan Boat Company,** P.O. Box 186, Chelan 98816 (682-2224), runs one round-trip to Stehekin daily April 15 to October 15, leaving at 8:30am. The dock is one mi. south of Chelan on U.S. 97. Regular service takes passengers only. (Boats Oct. 16-May 15 Mon., Wed., Fri., and Sun. $14.50, round-trip $21; ages 6-11 ½-price; under 6 free.) The new **Lady Express** cuts the trip time in half, but almost doubles the price: one way $24, round-trip $38 (times same as above).

A lodge, a ranger station, and a campground cluster around Stehekin. An un-paved road and many trails probe north into the south unit of the **North Cascades National Park.** A shuttle bus ($4) operates along the Stehekin River Rd., linking Stehekin and the lakeshore to the national park. (Buses leave Stehekin Landing at 7:30am, 9am, and 2pm.) All walk-in campgrounds in North Cascades are open May through October (free). An excellent resource for the entire Stehekin area is *The Stehekin Guidebook* (free).

Backcountry use permits are mandatory in the park throughout the year and are available on a first-come, first-served basis. Pick one up at the Chelan or Stehekin ranger stations. For more information, see North Cascades National Park.

Grand Coulee Area

A long time ago (18,000 years, to be exact) the weather warmed, and a little gla-cier blocking a lake in Montana slowly melted and gave way. The result was a wall of water which swept across eastern Washington, gouging out the loess and basalt to expose the granite below. The whole process, is believed to have taken one month, carved massive canyons called "coulees." The entire region is now known as the Chanelled Scab Lands. Geologists, who usually assume that all change takes place gradually, were at first baffled by the Coulees. Today, the Coulees are acknowledged as striking evidence of a violently rapid geological transformation. The largest of the coulees is named, appropriately enough, Grand Coulee. Now that the Grand Coulee Dam is in place, it also contains the massive **Franklin D. Roosevelt Lake** and **Banks Lake.**

The area of the Columbia River from Banks Lake north to the Canadian border constitutes the **Coulee Dam National Recreation Area.** The hub of the works is at the Grand Coulee Dam and its surrounding cities—Grand Coulee, Coulee Dam, and Electric City. The **Grand Coulee Dam,** celebrated by Woodie Guthrie and oth-ers, was a local cure for Depression—7000 workers were employed for eight years (1934-42) in constructing the engineering marvel. Today the dam irrigates the previ-ously parched Columbia River Basin and generates much of the electrical power used in the Northwest.

At the **Visitors Arrival Center** (663-9265), on Hwy. 155 just north of Grand Cou-lee, you can see a 13-minute film featuring some fascinating 1930s footage of the dam's construction, accompanied by Woody Guthrie. The center also provides in-formation on fishing and motorboating on the two enormous lakes and can start you on a self-guided tour through the power plants. Guided tours of the dam leave from the top of the monolith on the half-hour every day in summer between 10am and 6pm. (Open daily 8:30am-10pm; Labor Day-Memorial Day 9am-5pm. Free.) Arrive before 1:30pm to find out what it's like at the base of an avalanche when the dam's spillway gates open, shooting thousands of gallons of the Columbia down the dam's face. Return to the dam at 10pm during the summer to view the truly wonderful, multimillion-dollar light show. The motel postcards in town fail to cap-ture its magnificence.

There is a **Safeway** in Grand Coulee at 101 Midway Ave. (633-2411; open daily 8am-10pm). The **post office** sorts your mail across the street. (Open Mon.-Fri. 8:30am-4:45pm, Sat. 8:30-11:30am. General Delivery ZIP Code: 99133.)

Accommodations, Camping, and Food

Center Lodge Motel, 508 Spokane Way (633-0770), in Grand Coulee. The rooms are big, airy, and built for munchkins—short beds, low showers, and tiny sinks. The current manager is an authority on windmills. Singles $25. Doubles $30.

Umbrella Motel, 404 Spokane Way (633-1691), in Grand Coulee. Smaller rooms, bigger beds, slightly cheaper. Singles $16. Doubles $18-20.

Campers should head to **Spring Canyon** (633-9441), two mi. east of Grand Coulee off Hwy. 174, a gorgeous setting on the banks of Franklin D. Roosevelt Lake, with 89 sites and a beach area. It often serves as an overflow for Steamboat park. Spring Canyon is wheelchair-accessible and has flush toilets. Be sure to wake up early; sprinklers begin at 11am. (Sites $6.) Other campsites east of Spring Canyon are accessible only by boat. Eight miles south of the dam on Hwy. 155 by the banks of Banks Lake, **Steamboat Rock State Park** (633-1304) has 100 sites set in striking scenery. Rock walls rise dramatically all around. (Flush toilets, pay showers, and wheelchair access. Sites $6-10.) Numerous **free camping areas** line Hwy. 155 south of Electric City; pull onto any of several unmarked dirt roads that lead to Banks Lake. Keep an ear out for rattlers (and we're not referring to Charo's maracas). The **Coulee Playland Resort** (633-2671), in Electric City 4 mi. from the Grand Coulee Dam, offers more amenities than the free campsites nearby, but be prepared to pay the price—$8 for tents, $11 for RV hookups. Boat tours of Banks Lake ($8.50) or Steamboat Rock ($12) depart from the resort three times daily. Call the State Parks Summer Hotline (800-562-0990) for more information.

You and Me Pizza, 19 Midway (633-2253), in Grand Coulee. The only homemade retail pizza in town. Enjoy the pepperoni pizza ($1.90), hefty hoagies ($3), and pitcher of soda pop ($1.75). On Tues., drop in 6-8pm for all the pizza you can gobble (with small soda $5). Open Mon.-Thurs. 3-8pm, Fri.-Sat. 11am-8pm; extra hours in summer.

Tee Pee Drive-In, 211 Midway (633-2111), in Grand Coulee. Cheap burgers ($1-2.60) become even cheaper if you win at Tee Pee Yahtzee—roll the same number on all 5 dice and your meal's free (your chances are 1 in 7776). Unfortunately, they don't give you the dice until after you order. Open Mon.-Fri. 10am-7pm, Sat. 10am-5pm.

Flo's Place, 315 Spokane Way (633-3216), in Grand Coulee. Country cooking served on plastic checkerboard tablecloths. Mel would be proud. Delicious omelette with choice of 3 ingredients, hash browns, toast and coffee $4.25. Nothing on the menu is over $5.50. Open Mon.-Sat. 5:30am-8pm; in winter Mon.-Sat. 5am-2:30pm.

Near Grand Coulee

Nespelem, 14 mi. north of Coulee Dam, is in the **Colville Indian Reservation.** The town's **Drum and Feathers Club Celebration** brings Native Americans from all over Washington to Nespelem during the first two weeks of July. Celebrating involves dancing, stick games, arts and crafts, and plenty of food. For a place to stay or a hearty snack, enter the raffle for such prizes as a 16-ft. tee pee or a half-side of beef.

South of Grand Coulee, near Coulee City, is **Sun Lakes State Park,** the site of **Dry Falls,** a chasm measureless to man and carved by the same waters that shaped the coulees. The falls were once 3½ miles wide. The **Dry Falls Interpretive Center** (632-5583) subjects the area's past to various modes of historical analysis. (Open Wed.-Sun. 9am-6pm; Oct.-April by appointment only.) Camping in the park is plentiful, with facilities for the disabled. (Standard sites $6.)

History and fishing enthusiasts should drive the 70-odd mi. northeast from Grand Coulee (along Hwy. 174, 2, and 25) to **Fort Spokane,** near Miles. The fort served as a military outpost in the late 19th century, housing the soldiers who tried to manage affairs between local Native Americans and the white settlers. Self-guided tours begin at the visitors center. (Open daily 9:30am-5pm.) The nearby **campground** features a beach and a fish cleaning station. (Sites $6.) Cool, eh?

Ellensburg

Once a candidate to become Washington's state capital, the town was virtually destroyed by fire in 1889. The downtown area has since then been carefully reconstructed to preserve the spirit of the past. Ellensburg is particularly proud of its blue agate gemstones, the largest of which (6 lbs.) is on display at the Kittitas County Museum. Ellensburg is also the home of one of the world's most obese psychedelic bands, the Screaming Trees. Ellensburg celebrates its history as a ranch-town with an annual rodeo, held on Labor Day.

Practical Information and Orientation

Visitor Information: Chamber of Commerce, 436 N. Sprague St. (925-3137). Open Mon.-Fri. 8am-5pm; Oct.-April Mon.-Fri. 9am-5pm.

Greyhound: 801 Okanogan St. (925-1177), at 8th Ave. Six buses per day to Seattle ($14), 2 to Walla Walla ($25), 3 to Spokane ($20), and 2 to Portland ($30). Open Mon.-Fri. 8:30am-5:30pm, Sat. 10:30am-4:45pm, Sun. 10:45-11:15am and 12:15-4:45pm.

Taxi: Kourtesy Kab, 925-2771.

Laundromat: College Coin Corner of Walnut and 8th (962-6000). Open daily 7am-10pm.

Pharmacy: Downtown, 414 N. Pearl St. (925-1514). 10% senior citizen discount. Open Mon.-Sat. 9am-6pm.

Washington State Patrol: 925-5303.

Hospital: Kittitas Valley Community, 603 S. Chestnut St. (962-9841).

Crisis Line: 925-4168.

Post Office: Corner of 3rd and Pearl (925-1866). Open Mon.-Fri. 9am-5pm. General Delivery ZIP Code: 98926.

Area Code: 509.

Ellensburg lies 36 mi. north of Yakima on I-82, and 100 mi. east of Seattle on I-90. It's a convenient reststop when crossing the state, but don't limit yourself to the chain of fast-food places near the freeway. The main drag (Main St., of course) runs north-south and intersects I-90 about a mile south of the downtown area. **Central Washington University** is in the northeast corner of Ellensberg, between 8th and 14th Ave. The visitor's guide has a walking tour of the historical district, but a quick jaunt down Pearl and Pine Streets will suffice.

Accommodations and Camping

Aside from KOA, the closest campground is in the Wenatchee National Forest, 20 mi. north on U.S. 97 (674-4411). Intrepid campers might also try the free (but few and very, very primitive) sites along the Yakima river in the canyon just south of town. Take Canyon Rd. out of Ellensberg for about four mi. During the rodeo, cheap rooms are available at Central Washington University (see Sights).

Harold and Wait's Motels, 601 N. Water, in Motel Square (925-4141). Two neighboring motels run out of the same office. The rooms at Harold's are nicer but the ones at Wait's have kitchens. Outdoor pool and free movies. Singles from $26. Doubles from $35.

Regalodge Motel, 300 W. 6th, in Motel Square (925-3116). Two blocks from the main drag. Spacious rooms are better than the shabby exterior would suggest. Indoor pool. Singles from $26. Doubles from $35.

Lighthouse Motel, 607 W. Cascade Way (925-9744), off 8th Ave., west of downtown. Horribly inconvenient without you own wheels. Dim but clean rooms with cable TV, A/C, and bath. Some doubles have kitchens, but they are often reserved for months at a time. Singles $24. Doubles $28.

Rainbow Motel, 1025 Cascade Way (925-3544). Closer than the Lighthouse, but by no means close. Ordinary rooms and outdoor barbecue area. A/C, color TV, and laundromat. Singles from $27. Doubles from $31.

KOA Kampground, 2½ mi. west of town down Cascade Way (925-9319), exit 106 off I-90, practically on the highway. Only camping in vicinity. Large area with laundry and game room. Sites $13.50, $2 extra per person after 2 people. Electrical hookup $2; sewer connection $1.50. Open April 1-Oct. 14.

Food

The Valley Café is the best place to eat in Central Washington; eat all your meals there.

Valley Café, 105 W. 3rd Ave. (925-3050). This wonderful art-deco café has been around since the 30s. The best values on the varied menu are the Mexican specialties (enchiladas $5.25). Superb breakfasts (Fri.-Sun. only) include 2 whole wheat pancakes for $1.65. The hot pastrami sandwich ($4.25) is the tastiest this side of Brooklyn. The fruit frappé ($2), or "smoothie," alone makes a trip to Ellensburg worthwhile. Lunch menu served all day. Open Mon.-Thurs. 11am-9:30pm, Fri.-Sun. 7:30am-9:30pm.

Casa de Blanca, 1318 S. Canyon Rd. (925-1693). Hefty servings of basic Mexican food ($4-6). Try the $4.50-6.75 combination plates for a smattering of everything. Lunch special $3.75. Open daily 11am-10pm.

Carlyle's Café, Pine and 4th St. Families overflow from the booths and teenyboppers crowd the barstools at this small restaurant. Plain food—but cheap and generous with portions. A full fish-and-chips dinner is only $4, chicken only $4.25. Open daily 7:30am-5pm.

Topper's Drive-In, 608 N. Main (962-1833). Just another cheap drive-in on the interstate of life, but the only one in town. Deluxe burger 99¢, 21 flavors of soft ice cream (89¢ large cone). Open Mon.-Sat. 7am-9pm.

Four Winds Bookstore and Café Rose, 202 W. 4th. A used bookstore bound neatly with an espresso bar. Coffee drinks range from $1.25-2.

Sights

The **Kittitas County Museum,** 114 E. 3rd Ave. (925-3778), at Pine St., is housed in an 1889 building with horseshoe-shaped windows. In addition to Native American artifacts and exhibits on ranching and the area's agricultural history, this veritable Uffizi of the west features an extensive gem and mineral collection. (Open Mon.-Fri. 1-5pm, Sat. 1-4pm. Free.) The **John Clymer Museum,** a tribute to the famous Western painter from Ellensberg, is currently at 406 N. Pearl. At an unspecified date it will move into the Ramsey Building. Part museum, part gallery, the exhibit displays Clymer originals (including some of his *Saturday Evening Post* covers) as well as the permanent collection of the Western Art Association.

Families gather for picnics on weekend afternoons in **Memorial Park.** Located on the east end of 7th St. near the rodeo grounds, the park awakens green thoughts in its green shade. But come Labor Day the park is stampeded by one of the nation's ten most popular **rodeos,** as 500 cattlefolk compete for $100,000 worth of prizes in steer-wrestling, bareback bronco-riding, and wild-cow milking. (Seats in the uncovered grandstand $6, in the covered grandstand $8 on Fri.; $10 Sat.-Mon.) For tickets—hot items indeed—write the Ellensburg Rodeo Ticket Office, P.O. Box 777, Ellensburg 98926. During the rodeo, Central Washington University provides spacious and clean accommodations within 3 blocks of the rodeo grounds. (Singles $21.50. Doubles $38.) For information and reservations (make them by July), write to the Conference Center, Courson Hall, Ellensburg 98926 (963-1141). Local motels fill up and rates increase accordingly.

The progenitor of the rodeo, the **Kittitas County Fair** still manages to compete with its progeny on the same weekend. The four days of livestock displays, art shows, and domestic goat-milking contests are tamer than the rodeo, and are free to boot. The **Annual National Western Art Show and Auction** hot-wires up the town in the third weekend of May with auctions and exhibitions. More off-beat attractions are the **Ellensberg Bull** that sits casually on a Pearl St. parkbench and **Dick and Jane's Spot** at 1st and Pearl. The house and grounds occupying this "spot" are one large piece of art. The confused design may not be to your (or anyone's) taste, but it's worth a look.

Olmstead Place State Park (925-1943) is the site of the area's oldest log cabin and a showplace for early agricultural equipment. Several 19th-century buildings remain, including a dairy barn and a granary. Take Old Vantage Highway east of town. The park is open daily 6:30am-dusk, the buildings are open Sat.-Sun. noon-4pm. Groups can arrange a tour for Mon.-Sat., by appointment only.

Yakima

An agricultural apotheosis tucked neatly at the foot of the Cascades, Yakima calls itself the "fruit bowl of the nation." Blessed with rich volcanic soil, 300 days of sunshine per year, and a fresh groundwater supply, the area seems to be home to more fruit stands than people. Yakima could be any small city in the American heartland except for the juxtaposition of this agricultural serving-platter and its next door neighbor, the snow-capped Mt. Ranier which hangs like a Hollywood backdrop to identify the setting as Washington rather than Kansas. Ideal for launching into more mountainous atmospheres, the Yakima Valley is also home to a thriving Native American reservation and several world-class wineries.

Practical Information and Orientation

Visitor Information: Yakima Valley Visitors and Convention Bureau, 10 N. 8th St. (575-1300), at E. Yakima. Maps of town and brochures on Yakima's charms. The *Yakima City and County Map* ($1) is useful, but the map in the free *Yakima Valley Visitors Guide* serves just as well. Open Mon.-Fri. 8am-5pm, Sat.-Sun. 9am-5pm.

Greyhound: 602 E. Yakima (457-5131). Buses halt in Yakima on the way from Seattle (3 per day, $18 one way). No service from Yakima to Mt. Rainier. Open Mon.-Fri. 8am-4pm; Sat.-Sun. 8am-12:45pm, 1:45-4pm.

Taxi: Yellow Cab, 122 S. 1st St. (857-6500). Open 24 hr. **Diamond Cab,** 904 S. 3rd St. (453-3113). Open 24 hr.

Car Rental: Economy Auto Rentals, 3811 Main St., Union Gap (452-5555), just outside town. $20 per day, 50 free mi. plus 25¢ each additional mi. Must be 21 with a credit card. **Agency Rent-A-Car,** 324 W. Yakima Ave. (575-0939). $25 per day, unlimited mileage, drivers under 21 are acceptable with proof of insurance and credit card.

Camping Supplies: Herman's Sporting Goods, 2801 W. Nob Hill Blvd. (248-4500). Open Mon.-Fri. 10am-9pm, Sat. 10am-6pm, Sun. 11am-5pm. **Svends's Mountain Sports,** 1212 W. Lincoln St. (575-7876). Open Mon.-Fri. 10am-7pm, Sat. 10am-5:30pm.

Laundromat: Glenwood, 418-A S. 48th (965-3926). Open Mon.-Sat. 8:30am-9pm, Sun. 10am-6pm.

Recorded Weather Information: 575-1212.

Road Information: 457-7100.

Crisis Line: 575-4200. 24 hr.

Senior Information and Assistance: 454-5475. Open Mon.-Fri. 8:30am-5pm.

Poison Information: 248-4400.

Pharmacy: Medicine Mart Downtown, 306 E. Yakima Ave. Senior citizen discount on all prescriptions. Open Mon.-Fri. 9am-6pm, Sat. 9am-1pm.

Hospital: Yakima Valley Memorial, 2811 Tieton Dr. (575-8000). Open 24 hr. **St. Elizabeth Medical Center,** 110 S. 9th Ave. (575-5060). Open 24 hr.

Police: 204 E. B St. (248-1010).

Post Office: 205 W. Washington Ave. (575-5823 or 575-5827). Open Mon.-Fri. 8:30am-5pm. General Delivery ZIP Code: 98903-9999.

Area Code: 509.

Yakima is 36 mi. south of Ellensburg on I-82, 100 mi. east of Mt. Ranier on U.S. 410 and 125 mi. north of Pendleton on I-97. A stopover for weary drivers, Yakima is oriented towards those with cars. The downtown area is the northeast portion of the city and is near the Yakima River. The main drag, Yakima Ave., is the divider of north and south streets. **Yakima Transit** buses trace ten convenient routes, operating Monday through Friday from 5:45am to 5:45pm, Saturday from 7:45am to 6:15pm. (Fare 35¢, senior citizens 15¢, children 20¢.) For specific route information, call 575-6175 (4:30am-7pm).

Accommodations and Camping

Finding a cheap bed in the fruit bowl of the nation is often the pits. Affordable places keep clear of downtown and conventions often swallow up every room in the city. Yakima's few campgrounds are overcrowded and noisy. Less expensive, more pleasant campgrounds are on Hwy. 12, west of town on the way to Mt. Rainier. Campgrounds with drinking water are $5; those without are free.

YWCA, 15 N. Naches Ave. (248-7796), downtown. Women over 17 only. Small and pleasant. The 9 single rooms (shared baths) are often full but they may let you sack out on the common room couch. $10 per night, $50 per week, $150 per month. $25 key deposit.

Motel 6, 1104 N. 1st St. (454-0080). More reliable and professional than the string of budget motels along 1st St. that blink in and out of business. Singles $26.90. Doubles $33.36.

Log Motel, 1715 S. 1st St. (575-9456). A little rundown but cheap and quiet, largely because of its distance from downtown (a brisk 25-min. walk). Singles $21.50. Doubles $34.

Yakima Sportsman State Park (575-2774), 3 mi. east of town at 904 Keys Rd. Exit 34 off I-82. Bring insect repellent in spring, though insects may be the least of your troubles—beware of noise. Park open 6:30am-10pm. Sites $7.50, with hookup $10.

Food

There is little reason to set foot in a Yakima restaurant, unless you stay long enough to grow sick of fresh fruit. The *Yakima Valley Farm Products Guide*, distributed at the visitors bureau and at regional hotels and stores, lists local fruit sellers and U-pick farms. Peaches in season here often cost less per pound than they do per peach in other regions. U.S. 12 heading toward Naches has the best assortment of fruit stands, including the prominent **Cherry Lane Fruit and Gift** (653-2041), near the intersection with I-82.

Brunsbrae, 1813 Naches Heights Rd. (965-0873), and **Johnson Orchards,** 4906 Summitview Ave. (966-7479), are the 2 U-pick farms closest to town. The former specializes in cherries, the latter in apples. Farms generally stay open in summer from 8am to 5pm. Wear gloves and sturdy shoes, and bring as many empty containers as you can. U-picks are good deals and fun, but you can save almost as much by buying directly from the farms themselves. **Snokist Warehouse,** 18 W. Mead Ave. (453-5631), sells apples year-round. (Open Mon.-Fri. 8am-5pm.)

Kemper's, 306 S. 1st St. (453-6362). Gaudy purple drive-in where Elroy and Astro would feel at home. Standard burgers (deluxe cheese $1.19) and intriguing shakes (try the brandied peach, 90¢). True drive-in junkies will order a *sack* of fries (serves 6, $2.50). Open Mon.-Thurs. 9am-midnight, Fri. 9am-12:30am, Sat.-Sun. 10am-midnight.

Santiago's, 111 E. Yakima Ave. (453-1644). Named the best Mexican restaurant in the region by *Pacific Northwest* magazine in 1989, Santiago's combines excellent food with an ambience to please any Southwestern yuppie. Try a *chalupa* for lunch. Full dinners run in the $9-10 range. Their delicious (free!) salsa and chips are almost better than their entrees. Open for lunch Mon.-Sat. 11am-2:30pm, for dinner Mon.-Thurs. 5-10pm, Fri.-Sat. 5-11pm, Sun. noon-9pm.

The Brewery Pub (575-2922), on the north end of the train station. A large upscale pub serving only the ales of its owner, microbrewmeister Bert Grant. Pint of Grant's Scottish Ale $2.50, of Yakima cider $3. Small lunch menu varies. Open Mon.-Fri. 11:30am-11:30pm, Fri.-Sat. 11:30am-12:30am.

Sights and Activities

Most of the attractions of the Yakima Valley lie outside the city proper. Pick up one of the local handbooks or ask a native for tips on good car and bike loops. One of the prettiest bike trails runs along the river from Sherman Park in Nob Hill to the Selah Gap. **Toppenish**, 19 mi. southeast of Yakima, is the jump-off town for the **Yakima Indian Reservation.** The **Yakima Indian Nation Cultural Center,** 22 mi. south on U.S. 97 in Toppenish (865-2800), has a smorgasbord of events and information about the 14 tribes that once inhabited Yakima Valley. The **museum** here concentrates on the oral tradition of the Yakimas. (Admission $2, $5 family. Open Mon.-Thurs. 9am-5pm, Fri. 9am-9pm, Sat. 10am-9pm, Sun. 10am-6pm.)

The **Toppenish Powwow Rodeo and Pioneer Fair** (865-3996 or 865-5313) occurs during the first weekend of July on Division Ave. in Toppenish (fair admission $1, rodeo $5). Twenty-eight mi. west from Toppenish, the small town of **White Swan** hosts the **Tiinowit International Powwow and Treaty Celebration Day and Rodeo** during the first week of June. Both powwows feature games, dancing, live music, a rodeo, and fair food. Also in White Swan is the **Fort Simcoe State Park.** Established as a military post in 1856, the fort was inherited by the Yakima Indian Agency. The **Interpretive Center** is open Mon.-Fri. 8am-5pm, Sat.-Sun. 9am-6pm; Oct.-April Mon.-Fri. 8am-9pm. The park grounds are always open.

Worth seeing in Yakima itself is the **Yakima Valley Museum,** 2105 Tieton Dr. (248-0747). Known chiefly for its collection of horse-drawn vehicles, the museum also houses a re-creation of the office of Yakima's most famous native son, Justice William O. Douglas, and a display of Phil and Steve Mahre's skiing trophies. (Open Tues.-Fri. 10am-5pm, Sat.-Sun. noon-5pm, closed in January. Admission $2.50, senior citizens and students $1.25, families $5, under 10 free.)

Unfortunately, **Historic North Front Street** and **Yesterday's Village** have little to do with yesterday's history. Featuring somewhat expensive shops, this area offers the visitor no new information about Yakima—and fewer bargains. Of mild interest is **Track 29,** in between the previous two sites. The shops are all the same but each is located in a separate train car.

An electric trolley shuttles between Yakima and Selah (5 mi. north) for a scenic hour's round-trip; tours leave on the hour (11am-3pm) from the **Trolley Car Barn,** 507 S. 4th Ave. (575-1700; open May-Oct. Sat.-Sun. 11am-3pm; admission $3, ages over 64 and 6-12 $1.50, under 6 free). The **Yakima Valley Air Fair,** held during the last weekend in June at Yakima Municipal Airport, features antique planes. On a larger scale, the **Central Washington State Fair** is held in Yakima in late September. The nine-day event includes agricultural displays, rodeos, big-name entertainers, "regional specialties," and horse racing.

Bars like **The Phoenix,** 1219 N. 1st St. (248-8400), feature live country music nightly. The larger motels and hotels in town also present live entertainment, with cover charges running $1-3.

Wine Country

A television commercial a few years back showed a Frenchman with a glass of wine staring in disbelief at a globe, decrying "Washington State?" At one time, wine connoisseurs would have turned up their *nez* at pedestrian Washington labels. But the state is now the second largest producer of wine in the nation, and local vineyards have rapidly been garnering international acclaim.

The majority of wineries are situated in the Yakima, Walla Walla, and Columbia Valleys. These areas, just east of the Cascades, benefit from a rain shield that keeps the land naturally dry (and thus easily controlled by irrigation) with mineral-rich soil, bequeathed by ancient volcanoes. And, as almost every wine brochure points out, this region is at *exactly* the same latitude as Burgundy and Bordeaux.

Wineries abound in the small towns between Yakima and the Tri-Cities. Almost all offer tours and tastings and many have spectacular scenery as well. Common varieties are Chardonnay, Riesling, Chenin Blanc, Gewïrtztraminer, Merlot, Semillon and Cabernet Sauvignon. Among the most popular of the over 40 wineries in the region are **Chateau St. Michelle, Columbia Crest, Covey Run, The Hogue Cellars,** and **Stewart Vineyards,** but small new wineries pop up all the time. You can purchase *Touring the Washington Wine Country* ($1.50 plus 50¢ handling) from the Washington Wine Commission (write P.O. Box 61217, Seattle, WA 98121, Attn: Wine Brochure). There are also many other useful guides to be had free in visitor centers across the region. Of particular value are *The Grape Vine* and *Wine tour* which provide maps and information for the winegoer.

The following wineries are listed in geographical order from Yakima to the Tri-Cities. Almost all closely border I-82. Hours vary but most are open 10am-5pm, some with shorter hours on Sunday. Zillah: **Bonair, Covey Run, Horizon's Edge, Staton Hills, Zillah Oaks.** Granger/Sunnyside: **Cascade Crest Estates, Tucker Cellars, Stewart Vineyards.** Prosser/Grandview: **Chateau St. Michell, Minzerling Vineyards, The Hogue Cellars, Yakima River Winery.** Paterson (take Hwy. 122 from Prosser): **Columbia Crest, Mercer Ranch Vineyards.** Benton City: **Kiona Vineyards, Oakwood Cellars.** Pasco: **Preston Wine Cellars.**

Tri-Cities

The Tri-Cities lie at the juncture of the Columbia, Yakima and Snake Rivers, 100 mi. southeast of Yakima and 70 mi. north of Pendleton, Oregon on I-82. Pasco is the oldest and smallest (pop. 18,520) of the three cities, a railroad town settled in 1886. Across the Columbia are Richland and Kennewick. Richland (and Hanford) were built by the government in the 1940s as one of its secret atomic cities. Kennewick, separated from Richland by the Yakima river, is the largest (pop. 37,320) and newest city. It suffers from suburban sprawl but does have the largest covered shopping mall in eastern Washington. Richland, the site of the Hanford Nuclear Reservation, made national headlines a few years ago when its high school students voted overwhelmingly in favor of keeping both their name, the "Bombers," and their mascot, a mushroom cloud.

Practical Information

Visitor Information: Richland Chamber of Commerce, 515 Lee Blvd. (946-1651). Open daily 8am-noon, 1-5pm. **Greater Pasco Area Chamber of Commerce,** 129 N. 3rd (547-9755). Open Mon.-Fri. 9am-5pm. **Kennewick Chamber of Commerce,** 500 N. Morain #1200 (736-0510). Open Mon.-Fri., 8am-noon, 1-5pm.

Amtrak: W. Clark and N. Tacoma, Pasco (545-1554). Two trains daily, one each to Portland ($48) and Spokane ($25). Open Mon.-Wed. 5am-9pm, Thurs.-Fri. 5am-10:30pm, Sat.-Sun. 5am-7pm.

Greyhound: 115 N. 2nd St., Pasco (547-3151).

Ben Franklin Transit: 735-5100. Buses Mon.-Fri. 6am-7pm, Sat. 8am-7pm. No buses on holidays. Bus #120 runs an intercity loop between all 3 cities. #160 travels between Kennewick and Pasco, #225 between Richland and Pasco.

Taxi: Tri-Cities Deluxe Cab Co.: 547-7777.

Car Rental: AA Auto Rentals, 1900 W. A St., Pasco. (545-9296). $17.50 per day with 100 free mi. plus 20¢ per additional mi. Must be 21 with full insurance coverage and a credit card.

Laundromat: The Soap Opera, 1370 Jadwin Ave., Richland (946-1748). Open daily 7:30am-9:30pm.

Senior Information and Assistance: 783-0631.

Pharmacy: Payless, 215 N. 4th, Pasco (547-2231). 1268 Lee Blvd., Richland (946-4684). 101 N. Ely, Kennewick (783-1438).

Hospital: Kennewick General Hospital, 900 S. Auburn, Kennewick (586-6111).

Police: 1015 N. 5th St., Pasco (545-3421). 505 Swift Blvd., Richland (943-9161). 210 W. 6th Ave., Kennewick (582-5141).

Post Office: 3500 W. Court, Pasco (547-8481). General Delivery ZIP Code: 99301. 815 Jadwin Ave., Richland (943-1128). General Delivery ZIP Code: 99352. 525 S. Auburn, Kennewick (582-5000). General Delivery ZIP Code: 99336.

Area Code: 509.

Orientation

I-82 runs to the west of Richland and Kennewick, heading north to Yakima and south to Pendleton. U.S. 182 and U.S. 395 intersect I-82 (at Richland and Kennewick respectively) and cross the Columbia River into Pasco. There they meet up with U.S. 12 which heads southeast to Walla Walla. U.S. 395 continues northeast to Spokane. Hwy. 240 runs between Richland and Kennewick, on the west bank of the Columbia.

Accommodations

The best budget option (after the hostel) is the Bali Hi. Unlike the motels in Kennewick and Richland which are oriented toward tourists, the motels in Pasco tend to cater to the highway/trucker trade

Richland AYH Home Hostel, 194 Riverwood St., Richland (627-6411). Even without a *Let's Go* map to confuse you, you're bound to get hopelessly lost trying to find this place; call for directions. Four beds in a beautiful home in the midst of restoration. Owner often rents rooms to local students and conversations can be interesting. Nice view of the Yakima River. $8 per night.

Bali Hi Motel, 1201 George Washington Way, Richland (943-3101). From the Indian heads on the door to both the comfy chairs and refrigerators, all the little touches are taken care of. Tea and coffee makers in every room are an added bonus. Singles $29. Doubles $33. Must be 21.

Columbia Center Dunes Motel, 1751 Fowler St. (783-8181), in the Columbia Center Mall between Richland and Kennewick. Impersonal but comfortable, with refrigerators and A/C. Singles $25. Doubles $33.

Starlite Motel, 2634 N. 4th, Pasco. Small and off the beaten track. Very well managed. Mainly for truckers-in-the-know. Bag lunches upon request. Singles $22.

Motel 6, 1520 N. Oregon, Pasco (546-2010). This location draws more semis than station wagons but it's convenient to the airport and train station. Free movies and a pool. Singles $22. Doubles $28.

Food

If you stay in the Tri-Cities and don't eat at either Emerald of Siam or Casa Chapela you will not be welcomed back.

Casa Chapela, 107 E. Columbia Dr. (586-4224) and 2100 N. Belfair, both in Kennewick. Expect to wait for a table at this popular Mexican restaurant. Strolling Mariachi bands accompany such delectable treats as *Camarones Mexicanos* ($5), a shrimp appetizer, or *sopitos* ($6). Open Mon.-Thurs. 11am-10pm, Fri.-Sat. 11am-11pm.

Emerald of Siam, 1314 Jadwin Ave., Richland (946-9328) and 8300 Gage Blvd., Kennewick (783-6214), behind the Columbia Center Mall. Possibly the best Thai food east of Thailand and certainly the best in the Tri-Cities. Try the *Gaeing Pa-Nang Nuea* (beef with red curry paste in coconut, $7). For maximum enjoyment, have the lunch buffet ($5, children under 12 $2.50), and then move on to Casa Chapela. Open Mon.-Fri. 11:30am-2pm, Mon.-Sat. 5-9pm.

Giacci's, 94 Lee Blvd., Richland (946-4855), next to Howard Amon Park. Residents argue about the relative merits of Giacci's and the two restaurants listed above. A full dish of pasta is $7: try the linguini with sausage. A Giacci's Wedge ($7) of ham, salami, provolone and more is picnic-perfect. Open Mon.-Thurs. 11am-3pm, Fri.-Sat. 11am-5pm, 6-9pm.

Blackberry's, 5011 W. Clearwater Ave., Richland (735-7253). A popular local spot with occasional eccentricities. Full dinners $6-10. Try the liver and onions, $6. Open Mon. 7am-2pm, Tues.-Fri. 7am-9pm, Sat. 8am-9pm, Sun. 8am-2pm.

Sights

Whatever your politics, the Hanford Nuclear Reservation is the critical attraction. The **Hanford Science Center,** 825 Jadwin Ave., Richland (376-6374), next to the post office, is an exercise in justification, but an interesting one. (Open Mon.-Fri. 8am-5pm, Sat. 9am-5pm, Sun. noon-5pm. Free.) **The Fast Flux Test Facility (FFTF)** is the nation's most important test reactor, designed to test materials for fast breeder reactors. Its visitor center is 12 mi. north of Richland. **WPPSS Plant 2** is the outcome of a statewide nuclear energy plan that originally encompassed several WPPSS (pronounced Whoops!) plants but failed and lost all its shareholders' money. The visitor center (372-5860) is off Stevens Dr., 12 mi. north of Richland. (Open Thurs.-Fri. 11am-4pm, Sat.-Sun. noon-5pm.)

The Northern Pacific Railroad put Pasco on the map in 1886. The **historical district** is clustered around 4th and Lewis, the site of the open-air **Pasco Farmer's Market** (open Wed. and Sat. May-Nov.). The largest of its kind in agro-centric eastern Washington, the market attracts thousands every week. The **Franklin County Historical Museum,** 305 N. 4th Ave. (547-3714), sits next door with the usual collection of pioneer and Native American exhibits. It also houses good local archives. (Open Tues.-Sat. noon-4pm. Free.)

The first intrusion in this area by Europeans came in 1805 when Lewis and Clark mad a pit stop at what is now **Sacajawea State Park** (off Hwy. 12 towards Walla Walla). The interpretive center is open April 25-Sept. 15 Wed.-Sun. 10am-6pm. Other parks worth checking out are **Howard Amon Park** in Richland and **Columbia Park** in Kennewick, both bordering the Columbia River. These become jam-packed at the end of July when the **Columbia Cup Unlimited Hydroplane Race** hits town. The **Northwest Wine Festival** hold its Dionysian rites during October.

Walla Walla

The valley around Walla Walla was a hotbed of activity back in the days of the Oregon Trail. Fort Walla Walla, the only military base in the homeland of the Cayuse Indians, provided armed protection for pioneers, while the nearby Whitman Mission offered food and shelter. Today Walla Walla ("many waters," in the local Native American tongue) is a thriving agricultural center with a few tourist offerings: take in some local history, visit Whitman College (arguably the best private college in Washington), or sample the town's famous onions, known as "Walla Walla Sweets." Just keep any snickers about its name to yourself: locals have been enduring barbs for over a hundred years and their tempers may be wearing thin thin.

Practical Information and Orientation

Visitor Information: Chamber of Commerce, 29 E. Sumach St. (525-0850), at Colville. Pick up a street map and a copy of their *Food, Fun, and Lodging* guide. Open Mon.-Fri. 8:30am-5pm.

Greyhound: 315 N. 2nd St. (525-9313), at E. Oak St. One bus per day to Boise ($58.25), 2 to Spokane ($27.45), 2 to Seattle ($29.25), 3 to Portland ($29.95). Open Mon.-Fri. 8am-5:30pm, Sat. 8am-noon.

Bassett Transit: 800-342-0210. The cheapest and quickest mass transit (other than Lori's jalopy) to Seattle, Richland, and Yakima. The Seattle-Walla Walla route ($25 one way) takes only 6 hr., as compared to Greyhound's 9 hr. (and Lori's 2 days).

Valley Transit: 8 W. Poplar St. (525-9140). Five color-coded lines thoroughly cover Walla Walla and beyond. The accommodating drivers will drop you off anywhere along their route. Buses run Mon.-Fri. 6am-7pm, Sat. 9am-5pm. Fare 25¢.

Dial-A-Ride: 527-3779. Free transportation for the handicapped and for ages 60 and over. Call a day ahead. Vans run Mon.-Sat. 8am-4pm.

Taxi: A-1 Cab, 7 S. 4th Ave. (529-2525). 24 hr.

Car Rental: Chuck Lightfoot Husky, 2933 Isaacs Ave. (525-1680). The best deal in town. $27 per day, 100 free mi., 22¢ per each additional mi. Must be 21 with credit card or $350 deposit.

Hospital: St. Mary's Medical Center, 401 W. Poplar St. (525-3320). Open 24 hr.

Senior Citizen Services: The Senior Center (527-3775), open Mon.-Fri. 8:30am-5pm.

Post Office: 128 N. 2nd St. (522-6337), across from the Chamber of Commerce in a fine old building. Open Mon.-Fri. 9am-5pm. General Delivery ZIP Code: 99362.

Area Code: 509.

Walla Walla lies on U.S. 12 in southeastern Washington, at the junction with OR Hwy. 11, a 44-mi. connective artery leading to I-84 in Pendleton, OR. Walla Walla is 125 mi. east of Yakima and 160 mi. south of Spokane. The city is much easier to visit by car than by bus—the only bus from the north arrives at 11pm.

Accommodations and Camping

Walla squared has developed into a convention center; for some reason, business people love to call meetings at the foot of the Blue Mountains.

Whitman Annex Motel, 204 N. Spokane (529-3400). Have a ready excuse to retreat to the roomy, clean lodgings with A/C, TV, and a small bathtub, because the jolly management can discourse endlessly on the wonders of Walla Walla. Singles $22. Doubles $24.

City Center Motel, 627 W. Main (529-2660), 8 blocks from city center. Pleasantly landscaped grounds (including a pool), an exuberant proprietor, and that rare motel phenomenon: matching bedspreads and carpet. Free coffee. Singles $26.50. Doubles $34.50.

EconoLodge, 305 N. 2nd Ave. (800-368-4400). This clean, spacious motel is a scant half-block from the Greyhound station. A/C, pool, TV, and groovy artwork on walls. Singles $28. Doubles $36.

Tapadera Inn, 211 N. 2nd Ave. (800-722-8277), next to EconoLodge. A/C, continental breakfast, and TV with HBO. Smallish rooms. Singles $27. Doubles $37.80.

Walla Walla College, 204 S. College Ave. (527-2814). Take bus #1W. Nonstudents welcome. Dorm rooms $15 (including linen) are available June to mid-Sept. Call ahead 9am-5pm.

Fort Walla Walla Campground (527-3770), just southwest of downtown on Dalles Military Rd. A family place with spacious, quiet grounds. Coin-operated showers. Sites $8.50, with electricity and water $11. Open May 1-Oct. 1.

Umatilla National Forest (522-6290), 35 mi. southeast of town, off Hwy. 204. Maintains several developed campgrounds. For information, go to the Forest Service Ranger Station, at 1415 W. Rose St., a mile or so west of the city center. Sites $3-7.

Food

The food in Walla Walla peaks at average. For local produce try **Ascolano's** in the renovated Northern Pacific Depot, 416 N. 2nd St.

Jacobi's Café, 416 N. 2nd St., in the Depot. A large pleasant Italian café with outdoor and indoor seating. Excellent garlic bread. Entrees $5-7. Open Sun.-Thurs. 11am-9pm, Fri.-Sat. 11am-11pm.

Ice Burg, 616 W. Birch (529-1793). Your have never seen drive-thru lines this long. Good, cheap food induces locals to put up with 30-90 min. waits. Burgers start at $1.24, shakes $1.52, pints of soft ice cream $1.11. Open Mon.-Thurs. 7:30am-10:30pm, Fri. 7:30am-11pm, Sat. 11am-11pm, Sun. 11:30am-10pm.

Pastime Café, 215 W. Main St. (525-0783). The relaxed, homey atmosphere might lull you, but the 12-oz. steak and spaghetti special ($7) will perk your palate right up. The pasta is particularly good. Ravioli, $5.25. Open Mon.-Sat. 5:30am-midnight. Bar stays open until 2am.

Sights

The **Fort Walla Walla Museum Complex,** Dalles Military Rd. and 9th St. (525-7703), in the southwest corner of town, shelters such curiosities as a 19th-century jail and doctor's office. Those who have devoted their lives to the study of farm-equipment should not miss the full-scale replica of a 33-mule combine harvester. A complicated harness system called the "shadorey" hitch allowed one person to simultaneously control all 33 mules. In mid-July a pioneer-Indian rendezvous is held here. Events include a salmon bake, a mule-packing contest, a tomahawk throw, and (only in Walla Walla) a women's rolling-pin throw. (Open June-Sept. Tues.-Sun. 1-5pm; May and Oct. Sat.-Sun. 1-5pm, but may be open during the week for school tours; call ahead. Admission $2, ages 6-12 $1, under 6 free.)

Seven miles west of town on U.S. 12, the **Whitman Mission National Historic Site** (529-2761) presents the more dramatic side of the region's history. In 1836, the missionary Marcus Whitman (a statue of whom now stands in the Washington State Capitol Building) and his wife Narcissa (the first woman to cross America on the overland route) arrived in the area. Together they ministered to settlers who streamed along the nearby Oregon Trail and tried to convert the Native Americans to the beliefs and customs of Presbyterianism. This bit of history came to an abrupt end, when, in 1847, the Cayuse Indians slaughtered the Whitmans.

The **visitors center** at the mission site has a museum and is a good place to start walking the trails to Great Grove and the Whitman Memorial. (Open June-Aug. daily 8am-6pm; Sept.-May 8am-4:30pm. Admission $1, families $3, over 61 and under 17 free.) Pick up the *Walla Walla Gallery Guide* for easy walking tours of local art galleries. The second Wednesday of every month is "Gallery Night."

The **Sweet Onion Festival** is held in the last week of July in honor of the town's incredible, edible bulb. For information and sweet onion recipes, contact the Walla Walla Sweet Onion Commission, P.O. Box 644, Walla Walla 99362.

Pullman

One legend suggests that Pullman founder Bolin Farr named this town after his closest friend, George Pullman (of boxcar fame). Another claims that in 1887 the townspeople held a contest wherein the person who donated the most money to the public coffers would have it named after himself. According to this version, George Pullman sent a check for $25—along with a note that he not be bothered again.

Today, Washington State University (WSU), on the hills to the east of Main St., supplies the city with a *raison d'etre* and the *money d'etre,* and Pullman showers its gratitude on the Cougars, WSU's football team. Whether you're at the Cougar Drive-In, where students head for a malted and a burger, or the Cougar Land Motel, where their parents stay over commencement weekend, you'll find posters, stickers, and pennants spurring on the savage felines.

Practical Information and Orientation

Visitor Information: Pullman Chamber of Commerce, N. 415 Grand Ave. (334-3565). Enough brochures on "The Other Washington—The State!" to wallpaper the White House. Pick up a copy of *Pullman Dining and Lodging.* Open Mon.-Fri. 8am-5pm, Sat.-Sun. 10am-2pm. **WSU** has a **Visitor Information Center** in the campus police building on Wilson Rd. (335-3564), to which students are oblivious. Open 24 hr.

Greyhound: NE 115 Olsen (334-1412), at Grand. Buses to: Boise (2 per day, $30); Spokane (2 per day, $12); Seattle (2 per day, $40); Walla Walla (1 per day, $20). Open Mon.-Fri. 10am-5:30pm. No storage lockers available.

Pullman Transit: 725 Guy St. (332-6535). Three lines operate Mon.-Fri. 6:50am-5:50pm. Runs mostly between the WSU campus and downtown. Fare 35¢, ages under 18 20¢.

Taxi: Evergreen Taxi Inc., 332-7433. 24 hr. $1.75 for pickup, $1.40 per mi.

Car Rental: Budget Rent-A-Car, Pullman Airport (332-3511). $42 per day, 100 free mi. with 30¢ each additional mi. Must be 21 with major credit card.

Bike Rental: Blue Mountain Recreation and Cyclery, N. 131 Grand Ave. (332-1703). Good quality 10-speeds $10 per day, with $25 deposit or credit card. Used bikes only $5 per day, with $10 deposit or credit card. Open Tues.-Sat. 10am-5:30pm.

Laundromat: Betty's Brite and White, N. 1235 Grand Ave. (332-3477).

Senior Citizen Services: Pullman Senior Citizen Center, City Hall (332-1933).

Rape Crisis Information: Women's Center, 885-6616.

Crisis Line: 332-1505. 24 hr.

Child Care: The Chamber of Commerce (334-3565) keeps a frequently updated list of available babysitters.

Post Office: Lewiston Hwy. (334-3212). Open Mon.-Fri. 8:30am-5pm. General Delivery ZIP Code: 99163.

Area Code: 509.

Pullman lies at the junction of Hwy. 27 and 270, fewer than 10 mi. west of the Idaho border. U.S. 195, running from Spokane south to Lewiston, bypasses the city to the west. Walla Walla lies 100 mi. to the southwest, Spokane 70 mi. north. Pullman lies 9 mi. *vostok* of Moscow, Idaho.

Most of Pullman's enterprises lie along Main Street and Grand Avenue. Grand runs north to south; Main travels west to east, terminating at the WSU campus. The campus has digested the eastern half of town.

Accommodations and Camping

The large number of student travelers who gambol through town draws an encouraging selection of moderately priced, no-frills motels. Rooms are easy to find, except on weekends of home football games and during commencement (first week of May).

Regents Hall (335-3320), on the WSU campus. Call a week or two in advance for the best deal in town, although conventions often make rooms scarce in summer. A student ID (and $6.85) buys a dorm room double. Without student ID this package is $14.

Manor Lodge Motel, SE 455 Paradise (334-2511), at Main, 3 blocks from the Greyhound station. A clean and comfortable establishment in a great location. Friendly staff. Live high on the hog with your refrigerator, couch, and bathtub. Singles $20. Doubles $24.

The Hilltop Motor Inn (334-2555), off U.S. 195 (Colfax Hwy.) at the northwest edge of town. Not very practical for Greyhound travelers. Superb view of the town; it ain't called the hilltop for nothing. Clean, comfortable rooms with TV and bath. Singles $30. Doubles $33.

Cougar Land Motel, W. 120 Main (334-3535), smack dab in the center of town. Where WSU parents stay while visiting their cubs. Pool, rooms with a bathtub and refrigerator. Singles $29. Doubles $33.

Food

There are enough burgers, pizzas, and subs in Pullman to lard the stomachs of thousands of college students for ever and ever. Sanctuaries from student cuisine are few and far between.

Ferdinand's (335-4014), Troy Hall on WSU campus. Everything made on the premises with milk from WSU's dairy. Sweet basil, smoky cheddar and more prosaic cheeses $8.75 for a 30-oz. tin (their Cougar Gold may be the best attraction in Pullman). Try a cone of peanut butter ice cream ($1) or a large glass of milk (55¢). And yes, it's named after that gentle bull who loved to smell flowers. Open daily 9am-4pm; in winter 9:30am-4:30pm.

Cougar Café, N. 146 Grand Ave. (332-1132), around the corner from the Greyhound station. Framed pictures of famed Wazzu athletes splatter the walls of this mercifully uncrowded breakfast and lunch stop. Try the heaping stack of French toast for $3. Open Mon.-Fri. 5am-1:30pm, Sat. 6am-1:30pm, Sun. 7am-1:30pm.

The Pizza Answer, E. 231 Main (334-4417). Delicious, cheesy slices available for $1. 32-oz. pop 50¢. Mostly delivers to hungry Cougars. Mostly. Open daily 11am-4pm.

Couger County Drive-In, N. 760 Grand Ave. (332-7820), a 10-min. walk from downtown. Drive through or slide into a booth at this popular student hang-out. Burgers (from $2) and shakes (lots o' flavors, $1.10). Try the Cyclone D-soft ice cream mixed with candy (large $1.79). Open 10am-11pm.

Alex's Restaurante, N. 139 Grand Ave. (332-4061). Quiet, well-mannered, and nobly named, with good Mexican dinners ($8-10) and lunches ($3-4). Open Tues.-Thurs. 11:30am-2pm and 5-10pm, Fri. 11:30am-2pm and 4:30pm-1am, Sat. 4:30-11pm, Sun. 5-10pm.

Mandarin Wok Restaurant, N. 115 Grand Ave. (332-5863). Chinese food prepared with care and a minimum of MSG. Dinners are overpriced, but you can enjoy the same quality in the $4.50 lunch special (main dish, soup, eggroll, fried rice, and tea). The best Chinese food in the area, in an appropriately elegant setting. Open Mon.-Fri. 11:30am-1:30pm and 5-9pm, Sat. 5-9pm, Sun. 5-8:30pm.

Pizza Haven, E. 420 Main (334-2535). Hearty pizzas (from $3.75) and pastas (from $2.90). Draft 79¢. On Sun. and Wed. the all-you-can-eat pizza and salad deal includes a 20-oz. Pepsi to wash it down ($3.75). The pizza is thick and rich, but cannot stump the Answer. Open Sun.-Thurs. 11am-10pm, Fri.-Sat. 11am-midnight.

Sights and Entertainment

The steeply sloping campus of **Washington State University** in the east of town is Pullman's primary fixture. The second largest university in the state (enrollment 18,000), WSU specializes in agriculture and engineering. Call or stop by the **University Relations Office** in the French Administration Building, Room 442 (335-3581), which offers guided tours of the 100-year-old campus every weekday at 1pm during the school year (early Sept. to early May). Pick up a copy of *Museums and Collections at Washington State University.* All campus museums are free and open during the school year only. Johnson Hall houses both the **Entomological Collection** (335-5504) and the **Mycological Herbarium** (335-3749). Enjoy one million insect specimens and seventy thousand living fungi, respectively (open Mon.-Fri. 8am-5pm). The **Anthropology Museum** (335-3441), in College Hall, is a working part of the Anthropology Department, and current research projects are often on display. (Open Mon.-Thurs. 9am-4pm, Fri. 9am-3pm.) The **Museum of Art,** in the Fine Arts Building (335-1910), has a small permanent collection and rotating exhibits of local and international art. (Open Tues. 10am-4pm and 7-10pm, Wed.-Fri. 10am-4pm, Sat.-Sun. 1-5pm.)

The gentle terrain and broad views of Washington's Palouse region make the district ideal for exploration by bicycle or automobile. **Kamiak** and **Steptoe Buttes,** north of town off Hwy. 27, make for enjoyable day trips. Pack a picnic lunch and head for the hills.

For non-children, there are nearly as many bars as Cougar signs in the Palouse. **Pelican Pete's,** SE 1100 Johnson (334-4200), is the unanimous undergrad favorite. Wednesday night is "Happy Wheel Night," based on the dried-up gameshow Wheel of Fortune. Rainier Beer is 75¢. Mixed drinks $1.50. (Open 11am to whenever the action dies down, usually around 2am. Happy hour 3:30-6:30pm.) Just down the street from the Regents dorm are two other popular university hangouts. At **Cougar Cottage,** NE 900 Colorado (332-1265), true drafts are $1 and burgers and Mexican food range from $2-6. (Open daily 11am-2am.) The **Campus Cavern,** NE 1000 Colorado (334-5151), serves sandwiches and burgers for $3-4.

Spokane

Originally named Spokan Falls after the area's original residents, the Spokan-ee Indians, Spokane was the first pioneer settlement in the Pacific Northwest. After the Great Fire of 1889, Spokane quickly re-rooted in industries spawned by local natural resources. Today, with an economy still based on lumber, mining, and agriculture, the spunkiest city in Eastern Washington remains one of the Northwest's major trade centers. And its most successful native son, Representative Thomas Foley, now has a steady job as Speaker of the House in the other Washington (DC, that is).

In its own unwilling way, Spokane achieves urban sophistication without typical big-city hassles. The downtown thrives, though the pace is slow (not a soul crosses the street until the Walk sign flashes). The Expo '74 legacy includes Riverfront Park's museum and theater, as well as a number of elegant restaurants and hotels. Arboretums, gardens, abundant outdoor activities, and a spectacular series of bridges spanning the Spokane River and Falls celebrate wonders more ancient than concrete.

Practical Information and Orientation

Visitor Information: Spokane Area Convention and Visitors Bureau, W. 926 Sprague Ave. (747-3230). Overflowing with literature extolling every aspect of Spokane. Open Mon.-Fri. 8:30am-5pm, and most summer weekends 9am-3pm (depending on volunteer availability). **Travelers Aid Service,** W. 1017 1st (456-7169), near the bus depot. Kind staff, accustomed to helping stranded travelers find lodgings. Open Mon.-Fri. 1-5pm.

Amtrak: W. 221 1st St. (624-5144, after business hours 800-872-7245), at Bernard St., downtown. To: Chicago (1 per day, $196); Seattle (1 per day, $60); Portland (1 per day, $60). Depot open Mon.-Fri. 11am-3:30am, Sat.-Sun. 7:15pm-3:30am.

Greyhound: W. 1125 Sprague (624-5251), at 1st Ave. and Jefferson St., downtown. To: Seattle (5 per day, $33), Lewiston, ID (2 per day, $20), and Walla Walla (2 per day, $28). **Empire Lines** (624-4116) and **Northwest Stage Lines** (800-826-4058 or 838-4029) share the terminal with Greyhound, serving even more of Eastern Washington, northern Idaho, and British Columbia. Station open daily 6am-8pm and 1-3am.

Spokane Transit System: W. 1229 Boone Ave. (328-7433). Serves all areas of Spokane, including Eastern Washington University in Cheney. Fare 60¢, ages over 64 and disabled travelers 30¢. Free transfers valid for ½ hr. Coupon booklets, available at midday, good for discounts in local shops and restaurants. Operates until 12:15am downtown, 9:15pm in the valley along E. Sprague Ave.

Taxi: Checker Cab, 624-4171. 24 hr. **Yellow Cab,** 624-4321. **A-1 Taxi,** 534-7768.

Car Rental: U-Save Auto Rental, W. 918 3rd St. (455-8018), at Monroe. Cars from $19 per day with 100 free mi.; 20¢ per additional mi. $250 deposit or major credit card required. Must be 21. Open Mon.-Fri. 8am-6pm, Sat. 8am-5pm.

AAA Office: W. 1717 4th (455-3400).

Camping Equipment: White Elephant, N. 1730 Division St. (328-3100) and E. 12614 Sprague (924-3006). The Crazy Eddie's of camping stores, with every imaginable piece of equipment at bargain prices. Open Mon.-Thurs. and Sat. 9am-6pm, Fri. 9am-9pm. **Outdoor Sportsman,** N. 1602 Division St. (328-1556). Prices are even more insane. Open Mon.-Thurs. 9:30am-6:30pm, Fri. 9:30am-7pm, Sat. 9:30am-6pm, Sun. 11am-5pm.

Public Library: W. 906 Main St. (838-3361). Reliable source for historical information, bus schedules, and telephone books. Open Mon.-Thurs. 10am-9pm, Fri. (and winter Sat.) 10am-6pm.

Events Line: 747-2787. 24-hr. Recorded information on arts happenings in Spokane.

Laundromat: Ye Olde Wash House Laundry and Dry Cleaners, E. 4224 Sprague (534-9859).

Weather: 624-8905.

Crisis Hotline: 838-4428. 24 hr.

Drug Crisis Line: 326-9550. 24 hr.

AIDS Hotline: 456-3640.

Mental Health Center: 838-4651.

Youth Help: 624-2868. Helps find accommodations. 24 hr.

Senior Center: W. 1124 Sinto (327-2861).

Pharmacy: Hart and Dilatush, W. 501 Sprague (624-2111). 24 hr.

Hospital: 455-3131.

Ambulance: 328-6161. 24 hr.

Police: 456-2233. 24 hr.

Post Office: W. 904 Riverside (459-0230), at Lincoln. Open Mon.-Fri. 8:30am-5pm. General Delivery ZIP Code: 99210.

Area Code: 509.

Spokane lies 280 mi. east of Seattle by I-90. The **Spokane International Airport** is off I-90 southwest of town. Avenues run east-west parallel to the river, streets north-south, and both alternate one-way. The city is bifurcated north and south by **Sprague Avenue,** east and west by **Division Street.** Downtown is the quadrant north of Sprague and west of Division, wedged between I-90 and the Spokane River. Exits 279 to 282 serve the area. Street addresses are listed with the compass point first, the number second, and the street name third (e.g., W. 1200 Division). No one knows why.

Riverfront Park adjoins Spokane Falls in the heart of the heart of the city. Two blocks south of here, at Riverside and Howard St., all Spokane Transit System buses start and finish their runs.

Accommodations and Camping

Don't try to sleep in Riverfront Park; the Spokane police don't *like* it. A handful of hotels south of downtown are cheap but sleazy. Most camping areas are at least 20 mi. away. The hostel is certainly your best option.

Brown Squirrel Hostel (AYH), W. 1807 Pacific Ave. (838-5968), in Browne's Addition. To be safe, walk along Sprague rather than 1st St. to and from the Greyhound station. About 20 beds fill the 2nd story of a classic 3-level house, convenient to a Safeway and a drug store with real fountain service (try the egg cream). The rooms are cozy; before long you'll feel like a member of the manager's family—just don't use the family phone (use the phone 2 blocks away at the Safeway instead). Officially open 8-10am and 5-10pm, but stop in just about anytime. No curfew. Members $8, nonmembers $11. Linens, towels, and (if necessary) transportation to the airport or bus station provided.

Eastern Washington University (359-7022), 18 mi. from Spokane in Cheney. Take bus #24 from Howard and Riverside St. downtown. By car, take I-90 southwest 8 mi. to exit 270, then Hwy. 904 south; turn right on Elm St. and continue to 10th. Pleasant dorm rooms, rarely full. Program run by helpful students. Inquire at Morrison Hall in the summer, or Anderson Hall during the school year. Singles $9.70. Doubles $19.40. With student ID singles $7, doubles $14. Linen provided. Open year-round.

Town Centre Motor Inn, W. 901 1st St. (747-1041), at Lincoln St. in the heart of downtown, 4 blocks from the bus depot. Large, comfortable rooms decorated with garish oil paintings. Some rooms have refrigerators at no extra cost. Complimentary coffee served with the morning paper in the motel office. Save 15% by exchanging your US$ for CDN$ at one of the downtown banks beforehand as they accept it at par. Singles $30. Doubles $38.

El Rancho Motel, W. 3000 Sunset Blvd. (455-9400). On the edge of town, with easy access to freeway. Take 2nd Ave. west to Maple St., where Sunset cuts diagonally across the intersection. Follow Sunset approximately 15 blocks. Rooms have cable, free coffee, and A/C. Equipped with laundromat, pool, and children's play area. Singles $27.50. Doubles $40.

Motel 6, S. 1580 Rustle St. (459-6120), at exit 277 on I-90. In other words, far from downtown. TV and pool. Singles $30. Doubles $32. Call 2-3 weeks in advance for reservations.

Riverside State Park (456-3964), 6 mi. northwest of downtown on Rifle Club Rd., off Hwy. 291 or Nine Mile Rd. Take Division north and turn left on Francis. 101 standard sites in an urban setting. Kitchen and small museum in the park. Shower and bath. Facilities for the disabled. Sites $7.50.

Mt. Spokane State Park (456-4169), 35 mi. northeast of the city. Take U.S. 395 5 mi. north to U.S. 2, then go 7 mi. north to Hwy. 206, which leads into the park. Popular with winter athletes for its cross-country skiing and snowmobiling trails. Views of 3 states and Canada from the Vista House. 12 sites. Flush toilets, no showers, only cold water. Sites $7.

Smokey Trail (747-9415), 5 mi. west of the city. Take I-90 to exit 272. Follow Hallett Rd. east to Mallon Rd., then 1 mi. south. Warm up with hot showers and free firewood. Sites $12, RV hookups $15. Open May 15-Sept. 20.

Food

Besides supporting a number of small diners and cafés, Spokane works as a trading center for Eastern Washington's fresh produce. On Wednesdays and Saturdays from May to October, the **Spokane County Market** (456-5512) vends fresh fruit, vegetables, baked goods, and arts and crafts in Riverfront Park. The **Green Bluff Growers Cooperative** is an organization of 20-odd fruit and vegetable farms, 16 mi. northwest of town off Day-Mountain Spokane Rd. Many of the farms have "U-pick" arrangements, and nearby are free picnic areas with panoramic views. Peak season for most crops is from August to October. Write Green Bluff Growers, E. 9423 Green Bluff Rd., Colbert 99005, or look for a brochure downtown.

For a variety of interesting cuisine downtown, head to **The Atrium,** on Wale St. near 1st. Ave. **Europa Pizzeria,** one of the restaurants in this small brick building, bakes the best pizza in town. Across the river from Riverfront Park is the **Flour Mill,** an historical site that has been converted into a mall with the obligatory knick-knacks stores and quaint eateries.

Dick's, E. 10 3rd Ave. (747-2481), at Division. Look for the pink panda sign near I-90. Received a special mention in the prestigious *Let's Go: Did You Know?* Hall of Fame awards. A takeout burger phenomenon that has not grasped the principle of inflation. Burgers 93¢, fries 39¢, slice of pie 89¢, sundaes 58¢, soft drinks 39¢, etc., etc., etc. Take the Panda's advice and buy by the bagful. Always crowded but the battalions of workers move the lines along quickly. Open daily 9am-1:30am.

Auntie's Bookstore and Café, W. 313 Riverside (838-0206). Browse through the excellent selection of books, including extensive collections on regional history, gender studies, and religion, then compose your own sandwich for $3 and up. Lunch specials $4. Open Mon.-Sat. 9am-9pm, Sun. noon-5pm.

Coyote Café, W. 702 3rd Ave. (747-8800). This jazzy Mexican joint has *cerveza* signs on the walls, cacti in the windows, and $2.16 margaritas all day. You don't have to be a "supah genius" to enjoy the Wile E. coyote *chimichanga* ($6) and the coyote dog (chili, cheese, and onions; $4). Open Mon.-Thurs. 11am-11pm, Fri. 11am-midnight, Sat. noon-midnight, Sun. noon-10pm.

Knight's Diner, N. 2442 Division (327-5365). Take bus #6. A long red-and-black diner in an old train car. Western down-home cooking and hospitality. Hearty breakfasts and lunches ($2-4). Open Tues.-Sun. 6:30am-2pm.

Cyrus O'Leary's, W. 516 Main St. (624-9000), in the Bennetts Block complex at Howard St. A Spokane legend. Devour delicious food from a creative 25-page menu. Costumed staff (decked out in 1890s Wild West garb) serves enormous $6-12 meals. Sandwiches $3-5. Happy hour 4-6pm. Open Mon.-Thurs. 11:30am-11pm, Fri.-Sat. 11:30am-midnight, Sun. 11:30am-10pm.

Thai Café, W. 410 Sprague (838-4783). This tiny restaurant adds plenty of spice (or only a little, depending upon your preference) to Spokane's otherwise Americanized ethnic fare. Traditional dishes like *pad thai* and *gai pahd* cost only $4-6. Open Mon.-Fri. 11:30am-1:30pm and 5-8:30pm, Sat. 5-8:30pm.

Benjamins' Burger Inn (455-6771), in the Parkade Plaza. This popular and convenient alternative to Dick's sells larger, juicer—and more expensive—burgers ($2). Get a little crazy with the curly fries (75¢). Carrot cake $1.25. A bowl of chili $1.55. Open Mon.-Fri. 7am-6pm, Sat. 8am-5pm.

Señor Froggy, W. 603 3rd Ave. (624-6209) and N. 1918 Division (328-7280). Valiantly attempts authentic Mexican decor and flavor. Although the frog doesn't truly succeed on either count, it comes close enough considering the price and quick service. *Empanadas* (a savory Mexican turnover) 95¢, meaty tacos 69¢. Open Mon.-Thurs. 10:30am-11pm, Fri.-Sat. 10:30am-midnight, Sun. 10:30am-10pm.

The Great Harvest Bread Co., W. 816 Sprague (624-9370). A gourmet cafeteria that serves homemade soups and sandwiches, as well as a wide selection of freshly baked goodies. This is the place to stock up on fresh bread (3kg loaf $2.25) and moist muffins (75¢). Follow your nose. Open Mon.-Fri. 6am-6pm, Sat. 6am-5pm.

Milford's Fish House and Oyster Bar, N. 719 Monroe (326-7251). Don't be fooled by the dingy neighborhood—Milford's is one of the finest restaurants in the entire Pacific Northwest. And though it may well sink your budget, the freshest seafood in town will certainly buoy your spirits. Choose from a placard of fresh specials ($10-14) which are rotated daily; each includes a bowl of clam chowder or a dinner salad along with bread and vegetables. Open Mon. 5-9pm, Tues.-Sat. 5-10pm, Sun. 4-9pm.

Sights and Activities

Spokane has few aspirations to flashy art or high-flown architecture. The city's best attractions are those that concentrate on local history and culture. The **Museum of Native American Cultures (MONAC),** E. 200 Cataldo St. (326-4550), sits virtually by itself atop a hill to the northeast of downtown, off Division St. The modern architecture houses a collection of Native North and South American art and artifacts. Although somewhat removed from the immediate attractions of downtown, the museum holds some interesting exhibits on the Northwest Territories. (Open Tues.-Sat. 10am-5pm, Sun. 11am-5pm. Admission $3, ages over 65 and students $2, families $7.) The **Cheney Cowles Memorial Museum,** W. 2316 1st Ave. (456-3931), near the hostel, also has exhibits on Native American culture and history, in addition to well-explicated displays on the animals and pioneers of Eastern Washington. One gallery of the museum is also given over to contemporary Northwest art. Every Wednesday at 7:30pm, except during the summer, a local artist lectures and shows his work for free. Alongside the museum sits the **Grace Campbell House** (456-3931). Owned in the 1890s by mining magnate Amasa Campbell and designed by then-renowned architect Kirkland Cutter (who also did the Monroe St. Bridge), the Tudor mansion exposes the high class indulgences of Spokane's upper crust. (Museum open Tues.-Sat. 10am-5pm, Sun. 2-5pm. Admission $2, senior citizens and students $1. House open Tues.-Sat. 10am-4pm, Sun. 2-5pm. Wed. free.)

Riverfront Park, N. 507 Howard St. (456-5512), just north of downtown, is clearly Spokane's center of gravity. If the park hadn't been built for the 1974 World's Fair, the populace would have nowhere to stroll on leisurely weekend afternoons. The **IMAX Theatre** (456-5511) boasts a 5½-story movie screen and a projector the size of a Volkswagon. The 45-minute film "To the Limit" will take you for a ride. (Admission Tues.-Sun. $4, senior citizens $3.50, ages under 18 $3. Open daily noon-9pm, shows on the hour.) The **Eastern Washington University Science Center** (456-5507) offers hands-on exhibits on computer technology and astronomy. (Open April 10-May 26 daily 9am-3pm; late May-early Sept. 11am-6pm. Admission $3, seniors $2.50, children $2.) One section of the park has all the "kiddie" rides—including the exquisitely hand-carved **Looff Carousel** (open daily 11am-9pm; 60¢ a whirl). A "Single Day Pass" (adults $9, children $8) covers the whole works. The park offers ice-skating in the winter ($2.50) and hosts special programs and events. The Day Pass also includes a free trip aboard the park's **Gondola Skyride Over the Falls,** which, as its name implies, travels from one part of the park over Spokane Falls to the north side of the river. (Open in summer daily 11am-9pm. Without Day Pass, admission $2.50, children $1.50.)

Hard-core Bingsters will be drawn to a past *Let's Go: Did You Know?* honorable mention, **Crosby Library,** E. 502 Boone St. (328-4220), at Gonzaga University. Here, the faithful display ole Bing's relics: gold records, awards, photographs, and a piece of his right index finger bone. Then look across to DeSmet's Hall, where

Bing tossed a piano off of the third floor (the real reason he "left" Gonzaga for show-biz). (Open Mon.-Thurs. 8am-midnight, Fri. 8am-5pm, Sat. 9am-5pm, Sun. 1pm-midnight. Free.)

Spokane's collection of two dozen parks includes tranquil, well-groomed **Finch Arboretum**, W. 3404 Woodland Blvd. Over 2000 species of trees, flowers, and shrubs are available for viewing 24 hours. **Manito Park**, on S. Grand Ave. between 17th and 25th Ave. (856-4331), south of downtown, encompasses a flower garden, tennis courts, a romantic duck pond, and the Dr. David Graiser Conservatory, which also houses many tropical and local plant species. (Open daily 8am-dusk; in winter 8am-3:30pm. Free.) Adjacent to Manito Park is the **Nishinomiya Garden**, a lush Japanese garden consecrating the friendship of Spokane and her Japanese sister city, Nishinomiya. (Same hours as Manito Park. Free.)

The state runs two parks near Spokane, and both merit a trip. **Riverside State Park** (456-3964 or 456-2499) embroiders the Spokane River with 7655 acres of vol-canic outcroppings, hiking trails (especially good in Deep Creek Canyon, the fossil beds of a forest that grew there seven million years ago), and equestrian trails (horse rental $9 per hr. by appointment only in nearby Trail Town; 456-8249). The park contains a large area for off-road vehicles that becomes prime cross-country ski ter-ritory in the winter. Also in the park is the **Spokane House Interpretive Center** (466-4747), site of the first structure built by whites in the Northwest, a fur trading post (1810). The center now traces the history of fur trading in the region. (Free.)

Mount Spokane State Park (456-4169) stands 35 mi. to the northeast of the city. An improved, toll-free road extends to the summit. Clear days afford views of the Spokane Valley and the distant peaks of the Rockies and Cascades. Mt. Spokane is a skiing center with free cross-country trails and $15-20 downhill ski packages. The area is also good for hiking, horseback riding (no rentals here), and camping (see Accommodations). The **U.S. Forest Service** (456-2574) has more information on the parks.

Turnbull National Wildlife Refuge (235-4723), 21 mi. south of Spokane, is a happy breeding ground for bird species of the Pacific flyway. Take the Four Lakes, Cheney exit off I-90, and go left on Badger Rd. Numerous blinds have been set up for photographing, and lucky visitors may catch a glimpse of trumpeter swans. (Open daily until dusk. $2 per vehicle.)

Don't leave Spokane without tasting a fine Eastern Washington wine. The **Arbor Cliff House**, N. 4705 Fruithill Rd. (927-9463), offers a tour of a national historical house, a view of the city, and free wine (daily from noon-5pm). To get there, take I-90 to the Argonne north exit, travel north on Argonne over the Spokane River, turn right on Upriver Dr., proceed one mi., and then bear left onto Fruithill Rd. Take a sharp right at the top of the hill and you are there.

Entertainment

Spokane's traditional tastes are reflected in the large number of bowling alleys and movie theaters gracing the city. A wide spectrum of live music satisfies aesthetic carnivores. The *Spokane Spokesman-Review's* Friday Weekend section and the *Spokane Chronicle's* Friday Empire section have the lowdown on area happenings. Dur-ing the summer, the city parks present a free **Out-to-Lunch** series at noon on week-days at various locations around town. Call 624-1393 for schedule information.

Spokane supports two minor league professional sports teams. The **Indians** paly ball at N. 602 Havana (535-2922) from June through August (tickets $7.50-8.50) while the **Chiefs** skate the Coliseum (328-0450) from October through March. All city-sponsored events are now ticketed by Select-A-Seat. Call 325-SHOW for infor-mation or 325-SEAT for reservations.

The Spokane Coliseum, N. 1101 Howard St. (456-3204). Rock concerts, rodeos, and other special events ($7-18.50).

The Opera House, W. 334 Spokane Falls Blvd. Home to the Spokane Ballet and the Spokane Symphony Orchestra (624-1200), this riverside complex also opens its stage to special per-formances, from rock concerts to chamber music.

Civic Theater, N. 1020 Howard St. (325-2507 for reservations, 325-1413 for information), opposite the Coliseum. Locally produced shows, ranging from off-off-Broadway to Spokane-based plays. Has a downstairs theater for local, more "risqué" productions. Tickets Fri.-Sat. $10, Wed.-Thurs. $8, ages over 64 and students $7.

Spokane Interplayers Ensemble, S. 174 Howard (455-7529). A resident professional theater which performs a broad range of plays. Seven productions a season, 20 public performances each.

Magic Lantern Theatre, S. 123 Wall St. (838-8276). Fantastic films, from American classics to such foreign features as Wim Wenders's *The Airfeet of Desire and Rocky Horror.* Bruce Lee flicks shown frequently as well. Admission $5, senior citizens $3, students $4.

Fox Theater, at the corner of W. Sprague and Monroe. Slightly dated first-run flicks $1.50. Evening shows only.

Outback Jack's, W. 321 Sprague Ave. (747-7539). The place-to-be among Spokane's younger crowd. A variety of drink specials and a relaxed atmosphere. Nothing to do with Australia, however. 25¢ drafts, 50¢ pints on Thurs. 8-11pm. Cover Mon.-Tues., and Thurs. $1. Hosts local bands on Fri. and Sat., cover $2.

Henry's Pub, W. 230 Riverside Ave. (624-9828). The place for live rock Wed.-Sat. nights. Cover charge varies from $1-3 depending on the band. Local and out-of-town bands such as the Peace Frogs, Pointed Sticks, and Final Exam slam and thrash here. Draft beer $1.75. Open Mon.-Fri. 11am-2am, Sat.-Sun. 4pm-2am.

The Onion Bar and Grill, W. 302 Riverside (747-3852). A bastion of yuppiedom; men in European suits act tough as they nurse frozen margaritas while playing pool in the back room. Different drink special each night of the week. Dinners under $7, frozen margaritas $3.50, drafts $1.85. Open Sun.-Thurs. 11:15am-1am, Fri.-Sat. 11:15am-2am.

Flaherty's, W. 514 Sprague Ave. (8383-8076). Caters to a slightly older crowd, but the change of pace is relaxing and the drinks relatively cheap. Drafts $1.50, bottles $2, pitchers $4. No drink specials or anything; just have a seat and drink your beer. Open daily 11am-2am.

Seasonal Events

On the first Sunday in May, Riverfront Park hosts its premature, annual **Blooms-day Road Race,** the second biggest race on the West Coast and the highlight of the **Lilac Festival,** a week-long hoopla of car shows, art fairs, house tours, and Special Olympics. The week (which seems to have very little to do with flowers) culminates in a torch-lit parade. For information on these and other events, contact the Chamber of Commerce. In August, downtown salutes the flag in the **Main Street USA** celebration. The annual **Bach Festival** at the end of January is the highlight in a series of Connoisseur Concerts given at W. 310 5th Ave. (call 747-6443). During the Independence Day weekend, friendly citizens of Spokane celebrate a Lehreresque **Neighbors Day** at Riverfront Park. Events include art fairs, an antique car show, and fireworks at sundown.

WESTERN CANADA

US$1 = CDN $1.14	CDN$1 = US$0.88
AUS$1 = CDN $.93	CDN$1 = AUS$1.08
UK£1 = CDN $2.19.	CDN$1 = UK£.46
NZ$1 = CDN $.71	CDN$1 = NZ$1.51

Prices are given in Canadian dollars, unless otherwise specified.

BRITISH COLUMBIA

Larger than California, Oregon, and Washington combined, British Columbia attracts so many visitors that tourism has become the province's second largest industry (after logging). Although Canada's westernmost province does offer excellent skiing year-round, most tourists arrive in the summer and flock towards the beautiful twin cities of Vancouver and Victoria, as well as the pristine lakes and beaches of the Okanagan Valley.

As you head north, the ratio of clouds to crowds increases. The thick forests, low mountains, and occasional patches of high desert are interrupted only by such supply and transit centers as Prince George and Prince Rupert. Farther north, even these outposts of civilization defer to thick spruce forests, every so often tainted by the touch of the voracious logger or blackened by lightning fires.

Originally claimed for Great Britain by Captain James Cook in 1778, British Columbia retains vestiges of its days under the Union Jack without forgetting its Native roots. Victoria's populace carries on afternoon tea-time in the finest English tradition, while Native Americans along the Pacific Coast perpetuate age-old customs. Refugees from across the globe mix freely in Vancouver, and such weathered towns as Barkersville (currently being restored) pay homage to the miners and loggers of the late 19th century who wrested their livelihood from the wilderness.

The Canadian and British Columbian governments have a better-than-average record of preserving these treasures: almost 6000 sq. km of land fall under either provincial or federal protection. The extensive park system makes enjoying BC fairly easy, and the 3 Ws (wood, water, washrooms) are never far away.

Practical Information

Capital: Victoria.

Visitor Information: Ministry of Tourism and Provincial Secretary, Parliament Bldgs., Victoria V8V 1X4, (604-387-1642). Ask especially for the *Accommodations* guide, which lists prices and services for virtually every hotel, motel, and campground in the province. Branches in **Seattle,** P.O. Box C-34971, Seattle, WA 98124-1971 (604-387-1642); **Los Angeles,** 2600 Michelson Dr., #1050, Irvine, CA 92715 (714-852-1054); and **San Francisco,** 100 Bush St., #400, San Francisco, CA 94104 (415-981-4780).

Canada Parks Service: Write the Sr. Communications Officer, 220 4th Ave. SE, P.O. Box 2989, Station M, Calgary, AB T2P 3H8, or call **BC Parks** at 604-387-5002.

Time Zone: Mostly Pacific (1 hr. behind Mountain, 2 behind Central, 3 behind Eastern). Small eastern section is Mountain (1 hr. behind Central, 2 behind Eastern).

Traffic Laws: Mandatory seatbelt law.

Postal Abbreviation: BC.

Drinking Age: 19.

Emergency: 911.

Area Code: 604

Impractical Information

Motto: *Splendor sine Occasu* (Splendor without Diminishment).

License Plate Slogan: *Beautiful British Columbia.*

Year of Royal Naming: 1858, by Queen Victoria.

Year to Join Confederation: 1871

Provicial Flower: Pacific Dogwood

Provincial Tree: Douglas Fir

Provincial Bird: Heron

Provincial Stone: Jade

Travel

British Columbia is Canada's westernmost province, covering over 890,000 square km, bordering four U.S. states (Washington, Idaho, Montana, and Alaska) and three Canadian jurisdictions (Alberta, the Yukon Territory, and the Northwest Territories). Vancouver, on the mainland, can be reached via interstate highway from Seattle; Victoria, on Vancouver Island to the southwest of Vancouver, requires a ferry trip from Anacortes, Port Angeles, Seattle, or the Tsawwassen Terminal near Vancouver. However you travel, get used to thinking in terms of distances of kilometers in three or four digits.

Road travel throughout the province varies with the immensely diverse terrain. If you decide to take your own vehicle, avoid potential hassles by obtaining a **Canadian nonresident interprovince motor vehicle liability card** from your insurance company before leaving. Border police may turn you away if you are not properly insured. In the south, roads are plentiful and well-paved, but farther north, both asphalt and towns seem to have been blown away by the Arctic winds. Above Prince George, travel along the two major roads—the Alaska Hwy. and the Cassiar Hwy.—is hindered by stretches of "chip-seal," a cheaper and substantially rougher version of asphalt. Much of British Columbia is served by **Greyhound** (662-3222 in Vancouver) although **Pacific Coastal Lines (PCL)** has a monopoly on transport on Vancouver Island.

The Coquihalla Highway (Hwy. 5, more popularly known as "The Coca-Cola") was completed in 1986 to carry tourists comfortably from Hope, near Vancouver, to Kamloops, a city roughly halfway between Vancouver and Alberta's Banff and Jasper National Parks. The Coquihalla Highway costs $10, but is a much more direct route and constitutes a substantial time savings. Unfortunately, the terrain is very hilly and has assassinated more than one transmission. If you don't think your car is up to snuff, you can always enjoy the Fraser River Canyon's scenery via the Trans-Canada Highway instead. The Yellowhead Highway (also Hwy. 5) brings you from Kamloops on to Jasper.

For information about crossing the U.S.-Canada border and for customs regulations, see For International Visitors in the General Introduction.

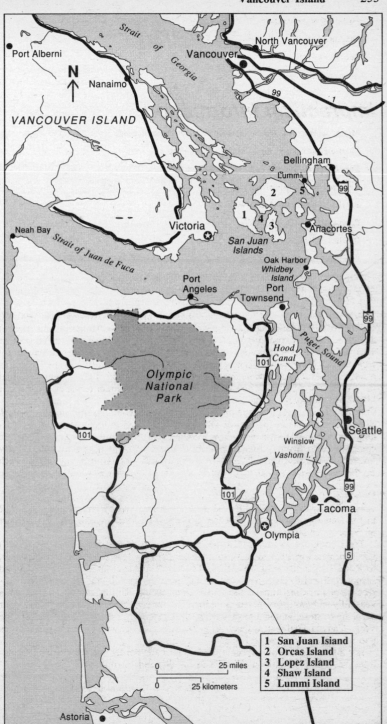

N

Port Alberni

Nanaimo

VANCOUVER ISLAND

Strait of Georgia

Vancouver

North Vancouver

99

1

Bellingham

Lummi

5

2

1

4

3

Victoria

*San Juan
Islands*

Anacortes

Oak Harbor

*Whidbey
Island*

Port
Townsend

99

Neah Bay

Strait of Juan de Fuca

Port
Angeles

*Hood
Canal*

Puget Sound

Olympic
National
Park

101

Seattle

Winslow

Vashom I.

99

101

Tacoma

Olympia

5

101

1	San Juan Island
2	Orcas Island
3	Lopez Island
4	Shaw Island
5	Lummi Island

0 ————— 25 miles

0 ————— 25 kilometers

Astoria

Vancouver Island

Named after Captain George Vancouver, the first white man to circumnavigate the island (he did it accidentally in 1787 . . . while looking for passage to China) Vancouver Island stretches almost 500km along continental Canada's southwest coast and is one of only two places in Canada to penetrate south of the 49th parallel (London, Ontario is the other). The cultural center of the island is Victoria, the province's capital city, on the extreme southern tip. Toasted by frequent sunshine (though residents deny it and, in a negative publicity campaign like their southern neighbors in "lesser Seattle," pretend to celebrate a "rain festival" Jan. 1-Dec. 31), the city attempts to preserve its British charm. Elsewhere, the Native Americans who first walked the northern reaches of the island have left their tradition behind in the locals' respect for nature, love of hiking, and vendetta against fish.

Victoria

The sun may have set on the British empire years ago, but, like a heroic soldier in the Falklands War, Victoria still lives the dream. The 90-minute ferry trip between Vancouver and Victoria imitates an English Channel crossing, and as you step ashore in the Inner Harbour, you will be greeted by double-decker buses, festively decorated with the Union Jack. In kilt and sporran, a bagpiper plies his street trade at the corner of the Parliament Buildings, stately stone edifices worthy of Westminster. The ivy-shawled Empress Hotel, also named for the dour queen, gazes regally at its own image in the water. On warm summer days, the more Anglophilic residents sip their noon teas on the lawns of Tudor-style homes in the suburbs, while downtown, horse-drawn carriages clatter around Bastion Square.

Despite Victoria's refined image, today's citizens are not at all ashamed of the town's ornery prospectors who swilled beer in front of rowdy brothels on their way to the Cariboo mines during the 1858 gold rush. Hudson's Bay Company moved its western headquarters to the southern tip of Vancouver Island after the site of its former headquarters in Astoria, Oregon was declared U.S. property. When the Canadian Pacific Railway reached the Pacific Coast, Victoria coaxed an additional stretch across the Strait of Juan de Fuca from Vancouver, and the city stole Vancouver's distinction as Canada's western railroad terminus. In 1869, Victoria was named the capital of British Columbia, partially on the assumption that the promised railroad would cause the city to expand further. The railroad dream was never fully realized, and Victoria did not undergo the adornments of industrialization. Instead of pollution, ugly factory chimneys, and Margaret Thatcher, Victoria has 250,000 well-heeled citizens delighting in the thankfully un-British annual rainfall of only 27 inches.

Practical Information and Orientation

Visitor Information: Tourism Victoria, 812 Wharf St., Victoria V8W 1T3 (382-2127), in the Inner Harbour. Piles of pamphlets that must have decimated entire BC forests. Open daily 9am-8pm; in winter 9am-5pm.

VIA Rail: 450 Pandora St. (383-4324 for departure/arrival information; 800-665-8630 for general information and tickets). Near the Inner Harbour.

Bus Service: Pacific Coast Lines (PCL) and its affiliate **Island Coach Lines,** 700 Douglas St. at Belleville (385-4411). Connects all major points and most minor ones, though fares can be steep. The station has lockers at $1.25 per 24 hr.

Greyhound Depot: 710 Douglas St., at Belleville St. (385-5248), behind the Empress Hotel. Gotcha. This is an information booth only, as Greyhound offers no service on the island or to Vancouver. Buses run exclusively out of the Vancouver terminal (see Vancouver).

BC Ferry: 656-0757 for a recording, 386-3431 for a person. Between Swartz Bay (Victoria) and Tsawwassen (Vancouver) 14 per day 7am-9pm (bike $2.10, car $17, plus $4.75 per person). Between Horseshoe Bay (Vancouver) and Nanaimo 10 per day 7am-9pm, same rates. Take bus #70, fare $1.

Washington State Ferries: 381-1551. From Sidney to Anacortes, WA, via the San Juan Islands: 1 per day in winter, 2 in summer. Buy your ticket straight through to Anacortes and stop over in the San Juans for as long as you like; you can rejoin the ferry at any point as long as you continue traveling eastward. Passengers $7.50; car and driver $35; ages over 64 and 5-11 $4; under 5 free. Fares do vary by season (call for exact rates and schedules). Take bus #70, fare $1.

BC Stena Line: 390 Belleville St. (386-1124; off-season 388-7397). Round-trip cruises from Pier 48 in Seattle, WA to Victoria aboard the ritzy *Crown Princess Victoria* or *Vancouver Island Princess* (in summer 3 per day, $30, $40 round-trip; in winter 1 per day, rates reduced).

Black Ball Transport: 430 Belleville St. (386-2202). Connects Victoria with Port Angeles, WA. Mid-May to late Sept. 4 per day; early Oct.-late Nov. and mid-March to mid-May 2 per day. Fare $6.80, car and driver $27.80, ages 5-11 $3.40.

Victoria Regional Transit: 382-6161.

Car Rental: A.D.A. Rent-A-Used-Car, 752 Caledonia Ave. (388-6230). $15 per day plus 10¢ per km. Must be 21. $250 deposit for 1 week rental, $150 for 1 day; confirmation of employment or university ID requested. Open Mon.-Sat. 8am-5pm. **Budget Discount Car Rentals,** 727 Courtney St. (388-7874). Not to be confused with the far more expensive Budget Rent-A-Car on the same block. Must be 21 with a major credit card. Used cars in excellent condition from $15 per day plus 10¢ per km. Open daily 7:30am-7pm.

Canadian Automobile Association: 382-8171. Full benefits for AAA members.

Taxi: Victoria Taxi, 383-7111. **Westwind,** 474-4747.

Bike Rental: Explore Victoria, 1007 Langley St. (381-2453; 382-9928 off-season). 18-speed mountain bikes $5 per hr., $15 for 24 hr. $20 deposit per bike. Open daily 9am-6pm. **Harbour Scooters,** 1223 Wharf St. (384-2127). 18-speed mountain bikes $18 per day. Open daily 9am-6pm.

Scooter Rentals: Harbour Scooters (see above). $25 per day, with credit card or $25 deposit.

Camping Supplies and Rentals: Jeune Brothers, 570 Johnson St. (386-8778). 2-person tent $15 for 3 days, $23 per week. Open Mon.-Sat. 9:30am-5:30pm, Sun. 11am-5pm.

Library: (382-7241), 735 Broughton at Courtney. Open Mon., Wed., Fri.,Sat., 9am-6pm; Tues., Thurs. 9am-9pm.

Jazz Hotline: 628-5255.

Laundromat: 812 Wharf St., 1 floor below Tourism Victoria. Also has pay showers.

Crisis Line: 386-6323.

Rape Crisis: 383-3232. Open 24 hr.

Gay and Lesbian Information: 361-4900. Volunteer staff, so hours are indeterminate.

Handicapped Services: 382-4488 or 727-7811.

Tourist Alert Board, 380-6136. If you need to reach someone in an emergency and don't know where to find them, this number will put a message at every tourist office in the city and at major tourist attractions.

Poison Control: 595-9211. Open 24 hr.

Pharmacy: London Drugs, 900 Yates St. (381-1113), at Vancouver, in the Wilson Centre. Open Mon.-Sat. 9am-10pm, Sun. 10am-6pm.

Police: 625 Fisgard at Government St. (384-4111). Staff sergeant on duty 24 hr.

Post Office: Postal Station E, 1230 Government St. (388-3575), at Yates. Open Mon.-Fri. 8:30am-5pm. Postal Code: V8W 2L9.

Area Code: 604.

Ferries and buses connect Victoria, on Vancouver Island's southern tip, to many cities in British Columbia and Washington (see Practical Information above). The city of Victoria enfolds the Inner Harbour; **Government Street** and **Douglas Street** are the main north-south thoroughfares. Traditional tourist attractions crowd this area, and locals are few and far between. Residential neighborhoods form a semicircle around the Inner Harbour, the more popular and wealthy weighting the beaches in the east. **Victoria Regional Transit** (382-6161) serves the whole city seven days per week, with major bus connections at the corner of Douglas and Yates St. downtown. Travel in the single-zone area costs $1, multi-zone (north to Sidney and the Butchart Gardens) $1.25. Daily passes for unlimited single-zone travel are available at the visitors center and 7-11s for $3 (ages over 65 and under 12 $2). Transit maps and a riders' guide come free from Tourism Victoria (see Practical Information).

Accommodations

Victoria Youth Hostel (IYHF), 516 Yates St., Victoria V8W 1K8 (385-4511), at Wharf St. downtown. Big, modern, and spotless. Extensive kitchen and laundry facilities. 102 beds. Two-family rooms with 4 beds each. Open Sun.-Thurs. 7:30-midnight, Fri.-Sat. 7:30am-2am. Members $10, nonmembers $15.

University of Victoria (721-8395), 20 min. northeast of the Inner Harbour by bus; take #7 or 14. Private rooms with shared baths. Coin-operated laundry machines. Register in the Housing Office, near the Coffee Gardens entrance that faces Ring Rd. Registration 7:30am-midnight. Singles $22. Doubles $36.25. Breakfast included. Reservations advisable. Open May-Aug.

Salvation Army Men's Hostel, 525 Johnson St. (384-3396), at Wharf St. Men only. Modern, immaculate, and well run on a first-come, first-sleep basis. Dorms open daily at 4pm. You need a late pass if you plan on returning after 11pm. Dorm beds $6, private rooms $10. Meals $1.50 extra.

YWCA, 880 Courtney St. (386-7511), at Quadra, within easy walking distance of downtown. Women only. Heated pool and private rooms with shared baths. Check-in 11am-6pm. Check-out 6-11am. Singles $28.60. Doubles $42.90.

Battery Street Guest House, 670 Battery St. (385-4632), 1 block in from the ocean between Douglas and Government St. Dutch spoken in this spacious home. Non-smokers only. Singles from $35. Doubles from $55.

Cherry Bank Hotel, 825 Burdett Ave. (385-5380), at Quadra St., 2 blocks from the visitors center. 90-year-old B&B, very traditional. Spotless rooms along winding corridors. *Trivial Pursuit* played incessantly in the lounge—they even advertise it outside. Singles from $34.50. Doubles from $41.

Jamie's Bay Inn, 270 Government St. (384-7151), at Toronto St., just 2 blocks south of the Parliament Buildings. Near everything, but quiet and relatively inexpensive nonetheless. The rooms are light and airy. TV, soft beds. Singles $29, with shared bath. Doubles $37, with private bath $52. Reservations absolutely necessary July-Sept.

Victoria Backpackers Hostel, 1418 Fernwood Rd. (386-4471). Take buses #1, 10, 11, 14, 27, or 28 to Fernwood. Shared rooms $10, private $20. Doubles $30. No curfew.

Camping

The few grounds on the city perimeter cater largely to RV drivers who are loaded. Be forewarned that many campgrounds fill up in July and August; reservations are wise.

McDonald Park (655-9020), less than 3km south of the Swartz Bay Ferry Terminal, 30km north of downtown on Hwy. 17. Makes "slightly rural" seem like first class. No showers, and no beach access. Government-run. 30 tent and RV sites $6.

Thetis Lake Campground, 1938 Trans-Canada Hwy. (478-3845), 10km north of the city center. Serves traffic entering Victoria from northern Vancouver Island. Sites are peaceful and removed, maybe too removed—it's a long walk to the bathroom. Metered showers and a laundromat. Sites $10, plus 50¢ per person. Full hookups $12.50.

Fort Victoria Camping, 127 Burnett (479-8112), 7km NW of downtown off the Trans-Canada Hwy. Free hot showers. Laundromat. Sites $13.50, with full hookups $18.50.

Goldstream Park, 2930 Trans-Canada Hwy. (387-4363). Government-run, set in a deeply forested area along a river, 20km northwest of Victoria. Great short hiking trails, swimming, and fishing. In November, the river is crowded with salmon returning to their roots. Flush toilets and firewood available. 150 gorgeous (albeit gravelly) sites ($10). The nearby **Freeman King Visitor Centre** relates the history of the area from glaciers to the welfare state. Naturalists will take you for a walk, or roam down the self-guided nature trail. (Center open in summer daily 8:30am-4:30pm; in winter by appointment only.)

Weir's Beach Resort, 5191 William Head Rd. (478-3323), 24km west on Hwy. 14. You pay for the great beach location. Metered showers and a swimming pool. Sites $13.50, with full hookups $18.

French Beach, farther west on Hwy. 14, nearly 50km out. Right on the water, the park has 70 sites with pit toilets, swimming, and hiking trails. No showers. Sites $8.

Food

Victoria's predilection for anachronisms is perhaps best evidenced by its eating habits. Victorians actually do take tea—some only on occasion, others every day, and no visit to Victora would be complete without participating in the ceremony at least once. And don't embarass yourself by asking for lemon with your tea; clear or milk only, please.

As in every big city, ethnic diversity in Victoria is a recipe for flavorful restaurants. **Chinatown,** west of Fisgard and Government streets, fills the air with a tantalizing bouquet of exotic aromas, with more West-coast offerings taking over by the time you get to Wharf St. If you feel like cooking, head down to **Fisherman's Wharf,** four blocks west at the corner of Harbour and Government St., between Superior and St. Lawrence Streets. On summer mornings, you can buy the day's catch straight off the boats.

The Blethering Place, 2250 Oak Bay Ave. (598-1413), at Monterey St. in upright Oak Bay. "Blether" is Scottish for "talk volubly and senselessly"—a fact of little relevance for this superb tearoom frequented by mousey elementary school teachers. Afternoon tea served with scones, Devonshire cream tarts, English trifle, muffins, and sandwiches all baked on the premises ($5.50). Ploughman's Lunch ($6) is a meatier alternative. Dinners $10. Open daily 8am-10pm.

Flying Rhino Diner, 1219 Wharf St. (381-5331), just down the street from Tourism BC and Bastion Sq. Not your standard diner fare. The vegetarian sandwiches ($5), nut burgers, and homemade soups here are quite good. Open Mon.-Fri. 8am-8pm, Sat. 10am-6pm, Sun. 10am-4pm.

Goodies, 1005 Broad St., 2nd floor (382-2124), between Broughton and Fort. Build your own omelette for $4.45 plus 65¢ per ingredient, or choose from a list of sandwiches like the "Natural High" (mushroomm and avocado, $5-7). Tex-Mex dinners $8. Breakfast served until 3:30pm, $1 discount on omelettes Mon.-Fri. 7-9:30am. Open daily 7am-9pm.

Lin Heung, 626 Fisgard St. (385-1632), in Chinatown, just across from the police station. Victorians wait in line for pork buns straight from the oven. The seafood is fresh and plentiful. $8 minimum. Open Wed.-Mon. 11am-9pm.

Saigon Café, 1692 Douglas St., at Fisgard. Try the prawn and pork soup ($4.10) or chicken curry with rice noodles ($4.50). No frills. Open Mon.-Sat. 11am-8pm.

Eugene's, 1280 Broad St. (381-5456), just up the street. Vegetarian souvlaki $2.50, dinners $5. *Spanakopita* or *Bougatsa* a nice change for breakfast. Eugene claims that you can "call when you leave and it will be ready on your arrival." Ring from a pay phone next door and freak Eugene out. Open Mon.-Fri. 8am-10pm, Sat. 10am-9pm.

Las Flores, 536 Yates St. (386-6313), a steroid-free Olympian's stride from the hostel. Filling burrito/enchilada combos for $8. Loud sound system reveals striking similarities between Mexican Top-40 and the stuff they play over at Eugene's.

Scott's Restaurant, 650 Yates St. (382-1289), at Douglas St. Real diner feel; you just *know* they serve a mean chicken à la king. "Breakfast 222" (2 hotcakes, 2 eggs, 2 sausages—pretty clever) for $3.75. Daily dinner specials a good bet ($4.85-6). Open 24 hr. (natch).

Sorrento Café and Deli, 636 Yates St. (381-3132). Another of the many cheap establishments along Yates St. The House special pizza easily feeds two for $11.25. Large slice $2. Open Mon.-Sat. 7:30am-11pm, Sun. 3-10pm.

James Bay Tearoom, 332 Menzies St. at Superior (382-8282). Portraits of Queen Victoria, King George V, Chuck and Di, Winston Churchill and a royal family tree from A.D. 900 set the scene for regal afternoon tea, daily 1-4:30pm. The place is crowded until 2:30pm. Open Mon.-Sat. 7am-9pm, Sun. 8am-9pm.

Willow's Galley, 2559 Estevan St. (598-2711), at Willow's Beach in Oak Bay, 6km east of the Inner Harbour. Take bus #1. Best $3 burger in town with chips ($1.25) wrapped in newspaper. Blueberry yogurt and vanilla ice cream combo cone $1. Eat on the lovely beach nearby. Open Tues.-Sat. 11am-7pm, Sun. noon-7pm.

Sights and Activities

Victoria is a small city; you can wander the Inner Harbour, watch the boats come in, and take in many of the city's main attractions—all on foot. The elegant residential neighborhoods and the city's parks and beaches, farther out are accessible by car and public transportation.

The first stop for every visitor should be the **Royal British Columbian Museum,** 675 Belleville St. (387-3014 for a tape, 387-3701 for a person). Arguably the best museum in Canada, it chronicles the geological, biological, and cultural histories of the province and displays detailed exhibits on logging, mining, and fishing. The extensive exhibits of Native American art, culture, and history include full-scale replicas of various forms of shelter used centuries ago. The gallery of Haida **Totem Art** is particularly moving. **Open Ocean** is a tongue-in-cheek re-creation of the first descent in a bathysphere. (Open daily 9:30am-7pm; Oct.-April 10am-5:30pm. Admission $5; senior citizens, disabled people, students with ID, and ages 13-18 $3; ages 6-12 $1. Free Mon. Oct.-April. Hang on to your ticket: it's good for two days). Fascinating free films about British Columbia's heritage run in the summer from 11am to 3:30pm in the museum's Newcombe Theatre. Behind the museum, **Thunderbird Park** is a striking thicket of totems and longhouses, backed by the oxydized-copper towers of the Empress Hotel.

Also on the grounds of the museum is **Helmcken House,** a Heritage Conservation building, part of which dates from 1852. Originally the home of Dr. John Helmcken, the medic for Fort Victoria, the house still contains many of the family's furnishings and displays some of the doctor's medical instruments. Needlework and paintings in the house, done by members of the family's first Canadian generation, will bore all but domestic-history buffs. (Open daily 10am-4pm. Free.)

Across the street from the front of the museum are the imposing **Parliament Buildings,** 501 Belleville St. (387-6121), home of the provincial government since 1859 (currently Bill Van Der Zalm's right-wing Social Credit party). The 10-story dome and Brunelleschi-esque vestibule are gilded with almost 50-oz. of gold. It seems the architect who won the competition for the buildings' design lied on his entry form, claiming to be a partner in a prestigious firm. Free tours leave from the main steps daily 9am-5pm, departing every 20 minutes in summer, every hour in winter. If you ask your guide to explain the *exact* relationship between Canada and the British monarchy, she will become visibly flustered and slip out of her ever-so-slight English accent.

Surrounding the Parliament buildings along Belleville and Menzies St. are a number of less-than-unique tourist-traps. **Undersea Gardens,** (382-5717) takes you underwater in a plexiglass corridor to view denizens of the deep (and not-so-deep). There is also a live scuba show every hour. (Admission $5.50, open daily 9am-9pm.) Just next door is the **Royal London Wax Museum** (388-4461) where, ironically, the main attraction is the wax sculpture of Mme. Tussaud herself (admission $5.25, open 8:30am-10:30pm daily, 388-4461). **Sea World** 1327 Beach Dr. at the Oak Bay Marina (598-3373), offers what you'd expect from a place called Sea World, and not much more. (Open daily 10am-9pm.)

Just north of Fort St. on Wharf is **Bastion Square,** which earned Victorians the Vincent Massey award for excellence in urban environment in 1971. In the square the **Maritime Museum,** 28 Bastion Sq. (385-4222), exhibits ship models, nautical instruments, and a 13m Native American canoe that left from Victoria in 1901 for a daring (but ultimately doomed) trip around the world. (Open Mon.-Sat. 10am-4pm, Sun. noon-4pm. Admission $4, senior citizens $3, students $1, ages under 6 free.) Free art exhibits occasionally appear between noon and 1:30pm.

Around the corner on Wharf St. is the **Emily Carr Gallery**, 1107 Wharf St. (387-3080). Carr was a respected BC artist who painted at the beginning of the century. Her originality lay in her synthesis of British landscape conventions and Native American style. This collection includes many of her paintings of Native totems and lifestyles, conscious attempts to preserve what she saw as "art treasures of a passing race." Also on display are photographs and manuscripts of other period artists, politicians and prominent citizens. Free films on Carr's life and work show at 2:30pm. (Open Mon.-Sat. 10am-5pm. Free.)

North on Fisgard St., the Government St. entrance to the now-tiny **Chinatown** is marked by the large "Gate of Harmonious Interest." A hundred years ago, Victoria's Chinatown covered a great deal of this region. Today, the area is just as tailored as the rest of the city. Still, the great restaurants and inexpensive trinket shops make Chinatown a rewarding place for a meal and a constitutional.

South of the Inner Harbour, **Beacon Hill Park** surveys the Strait of Juan de Fuca (take bus #5). Here you can picnic amidst the park's flower gardens, 350-year-old garry oaks, and network of paths.

East of the Inner Harbour, **Craigdarroch Castle,** 1050 Joan Crescent (592-5323), embodies Victoria's wealth. Take bus #11 or 14 to Oak St. and transfer to #1 or 2. The house was built in 1890 by Robert Dunsmuir, a BC coal and railroad tycoon, in order to tempt his wife away from their native Scotland. His former home is packed with Victoriana, and the interior detail is impressive. The tower has a mosaic floor and the dining room a built-in oak sideboard. (Open daily 9am-7:30pm; in winter 10am-5pm. Admission $4, seniors and students $3.)

One block back towards the Inner Harbor on Fort St. at 1040 Moss is the **Gallery of Greater Victoria** (384-4101), never the same museum twice. The museum has no permanent collection, save a wooden Shinto Shrine, and instead hosts an endless succession of temporary exhibits culled from local and international sources. (Open Mon.-Sat. 10am-5pm, Thurs. 'til 9pm, Sun. 1pm-5pm. Admission $3, seniors $1.50.)

Heading in the opposite direction from the Inner Harbour, hop on bus #14 or take Bay St. west off Government and stop just before crossing the Point Ellice Bridge at the **Point Ellice House,** 2616 Pleasant St. (385-5923). Read that one more time. Tall trees shelter the house from the depressed industrial area around it. Another Heritage House, the 1861 Point Ellice is decorated exactly as if the elitist oppressor residents had just stepped out for a spot of croquet. The dining table is set, the chess set stands ready in the drawing room, and cast-iron pots and period kitchen utensils are strewn about the kitchen. Guided tours are provided. (Open July-Sept. 5 Thurs.-Mon. 10am-5pm. Free.)

Across the bridge, you'll find **Craigflower Heritage Site,** at the corner of Craigflower and Admirals Rd. (387-3067; take bus #14), a complex of historical buildings on a farm built by Hudson's Bay Company in the 1850s. Craigflower is more rustic than Point Ellice, though the kitchen is equipped with all the Cuisinart equivalents of its day. (Open Wed.-Sun. 10am-3:45pm. Free.) At **Fort Rodd Hill National Historic Park,** on Ocean Blvd. (388-1601), off Hwy. 1A, old defense batteries and **Fisgard Lighthouse,** the first of Canada's west-coast beacons, compete for attention with excellent views of the strait. Take bus #50 or 61 to Western Exchange, transfer to #60, get off at the end of Belmont St., and walk along the path to the park. There's no service on evenings, Sundays, or holidays. (Park open daily 8am-sunset.)

Almost worth the exorbitant entrance fee are the stunning **Butchart Gardens,** 800 Benvennto, 22km north of Victoria (652-5256 for a recording, 652-4422 for a person Mon.-Fri. 9am-5pm). Begun by Jennie Butchart in 1904 in an attempt to reclaim the wasteland that was her husband's quarry and cement plant, the gardens are a maze of pools and fountains. Rose, Japanese, and Italian gardens cover 50 acres in a blaze of colors. From mid-May through September, the whole area is lit at dusk, and the gardens, still administered by the Butchart family, host variety shows and cartoons. Saturday nights in July and August, the skies shimmer with fireworks displays. Seventy thousand Christmas lights compensate for the lack of vegetation in December. Take bus #74 right into the Gardens, or #70 and walk one km. The last #74 from the Gardens to the Inner Harbour is at 8:30pm, so there is a free **Livery Service** to the #70 bus stop until 11pm. Ask for a **Livery Pass** when you buy your ticket. Motorists should consider an approach to Butchart Gardens via the **Scenic Marine Drive,** following the coastline along Dalles and other roads for a 45-minute ride. The route passes through sedate suburban neighborhoods and offers a memorable view of the Olympic Mountains across the Strait of Juan de Fuca. (Gardens open May-June and Sept. 9am-9pm; July-Aug. 9am-11pm; March-April and Oct. 9am-5pm; Jan.-Feb. and Nov. 9am-4pm; Dec. daily 9am-8pm. Admission in summer $9.50, ages 13-17 $5, ages 5-12 $1; otherwise, prices vary with the number of flowers in bloom.) Hang on to your ticket: readmission within 24 hours only $1.

Entertainment and Seasonal Events

Nightlife in Victoria doesn't really get off the ground until Thursday night, but once under way the entire city grooves to the rhythms of jazz, blues, country, rock, folk and more jazz. You can get an exhaustive listing of what's where in the free weekly *Monday Magazine* (released every Thursday), available at visitor information centers, the hostel, most hotel lobbies and tourist attractions. On Tuesdays movies at Cineplex Odeon theatres are half-price ($3.75).

The **Victoria Symphony Society,** 846 Broughton St. (385-6515), performs regularly under conductor Peter McCoppin, and the **University of Victoria Auditorium,** Finnerty Rd. (721-8480), plays home stage to a variety of student productions. The **Pacific Opera** performs at the McPherson Playhouse, 3 Centennial Sq. (386-6121), at the corner of Pandora and Government St. During the summer, they undertake a popular musical comedy series.

Harpo's Cabaret, 15 Bastion Sq. (385-5333), at Wharf St. Specializes in garage rock and reggae but occasionally sells out to classic rock tunes. Open Mon.-Sat. 9pm-2am; cover around $5.

The Forge, 919 Douglas St. (383-7137), at Courtney, in the Strathcona Hotel. They "don't admit anyone over 25." Hardcore and speed-metal bands. Our dear Queen would not have been amused. Open Mon. and Fri.-Sat. 7:30pm-2am, Tues.-Thurs. 8pm-2am.

Rumors, 1325 Government St. (385-0566). Gay and lesbian clientele; drinking and dancing. Open Mon.-Sat. 9pm-3am.

The **Folkfest** in late June celebrates Canada's birthday (July 1) and the country's "unity in diversity" with performances by politically correct and culturally diverse musicians. The **JazzFest,** sponsored by the Victoria Jazz Society (381-4042), also culminates on Canada Day. The **Classic Boat Festival** is held Labor Day weekend and displays pre-1955 wooden boats in the Inner Harbour. Free entertainment accompanies the show. Contact the visitor and convention bureau (382-2127) for more information on all Inner Harbour events.

Near Victoria

Victoria is the staging area for any number of excursions into the undeveloped areas of Vancouver Island. Roads on the southeastern part of the island are the most heavily trafficked, and are therefore the best hitching areas; public transportation clings to the larger towns and cities. Vancouver Island's population clusters near Victoria and along the eastern coast, facing the Georgia Strait and the mainland. The island's scalloped fringe was gouged out by glaciers moving down from the mountains. Mining once attracted many settlers but has since been replaced by logging. The fishing industry thrives; some of the world's largest salmon have met their maker here.

Excellent beaches outline the southwestern corner of the island. Farther north on the west coast, ancient fjords and mountains make this side inaccessible. West of Victoria on Hwy. 14 lies the town of **Sooke,** whose famous **All Sooke Day,** held in mid-July, draws lumberjacks from the whole island to compete in logging events. The **Sooke Region Museum,** on Hwy. 14 (642-6351), just beyond the Sooke River Bridge, delivers an excellent history of the area. (Open daily 10am-6pm; Oct.-April 10am-5pm. Free.) To get to the **Sooke Travel Infocentre,** 2070 Phillips Road (642-6112), take #50 bus to the Western Exchange and transfer to #61.

Just off the southeastern coast of Vancouver Island lies Canada's answer to the San Juans: **The Gulf Islands.** Although there are dozens of islands in the group, of which five are serviced by BC Ferries (call 656-0757 for details), the three principal members of the chain are **Salt Spring, Pender,** and **Mayne.** Pick up a free copy of *The Gulf Islander* on the ferry to Victoria for a complete listing of what's going on. For more information, call the **tourist information centres** in: Salt Spring (537-5252), Pender (629-6550), Mayne (539-5311), Galiano (539-2233) or Saturna (382-3551).

About 70km north of Victoria on Hwy. 1 lies the town of **Chemainus.** When the closure of the town's sawmill threatened economic disaster in 1980, an ambitious revitalization program, centered on a series of more than 30 enormous murals of the town's history, helped turn things around. In mid-July **Chemainus Daze** offers arts and crafts and a chance to meet with the mural artists. The **Horseshoe Bay Inn,** 9576 Chemainus Rd. (246-3425) at Henry has singles for $28, doubles $35. The **Senior Drop-In Centre,** on the corner of Willow and Alder (246-2111), is open daily 10am-4pm with coffee, tea and muffins for anyone who drops in. Call the **Chamber of Commerce** in Chemainus at (246-3944) for more information.

North of Sooke are some of the handsomest beaches on the southern island. Hwy. 14 continues along the coast to **Port Renfrew,** at the southeastern end of the **West Coast Trail.**

Pacific Rim National Park

The eclectic mixture of terrain comprising Pacific Rim National Park seems united by name only. The three units of land and sea that form the park are separated from each other by several kilometers. Taken as a whole these three regions embody an astonishing variety of wilderness. Separating the landlubbers from the old salts are the **Broken Group Islands** in Barkley Sound, accessible only to boaters and kayakers. **Long Beach** offers broad vistas of Sitka spruce and Western red cedar near a beach over 20km long and the kinder, gentler trails contrast with those found on the **West Coast Trail.** Constructed in 1907 to give shipwrecked sailors a path to civilization, this is the most demanding and potentially dangerous section of the park. The trail can be traversed only on foot, and takes anywhere from 5-9 days. About halfway along the trail near **Clo-oose** (pronounced KLO-ooze) is the **Carmanah Valley** where Douglas Firs tower over 90m above the forest floor, the tallest in the world. This route is for serious hikers only; the wilderness does not take kindly to ignorance or mishaps.

Barkley Sound arrogantly intrudes between Bamfield and Port Albion, and here you'll find the **Broken Group Islands** unit of the park. Accessible only by boat, these islands are almost literally untouched.

The 23 km **Long Beach** breaks up the 41 km between Uchuelet (pronounced you-CUE-let) in the south and Tofino in the north. Long Beach has several camping facilities (see Accommodations and Camping).

Each spring, you can view some of the 20,000 gray whales which commute past the park. There are also less imposing forms of wildlife: sea lions, black-tailed deer, black bears. Dress for wet weather here; even the mosquitoes wear raincoats.

Practical Information

Visitor Information: Long Beach (726-4212) 3 km into the Long Beach Unit of Hwy. 4. **West Coast Trail:** Pachena Bay (728-3234) or Port Renfrew (647-5434), both open daily 9am-5pm mid-May-Sept. 30. **Tofino** (725-3414), 315 Campbell St. **Uchuelet:** 1620 Peninsula Rd. (726-4641).

Ferry: Alberni Marine Transportation, Inc., P.O. Box 188, Port Alberni, V9Y 7M7 (723-8313). Operates the *M.V. Lady Rose* year-round to Bamfield (3 per week, $13, round-trip $25) and Ucluelet (3 per week, $16, round-trip $32).

Hospital: 261 Neill St., Tofino (725-3212).

Coast Guard: 725-3231.

Emergency: RCMP (725-3242), in Tofino.

Area Code: 604.

Accommodations and Camping

This is campground country. There are no hostels around and cheap beds are rare.

Uchuelet Lodge Hotel (726-4324) in Uchuelet on Main St. Shared bath, no phone, no TV. Singles from $25. Doubles from $30.

Dolphin Motel (725-3377), 3km south of Tofino near beach. Shared bath, TV. Singles $35, doubles $38.

Tin Wis Guest House (725-3402), on MacKenzie Beach, 2km south of Tofino (725-3402). Small but clean rooms with bunk beds. $25 for a room with two beds lacking bedding, $30 with bedding. Reservations necessary in July.

Green Point Campground (726-4245), 10km north of the park information centre. The 94 sites, equipped with hot water, flush toilets, and fireplaces, swarm with campers and mosquitoes in July and Aug. Ranger-led programs nightly. Lines form at 7am. Sites mid-June to Aug. $10.50, Sept.-March $5, April to mid-June $8.50.

Schooner Campground, at the northern end of Long Beach. A km-long trail drastically reduces demand for this backpacker's Valhalla, supplied with cold water and outhouses. Unfortunately, high tides threaten the grounds every other week during the winter. Sites $5.

Ucluelet Campground, at Ucluelet Harbor (726-4355). Showers and toilets. $14 per site, electricity $2, water $1, sewer $1.

Food

Long Beach Fish 'n' Chowder, 921 Campbell St. (725-3244), outside Tofino. No aspirations to elegance, but plenty of mariners' paraphernalia on the wall to keep you entertained while you wait for the clam chowder ($2.25). Three pieces of French toast $4.20. Open Mon.-Thurs. 8am-3pm, Fri.-Sun. 8am-7pm.

Alleyway Café, at Campbell and 1st (725-3105), in Tofino. Small, clean, and colorful. Try a clamburger (if you dare, $5), the unique taco-in-a-bowl ($4), or inflicting sharp objects on the inflatable cacti that line the windows. Open Sun.-Thurs. 10am-8pm, Fri.-Sat. 10am-9pm.

Common Loaf Bake Shop, 131 1st St. (725-3915), in Tofino. Everything here is dense, delicious and satisfying. The chocolate chunk cookie (60¢) and coffee date-nut bread (70¢) are uncommonly good. Open Mon.-Sat. 8am-8pm, Sun. 8am-7pm.

The Gray Whale, 1596 Peninsula St. (726-7336), in Ucluelet. Polish off a pizza sub ($2.49) with a blue bubble gum milkshake ($2). Open daily 11am-8pm.

Sights and Activities

Whale watching is the premier outdoor activity on Long Beach from mid-March to mid-April. Local mariners will gladly take you on a three-hour ride to observe the grays closely (about $30). Smooth rides in large boats are available, but the real thrill-seekers venture out in **zodiacs,** hard-bottomed inflatable rafts with massive outboard motors that ride the swells at 30 knots.

Educational programs run every night at **Green Point Campground** (726-4245), 15km south of Tofino. Park officials often lead morning beach-exploration trips, pointing out all sorts of bizarre tide pool life forms. **Radar Hill,** a few km north of Green Point, is connected to the highway by a short paved road and is an excellent lookout point. Learn about the indigenous wildlife at the **Wickaninnish Centre**

(726-4212), 3km off Hwy. 4 just past the park entrance. (Open daily mid-May to Labor Day. Free.)

Most visitors take advantage of the park's magnificent **hiking trails.** Pick up a *Hiker's Guide* for the Long Beach unit at the visitors center for a list of nine hikes ranging from 100m to 5km in length. When the rain finally overwhelms you, seek refuge in the Native American art galleries in Ucluelet and Tofino. Ucluelet's **Du Quah Gallery,** 1971 Peninsula Rd. (726-7223) is more modest than Tofino's **Eagle Aerie Gallery,** 350 Campbell St. (725-4412), which protects unusual and striking paintings behind $17,000 carved wooden doors. **Second Circle Native Arts and Museum,** Campbell St at 3rd St., contains a small but varied collection of artifacts and handicrafts. (Open daily 10am-6pm. Free.)

Central and North Vancouver Island

Vancouver Island is like New York State; there's the city (Victoria) and then there's the rest. The Trans-Canada Hwy. ends its 4984-mi. course at Duncan and becomes Rte. 19, which runs up the eastern coast of the island. Just north of Duncan is the charming town of Nanaimo. The largest city in the central region, Nanaimo's heritage combines Native Americans, Welsh coal-miners, and Anglo-Canadian pastry chefs. Beyond Nanaimo, the towns gradually shrink. Port Alberni, at the tip of the Alberni Inlet, and Campbell River, along Rte. 19, are are homebases for excellent fishing or hiking. Campbell River guards the entrance to triangle-shaped Strathcona Provincial Park. Hornby Island, off the eastern side of the island, is a remarkable post-hippie settlement. And continuing along Rte. 19 into the northern third of Vancouver Island, known to the residents as "North Island," one notices an abrupt shift from Peugeots to pickups, Bacardi to Black Label, crumpets to clamburgers. Fishing and logging dominate the economy, and rivers and mountains mark the land.

Nanaimo

Nanaimo's 50,000 inhabitants are perhaps the most amiable folk on Vancouver Island. In the 19th century, Robert Dunsmuir's path to riches led through Nanaimo's coal mines; the supply is still there, but demand for the coal industry floundered after WWII. BC's first settlement has since shifted its focus from coal to logging and fishing. As logging turned to pulp throughout the province, Nanaimo (like the rest of BC) turned to tourism to supplement its revenue. The combination of affable, outgoing people, easy access by car or ferry, and a slow-paced, relaxing atmosphere has drawn vacationers (especially anglers) from all parts of the continent. The community's citizens have immigrated from lands as varied as England, China, Finland, and Poland, but they are now bound together by their willingness to flash welcoming smiles and show off their city to anyone who drives, hikes, or sails by.

Practical Information and Orientation

Visitor Information: Travel Infocentre, 266 Bryden St. (754-8474), on the Trans-Canada Hwy., just northwest of downtown. Mine of information on all of Vancouver Island. Call ahead for accommodation referrals. Open daily 8am-7pm.

BC Ferry: 680 Trans-Canada Hwy., Nanaimo V9S 5R1 (753-6626 for recorded info, 753-1261 for a person). To Vancouver 10 per day 7am-9pm (passenger $4.75, car and driver $21.75). Ferries leave from terminal at the northern end of Stewart Ave. (Take bus #2.) Check in 15 min. before departure.

Island Coach Lines: Comox and Terminal (753-4371), behind Tally Ho Island Inns. To: Victoria (6 per day, one way $10.50); Port Hardy (2 per day, one way $45); and Port Alberni (3 per day, one way $7.50, with connecting service to Tofino and Ucluelet).

Car Rental: Rent-A-Wreck, 41 Nicol St. (753-6461). Very used cars start at $25 per day plus 14¢ per km. Must be 21 with a major credit card. Open Mon.-Sat. 8am-6pm, Sun. 10am-4pm.

Bus Information: 390-4531. Terminal at Front and Wharf.

Laundromat: corner of Nichols and Robins at the Payless Gas Station. Open 24 hr.

Crisis: 754-4447.

Youth Crisis: 754-4448.

Pharmacy: London Drugs (753-5566), in Harbour Park Mall at Island Hwy. and Terminal Ave. Open Mon.-Sat. 9am-10pm, Sun. 10am-6pm.

Hospital: 1200 Dufferin Crescent (754-2141). Open 24 hr.

Police: 303 Pridaux St. at Fitzwilliam (753-2345).

Fire: corner of Fitzwilliam and Milton (753-1234).

Post Office: 60 Front St., at Church St. Open Mon.-Fri. 8:30am-5pm. Postal Code: V9R 5J9.

Area Code: 604.

Nanaimo lies on the eastern coast of Vancouver Island, 111km north of Victoria on the Trans-Canada Hwy., 391km south of Port Hardy via Hwy. 19. The twain meet downtown at the waterfront and become the major roads in town. The ferry terminal is 2km north of the junction on Stewart Ave.

Ten bus routes serve the area, although almost everything is within walking distance of downtown. Fare is 65¢ (exact change) or $1.80 for a day pass.

Accommodations

Nicol St. Mini-Hostel (IYHF), 65 Nicol St. (753-1188), 7 blocks SE of the Island Bus Lines Depot. If you're coming into Nanaimo from the south, ask the driver to let you off by the Nichol St. Hostel, and save yourself a walk. Great management and a dog that thinks it's a pony. Members $10, non-members $12. Laundry (wash and dry) $2.50. Open May-Sept.

Thomson Hostel (IYHF), 1660 Cedar Hwy. (722-2251), 10km south of Nanaimo. Take bus #11, or take the free shuttle from the bus depot free pickup at bus depot at 9pm. Accommodates 12 in 4 bedrooms, in addition to camping space. Kitchen facilities. Ping-pong table, billiards, and piano. Register between 9am and 11pm. Members $10, nonmembers $12. Laundry facilities $1.50. Open year-round.

May House Bed & Breakfast, 2415 Cosgrove Crescent (758-1423). The cheerful folks who live here will take all guests from the ferry, bus, or train terminals to their house with a fantastic view of Departure Bay. Laundry facilities are available, and coffee brews 24 hr. Singles $28. Doubles $38.

Colonial Motel, 950 Terminal Ave. (754-4415), on the Trans-Canada Hwy. Immaculate rooms. A popular nook for fishermen; the management will happily schedule you on a charter. Singles $32.95. Doubles $37.95.

Big 7 Motel, 736 Nicol St. (754-2328), downtown. Typical loud, kitschy motel decor, but the rooms are in good shape. Waterbed units available for those who don't want to give up that seasick feeling after a long day of open-ocean fishing. Singles $34. Doubles $36.

Camping

No commercial campgrounds are within walking distance of downtown, but plenty line the highway to the north and south.

Westwood Lake (753-3922), west of town off Jingle Pot Road. Full facilities. 75 sites. $10, $12 with hookups. Take bus #5.

Jingle Pot (758-1614), west on Island Hwy. off Jingle Pot Road. 60 sites $9, $12 with hookup. Full facilities.

Brannen Lake Campsite, 4228 Biggs Rd. (756-0404), 6km north of ferry terminal. Follow the signs from Hwy. 19. Definitely worth the trip. Clean bathrooms with hot showers (25¢). Remote, quiet sites layered with a lush cushion of green grass. Helpful staff. Sites $10, hookups $12.

Food

Look out Ring Dings and Susie Q's, here comes the **Nanaimo Bar,** three layers of sinfully delicious graham crackers, butter, and chocolate. Residents take great pride in their hometown concoction; a 1986 contest uncovered nearly 100 separate recipes. Most of the neighborhood restaurants and bakeries offer their own special rendition and the conscientious traveler will sample several. Leaving the city without trying a Nanaimo Bar is like hitting a home run and forgetting to touch third.

Up Stewart Ave., hungry travelers waiting to grab a boat to Vancouver can stop in at the **Nanaimo Public Market,** where food stands serve the finest in British cuisine: fish and chips. (Open daily 9am-9pm; Sept.-June 9am-6pm.)

The Scotch Bakery, 87 Commercial St. (753-3521). The acknowledged headquarters of Nanaimo Bar afficionados (70¢). Don't ignore the chocolate macaroons (60¢) or sausage rolls (90¢) either. Open Mon.-Fri. 8:30am-5:30pm, Sat. 8:30am-5pm.

New York Style Pizza, 426 Fitzwilliam (754-0111), at Richards. Offers visual amenities like classy framed posters of Gotham and Louis Armstrong, though the pizza doesn't taste anything like Ray's of Greewich Village. Live jazz Sun. nights. 6" pizza $3, pasta specials $7. $3 minimum. Open Tues.-Thurs. 11:30am-9pm, Fri.-Sat. 11:30am-10pm.

Doobee's, Church and Commercial St. (753-5044). Delicious sandwiches $3-4. Sidewalk tables, sunshine, harried pedestrians, 75¢ espresso, and $1.25 cappuccino will keep you singing. Shoobee doobee doo. Open Mon.-Fri. 7am-9pm, Sat. 9am-5pm.

Nanaimo Harbour Lights Restaurant, 1518 Stewart Ave. (753-6614). The owner, ex-NHL referee Lloyd Gilmour, is more than willing to "talk puck" with any interested party. Surf-and-turf entrees also let you face off with the salad bar ($9-12). Lunches $6. Open Mon.-Thurs. 11:30am-3pm and 5-9pm, Fri.-Sat. 11:30am-3pm and 5-10pm.

Sights

The **Nanaimo Centennial Museum,** 100 Cameron St. (753-1821), next to the bus terminal, illuminates all aspects and eras of Nanaimo history with fossilized remains of plants and animals, Coastal Salish masks and totems, and a full-scale walk-through model of a coal mine, as well as intimate detail about the explosion of 1897 that killed 148 workers. It particularly pays tribute to the contribution the imported coolie labor made to the community's vitality and the long struggle of Chinese-Canadians for equality. Not 300m from the musuem on the water's edge is the **Bastion.** Constructed by the Hudson's Bay Company as a storehouse and safehouse against Native attacks, the Bastion now houses a *museum.* A six-pound cannon discharges daily at noon. Both the museum and the Bastion are open daily 10am-5pm.

2½ km north of town is the **Nanaimo Art Gallery** (755-8790). Lacking a permanent collection, the Gallery features various transient exhibitions focusing on both local and international art and culture. Bus #6 will save you the 30-minute walk uphill. About one km further west up Harewood St. by the city reservoir is the Morrell Nature Sanctuary. The trails, flat and wonderfully tranquil, are a perfect place for getting lost.

Three kilometers south of town on Hwy. #1 (also Hwy. #19) is the **Petroglyph Park Provincial Park** (yes, that's really the name). Hundreds of generations of Salish Shamans have carved figures of various animals and mythical creatures into the soft sandstone. Rubbings can be made from concrete replicas at the interpretive center at the base of the trail leading to the petroglyphs.

Departure Bay washes onto a pleasant beach in the north end of town off Stewart Ave. **Kona Buds** (758-2911), right on the beach, rents sailboards, canoes, bicycles, jet skis, and wet suits for under $10 per hour. They also run a shop downtown at the corner of Commercial and Albert. (Open Mon.-Sat. 10:30am-5:30pm.) **Newcastle Island Provincial Park** has campsites for $8 (no hookups), pit toilets, and fantastic swimming beach. There's no auto access to the park, however, so unless you're feeling like Mark Spitz, you'll have to shell out the $3.50 (round-trip) for the ferry (runs every hour on the hour daily 10am-9pm). The park

The annual **Nanaimo Festival** (formerly Shakespeare Plus) presents plays about the city's history in late June and early July. All plays take place at Malaspina College; ticket prices range from $6-12. For reservations, contact the festival at P.O. Box 626, Nanaimo V9R 5L9 (754-7587), or stop by the office above the Travel Infocentre.

The week-long **Marine Festival** is held during the second week of July. Highlights include the Silly Boat Race and the renowned **Bathtub Race.** Bathers from all over the continent race porcelain tubs with monstrous outboards from Nanaimo to Vancouver across the 55km Georgia Strait. The organizer of this bizarre but beloved event is the **Loyal Nanaimo Bathtub Society,** P.O. Box 656, Nanaimo V9R 5L5 (753-7223). They hand out prizes to everyone who makes it across, and ceremoniously present the "Silver Plunger" trophy to the first tub that sinks. Go figure.

Port Alberni

Port Alberni is at the geographical heart of Vancouver Island. Though it is sometimes thought of as the used-car dealership capital of the world, salmon fishing, not used cars, provide the economic thrust for this small city of 20,000. This fact is, unfortunately, supported by the town's odor.

Practical Information

Tourist Information: Site 215, C-10, R.R. 2 Pt. Alberni V9Y 7L6 (724-6535).

Bus Service: Island Coach Lines, 5065 Southgate (724-1266), at Victoria Quay. Flag stop at the 7-11 much closer to town and motels (see Accommodations).

Transit: 723-3341. Terminal on 10th Ave. past the Echo Centre.

Medical Services: 723-2444.

Police: 723-2424.

Area Code: 804.

Accommodations and Camping

Redford Motor Inn, 3723 Redford St. (724-0121), at the jct. of Hwy. 4 and 4A by the 7-11. Cable TV, free local calls. Singles $36. Doubles $38.

Westbay Hotel (723-2811), 13km west on Hwy. 4. Harder to get to and baths are shared, but lower prices compensate. Singles $25. Doubles $30.

Somass Motel, 5279 River Rd. (724-3236). A motel is a motel is a motel. Singles $34. Doubles $39.

Lakeshore Campground (723-2030), on Sproat Lake. Showers, toilets, laundry. Sites $10; no hookups (but they're working on it—call ahead).

Dry Creek Park Public Campground, 4850 Argyle St., off 3rd Ave. (723-6011). 30 sites. Showers, flush toilets. Sites $10, electricity $1. Open May-Sept.

Food

Alberni Delicatessen, 4780 Tebo St. (723-6812), 5km south of the town center. A remarkably varied selection. Sandwiches from $5. Open Mon.-Sat. 10am-6pm.

Out to Lunch, 2966 3rd Ave. (724-6344) in the north end. Great stuff for 6 bucks.

Sights and Activities

The **Alberni Valley Museum** (723-2181), at the corner of 10th Ave. and Wallace St. in the Echo Center, has a better-than-average collection chronicling the central island Natives. Of particular interest are the interactive logging exhibits: if you've never wielded a logger's pike, here's your chance. The **Sproat Lake Provincial Park,** 8km north of town on Hwy. 4, features **petroglyphs** as well as the **Martin Mars Flying Tankers,** the largest pieces of airborne fire-fighting equipment in the world (on display when California isn't borrowing them).

Port Alberni's answer to "the Circus of the Stars" is its **NHL Salmon Derby,** held every Simcoe Day (the first Monday in August). NHL greats and not-so-greats raise money for local charity by hooking 30- to 60-pound salmon, instead of Wayne Gretsky.

Hornby Island

In the 1960s, large numbers of young Americans fled the draft, only to settle on quiet Hornby Island, one of the two small chunks of land off Vancouver's eastern coast, halfway between Nanaimo and Campbell River. Today, Hornby Island and her sister, **Denman,** comprise an interesting mélange of the descendants of pioneering families circa 1850 and hippie-holdovers who offer spiritual awareness readings and "grow their own." Living in a curious symbiosis, the two groups share a thinly-veiled disdain of tourists.

Practical Information

Tourist Information: Denman/Hornby Tourist Services, Denman Island V0R 1T0 (335-2293). On Hornby, go to the Post Office.

Ferries: BC Ferries, from Buckley Bay on Hwy. 19. 18 sailings daily. $7.50 with car, $3.50 walk-on.

Taxi: 335-0521.

Bike Rental: Zucchini Ocean Kayak Centre, at the Co-op (335-2033). Bikes $5 per hr., $20 per day. Kayak/windsurf $20 per 4 hr., $30 per day. Wetsuit $10 per 4 hr., $20 per day. Open daily 10am-6pm.

Ambulance: 338-9112.

Police: 338-6522.

Post Office: At the Co-op at the terminus of Central Rd. (335-1121), on the eastern shore of the island. Postal Code: V0R 1Z0.

Area Code: 604.

Orientation

Island Coach Lines has a flag stop at **Buckley Bay,** where the ferry docks. It's a 10-minute ride to Denman where you have to disembark and make the 11km trek across Denman to the docks for another 10-minute ride to Hornby. Ask around for a lift across, but make sure your hair is combed—islanders can be somewhat reticent. Once on Hornby, there are only two roads to worry about: **Shingle Spit Road** and **Central Road,** separated by the docks. Central Rd. extends to the eastern shore where all the "action" is. If you are without wheels, find a friendly face on the ferry—it's 15km away and there's no public transit.

Accomodations, Camping, and Food

If you plan on spending more than a day here, bring a tent and food. Although what the island does have to offer is enticing, the selection is extremely limited.

The Thatch 335-0136), right at the ferry docks. A versatile establishment—pub/restaurant/laundromat/hotel/campground. The pub fare is standard but reasonably priced; the restaurant has breakfast plates from $4 (restaurant open daily 9am-9pm). Rooms at the hotel run $65 per night for doubles (there are no singles). Campsites $12 per night, $15 with hookups.

Tribune Bay (335-2359), at the Co-op at the eastern end of Central Rd. 120 sites, $13.50 per night. 8 sites with hookups, $16. Right on the wonderful Tribune Bay. Coin-op showers. Open Easter-Labor Day.

The Joy of Cooking (335-1487), by the Co-op. Serves up BC-style sushi in the form of Nori Rolls: smoked salmon, rice and other stuff wrapped in seaweed ($2.50). More pedestrian fare also prepared with glee. Open daily 8:30am-8pm.

The Co-op (335-1121), at the end of Central Rd. by Tribune Bay. The eye of Hurricane Hornby. Well-stocked grocery store with a deli. Open daily 9am-7pm.

Sights and Attractions

With its light traffic and paved roads, consider acquainting yourself with Hornby Island on bike (for bike rental, see Practical Information). Low tide at **Tribune Bay** and **Whaling Station Bay** uncovers over 300m of the cleanest, finest sand on Vancouver Island. Tribune, lapping at the base of Central Rd., is the more accessible of the two. Whaling Station Bay is about 5km farther north.

On the way to Whaling Station Bay from Tribune Bay is Helliwell Rd., the cutoff for **Helliwell Provincial Park**. A well-groomed trail takes you on a one-hour hike through old-growth forest to bluffs overlooking the ocean. Cormorants are everywhere, diving like lawn-darts into the ocean to surface moments later with trophy-quality fish, and bald eagles cruise amidst the sea breezes.

The **Hornby Festival** draws musicians, comedians, and artists from all over Canada for ten days in early August. Call the Hornby Festival Society at 335-2734 for details.

Campbell River

Although 67km south of the acknowledged boundary of North Island, Campbell River is close enough in spirit to be included among its northern neighbors. Its tourist-based economy is geared toward fishing, skiing, kayaking, scuba diving, and mountain climbing.

The promise of a "Northwest Passage," the fabled Arctic waterway connecting the Atlantic and Pacific Oceans, brought Captain George Vancouver up the Discovery Passage in 1792. News of the enormous salmon regularly plucked from the river by Cape Mudge Natives sparked a tremendous influx of sport fishermen at the turn of the century. And today every pamphlet, billboard, and menu proclaims Campbell River "Salmon Capital of the World."

Practical Information and Orientation

Visitor Information: Travel Infocentre, 923 Island Hwy. (286-0764). A paragon among island Infocentres. Open daily 8am-8pm; in winter Mon.-Fri. 9am-5pm, Sat. 10am-5pm.

Buses: Island Coach Lines (287-7151), corner of 13th and Cedar, in the NE margin of town. To Port Hardy (1 per day, $32.55) and Victoria (5 per day, $25.60).

Transit: 287-7433. The 4 different lines converge downtown at the Tyee Plaza. Fare 65¢.

Car Rental: Rent-A-Wreck, 1355 N. Island Hwy. (287-8353), in the Esso station. Must be 19 with major credit card. Chevettes $23 per day plus 15¢ per km. Open Mon.-Fri. 8am-5:30pm, Sat. 8am-5pm.

Taxi: Al's Taxi (287-7666).

Laundromat: Campbell River Laundromat and Dry Cleaning, 1231 Island Hwy. (286-6562), in the Tyee Mall. Open Mon.-Fri. 9am-10pm, Sat. 9am-6pm.

Women's Center: 10th and Cedar (287-3044).

Crisis Line: 287-7743.

Hospital: 375 2nd Ave. (286-1155).

Police: corner of Alder and St. Anne's, (286-6221).

Post Office: on Beech, at Alder. Open Mon.-Fri. 8:30am-5:30pm. Postal Code: V9W 4Z8.

Area Code: 604.

Campbell River is a crossroads in the middle of Vancouver Island's eastern coast, 240km equidistant from Victoria at the southern tip and Port Hardy at the northern end. Highway 19, the town's principal artery, runs along the waterfront.

Accommodations and Camping

You may be hard pressed to find a room under $30 during the height of the July fishing season. The few campgrounds in town are overpriced and aesthetically bleak. Stop at any one of the cheaper spots a few kilometers west on Hwy. 28 or north and south on Hwy. 19.

Vista Del Mar, 920 S. Island Hwy. (923-4271). If you're coming in from the south, ask the bus driver to drop you off here. From the north, take transit bus #3, Highway, to Ocean Grove. Overlooks the briny waters of Georgia Stait. Well-maintained, with plenty of amenities for fisherfolk—boat ramp, fishing guides, and a freezer for the day's catch. Singles $34. Doubles $40.

Willow Point Bed & Breakfast, 2460 S. Island Hwy. (923-1086). Conservative atmosphere with tidy rooms. Singles from $35. Doubles from $40. Reservations necessary.

Friendship Inn Motel and RV Park, 3900 N. Island Hwy. (287-9591). An adequately appointed amalgam of hotel and campgrounds. Rooms include full bath and telephone. Singles $32. Doubles $38. Campground with hot showers (25¢ per 9 min.); RVs only. 28 sites with full hookup $14.

Parkside Campground (287-3113), 5km west of Campbell River on Hwy. 28. Appealing wooded sites in private, quiet surroundings. Free hot showers in clean bathrooms; laundromat. Sites $10, full hookups $15.

Food

If your angle on the angling turned out somewhat obtuse, you can buy what you need at **Overwaited Food and Drugs** at 13th and Elm. (Open daily 9am-9pm.) For a town of its size, Campbell River has disappointingly few innovative eateries, and fast-food joints litter the highway. Look for a place that serves the area's obvious specialty: **fresh baked salmon.**

Café California, 969 Alder St. (287-7999). Commodifies Mexican food, but its varied menu of filling entrees includes the "catch of the day." Lunch entrees around $6. Open Mon.-Thurs. 11am-10pm, Fri.-Sat. 11am-11pm, Sun. 4:30-9pm.

Del's Burgers, 1423 N. Island Hwy. 31 shades of milkshake ($1.50) liven up an otherwise unexceptional burger shack right out of *Happy Days.* Open daily 8am-midnight; in winter 9am-10pm.

Royal Coachman Neighbourhood Pub, 84 Dogwood St. (286-0231). Dartboards and 13 types of draught make this a fun place to be. Pub-fare lunches from $5. Open daily 11am-midnight.

Susi's Seafood, 560 11th Ave. (287-2457), off Hwy. 19. Rest assured that your seafood will be fresh—you can watch your shellfish squirm in the salt-water tanks before their corpses are laid to banquet at your behest. Take-out only; grab a crab ($3.75 per lb.) or clasp some clams ($2.25 per lb.) and have a cookout elsewhere. Open daily 10am-6pm.

Sights and Activities

Plenty of 15-kilo Tyee salmon hop off the hooks annually in Campbell's waters. You can shell out a small fortune (well, at least $50) paying for guides and charters, but amateur fishermen reap deep-sea prizes from the new **Discovery Pier** (fishing charge $1) in Campbell Harbor. The pier has 200m of boardwalk planks and an artificial, underwater reef built to attract astigmatic fish. Attendant fishermen rent full outfits for under $15.

National Geographic once praised Campbell River's **scuba diving** as "second only to the Red Sea." Experienced divers should not miss out on the aquatic delights, especially the octopi that wave hello frequently during night dives. A few stores along the waterfront offer outrageously expensive rentals.

Nearby **Strathcona Provincial Park** is a veritable varicose vein network of hiking trails, ranging from short strolls to challenging overnight routes. These are all described in a free Strathcona pamplet available at the Infocentre. The most convenient place to embark on a hike is the Ironwood Mall, origin of **Nunns Creek Park Trail,** a short, serene walk not connected to Strathcona Park.

No visit to the self-proclaimed "Salmon Capital of the World" would be complete without the requisite **Salmon Hatchery Tour** (287-9564), on the Quinsam River, a seven-km walk or drive from town (no public buses venture upstream to the hatchery). An audio-visual display and live viewing introduce you to happy little fingerlings that one day will be entrees or trophies. (Open daily 8am-4pm.)

One hundred seventy-one km north of Campbell River up Hwy. 19 is the town of **Sayward** whose main (only) claim to fame is the **Valley of 1000 Faces** (282-3303). Inside this five-acre enclosure lurks a logger's nightmare: 1000 neatly cut logs, each slab of wood with a face painted on it. The park also displays *the* Sasquatch, a half-man/half-ape creation (kids may be a bit leery). The entire park was created by an elderly Native woman named Hetty. (Open May 1-Sept. 1; donations only.)

Port Hardy

Port Hardy is in a certain sense the modern Canadian equivalent of Liverpool. The unassuming town was completely content to be a quiet logging and fishing community until the BC ferry established the city as the drop-off point for visitors heading south from upper BC and Alaska. Virtually overnight, Port Hardy etched a name for itself as a major transportation port, evidenced by the city welcome sign, carved out with a chainsaw. Unlike Liverpool, it remains a mild coastal town, an excellent place for ferry passengers to spend the night.

Practical Information and Orientation

Visitor Information: Travel Infocentre, 7250 Market St. (949-7622). Take Hardy Bay Rd. off Hwy. 19 to Market St. Pick up a restaurant menu guide and tour maps. Open daily 9am-6pm.

Buses: Island Coach Lines, Market St. (949-7532), across from the Travel Infocentre. To Victoria 1 per day, one way $50.75.

Ferry: BC Ferry (949-6722), 3km south at Bear Creek. Service between Prince Rupert and Port Hardy every other day (one way $56).

Taxi: North Island Taxi, 949-8800.

Laundromat: Payless Gas Co., on Granville St. (949-2366). Open 24 hr.

Crisis: 949-6033.

Coast Guard: 974-5413.

Hospital: 949-6161.

Emergency: Police, 7355 Columbia (949-6335). **Ambulance:** 949-7224.

Postal Code: V09 2P0.

Area Code: 604.

On the northern tip of Vancouver Island, Port Hardy serves as the southern terminus for ferries carrying passengers down from Prince Rupert and Alaska. Highway 19 runs south from the center of downtown.

Accommodations and Camping

Despite the fact that many of the people arriving via ferry bring along RVs, the demand for hotel rooms is just as high as you would expect in any port town.

Airport Inn (949-9424). Take Byng Rd. off Hwy. 19 toward the airport. Once the cheapest rooms in town. Cable TV. Restaurant downstairs. Singles $46. Doubles $48. Kitchen units $6.

Pioneer Inn (949-7271), off Hwy. 19 on Old Island Hwy., 2km south of town. Next to a salmon hatchery, if that makes any difference. Laundry facilities and a dining room. Singles $42. Doubles $48.

Quatse River Campground, Hardy Bay Rd. (949-2395), across from the Pioneer Inn. Quiet, wooded setting with private sites. Toilets come in a choice of flush and pit. Showers and laundromat. Sites $8, full hookups $11.

Wildwoods Campsite (949-6753), on the road from the ferry, within walking distance of the terminal. Comfortable sites lined with pine needles. Plenty of spaces crammed into a relatively small forest area, but well-designed to afford maximum privacy. Hot showers, but expect a line in the morning. Sites $8, with car $10, with hookup $12.

Food

Port Hardy maintains its excellent cuisine in the face of growing ferry traffic. A brigade of superb budget restaurants serve dinners for under $10.

Brigg Seafood House (949-6532), at Market and Granville St. Seafood served in a large old house. Their "you catch it, we'll cook it" service can get you dinner with all the trimmings for $5. Children's menu available. Bistro dinners from $7. Open Sun.-Wed. 11:30am-3pm and 5-10pm, Thurs.-Sat. 11:30am-3pm and 5:30-11pm.

Sportsman's Steak & Seafood House (949-7811), on Market St. across from the Infocentre. Lunch sandwiches stuffed with meat from $4. Salad bar is well-stocked. Surf-and-turf entrees under $9. Open daily 11:30am-2pm and 5pm-"whenever."

Carrot's (949-8525), at the Best Western on Granville St. Tons of pasta dishes in the $6 range. Spicy dijon chicken $9. Open daily 8am-10:30pm.

Snuggles (949-7575), at the Pioneer Inn on Old Island Hwy. Must be 19. A good place to bring a paramour without having to hock your mom's wedding ring. Live entertainment and live cooking; watch the chef whip up your meal. Salads $4-6, entrees from $11. Open Mon.-Thurs. 5:30-10pm, Fri.-Sun. 5-11pm.

Sights

For a peek at vignettes of city history, head to the **Port Hardy Museum,** 7110 Market St. (949-8143), near the Infocentre. The small library/museum holds early Native artifacts and some yellowed photographs; not very heady stuff, but it's free. Port Hardy's most prized possession is the **Welcome to Port Hardy** sign on Market St. It was carved with the sculptor's ultimate chisel: a chainsaw. After you've snapped a picture of yourself in front of this bewilderingly overrated post, stroll along the seawall to absorb the town's coastal beauty.

Port McNeill, 65km south of Port Hardy on Hwy. 19, runs fishing charters booked through the Travel Infocentre along the highway or at the ferry dock booth. **Bud's Charters** (956-4781) has a half-day, four-person excursion for relatively low prices. The **BC Ferry** (956-4533) sells rides to nearby **Alert Bay** (40 min.), a renowned area for spotting pods of orcas (killer whales). One of the world's largest totem poles (58m) bestrides the nearby Nimpkish Natives' reserve. For more information on the small village, stop by the **Travel Infocentre** on Fir St. (974-5213).

Vancouver

Canada's third largest city (after Toronto and Montreal), comes as a pleasant surprise to the jaded metropolis-hopping traveler. Tune out the language, and Vancouver could be a North American Sweden or Switzerland: the transit system is immaculately efficient, the sidewalks are largely spotless, and even the seediest areas are basically safe. Although you will find some fantastically dingy back alleys, the

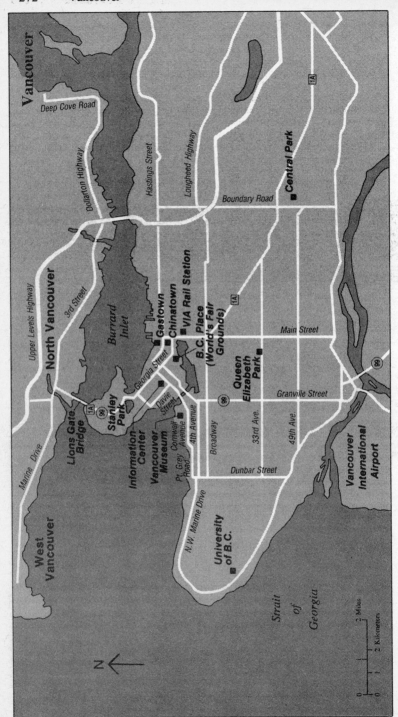

streets are broad, clearly laid out, and well marked. Vancouver's citizens display a rare humility, at times approaching naïvete—traits rare in a city this size.

Vancouver is fast joining the post-industrial age: the unemployment rate has fallen by half in recent years, and electronics and international finance have largely replaced timber and mining as the city's economic base. A growing wave of Chinese immigration, largely from Hong Kong, is turning Vancouver increasingly towards the Far East; cynics say their city is becoming "Hongcouver," and predict racial tensions will rise. To others, Vancouver is the very model of a modern multi-ethnic metropolis. The question is still up in the air, but Mayor Gordon Campbell promises that his city will "not become like a city in the United States." (Well!)

The range of things to do here is astounding. You can go for nature walks among 1,000 year old virgin timber stands, wind-surf, take in a modern art exposition or get wrapped up in a movie at the most technologically advanced movie theatre in the world—and never leave downtown. Filled with beaches, parks, and endless amounts of fun and uplifting activities, the cultural vortex that is Vancouver has swallowed hordes of unsuspecting vacationers. If you insist on purchasing a return trip ticket in advance, be sure to allot yourself ample time to fully appreciate this marvelous city.

Practical Information

Visitor Information: Travel Infocentre, 1055 Dunsmuir St. (683-2000), near Burrard St., in the West End. Help with tickets, reservations, and tours. Open daily 8am-6pm. If the racks of literature don't answer all your questions, the staff certainly will.

BC Transit Information Centre: 261-5100. Fare $1.25, exact change. Day passes ($3.25) available at all 7-11 stores or Waterfront stop.

Parks and Recreation Board: 681-1141.

The Gray Line: 900 W. Georgia St. (681-8687), in Hotel Vancouver. Expensive but worthwhile city tours with a number of package options. Basic tours leave daily and last 3½ hr. ($29.50, children $15). Reservations required.

Taxis: Yellow Cab, 681-3311. **Vancouver Taxi,** 255-5111.

Car Rental: Rent-A-Wreck, 180 W. Georgia St. (688-0001), in the West End, and 1085 Kingsway (876-5629), at Glen. From $35 per day; 150km free plus 15¢ per additional km. Must be 19 with credit card. Open Mon.-Fri. 8am-9pm, Sat. 8am-6pm, Sun. 9am-5pm. Kingsway location open Mon.-Fri. 8am-7pm, Sat. 9am-5pm.

Bike Rental: Bayshore, 745 Denman St. (688-2453). Convenient to Stanley Park. Practically new bikes $5.60 per hr., $20 per day.

Road Conditions: 660-9775. 24 hr.

Bicycling Association of BC: 1367 W. Broadway, #332, Vancouver V6H 4H9 (731-7433 events line, 737-3034 office). One-page cycling map of city; more detailed maps available through the mail. Open Mon.-Fri. 9am-5pm.

Camping Equipment Rentals: Sports Rent, 2560 Arbutus St. (733-1605), at Broadway. Take bus #10 or 14 from Granville Mall. Backpacks ($8 per day, $20 per week), 2-person tents ($15 per day, $40 per week), and every other kind of camping or sports equipment imaginable. Open Mon.-Wed. 8am-7pm, Thurs.-Sun. 8am-9pm.

Scuba Rentals: The Diving Locker, 2745 W. 4th Ave. (736-2681). Complete outfit $50 first day, $25 every day thereafter. Open Mon.-Thurs. 9:30am-7pm, Fri. 9:30am-8pm, Sat. 9:30am-7pm.

Public Library: 750 Burrard St. (665-2280 or 665-2276 for a recording), at Robson St., downtown. Open Mon.-Thurs. 9:30am-9:30pm, Fri.-Sat. 9:30am-6pm; Oct.-March also Sun. 1-5pm.

Arts Hotline: 684-2787.

Weather: 666-1087.

Distress Line: Vancouver Crisis Center, 733-4111. 24 hr.

Women's Services: Rape Crisis Center, 875-6011. **Rape Relief Center,** 872-8212. Both 24 hr. **Battered Women's Support Services,** 2515 Burrard St. (734-1574). Open Mon. and Fri. 10am-2pm, Tues.-Thurs. 10am-4pm. 24 hr. **Emergency:** 872-7774. **Women's Resource Center,** 1144 Robson St. (685-3934), in the West End between Thurlow and Bute St. Open Mon.-Fri. 10am-2pm; in winter Mon.-Fri. 10am-4pm, Sat. 1-4pm.

Senior Citizens Information and Support Network: 531-2320 or 531-2425.

BC Coalition of the Disabled: 875-0188.

Gay and Lesbian Switchboard: 1-1170 Bute St., 684-6869. Counseling and information. Open Mon.-Fri. 7-10pm, Sat.-Sun. 4-10pm.

AIDS Vancouver: 872-6652.

Poison Control: 682-5050.

Pharmacy: Shoppers Drug Mart, 279 Broadway at Carnarvon (733-9128). Open daily 9am-9pm.

Police: Main and Powell (665-3321).

Post Office: Main branch, 349 W. Georgia St. (662-5725). Open Mon.-Fri. 8am-5:30pm. Postal Code: V6B 3P7.

Area Code: 604.

Getting There

Vancouver is located in the southwestern corner of the British Columbia mainland, across the Georgia Strait from Vancouver Island and the city of Victoria. **Vancouver International Airport,** on Sea Island 11km south of the city center, makes connections to major cities on the West Coast and around the world. To reach downtown from the airport, take Metro Transit bus #100 to 70th Ave. Transfer there to bus #20, which arrives downtown heading north on the Granville Mall. The private **Airport Express** bus leaves from airport level 2 every 15 minutes between 6:15am and 12:30am and heads for downtown hotels and the Greyhound station ($6.75 per person; 266-0376 for info).

Greyhound makes several runs daily between Seattle and Vancouver. The downtown Greyhound station gives easy access to the city's transit system. Catch bus #11 heading north on Nanaimo St.; it travels through Vancouver's Chinatown, arriving downtown along Pender St. heading west. **VIA Rail** runs one train per day on the famed Trans-Canada Railway, bound for the eastern part of the continent. **BC Rail's** station in North Vancouver launches trains toward northern British Columbia. **BC Ferries** regularly connects the city of Vancouver to Vancouver Island and the Gulf Islands. Ferries leave from the Tsawwassen terminal, 25km south of the city center. To reach downtown from the ferry terminal, take bus #640 to the Ladner Exchange and transfer there to bus #601. The bus arrives downtown on Seymour St.

Greyhound: 150 Dunsmuir St. (662-3222), downtown at Beatty St. Service to the south and across Canada. Open daily 5:30am-midnight. To: Calgary (4 per day, $73), Banff (4 per day, $67.35), Jasper (3 per day, $63.20); and Seattle (7 per day, US$20, CDN$23).

Pacific Coach Lines: 150 Dunsmuir St. (662-3222). Serves southern BC, including Vancouver Island, in conjunction with Greyhound. To Victoria $16.50, including ferry.

VIA Rail: 1150 Station St. (1-800-665-8630 or 669-3050). To Jasper (3 per week, $63.50), Edmonton (3 per week, $136). Open Mon. and Sat. 7:30am-9:30pm; Tues.-Wed., Sun. 7:30am-3pm; Thurs. 3pm-9:30pm; Fri. 10am-5:30pm.

BC Rail: 1311 W. 1st St. (984-5246), just over the Lions Gate Bridge in North Vancouver. Take the SeaBus downtown to North Vancouver, then bus #239 west. Daily to: Garibaldi

($9), Williams Lake ($44.50), Prince George ($61), Whistler ($11), and points north. Open daily 7am-9pm.

BC Ferries: to Victoria, the Gulf Islands, Sunshine Coast, Inside Passage, Prince Rupert, and the Queen Charlotte Islands. General information 669-1211, recorded information 685-1021, Tsawwassen ferry terminal 943-9331. Mainland to Vancouver Island ($4.75, car and driver $21.75, motorcycle and driver $12.75, bicycle and rider $6.85; ages 5-11 ½-price). The terminal serving Victoria is actually located in Swartz Bay, north of Victoria. (See Getting There in Victoria for more information.)

Bicyclists will find many excellent routes both in the city itself and outside it—in the Fraser River Canyon, along the shore of Georgia Bay, on the Gulf Islands, and on Vancouver Island. The Bicycling Association of BC (see Practical Information) can recommend specific trips, and Tourism BC publishes a thorough pamphlet on bicycling. Note that the George Massey Tunnel on Hwy. 99, under the Fraser River, is closed to bicycles.

Getting Around

Vancouver's various neighborhoods are better fused than in the past, when marsh waters connecting False Creek with Burrard Inlet would detach the downtown peninsula at high tide. Landfill has brought residents closer together, but the profusion of waterways can still confuse the most diligent map readers. Most of the city's attractions concentrate on the city center peninsula and the larger rhino-snout-shaped land to the south. The residential area of the city center peninsula, bounded by downtown to the east and Stanley Park to the west, is known as the **West End.** The western portion of the southern peninsula from around Alma Ave. west to the University of British Columbia campus is **Point Grey,** while the central area on the same peninsula from the Granville Bridge to Alma Ave. is "Kitsilano," or "Kits" to the cognoscenti.

Don't try to make any distinction between streets and avenues in Vancouver—there is no apparent standard, and even maps usually omit the surname. The one exception to this madness is the numbered arterials, which are always *avenues* in Vancouver proper (running east-west), and always *streets* in North Vancouver (running every which way but loose). Downtown, private vehicles are not allowed on Granville between Nelson and West Pender St., which is referred to as the **Granville Mall.** Both **Chinatown,** stretching east-west between Hastings and East Pender from Garrel Ave. to Gore Ave., and **Gastown,** on Alexander as it runs into Water St., are easily reached on foot from the Granville Mall.

Vancouver's **Metro Transit** covers most of the city and suburbs, with direct transport or easy connecting transit to the city's points of departure: Tsawwassen, Horseshoe Bay, and the airport (see Getting There for specific lines). Often one bus will run along a route in one direction while a bus of a different number will run in the other direction; ask a local or bus driver for assistance.

If you have a car, consider using **Park 'n' Ride** from New Westminster to circumvent the city's perpetual rush hour. Exit Hwy. 1 at New Westminster and follow signs for the Pattullo Bridge. Just over the bridge, you'll see signs for the Park 'n' Ride lot to your right, between Scott Rd. and 110th Ave. A fare bus will be waiting where you can purchase one-way tickets for the bus, SkyTrain, and SeaBus, or one-day passes for $3.50. Parking is free, and taking the SkyTrain downtown is faster than driving.

You can ride in Metro Transit's central zone one way for $1.25 (senior citizens and ages 5-11 65¢) at all times. During peak hours (6:30-9:30am and 3-6:30pm), it costs $1.75 (senior citizens and ages 5-11 90¢) to travel two zones. During off-peak hours, passengers pay only the one-zone price. Day-passes are $3.50, and transfers are free. Single fares, passes, and transfers are also good for the SeaBus and SkyTrain (running southeast from downtown to New Westminster). Timetables are available at 7-11 stores, public libraries, city halls, community centers, and the Vancouver Travel Infocentre (see Practical Information). To retrieve **lost property** in

Metro Transit's possession, call 682-7887 (Mon.-Fri. 9am-5pm); otherwise stop by the lost property office at 611 W. Hastings, in the Harbour Centre Building.

Metro Transit's **SeaBus** operates from the Granville Waterfront Station, at the foot of Granville St. in downtown Vancouver, to the Lonsdale Quay at the foot of Lonsdale Ave. in North Vancouver. The fares are the same as one-zone bus fares, and all transfers and passes are accepted. While waiting, study *The Buzzer,* Metro Transit's weekly pamphlet on transit updates and community events, available wherever transit timetables are distributed.

Driving in car-crazy Vancouver is a serious hassle. Rush hour begins at dawn and ends at dusk. Beware of the 3-6pm restrictions on left turns and street parking. If you can find no parking at street level, look for underground lots and be prepared to pay stratospheric prices. (Try the lot below Pacific Centre at Howe and W. Georgia St., sometimes called "Garageland.") One-way streets are a curse throughout the city, but many maps have arrows indicating directions. The free Tourism BC maps don't cover the area outside the city center in detail; purchase the larger-scale street map, available from the Infocentre for $2.

Accommodations

Greater Vancouver is a rabbit warren of bed and breakfast accommodations. Cheaper than their American equivalents (but still not as affordable as English B&Bs), these private homes are usually comfortable and have personable proprietors. Rates average about $25 for singles and $35 for doubles. The visitors bureau has a four-page list of B&Bs. Several private agencies also match travelers with B&Bs, usually for a fee; get in touch with **Town and Country Bed and Breakfast** (731-5942) or **Best Canadian** (738-7207). Always call for reservations at least two days in advance.

Vancouver International Hostel (IYHF), 1515 Discovery St. (224-3208), in Point Grey on Jericho Beach. Turn north off 4th Ave., following the signs for Marine Dr., or take bus #4 from Granville St. downtown. Comely location on beach and park, with a superlative view of the city from False Creek. Over 350 beds, massive dorm rooms, good cooking facilities, and occasional opportunities to spend a few hours cleaning in exchange for a room. TV room inside, and plenty of grassy space outside for Ravi to practice his Chippendale's dance moves. Three-day limit enforced in summer, but flexible otherwise. Eight family rooms. Midnight curfew strictly enforced, as is the lights-out rule for the entire building. Laundry facilities. Rents top quality mountain bikes for $16 per day. Members $10, nonmembers $12. Bedding $10.

Globetrotter's Inn, 170 W. Esplanade in North Vancouver (988-5141). Could use a vacuuming, but much nicer than Vincent's (see below) and as close to downtown as the hostel. Take the SeaBus to Lonsdale Quay, then walk 1 block east to W. Esplanade and Chesterfield. Kitchen facilities and shared baths. $12 per night, private singles $25. Doubles $30.

Vincent's Backpackers Hostel, 927 Main St. (682-2441), next to the VIA Rail station, under a big green store called "The Source." Take bus #3 (Main St.) or #8 (Fraser). Not quite as clean or as structured as the IYHF hostel, but more colorful, cheaper, and within walking distance of downtown. Kitchen, fridge, TV, stereo, and the music of Greyhounds gleefully revving their engines until late at night. One washer, one dryer. Rents mountain bikes for $8 per day. Office open 8am-midnight. Check in before noon for best shot at a bed. Shared rooms $8. Singles with shared bath $16. Doubles with shared bath $20.

YWCA, 580 Burrard St. (800-633-1424 or 662-8188), downtown at Dunsmuir, 7 blocks from the bus depot. Women, male-female couples, families, and men (when the YMCA's full). Recently remodeled and clean, but expensive. High-quality sports facilities for female guests over 15 years old (free). Kitchens on every other floor, and cafeteria in basement. Staff on duty 24 hr., but building locked at midnight—buzz for entry. No male visitors ordinarily allowed upstairs. Some singles smaller than others, so ask to see a few before choosing. Four-week max. stay. Singles $34. Doubles $49. Extra bed $10. 10% discount for YWCA members, senior citizens, and groups. Weekly and monthly rates available Sept.-June.

YMCA, 955 Burrard St. (681-0221), between Smithe and Nelson, 4 blocks south of the YWCA. Newly renovated. Concerned staff on duty 24 hours. Pool, gymnasiums, ball courts, and weight rooms (free). All rooms have shared washrooms and showers. Cafeteria open

Mon.-Fri. 7am-4pm, Sat. 8am-2pm. Singles $27. Doubles $46. Weekly and monthly rates available Oct.-April.

Salvation Army, 500 Dunsmuir St. (681-3405). Men only. Dorm beds $8 per night. Check-in 5-11pm, but get there before 5:30pm. No reservations. 11pm curfew.

Dufferin Hotel, 900 Seymour St. (683-4251), at Smithe. Clean rooms, color TV. Safer than many other hotels in the area. No visitors after 11:30pm. Check-out 1pm. Singles $50. Doubles $60. $5 less in winter.

Nelson Place, 1006 Granville (681-6341), at Nelson St., 1 block from the Dufferin. Borders on Vancouver's small and tame red-light district. Great access to downtown. Small but tame rooms with TV and bath. Singles $40. Doubles $45. $5 less in winter.

Sylvia Hotel, 1154 Gilford St. (681-9321), 2 blocks from Stanley Park in a quiet residential neighborhood. Magnificent singles $40. Doubles $48. Additional cots $8. Reservations recommended.

University of British Columbia Conference Centre, 5959 Student Union Mall, Walter Gage Residence (228-2963), at the end of Vancouver's largest peninsula. Take bus #4 or 10 from the Granville Mall. Draws swarms of conventioneers in summer. Check-in after 2pm. Singles $28. Doubles $45. $5 per additional person.

Simon Fraser University, in Burnaby (291-4503), 20km east of the city center. 190 singles and 9 doubles available May-Aug. Shared bath. Call Mon.-Fri. 8:30am-4:30pm. Check-in 2-4:30pm. Check-out 11am. Singles $17. Doubles $37. With linen and towels: singles $26, twins $42. No reservations necessary.

Horseshoe Bay Motel, 6396 Bruce St., in W. Vancouver/Horseshoe Bay (921-7454). Perfect location for people using the BC Ferry. Showers with baths. Singles $60. Doubles $65. In winter singles $45, doubles $50. Kitchen units $10.

Camping

Greater Vancouver has few public campgrounds; one must resort to expensive, private ones. The visitors bureau has a complete list of campgrounds outside Vancouver; many are for RVs only. **Sports Rent** offers tents (see Practical Information), but the cost makes it more sensible to spend the money on a bed at a hostel. The town of **White Rock,** 30 minutes southeast of Vancouver, has campgrounds that allow tents. Take bus #351 from Howe St. downtown.

Richmond RV Park, 6200 River Rd. (270-7878), near Holly Bridge in Richmond. Take Hwy. 99 to Westminster Hwy., then follow the signs. Unquestionably the best deal within 15km of downtown. Sites offer little privacy, but the great showers and soothing staff are sure to wash your cares away. Sites $13, with hookups $16-18. Open April-Oct.

Hazelmere RV Park and Campground, 18843 8th Ave. (538-1167), in Surrey. Off Hwy. 99A, head east on 8th Ave. Quiet sites on the Campbell River with beach access. Sites $14, with hookups $16. Each additional adult $2. Showers 25¢.

ParkCanada, 4799 Hwy. 17 (943-5811), in Delta, about 30km south of downtown Vancouver. Take Hwy. 99 south to Tsawwassen Ferry Terminal Rd., then go east for 2.5km. The campground, located next to a giant waterslide park, has flush toilets and free showers, though the lines may be long. Sites $12, with hookups $18.

Dogwood Campground, 15151 112th St. (583-5585), 31km east on Hwy. 1 in Surrey. Flush toilets and pay showers. Sites $14, with hookups $20.

Food

Steer clear of restaurants hawking "Canadian cuisine"—nobody really knows what Canadian cuisine is. The city's best offerings are the diverse ethnic gastro-centres and the older natural-foods culinaria. In North America, Vancouver's **Chinatown** is second in size only to San Francisco's. The East Indian neighborhoods along Main, Fraser, and 49th St. synthesize the spicy dishes of the subcontinent. Groceries, shops, and restaurants cluster around E. Pender and Gore St.

Eateries in the **West End** and **Gastown** compete to extract the highest prices in the city; the former caters to executives with expense accounts, while the latter suckers tourists fresh off the cruise ships. Many of the greasy spoons along Davie and Denman St. stay open late or around the clock. Near the IYHF hostel, **Buy-Low Foods** (597-9122), in Jericho Village at the corner of 4th and Alma, will help keep costs down. (Open Mon.-Fri. 9am-9pm.)

The **Granville Island Market,** under the Granville Bridge, off W. 4th Ave. across False Creek from downtown, intersperses trendy shops, art galleries, and restaurants with countless produce stands selling local and imported fruits and vegetables. Take one of the many buses that run south on Granville and cross the Granville Bridge; get off at W. 4th St. and walk 6 blocks back down the hill. Otherwise, stay on the bus to Broadway and Granville Exchange and change to bus #51; it will take you directly to the island. The range of delicacies offered by the stalls at the north end of the island will blow your mind. Slurp cherry-papaya yogurt soup (from an edible sugar waffle bowl), indulge in kosher-style cheese blintzes and potato knishes, or pick up some duck or shrimp stock to take back to the hostel's stew pot. The bakeries also sell day-old bread and bagels at half-price. Picnicking sparks spontaneously in the parks, patios, and walkways that surround the market. (Market complex open daily 9am-6pm; Labor Day-Victoria Day Tues.-Sun. 9am-6pm.)

The Naam, 2724 W. 4th Ave. at Stephens (738-7151), in the Kits area. Take bus #4 or 7 from Granville. Vancouver's oldest natural-foods restaurant. With a fireplace and patio, the Naam is a truly delight. Tofu-nut-beet burgers ($5), spinach enchiladas ($8), and salad bar ($1.25 per 100g). Open 24 hr.

Dos Amigos Tapas, 3189 W. Broadway (731-5444), at Trutch. Not much Spanish ambience (it used to be a Swensen's), but the food is unadulterated. Order 3 or 4 dishes in true tapas tradition. Melon and smoked ham $3.75, marinated mushrooms $2.75, deep-fried squid $4. Open Tues.-Thurs. 11:30am-10:30pm, Fri.-Sat. 11:30am-11pm.

Dar Lebanon Palace, 678 W. Broadway (873-9511), at Heather. Take bus #10 or 14 from Granville. Dinners can be pricey (beef or lamb shish kabob with rice and veggies for $12), but lunches are more reasonable (pita sandwiches $5, stuffed grape leaves $4.50). Anything can be ordered to go. Open daily 10am-midnight.

The Sitar, 564 W. Broadway at Ash (879-4333). Take bus #10 or 14 from Granville. Standard Indian food in a standard Indian setting sometimes enhanced by the presence of pimply ex-MTV star Bryan Adams. *Tandoori* chicken $8, *mulligatawny* $2.50, full dinners $11. Open Mon.-Fri. 11:30am-10pm, Sat. noon-10pm, Sun. 4-10pm.

Singapore Restaurant, 546 W. Broadway (874-6161). Take bus #10 or 14 from Granville. The mix of Malaysian, Chinese, and Indian cuisine corresponds to the tangled demography of Singapore. The spartan surroundings are also redolent of Singapore. Fried noodles $5.50, prawns and ginger $9, beef or chicken *satay* $1 each. Open Mon.-Fri. 11am-2:30pm and 5-10pm, Sat. 11am-10pm, Sun. noon-10pm.

The Vegetable Patch, 1485 Broadway at Granville (738-5233). Veggie sandwich and soup $5. Open Mon.-Fri. 7:30am-4pm, Sat. 10am-4pm.

Bill Kee Restaurant, 8 W. Broadway (874-8522 or 879-3222). Take any bus to the Broadway and Granville Exchange, then bus #9 east on Broadway. Cleaner and more pleasant than most of the city's Chinese joints. Fantastic Cantonese food straight from Hong Kong. Most dishes $5-8.50. The wonton soup is a meal in itself ($2.25). Take-out and free delivery. Open Sun.-Thurs. 10:30am-2am, Fri.-Sat. 10:30am-3am.

The Flamingo, 3469 Fraser, north of 19th (877-1231). Vibrant and elegant. Regal Dim Sum ($2-6), but dinners only a Tai-pan could afford ($20-35).

Isadora's Cooperative Restaurant, 1540 Old Bridge Rd. (681-8816), on Granville Island, 1 block on your right immediately after entering the shopping area. This natural-food restaurant sends its profits to community service organizations. Sandwiches $7, dinner entrees $10, Bamfield burger made with filet of rock sole $6.25. Open Mon.-Thurs. 7am-10pm, Fri. 7am-11pm, Sat. 9am-11pm, Sun. 9am-10pm. Closed Mon. evenings in winter.

Sirloiner, 1517 Anderson St. on Granville Island (681-2127). If a tight budget has you craving animal protein, their $11 all-you-can-eat steamship round buffet should help. Open Mon.-Thurs. 11:30am-11pm, Fri.-Sat. 11:30am-midnight, Sun. 10:30am-10pm.

Frannie's Deli, 325 Cambie (685-2928), at W. Cordova St. In the heart of downtown, near Gastown. Doesn't look like much from outside (or inside), but your stomach is the better judge. A variety of sandwiches, including a $3 vegetarian. A gathering place for casually dressed Canadian capitalists. Open Mon.-Sat. 6:30am-6:30pm.

The Souvlaki Place, 1807 Morton (689-3064), at Denman St., near Stanley Park. A Greek establishment with an inspiring view of English Bay. *Souvlaki* $4.25; yogurt, honey, and pita $2.75. Open daily 11:30am-11pm.

The Green Door, 111 E. Pender St. (685-4194), in central Chinatown. Follow the garbage trucks down the alley off Columbia St. to find the hidden entrance. This legendary, wildly green establishment takes a prominent place in the copious annals of Vancouver hippie lore. Huge portions of slightly greasy Chinese seafood ($5.50). Open daily noon-10:30pm; Oct.-May Wed.-Mon. noon-10pm.

The Only Seafood Café, 20 E. Hastings St. (681-6546), at Carrall St. on the edge of China-town, within walking distance of downtown. Large portions of great seafood at decent prices, and a reputation that has spread throughout the Northwest. They've been around since 1912, and they *still* don't have a rest room. Fried halibut steak $9. Open Mon.-Thurs. 11am-9:30pm, Fri.-Sat. 11am-10pm.

A Taste of Jamaica, 941 Davie St. (683-3464), downtown. Come back to Jamaica with reggae, Jamaica posters, and red, green, and yellow seat covers. Ox-tail stew $6, goat or lamb curry $6. The homemade ginger beer is a local favorite ($1.50). Open Mon.-Sat. 11am-11pm, Sun. 5-11pm.

Stephos, 1124 Davie St. (683-2555). Much more elegant than The Souvlaki Place, and the prices are only slightly higher. Full *souvlaki* meal $6-10, hummus and pita $3.50, baklava $2.50. Open Mon.-Sat. 11:30am-11:30pm, Sun. 4:30-11:30pm.

Fresgo Inn, 1138 Davie St. (689-1332), in the West End between Bute and Thurlow St. Cafeteria-style food subjected to multiple heat lamps. Subs $6; 2 eggs, 2 pancakes, 2 sausages, and 2 strips of bacon $2.75. Open Mon.-Sat. 8am-3am, Sun. and holidays 9am-midnight.

Did's Pizza, 622 Davie St. (681-7368), near Seymour St. The clintele is as tame as the graffiti and loud music are wild. The pizza is excellent—thin crust, with just the right amount of semi-coagulated grease. $3 per slice. Open Mon.-Sat. 11am-3:30am, Sun. 5pm-1am.

Nick's Spaghetti House, 631 Commercial Dr. (254-5633), on the main drag of the Italian district. Take bus #20. An old restaurant under new management. Standard Italian food in a traditional atmosphere. The spaghetti is *magnifico* ($8.50). Open Mon.-Thurs. 11:30am-11pm, Fri. 11:30am-midnight, Sat. 4pm-midnight, Sun. 4-10pm.

Joe's Café, 1150 Commercial Dr. A unique cross between cappuccino bar and pool hall, Joe's is something of a nexus for students and artists living in the area. Absolutely nothing with any nutritional value here. Usual array of coffee drinks $1-2. Open daily 10am-midnight.

Arriva Ristorante, 1537 Commercial Dr. (251-1177), up the hill from Nick's, on the same bus line. Italian cuisine for that special night out. The interior is elegant but unpretentious, the service impeccable. Subtle spectrum of vegetarian, meat, and seafood sauces for the $8 pasta. Dinners $10-15. Open Mon.-Fri. 11:30am-3pm and 5-10:30pm, Sat.-Sun. 5-10:30pm.

Café Madeleine, 3763 W. 10th (224-5558), out toward UBC. Take bus #10 or 14. Pleasant and nuclear-free. The sandwiches, burgers, and big breakfasts (all $6) are overpriced but fill-ing. Open Sun.-Thurs. 8am-10pm, Fri.-Sat. 8am-midnight.

Sights and Activities

Vancouver has got a *lot* of sights and activities.

World's Fair Grounds and Downtown

Expo '86 was the first world's fair to be held in two different locations. The **main grounds,** between Granville and Main St., are now devolving into office space, hous-ing for senior citizens, and a cultural center. The Canada Pavilion, now called **Can-ada Place,** is about ½ km away and can be reached by SkyTrain from the main Expo site. The vast pavilion is a conventioneer's dream and an agoraphobe's nightmare; its roof, constructed to resemble gigantic sails, dominates the harbor. The shops and restaurants inside are outrageously expensive, but fun to look at. The promenades around the complex are terrific vantage points for snapshots of West Vancouver, or for gawking at one of the more than 200 luxury liners that dock here annually. There's a tour information booth in front of Canada Place (688-8687; open Mon.-Fri. 10am-5pm).

Also under the sails is the five-story **CN IMAX Theatre** (682-4629). The flat screen doesn't draw you in as much as a domed IMAX screen, but has unsurpassed image clarity with no peripheral distortion. So there. (Tickets $5.50-8. Open daily noon-9pm.)

The real big-screen star of Expo '86 is the **Omnimax Theatre,** part of the **Science World** complex at 1455 Quebec St. (687-7832) on the Main St. stop of the Sky Train. From asteroids to zephyrs, you will find yourself delightfully sucked into this celluloid wonderland. This 27m sphere is the largest, most technologically advanced theatre in the world. Science World also features less illusory hands-on exhibits for children. Admission to both is $10, or $6.50 for just Science World. Tickets for the Omnimax alone cannot be purchased. Call 875-6664 for show times.

One block south of Chinatown on Main St. at 777 S. Pacific Blvd. is **BC Place Stadium.** Vancouver's so-called "mushroom in bondage" is home to the Canadian Football League's BC Lions. Don't miss the **Terry Fox Memorial** at the entrance to the stadium, erected in honor of the Canadian hero who, after losing his leg to cancer, ran 3318 mi. across Canada to raise money for medical research. Because of his efforts, a nation of only 26 million people raised over $30 million (that's more than $1.15 per Canuck).

Newly renovated, the **Lookout!** at 555 W. Hastings St. (683-5684), offers fantastic 360° views of the city. It's expensive ($5, seniors $3) but your ticket is good for the whole day, so you can leave and come back for the romantic night skyline. Open daily 9am-10pm.

The **Vancouver Art Gallery,** 750 Hornby St. (682-5621), in Robson Sq., has a small but well-presented collection of classical and contemporary art and photography. British Columbian Emily Carr's surreal paintings of trees and totem poles are displayed in abundance, along with an entire floor devoted to the works of other Canadian artists. The Gallery compensates for its limited holdings with innovative exhibitions. Free tours are frequently given for large groups; just tag along. (Open Mon.-Wed. and Fri.-Sat. 10am-5pm, Thurs. 10am-9pm, Sun. noon-5pm. Admission $2.75, seniors and students $1.25. Free Thurs. 5-9pm.)

A few smaller, wackier museums are fun to visit. The **BC Sugar Museum,** 123 Rogers St. (253-1131), 1 block west of Clark Dr., at the foot of Rogers on Burrard Inlet, traces the zany history of one sugar company's development since its inception in 1890. The museum is full of old sugar-making equipment, plus goofy letters and photographs related to the industry and those involved in it. Phone ahead for groups larger than 5 people. (Open daily 9:30am-3:30pm. Free.) The **Beatles Museum,** 456 Seymour St. (685-8841), in RPM records at Pender St., is a Fab Four fanatic's fantasia. Since all the stuff's for sale, the place doesn't qualify as a real museum, but browsers are welcome and the curator tells some great stories. (Open Mon., Wed., and Sat. 10am-6pm, Thurs.-Fri. 10am-9pm, Sun. noon-5pm.)

Gastown and Chinatown

Gastown is a revitalized turn-of-the-century district viewed with disdain by most locals as an expensive tourist trap. The area is named for "Gassy Jack" Deighton, the glib con man who opened Vancouver's first saloon here in 1867. His statue now stands at the intersection of Water, Powell, and Alexander St. In 1886, a fire leveled 1000 buildings, including the infamous saloon, in 45 minutes. In the 1960s, community groups led the fight for restoration. Today the area is overflowing with craft shops, nightclubs, restaurants and boutiques. Many cater exclusively to tourists, but the area can still be fun, especially along **Water Street.** If you find you're really bored, you can stop every 15 minutes and listen to the steam-powered clock on the corner of Cambie and Water St. It's the only one on the continent.

Gastown is a fair walk from downtown or a short ride on bus #22 along Burrard St. to Carrall St. It is bordered by Richards St. to the west, Columbia St. to the east, Hastings St. to the south, and the waterfront to the north.

Chinatown, just east of Gastown, is within walking distance of downtown. You can also take bus #22 on Burrard St. northbound to Pender and Carrall St., and return by bus #22 westbound on Pender St. The area is rundown and some consider it unsafe. At night, women traveling alone should exercise caution. A safer (albeit expensive) way to see this huge area is through Gray Line Tours (see Practical Information).

Parks

Stanley Park

Founded in 1889, **Stanley Park,** at the westernmost end of the center peninsula, is testament to one man's urban foresight. Surrounded by a seawall promenade, the thickly wooded park is crisscrossed with cycling and hiking trails and remains one of the city's most popular attractions. Within the boundaries of the park are odd restaurants, extraordinary tennis courts, the Malkin Bowl (an outdoor theater), and fully equipped beaches where you can even swim. The **Brockton Oval,** located on the park's small eastern peninsula of Brockton Point, is a cinder running track, with hot showers and changing rooms. Nature walks are given May-Sept. Tues. at 10am and July-Aug. at 7pm. They start from the Lost Lagoon bus loop (in the morning in May, June, and Sept.) or from Lumberman's Arch Water Park (all other times). **Lost Lagoon,** a marshy lake next to the Georgia St. entrance, bristles with a number of fish and bird varieties, including the rare trumpeter swan. Stranger aquatic species practice for their Red Cross tests at the **Vancouver Aquarium** (682-1118), on the eastern side of the park, not far from the entrance. The British Columbian, Tropical, and Amazonian Halls are named for the environments they skillfully replicate. The marine mammal complex features orca and beluga whales in a sideshow revue. The aquarium stages several performances per day; you'll have to settle for fish flicks on rainy days. (Open daily 9:30am-8pm; in winter 10am-5:30pm. Admission $5.75, senior citizens and ages 13-18 $4.75, under 12 $3.25.) Stanley Park's small, free **zoo** next door is worth visiting just to see the monkeys pelt the hapless harbor seals with apple cores. (Open daily 10am-5pm.) Perhaps the best way to see the park is on bike (see Bike Rental under Practical Information). If you don't feel like biking or hoofing your way around the park, horse-drawn carriages will take you on a 50-minute tour (every ½ hr., daily 11am-4pm, $10). Call 681-5115 for more details.

Vanier Park

During the summer, a tiny **ferry** (684-7781) carries passengers from the Aquatic Centre across False Creek to Vanier (*not* pronounced Van-ee-YUR) Park and the museum complex located there. (Ferries daily, every 15 min. 10am-8pm. Fare $1.25.) Another ferry runs from the Maritime Museum in Vanier Park to Granville Island. (Fare $2.50.) Vanier Park can also be reached by bus #22, heading south on Burrard St. from downtown. Once you reach the park, visit the circular **Vancouver Museum,** 1100 Chestnut St. (736-7736), guarded by an abstract crab fountain. The museum displays artifacts from Pacific Northwest Native American cultures and several rotating exhibits. Down in the basement lurks Glenn Gould's piano, now considered a national treasure. (Open Mon.-Fri. 10am-9pm, Sat.-Sun. 10am-5pm. Admission $5, seniors, students, and kids under 13 $2.50, families $12.) The museum also sponsors a number of free outdoor concerts, dance performances, and workshops during the summer. Call for details.

Housed in the same building, the **H. R. MacMillan Planetarium** (736-3656) sometimes runs four different star shows per day. Laser shows set to rock music illuminate the roof Tues.-Sun. at 8:30pm. (Star shows $4.25, laser shows $5.25.) The adjacent **Gordon Southam Observatory** is also open to the public, weather permitting. (Open Fri. 7-11pm, Sat.-Sun. noon-5pm and 7-11pm—but call ahead at 738-2855 to make sure. Free.)

The **Maritime Museum** (737-2211) is also part of the complex in Vanier Park. Mercifully non-military in its emphasis, the museum's exhibits photographs and models trace the growth of Vancouver's harbor and port. An exception to the pacifist atmosphere is the well-restored *St. Roch.* This 1928 Royal Canadian Mounted Police Arctic Patrol Service Vessel gained its fame during WWII, when it became the first ship to negotiate the Northwest Passage. The boat is displayed in its towering entirety, and guided tours are given daily. (Open daily 10am-5pm. Admission $3, seniors, students, and children under 13 $1.50, families $6. Wed. 5-9pm free. Combination tickets to both the Maritime Museum and the Vancouver Museum available.) The Maritime Museum displays more wooden boats in the **Museum Harbour,** on the water. You can wander free of charge 24 hr. The museum holds a "shanty sing" on the dock every Wednesday evening in the summer.

More Parks

Another adored city park is the **Van Dusen Botanical Garden,** 37th Ave. and Oak St. (266-7194). Take bus #17 from Granville Mall. Floral collections of this 55½-acre beauty range from a Sino-Himalayan garden to a growth of heather to an indoor exhibit of Japanese bonsai trees. The garden also serves as a setting for summer concerts and craft shows, and special days for senior citizens and the disabled. (Open daily 10am-dusk; in winter 10am-4pm. Admission $3.75, seniors and children $2, families $11.)

Overlooking the city center, **Queen Elizabeth Park,** at 33rd Ave. and Cambie St. (872-5513), metamorphosed from a quarry into an ornamental sunken garden. Take bus #15 from Burrard St. Atop the hill, the **Bloedel Conservatory** gathers a spray of tropical plants and birds together into a geodesic dome. (Open in summer daily 10am-9pm; otherwise 10am-5:30pm. Admission $2.30, seniors and ages 6-18 $1.15.)

The **Dr. Sun Yat-Sen Classical Chinese Garden,** 578 Carrall St. (662-3207), is yet another quiet place to escape from the city. Designed and built by artists brought to Vancouver from China, the garden brandishes many imported plantings and carvings. (Open daily 10am-8pm; Oct.-Apr. 10am-4:30pm. Admission $3, seniors, students, and children $2, families $6.)

Beaches

For a large city, Vancouver has a remarkable collection of bacteria- and medical waste-free beaches. Even if you don't dip a foot in the cold northern Pacific, you can join the West Coast spirit by participating in Sport BC's weekly **Volleyball tournament,** with all levels of competition. Scare up a team at the hostel, then call 737-3096 to find out where to go to make people eat leather. All of Vancouver's beaches have lifeguards from Victoria Day to Labor Day daily from 11:30am to 9pm.

Follow the western side of the seawall south to **Sunset Beach Park** (738-8535), a strip of grass and beach that extends south all the way to the Burrard Bridge. At the southern end of Sunset Beach is the **Aquatic Centre,** 1050 Beach Ave. (665-3424), a public facility with a 50m indoor saltwater pool, sauna, gymnasium, and diving tank. (Open Mon.-Thurs. 7am-10pm, Sat. 8am-9pm, Sun. 11am-9pm; pool opens Mon.-Thurs. at 7am. Gym use $3, pool use $2.40.)

Kitsilano Beach, known to locals as "Kits," on the other side of Arbutus St. from Vanier, is a local favorite with its heated saltwater outdoor pool (731-0011; open in summer only). The pool has lockers and a snack bar. (Beach open daily 7am-8:45pm; Oct.-May Mon.-Fri. noon-8:45pm, Sat.-Sun. and holidays 10am-8:45pm. Admission to the pool $1.40, seniors and children 70¢, families $2.70.)

Jericho Beach, to the west, though harboring the massive youth hostel (see Accommodations), tends to be less heavily used than Kits Beach (and has free showers). North Marine Dr. runs along the beach, and a great cycling path at the edge of the road leads up to the westernmost edge of the UBC campus. Bike and hiking trails cut through the campus and crop its edges. As you enter the campus, several marked trails lead down to the unsupervised **Wreck Beach,** a nudist hang-out; though police may sneak a peak, they generally turn a blind eye to the various *recreational* activities there.

Universities

The high point of a visit to the **University of British Columbia (UBC)** is the university's **Museum of Anthropology,** 6393 NW Marine Dr. (228-3825). To reach the campus, take bus #4 or 10 from Granville. The museum's collection is housed in a dramatic glass-and-concrete building whose high ceilings and powerful lines provide an appropriate environment for totems and other massive sculptures by the Native peoples of the Pacific Northwest coast. *Raven and the First Men,* a contemporary carving by Haida artist Bill Reid, integrates traditional mythologies and modern forms. The $1 *Guide to the UBC Museum of Anthropology,* available at the entrance desk, sorts out the cultural threads of the various nations that produced these works; much of this information does not appear on exhibit labels. Hour-long guided walks will help you find your way through the maze of times and places. (Open Tues. 11am-9pm, Wed.-Sun. 11am-5pm. Admission $4, seniors and students $2, ages 6-12 $1. Tues. free.)

Behind the museum, in a weedy courtyard designed to simulate the Pacific coastal islands, the **Outdoor Exhibit** displays memorial totems and a mortuary house built by the Haida nation. Each carved figure represents one aspect of the ancestral heritage of the honored dead. Even if you don't make it inside the museum itself, don't miss this silent soliloquy of this little-known culture.

Curators of the **Nitobe Memorial Garden** (228-3928), to the south of the museum across Marine Dr., have fashioned a small immaculate garden, in traditional Japanese style. (Open daily 10am-8pm; Sept.-June 10am-5pm. Admission $1.25, students 50¢. Free in winter Mon.-Fri. 10am-3pm.) The **Asian Centre,** 1871 West Mall (228-2746), near the gardens, often has free exhibits of Asian-Canadian art. The Asian Centre Library contains the largest collection of Asian materials in Canada. (Open Mon.-Fri. 9am-5pm. Call for a schedule of events.)

All of UBC's gardens fall under the official rubric of the **Botanical Garden** (228-4208). The **Main Garden,** which is in the southwest corner of the campus at 16th Ave. and SW Marine Dr. (note that the entrance and visitor parking area are on Stadium Rd., north of the West Mall), may not be worth the bother, especially to the non-horticulturist. Although pebbles outnumber pistils, the **Physick Gardens** are fascinating; signs alert you to the poisonous nature of some of the plants. In the 30-acre **Asian Garden,** through the tunnel and across the street, quiet paths lead past blue Himalayan poppies and rhododendrons. For general and tour information on all the gardens, call the Botanical Garden office weekdays 8:30am-4:30pm. (Open daily 10am-8pm. Admission $2 per garden, Wed free.)

Large maps at entrances to UBC's campus indicate other points of interest and bus stops. In addition to its gardens, UBC also has a public swimming pool in the **Aquatic Centre** (228-4521), a free **Fine Arts Gallery** (228-2759), free daytime and evening concerts (228-3113), and a museum of geology (228-5586). (Museums and pool open Mon.-Fri. 8:30am-4:30pm.) To arrange a walking tour of the campus between May and August, call 228-3131.

Vancouver's other major academy is the relatively new and somewhat isolated **Simon Fraser University (SFU).** Built in 1965, the campus is beautiful, with the architecture and landscaping complementing each other perfectly. The **Main Mall** and **Academic Quadrangle** alone are worth the 35-minute bus ride to the top of "the hill." Take bus #10 or 14 to Kootenay Loop, then the #135-SFU. The **Athletic Services Deptartment** (291-3611) can fill you in on the details of using the university's gyms and pools, and the **Outdoor Recreation Office** (291-4434; open Mon.-Fri. 10am-4pm) will give you maps for the numerous hiking trails around the campus. Free **walking tours** leave the Administration Bldg. every hour on the half-hour daily 10:30am-3:30pm. Call 291-3439 or 291-3210 if you have any questions.

The Pub in th Main Mall has the cheapest beer on the lower mainland, as well as great company. (Open Mon.-Fri. 9pm-midnight, Sat.-Sun. 9pm-4am.) To find out what else is happening around campus, grab the free weekly *The Peak,* including an extensive arts section on city happenings, from drop-boxes scattered around campus.

Shopping

Granville Mall, on Granville Ave. between Smithe and Hastings St., is one of the few open-air pedestrian malls in Vancouver. Vehicles other than buses are prohibited. From Hastings St. to the Orpheum Theatre, most shops and restaurants on the mall capitulate to young professionals and business executives on their lunch hours. Beyond W. Georgia St., the mall takes an adolescent twist as expensive department stores defer to theaters, leather shops, and raucous record stores.

A few blocks to the west, the **Harbour Centre,** 555 W. Hastings St., flaunts a snazzy mall with distinctly non-budget restaurants, and a **skylift** for exceptional cityscapes. (See Sights and Activities: Downtown.) If you are dying to fill your matching luggage set with chic purchases, head to the ritziest mall west of Long Island: the **Park Royal Shopping Centre** on Marine Dr. in West Vancouver. Take bus #250, 251, or 252 on Georgia St. downtown. Graced with pseudo-European delicatessens and shops, the **Robsonstrasse** shopping district, on Robson St. between Howe and Broughton St., invites its patrons to spend their money under kaleidoscopic awnings. **Pacific Centre,** 700 W. Georgia St., is proud to be one of Vancouver's newest malls. It is located at the Granville SkyTrain station.

Entertainment

To keep abreast of the entertainment scene, pick up a copy of the weekly *Georgia Straight* or the new bimonthly *Boulevard,* both free at newsstands and record stores. The 25¢ *Westender* lists entertainment in that lively neighborhood and also reports on community issues, while the free *Angles* serves the city's gay community. Believers in the New Age should peruse the free *Common Ground,* a quarterly with listings and advertisements for restaurants, services, events, bookstores, and workshops. Music of all genres can be heard in Vancouver's pubs and clubs; both *Georgia Straight* (an allusion to the body of water between mainland BC and Vancouver Island) and the *Westender* have the full rundown.

Basin St. Cabaret, 23 West Corova St. (688-5351). Bluesy jazz nightly. Local talent who play "cause they love the music" jam from 9pm-2am. Add cheap beer (pint $3, glass $1.50), a dance floor, and a terrace over the back alley—this new club is one of the hippest in Vancouver. No cover.

Blarney Stone Inn, 216 Carrall St. (687-4322). Live Irish music, restaurant, and dance floor. Lunch $5, dinner around $12. Cover $3. Open Mon. 11:30am-5pm, Tues.-Fri. 11:30am-2am, Sat. 5pm-2am.

Town Pump, 66 Water St. (683-6695), a few blocks away from the Blarney Stone in the center of Gastown. College students and businesspeople frequent the Pump for live music nightly from jazz to reggae. Snack menu available all day, burgers $6. Open Mon.-Sat. 11:30am-2am, Sun. 11:30am-midnight. When the big names show up, tickets are $10-15 at the door.

Darby D. Dawes, 2001 MacDonald St. (731-0617), at W. 4th Ave. near Kits Beach. A neighborhood pub with famous Sat. afternoon rock jam sessions. Bring your axe. Full meals served daily 11:30am-7pm, snacks until 10pm. Entertainment Fri.-Sat. 8pm-1am, Sun. 8pm-midnight.

The Railway Club, 579 Dunsmuir St. (681-1625). Lively jazz sessions Sat. 3-7pm. Get there before the band in the evening and duck the cover ($2-5). Open Mon.-Sat. noon-2am, Sun. 7pm-midnight.

The Gandy Dancer, 1222 Hamilton St. (684-7321), in the warehouse district. Enter on the side facing Pacific Blvd. Most innovative of the dozen gay and lesbian clubs in the city. Tues. and Wed. occasionally feature amusing contests; Fri. for men only. Open daily 7:30am-2am.

Castle Pub, 750 Granville St. (682-2661). Quiet gay and lesbian pub. Frequently sponsors benefit receptions for local charities. Open Mon.-Sat. 10am-midnight.

The **Vancouver Symphony Orchestra (VSO)** plays in the refurbished **Orpheum Theater,** 884 Granville St. (280-4444). The VSO ticketline is 280-3311. The 52-year-old **Vancouver Bach Choir** (921-8012) sometimes performs with the VSO in the Orpheum. Smaller groups, such as the *Warblin' Rosen Trio,* appeal to a variety of musical tastes—check the *Westender* for listings.

Robson Square Media Centre, 800 Robson St. (660-2487), sponsors events almost daily during the summer and weekly the rest of the year, either on the plaza at the square or in the centre itself. Their concerts, theater productions, exhibits, lectures, symposia, and films are all free or nearly free. The centre's monthly brochure *What's Happening at Robson Square* is available from the visitors bureau or businesses in the square.

Vancouver also has an active theater community. The **Arts Club Theatre,** Granville Island (687-1644), hosts big-name theater and musicals, and the **Theatre in the Park program,** in Stanley Park's Malkin Bowl, puts on a summer season of musical comedy. Call 687-0174 for ticket information. The annual **Vancouver Shakespeare Festival** (June-Aug. in Vanier Park) often needs volunteer ticket-takers and program-sellers, who may then watch the critically acclaimed shows for free. Call 734-0194 for details. **UBC Summer Stock** (228-2678) puts on four plays during the summer at the Frederick Wood Theatre.

The **Ridge Theatre,** 16th Ave. and Arbutus (738-6311), often shows European and non-mainstream films. (Tues. free; other nights $6.) The **Hollywood Theatre,** 3123 W. Broadway (738-3211), also runs artsy films, but mixes a heavy dose of Joel Silver into their schedule. (Tickets $3. Doors open at 7pm.) **Vancouver East Cinema,** 2290 Commercial Dr. (253-5455), at E. 7th Ave., screens documentaries and art films for $5.50. **Cinema Simon Fraser,** Images Theatre, SFU (291-4869), charges $2.50 for a variety of films, Joel Silver's and otherwise. (Open Sept.-May.) The **Paradise,** 919 Granville (681-1732), shows double features of first-run movies (triple features on weekends) for $2.50.

Vancouver's universities never cease acting culturally. The **SFU Centre for the Arts** (291-3514) offers both student and guest-professional theater, primarily from September to May. For **UBC's** activities, call Public Events Information at 228-3131 or pick up a free copy of *Ubyssey.* UBC's film series rolls high-quality movies Thursday and Friday nights for $1.50.

Seasonal Events

Attend one of Vancouver's annual fairs, festivals, or celebrations to confirm rumors of the city's cosmopolitan nature. The famed **Vancouver Folk Music Festival** is held in mid-July in Jericho Park. For three days the best acoustic performers in North America give concerts and workshops. Tickets can be purchased for each event or for the whole weekend. Buy a whole-weekend ticket before June 1 to receive a $5 discount. For more details, contact the festival at 3271 Main St., Vancouver V6V 3M6 (879-2931).

Experience the area's Native folk culture at the **First People's Cultural Festival,** held each June at a different area reserve. A full day of traditional dance and crafts is capped with a salmon barbecue. (Admission $10.) Proceeds benefit the Urban Native Education Centre, 285 E. 5th St. (873-3761); call the information center for more information. The festival is *really* popular so book accommodations at least a month in advance (particularly at the hostel) if you plan to be in town. The annual **jazz festival** (682-0706) in late June, featuring bands like Randy Wanless's Fab Forty, is totally hot. Call 682-0706 for details.

Vancouver's Chinese community fêtes its heritage on **Chinese New Year** (usually in early to mid-Feb.). Fireworks, music, parades, and dragons highlight the celebration. The **Folkfest** (736-1512) in early June features two weeks of multicultural merriness in Gastown and Robson Sq. All the festivities are free. Italians and Greeks whoop it up in July and the last week of June, respectively. Food stands, musical performers, carnivals, and more food stands cluster around each community's center.

Vancouver celebrates its relationship with the sea several times per year. The Maritime Museum in Vanier Park (see Sights and Activities) hosts the annual **Captain Vancouver Day** (736-4431) in mid-June to commemorate the 1792 exploration of Canada's west coast by Captain George Vancouver. Thrills include free boat tours of the harbor, a miniature boat battle, boat model building, hot air balloon rides, and appearances by the **Shanty Singers.** In mid-July, the **Vancouver Sea Festival** (684-3378) schedules four days of parades, concerts, sporting events, fireworks, and salmon barbecues. All events take place in English Bay and are free, but you have to pay for the salmon. The headline attraction is the notorious **Nanaimo to Vancouver Bathtub Race,** a journey across the rough waters of the Strait of Georgia for Gilgameshes with rubber duckies.

Near Vancouver

For a secluded and esoteric park, head out across the Lions Gate Bridge from Stanley Park along North Marine Dr. to **Lighthouse Park.** As a bicycle daytrip, the ride is fantastic, but not to be undertaken lightly. It's a 50km round trip, and the inclines can be daunting. This is not for puny pedalers. Bus #250 from downtown will take you right to the park's entrance.

Once there, numerous trails will take you all over the 185-acre preserve with peaceful views of the waters. There is also one of the few remaining manned lighthouses on the point, and guided tours (the only way you can get to see the lighthouse) ascend on the hour Wed.-Sun. 11am-5pm (free).

Puff along on the **Royal Hudson Steam Locomotive** (688-7246), operated by 1st Tours. After a two-hour journey along the coast from Vancouver to Squamish (the gateway to Garibaldi Provincial Park), passengers are loosed for 90 minutes to browse in town before they head back. (Excursions May 21-July 16 Wed.-Sun.; July 19-Sept. 4 daily; Sept. 6-24 Wed.-Sun. Fare $24, seniors and youths $20, children $14.) The train departs from the BC Rail terminal, 1311 W. 1st St., across the Lions Gate Bridge in North Vancouver. Reservations are required.

To the east, the town of **Deep Cove** maintains the salty atmosphere of a fishing village. Sea otters and seals frolic on the pleasant Indian Arm beaches. Take bus #210 from Pender St. to the Phibbs Exchange on the north side of Second Narrows Bridge. From there, take bus #211 or 212. **Cates Park,** at the end of Dollarton Hwy. on the way to Deep Cove, has popular swimming and scuba waters and is a good destination for a day bike trip out of Vancouver. Bus #211 also leads to **Mount Seymour Provincial Park.** Trails leave from Mt. Seymour Rd., and a paved road winds the 8km to the top. One hundred campsites ($7 per site) are available, and the skiing is superb.

For a less vigorous hike that still offers fantastic views of the city, head for **Lynn Canyon Park.** The suspension bridge here is free and uncrowded, unlike its more publicized twin in Capilano Canyon. Often called a rip-off by Vancouverites, the Capilano bridge charges the gullible tourist $4.50 just to walk across. Try Lynn instead; besides, it's 6m longer. Take bus #228 from the North Vancouver SeaBus terminal and walk the ½km to the bridge. While there, take in the concise exhibits of the **Lynn Canyon Ecology Centre** (987-5922; open daily 10am-5pm; free).

Grouse Mountain is the ski resort closest to downtown Vancouver and has the crowds to prove it. Take bus #246 from the North Vancouver SeaBus terminal; at Edgemont and Ridgewood transfer to bus #232, then the "supersky ride." The $10 aerial tramway runs from 9am to 10pm. The slopes are lit until 10:30pm from November to May, and the tram ride is popular with sightseers in summer. On sunny days, helicopter tours leave from the top of the mountain, starting at $25 per person. For more information contact Grouse Mountain Resorts, 6400 Nancy Greene Way, North Vancouver V7R 4N4 (984-0661, ski report 986-6292). Ski rental is available for $16.50 per day; no deposit is required. Adult lift tickets are $22.

The **Reifel Bird Sanctuary** on Westham Island, 16km south of Vancouver, is just northwest of the Tsawwassen ferry terminal. Bus #601 from Vancouver will take you to the town of **Ladner,** 1½ km east of the sanctuary. Two hundred thirty species of birds live in the 850 acres of marshlands, and spotting towers are set up for long-term birdwatching. (Open daily 9am-4pm.) For information contact the **BC Waterfowl Society** at 946-6980.

Fifty kilometers north of Vancouver (on the way to Whistler) is the **BC Museum of Mining** in Britannia Beach (688-8735 or 896-2233). An electric mine train pumps passengers through an old copper artery into the mountain that poured out the most metal in the British empire: 1.3 billion pounds. (Open mid-May to June Wed.-Sun. 10am-5pm; July-Labor Day daily 10am-5pm; Sept. Sat.-Sun. 10am-5pm. Admission $6, seniors and students $3.50.)

Golden Ears Provincial Park is 50km east of the town of Haney. Turn north on 224th St. and follow it 4km until it ends, then turn right and proceed for 8km. The roads are not well marked, but all roads lead to Golden Ears. Inside the park, the **Cultus Lake Campground** operates 346 tentsites ($10 per site). The park itself has myriad hiking trails, including some short ones leading to waterfalls.

Whistler

Thanks to a sporting enthusiasm from both the federal and provincial governments in the form of massive subsidies, the resort communities of Whistler now boast the best winter (and summer) skiing in North America, surpassing even Vale, CO in number of skier days and, by most accounts, the quality of its runs.

Clusters of development are strung out along a 7km stretch of Hwy. 99, with **Whistler Creek** in the north end by Alpha and Nita Lakes. Six kilometers north is **Whistler Village,** off Village Gate Blvd., which embraces the Whistler Convention Centre and overpriced skier services galore. Built all at once, this area looks and feels like a Disneyworld "Skiland."

Practical Information

Tourist Information: Tourism Office (932-5528), in Whistler Creek right on Hwy. 99 across the road from the Husky gas station. Look for the log cabin building. Open daily 9am-5pm. There are two kiosks in Whistler Village, chock full of pamphlets. Open daily 10am-6pm.

Buses: Maverick Coach Lines Ltd. (800-972-6301 or 255-1171), at the Greyhound depot in Vancouver. From Vancouver, 5 per day, $11. There's a flag stop at the Husky Station with a loop through Whistler Village.

Taxi: Whistler Taxi (932-5455).

Car Rentals: Avis Rent-A-Car (938-1331), at Fairways Hotel in Whistler Village. Must be 19 with major credit card. From $35 per day plus 15¢ per km.

Bike Rental: Mountain Bike Rental, in the Whistler Village complex (932-3659). $6 per hr., $30 per day. Open daily 9am-7pm. **Blackcomb Lodge** (932-3141). $7 per hr., $25 per day.

Laundromat: (932-3980). Across from the Tourist Office on Sarajevo Dr. Open Mon.-Sat. 1-9:30pm, Sun. 10am-9:30pm.

Post Office: 8000 Hwy. 99 (932-5012). Open Mon.-Fri. 8:30am-5:30pm. General Delivery Postal Code: VON 1BO.

Police: RCMP 8000 Hwy. 99 (932-3044), on Village Gate Blvd. in Whistler Village.

Accommodations and Camping

Don't buy *anything,* let alone lodging, in Whistler Village if you can possibly help it. Unfortunately, sometimes you're stuck: the only pharmacy is the Pharmasave in the village. There are no budget accommodations in the village. There are lots of good deals, however, in Whistler Creek.

Whistler Youth Hostel (CYHA) (932-5492), on the western shore of Alta Lake between Whistler Creek and Whistler Village. Probably one of the best hostels in North America. The easiest way to get to and from the hostel from Vancouver is by train, as there is a flag stop immediately behind the hostel ($12). By car, take the Alta Lake Road cut-off from Hwy. 99 2km north of Whistler Municipality Sign (1km south of Whistler Creek) and follow the signs. By bus is more difficult: get off at the Husky station, walk down Lake Placid Dr. to the train tracks, then follow the tracks to Chaplinville Rd. (it's unmarked, but it's the only road that meets the tracks). Head west to Alta Lake Rd., then north and follow the signs. It'll be tempting to just continue along the tracks, but *don't:* freight trains come through at random intervals and beyond Chaplinville there's no escape but a tumble down a steep, rocky bluff into the lake. Members $10, nonmembers $12. Laundry and extensive kitchen facilities and lockers (you can rent a lock for $1 per day, $5 per week).

Backpacker's Hostel, 2124 Lake Placid Dr. (932-1177), right behind the Husky Station. In cahoots with Vincent's in Vancouver, but much nicer (though a bit cramped). Kitchen facilities, TV, and VCR. Dorm beds $12 per night.

Fireside Lodge (932-4545), 3km south of Whistler Village in Nordic Estates. Kitchen and laundry facilities. $15 per person, bedding required.

KOA Campground (932-5181), 2km north of Whistler Village off Hwy. 99. Should be called Kampgrounds of Kanada; laundry facilities, hot tub, and sauna. $15 per site, electricity $2.

Food

The restaurants in Whistler Village all cost a fortune. You're better off getting your own fixin's at **Food Plus** (932-6193; open 24 hr.) on Lake Placid Rd. across from the tourist office. It's cheaper than the Husky Station grocery, and has a better selection.

Southside Deli, on Lake Placid Rd. (932-3368), on the Husky Station side of Hwy. 99. Great breakfasts—try a Bacon, Egg, Lettuce, Cheese and Ham sandwich for $6.25. Open daily 6am-4pm.

Florentyna's (932-4424), across the street from Southside Deli. Upscale decor and prices to match. Decent tortellini $9.50. Open daily 5pm-midnight.

Sights and Activities

In the winter, the whole world comes here to ski, and with good reason. Whistler Mountain boasts the largest vertical drop of any ski mountain in North America (7000 ft.) and platoons of quad-chairs to get you to the top. Blackcomb Mountain in Whistler Village (just follow the signs) has offered **summer skiing** on the 200m thick **Horstmere Glacier** only since 1988 and already has the best skiing between June and October in the Northern Hemisphere. It can be pricey, though: $20 for rentals, $28 for a lift ticket. Bring a camera for the thrill of taking home shots of skiing in July—in the morning that is—conditions get mushy by 11:30am. Rental shop opens at 7am, lifts at 8am.

If you prefer seeing to skiing, the 45 minute series of chair lift rides to the summit is spectacular ($12, $9 with a hostel card). For an additional $4 you can take a mountain bike to the top and ride the dirt trails down (see Bike Rental under Practical Information). For information on all Blackcomb facilities call 932-3141.

For less expensive fun, pick up a map of the various hiking/biking trails at any tourist office, or enjoy a summer barbecue with the volleyball net and hibachi stands of Alpha Lake Park (on Alpha Lake), off Lake Placid Rd.—the glacial water is bracing. The hostel, located on Alta Lake, is perfect for swimming, windsurfing, and canoeing (particularly in the public canoe available for free).

About 4km south of Whistler Creek is the **Whistler Museum and Archives** (932-2019). The museum is a nice stop if you have time, but isn't really worth the effort if you have to sweat to get there. (Open July-Sept. Wed.-Sun. 10am-4pm; otherwise weekends 10am-3pm).

Near Whistler

Just 64km north of Vancouver and just south of Whistler is the 195,000 hectare **Garibaldi Provincial Park.** With three lakes, dozens of hiking trails of all levels, fishing and camping facilities, this is a park-and-a-half. You can get general maps from the Tourist Office, or more detailed information from the Garibaldi/Sunshine Coast District Office on Alice Lake Rd. off Hwy. 99, just north of Squamish. Write to them at Box 220 Brackendale, BC V0N 1H0 (604-898-3678).

Twenty-five kilometers north of Whistler near Pemberton is **Nairn Falls Provincial Park.** The 88 sites ($8 each) include toilets, showers and water. Open May-Oct.

Fraser River Canyon

Simon Fraser, Canada's solo equivalent of Lewis and Clark, braved 1300km of turbulent water to reach Vancouver from Mt. Robson in 1808. Today a far easier path (the Trans-Canada Hwy.) snakes down the Fraser River between the towns of Hope and Cache Creek. The 200km of coiling rapids are tamer than the Infocentre pamphlets would have you believe, but the sheer size of the steeply sloping, pine-scented canyon qualifies it as the most striking patch of mountains in the province.

In the original "Rambo" movie, *First Blood,* Sylvester Stallone singlehandedly destroyed **Hope**—shooting up cars, blowing up buildings, and maiming a dozen policemen. For some reason (perhaps the box-office gross), this has started a trend of on-location filmings in this small town of 3500. In the past three years, *Shoot to Kill,* with Sidney Poitier and Kirstie Alley, and the bomb *Fire with Fire* (with no memorable stars) were also filmed in Hope.

Even without hordes of gaffers and key grips, Hope, located 150km east of Vancouver and 190km south of Cache Creek, remains the most populous town along the Fraser Canyon. The **Travel Infocentre,** 919 Water Ave. (869-2021), on the main thoroughfare, disseminates exhaustive information on the town and the entire Fraser River Canyon region. (Open daily 8am-8pm; Labor Day-June 25 Tues.-Thurs. 9am-5pm, Fri.-Mon. 8am-8pm.) Try the **Flamingo Hotel** (869-9610), east of town, where singles are $25, doubles $30, and kitchens $5 extra. The town operates a large campground, **Coquihalla River Park,** at 800 Kawkawa Lake Rd. (869-5671), off Hwy. 3 via 7th Ave. Many sites have full hookups and metered showers which make every drop count. (Sites $10.) Hope has its share of fast-food joints, but **Ryan's,** at the junction of the Trans-Canada Hwy. and Hwy. 3 (869-5716), puts great chicken pot pies on your table with more deliberation ($6). (Open daily 6am-10:30pm.) The **RCMP** in Hope (869-5644) is at 670 Hope-Princeton Hwy., just off Hwy. 3.

For a closer look at the Fraser River, set out on the moderate **hiking trails** that lead from trailheads near Hope. The 20-minute, mosquito-ridden **Rotary Trail** starts off at Wardle St. and runs into the confluence of the Fraser and Coquihalla Rivers. If you are looking for something a bit more challenging, climb to the summit of **Thacker Mountain.** To reach the foot of the path, cross Coquihalla River Bridge, make two quick lefts across the creek, then a right onto the road leading to a housing development. The car park at the road's end marks the beginning of a 5km gravel path to the peak, which features clear views of Hope and the Fraser River.

The Gold Rush town of **Yale** boasted a population of 20,000 in 1858, the largest west of Chicago and north of San Francisco but cursed by its name, the town has floundered while the population has dwindled below 250. Yale's inexpensive hotels are (not surprisingly) very close to Hell's Gate and the town itself is just 30km north of Hope on the Trans-Canada Hwy. Find out every last bit there is to know about the town at the **Yale Historical Society** (863-2324), next to the church at Park and Fraser (open daily June-Sept.). Overnight guests should try the **Fort Yale Motel,** on the Trans-Canada Hwy. (863-2216), an air-conditioned abode with disabled access, near several budget restaurants. (Singles $26. Doubles $30.) **Snowhite Camp-**

site (863-2252), 5km south on the highway, provides shady sites with coin-operated showers and rakish plaster dwarves. RV facilities. (Sites $9, with hookups $12. Open April-Sept.) Noise from the nearby railroad tracks will plague you no matter where you stay in Yale—be thankful that the trains are short.

Simon Fraser's pioneering jaunt down his namesake river bypassed Yale altogether, but he likened one particularly tumultuous stretch of rapids to the "Gates of Hell." A resort area 25km north of Yale on the Trans-Canada Hwy., **Hell's Gate**, even as viewed from afar, makes Fraser's successful trip seem miraculous indeed. When melting snow floods the river in spring, the 60m-deep water rushes through the narrow gorge with such force that the air around it vibrates and sizzles.

Ever since convicted child murderer Charles Olsen was recaptured near Hope in 1985, locals have been very reluctant to pick up hitchhikers. You could easily wait two hours for a ride, and there's no transit to Hell's Gate. You can rent a car at **Gardner Chev-Olds** in Hope at 945 Water St. (869-9511), next to the infocentre ($25 per day with free 100km plus 15¢ per additional km; open Mon.-Sat. 8:30am-6pm).

Hardcore campers will enjoy **Gold Pan River Campground**, 16km west of **Spences Bridge**. The 12 sites ($6) offer no privacy but are only meters away from the rushing **Thompson River**. The less intrepid should opt for **Skihist Provincial Park Campground**, 12km east of **Lytton**. The 50 sites ($8) are protected by gates which are locked 11pm-7am; water and flush toilets are provided (leave yours at home).

According to a popular local legend, two ornery bandits robbed a freight wagon during the 19th-century Cariboo Gold Rush, but were not quick enough to escape the long arm of the Canadian mounties. One of the two was so badly wounded, he barely had time to cache his treasure near a small creek. Residents have yet to find the treasure, but **Cache Creek**, 80km west of Kamloops, grew up around the legend. Visitors can learn more about the town through the **Travel Infocentre** (457-9118), but there is little to do there besides sleep and refuel and bury some gold. Impossible to overlook, the **Castle Inn** (457-9547) is the garish gray medieval castle perched incongruously alongside the highway. The hotel's large, air-conditioned singles start at $25; the **Dairy Queen** next door is one of the few cheap eats in town. The closest campground is **Brookside Campsite** (457-6633), just east on Hwy. 1; showers are free, and there is an adjacent store. (Sites $8, with hookups $11. Open May-Oct.)

Okanagan Valley

Known throughout Canada for its bountiful fruit harvests, the Okanagan Valley lures visitors with summer blossoms, sleepy towns, and tranquil lakes. The towns' Native American names, like Kelowna, Penticton, and Naramata, bespeak the region's heritage. Although high-powered tourists will be bored by the long stretches of empty road and the slow Okanagan pace, tourists with cars can explore the subtle pleasures along lake-lined Hwy. 97 of camping in an orchard bursting with newly-ripened cherries, eating the fruit at a family stand, sampling the wines at a local winery, or fishing in one of the pristine lakes. Bus travelers will have to settle for the larger Okanagan towns of Penticton and Kelowna, where the din of heated pools, waterslides and luxury hotels drowns out the silence of the surrounding countryside.

Penticton

Native American settlers named the area wedged between the Okanagan and Skaha Lakes *Pen-tak-tin,* "a place to stay forever." Today those same settlers would spin in their graves if they knew the extent to which their eternal paradise has been usurped by weekend tourists. Hot weather, sandy beaches, and proximity to Vancouver, Seattle, and Spokane have ushered in the Tourist Age. Budget travelers may find it a strain to spend a weekend here, let alone forever. Prices, however, don't seem to hinder the sun-worshipers who visit in summer; the guano-covered beaches bulge with scantily clad men and women. The warm, clean water and sprawling beaches of the Okanagan and Skaha Lakes make for ideal sailing and fishing conditions.

Practical Information and Orientation

Visitor Information: Chamber of Commerce, 185 Lakeshore Dr. (492-4103). Take Riverside Dr. north off Hwy. 97, then right on Lakeshore. A copia of travel brochures and an attentive staff. Open daily 8am-8pm; Sept. to mid-June Mon.-Fri. 9am-5pm, Sat.-Sun. 10am-4pm. In summer, the city also sets up **Information Centres** along Hwy. 97 N. and S. While not as expansive as the main office, they carry an ample supply of literature. Open mid-June to Sept. daily 9am-6pm.

Greyhound: 307 Ellis (493-4101). To: Vancouver (5 per day, $31.95); Vernon (5 per day, $9.85); Kelowna (6 per day, $5.40). Open Mon.-Fri. 5:45am-12:45am.

Buses: Penticton Transit Service, 301 E. Warren Ave. (492-5602). Bus service around the city for 65¢ per ride. The Chamber of Commerce carries complete schedules. Service also available to nearby Naramata.

Taxi: Rainbow Taxi, 492-6700.

Car Rental: Budget Rent-A-Car, 1597 Main St. (493-0212). From $13 per day plus 16¢ per km. Must be 21 with major credit card.

Bike Rental: Riverside Bike Rental, 75 Riverside Dr. (493-1188), at Lakeshore Dr. Mountain bikes $6 for 1st hr., $4 per additional hr. Tandems $9 per hr. Open May-Sept. daily 8am-dusk.

Weather: 492-0539.

Women's Shelter: 493-7233.

Hospital: 550 Carmi Ave. (492-4000). **Ambulance:** 493-1020.

Police: 1101 Main St. (492-4300).

Post Office: Corner of Namaimo Ave. W and Winnepeg St. (492-5717). Postal Code: V2A 6J8.

Area Code: 604.

Penticton lies in southcentral British Columbia, 400km east of Vancouver on Hwy. 97. It is the southernmost stomping ground of the tourist region of Lake Okanagan, the warmest and driest of the trio that includes Kelowna on the north end and Vernon in the middle. Lake Okanagan borders the north end of town, while the smaller Skaha Lake lies to the south. Main Street (Hwy. 97) bisects the city from north to south.

Accommodations

Because Penticton is a full-time resort city, hotels here charge more than those in the surrounding towns. Singles rarely come cheaper than $35, especially after Canada Day. Campgrounds convenient to town are scarce and expensive.

Peach Bowl Motel, 1078 Burnaby Ave. (492-8946). Decent rooms in a decent location (2 blocks from the beach) at a great price. Management the very model of hotel hospitality. Singles $30, doubles $35. Off-season, singles $25. Doubles $30. Kitchens $5 extra.

Three Gables Hotel, 353 Main St. (492-3933), in the heart of Penticton, only 5 min. from the depot and the beach. The newly renovated rooms are spaciously appealing. Showers, cable TV, and A/C. Singles $40. Doubles $50. Triples $65. $5 per additional person.

Kozy Guest House, 1000 Lakeshore Dr. (493-8400). Great location on Okanagan Lake Beach. The prices are low for Penticton. Each room features a revolutionary revolving television invented by the owner; you can watch it even from the bathroom. Showers in every room. Singles and doubles $40. Off-season, singles $25, doubles $35. Kitchens $20 extra.

The Pines Motel, 1896 Main St. (492-3115). The friendly manager is prepared to haggle. The location on Hwy. 97 is convenient for passers-through, not for beach bums. Traffic noise does not die down until 11pm. Singles $42. Doubles $46. Kitchens $12 extra.

Ti-ki Shores, 914 Lakeshore Dr. (492-8769). Take advantage of the Okanagan Lake Beach across the street or the hotel's heated pool. Units are clean and luxurious. Singles and doubles $49. Off-season $25.

Camping

Since you will be paying through the nose anyway, you might as well try to find a campground on the shores of Okanagan Lake. Make reservations well in advance; open sites are a rare find in July and August.

Wright's Beach Camp, Site 40, Comp. 4, R.R. 2 (492-7120). Directly off Hwy. 97 on the shores of Skaha Lake at the south end of town. Nearby traffic is often noisy. Adequate wash-rooms and showers. Sites $16, hookups $3. Make reservations at least 1 week in advance.

South Beach Gardens, 3815 Skaha Lake Rd. (492-0628), across the street from the beach, east of the Channel Parkway. Fully equipped sites $17-18. Unserviced $13.

Park Royal RV Park, 240 Riverside Dr. (492-7051), off Hwy. 97. 10 shaded tenting sites ($16) with extensive facilities.

Food

Although intransigent budget travelers may have to swallow their pride and sell out to McDonalds or Burger King, there are a few local sandwich shops that provide workable alternatives.

Judy's Deli, 129 W. Nanaimo (492-7029). Healthy beachgoers stop here for hearty home-made soups ($1.25-1.50) and butter-laden sandwiches ($2-2.50). Open Mon.-Sat. 9am-5:30pm.

Taco Grande, 452 Main St. (492-7440). Typical speedy burrito joint. Most dishes $1.75-4, but a superior breakfast special—2 eggs, 3 sausages, hash browns, toast, and coffee ($3). Plain gringoburger $2. Open daily 9am-11pm.

Elite Restaurant, 340 Main St. (492-3051). Serving quality meals since 1927. Menus appear to be the same ones used for 60 years; unfortunately the prices have met modernity. Burgers $3.50-5, sandwiches $3-6. Lunch special of soup du jour and sandwich ($3). Dinner special of entree, salad or soup, bread roll, pudding or jello, and tea or coffee ($7). Open daily 6am-midnight.

Sights and Seasonal Events

Not surprisingly, much of the Penticton tourist trade revolves around the Okanagan Lake. An arid summer and lakesport facilities make Penticton a popular tanning hangout for a chic young crowd. Try to get off the guano and into the water. **Sail Inland** (492-2628 or 493-8221) arranges cruises, charters, and lessons. **The Marina,** 293 Front St. (492-2628), offers rentals of ski boats and fishing equipment. **Roli's** (493-0244), on the beach next to the Penticton Lodge (the mammoth hotel on the hill), offers windsurfing rentals and lessons. Rentals start at $11 for the first hour. The *Casabella Princess,* 45 E. Lakeshore Dr. (493-5551), gives pleasant paddlewheel cruises on the Okanagan for less active water-worshipers ($8.50, seniors and students $6.50).

For a sample of local culture take a trip to the **Art Gallery of the South Okanagan,** 11 Ellis St. (493-2928), at Front St. This lovely beachfront gallery exhibits on the local and international levels; it also claims to be the world's first solar-powered art gallery. The best part is, it's absolutely free. (Open Tues.-Fri. 11am-5pm, Sat.-Sun. 1-5pm.) The **Penticton Museum** (a.k.a. the **R.N. Atkinson Museum**) at 785 Main St. (492-6025) presents a potpourri of Western Canadiana, tracing the history of the region with Native artifacts and wildlife displays. (Open Mon.-Sat. 10am-5pm.)

Masquerading as an East African wildlife preserve, the **Okanagan Game Farm,** (497-5405) on Hwy. 97 just south of Penticton, covers 560 acres and protects 130 animal species from the boisterous summer visitors on the lake. All creatures roam free from fences and bars. Cars can drive throughout the park, and animal checklists should amuse the kiddies. (Admission $6, ages 5-15 $4. Open 8am-dusk.)

During spring (the best season to visit), the colorful **Blossom Festival,** held in April, welcomes the fresh flowers blooming in hundreds of apple, peach, and cherry orchards. The city shifts into full gear with the **Peach Festival** at the end of July and the torturous **Ironman Canada Triathlon** in August. The Peach Festival offers recreational and aquatic activities for all ages, while the nonstop triathlon commits true athletes to 4km of swimming, 180km of bicycling, and 45km of running (holy cow). The mists and mellow fruitfulness of fall mark the ripening of the wine season. There are five wineries within easy driving distance of Penticton; the closest one, **Casabello Wines,** 2210 Main St. (492-0621), offers regular tours and free tasting. Nearby, **Apex Alpine,** 185 Lakeshore Dr. (collect 492-4181), provides winter diversion with six ski lifts, 35 runs, and a 670m vertical drop.

Kelowna

Gravitating towards Ogopogo, Kelowna's Loch Ness monster, summer events in this pleasant resort cluster about the lake. However, the renowned 81-year-old Kelowna Regatta, traditionally the summer's centerpiece, came to a screeching halt in 1988 after two riots deranged the extravaganzas. That summer, events from watersports to air shows quickly evolved into something quite different from family-oriented fun; tear gas was even called into play. The next year's riot was in fact better organized than the regatta itself. Signs as far away as Vancouver advertised the event and trucks filled with rocks drove in just for the "festivities." The city of Kelowna has since discontinued its annual celebration. Despite this setback, Kelowna still tempts tourists with a diverse dining scene, dozens of reasonable motels, excellent beaches, and enough free wine to make you forget there ever was a regatta.

Practical Information and Orientation

Visitor Information: Travel Infocentre I, 544 Harvey Ave. (861-1515). Large office plastered with brochures on local tours and events. The staff smiles. Open daily 8am-8pm; Labor Day-late June 9am-5pm. **Infocentre II, (The Adventure Continues)** is playing 500m north of the airport (765-0338). More brochures and beaming smiles. Same hours as the first one.

Greyhound: 2366 Leckie Rd. (860-3835). To: Calgary (2 per day, $53.80); Banff (2 per day, $39.30); Cache Creek (2 per day, $20.80); Kamloops (2 per day, $14.30).

Buses: Kelowna City Bus Transit (860-8121). Limited service to the beach, downtown, shopping centers, and Greyhound. All the buses stop downtown at the intersection of Ellis St. and Bernard Ave. Fares start at 70¢, seniors (BC only) and students 55¢ for 1-zone travel. A 1-zone Day Pass costs $1.90 (BC seniors and students $1.40).

Car Rental: Rent-A-Wreck, 2702 Hwy. 97 N. (763-6632). From $25 per day plus 14¢ per km. Must be 21 with credit card.

Bike Rental: Sports Rent, 3000 Pandosy St. (861-5699). Mountain bike rentals $5 per hr., $15 per day or $30 per 3 days. Open daily 9am-6pm.

Weather: 765-4027.

Crisis Hotlines: Adults 763-9191; teens 763-3366.

Emergency: 911.

Police: 762-3300.

Post Office: 471 Queensway Ave. (762-2118 or 763-4095). Open Mon.-Fri. 8:30am-5pm. Postal Code: V1Y 7N2.

Area Code: 604.

Downtown Kelowna crams against the eastern side of Lake Okanagan. **Highway 97**, which becomes Harvey Ave. downtown, runs directly through the city and crosses the lake on a 620m floating bridge, the largest of its ilk in Canada. The highway leads directly north to Salmon Arm and south to Penticton. In the downtown area, streets are plotted according to an ordered grid system. Imagine that.

Accommodations and Camping

Rooms in Kelowna can be as elusive as the Ogopogo. The newly-founded hostel is the best option. Call well in advance for reservations in both the summer and winter, when many hotels fill up with monthly renters. Rates often take a dive during the off-season.

Kelowna Backpackers Hostel, 2343 Pandosy St. (763-6024). In the heart of downtown Kelowna, this recently opened hostel offers beds and breakfasts at hostel prices. Kitchens facilities, TV, and free local phone calls. Shared rooms $10, doubles $30.

Rainbow Motel, 1810 Gordon Dr. (763-3544), 2 blocks off Hwy. 97. Some of the lowest prices in town. All rooms have A/C and cable TV; some have refrigerators. Singles from $32. Doubles from $34. Kitchens $5 extra.

Ponderosa Motel, 1864 Harvey Ave. (860-2218). About as homey and secluded as a roadside motel can be—friendly rooms and tidy management. Only 16 units, so call ahead. Singles from $34. Doubles from $38. Kitchens available.

Kenogan Motel, 1750 Gordon Dr. (762-3222) at Harvey Ave. Peeling paint and abused furniture, but everything functions. Singles $30, $5 per additional person.

Quo Vadis Motel, 3199 Lakeshore Rd. (763-4022). Too expensive for the single traveler, but king-sized beds in singles can easily sleep two (6 if you're all close chums). Gargantuan TV in room. Heated swimming pool. Singles and doubles from $45. Kitchenettes available.

Kelowna has two major camping areas, one on the east side of the river and one on the west. For reasons known only to Ogopogo, the western campgrounds are less expensive than their eastern neighbors. Traveling west along Hwy. 97 across the floating bridge, take a left on Boucherie Ave. and continue for a few kilometers to campground country. **Happy Valley** on Pritchard St. (768-7703; $14), **Billabong Beach** on Boucherie Ave. (768-5913; $11), and **Green Bay** on Green Bay Rd. (768-5913; $15) all offer sandy services and sophisticated beaches. Happy Valley tends a cherry orchard where happy visitors are happily welcome to pick as many cherries as they wish. Green Bay operates cabins where four can sleep for $40 per night.

Food

Although beef still reigns supreme in Kelowna (seafood flounders in a distant second), the town is beginning to discover the delights of lighter fare. Try cruising the backstreets for mouth-watering bakeries and ice cream shops. There is a **Safeway** supermarket on Richter and Bernard (open daily 8am-10pm).

Jonathan L. Segals, 262 Bernard Ave. (860-8449). Stay cool on the roof overlooking the lake while pecking at some of Kelowna's best food. An original menu features everything trendy from tofu burgers ($4) to pizza bagels ($2). Sandwiches and burgers $4-6. "Open 11:30am-Late!" it says—at least 1-2am on weekends.

Roxy's Cafe, 1630 Ellis St. (763-1000). High ceilings, tall drinks, and a lunatic menu ensure popularity with locals. Moderately priced burgers ($4-6) and salads ($3-6). Open Mon.-Thurs. 11:30am-9pm, Fri.-Sat. 11:30am-midnight, Sun. 5-9pm.

Earl's Hollywood on Top, 211 Bernard Ave. (763-2777). Turn north on Bernard just east of Okanagan Lake off Hwy. 97. This area favorite serves up Hollywood Ribs ($11) as well as other beef and fresh seafood dishes. Outdoor dining. Open Sun.-Thurs. 11:30am-11pm, Fri.-Sat. 11:30am-midnight.

Poor Boys, 450 Bernard. Hums 7 days a week. Your choice of liver and onions, meatloaf, Cornish game hen, or halibut and chips $5, $4.45 for seniors. Draft beer $1.25. Soup and sandwich lunch special $3. Open Mon.-Sat. 8am-10pm, Sun. 10am-8pm.

Sights

In Kelowna, the term "vineyards" translates into "four wineries and four free wine-tasting rooms." **Calona Wines,** 1125 Richter St. (762-9144), 6 blocks directly off Hwy. 97, is the second largest winery in all of Canada and gives free guided tours on the half-hour, between 9am and 4pm in the summer. Sample as many wines as you wish, then stumble into the gift shop. (Open daily 9am-6pm; in winter Mon.-Sat. 10am-5pm, Sun. 11am-5pm.) Other wineries near the city include **Grey Monk Estate Cellars,** 5450 Lakeshore Dr. (766-3168), north of Kelowna (tours given daily noon-3pm on the hour; free), the **Cedar Creek Estate Winery** (764-8866) south of town; and **Mission Hill Vineyards,** corner of Boucherie Rd. and Mission Hill (768-5125), to the west (tours given daily 10am-7pm on the hour; free). True connoisseurs should arrive in early October for the annual **Okanagan Wine Festival,** which features fashion shows, craft fairs, and, of course, an evening of serious wine tasting.

Younger sippers or those who prefer their grapes that way should visit the **Sun-Rype Fruit Juice Factory,** at 1165 Ethel St. in Kelowna (762-2604). This Canadian company has been harvesting plants since 1889, and from June through September they'll show you how it's done at no charge. (Open Mon.-Fri. 9am-3pm.) The **Hiram Walker Okanagan Distillery,** in nearby Winfield on Jim Bailey Rd., produces over 50 potent potables, including Canadian Club whisky, offers free tours and tastings five times per day (Mon.-Fri.) during the summer. Call ahead (763-4922) to arrange a tour.

With the loss of the regatta, summertime visitors searching for seasonal entertainment will have to settle for the less rowdy theatrical tradition of the **Sunshine Theatre.** The established ensemble presents professional dramas from late June to late August in the air-conditioned **Kelowna Community Theatre.** For more information write to Sunshine Theatre, P.O. Box 443, or call 763-4025.

Water buffs willing to risk an encounter with Ogopogo can rent canoes from **Lee Outfitters,** S1-C6 R.R. #1, Glenmore Rd. (762-8156). Waterskiers, fishermen, and families wishing to cruise on the Okanagan will find everything they need at **Kelowna Marina,** P.O. Box 1167 (762-3128). Bring your bathing suit and gobs of that white stuff lifeguards wear on their noses.

Kelowna definitely focuses on the outdoorsy crowd, but rained-in geologists can visit the **Kelowna Museum,** 470 Queensway (763-2417), for a cross-section of the city's natural history; the **Kelowna Art Gallery** (762-2226) is in the same building. Free **walking tours** of Kelowna's art galleries leave from the Chamber of Commerce; call 763-9803 to arrange one.

Southeastern British Columbia

Revelstoke

Named after the British banker who supplied the money to build a much-needed railroad into the wilderness, 19th-century Revelstoke was once a town straight out of a Peckinpah film, with dust-encrusted maniacs maiming each other amid the gold-infested Selkirk Mountains.

Slung between the impressive snow-capped peaks of the Selkirk and Monashee Mountains, the town attracts mainly an older, Winnebago-ensconced crowd. It is, however, trying to entice a younger set of skiers and hikers. A large-scale ski resort is in the works for Mt. MacKenzie, just 5km south of Revelstoke. The projected influx of money and tourism threatens to turn Revelstoke into another Banff—an unwelcome prospect to many who actually live there. Until the déluge, however, Revelstoke remains quiet, beautiful, and unexploited.

Practical Information and Orientation

Visitor Information: Travel Information Centre, junction of Hwy. 1 and Hwy. 23 (837-3522).
Chamber of Commerce, 205 E. 1st St. (837-5345), downtown. Useful and convenient. For more information write to the Chamber, P.O. Box 490, Revelstoke V0E 2S0.

Greyhound: 1899 Fraser Dr. (837-5874), just off Hwy. 1. To: Calgary ($31.80); Vancouver ($40); Salmon Arm ($7.70). Open Mon.-Fri. 5:30am-7pm and 10pm-midnight.

Taxi: Johnnie's, 314 Townley St. (837-3000).

Car Rental: Tilden Car Rental, 301 W. 1st St. (837-2158). New cars at decent rates. $36 per day with 100 free km plus 10¢ per additional km. Must be 21 with credit card.

Bicycle Rental: Revelstoke Cycle Shop, 120 Mackenzie Ave. (837-2648). Rents mostly mountain bikes ($6 per hr. or $24 per day) and an occasional 10-speed. Open in summer Mon.-Sat. 9am-9pm, winter Mon.-Thurs. and Sat. 9am-5:30pm, Fri. 9am-8pm.

Ambulance: 374-5937.

Police: 320 Wilson St. (837-5255).

Post Office: 307 W. 3rd St. (837-3228). Open Mon.-Fri. 8:30am-5pm. Postal Code: V0E 2S0.

Area Code: 604.

Revelstoke borders the Trans-Canada Hwy., 410km west of Calgary and 575km east of Vancouver. The town itself is relatively small and can be easily covered on foot or by bicycle but Revelstoke National Park which encompasses the town is 263-square km. Mild temperatures, a relatively long growing season, and large amounts of rain endows this portion of the Columbia Mountains with lush vegetation and bountiful wildlife. Revelstoke and its easterly neighbor, Glacier National Park, contain a section of the Columbia Rain Forest. Pay a visit to the 800-year-old cedars and you will come to appreciate why residents are so concerned over the logging industry's "clear-cutting."

Accommodations and Camping

Numerous inexpensive hotels line Revelstoke's rim along the Trans-Canada Hwy. A quick detour into the town, however, will give you a bed for the same low price. Local campgrounds tend to favor the RV driver over the backpacker.

L & R Nelles Bed & Breakfast, Hwy. 23 (837-3800), 2km from the Trans-Canada Hwy. A bit more expensive than most bargain hotels, but the atmosphere could be bottled as a cure for homesickness. One night's lodging in this large family ranch includes a generous breakfast of bacon, eggs, hash browns, and coffee. Singles $30. Doubles $40. Each additional adult $15, child $10. No reservations necessary.

Hidden Motel, 1855 Big Eddy Rd. (837-4240). Take Hwy. 23 south from Trans-Canada Hwy., turn left on Big Eddy Rd. Cozy, comfortable family-operated hotel. Every room has its own stove, refrigerator, kitchen sink, and cable TV. Great for groups of up to 6. Singles and doubles $33. Each additional person $5. Senior citizen discount $2.

Frontier Motel, corner of Trans-Canada Hwy. and Hwy. 23 (837-5119). Twenty-eight small but adequate rooms. Tiny but functional color TV, sink, bath. Exuberant staff. Popular restaurant run by the same management next door. 24 hr. store. Singles $28. Doubles $37. Quads $40. Prices drop $3 in winter.

Smokey Bear Campground, Hwy. 1, 5km west of Revelstoke. Convenient location, but so close to the highway that logging trucks rumbling by at 2am may awaken light sleepers. Clean bathrooms, metered showers, laundromat, and amply stocked store. Both RVs and tents are welcome. Sites $10, each additional person 75¢. Electricity $2, sewer $1, fresh water 50¢. Open May-Oct.

Canyon Hot Springs, Hwy. 1 (837-2420), 35km east of Revelstoke on the border of Mt. Revelstoke National Park. The staff is pleasant, and the scenic location—near both Mt. Revelstoke and Glacier National Parks—is convenient for exploring the mountains. Caters more to RVs than to backpackers. Sites $12. Group rates available on request. Open May-Sept.

Food

The downtown dining scene is dominated by Chinese and Italian restaurants. You'll have to head many kilometers to the west along Hwy. 1 for a Whopper or a box of McDonaldland Cookies.

Annie's Kitchen, 1401 Victoria Rd. (837-2042). Baseball-cap-and-plaid-shirt sporting customers pack in for the large portions. The $3 breakfast special includes a cup of toe-curlingly strong coffee. Muffins and bottomless cup of coffee $2. Soup and sandwich $3.50. Open daily 6am-9pm.

Manning's Restaurant, 302 MacKenzie Ave. (837-3253). The best Chinese food in town, plus a wide array of continental dishes. Reasonably priced. Beef and broccoli ($6.25), sweet and sour spareribs ($6), 8- or 12-oz. steaks ($1 per oz.). Open Mon.-Sat. noon-10pm, Sun. 4pm-9pm.

Frontier Restaurant, at the junction of Hwy. 1 and Hwy. 23 (837-5119). The Frontier dishes out large helpings of the "Ranchhand," ½-lb. of beef with the works ($6). Tenderfoots may prefer the sparer "bareback" ($4.25). Open daily 6am-9pm.

Brenda's, 104 Connaught (837-3030), in the Macleod's Bldg. Brenda whips up good, homemade food that the locals love. Self-service lunch and breakfast specials $2-4.

A.B.C. Family Restaurant, Victoria St. (837-5491). Link in a chain of "family" restaurants, but maintains an original atmosphere nonetheless. Huge menu ranges from $6-9 for dinner entrees. Try the croissant lunch ($4.75), and don't pass up a slice of fresh pie ($2-3). Open daily 6am-10:30pm.

Burger Junction, 1601 Victoria Rd. (837-2724). Better than average fast food burgers ($2-4). An Arctic Swirl ($2.75) is icing on the cake. Open daily 10am-10pm; in winter Mon.-Sat. 10:30am-7:30pm.

Sights

All tourism in town revolves around the **Revelstoke Dam,** 5km north of Hwy. 1 on Hwy. 23 (837-6515 and 837-6211). Don't think that if you've seen one dam, you've seen them all. The dam's **visitor centre** underscores the dam's mechanical marvels by means of a free tour via shortwave radio receiver. Take the elevator to the top of the dam for an impressive view. (Open daily mid-March to mid-June 9am-5pm; mid-June to mid-Sept. 8am-8pm; mid-Sept. to Oct. 29 9am-5pm. Disabled access.) The **Revelstoke Museum and Archives** (837-3067), 315 1st St. W., like most other small town museums, resides in an old government building (the post office) and advertises a modest ensemble of local turn-of-the-century artifacts. Note the extensive collection of early 20th-century photography. (Open June-Aug. Mon.-Sat. noon-9pm; May, Sept., and Oct. Mon.-Fri. 1-5pm; Nov.-April Mon., Wed., and Fri. 1-4pm.)

Mt. Revelstoke National Park has many of the scenic attractions one expects from the Canadian national parks. Despite its relatively small size (260 sq. km), the park produces plenty of flora and fauna to amuse biologists and nature lovers. Thirty-five km of established trails lead to many excellent **fishing** lakes—apply at the park information center for a permit. Those not wishing to climb to the summit of Mt. Revelstoke can take a winding scenic road all the way to the peak. **Summit Road** leaves the Trans-Canada Hwy. 1.5km east of Revelstoke and takes about an hour to drive. Ask the **park superintendent,** 313 3rd St. W. (837-5155), about the park's other pleasures.

Two special **boardwalks** just off Hwy. 1 on the eastern border of the park allow visitors to explore the local brush in depth. One trail leads through "acres of stinking perfection"—skunk cabbage plants deep and wide which grow to heights of over 1.5m. The other wanders into a forest full of giant cedar trees, some over 1000 years old.

Revelstoke has tried some curious variations on the downhill theme to spice up its winter ski season. **Mount Mackenzie,** P.O. Box 1000 (collect 837-9489), 5km outside of town, gives you a chance to climb deep bowls of powdered snow in motorized Snow Cats. Experts (rich experts, that is) may want to try **Helicopter Skiing,**

P.O. Box 1409, Golden (344-5016, call collect), in the Selkirks. **Cross-country** skiers can find more than enough snow and trails in the nearby national parks to keep them busy all winter long. Contact **Ski Revelstoke**, P.O. Box 1479 (837-3538), for more information. Summer vacationers might wish to contact **Monashee Outfitting**, P.O. Box 2958 (837-3538), which sponsors just about every outdoor activity possible, including horse rides, fishing trips, hunting trips, and gold panning.

Near Revelstoke

Salmon Arm is a small, honky-tonk town just like thousands of others, but its setting is extraordinary. Lake Shuswap, right next to downtown, is sublime and the mountains which cradle the town are absolutely spectacular, especially when the leaves change in autumn.

Stay at the **Cindosa Bed and Breakfast**, 3951 40th St. NE (832-3342), and the Cindosas will pamper you with nice beds and fantastic, home-cooked breakfasts (with ingredients from from the farm out back). They will even pick you up at the bus station. Singles $25. Doubles $35. Each additional person $10. **Glen Echo Resort**, R.R. #2, Site #3 (832-6268), 7 mi. west on Hwy. 1, is the campsite nearest to town, and is smack on the lake, with a sandy beach and excellent swimming all summer long. Gregarious owner. (Sites $8. Open Victoria Day-Thanksgiving.)

Despite its name, Salmon Arm's culinary establishments showcase neither fish nor limbs. Restaurants offer standard surf 'n'turf fare with a definite emphasis on the turf. Try **Mr. Mike's** (832-8428) on Hwy. 1 across from the waterslide. The salad bar is a vegetable frenzy with 65 items. All-you-can eat lunch ($5) and dinner ($6) which includes dessert. Open daily 11am-9pm. The **Eatery,** at 361 Alexander St. (832-7490) serves "Big Magilla"sandwiches (turkey, roast beef, and lamb, $3.85) along with other gargantuan concoctions. Open Mon.-Thurs. and Sat. 6am-5pm, Fri. 6am-9pm.

While in town, you can fish or swim in **Lake Shuswap** or go white water rafting on nearby **Adams River.** You can also hike out to **Margaret Falls,** just west of town. Follow the signs for Heral Park off Hwy. 1. A 10km detour and a short hike on the well-manicured slopes will bring you to the striking set of falls.

The **Travel Infocentre**, Box 999 (832-6247), is just off the Trans-Canada Hwy. in the center of town. You can wash out your grubbies at the **Maytag Laundromat**, 456 Trans-Canada Hwy. in the the Smitty's shopping center (832-5500. Open daily 6am-11pm). Emergencies in Salmon Arm are answered by the **ambulance** (374-5937); the **hospital** is at 601 10th St. NE (832-2182) and the **police** are at 501 2nd Ave. NE (832-6044). Address letters to **postal code** V1E 4M6. The **area code** is 604.

Glacier National Park

For a $5000 salary bonus and immortality on the map, Major A.B. Rogers discovered a route through the Selkirk Mountains which finally allowed East to meet West in Canada's first transcontinental railway. Completed in 1885, the railway was a dangerous enterprise; over 200 lives were lost to avalanches during its first 30 years of operation. Today, **Rogers Pass** lies in the center of Glacier National Park, 1350 square kilometers that commemorate the efforts of Rogers and other hardy frontiersmen toward uniting British Columbia with the rest of Canada.

Avalanches, grizzly bears, and harsh winters conspire to render Glacier National Park a beloved stomping ground for rugged outdoor enthusiasts. With over 140km of challenging trails, Glacier provides plentiful hiking and camping for those who wish to rough it in the Selkirks. For the hiker on wheels, the Trans-Canada Highway bisects the park into a pleasant 45-minute drive, complete with spectacular views of over 400 glaciers. The best time to visit Glacier is from mid-June to late September, when the climate is relatively mild; unfortunately, during the summer months rain falls one out of every two days.

Hikers not directly descended from Sir Edmund Hilary should avoid the park in winter, as near-daily snowfalls and the constant threat of avalanches often restrict travel to the Trans-Canada Hwy. Preemptive snowslides, often induced by the Canadian Armed Forces and their 105mm howitzers, can block the highway itself.

Practical Information and Orientation

Visitor Information: Park Administration Office, 313 3rd St. W. (837-5155), west of the park in Revelstoke. Knowledgeable staff ready to answer any questions about the Canadian National Parks. Open Mon.-Fri. 8am-4pm. Write the Superintendent, P.O. Box 350, Revelstoke V0E 2S0. **Rogers Pass Centre,** located along the Trans-Canada Hwy. in Glacier National Park, has enough computerized information, large scale models, and photographs on the history of Glacier to warrant a visit. Do not miss the free 25-min. movie *Snow War,* which is shown on the hour and includes a chilling scene from an actual avalanche rescue. Open daily 8am-9pm; in winter 9am-5pm.

Greyhound: 837-5874.

Emergency: 837-6274.

Area Code: 604.

Glacier lies right in the path of the Trans-Canada Hwy., 262km west of Calgary and 723km east of Vancouver.

Accommodations, Camping, and Food

The pickings for indoor lodging in the park are mighty slim. The **Best Western Glacier Park Lodge,** Trans-Canada Hwy., The Summit, Rogers Pass (837-2126), has the only beds in town. Rooms are nice, with comfortable beds and clean bathrooms. Not surprisingly, these amenities make the lodge too expensive for the average budget traveler: singles $75, doubles $80 during peak summer months, with children under 12 free and a 10% discount for senior citizens.

Glacier National Park has three campgrounds: **Loop Brook, Mountain Creek,** and **Illecillewaet** (ILL-uh-SILL-uh-watt). Backcountry camping is also permitted, but be sure to register beforehand with the warden service and pitch your tent at least 3km from the highway. All three open in mid-June and close by the end of September, though Illecillewaet stays open in winter without plumbing. Winter guests must register at the **Administration Office** at Rogers Pass. Be forewarned, however, that 10-foot snow drifts in November make camping a survival sport. Unserviced sites at Mountain Creek, the largest of the three campgrounds, cost $6.50. Similar sites at the other two run $8.50 per night. The brochure *You Are In Bear Country* at Rogers Pass will be of use if you prefer not to become a late-night snack for a Smoky-become-Freddy. During the summer the camps have bathrooms with fresh cold water, but no showers. Park passes are $20 per year, with a daily rate of $3 per car (4 days $6). The only restaurant in the area is at the Best Western, where prices are certainly not budget and proper attire is required.

Sights

The Trans-Canada Hwy.'s numerous scenic turn-offs are embellished by picnic facilities, bathrooms, and historical plaques. For a more detailed description of the various hiking trails, contact the Park Administration Office or pick up a copy of *Footloose in the Columbias* at the Rogers Pass Information Centre. The highest concentration of hiking trails can be found near the Illecillewaet campground, 3.4km west of Rogers Pass. Seven well-marked trails provide spectacular views of the area's mountains and glaciers. From early July to late August, the Rogers Pass Information Centre runs daily interpretive tours through the region beginning at 10am. Come prepared for one of these 4-6 hour hikes with a picnic lunch, a rain jacket, and a sturdy pair of walking shoes. The park also promotes skiing, snowshoeing, and, on a trial basis, mountain biking. Talk to a park official, however, before propelling yourself in such fashion.

Northern British Columbia and the Yukon

The sheer physical beauty of the Yukon and Northern British Columbia amply rewards those willing to put up with nasty weather, poor road conditions, and the loneliness of a land that averages one person per 15 square kilometers. Native Americans gave this area its name when they called the Yukon River "Yuchoo," or Big River. The first region of North America to be settled (some 20,000 years ago), the Yukon and Northern British Columbia remain largely untouched and inaccessible.

The Cariboo Highway

The portion of Hwy. 97 known as the Cariboo Hwy. runs approximately 500km north-south between Cache Creek and Prince George. So uninteresting is most of the route that stops carry official names such as "100 Mile House" and "108 Mile Ranch." There is no reason to stop anywhere along the route, aside from an occasional fill-up or photo opportunity . . . or sheer fatigue.

Should you find yourself pulling over, your best bets are the towns of **Williams Lake**, at Mile 155 (signposts are always the last to go metric) or **Quesnel** (pronounced kwuh-NEL) at the half-way point between Williams Lake and Prince George.

In Williams Lake, you can secure a roof over your head at the **Valley View Motel** (392-4655), right off the highway. Air-conditioned singles are $30, doubles $32. Just next door is the **Lakeside Motel** (392-4181), with singles for $25, campsites for $7.50, and full hookups for $13.50. In **Quesnel**, try the **Wheel Inn Motel**, 146 Carson Ave. (992-8975) with singles for $26. **Roberts Roost Campground**, 3121 Gook Rd. (747-2015), is in **Dragon Lake**, 8km south of Quesnel. Open April to October, the campground has showers, flush toilets, laundry facilities, and a swimming beach. (Sites $11, full hookup $15.)

The Williams Lake **Travel Infocentre** on the highway (392-5025; open daily 8am-8pm, Mon.-Fri. 9am-5pm Labor Day-Victoria Day) can give you the poop on activities and events in the area, including the **Williams Lake Stampede**, held during the first weekend in July. In Quesnel, the **Infocentre**, at 703 Carson Ave. in Le Bourdais Park, has similar services (992-8716; open 8am-8pm daily, closed Labor Day-Victoria Day). Ask about the town of **Barkerville**, 80km east, where the Yukon Gold Rush lives again. The town clings precariously to the map by luring tourists with wild-west costumes, period buildings, and gold-panning. Check with the Quesnel Travel Infocentre or the Visitor Services Officer, Barkerville V0K 1B0 (994-3332), for a schedule of the town's shenanigans. For reasonably complete coverage of the entire Cariboo region, pick up a free copy of *Cariboo Calling,* published by the 100 Mile Free Press each year and available at just about any hotel or tourist attraction between Clinton and Williams Lake.

Prince George

Named for the British Prince whom Shelley described as "mud from a muddy spring," Prince George was not incorporated until its infusion with railway workers in 1915. Today, the town prides itself on its spontaneity and originality; during February's Mardi Gras festival, elaborately costumed locals compete in a golf tournament—in the snow. The rest of the time, the town has a strange, almost eerie, feel to it. The 50-square-block downtown is made up mostly of one-story buildings in various states of disrepair. A few modern, 15-story office buildings perch around the edge of the area, confusing the picture. The streets are broad and virtually devoid of cars or people, and yet the city proudly publicizes the fact that it has installed parking structures supplying 5000 spaces. It seems as if everything grew rapidly, only to have its citizens quickly and mysteriously skip town. Perhaps Prince George's 68,000 residents simply spend all their time in the suburbs, enjoying the city's 100 parks and 60 baseball diamonds.

Practical Information and Orientation

Visitor Information: Travel Infocentre, 2 locations—1198 Victoria St. (562-3700), at 15th Ave., and the junction of Hwy. 16 and 97 (563-5493). Both open May-Sept. Mon.-Fri. 8:30am-8pm, Sat.-Sun. 9am-8pm. The latter remains open in the off-season Mon.-Fri. 9am-5pm. Pick up a free, detailed map of the city.

Trains: BC Rail (561-4033), at the end of Terminal Blvd., 2km south on Hwy. 97. To Vancouver (1 per day in summer, 3 per week in winter, $65.60) along one of British Columbia's most eye-popping routes. Reservations recommended. **VIA Rail**, 1300 1st Ave. (564-5233), at the foot of Quebec St. To: Edmonton, AB (3 per week, $77.50); Jasper, AB (3 per week, $47), and Prince Rupert (3 per week, $62). Seniors and students 1/3 off. Terminal open Tues.-Thurs. 5pm-1am.

Greyhound: 1566 12th (564-5454), across from the Infocentre. Buses to: Whitehorse, YT (1 per day, $145.05); Edmonton, AB (2 per day, $62.10); Vancouver (3 per day, $62.85); Prince Rupert (2 per day, $60.10); and Dawson Creek (2 per day, $34.95). Open Mon.-Sat. 5:30am-midnight, Sun. 5:30-10:15am, 3:15-6pm, and 8:30pm-midnight.

Public Transportation: Prince George Transit, 1039 Great St. (563-0011). Limited service around the downtown area, but everything's within walking distance anyway. Fare 75¢, senior citizens 50¢, students 60¢. Runs Mon.-Sat. 8:30am-5pm.

Taxi: 564-4444.

Car Rental: Rent-A-Wreck, 1956 3rd Ave. (563-7336). $17 per day, plus 11¢ per km. Must be 21 with credit card. Open Mon.-Fri. 8:30am-5:30pm, Sat. 9am-5pm. **Tilden**, 1350 7th Ave. (564-4847). $35 per day, plus 12¢ per km. Weekend special $15 per day and 15¢ per km. Must be 21 with credit card. Open Mon.-Fri. 7:30am-5:30pm, Sat. 8am-5pm, Sun. 8am-4pm.

Library: 887 Dominion (563-5528 for a machine, 563-9251 for a person). Open Mon.-Thurs. 10am-9pm, Fri.-Sat. 10am-5:30pm.

Laundromat: The White Wash Laundrymat, at 2nd and George (563-2300). Open daily 6am-9pm.

Highway Conditions: 564-2524.

Crisis Center: 563-1214.

Pharmacy: 5th Avenue Pharmacy, at 5th and Dominion. Open Mon.-Sat. 10am-10pm.

Hospital and Ambulance: Prince George Regional Hospital, 2000 15th Ave. (564-4558).

Police: RCMP, 1325 5th Ave. (563-1111).

Post Office: 1323 5th Ave. (561-5184). Open Mon.-Fri. 8:30am-5pm. Postal Code: V2L 4R8.

Area Code: 604.

Prince George lies roughly equidistant from four major Canadian cities: 780km northeast of Vancouver, 720km southeast of Prince Rupert, 735km west of Edmonton, and 790km northwest of Calgary. The airport is at the eastern end of town, a $6 cab ride from downtown. Both the VIA Rail and Greyhound stations are centrally located, within walking distance of hotels and restaurants.

Accommodations and Camping

Queensway Court Motel, 1616 Queensway St. (562-5068), near downtown. Take Queensway north off Hwy. 97. Standard hotel rooms, but reasonably inexpensive. Singles $30. Doubles $34.50.

Spruceland Inn Ltd., 1391 Central St. (563-0102), at the junction of Hwy. 97 and 15th Ave. near the Infocentre. Costs a bit more than the run-of-the-mill budget hotel, but it has an indoor pool, excellent large rooms, and central location. Singles $46. Doubles $52. Make reservations well in advance.

The National Hotel, across from VIA station. If the loud voices of the semi-permanent residents don't keep you awake, the throbulating music from the bar below will. The redeeming quality of this hotel is the amazing price. Singles with shared bath $18. Doubles $32.

South Park Trailer Park, on Hwy. 97 (963-7577), 5km south of Prince George. Somewhat bare sites, but removed from the highway. The bathrooms are clean but woefully inadequate, with only one toilet and one coin-op shower—expect a shower line in the morning. Sites $9, with hookups $11.

Red Cedar Inn, on Bear Rd. (964-4427), 8km west off Hwy. 16. Low prices, but the sites are so close to the highway that you can see the whites of the eyes of drivers passing by. Sites $9, with full hookup $11.

Spruceland KOA, on Hwy. 16 (964-7272), immediately across from Red Cedar Inn. The goodies expected from a KOA: heated pool, free showers, laundry room, and store. Sites $13, with full hookups $18.

Food

Prince George serves middle-of-the-road cuisine: average plates for average prices. Two days out of town you will not remember when, where, or how much you ate. The hyperkinetic eateries lined up along Central St., west of downtown, are not such a bad option considering the bleak culinary landscape.

Earl's, 15th Ave. and Central St. (562-1527). Part of a Canadian chain, but well worth a visit. On your way in, dodge droppings from the countless *papier mâché* parrots overhead. Burgers, fish, creative sandwiches (all around $6), and steaks ($10-12). Open Mon.-Thurs. 11:30am-midnight, Fri.-Sat. 11:30am-1am, Sun. 11:30am-10pm.

Nick's Place, 363 George St. (562-2523). Bare bulbs on the walls make it difficult to see what you're eating. Large dish of surprisingly good spaghetti $5.50. Open Mon.-Sat. 11am-3:30pm, Sun. 4-11pm.

Royal Jade Restaurant, at 3rd and Dominion (562-8888). Standard breakfast with eggs, bacon, and toast $2.25. Lunch and dinner are exclusively Chinese ($5 per dish). Open Mon.-Sat. 8am-7pm, Sun. 8am-2pm.

Pastry Chef Bakery (564-7034), across from Nick's. 30% off day-old goodies. Open Mon. 10am-5pm, Tues.-Thurs. and Sat. 9am-5:30pm, Fri. 9am-6pm.

Niner's Diner, at the corner of 5th and George (562-1299). Expensive dinners ($11-15) but great nachos ($6) and artfully kitschy decor. Open Mon.-Thurs. 11:30am-11pm, Fri.-Sat. 11:30am-midnight, Sun. 11:30am-10pm.

Sights and Seasonal Events

Cottonwood Island Nature Park, a 3km walk from downtown along Patricia Blvd., has plenty of comfortable walking trails. For a bird's eye view of the rich landscape, climb to **Connaught Hill Park,** off Queensway on Connaught Dr. **Fort George Park,** at the eastern end of 20th Ave., houses the **Fort George Regional Museum,** which has accumulated a wooden life preserver, a collection of primitive chain saws, and $1.25 rides on an original steam-engine train. (Open Tues. noon-8pm, Wed.-Sun. noon-5pm; Sept. 16-May 14 Mon.-Fri. 10am-3pm. Admission $1.25, senior citizens and children 75¢.)

For a closer look at the machinations of the modern forest industry, the **Canfor-P.G. Pulp and Paper Mills** offers scintillating three-hour **mill tours** Monday-Friday. A mill bus picks up whomever is interested at the Infocentre on Victoria St. at 1pm. Times may vary, so call the center in advance.

A half-hour drive from downtown will bring visitors well into the British Columbian wilderness, full of excellent fishing and hunting opportunites. **Bobsports,** 680 Victoria St. (562-2222), sells a complete line of equipment for both pursuits. No bobsleds, though. (Open Mon.-Thurs. and Sat. 9am-6pm, Fri. 9am-9pm.) Forty-three km north of downtown on Mitchell Rd. is the **Huble Farm.** Originally a homestead, the farm seized the chance to become a trading center for travelers making the portage across the continental divide between the Fraser and Peace Rivers. Today, Old Man Huble's place is a museum devoted to the life of the western *courier-de-bois* (open July 1-Sept. 1 daily 9am-5pm).

The close relationship between Prince George and its railways is chronicled at the **Prince George Railway Museum** (563-7351). The museum, on the north side of the ironically obstructing tracks, is difficult to reach. To get there, you must cross the ties at the Grand Trunk Pacific Bridge, then double back west about one km. (Open May 20-Labor Day daily 9am-5pm).

Prince George's Napoleonic events and festivities "range from the sublime to the ridiculous and beyond." A perfect example of this is **Mardi Gras,** which lasts 10 days in February or March and features such events as Sno-golf, softball in the snow, and the goofiest test of physical agility—knurdling (jousting with padded poles). Summer events include a rodeo and triathlon. Prince George's **Oktoberfest** is the biggest event of the fall, and includes exactly what you'd expect it to: beer, bands, and braided blondes.

Prince Rupert

Wealthy entrepreneur Charles Hays dreamt of completing a second trans-Canada railroad, ending at then-uninhabited Kaien Island. Hays bought himself a ticket to England to drum up the money—aboard the S.S. *Titanic.* Although Hays's fundraising and design plans lie peacefully with him on the Atlantic floor, the Grand Trunk Pacific Railway eventually established a company city on the island. They named it Prince Rupert, after the second cousin of Charles II. Poor Hays is today remembered only by a statue downtown.

Practical Information and Orientation

Visitor Information: Travel Infocentre, 1st Ave. and McBride St. (624-5637). Hwy. 16 turns into McBride at the edge of town. Brochures a-plenty, including extensive information on Alaska for visitors heading north up the Marine Hwy. Free museum displays relics of ancient Native American tribes. Open Mon.-Sat. 9am-9pm, Sun. 9am-5pm; mid-Sept. to mid-May Mon.-Sat. 10am-5pm.

Flights: Air BC, 700 2nd Ave. W. (624-4554). Three flights per day to Vancouver (one way $221). **Canadian Air** (624-9181), on the bottom floor of the mall on 2nd Ave., offers the same service at the same price.

VIA Rail: 627-7589. Take the ramp down from the corner of 1st Ave. and 2nd St. If you weigh more than 2 tons, find an alternate route. Service to Vancouver ($152 one way) and Prince George ($59 one way), 3 times per week. Open Mon., Wed., Thurs., Sat. 9am-3pm.

Greyhound: 822 3rd Ave. near 8th St. (624-5090), across from Overwaitea. Two buses per day to Prince George ($60.10). Open Mon.-Fri. 8am-8pm, Sat. 8am-noon and 4-8pm, Sun. 9:30-11am and 6:30-7:45pm.

Alaska Marine Highway: Ferries north from Prince Rupert into the Alaskan Panhandle. To: Ketchikan (US$32, with car US$62), Wrangell (US$47, with car US$96), Petersburg (US$58, with car US$123), Juneau (US$87, with car US$182), and Haines (US$101, with car US$207).

BC Ferry: 624-9627. Take Hwy. 16 west until it ends at the ferry terminal. Service to: the Queen Charlotte Islands (6 per week, $15, with car $73), Vancouver, and Port Hardy (4 per week, $68, with car $210). Reservations required at least 3 weeks in advance for vehicles.

Local Transportation: Prince Rupert Bus Service, 624-3343. Limited service around downtown. Operates Mon.-Sat. Fare 75¢, seniors 45¢, students 55¢.

Library: On McBride at 6th St. (627-1345). Open Mon.-Thurs. 10am-9pm, Fri. 10am-5pm, Sat. 9:30am-5:30pm; in winter Sun. 2-5pm.

Laundromat: King Koin Laundromat at 7th and 2nd Ave. Open daily 7am-11pm.

Pharmacy: Shoppers Drug Mart, corner of Fulton and 3rd Ave. W (624-2151). Open Mon.-Fri. 9:30am-9pm, Sat. 9:30am-7pm, Sun. 11am-6pm.

Emergency: 911.

Police: RCMP, 100 6th Ave. (624-2136).

Post Office: 2nd Ave. and 3rd St. (627-3085). Open Mon.-Fri. 9am-5:30pm. Postal Code: V8J 3P3.

Area Code: 604.

The only major road into town is the versatile **Highway 16,** which becomes McBride at the city limits and then curves left to become 2nd Ave. downtown. Prince George is 720km to the east.

Accommodations, Camping, and Food

Nearly all the hotels are located within the 6-block-square area circumscribed by 1st Ave., 3rd Ave., 6th St., and 9th St., but very few are available for less than $40, and those that are tend to be of the over-the-tavern variety. Everything fills up when the ferries dock, so call a day or two ahead, no matter where you intend to stay.

Pioneer Rooms, 167 3rd Ave. E (624-2334), in the big green building. Squeaky-clean with great management and a less rough-edged clientele than at the other budget lodgings. Singles $15-20. Doubles $25-30.

Oceanview Hotel, 950 1st Ave. W. (624-6259). Guests of the loud music and hard liquor sort. One bathroom per floor. Singles 23. Doubles $25, with bath $33.

Commercial Hotel, 901 1st Ave. W. (624-6142). The spartan rooms seem clean, although it's hard to tell in the dim light. Singles $20. Doubles $25.

Aleeda Hotel, 900 3rd Ave. W. (627-1367). Cheapest of the more expensive places in town. All the standard amenities. Singles $42. Doubles $55.

Park Ave. Campground, 1750 Park Ave. (624-5861), less than 2km east of the ferry terminal via Hwy. 16, this is the only campground actually in town. The sites are by no means private, but the hot showers and short walk to the ferry terminal make this a welcome stopover for weary ferry passengers. Tentsites $11. RVs $13.

Prudhomme Lake Campground, 16km east on Hwy. 16. A province-managed spot with toilets and drinking water. 24 sites at $8 each.

New Moon, 630 3rd Ave. (627-7001). One of the better Chinese restaurants on the Alaska Marine Highway. Daily lunch specials ($6) include soup, tea, and dessert. All-you-can-eat smorgasbord featuring (drumroll, please . . .) barbecue ribs (served Mon.-Fri. noon-1:30pm, Fri.-Sun. 4:30-8pm) $7.75. Open Mon.-Thurs. 11am-midnight, Fri.-Sat. 11am-3am, Sun. 11am-11pm.

Green Apple, 301 McBride St. (627-1666). Huge servings of fish and chips $6. Open Mon.-Sat. 11am-9:30pm, Sun. noon-8pm.

Bogey's Bistro, at the corner of 2nd Ave. and 6th St. (624-6711). Fairly elegant, even with the big-screen TV. the Pita Reuben ($7) is a nice alternative to burgers. Open daily 11:30am-2:30pm.

Cu's Steak and Seafood, 816 3rd Ave. (624-3111). You guessed it. Steaks from $12, seafood from $11. Burgers $3.50-5. Open Mon.-Thurs. 11am-10pm, Fri.-Sat. 11am-11pm, Sun. 4-10pm.

Sights and Activities

Although it offers neither mind-blowing sights nor a high-powered tourist industry, Prince Rupert is graced with genuine Canadian amiability. Let your friends at the Travel Infocentre give you a walking tour map spanning the 15 downtown blocks. The tour includes all that can be considered sights—namely the Infocentre's free museum, a tiresome wealth of totem poles, the carefully manicured Sunken Gardens, and a Native American carving shed. Also meeting at the Infocentre are three-hour guided archeological boat tours. For $15 a local expert will take you across the waves to nearby Digby Island, the site of an ancient Native settlement, then across to the modern community of Metlakatla and back to Prince Rupert. Tours leave from the Infocentre daily at 1pm. No reservations required.

Restored to its original 1911 form is the **Kwinitsa Station** (627-1915) across from the VIA Rail station. This small, free museum has a coherency rare in small-town museums and breathes life into a vanished era. The videotape on the second floor is especially interesting. Open June 10-Sept. 1 Mon.-Fri. 9am-7pm, Sun. 11am-7pm.

The **Mt. Hayes Gondola** (624-2236 or 624-6263) will take you to waving-distance of Alaska. Walk or drive 2 km to the end of Wantage Rd., off Hwy. 16, and watch for eagles and other birds of prey. (Open Wed., Thurs., Sun. noon-9pm, Fri.-Sat. noon-midnight. Admission $6, seniors and children $4.)

Sixteen km farther east along Hwy. 16 sits **Diana Lanke Park,** a picnic area set against an enticing lake—especially alluring in the lazy oven of summer.

Queen Charlotte Islands

Just 130km off the coast of Prince Rupert float the Queen Charlotte Islands, an archipelago with over 150 members. Sometimes referred to as the "Canadian Galopagos," these remarkable islands were one of the only two regions in Canada not renovated by glaciers during the last ice age (the other is the southern tip of Vancouver Island). The islands' 6000 residents—over half of whom live in Masset and Queen Charlotte City on Graham Island—coexist with the world's only known Golden Spruce tree, a yellow-flowering perennial daisy, a quarter of Canada's Pacific Coast bird species, and one particularly potent (and illegal) strain of hallucinogenic mushroom.

Sailor Juan Perez first discovered the islands in 1774, but not until four years later did Captain George Dixon inscribe them on the map, lending them the name of his beloved ship. Little has changed since the first encroachments by European settlers over 200 years ago.

The islands' Natives, the Haida (pronounced HIGH-duh), which have outlasted other First Nations in maintaining the integrity of their civilization, make up a large percentage of the population, and an even larger proportion of the islands' many artists. The land itself is heavily forested and largely mountainous. The beaches tend to be rocky and the water cold, but kayakers and anglers heap unending praise on the archipelago. When traveling about these "small" islands keep in mind that cities on Graham and Moresby Islands are not within walking distance of each other, and there is no public transportation. Try to find fellow travelers willing to form a popular front to share the astronomical car rental fees, or be prepared to bike the 110km between Queen Charlotte City on the south shore of Graham Island and Masset on the north.

Queen Charlotte City

Registered in 1908, Queen Charlotte City grew up around a sawmill and still relies on logging as its major industry, as the bare hills that surround the town can testify. Only now teetering on the brink of modernity, the town has so far been immune to the pesky virus of development. Some residents feel that they are being held back by lack of government funds, while others are satisfied with simply preserving their slow-paced lifestyle and watching Italian soap operas subtitled in Canadian on their satellite-dish TVs.

Practical Information and Orientation

Visitor Information: Travel Infocentre, 559-4742. Follow 3rd Ave. east out of town 1km, in a jewelry store. Buy the $4 *Guide to the Queen Charlotte Islands* and let the unusually perspicacious staff highlight, annotate, and amplify the already comprehensive book. Hours vary with the ferry. For a morning ferry, open 6am-5pm; for an evening ferry open 9am-9pm.

Kallahin Travel Service: 559-8455 or 559-4746, upstairs from Rainbows. Arranges all sorts of boat charters and special trips to the islands.

BC Ferry: Terminal in Skidegate Landing (559-4485), 5km east. To Prince Rupert (6 per week, $15, with car $73). Reservations at least 3 weeks in advance required.

Interisland Ferry: (559-4485). Runs between Skidegate Landing on Graham Island and Alliford Bay on Moresby Island (12 trips per day, $1.60, with car $6.80).

Budget Car Rental: 3219 Wharf St. (559-4675), in the same building as Sears and Dutch Oven. $53 per day plus 25¢ per km. Must be 21 with credit card. Open Mon.-Fri. 9am-3pm, Sat. 9am-1pm.

Bike Rental: 559-4653, knock three times on the black plywood shack on 3rd Ave. in the center of town. Older mountain bikes $16 per day, $50 deposit, helmets and saddlebags included (no hourly rental). Also offers day-long bike tours for $60 per person, 2 person minimum. Open Tues.-Sat. 11am-6pm.

Laundromat: 121 3rd Ave. (559-4444). Open Mon.-Sat. 9:30am-6pm, Sun. 11am-5pm.

Hospital: 3rd Ave. (559-8466), in the east end of town.

Emergency: Police (RMCP), 3211 Wharf St. (559-4421). **Ambulance,** 559-4506. **Fire,** 559-4488.

Post Office: in the City Centre Bldg. on 2nd Ave. (559-8349). Open Mon.-Fri. 8:30am-5:30pm, Sat. 8:30am-12:30pm. Postal Code: V0T 1S0.

Area Code: 604.

Queen Charlotte City tumbles inward from the water at the southern end of **Graham Island.** The city stretches for 2km along 3rd Ave., which turns into Hwy. 16 to the east, leading to Tlell, Port Clements, and Masset.

Accommodations and Camping

Spruce Point Lodging, (559-8234), on the little peninsula across from the Chevron station at the west end of town. Brand-new hostel beds in a co-ed dorm for $12.50. Laundry and cooking facilities. Also operates a bed and breakfast next door (singles $45, doubles $50).

Premier Hotel, 3101 3rd Ave. (559-8451). Friendly staff and eclectic decor. Singles with shared bath from $25. Doubles with balconies from $45.

Bellis Lodge (557-4434), in Tlell, 40km north of the ferry terminal. Hostel beds and kitchen facilities, but the nearest supplies are 19km to the north. Members $12, nonmembers $17.

Haydn Turner Park Campsite, at the west end of 4th Ave. $8 sites with toilets and water.

Joy's Island Jewellers, 3rd Ave. at the east end of town. Makes a few tentsites available in the yard next door ($3.50). Showers are a whopping $5, but a private well, which provides some of the best drinking water on the islands, is a real gem.

Food

Margaret's, 3223 Wharf (559-4204). You can't go wrong with Margaret's $5.50 sandwich specials, including soup and fries. Open Mon.-Sat. 6:30am-3pm, Sun. 9am-3pm.

Claudette's Place, 233 3rd Ave. (559-8861) just west of town center. Great Denver Omelette ($6) and enormous halibut steaks (they'd better be for $14). Open daily 8am-10pm.

Dutch Oven Bakery and Deli, on Wharf St. (559-4645), next to Margaret's. Light snacks, including meatpies ($2.45) and carrot muffins (75¢). Open Tues.-Wed. and Fri.-Sat. 10am-5pm.

Kathy's (559-4231), in Skidegate Mission. This converted RV in the center of town is applauded many times over for its octopus burger ($4). Open Wed.-Mon. noon-6pm.

Sights

Contemporary Haida artwork sparkles on display at **Rainbows Art Gallery and Gift Shop,** on 3rd Ave. at Alder (559-8420), a gallery of silver, gold, and argillite (black shale) carvings. (Open Mon.-Sat. 9am-6pm.)

Skidegate Mission, known as "the village," is a cluster of small houses with big TV satellite dishes located 2km east of the landing. In summer, head down to the village on Thursday nights for the **seafood feast** at Old Skidegate Hall, a $20 extravaganza (children under 13 $10) featuring the biggest and best of the week's catch. Dinner starts at 6pm, but locals arrive 30 minutes early. Halfway between Skidegate

Landing and Skidegate Mission is the **Queen Charlotte Islands Museum** (559-4643), presenting a large collection of argillite carvings and other relics of Haida history. (Open Tues.-Sat. 9am-5pm. Admission $2.)

Heading northwest to Pt. Clements (pronounced kluh-MENTS) for 50km will lead you to a 5km dirt road ending in a trailhead. From there it's a five-minute hike to the world's only known mature **Golden Spruce,** an albino-like tree whose needles have been bleached by sunlight. Go in the morning for best viewing. When you've finished marveling at it, head to the **museum** at the south end of Pt. Clements (557; open Mon.-Fri. 1-5pm; admission $1) to inspect a vast collection of tools designed to chop it down.

In Queen Charlotte City, just south of town, is the city dump. The garbage is no thrill, but the 40-plus bald and golden eagles and half-dozen black bears that congregate there nightly are a real sight. Go in a car, as garbage bears are capable of trashing any tourist.

Masset

Bordered by a wildlife sanctuary to the north, an ancient village to the west, and ebbing tides to the south, Masset, with a population of 1600, is the largest metropolis on the islands. In 1909, the Graham Steamship, Coal, and Lumber Company built "Graham City" at the north end of Graham Island, but the city later became "Masset," in honor of the Native Massett Haida who laid first dibs on the area.

Old Massett Village, 2km west of town at the terminus of Hwy. 16, is hustlin' and bustlin' with 600 descendants of the original tribe. The alleys are lined with Haida housefront/storefronts selling an array of carvings. Be sure to walk all the way to the peninsula's tip for some of the island's finest ocean views. At the jumbled **Ed Jones Haida Museum,** old photographs and Native artwork now fill what was once a two-room schoolhouse for Haida children.

Red-breasted sapsuckers, orange-crowned warblers, glaucous-winged gulls, great blue herons, red tufted Rosens, and binocular-toting tourists converge on the **Delkatla Wildlife Sanctuary,** off Tow Hill Rd. The best paths from which to sight the 113 airborne species leave from the junction of Trumpeter Dr. and Cemetery Rd. The **Golden Spruce** itself can be reached more easily via paved Hwy. 16, running south from Masset. (See Queen Charlotte City.)

Practical Information and Orientation

Visitor Information: Travel Infocentre, Old Beach Rd. (626-3982), at Hwy. 16. Plenty of local history and trail maps for choice birdwatching. Open July-Aug. The **Masset Village Office** on Main St. will give you further information, as can the **Chamber of Commerce,** Box 38, Masset V0T 1M0 (626-5211).

Car Rental: Budget Rent-A-Car, Collison Ave. (626-5571). Must be 21 with credit card. $53 per day plus 25¢ per km.

Taxi: Island Taxi, 557-4230.

Ambulance: 626-3636.

Police: 626-3991, on Collison Ave.

Postal Code: V0T 1M0.

Area Code: 604.

Masset is at the north end of Graham Island along Hwy. 16. Collison Ave. (fortunately, not "collision") is the main drag. Old Massett Village lies 2km farther down the road.

Accommodation, Camping, and Food

It's something of an understatement to say your options in Masset are limited. **Naikoon Park Motel,** on Tow Hill Rd. (626-5187), close to the beach and Naikoon Provincial Park, charges $35 for singles and doubles. **Masset-Haida Lions RV Site**

and Campground, on Tow Hill Rd. next to the Wildlife Sanctuary, is the town's only campground and has metered showers, flush toilets, and gravelly sites. (Sites $8, electricity $2; open late May-late Sept.) **Naikoon Provincial Park** dominates the eastern half of Masset's peninsula and maintains two campgrounds. **Agate Beach** is 20km east of Masset on the northern edge of the park, and **Misty Meadows** is just outside of Tlell in the southeast corner of the park. (Both charge $8 for sites with toilets and water.)

The **Pizza Place,** on Orr St. (626-5493), comes closest to offering a local specialty in the form of "Pizza with Pizzazz." (Open Mon.-Sat. 11:30am-midnight.) Break the diet next door at the city's only dough outlet, the **Dutch Oven Bakery** (626-3283; open Tues.-Sat. 9am-5:30pm).

The Cassiar Highway

Most travelers journey between British Columbia and Alaska via the Alaska Hwy. or aboard Alaska Marine Hwy. ferries. But a third and largely ignored route traces 750km of **Highway 37,** commonly known as the Cassiar Highway. This lonely road slices through spectacular extremes of burnt forest, logged wasteland, and virgin wilderness from Hwy. 16 (between Prince George and Prince Rupert) to Mile 655 of the Alaska Hwy. (near the Yukon border). Long stretches of unpaved road, swirling dust, and flying rocks can chip windshields, crack headlights, and generally gum up the car's works. Nevertheless, the Cassiar is a good way to cut hundreds of km off the Alaska Hwy. Gas stations are few and far between, so bring along a spare tire and an emergency gas supply.

The road is divided into three sections. From Hwy. 16, the intrepid motorist follows 172km of paved road to **Meziadin Junction.** The **Rest and Be Thankful Café** allows the dazed driver to do just that, featuring dinner specials and fresh berry pies. The cabins next door run the gamut from about $25 for a single bunkhouse bed to $65 for two single beds and a double bed all in one big room.

A 340km trek across hard-packed dirt will take you on to **Dease Lake.** Here the **Boulder Café** defies budget travelers' intuitions, serving prohibitively expensive breakfasts but reasonable dinners. (Open Mon.-Sat. 6am-10pm, Sun. 7am-10pm.) **The Grayling** has well-kept singles for about $32.

The final leg of the trip is the most scenic, each turn of the paved road to the Alaska Hwy. revealing a new lake or mountain. These last 237km reward the adventurer with one of the best (and best-named) restaurants on the Cassiar: **Yukon Ma's Cafe.** Try the salisbury steaks then cleanse the palate with a few burgers.

A Complete Guide for Highway 37, available at the **Terrace Infocentre,** offers a partial list of the many facilities and campgrounds on the route. Hitchhikers on the Cassiar, as usual, will find locals and truckers friendly and RV drivers unfriendly.

Skeena Valley

The Gitksan tribe once used the Skeena River as a convenient route from the coast into the mainland mountains. Dubbed *K-shian* (water of the clouds) by the trading Natives, the river flows west from Hazelton and empties into the Pacific at Prince Rupert, all the way carving out the foggy Skeena Valley.

Gitksan villages dot Hwy. 37, which follows the river through the valley to Prince Rupert. "Gitksanomics" (the tribal economy) depends on the trickle-down theory of handicraft sales from passing motorists. Craft shops and totem poles grow quicker than dandelions on the roadsides of **K'san** and **Kitwanga** villages.

In the heart of the Skeena Valley at the intersection of Hwy. 16 and 37, **Terrace** is a perfect stopover on the way to or from Prince Rupert ferries. The **Travel Infocentre,** 4511 Keith Ave. (635-2063), provides ample background on the Skeena's colorful history, as well as information on the nearby Native villages. (Open daily 9am-8pm.) If you plan to spend the night, the **Cedars Motel,** 4830 Hwy. 16 (635-

2258), has some of the cheapest (and only) rooms in town (singles from $29) and an adjoining restaurant. Campers can sleep under the stars at **Ferry Island Campground** (638-1174), 3km east of Terrace on Eby St., off Hwy. 16. Its pit toilets, drinking water, and electrical hookups make a night in the wilderness just that much cozier. (Open Victoria Day-Labor Day. Sites $9, electricity $2.)

Dawson Creek

Do not confuse drab Dawson Creek, BC with Dawson City, former capital of the Yukon. While the latter is worth seeing to relive the gold-mining era, the former should be used only to get out and scrape the bugs off your windshield. Dawson Creek's major distinction is the cairn marking Mile Zero on the Alaska Highway, the major access road to the Land of the Midnight Sun. Dawson Creek gets the last laugh, however, as it has a monopoly on civilization in a hundred-km radius.

McLeod Lake, about 100km into the trip between Prince George and Dawson Creek, has a campground, a few hotels, and little else. Unless the monotony of the drive has weighted your eyelids to the point where you need to rest, knock off the next 160km to **Chetwynd**—home of the **Country Squire Motor Inn** (788-2276; 5317 S. Access Rd.) and the **Pinecone Motor Inn** (788-3311; 5224 53rd Ave.). Both hotels lie directly on the highway as you enter from the south, and both offer the same basic necessities: rooms with bathrooms and a restaurant downstairs that serves decent food. Singles run about $42. The **Chetwynd Court Motel** (788-2271; 5104 N. Access Rd.) is in the city center and has singles from $38.

Overnight guests in Dawson Creek looking for econorama lodgings should try the **Cedar Lodge Motel,** 801 110th Ave. (782-8531; singles $25). Another option is the **Peace Villa Motel,** 1641 Alaska Ave. (782-8175). Behind the neo-Victorian exterior you'll find large, clean rooms, nice bathrooms, and a friendly staff bearing free coffee. (Singles from $36.) RV drivers should head for **Tubby's RV Park,** 20th St. and Hwy. 97 (782-2584); tenters should try **Mile 0 City Campground,** 1km west of the Alaska Hwy.'s starting point (782-2590). Tubby's has an industrial, RV feel, with its 71 sites (open May-Oct.), while Mile 0 manages a generally greener atmosphere. Both have showers and rent sites for $9.

The best place for nourishment in Dawson Creek is the **Stagecoach Restaurant,** 1725 Alaska Ave. (782-8419), at Mile 0 of the Alaska Hwy. McDonald's Golden Arches beckon at 11628 8th St., just down Hwy. 2.

Greyhound, 1201 Alaska Ave. (782-3131), in Dawson Creek runs buses to Whitehorse, YT (1 per day, $112.65), Prince George (2 per day, $35), and Edmonton, AB (2 per day, $51.15). In an emergency, contact the **police** at Alaska Ave. and 102nd (782-5211), or call the **ambulance** (782-2211). The **tourist information centre,** 900 Alaska Ave. (782-9595), in the old train station just off Hwy. 97, brandishes brochures that promote the few areas of interest in Dawson Creek. (Open daily 8am-8pm). The **post office** is at 11622 7th St. (782-2322), and the **postal code** is V1G 4J8. The **King Koin Laundromat,** 1220 103rd Ave. (open daily 8am-9pm) is around the koiner.

The Alaska Highway

Built during WWII, the unpredictable Alaska Highway maps out an astonishing 2647km route between Dawson Creek, BC, and Fairbanks, AK. One probably apocryphal story maintains that all the bends and dips in the road were created intentionally to prevent Japanese fighter pilots from landing during the war. The route is barren of any trace of civilization, just as it was when 19th-century prospectors first planted mileposts arbitrarily amid the arctic winds. Do not use the mileposts as official calibration standards, but rather as a general guide; the new kilometer posts, though not as frequent, are more accurate. **Fort Nelson,** 480km north of Dawson Creek, is the last city of any note before Whitehorse. The **Pioneer Motel Ltd.,** at Mile 300 (774-6459), convenient to the highway, rents singles for $32, doubles for

$36, and kitchenettes for $4 extra. Campers should continue another kilometer to **Westend Campground** (774-2340), a veritable oasis in the middle of the Yukon with hot showers, a laundromat, and a free car wash. Sites are $9. Fort Nelson cuisine consists of nothing more than standard hotel restaurant fare.

Just past Fort Nelson, road conditions take a turn for the worse. Pavement gives way to "chip-seal," a layer of packed gravel held in place by hardened oil. In the dry summer, dust and rocks fly freely, virtually guaranteeing shattered headlights and a chipped windshield. All drivers should fit their headlights with plastic or wire-mesh covers. Most locals protect their radiators from bug splatter with large screens mounted in front of the grill. As if to compensate for the deteriorating road conditions, the scenery picks up considerably after Fort Nelson. The stone mountains shooting up every few kilometers are especially dramatic. The spruce timberlines are low in altitude and razor sharp, leaving only cold gray rock to meet the sky above. Near the BC-Yukon border, the road winds through vast areas of land scorched by forest fires; gray arboreal skeletons with only small patches of color stretch as far as the eye can see in all directions. At night, this area offers prime viewing of the northern lights, as there are no city lights to clutter the sky.

Small hotels, plain but expensive, pockmark the remainder of the highway every 80 to 160km. Campers' needs are pampered by the provincial parks that spring up along the road. **Stone Mountain Campground,** about 160km past Fort Nelson, is a park campsite set in the scenic paradise beside Summit Lake. Each park has sites with toilets and fresh water available for $5 per night. Great views invite photographic framing now and again along the remainder of the drive to Whitehorse; the long journey is nonetheless quite taxing.

Pick up the exhaustive listing of *Emergency Medical Services* and Canada Highway's *Driving the Alaska Highway* in a visitors bureau, or write the Department of Health and Social Services, P.O. Box H-06C, Juneau, AK 99811 (907-465-3027). The free pamphlet *Help Along the Way* lists emergency numbers along the road from Whitehorse to Fairbanks.

Whitehorse

Whitehorse's population exploded to 13,000—nearly half of the Yukon's total population—when in 1942 the U.S. Army built the Alaska Highway to defend against the Japanese. The Yukon's capital maintains its century-old gold-rush architecture and continues to exude the self-reliant individualism of that time. Today, the descendants of the original gold miners coexist with Native Americans who have lived in this region for 20,000 years.

Practical Information and Orientation

Visitor Information: Visitor Reception Centre, 302 Steele St. (667-2915), in the T.C. Richards Bldg. at Steele and 3rd Ave. Since there are only 7 official reception centers in the entire Yukon, each one comes stocked with an astounding amount of literature. The center also offers free audiovisual shows downstairs. Open May-Sept. daily 8am-8pm. The **Parks Canada Building,** South Access Rd. and 2nd Ave. (667-4511), next to the *S.S. Klondike,* stores information on the history of the Yukon's sternwheeler river boats. Free boat tours are given daily. Open May-Sept. daily 9am-7:30pm.

Flights: Canadian Airlines (668-4466, for reservations 668-3535). To: Calgary (2 per day, $433), Edmonton (2 per day, $372), and Vancouver (3 per day, $372).

Greyhound: 3211 3rd Ave. (667-2223). To: Vancouver (1 per day, $142), Edmonton (1 per day, $142), and Dawson Creek (1 per day $110). There is *no* Greyhound service to Alaska. Open Mon.-Fri. 8am-noon and 1-5:30pm, Sat. 9am-noon, Sun. 5:30-9am.

Alaskan Express: in the Greyhound depot (667-2223). Buses run late May to mid-Sept. To: Anchorage (2 per week, US$140), Haines (2 per week, US$71), and Fairbanks (2 per week, US$129).

Norline: in the Greyhound depot (668-3355). Operates bus service to Dawson City (3 per week in summer, 2 per week in winter; $66).

Local Transportation: Whitehorse Transit, 668-2831. Limited service downtown 6am-7pm. Fare $1, seniors 50¢, children and students 75¢.

Taxi: Yellow Taxi, 668-4811. **Yukon Taxi Service,** 668-6830.

Car Rental: Norcan Leasing, Ltd., 8 Alaska Hwy. at Mile 917 (668-2137). Must be 19 with credit card. Cars from $44 per day with 25¢ per km.

Bike Rental: The Bike Shop, 6th Ave. and Ray St. (667-6501). Mountain bikes for $19 per day. Open daily 10am-6pm.

Library: 2nd Ave. at Hawkins. Open Mon.-Fri. 10am-9pm, Sat. 10am-6pm, Sun. 1-9pm.

Crisis Line: 668-9111.

Pharmacy: Shoppers Drug Mart, in the mall at Main St. and 3rd Ave. Open Mon-Fri. 9am-9pm, Sat. 9am-6pm, Sun. 11am-5pm.

Hospital: 668-9333, on the east side of the Yukon River on Hospital Rd., just off Wickstrom Rd.

Ambulance: 668-9333.

Police: 4th and Eliot (667-5555).

Post Office: 3rd and Wood, in the Yukon News Bldg. General Delivery Postal Code for last names A-L is Y1A 3S7, M-Z Y1A 3S8. Open Mon.-Sat. 7am-7pm.

Area Code: 403.

To reach Whitehorse by car, take the downtown exit off the Alaska Highway. Once there, park the car and use your feet; downtown is relatively compact. The airport is to the west, a short cab ride away, and the bus station is on the northeastern edge of town, a few minutes' walk from downtown.

Accommodations and Camping

Call the **Yukon Bed and Breakfast Association** (633-4609) to reserve a room in a Klondike household. Singles average $30 and doubles $40, plus $15 per extra person. Hotels often exploit their guests' joy at finding a town with more than 100 residents and pets—singles average $50. Camping in Whitehorse can be a problem since there is only one RV campground and one tenting park near the downtown area. Tenters praying for a hot shower should find their way to the group of campgrounds clustered 10-20km south of town on the Alaska Highway.

Fourth Avenue Residence (IYHF), 4051 4th Ave (667-4471). Offering long- and short-term housing, the residence boasts cooking and laundry facilities, good security, and free use of the city pool next door. Extremely well run. Hostel beds $13.50, nonmembers $15. Private singles $38. Doubles $42.

Chilkoot Trail Inn, 4190 4th Ave. (668-4190). Clean rooms enlivened by TV, private bath, and lots of highway noise. Singles $45. Doubles $55, with kitchenette $60.

Fort Yukon Hotel, 2163 2nd Ave. (667-2594), near shopping malls and Greyhound. Rooms are old but untarnished. Singles from $24. Doubles from $39.

Pioneer Trailer Park, at Mile 911 on the Alaska Highway (668-5944). Food store, laundromat, RV repair shop, isolated tentsites, showers, and a car wash. Not bad for the middle of the wilderness, though the tent sites are an inconvenient 3-min. walk from the washrooms. This is the closest campground to Whitehorse that has showers for tenters, but they cost 25¢ per min. Sites $6, with hookups $13. Open May-Sept.

Robert Service Campground, 1km out South Access Rd. A convenient stop for tenting folk, but provides almost as few amenities as it did when Robert Service (the bard of the Yukon) visited here in the 19th century. Drinking water must be boiled 10 min. before consumption. There are toilets, but no showers. Sites $4.

Sourdough City RV Park, 2240 2nd Ave. (668-7938), across from Greyhound. All the earmarks of a post-romantic Utopia, with RVs stretching as far as the eye can see. 103 full hookup sites, laundromat, showers, and a courteous staff. Complete hookups $16. Open May-Sept.

Food

Do not be disillusioned by the dilapidated exteriors of many Whitehorse gastrocenters; the insides are usually well-worn but cozy. The high prices are reasonable by Yukon standards.

No Pop Sandwich Shop, 312 Steele (668-3227). Very popular with Whitehorse's small suit-and-tie crowd. The Beltch (BLT and cheese, $4) and veggie burger ($3.75) are worth trying. Open Mon.-Sat. 9am-9pm.

Talisman Café, 2112 2nd Ave. (667-2736). Good food in a nondescript environment. Get all 4 food groups in the Russian *peroshki* ($8). Burritos $5 and breakfasts $5.50. Open Mon.-Fri. 6am-11pm, Sat. 8am-10pm

Mom's Kitchen and Donut Shop, 2157 2nd Ave. (668-6620), at Alexander. Serves all meals, but breakfast is a specialty when Mom whips up some pretty good omelettes ($4.75-8). Lunch on a "Burger Supreme" with *everything* $8.45. Open Mon.-Fri. 6:30am-8pm, Sat. 6:30am-4pm, Sun. 6:30am-2pm.

The Bistro, 205 Main St. (668-7013), at 2nd Ave. Expensive Canadian cuisine and a finale of delectable desserts. The Canuck croissant sandwich (sliced smoked salmon and onion) is $8 and the carrot cake $2.50. Open Mon.-Thurs. 8:30am-5pm, Fri. 8:30am-7pm, Sat. 8:30am-5pm.

Sights

Considering the size of its city, the Whitehorse welcoming committee has put together an astonishing array of scheduled tours and visitor activities. The **Yukon Museum Association,** 3126 3rd Ave. (667-4704), sponsors "Heritage Walks"—free daily tours of downtown Whitehorse, which leave from the office next to the visitors center. The **Yukon Conservation Society,** 302 Hawkins St. (668-5678), arranges hikes Monday through Friday during July and August to explore the Yukon's natural beauty. **Yukon Native Products,** 4230 4th Ave. (668-5935), sells traditional goods; tour the garment factory to see how far Klondikes will go to keep warm in the frigid winters. (Open Mon.-Sat. 7:30am-8pm, Sun. 10am-4pm; tours given Mon.-Sat. at 10:30am and 3:30pm.) If you're touring on your own and have any questions, ask the **Red Serges**—students dressed as turn-of-the-century North West Mounted Police officers (about a dozen of these pseudo-mounties roam the city daily from 10am-6pm).

The restored *S.S. Klondike,* on the South Access Rd. (667-4511), is a permanently dry-docked sternwheeler recalling the days when the Yukon River was the city's sole artery of survival. Pick up a ticket for a free guided-tour at the information booth at the entrance to the site's parking lot. (Open May-Sept. daily 9am-6pm.) The **Whitehorse Rapids Dam and Fish Ladder,** at the end of Nisutlin Drive (667-2235), 2km southeast of town, allows salmon to bypass the dam and continue upstream on the world's longest salmon migration. (Open mid-July to Aug. daily 8am-10pm. Free.)

Visitors missing local culture will find it at the **MacBride Museum,** 1st Ave. and Wood St. (667-2709). The exhibit features memorabilia from the early days of the Yukon, including photographs of Whitehorse as a tent city. (Open mid-May to early Oct. daily. Admission $3, senior citizens and students $2, families $6.) The **Old Log Church Museum,** 303 Elliot St. (668-2555), at 3rd, has converted its pews into a museum that fully explicates the history of missionary work in the territories. Built by its pastor, the church required only three months of labor; sub-zero weather has a way of motivating people. (Open late May to mid-June Mon.-Fri. 9am-5pm; mid-June to late Aug. Mon.-Sat. 9am-8pm, Sun. noon-4pm. Admission $2, children $1.) Similarly, the incredible three-story **Log Skyscrapers** at 3rd Ave. and Lambert St. were built singlehandedly in the 1970s by a local septuagenarian.

There are two stage shows in town, each of which takes a different angle in an attempt to re-create the ethos of the Stampede of '98. The **Frantic Follies,** produced by Atlas Tours, 2nd Ave. and Wood St. (668-3161; open daily 9am-6pm), is a vaudeville revue featuring banjo pickin' men, cancanning women and—say it ain't so—WWII tunes. (Admission $15, children under 12 $7.50, shows 7:30pm and

9:30pm nightly). The **Eldorado Show,** nightly at 8pm in the Gold Rush Inn, 411 Main St. (668-6472), puts on a two-hour melodrama with original musical numbers in the style of the gold rush era. Stephen Sondheim would wince. (Tickets sold in the the lobby, $14, children under 12 $7.) Vacationing scholars are welcome to browse and research at the **Yukon Archives,** in the Yukon Government Administration Building, 2140 2nd Ave. (667-5321).

Two-hour river tours are available on two different lines. The **Youcon Kat** (668-2927) takes you on a jaunt downstream from the hydroelectric dam from June to Sept. Boats leave daily at 1 and 3pm from the ramshackle pier at 1st and Steele. ($14, senior citizens $11, children $7.) **Schwatka Tours,** run by Atlas Tours (668-3161), run upstream from the dam through what's left of the rapids (the dam raised water levels almost 10m). Get directions and tickets in advance at Atlas tours, about 4km out of town (tours 2pm and 7pm daily, $13, children $6.50). The **Yukon Gardens** (668-7972), 3km southwest of town at the junction of the Alaska Hwy. and South Access Rd., blossom with 22 acres of indigenous northern wild flowers and plants. With only 71 frost-free days per year in this region, the Gardens grow some of the hardiest wildflowers and lichens in the world. (Open early June to mid-Sept. daily 9am-9pm. Admission $4.75, students $2.75.)

Dawson City

Gold. Gold! GOLD! Men have killed and died for it, nations have warred over it, and empires have crumbled for the lack of it. But of all the insanity ever inspired by a "lust for the dust," the creation of Dawson City must surely be ranked among the most ridiculous. For one glorious, crazy twelvemonth, from July 1898 to July 1899, Dawson City, on the doorstep of the Arctic Circle and a thousand miles from anywhere else, was the largest Canadian city west of Toronto and every bit as cosmopolitan as Seattle or San Francisco. Its 30,000-plus residents, with names like Swiftwater Bill, Skocum Jim, Arizona Charlie Meadows, Quickfingers Quitslund, and The Evaporated Kid, had each somehow dragged, pushed, sledded, or otherwise got 1000 lb. of provisions over the most difficult terrain on earth—all driven by one desire: to be rich beyond the dreams of avarice.

The towns along the various routes into the Klondike were inevitably named by the 70,000 or so who never made it: Hell's Mountain, Destruction City, and Death Gulch are the monuments to the forgotten thousands who failed. You didn't need to find gold to "succeed" in Dawson, you merely had to survive.

When the gold ran out in 1900, the city didn't prove as hardy as her inhabitants and quickly fell into ghost-town status. It wasn't until the early 60s that the Canadian federal government, recognizing the importance of Dawson, brushed away the tumbleweeds and began to restore the Arctic Eldorado to her former glory. The work has been slow, but the results to date have been worthwhile. There is no tacky Hollywood-goes-Yukon show biz here, but a faithful re-creation of one of the greatest gold rushes that ever was. And after more than three-quarters of a century, Dawson City is once again the jewel of the Yukon.

Practical Information and Orientation

Visitor Information: Visitor Reception Centre, Front and King St. (993-5566). Daily historic slide shows and movies, as well as extensive information on local history. Open May-Aug. daily 9am-9pm, Sept. 9am-8pm. **Tourist radio** (96.1 FM) has weather, road conditions and seasonal events.

Buses: Norline Coaches Ltd., 3211A 3rd Ave. (668-3355). The only scheduled service to Dawson City. Buses leave from Whitehorse and connect to Fairbanks 3 times daily.

Library: At the corner of 5th and Princess (993-5571). Open Mon.-Thurs. 9:30am-9pm, Fri. noon-7pm, Sat. 8am-4pm, Sun. noon-8pm.

Laundromat: At the corner of Front and York (993-5384). Wash yourself at the coin-op showers or bathe in the real soda fountain. All open Mon.-Fri. 8am-7pm, Sat.-Sun. 10am-6pm.

Pharmacy: Arctic Drugs (993-5331) on Front St. next to the visitors center. Open Mon.-Fri. 9am-8pm, Sat.-Sun. 9am-6pm.

Emergency: 993-5333.

Police: RCMP (993-5444) on Front St. in the south end of town north of Craig St.

Post Office: 5th Ave. and Princess St. (993-5342). Open Mon.-Fri. 8:30am-12:30pm and 1:30-5:30pm, Sat. 8:30am-12:30pm. Postal Code: Y0B 1G0.

Area Code: 403.

To reach Dawson City, take the Klondike Hwy. 533km north from Whitehorse, or follow the Top of the World Hwy. about 100km east of the Alaskan border. The city itself can easily be covered by foot in only a few hours.

Accommodations and Camping

Predictably, hotel rooms are more expensive in Dawson City than elsewhere. Consider camping or inquire about the hostel-type rooms which were under construction at 3rd and Harper in July 1990 (they should be in operation by the summer of 1991).

Mary's Rooms, at 3rd Ave. and Harper (993-6013). The word "dump" springs to mind, but upon further inspection, you'll find the place tolerable. Singles $39. Doubles $45. All with shared bath.

Westminster Hotel, at 3rd and Queen (993-5463). Respectable rooms. Proprietor looks like an authentic sourdough. Singles $40. Doubles $60, with shared bath.

Dawson City Bed and Breakfast, 451 Craig St. (993-5649). Fantastic rooms with wonderfully accommodating management. Singles $49. Doubles $55, shared bath. Make reservations at least a week in advance, 2 weeks if you want a weekend.

Klondike Kate's Motel, at 3rd and King (993-5491). Individual cabins give you that lonely-prospector feeling. Singles $55. Doubles $65. Private bath.

Gold Rush Campground, 5th and York St. (993-5247). Gold rush has a monopoly on RV sites, so it is wise to phone ahead. Campsites are fairly crowded and too rocky for tenters. Laundromat, grocery store, showers, dump station, and car wash. The management is extremely helpful. Sites $10, electric hookhps $15, full hookups $17.

Yukon River Campground. Ride the ferry to the west side of Dawson City and take the first right. The ferry is free and operates every 45 min. or as needed, 24 hr. A heaven for budget travelers who want to return to nature. Remember, you must boil drinking water for 10 min. Toilets. RVs are welcome, but no hookups are available. Sites $5.

Food

There's not a lot around, but for the most part prices are reasonable by northern standards. The number of Québecois running eateries this far from *la belle province* is astonishing.

Klondike Kate's (993-6527) by Klondike Kate's Motel (no affiliation). Veggie sandwich ($5.25) should keep scurvy at bay and the K.K. Breakfast Special ($4) is the best am deal in town. Open May 18-Sept. 18 7am-11pm.

Nancy's, Front and Princess St. (993-5633). The sweet-tooth's choice. Homemade pastries and breads. Sourdough breakfast with 2 pancakes, juice, and coffee $4. The house specialty is the salmon dinner with Hollandaise sauce ($14). Open daily June-Aug. 7am-9pm.

'98 Drive In, Front St. (993-5226). Styled after a 1950s American drive-in, but named for the 1898 Klondike Gold Rush. Monster buffalo burgers $8.25, deluxe burgers $5. Menu includes ice cream and homemade fries. Open daily May-Aug. 11am-9pm, Sept 11am-8pm.

Sights and Entertainment

Perhaps to compensate for the cost of everything else, Dawson City sponsors a huge variety of free tours and sights. A good way to keep track of it all is to pick up the **Dawson City Passport** for $2 at the visitors center. Free **walking tours** leave from the center five times daily and from the Commissioner's Residence twice daily. The guides are extremely well informed, and these tours are the best way to appreciate Dawson City.

Make time to catch the **Robert Service Readings,** in front of the very cabin on 8th Ave. at Hanson where the Bard of the Yukon penned such immortal ditties as "The Cremation of Sam McGee" and "The Shooting of Dan McGrew." Two shows daily (the best readings north of Pt. Madison), 10am and 3pm.

Just down the street is the re-located **Jack London Cabin.** London's life and times are recounted with memorabilia daily at 1pm. Tours of Arizona Charlie's marvelously restored **Palace Grand Theatre** are given daily, and you can catch the award-winning half-hour documentary **City of Gold,** which sparked the federal government's interest in Dawson, at 2:30pm. Also in the Palace Grand are the **Gaslight Follies** (993-5575). An original melodrama and a vaudeville revue alternate Wed.-Mon. at 8pm. This duo form the best period show in the Yukon. (Tickets $10 and $12.)

The **Dawson City Museum,** on 5th south of Church (993-5007), holds temporary shows by local artists and offers free hour-long tours of its extensive mining exhibits. (Open daily 10am-6pm, admission $3; tours given by request.)

Nightlife in Dawson is dominated by **Diamond Tooth Gertie's,** at 4th and Queen, Canada's only legal gambling hall. For a $4 cover you can try your hand at roulette, Red Dog, Blackjack, Texas Hold'em, or just take in one of the four nightly floor shows—a good bet. Open nightly 8pm-2am.

If you're interested in learning about the modern gold mining operations (last year's take was 40,000 ounces) or panning on your own, check in with **Gold City Tours,** on Front St. (993-5175). The five-hour tours cost $31. The dredges are 8km out of town, so unless you have you own car, this is about your only option. (Open daily 9am-6pm.) Don't hitchhike or you, too, may become The Evaporated Kid.

Dempster Highway

Named after one of the most courageous and bush-wise officers to wear the RCMP red, Sergeant W.J.B. Dempster, the 741km (460 mi.) Dempster Highway is the only road leading into Canada's isolated Mackenzie Delta communities of **Fort McPherson, Tuktoyaktuk,** and **Inuvik** (pronounced in-NEW-vik).

This is not a drive to be taken lightly. Despite the service centers and camp-grounds along the way, there will be long stretches where you'll be on your own. Hitching the route is strongly discouraged. Prepare to wait whole days. Thankfully, however, the frequency of rides is inversely proportional to length.

There are numerous points of interest, not the least of which is the 150,000-strong **Porcupine Caribou Herd** that migrates across in the fall. The animals take four-and-a-half days to cross the road, and have the right-of-way.

There are two **ferry crossings** on the route, at the **Peel River** and at **Arctic Red River,** both free. Operation depends on the weather; call 800-661-0752 for current status. **The Dempster** is indispensible and available at the tourist infocentres in Whitehorse and Dawson City, and is a must for anyone venturing out along the highway.

For current road conditions and up-to-date maps and information, contact the **Western Arctic Visitors Centre** (Front St. at King, 993-6506; open June-Aug. daily 9am-9pm) in Dawson City, YT. **Gold City Tours** (Front St., 993-5175), in Dawson City, provides bus service along the Dempster from Dawson City to Inuvik twice weekly ($180) via Arctic Red River ($30) and Fort McPherson ($45). Open daily 9am-9pm.

ALBERTA

The icy peaks and turquoise lakes of Banff, Jasper, Yoho, and Kootenay National Parks preside as Alberta's most prominent landscapes. The vast Columbia Icefield, straddling the parks as well as the Alberta/British Columbia border, feeds three of the world's largest bodies of water. As the Athabasca, Saskatchewan, and Columbia Glaciers melt, their waters flow into three river systems: The Mackenzie flows to the Arctic Ocean, the Saskatchewan reaches the Atlantic Ocean through Hudson Bay, and the Columbia empties into the Pacific.

But there is more to Alberta than Banff and Jasper—plenty more farmland, prairie, and oil fields, that is. Rural Alberta includes kilometer after kilometer of seldom-traveled roads, thousands of prime fishing holes, world-renowned dinosaur fossil fields, and intriguing remnants of Native American culture. The southern section of the province features several fascinating attractions, including **Waterton-Glacier National Park, Head-Smashed-In Buffalo Jump,** and the **Frank Slide,** as well as Alberta's humble capital, Lethbridge.

Petrodollars have brought gleaming, modern cities to the prairie. Calgary caught the world's eye when it hosted the XV Winter Olympics, and is perenially host to the wild and wooly Stampede. Edmonton, slightly larger than its southern rival, is home to the world's largest shopping mall, and, until 1988, Wayne Gretzky.

More than half of the province lies to the north of Edmonton. This is the uninhabited land of the midnight twilight. Since the north is void of any substantial cities, the ethereal charm of rural towns must support you as you venture farther toward the pole.

Travel

Highway 16 connects Jasper with Edmonton, while the **Trans-Canada Highway** (Hwy. 1) runs right through Calgary and then continues 120km west to Banff. **Highway 3** connects Medicine Hat with Vancouver, BC, passing a plethora of historical signposts along the way. The extensive highway system makes possible many bus connections between the major points of interest. Use Calgary as a travel hub. **Greyhound** runs from Calgary to Edmonton to Jasper, as well as from Calgary to Banff. **Brewster,** a subsidiary of Greyhound, runs an express bus between Banff and Jasper. Calgary and Edmonton have the two major airports in Alberta.

You must leave the Trans-Canada Hwy. to explore rural Alberta—a feat easier said than done. Writing-On-Stone Provincial Park and Elk Island National Park, two of the province's most intriguing destinations, lie off of the usual tourist trail. **Hitching** in such areas is a hit-or-miss proposition. If you can get a ride, it'll probably last a long time, but you might have to wait an eternity between lifts. To reach out-of-the-way (but highly worthwhile) sights, consider renting a car from **Rent-A-Wreck,** a Canadian-based company that rents cars that aren't really wrecks for very reasonable rates.

Another option is **Exitreks** (403-269-1464), a new company run by enthusiastic Albertans eager to show off the isolated campgrounds and forestry trunk roads of their province. Exitreks conducts six-day tours and occasional shorter tours. For information and tour itineraries, write Exitreks Ltd., #208, 604 1st St. SW, Calgary T2P 1M7.

More adventurous and independent travelers should have no problem discovering alternative methods of transportation in Alberta. From the glaciers of Jasper National Park to the huge northern lakes, the Ice Age designed the province with the hiker, ice climber, canoeist, and bicyclist firmly in mind. **Hikers, mountaineers,** and **ice climbers** will find the most, and the best, terrain in Banff's Canadian Rockies, Jasper National Park, and Kananaskis Country. **Canoeing centers** frequent the lakes of northern Alberta and the Milk River in the south. Bicyclists love the Ice-

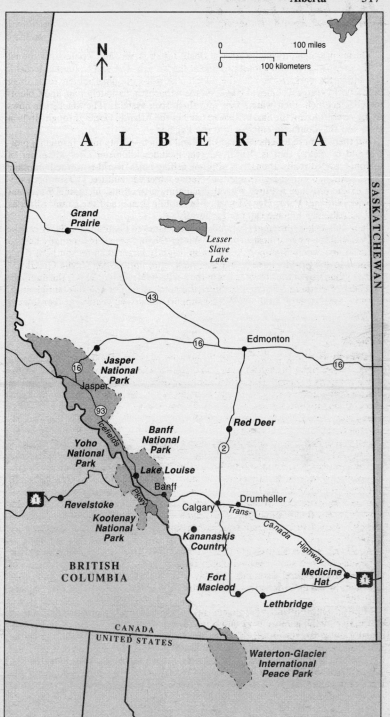

fields Parkway, but they can travel easily on the wide shoulders of other Alberta highways as well. Some highway segments, such as the Trans-Canada between Banff and Calgary, have special bike routes marked on the right-hand shoulder of the road. Consider bringing a mountain bike instead of the usual 10-speed. You and your bike will have an easier time on the rough rural roads; in the Rockies, you can bike through the backcountry. The national parks have made an effort to improve the situation by setting up hostels between Banff and Jasper and by establishing campsites that accept only hikers and bicyclists. Lone Pine Publishing, 9704 106 St., Edmonton T5K 1B6, prints an extensive array of guides to exploring Alberta (such as *Canoeing Alberta* by Janice MacDonald and *Camping Alberta* by Joanne Morgan). Other information sources include **Travel Alberta** and the **Alberta Wilderness Association.**

Practical Information

Capital: Edmonton.

Visitor Information: **Travel Alberta,** 15th floor, 10025 Jasper Ave., Edmonton T5J 3Z3 (800-661-8888, in AB 800-222-6501). Information on Alberta's provincial parks can be obtained from **Recreation and Parks,** #1660, Standard Life Centre, 10405 Jasper Ave., Edmonton T5J 3N4 (427-9429). For information on the province's national parks (Waterton Lakes, Jasper, Banff, and Wood Buffalo), contact **Parks Canada,** Box 2989, Station M, Calgary T2P 3H8 (292-4440). The **Alberta Wilderness Association,** P.O. Box 6389, Station D, Calgary T2P 2E1, carries information on off-highway adventures.

Time Zone: Mountain (2 hr. behind Eastern).

Postal Abbreviation: AB.

Drinking Age: 18.

Traffic Laws: Mandatory seatbelt law.

Emergency: 911.

Area Code: 403.

Impractical Information

Provincial Bird: Great Horned Owl. Chosen in 1977 by Alberta schoolchildren in a province-wide vote.

Provincial Flower: Wild Rose.

Provincial Tree: Lodgepole Pine.

Provincial Headdress: Baseball Cap.

Edmonton

While Calgary generates inspiring views and news, Edmonton overlooks a depressing river, a bland setting, and unelevating skyline. And though it is Alberta's capital and most populous city, Edmonton was overlooked by the Olympic Committee during one of its typically abominable winters.

The northernmost major city in North America is not pouting, however. The Gretsky-less Edmonton Oilers managed to win the 1990 Stanley Cup (their fifth in seven years). The city boasts a broad range of museums, galleries, and musical events, and the greatest number of theaters per capita in the world. Furthermore, Edmontonians claim a dubious sense of pride in their "West Ed" Mall, trumpeting it as the "World's Largest Indoor Mall."

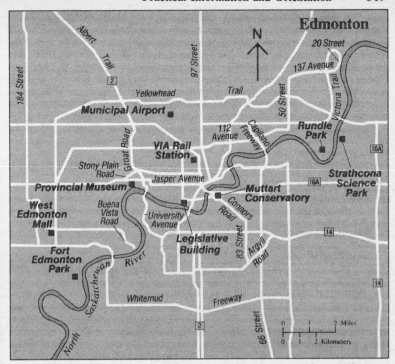

Beyond this, however, lies Edmonton's fundamental drabness. Fort Edmonton Park, the Provincial Museum, and the Muttart Conservatory have limited allure and are overshadowed as tourist attractions by the massive Mall from Hell.

Raised by the Klondike gold rush and the railroad, Edmonton was born in 1795 as the site of a Hudson's Bay Company trading post. Fur trapping and trading accounted for most of Edmonton's early industry until 1905, when the Canadian National Railway decided to lay its tracks through Alberta's soon-to-be-capital city. Leduc, just south of the city, hit black gold (oil, that is) in 1947, and Edmonton has felt the pleasures and pangs of the fluctuating industry ever since.

Practical Information and Orientation

Visitor Information: Edmonton Tourism, 9797 Jasper Ave. (422-5505). Information, maps, brochures, and directions. Helpful staff. Open daily 8:30am-4:30pm; in winter Mon.-Fri. 8:30am-4:30pm. Also at **Gateway Park,** on Hwy. 2 south of the city. Open daily 8am-9pm; in winter Mon.-Fri. 8:30am-4:30pm, Sat.-Sun. 9:30am-5pm. Edmonton operates two smaller offices on Hwy. 16 during the summer. One is in the western section of the city near 190 St., and the other is in the east by 23 Ave. Both open daily 10am-6pm. For paraphernalia on the rest of the province, head to **Travel Alberta,** 10015 102 St. (427-4321), on the 5th floor.

VIA Rail: 10004 104 Ave. (422-6032, for reservations 800-501-8630), in the CN Tower, easily identified by the huge red letters on the building. More expensive than the bus: $57 (students $51) to Jasper and $136 (students $122) to Vancouver. Open Mon., Wed.-Thurs., Sat. 9am-4:30pm; Tues., Fri., Sun. 6:30am-2pm, 5pm-12:30am.

Edmonton Transit: 423-4636 for schedule information. Buses and light rail transit (LRT) run frequently and all over the sprawling city. As in Calgary and Portland, you can ride free on the LRT if you stay in the downtown area (between Corona Station, at 107 St. and Jasper Ave., and Churchill Station, at 99 St. and 102 Ave.). Mon.-Fri. 9am-3pm and Sat. 9am-6pm. Otherwise the fare for bus and LRT is $1.25, ages over 65 and under 15 60¢. No bikes allowed on the transit system. For more information, stop by the **Downtown Information Centre,** 100 A St. and Jasper Ave. (Open Mon.-Fri. 9am-5pm, Sat. 8am-5pm, Sun. and holidays 9am-5pm.)

Greyhound: 10324 103 St. (421-4242). A bus leaves for Calgary nearly every hour 8am-8pm (one way $22). Buses to Jasper (4 per day, $32.20) and Vancouver (3 per day, $84). The daring can take the bus to Yellowknife, capital of the Northwest Territories, for a mere $136.25. Open Mon.-Fri. 6:30am-10pm, Sat.-Sun. 5:30am-12:30am.

Car Rental: Rent-A-Wreck, 10140 109 St. (423-1755). Rates start at $25 per day with 100 free km. Must be 21. Credit card or cash deposit required ($300, ages under 25 $600). Visitors from overseas must show a passport. Open Mon.-Fri. 7:30am-7pm, Sat.-Sun. 9am-5pm. A little more money will rent a sprightlier auto at **Thrifty,** 10036 102 St. (428-8555). Rates start at $33 per day with 100 free km plus 12¢ per km. Must be 25 with credit card.

Bike Rental: Campus Outdoor Centre, at the University of Alberta, 116 St. and 87 Ave. (492-2767). Mountain bikes only, $15 per day. Camping equipment also available.

Weather Information: 468-4940.

Hospital: 10216 124th St. (482-6925).

Emergency: 911.

Police: 423-4567.

Post Office: 9808 103A Ave. (495-3100), adjacent to the CN Tower. Open Mon.-Fri. 8am-5:45pm. Postal Code: T5J 2G8.

Area Code: 403.

Although Edmonton holds the distinction of being the northernmost major city in North America, it's actually in the southern half of Alberta, making it an easy 3½-hour drive from Calgary on Hwy. 2 and a four hours from Jasper on Hwy. 16. The city is well-served by bus, train, and plane. But while Greyhound and VIA Rail let you off downtown, the **airport** sits far south of town, a prohibitively expensive cab fare away. You might be able to find an airport shuttle bus taking travelers to downtown hotels; try to hop on.

While Calgary conveniently divides itself into directional quadrants, Edmonton figures adults should be able to figure out such trivialities unaided. The system sounds simple enough: **Avenues** run east-west, numbers increasing as you travel farther north, and **streets** run north-south, with the higher numbers at the west end of town. But the meandering North Saskatchewan River complicates matters. While 99 Ave. and 109 St. are on the north bank of the river, 99 Ave. and 71 St. are well into the south bank. Jasper Ave., the city's central thoroughfare, is just another name for 101 Ave. Transit maps are available all over town.

Accommodations

The liveliest place to stay in Edmonton is the hostel, though you'll have more privacy at St. Joseph's College or the University of Alberta.

Edmonton International Youth Hostel (IYHF), 10422 91 St. (429-0140), off Jasper Ave. The laid-back staff will play poker or canasta with you right up to the midnight curfew—and often beyond. They also provide information on Edmonton and the rest of Alberta (especially the wild North). The conspicuous absence of a living room television drives guests to converse or make friends. Everyone is required to do some kind of chore, like vacuuming or cleaning the stove. The area surrounding the hostel is not the finest; to be safe, walk via Jasper Ave., which is always busy and well-lit. Lockout 10am-5pm. Beware: the curfew is strictly enforced—if you stay out past midnight, you will spend the night discussing dialectic materialism with the night cashier at one of the exciting 24-hr. convenience stores on Jasper Ave. Members $9, nonmembers $13. Space usually available, even during the summer.

St. Joseph's College, 114 St. at 89 Ave. (492-7681), in the University of Alberta neighborhood. Office on 2nd floor, #223. Several buses, including bus #43, blow through the area. The rooms here are smaller, less institutional, and cheaper than those at the nearby university. Shaded lawn out front. In summer, make reservations—rooms fill up fast. Singles $17. Doubles $24 (limited number of them). Breakfast $4.

University of Alberta, 87 Ave., between 112 and 114 St. (492-4281), on the ground floor of Lister Hall. The university is crowded in the summer, but they always seem to have a free room somewhere. Classic institutional rooming units with beds and desks permanently fastened to the wall. Three sterile and quiet high-rise dorms. Singles $16.50. Doubles $22. For nonstudents singles $25, doubles $34.

YWCA, 10305 100 Ave. (429-8707). Men not allowed on the residential floors. Women sleep in quiet rooms, many with balconies. Free use of pool and unlimited local calls for $1 per day. Dorm-style bunks $7. Singles $20, with bath $25. Key deposit $5. Elevator card deposit $15.

YMCA, 10030 102A Ave. (421-9622). Close enough to the bus and VIA Rail stations to produce convenience without paranoia. A lively, clean building with rooms availing both men and women. Deluxe rooms on the newly renovated 4th floor. Singles $21, deluxe $27.50. Doubles $30. Bunk beds $10 per night (3 beds in 1 room, with lockers; 2-night max. stay).

Mayfair Hotel, 10815 Jasper Ave. (423-1650). If you're in the money, treat yourself to an evening in this elegant, recently renovated downtown bed and breakfast. Worth every penny. Singles $50, $5.25 per additional person. Corner rooms $66. Suites $60.

Hotel Cecil, 10406 Jasper Ave. (428-7001). Kindler, gentler, and in a safer location than most hotels-above-taverns. Singles $18, with bath $21. Key deposit $5. The hotel locks its doors at 11pm; you must identity yourself to be let in.

Food

One might hypothesize that citizens of Edmonton—the self-labeled "City of Champions"—kick-off their day with a bowl of Wheaties, the "Breakfast of Champions." Little evidence can be found to support this theory, however; Edmontonians prefer a more eclectic morning meal. In fact, should Edmonton redesign the culinary culture of the West, it would probably reduce everything to pancakes, bacon, and eggs. The city's restaurants have trouble with more substantial repasts. Both **downtown** and **Old Strathcona,** a region along 82 (Whyte) Ave. between 102 and 105 St., ooze with a high number of eateries.

For a quick and inexpensive meal, zip into one of Edmonton's numerous cafeterias. Lunch with politicians in the main cafeteria of the **Alberta Legislature Building** (open Mon.-Fri. 7am-3:30pm). Or try private sector economy at the cafeterias in the **YWCA** (men allowed; open Mon.-Thurs. 7am-7pm, Fri. 7am-6pm, Sat.-Sun. 8am-4pm) and the **YMCA** (open Mon.-Fri. 7am-6:30pm). The YMCA offers the cheapest breakfast special—ham, eggs, toast, and hash browns for $2.29—while the YWCA allows you to create your own menu at the sandwich bar for $3.

Real Pizza & Steaks, 9449 Jasper Ave. (428-1989). Real pizza and steaks. Superb blueberry pancakes (no wimpy soft berries—just good, thick ones) for $3.25. Good breakfast special (2 eggs, toast, bacon, and hash browns) for $3. Open 24 hrs.

Uncle Albert's Pancake House, 10370 82 (Whyte) Ave. (439-6609). One of 5 Edmonton locations. As the name suggests, pancakes reign here. Come in any Tues. in July during the Klondike days for pancakes and sausage—only 49¢. Even if you can't make it on a Tues. in July, Unlce Al still greases a good griddle ($3 for a stack of 5). Open daily 7am-8pm.

Patisserie Kim's Café, 10217 97 St. (422-6754). No frills here, just fast cheap food. For $2 dine on 2 eggs, hash browns, toast, and coffee, or a hamburger and fries. Not the safest location, but the law courts are just across the street. Open Mon.-Sat. 6:30am-6pm, Sun. 7am-6pm.

The Silk Hat, 10251 Jasper Ave. (428-1551). One of Edmonton's classic original restaurants, the Silk Hat still provides jukeboxes at each dimly lit booth. The daily sandwich special (about $4.50) even comes with dessert. Wash it all down with a mug of Molson ($1.25). This being Edmonton, breakfast served all day. Open Mon.-Fri. 6:30am-8pm, Sat. 6am-8pm, Sun. 11am-7pm.

Flip Side Café, 8405 112 St. (432-1371). Frequented by U. of A. students and such traveling academic superstars as Morris Zapp. Sandwiches in the $2.50 range—but meager portions. Check for happy hour beer specials—$2.25 for a 20-oz. mug., $6.25 for a 64-oz. pitcher. Open daily 7am-10pm.

9th St. Bistro, 9910 109 St. (424-7219). Hearty soups and creative sandwiches $5-7. The linguini with shrimp curry is a must-eat ($8). Cheap beer ($2.55 per Bud). Wayne Gretzky might have eaten here (but probably didn't). Open Sun.-Fri. 11am-1am, Sat. 11:30am-1am.

New York Bagel Café, 8209 104 St. Part of a continental trend towards subjecting the bagel to all kinds of unnecessary and humiliating encumbrances—for instance, chicken liver pâté. 007 fanatics can contemplate a James Bond favorite—bagel with malasol Beluga caviar ($22.60). Wash it all down with a pineapple or raspberry milk cocktail ($3), then choose from the 9 types of coffee.

Sights

The "oh-my-god-that's-*obscenely*-huge" **West Edmonton Mall** (444-5200 or 800-661-8890), stalks the general area of 170 St. and 87 Ave. The cosmos' largest conglomeration of retail stores under one roof, The Mall will always be the talk of the town. Though It keeps Edmontonians warm during the sub-zero winters, It leaves most tourists with a cold impression of the town.

When It first landed, the massive sprawl of mall seized 30% of Edmonton's retail business, effectively suffocating the downtown shopping district.

Enclosing a water park, an amusement park, and dozens of hopelessly caged exotic animals, the world's biggest Mall sccms even bigger thanks to mirrors plastered on nearly every wall. Among Its many achievements, The Mall boasts twice as many submarines as the Canadian Navy, a full-scale replica of Columbus' *Santa Maria,* and **Lazermaze,** the world's first walk-through video game. You can get to The Mall via bus #10. (Hours vary from store to attraction, so call ahead if you plan to go late in the day.)

For an almost refreshing change, head downtown to **Eaton's Mall,** 102 St. and 102 Ave. Owned and operated by the 555 Corporation, the same company responsible for the "West Ed." Mall, Eaton's Mall is smaller, keeps no caged animals and is far superior in architecture and design. Lined by colorful plants, Eaton's is a much more pleasant place to browse through than its monstrous uncle.

After sampling the "pleasures" of the late 20th century at the malls, the late 19th century will seem a welcome relief as you head for **Fort Edmonton Park,** off the Whitemud Freeway near the Quesnell Bridge. At the end of the park (farthest from the entrance) sits the fort, a 19th-century "office building" for Alberta's first entrepreneurs, the ruthless whiskey traders. Between the fort on 1846 St. and the park entrance are three long streets (1875 St., 1905 St., and 1920 St.), each bedecked with period buildings—apothecaries, blacksmith shops, and barns—from the streets' respective years. Appropriately clothed park volunteers greet visitors with the inquisitiveness of a 19th-century schoolmarm or the geniality of a general-store owner. Watch these vicars of things past conduct their daily business, or pick their brains with questions about stagecoaches or 19th-century loos. Be warned that the quaint stores and restaurant charge up-to-date prices. Hungry souls can get back to the entrance via a miniature train, a restoration of a genuine rail car, which choochoos the length of the park. (Open Victoria Day-Labor Day daily 10am-6pm; May-June 9:30am-4pm; Labor Day-Thanksgiving Sun., Mon., and holidays 10am-6pm. Admission $5, seniors and ages 13-17 $3.75.) The park is accessible by bus #123 or 32.

While visiting the fort, stop in at the **John Janzen Nature Centre** and pet the salamanders. (Open Mon.-Fri. 9am-6pm, Sat.-Sun. 11am-6pm.) Then, sprint across Hwy. 2 to the **Valley Zoo,** at 134 St. and Buena Vista Rd. (483-5511). The zoo may not compare with Calgary's, but it does flaunt more species than The Mall. The zoo originally followed a storybook theme but has since burst the strictures of narrative to offer a more intercontinental selection of species. (May-Sept. 5 open daily 10am-6pm; admission $3.50, seniors $2.75, youths $1.75. Sept. 8-March 27 open Sat.-Sun. noon-4pm; admission $2, seniors and youths $1.50.)

Lest you think Edmonton has gone overboard with re-created history, fear not: the four Giza-like, glass pyramids across the river are hi-tech greenhouses covering the **Muttart Conservatory,** 626 96A St. (428-5226 for a recording). In summer and winter, this botanical garden's choose-your-own weather chamber can simulate heat, humidity, and aromas in its Tropical Pavilion. Migrate to the more soothing climates of the Temperate and Arid Pavilions, lush with flowers, bushes, and trees.

(Open daily 11am-9pm; Sept.-May Sun.-Wed. 11am-9pm, Thurs.-Sat. 11am-6pm. Admission $4, seniors and ages under 18 $2.25.) Bus #51 whisks you to Muttart.

The **Alberta Legislature Building,** 97 Ave. and 109 St. (427-7362), is as stately and ornate as any capitol building in Alberta. Indeed, there is a point on the top floor where water sounds as if it's pouring down torrentially from above (an echo from the fountain 3 floors below). You can sample this "Ripley's Believe It or Not" effect yourself on the free, thorough tour of the building, given every half hour. (Open Mon.-Fri. 9am-8:30pm, Sat.-Sun. 9am-4:30pm; Labor Day-Victoria Day Mon.-Fri. 9-11:30am and 1-4pm, Sat.-Sun. noon-4pm.) The legislature is in session from early March to late May and again during October.

On a sunny summer day, as the Legislature Building's lunch bell rings, most of the city joins in front of this grand political palace. A spectacular network of fountains and pools stretches before the building's steps. To escape the sun and crowds, enter the Government Centre Pedway, an underground walkway that connects the Legislature Building with other government offices. The **Alberta Pedway Display,** 9804 107 St. (427-7362), features exhibits on Alberta's history, wildlife, inhabitants, technology. (Open daily 10am-4pm; Labor Day-Victoria Day Mon.-Fri. 10am-4pm. Free.) If you'd prefer to observe Edmonton from above the city, check out the **AGT Vista 33** on the 33rd floor of the Alberta Telephone Tower, 10020 100 St. (493-3333). Although the Vista 33 lacks the height and majestic mountain view of the Calgary Tower, this lookout spot costs much less and also includes a small **telephone museum.** The homesick can dial up their local area code and light a bulb in their hometown (yawn). A number of other hands-on displays might make this elevator trip well worth the nominal admission fee. (Open daily 10am-8pm. Admission 50¢, senior citizens and pre-schoolers free.)

A walking tour of the city at street level might suit those who fear heights (or depths). You can retrace the steps of Alberta's pioneers along **Heritage Trail.** The self-guided tour begins at 100 St. and 99 Ave. and saunters past the Legislature Building, Edmonton's first schoolhouse, and other historic landmarks. Just follow the red brick road. Another self-guided tour, the **Walking Tour of Old Strathcona,** starts at 8331 104 St. (433-5866) in the Old Strathcona Foundation Building. (Open Mon.-Fri. 8:30am-4:30pm.) Track the history of this area from its incorporation as a town in 1899 through its union with Edmonton in 1912. **Royal Tours of Edmonton** (425-5342) and **U-C Tours** (921-2104) will show lazy people the sights from behind bus windows.

Both of these tours stop at the **Provincial Museum of Alberta,** 12845 102 Ave. (453-9100), which caches all kinds of Albertan artifacts, from threshers and plows to Native American clothing and stone tools. Despite the impressive collection, the museum fails to create a very convincing impression of either pioneer or Native life. The museum does, however, contain one of the only photographs of Edmonton's downtown taken before modernization spiked the area with skyscrapers. (Open daily 9am-8pm. Free.) Take bus #1 or 2. The museum recently opened up another exhibit entitled **Traces of the Past,** displaying dinosaur fossils. (Open daily 9am-8pm; Labor Day-Victoria Day Tues. and Thurs.-Sun. 9am-5pm, Wed. 9am-8pm.)

Pick up your nightstick and throw on your badge at the **Police Museum,** 9620 103A Ave. (421-2274), on the third floor of the police station. While real cops track nefarious no-gooders downstairs, the museum explains the history of law enforcement in the province, from the Royal Canadian Mounted Police to the Alberta Provincial Police to Edmonton's finest. See uniforms and radar sets used in the pursuit of criminals and the preservation of justice. (Open Tues.-Sat. 10am-3pm. Free.)

Strathcona Science Park, at the city's eastern edge 1km south of Hwy. 16, features the **Strathcona Archaeological Centre** (427-9487), established near the site of a recently unearthed Native American settlement. Cluttered with tepee rings and buried stone tools, the site was discovered in 1976 by construction workers preparing to raze the area. The the site was later found to be more than 5000 years old. The small archeological center and its alert staff explain the Native Americans' periodic peregrinations through the area. Outside the museum, a hiking trail leads to the site of the archaeological excavation in progress. (Open Victoria Day-Labor Day

10am-6pm. Free.) Bus #20 or 28 will take you from the center of Edmonton to Rundle Park, a half-hour walk across the river from Strathcona Science Park.

Entertainment and Activities

Led by Wayne Gretzky, the **Edmonton Oilers** skated off with four of five consecutive Stanley Cups in the eighties. The team, *sans* Gretsky, continued their NHL domination into the nineties last year by beating the Boston Bruins to win the 1990 Stanley Cup. They play from October through April in the **Northlands Coliseum,** 115 Ave. and 79 St. (471-2191). The "City of Champions" also holds its **Edmonton Eskimos** in high regard. The Eskimos, winners of the Canadian Football League's 1988 Grey Cup, tackle their competition at **Commonwealth Stadium,** 11000 Stadium Rd. (429-2881).

Edmonton caters to the sports participant as well: kilometer after kilometer of paved bike trails and unpaved hiking/skiing trails weave through the river valley within the city limits. **Milk Creek Ravine Park,** on the river's south bank bounded by 82 (Whyte) Ave. and 91 and 98 St., has an extensive network of running trails. For a splash, the **Mill Woods Recreation Centre,** 7207 28 Ave. (428-2888), offers a wave pool as well as a number of calmer outdoor activities.

For a real splash, head to one of the bars in the downtown area. Homesick Brits hold support groups at **Sherlock Holmes,** 10012 101A Ave. (426-7784), an English-style pub which is known for its sing-along songfests and passel of staple British ales on tap. There's also a new Sherlock Holmes in The Mall, on Bourbon St. Country fans should mosey on over to **Cook County Saloon,** 8010 103 St. (432-0177), while Charlie Parker aficionados will dig **Yardbird Suite** at 10203 86 Ave. (432-0428). The **Sidetrack Café** at 10333 112 St. (421-1326) and **Blues on Whyte** at the Commercial Hotel, 10329 82 Ave. (439-3981), are the best blues clubs in the city. And check the free *The Edmonton Bullet,* theater, film, and music listings.

Save at least one night for a visual fest at the **Space Sciences Centre,** 11211 142 St. (452-9100 for a person, 451-7722 for a recording). Spectacular shows air either on the IMAX giant wraparound screen or in the Margaret Ziedler Star Theatre. The IMAX theatre screens thrilling films such as "Seasons," which yokes Vivaldi's *Four Seasons* to enormous images of nature's transformations. Rock laser shows, blare music ranging from Elton John to U2. (Open daily. IMAX movies $6, children $3. Laser shows in Star Theatre $5, children $3.50.) Buses #11, 22, and 37 rocket past the Space Sciences Centre.

For a more cerebral evening, buy tickets to the **Princess Theatre,** 10337 82 (Whyte) Ave. (433-0979, for a recording 433-5785). The movies here change every night, concentrating on popular reruns such as *The African Queen* and *The Gods Must Be Crazy.* Watch for the Princess's film festival in June. Schedules are available at the theatre and at dozens of stands around town. (Tickets $4.50, senior citizens $2.) The **National Film Theatre** screens everything from *Nanook of the North* to *Scott of the Antarctic* in the Edmonton Art Gallery Theatre, 2 Winston Churchill Square. (Admission $4.)

Seasonal Events

Edmonton, presumably jealous of Calgary's success with the Stampede, conjured up its own summertime carnival a few years back. Held for 10 days in mid-July, **Klondike Days,** like the Stampede, occasions the painting of cartoon figures on storefront windows and causes an epidemic of free (or nearly free) breakfasts. Edmonton even tries to rival Calgary's chuckwagon race with its very own pig races. The event recalls the Yukon gold rush around the turn of the century when Edmontonians lured treasure-seekers through their city, advertising the specious "Klondike Trail" from Edmonton to Dawson City. Prospectors found the trail a much more difficult path than the traditional Alaska route, and to some it proved impassable. Stymied gold-hunters turned back to settle in Edmonton, boosting the population from 2000 to 50,000. Despite its dubious heritage, the festival has grown popular by hosting such stimulating events as the Fun Tub Race and the Hairiest Chest Competition. Write to Edmonton's Klondike Days Exposition, P.O. Box 1480, Edmonton T5J 2N5, or call 471-7210 for information.

Each August, alternative entertainment happenings dominate the Old Strathcona District along 82 (Whyte) Ave. The **Fringe Theatre Event** (432-1553) features 150 alternative theater productions in area parks, theaters, and streets. During an earlier August weekend, the **Edmonton Folk Music Festival** brings country and bluegrass banjo-pickin' to the city. In late June and early July, take in the **Jazz City International Festival,** which jams together ten days of club dates and free performances by some of Canada's (and the rest of the world's) most noted jazz musicians. This musical extravaganza often coincides with a visual arts celebration called **The Works.**

Near Edmonton

For those without the means or desire to trek west or north, wilderness beckons a mere 35km east of Edmonton at **Elk Island National Park.** In 1906, civic concern prompted the establishment of the park in order to protect endangered herds of elk. Since then, all sorts of exotic mammals (plains bison, wood bison, moose, hikers) have moved in, but some might consider the park "for the birds": 240 species share the airspace over Lake Astotin. And while black bears and grizzlies may terrify tourists in Banff and Jasper, you'll have to deal with a different threat at Elk Island—bison. Pick up your copy of *You Are in Bison Country* at the Park Information Centre, just off Hwy. 16 and learn that bison are dangerous; in fact, they're faster than horses and five times bigger than Andre the Giant (and that's pretty big). The lakeshore is the center of civilized activity in the park. The **Astotin Interpretive Centre** (922-5790) answers questions, screens films, and schedules activities daily. It also explains that Elk Island is not one of the many water-bound forests in Lake Astotin, but rather "an island of forest amidst a landscape of man." (Open Thurs.-Tues. 11am-6pm; in winter Sat.-Sun. 11am-6pm.) Soviet defectors can feel at home in a replica of a thatched-roof **Ukranian pioneer home.** (Open mid-May to Labor Day Fri.-Tues. 10am-6pm.)

Backcountry camping is allowed in certain areas with a free permit, obtainable at the information center. If you want a shower and the prospect of 100-plus neighbors excites you, set up camp at the **Sandy Beach Campground,** off Hwy. 16 (992-6387; no reservations accepted). Swimming is not recommended at the beach, because if the leeches don't get you, the "swimmer's itch" probably will. The snack bar near the campground flings buffalo burgers at those who forgot to pack a lunch. The park also features 12 well-marked hiking trails, most from 3-17km in length, which double as cross-country and snowshoeing trails in the winter.

Continue east on Hwy. 16 all the way to the Soviet Ukraine—not quite the land of *glasnost* itself, but the **Ukranian Cultural Heritage Village,** a living tribute to one of Alberta's strongest ethnic groups. Like Fort Edmonton Park, it features the requisite historic buildings (including a hardware store), and its staff of "interpreters" carries on early 20th-century chores and guided tours. (Open Victoria Day-Labor Day daily 10am-6pm. Free.)

Western Alberta

Jasper National Park

Before the Icefields Parkway was built, few travelers dared to venture north from Banff into the untamed wilderness of Jasper. But those few who made it raved. The completion of the parkway in 1940 paved the way for all to appreciate Jasper's astounding beauty; today the yearly influx of vehicles (and tourists) is estimated to be over a million.

In contrast to its glitzy southern peer, Jasper's landscape insulates its inhabitants' tranquility. Even the townsite, a clustering of buildings dropped into 10,000 square km of virgin wilderness, remains serene. Jasperites gladly share their territory with wildlife, and pride themselves on the vast network of trails that penetrate some of the Rockies' most captivating scenery.

Be sure to set aside a couple of days to wander through the backcountry (which requires a free permit available at the Park Information Centre). At the very least, shut off you car's engine for a few hours and take a dayhike.

Practical Information and Orientation

Visitor Information: Park Information Centre, 500 Connaught Dr. (852-6176). Trail maps and information on all aspects of the park. Open June 14-Labor Day daily 8am-8pm; in spring and fall 9am-5pm. **Alberta Tourism,** 632 Connaught Dr. (in AB 800-222-6501). Open June-Sept. daily 8am-8pm; May Sun.-Thurs. 9am-6pm, Fri.-Sat. 9am-7:30pm. **Jasper Chamber of Commerce,** 634 Connaught Dr. (852-3858). Open Mon.-Fri. 9am-noon, 1-5pm. For further information, write to Park Headquarters, Superintendent, Jasper National Park, 632 Patricia St., Box 10, Jasper T0E 1E0 (852-6161).

VIA Rail: 314 Connaught Dr. (800-561-8630 or 852-4102). Lines run Tues., Fri., and Sun. only. To: Vancouver (1 per day, 16 hr., $98), Edmonton ($57), and Winnipeg ($166). Prices 1/3-off for senior citizens and students. Coin-operated lockers $1 for 24 hrs. Open daily 8am-10:30pm, shorter hours in off-season.

Greyhound: 314 Connaught Dr. (852-3926), in the VIA station. To Edmonton (14 per day, $32.20 one way) and Kamloops ($34.15 one way).

Brewster Transportation and Tours: 852-3332, in the VIA station. To Banff (full-day tour $49, daily 5½-hr. express $29) and Calgary (1 per day, 8 hr., $38).

Car Rental: Jasper Car Rental, 626 Connaught Dr. (852-3373). $40 per day with 50 free km, 22¢ per additional km. Must be 21 with credit card. Reduced rates for multi-day rental. **Tilden Car Rental,** in the bus depot (852-4972). $43 per day with 100 free km. Must be 21 with credit card. $2500 insurance deductible for drivers under 25.

Scooter Rental: Jasper Scooter Rental (852-5603), across the tracks from Texaco and above Dick's Auto. Rentals $7 per hr., $39 per day. Open daily 9am-9pm.

Bike Rental: Free Wheel Cycle, 600 Patricia St. (852-5380). Enter through the alley behind Patricia St. Mountain bikes $4 per hr., $10 per half-day, $17 per day. One-way rental to Banff 5 days, $20 per day (with Park n' Pedal in Banff, 762-3190). Must have valid ID (driver's license or credit card) for deposit. Open Mon.-Sat. 9am-9pm, Sun. 10am-8pm; April-July 1 and Labor Day-Oct. 9am-6pm. **Whistler's Youth Hostel** also rents mountain bikes. IYHF members $16 per day. Nonmembers $25 per day.

Hospital: 518 Robson St. (852-3344).

Ambulance and Fire: 852-3100.

Emergency: 852-4848.

Police: 600 Pyramid Lake Rd. (852-4848).

Post Office: 502 Patricia St. (852-3041), across from the townsite green. Open Mon.-Fri. 9am-5pm, Sat. 9am-3pm; Sept.-June Mon.-Fri. 9am-5pm. Postal Code: T0E 1E0.

Area Code: 403.

All of the above addresses are in Jasper Townsite, which is located near the center of the park, 362km southwest of Edmonton and 287km north of Banff. **Highway 16** conducts travelers through the park north of the townsite, while the **Icefields Parkway** (Hwy. 93) connects to Banff National Park in the south. Buses run to the townsite daily from Edmonton, Calgary, Vancouver, and Banff. Trains arrive from Edmonton and Vancouver. Hitching between Jasper and Banff is difficult as most cars are driven by tourists wary of picking up hitchhikers. Renting a bike is the most practical option for short jaunts within the park. Bikes can also be rented for one-way trips between Jasper and Banff (see Bike Rental).

Accommodations

Hotels in Jasper Townsite are too expensive to recommend as budget options. You may, however, be able to stay cheaply in a bed and breakfast, some without breakfast (Singles $20-30. Doubles $25-35. Triples $35-40. Quads $30-55.) Most are located right in town near the bus and train stations. Ask for the *Approved Accommodations List* at the Park Information Centre. Since few visitors know of the list, space is often available on short notice. Four of the three dozen homes on the list appear below. If you'd like to get away from the townsite and have some sort of transportation (preferably with wheels), head for a hostel (listed below from north to south). Reservations, as well as information on closing days and on the winter "key system," are channeled through the Edmonton-based Southern Alberta Hostel Association (439-3089).

Lena Hollenbeck, 716 Connaught Dr., P.O. Box 1052 (852-4563). Centrally located. Two rooms with double bed in each; one room with twin beds. Courtesy coffee/tea, use of BBQ, living room with color TV. Expect to find lively international conversations between guests. Ms. Hollenbeck will make you feel at home. Doubles $25 ($20 for one person). Two twin beds $30.

Betty Ens and Ed Simpson, 718 Connaught Dr., Box 816 (852-3640 or 852-6122). Three rooms with private or semi-private entrances (they will give you a key to come and go as you please). Singles $20. Doubles $30. Each additional person $5.

Gordon and Darlene Middleton, 732 Patricia St., P.O. Box 921 (852-3783). Three blocks from bus and train. The Middletons have been in Jasper for 30 years. TV room for common use. Each of the 2 singles converts into a double. Singles $25. Doubles $35. Each additional person $5. Kitchen $5. Complete suite $70. Year-round accommodations.

Mrs. G. Concim, 312 Patricia St., P.O. Box 1005 (852-3744). $25 for twin beds, $30 for 2 people. $5 each additional person and for kitchen facilities. Year-round accommodations.

Maligne Canyon Hostel (IYHF), 11 km. east of townsite on Maligne Canyon Rd. (852-3584). Located near it namesake. Small cabins in a very natural setting. Members $6, non-members $10. Closed Wed.

Whistlers Mountain Hostel (IYHF), on Sky Tram Rd. (852-3215), 7km south of the townsite. Closest to the townsite, this is the park's most modern (and crowded) hostel. Although usually full in summer, the staff tries to hold a few beds for those who complete the uphill hike from town. Crazy Galton-types can take the virtually vertical trail behind the hostel that leads to the Skygram station at the top of the mountain (hike takes about 3 hr.). Accommodates 69. Members $10, nonmembers $14.

Mt. Edith Cavell Hostel (IYHF), on Edith Cavell Rd., off Hwy. 93A. The road is closed in winter, but the hostel welcomes anyone willing to ski the 11km from Hwy. 93A. Really. Accommodates 32 visitors. Members $6, nonmembers $10. Open mid-June Oct. Closed Thurs.

Athabasca Falls Hostel (IYHF), on Hwy. 93, 30km south of Jasper Townsite, 500m away from Athabasca Falls. Members $7, nonmembers $11. Closed Tues.

Beauty Creek Hostel (IYHF), on Hwy. 93, 78km south of Jasper Townsite. Next to the handsome Sunwapta River. Accommodates 24. Accessible through a "key system" in winter (groups only). Members $6, nonmembers $10. Open May to mid-Sept., closed Tues.

Camping

The campsites below are listed from north to south. For campground updates, listen to 1450AM near the townsite.

Pocahontas, on Hwy. 16, at the northern edge of the park, 50km east of Jasper. Closest campground to the Miette Hot Springs. 140 sites. Sites $9. Open mid-May to early Sept.

Snaring River, 16km east of the townsite on Hwy. 16. 60 sites, 10 of which are walk-in tentsites. A small, primitive campground (outhouses, waterpumps). Sites $6. Open May 15-early Sept.

Whistlers, on Whistlers Rd., 3km south of the townsite. If you're intimidated by the wilderness, the humans occupying the 781 neighboring sites will keep you company. Hot and cold running water, showers, water, full hook-ups for RVs. Sites $12-16.

Wapiti, on Hwy. 93, 2km south of Whistlers. A magnet for RV visitors. A whopping 345 sites. Sites $9-12. Showers. Open mid-June to early Sept.

Wabasso, on Hwy. 93A, about 20km south of the townsite. 238 sites, 6 of which are walk-in tentsites. Sites $6.50. Open mid-June to early Sept.

Mount Kerkeslin, on Hwy. 93, about 35km south of Jasper Townsite. 42 sites. Sites $6. Open May 15-Sept. 7.

Honeymoon Lake, on Hwy. 93, about 50km south of the townsite. 35 sites. Sites $6. Open June 9-Sept. 14.

Jonas Creek, on Hwy. 93, about 70km south of the townsite. 25 sites, 12 of which are reserved for tents. Sites $6. Open May 19-late Sept.

Columbia Icefield, on Hwy. 93, 103km south of the townsite, at the southern border of the park. Not on the Athabasca Glacier, but close enough to receive an icy breeze on the warmest summer night. Crowded nevertheless. 33 tentsites. Sites $6. Open May 19-late Sept.

Wilcox Creek, on Hwy. 93, at the southern park boundary. 46 sites. Best spot for RVs. Sites $6-8. Open June 9 to mid-Sept.

Food

It's a good idea to stock up on food at a local market or bulk foods store and head for the backcountry. For around-the-clock grocery supplies, stop at **Wink's Food Store,** 605 Patricia St., or **Super A Foods,** just up the street. **Nutter's,** also on Patricia St., offers bulk grains, nuts, dried fruits, and (if you're tired of munching on granola) candy. They also sell deli meats, canned goods, and freshly ground coffee. (Open Mon.-Sat. 9am-10pm, Sun. 10am-9pm.)

Mountain Foods and Cafe, 606 Connaught Dr. (852-4050). Claim a table before you order at this popular streetside cafe. The menu has both hot and cold sandwiches, soups and desserts—all of them nutritious. Cold sandwiches $3. Pita melt with avocado, turkey, and tomato $5. Hearty bowl of lentil soup $1.75. Frozen yogurt $1.35. Prepare for the millenium (and sooth your soul) by stocking up on bulk grains and holistic books. Open daily 8am-10pm.

Jasper Bakery, on Patricia St. (852-4881). A small, café-style bakery that serves a delicious variety of baked goods (75¢-$2). Open daily 7am-11pm.

Scoops and Loops, 504 Patricia St. (852-4333). Average food at great prices. Croissant sandwiches ($2.50) and bran muffins (50¢) are fine for lunch, but definitely save room for dessert. Monstrous selection of hard and soft ice cream, pies, and pastries. Open daily 10am-10pm.

Dano's Ice Cream, Patricia St. (852-4945). Though a bit expensive, their custom-blended fruit ice cream and yogurt is delicious ($2-3.50). Open daily 10am-9:30pm.

Uptown Café, 607 Patricia St. (852-3758). A small, "fresh food" restaurant next to Sam's Gym. Samdwiches with potato salad $4.95. Slurp a fresh fruit smoothie ($3) while bicep-pumping music knocks down the walls. Open daily 8:30am-5pm.

Sights and Activities

An extensive network of trails connects most parts of Jasper, many paths starting at the townsite. Information centers distribute free copies of *Day Hikes in Jasper National Park* and a summary of longer hikes. Three ecological zones are represented in the park. The **montane zone** in the valley bottoms bristles with Lodgepole pine, Douglas fir, White spruce, and Trembling aspen. Subalpine fir and Engelmann spruce inhabit the middle **subalpine zone** and comprise 40% of the park. Small, fragile plants and wildflowers struggle for existence in the uppermost, **alpine zone,** making up another 40% of Jasper. Hikers should always remain on the trail in the alpine area to avoid trampling endangered plant species.

Kick off any foray into the wilderness with a friendly conversation at the Park Information Centre in the townsite. Experts will direct you to appropriate hiking and mountain-biking trails. The Icefield Centre, on Hwy. 93 at the southern entrance to the park (see Icefields Parkway), provides similar services.

Mt. Edith Cavell, named after a German nurse executed in WWI for assisting the Allies, will shake you to the bone with the thunderous sound of avalanches off the Angel Glacier. Take the 1½km loop trail **Path of the Glacier** or the 8km hike through **Cavell Meadows.** Mt. Edith Cavell rears her enormous head 30km south of the townsite on Cavell Rd. **Maligne Lake,** the largest glacier-fed lake in the Canadian Rockies, has vivid turquoise water and every conceivable water sport. Trails leave from the chalet and warden station. Drive 50km southeast from the townsite on Maligne Lake Rd. One unique feature of Jasper National Park is **Medicine Lake,** 30km east of Jasper Townsite. Water flows into the lake, but there is no visible outlet. The trick? The water flows out through a series of underground caves, emerging in such areas as **Maligne Canyon,** 11km east of the townsite on Maligne Canyon Rd. (pretty sneaky, huh?) Although squirrels can jump across the narrow 46m-deep gorge, don't even attempt it or you'll join those who have plummeted to their deaths.

The key to finding a secluded **fishing** spot is to go someplace inaccessible by car; remember, any place to which you can drive, so can 10,000 other people. One suitably remote area is **Beaver Lake,** located about 1 mi. from the main road at the tip of **Medicine Lake**. The lake is beautiful, never crowded, and even novice firshermen can catch dinner. Rent equipment at **Currie's,** 622 Connaught Dr. (852-5650) (rod, reel, permit, and worms $12; 1-day boat rental $20); hitchhike out to the tip of Medicine Lake and follow the signs from there.

Not to be outdone by Banff, Jasper has a gondola of its own. Rising 2½km up the side of Whistlers Mountain, the **Jasper Tramway** (852-3093) affords a panoramic view of the park. (Fare $8, ages 5-14 $3.75, under 5 free. Open mid-April to Sept. 4 8am-9:30pm; Sept. to mid-Oct. 9am-4:30pm.) A steep 10km trail starting from the Whistlers Mountain Hostel also leads up the slope; to spare your quadriceps take the tram ride down ($3.50). No matter which way you go, be sure to bring along a warm jacket and sunglasses to withstand the rapidly changing climate at the peak.

Guided trail rides are available for high prices. One-and-a-half-hour rides cost $20 at the Jasper Park Lodge (852-5794), 5km north of the townsite on Hwy. 16. Guided rides at Pyramid Lake are $12.50 per hour (852-3562).

Whitewater Rafting (Jasper) Ltd. runs several rafting trips from $32-50 (less expensive with bigger groups). Register at the Texaco station or phone 852-7238. **Boat rental** is available at Pyramid Lake (852-3536; canoes and rowboats $8 per hr., $5 per each additional hr.; motorboats $15 per hr., $14 each additional hr.; $20 deposit or a valid ID), and Maligne Lake (852-3370; canoes $6 per hr., $3 per additional hour; rowboats $25 per day; ID required for deposit). For a less exhausting tour of Maligne Lake, **Maligne Lake Scenic Cruises** offers narrated cruises in cozy, heated tour boats. Reservations recommended; write P.O. Box 280, or stop in at 626 Connaught Dr.

After dipping in Jasper's glacier-fed waters, revive your numbed body at **Miette Hot Springs,** north off Hwy. 16 along the clearly marked, 15km Miette Hotsprings Rd. The 1986-vintage building houses lockers and two pools (one of which is wheelchair accessible). Devoid of nutrient-filled additives and rotten-egg reek, the pools are heated via external pipes through which the spring water is pumped. Unfortunately, the 40°C (102°F) water is off-limits in winter. (Open June 19-Sept. 7 8:30am-10:30pm. Admission $2, $2.25 for kids. Suits $1, towels 75¢, lockers 25¢.) Rotten-egg-lovers can wallow in the sulphur-soused spring itself; a short trail leads south from a picnic area near the modern pool complex to one of the steamy outlets. Don't drink the water—it's 55°C (131°F) and full of unnamed and untamed microscopic organisms.

More curious hikers should attempt the three-faced **Mystery Lake Trail,** leading east and uphill from the pools. The trail transforms from paved path to dirt road to serious trek along the 11km to Mystery Lake. Be warned that you will need to cross a major river at a ford along the trail—with frequent flooding, however, the ford becomes unpassable.

Winter may keep you away from the springs, but you can always generate heat on the slopes of **Marmot Basin,** near Jasper Townsite. A full-day lift ticket costs $25, half-day $18. For information, write "A Marmot Experience," Box 1570, Jasper TOE 1E0 (800-661-1931 or 852-4242). Ski rental is available at **Totem's Ski Shop,** 408 Connaught Dr. (852-3078). The full package (skis, boots, and poles) runs

$12.50 per day. (Open daily 9:30am-10pm; Labor Day-Victoria Day 8am-6pm.) There is also cross-country skiing at Maligne Lake from November through May.

It's all downhill from Maligne Lake with **Downhill Bicycle Tours.** For $39, you can peddle an easy 35km from Maligne Lake—the trip includes 2½ hours of riding and 2½ hours of coasting. Call the Jasper Travel Agency (852-4400) for reservations.

If even this is too strenuous, you can follow a guided tour on a cassette (rental $10.95, purchase $12.95) from **Rocky Mountain Auto Tours,** at 612 Connaught Dr. You will probably have to get out of the car to get the tape, however.

Icefields Parkway

A glacier-lined, 230km road connecting Jasper Townsite with Lake Louise, the Icefields Parkway (Hwy. 93), called the "window on the wilderness," snakes past dozens of ominous peaks and glacial lakes. Whether driving or biking, set aside at least three days for the parkway. The challenging hikes and endless vistas are never monotonous. Thanks to the extensive campground and hostel networks which line the parkway, drawn-out trips down the entire length of Jasper and Banff National Parks are convenient and affordable. (See Accommodations and Camping under each park.) All points on the parkway are within 30km of at least one place where you can roll out your sleeping bag.

Before setting your wheels on the road, pick up a free map of the Icefields Parkway, available at park information centers in Jasper and Banff. The pamphlet is also available at the **Icefield Centre,** at the boundary between the two parks. The center sits in sight of the **Athabasca Glacier,** the most prominent of the eight glaciers which flow into the 325-square-km Columbia Icefield. The Icefield is one of the largest accumulations of ice and snow south of the Arctic Circle. Its snow continuously feeds eight major glaciers and its melt water runs into streams and rivers that terminate in three different oceans—north to the Arctic, east to the Atlantic, and west to the Pacific Ocean. Summer crowds have snowball fights on the vast icefields to the side of the road. **Brewster Transportation and Tours** (762-2241) carries visitors right onto the glacier in snowfaring monster trucks, called "Snocoaches." You pay $15 (ages 6-15 $5) for the facinating, 75-minute trip. (Tours given May 1-Oct. 15 daily 9am-5pm; Oct. daily 10am-4pm.)

If you have the time—and a burning curiosity about the geological history of the glaciers—sign up for a guided interpretive hike on the Athabasca. A three-hour hike called "Ice Cubed" costs $12 (ages 8-17 $6), and the five-hour "Icewalk Deluxe" is $16 (children $8). Hikes are conducted from June 29 to Labor Day. Write **Athabasca Glacier Icewalks,** Attention: Peter Lemieux, Box 2067, Banff T0L 0C0 (or call 762-5385).

The next best thing to actually journeying out onto the glacier is the 13-minute explanatory film inside the cozy **Icefield Centre.** (Open mid-June to Aug. daily 9am-7pm; mid-May to mid-June and Sept. 9am-5pm.) Although the centre shuts down in winter, the parkway closes only after heavy snowfalls, and then only until the plows clear the way.

If you only have time for a quick hike, try the **Parker Ridge Trail.** The 2.4km hike (one way) guides you away from the parkway, past the treeline, and over Parker Ridge. At the end of the trail awaits a postcard view of the Saskatchewan Glacier. The trailhead is located 1km south of the **Hilda Creek Hostel,** which is itself located 8.5km south of the Icefields.

Hinton

Don't follow the road signs to Hinton; just roll down your window and follow the smell. A large pulp mill in Hinton hurls a most egregious odor which can be smelled for miles around. In spite of this, Hinton, 29km east of Jasper's eastern gate, is an excellent place to stop over on your way to or from the national park.

It is also a good place to stock up on groceries; many Jasperites do their weekly shopping here.

For such a dull, smelly twon, Hinton presents a surprising number of bona fide attractions. See what it's like for a bishop to *really* take a queen when, three times during the summer months, citizens of Hinton act out the roles of chessboard warriors during **Live Chess Theatre.** On Tuesday afternoons at 10am, the **Obed Mountain Coal Company** gives tours of its mine. The **Cardinal River Coal Company (CRC)** also gives tours—four-hour stints with lunch included. Once your olfactory senses have been numbed, consider taking a tour of the **Weldwood Mill** (call 865-2251 for information). The town's modern **Recreation Complex** (865-4412) contains two indoor ice rinks, indoor pool, sauna, jacuzzi, squash and racquetball courts, and a cafeteria. But wait, the fun continues with a late-night nordic expedition at the **Athabasca Look-out Nordic Center,** which boasts one of the few lighted cross-country ski trails in Alberta. Call the visitors center for information.

You can choose from a catalog of a dozen local inns and lodges. The **Timberland Hotel** (865-2231), conveniently next door to the Tourist Info Centre, is the cheapest of the bunch, offering singles starting at $26.25 and doubles from $31.50. The floorboards may creak, but the rooms are clean and well-tended. **L & W's Pizza,** on the other side of Hwy. 16 (865-4892), has take-out, delivery, and sit-down meals. Burgers $1.95, with cheese $2.20. Fries $1.25. Small chees pizza $6.50. Open daily 10am-1am. Or try **Vegas Pizza** (small cheese $4) at the Hill Shopping Mall (865-4116; open Mon.-Wed. 11am-midnight, Thurs.-Sat. 11am-2am, Sun. 4pm-midnight).

Those desperate to put their tents and RVs to use can find a (temporary) home at the **Hinton Campground** (865-4412; just past the Tourist Info Centre on Switzer Dr., under the train tracks). The 65 sites here offer modern amenities for a reasonable $7, and you'll be right next door to the **Hinton Community Centre,** a convention center and arena for some of Hinton's bingo games. For a more complete escape from civilization, drive 20km north to **William Switzer Provincial Park** (865-5600). Open year-round, this secluded adventure area contains seven campgrounds with a total of 196 sites ($7 per night). The streams in the area provide excellent trout fishing and canoers will enjoy floating down Jarvis Creek, which links the park's five major lakes. (For more information write to William A. Switzer Provincial Park, P.O. Box 1038, Hinton, T0E 1B0.)

The Trudy-less **Tourist Information Centre** (865-2777) on the south side of Hwy. 16 in Green Sq., has a cordial and enthusiastic staff eager to sell you on Hinton as they pass out brochures. Open Mon.-Fri. 9am-5pm, Sat.-Sun. 10am-6pm; July and August daily 8am-8pm.

Banff National Park

Yellowstone and Yosemite rolled into one, Banff is Canada's most sublime and well-loved national park. Its snowcapped peaks and turquoise lakes are among the grandest sights in the entire Rockies. Free-roaming wildlife is plentiful; moose rule the marshes of Bow River Valley and bighorn sheep reign on the rocky slopes. Be aware that Banff's wildlife is protected by Canadian law, which states that it is illegal to feed, entice, or molest any animal.

The townsites of Banff and Lake Louise re-create the atmosphere and prices of a European resort. A deluxe suite at the Banff Springs Hotel costs $735 per night plus $15 per pet. Visitors can relax in an old-fashioned hot sulphur pool while wearing 1914-style bathing suits or ride a gondola to one of Banff's peaks.

Practical Information and Orientation

Visitor Information: Banff Information Centre, 224 Banff Ave. (762-3777). Open daily 8am-10pm; Oct.-May 10am-6pm. **Lake Louise Information Centre** (522-3833). Open mid-May to mid-June daily 10am-6pm; mid-June to Aug. 8am-10pm; Sept.-Oct. 10am-6pm.

Park Headquarters: Superintendent, Banff National Park, Box 900, Banff T0L 0C0 (762-3324).

Greyhound: operates out of the Brewster terminal. To Lake Louise (5 per day, $5.05) and Calgary (6 per day, $10.45). The Lake Louise buses continue to Vancouver ($67).

Brewster Transportation: 100 Gopher St. (762-6767), near the train depot. Monopoly on tours of the area, and runs 1 express daily to Jasper ($29). Does not honor Ameripasses. Depot open daily 7am-midnight.

Car Rental: Banff Used Car Rentals, junction of Wolf and Lynx (762-3352). $34 per day with 150 free km plus 10¢ per additional km. Must be 21 with major credit card. **Avis,** 209 Bear St. (762-3222). $50 per day with 100 free km plus 19¢ per additional km. Ask about IYHF member discount.

Moped Rental: Mountain Mopeds, 451 Banff Ave. $8.50 per hr., $30 per 4 hr., $45 per day. ID and $100 deposit required. Open daily 10am-8pm.

Bike Rental: Spoke 'n' Edge, 315 Banff Ave. (762-2854). 3, 5, and 10-speeds. $2.50 per hr., $10 per day; mountain bikes $4 per hr., $16 per day. **Bactrax Rentals,** 339 Banff Ave. (762-8177). Mountain bikes $3.50 per hr., $15 per day. Open daily 8am-8pm.

Hospital: Lynx and Wolf St. (762-2222).

Emergency: In Banff 762-4333, at Lake Louise 522-3811.

Police: 762-2226, between Lynx St. and depot.

Post Office: Corner of Buffalo and Bear St. (762-2586). Open Mon.-Fri. 9am-5:30pm. Postal Code: T0L 0C0.

Area Code: 403.

Banff National Park hugs the Alberta-British Columbia border, 120km west of Calgary. The **Trans-Canada Highway** (Hwy. 1) runs east-west through the park, the Icefields Parkway is the spine which connects Banff and Jasper National Parks. Greyhound links the park to major points in British Columbia and Alberta. Civilization in the park centers around the townsites of Lake Louise and Banff. Lake Louise is 55km northwest of Banff on Hwy. 1. Buses and the daily train are expensive. If you're hitching, expect plenty of competition.

Accommodations

Although the budget traveler may have difficulty finding an affordable restaurant in town, inexpensive lodging is abundant. Fifteen residents of the townsite offer rooms in their own homes—many year-round, and the majority in the $20-40 range. Ask for the *Banff Private Home Accommodation* list at the Banff Townsite Information Centre.

Banff International Hostel (IYHF), Box 1358, Banff T0L 0C0 (762-4122), 3km from Banff Townsite on Tunnel Mountain Rd., among a nest of condominiums and lodges has the look and setting of a modern-day ski lodge. In winter, a large fireplace warms the lounge area for cross-country and downhill skiers. A hike from the center of the townsite, but the modern amenities and friendly staff make the trek worthwhile. Ski and cycle workshop. Laundry facilities. TV. Wheelchair-accessible. Clean quads with 2 bunk beds. Registration 6-10am and 4pm-midnight. Members $12, nonmembers $17. Linen provided.

Banff YMCA, 102 Spray Ave. (762-3560). Welcomes both men and women. Antiseptic white everywhere confirms that this was once a hospital Immaculate rooms, are, of course, germ-free and clean. After midnight you have to identify yourself to be let in. Blankets for rent. Singles $38, doubles $46, bunks $14.

Hilda Creek Hostel (IYHF), 8.5km south of the Icefield Centre on the Icefields Parkway. Features a primitive sauna that holds about 4 people—uncomfortably. In the morning, guests must replenish the water supply with a shoulder-bucket contraption. Accommodates 21. Members $7, nonmembers $12. Closed Thurs. night.

Rampart Creek Hostel (IYHF), 34km south of the Icefield Centre. Has a wood-heated sauna, larger than Hilda Creek's. Accommodates 30. Members $7, nonmembers $12. Closed Wed. night.

Mosquito Creek Hostel (IYHF), 103km south of the Icefield Centre and 26km north of Lake Louise. Fireplace and sauna. Accommodates 38. Members $7, nonmembers $12. Closed Tues. night.

Corral Creek Hostel (IYHF), 5km east of Lake Louise on Hwy. 1A. The hostel nearest Lake Louise. Accommodates 50. Members $7, nonmembers $12. Closed Mon. night.

Castle Mountain Hostel (IYHF), on Hwy. 1A (762-2637), 1.5km east of the junction of Hwy. 1 and Hwy. 93. Recently renovated. Accommodates 36. Members $8, nonmembers $13. Closed Wed. night.

The Banff Springs Hotel, Spray Ave. (762-6895). A hotel marvel. A bit of a splurge at $735 for a suite for a night, but you can stay in someone else's room for only $15 per night if you masquerade as a pet.

Camping

There are a lot of happy campers in Banff. Human visitors throng tentsites nightly throughout the summer and an occasional black bear meanders by to create a little excitement. Some of these campgrounds raise their prices during the "premium period" (late June-Labor Day). None will take reservations, so arrive early. Mosquito Creek, Lake Louise, Johnston Canyon, and Tunnel Mountain Village have the best facilities and are located closest to a townsite. The following are listed from north to south.

Cirrus Mountain, 24km south of the Icefield Centre, 105km north of Hwy. 1 on 93. 16 sites, $8. Open June 26-Sept. 8.

Waterfowl Lake, 57km north of Hwy. 1 on Hwy. 93. 116 sites, $8. Open mid-June to mid-Sept.

Mosquito Creek, 103km south of the Icefield Centre and 26km north of Lake Louise. Near the Mosquito Creek hostel. 32 sites (20 during winter), $8. Open June 19-Sept. 14.

Lake Louise. Not on the lake, but 221 sites for tents (and 163 for RVs). Sites $8.50, "premium period" $10.50. Open mid-May to mid-Sept.

Protection Mountain, 11km west of Castle Junction on Hwy. 1A. 89 sites, $8.50. Open June 23-Sept. 7.

Castle Mountain, midway between Banff and Lake Louise along Hwy. 1A. 44 sites, $7.50.

Johnston Canyon, 26km northwest of Banff on Hwy. 1A. The only campground besides Tunnel Mountain with showers. Excellent trail access. 140 sites, $9, "premium period" $11. Open mid-May to mid-Sept.

Two Jack Main, 13km northeast of Banff. 381 tentsites and flush toilets. Sites $6.50. Open mid-May to Aug.

Two Jack Lakeside, just south of Two Jack Main. 77 sites on a lake where the Polar Bear Club could hold summer training. Brrr. Sites $8.50. Open June 30 to Sept 7.

Tunnel Mountain Village, 1km past the International Hostel, closest to Banff townsite. A village indeed, with showers and 622 tentsites. Sites $9.50. Two other campgrounds at Tunnel Mountain reserved for RVs.

Food

For many, the wilderness calls to mind campfires, roasting marshmallows, and pork and beans. Bring along your favorite recipes, and you'll eat well here. On your way to the hiking trail or campground, make a quick stop at Banff's largest and cheapest supermarket, **Safeway,** 318 Marten St., at Elk St. (762-5378), open daily 8am-10pm. Banff's restaurants generally charge high prices for mediocre food. Fast food is expensive and slow. But the Banff International Hostel and the Banff YWCA do serve affordable meals. The hostel's cafeteria serves up wholesome breakfast specials for $3-5 from 7-9am. It also cooks dinners from 5-7pm. The **Spray Cafe,** at the Y, boasts an even bigger breakfast deal: two eggs, bacon, hashbrowns, and toast for $3.25. Open Thurs.-Tues. 8am-3pm. The other restaurants below also promise inexpensive meals, a relative term in a town which caters to monied international tourists.

Banff Townsite

Coriander Nature Food, Banff Ave. (762-2878), in the Sundance Mall, upper level. This place even smells healthy thanks to the freshly cut lilacs at each table. Take a break from that burger diet with Mexican beans and rice in a pita ($3, with tofu $4.50) or a sandwich on thick 7-grain bread ($4-6). For dessert, try a shake made from apple juice, blueberries, and strawberries ($3). Pick up vitamins and trail mix on your way out. Open Mon.-Sat. 10am-6pm, Sun. 11:30am-5:30pm.

Aardvark's, 304 Wolf St. (262-5500). This small pizza place does big business late at night, when the bars close. Excellent pizza anytime, though. Small $6-8, large $12-19. Chicken wings $5. Open Mon.-Sat. 11am-4am, Sun. 11am-3am.

Mr. J. Jolly's Sandwich and Coffee House (762-4788), hidden in the back of the Clock Tower Village Mall on Banff Ave. Serves cappuccino ($1.85), but the cellophane-wrapped sandwiches (from $3.75) more accurately represent the nature of this hole-in-the-wall. Open daily 9:30am-5pm.

Joe Btfsplk's Diner, 221 Banff Ave. (762-5529). This doofy moniker, pronounced bi-TIF-spliks, is named after the L'il Abner character. Overpriced and crowded, this mock 50s diner serves decent food. Burgers and specialty salads $6-7, and tasty treats (muffins 95¢, rice krispie squares $1.50). Open daily 8am-11pm.

Silver City, 110 Banff Ave. (762-3337). Though primarily a bar, Silver City lays out an all-you-can-eat buffet ($5) which is actually pretty good, for "bar food." Stick around and take in a live band Fri. and Sat. night. Open daily 9pm-2am.

Sights and Activities

Hike to the **backcountry** for privacy, beauty, over 1600km of trails, and trout that bite anything. The pamphlet *Drives and Walks* covers both the Lake Louise and Banff areas, describing day and overnight hikes. You need a permit to stay overnight in the backcountry, and you can get one free of charge from information centers and park warden offices. All litter must leave the backcountry with you; in addition, no wood may be chopped in the parks. Both the International Hostel and the Park Information Centre have copies of the *Canadian Rockies Trail Guide,* with excellent information and maps.

Canada's first national park (and the world's third) began in 1885 as Hot Springs Reserve, featuring the **Cave and Basin Hot Springs** nearby. In 1914, a resort was built at the springs. Refurbished as the **Cave and Basin Centennial Centre** (762-4900), the resort now screens documentaries and stages exhibits. Explore the original cave or relax in the hot springs pool where lifeguards wear sexy pre-World War I bathing costumes. The centre is southwest of the city on Cave Ave. (Centre open daily 10am-8pm; Sept. 1-early June 10am-5pm. Pool open early June-Sept. 1 only. Admission to pool $2, ages under 12 $1.25.) A particularly scenic walk lies just beyond the Cave and Basin in **Sundance Canyon.** Allow about an hour and a half for the uphill trail; take the Viewpoint Path at the end. If you find Cave and Basin's 32°C (90°F) water too cool, follow the rotten-egg smell to the **Upper Hot Springs pool,** a 40°C (104°F) cauldron up the hill on Mountain Ave. (Open June-Sept. daily 8:30am-11pm. Admission $2, ages 3-16 $1.25. Bathing suit rental at either spring $1, towel rental 75¢, and locker rental 25¢.)

Taking a gondola to the top of a peak is an expensive way to see the park, but saves your legs for hiking at the summit. The **Sulphur Mountain Gondola** (762-5438), right next to the Upper Hot Springs pool, lifts you up to one of the most amazing views in all the Rockies. (Open daily 9am-8pm. Fare $7.50, ages 5-11 $3, under 5 free.) The **Summit Restaurant** perched atop Sulphur Mountain serves an "Early Bird" breakfast special for $3. The **Sunshine Village Gondola** (762-6555) climbs to the 2,215m-high resort village. The village is a good base for high alpine hiking. (Open June 27-Sept. 7 Mon.-Thurs. 8:30am-7:30pm, Fri.-Sun. 8:30am-10:30pm. Fare $12, ages 6-12 $5, under 6 free.) If that's not high enough for you, jump on the Standish chairlift, which will carry you to the peak (elev. 2430m).

Brewster Tours offers an extensive array of guided bus tours in the park. If you have no car, these tours may be the only way to see some of the main attractions, such as the Valley of the Ten Peaks, the Great Divide, the Athabasca Glacier, Johnston Canyon, and the spiral railroad tunnel cut into a mountain (the trains are so long, you can see them entering and exiting the mountain at the same time). The tour-guide/drivers are professional, knowledgeable, and entertaining. If you were planning on taking the regular Brewster bus from Banff to Jasper ($29), you might want to spend $20 more to see the sights in-between. One-way is $49, round-trip (9½ hr.) is $68. A walk on the Columbia Icefields is $13 extra. Brewster does not accept credit cards. Tickets can be purchased at the bus depot. Call 762-6767 for more information.

If you'd prefer to look up at the mountains rather than down from them, all the nearby lakes will provide a serene vantage point. **Two Jack Lake** (near Banff) and **Moraine Lake** (near Lake Louise) can be explored by boat and canoe. On Two Jack Lake, rowboats cost $8.50 per hour, $42.50 per day; canoes $8 per hour, $40 per day; $20 deposit. (Open July-Aug. daily; June Sat.-Sun. only.) On Moraine Lake, canoes cost $10 per hour (522-3733; $20 deposit required, open daily in summer 8am-sundown). **Fishing** is legal virtually anywhere you can find water, but you must hold a National Parks fishing permit, available at the information center ($5 for a 7-day permit, $10 for an annual permit). Superb trout fishing awaits those willing to hike the 7km to **Bourgeau Lake.** Closer to the road, try **Herbert Lake,** off the Icefields Parkway between Lake Louise and the Columbia Icefield. **Lake Minnewanka,** adjacent to Two Jack Lake, provides excellent fishing in its infamous waters, rumored to be the home of an Indian spirit—half human, half fish. You can find out about this ancient myth during a 2-hour guided tour sponsored by **Minnewanka Tours Ltd.** (762-3473; $12, children $6). Try to snag the 50-lb. trout that has always gotten away.

The hilly road leading to Lake Minnewanka provides cyclists with an exhilarating trip, as do many other small paths throughout the park. Bicycling is also allowed on most trails in the Banff Townsite area. Remember to dismount your bike and stand to the downhill side if a horse approaches. Also be forewarned that the quick and quiet nature of trail bicycling is more prone to surprise a bear than is the tromping of hikers.

The palatial **Banff Springs Hotel,** Spray Ave. (762-6895) is perched high over the townsite. In 1988, this enormous 825-room castle in 1988 celebrated its 100th birthday with a series of posh parties and its own special brand of beer. You probably won't have enough money to spend the evening here, or even order dinner, but you can take in a beer, a basket of bread, and a fantastic view for about $3 in the café on the second floor. The hotel offers free guided tours of the grounds Tues.-Sun. at 10am. The tour, a good pastime for a rainy day, reveals fascinating secrets about the hotel and offers a grand opportunity to view lavish architecture and museum-quality artifacts. The hotel also offers horseback riding (daily 9am-5pm; $15 for 1 hr., $24 for 2 hr., $29 for 3 hr.; reservations recommended).

Other rainy day attractions include Banff's small but illuminating museums. The **Whyte Museum of the Canadian Rockies,** 111 Bear St. (762-2291), traces the mountain chain from its initial discovery and exploration through its metamorphosis into a world-famous tourist magnet. You'll learn that the sights in Banff have changed little in the last century; they have simply become more crowded. A gallery downstairs shows paintings of the mountains and their inhabitants. (Open daily 10am-6pm. Admission $2, senior citizens and students $1.) The nearby **Park Museum,** on Banff Ave. near the bridge, provides two floors of a taxidermist's dream or a preservationist's nightmare: all species indigenous to the park (and even some that aren't) stuffed and placed in glass cases. Come eyeball-to-eyeball with a motionless grizzly and look a gray wolf square in the eye (if he blinks, run). Built in 1903, the museum also contains a well-stocked reading room where you can discover the differences between buffalo and bison or caribou and moose. (Open daily 10am-6pm. Free.) Less than a block away, on the second floor of the Clock Tower Village Mall (112 Banff Ave.), the **Natural History Museum** rounds out Banff's archival troika. The complete tour includes a thrilling 20-minute video documentary focusing on volcanoes, namely Mt. St. Helens. On the way out be sure to appreciate the legend of Bigfoot by snickering at an eight-foot-tall "authentic" model of the spurious Sasquatch. (Open daily 10am-8pm; in winter 10am-6pm. Admission $2, senior citizens and children $1.)

The **Art of the Wild Limited,** at 110 Banff Ave., on the second floor of the clock Tower Mall (762-2999), is filled with incredibly life-like paintings of North American landscape and animals. Without several thousand disposable dollars, you can't buy anything, but the trip is free and worthwhile. Open Tues.-Fri. 10am-9pm, Sat.-Mon. 10am-6pm.

Banff's bartenders contend that "the real wildlife in Banff is at the bars." The **Barbary Coast,** upstairs at 119 Banff Ave. (762-4616; open Mon.-Sat. 11am-2am); **Melissa's,** 218 Lynx St. (762-5511; open Mon.-Sat. 11:30am-1am); and **Silver City,** (see Food) bear this out every night. Party animals swish their tails in line for as much as two hours in summer. Drinks average $3-4.

The culture industry moves into Banff every year for the summer-long **Banff Festival of the Arts,** producing drama, ballet, jazz, opera, and other aesthetic commodities. Pick up a brochure at the Visitor Information Centre or call 762-6300 for details.

Lake Louise

The crystal waters of Lake Louise, framed by snow-capped peaks, often serve North American filmmakers' need for Swiss alpine scenery, and on a clear day, the view from the lakeside chateau evokes images of St. Moritz. Unfortunately most visitors spend only enough time at the lake to snap a couple photos; few spend the time to experience the area as explorer Tom Wilson did in the 1880s, who wrote of its majesty, "I never in all my explorations...saw such a matchless scene."

To gain a deeper appreciation of the turquoise-blue lake and the surrounding glacier, consult the **Lake Louise Information Centre** (522-3833). (Open May 19-June 18 8am-6pm; June 19-Sept. 4 8am-10pm; Sept. 5-Oct. 9 10am-6pm.) The brand-new, $4.4 million complex is a museum in itself, with exhibits and a short film on the formation of the Rockies. Renting a canoe from the **Chateau Lake Louise Boat House** (522-3511) will give you the closest look at the lake ($15 per hour). In addition, several hiking trails begin at the water. As incentive, aim for one of the two teahouses, tucked away at the end of the 3.4km Lake Agnes Trail and the 5.3km Plain of Six Glaciers Trail. Be prepared to pay dearly for this mountainous meal—all the food must be brought up by helicopter. (Teahouses open in summer daily 9am-6pm.) **Timberline Tours** (522-3743) offers guided horseback rides through the area. The 1½-hour tour costs $20, and the daytrip $55 (lunch included). The **Lake Louise Gondola** (522-3555), which runs up Mt. Whitehorn, across the Trans-Canada Hwy. from the lake, provides another chance to gape at the landscape. (Open mid-June to late Sept. daily 9am-6pm. Fare $7, ages 5-12 $3.50. "One way hiker's special" $5.) Like its counterpart at Sulphur Mountain, Lake Louise's gondola offers a $3 breakfast deal; just make sure to purchase your lift ticket by 9:30am (breakfast served until 11am).

Calgary

When the North West Mounted Police set up shop here in the 1860s, Commander-in-Chief Ephrem Brisebois named the town after himself. He was subsequently ousted from power for abusing his authority, and Col. James MacLeod renamed the settlement "Calgary"—Scottish for "clear running water." The city now thrives on a less transparent liquid. Since the discovery of oil in 1947, Calgary has become a wealthy and cosmopolitan city—the oil may be crude, but the people are refined. Office buildings rise higher than the oil derricks, businessmen scurry

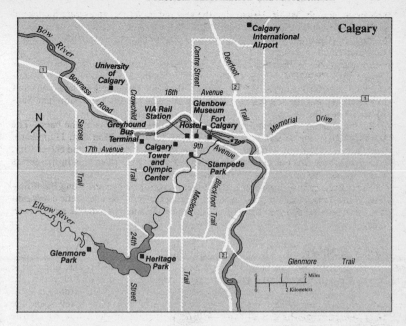

about in three-piece suits toting leather briefcases, and a newly built transport system soundlessly threads through the immaculate downtown streets.

Calgarians take pride in their well-oiled city. They proudly hold on to memories of hosting the XVth Winter Olympic Games. They are eager to brag that their Flames captured the 1989 Stanley Cup (remember, this is hockey country). They are inexplicably proud that bits of *Superman III* were filmed downtown (the filmmakers liked the effect of the mirrored buildings in the flying sequences). And of course, everyone puts on their cowboy hats, Wranglers, and western accents when the Stampede yahoos into town in July.

Practical Information and Orientation

Visitor Information: Calgary Tourist and Convention Bureau, 237 8th Ave. SE (263-8510). Call or write for help finding accommodations, especially around Stampede time. Open daily 8am-5pm. **Information centre** at the same address open daily 8:30am-7pm; Sept.-June Mon.-Fri. 8:30am-4:30pm. **Trans-Canada Highway office,** 6220 16th St. NE. Open daily 8am-9pm; Sept.-June 10am-5pm. **Airport office** open daily 7am-11pm. **Travel Alberta,** 455 6th St. SW (297-6574, in AB 800-222-6501), on the main floor, secretes information about the entire province. Open June-Sept. Mon.-Fri. 8:15am-4:30pm.

Greyhound: 850 16th St. SW (Outside Calgary 800-661-TRIP; within Calgary 265-9111). To Edmonton (10 per day, $22); frequent service to Banff ($10.45). Free shuttle bus from C-Train at 7th Ave. and 10th St. to bus depot. 10% senior citizen discount.

Calgary Transit: Information and Downtown Sales Centre, 206 7th Ave. SW. Bus schedules, passes, and maps. Open Mon.-Fri. 8:30am-5pm. Fare $1.25, ages 6-14 75¢, under 6 free. Exact change required. Day pass $3.50, children $2. Book of 10 tickets $10, children $6.50. **Information line** (276-7801) open Mon.-Fri. 6am-11pm, Sat.-Sun. 8am-9:30pm.

Taxi: Checker Cab, 272-1111. **Associated Cab** 276-5312. **Yellow Cab,** 250-8311.

Car Rental: Rent-A-Wreck, 2339 Macleod Trail (237-7093). Cars start at $33 per day with unlimited mileage. Must be 21 with major credit card. If under 25, there is a mandatory $10 per day surcharge for collision insurance. Open Mon.-Fri. 8am-7:30pm, Sat. 9am-5:30pm,

Sun. 10am-5:30pm. **Thrifty,** 117 5th Ave. SE (262-4400), airport (221-1961). Rates start at $44 per day with 150 free km, plus 12¢ per additional km. Must be 21 with major credit card. **Tilden,** 114 5th Ave. SE (263-6386), airport (221-1690).

Bike Rental: Sports Rent, 7218 Macleod Trail SW (252-2055). $15-20 per day. **Abominable Sports,** 640 11th Ave. SW (266-0899). Mountain bikes $15 per day; mopeds $20 per day.

Laundromat: Beacon Speed Wash & Dry (230-9828).

Time and Weather: 263-3333.

Gay Lines Calgary: 223 12th Ave. SW (234-8973), on the 3rd floor. Recorded phone message provides gay community information; peer counseling available at the office. Phone and office open Mon.-Sat. 7am-10pm.

Women's Resource Centre: 320 5th Ave. SE (263-1550), at the YWCA. For women of all ages seeking any kind of assistance. Open Mon., Wed. 9am-4:30pm; Tues., Thurs., 9am-9pm.

Sexual Assault Centre: 244-1353.

Drug Centre: 266-1605.

Hospital: Calgary General, 841 Centre Ave. E. (268-9111).

Ambulance Service: 261-4000.

Emergency: 911.

Police: 316 7th Ave. SE (266-1234).

Post Office: 220 4th Ave. SE (292-5512). Open Mon.-Fri. 8am-5:45pm. Postal Code: T2P 2G8.

Area Code: 403.

Calgary is accessible by several highways, including the Trans-Canada Highway. Planes fly into **Calgary International Airport** (292-8400 for the Transit Authority; 292-8477 for general information, daily 10am-9pm), approximately 5km to the northwest of the city's center. Cab fare from the airport to the city is about $20. Public transportation takes passengers directly to the northeastern-most stop of the C-Train for a mere $1.25. Bus #57 departs the airport every half-hour between 6:30-8am, 2:45-5pm, and 9:57-11:07pm. Unless you take a cab or have impeccable timing, you will probably end up taking the **Airporter Bus** (291-3848), which offers frequent and friendly service into downtown Calgary for $6.50. The bus serves six major downtown hotels—Delta Bow, International, Westin, Glenbow Inn, Palliser, and Skyline—though drop-offs are fairly flexible.

You'll find that Calgary is a well-planned city once you conquer your initial disorientation. The city is divided into quadrants: **Centre Street** is the great east-west divide, while the Bow River (with the adjacent Memorial Drive where the Bow actually bows) divides the north and south sections. The rest is simple: avenues run east-west, streets run north-south. Pay careful attention to the quadrant distinctions (NE, NW, SE, SW) at the end of each address. You can derive the street from an avenue address by disregarding the last two digits of the first number: thus 206 7th Ave is at 2nd St., and 2339 Macleod Trail is at 23rd St. Pick up a city map at convenience stores or at the Information Centre (see Practical Information).

Public transportation within the city is inexpensive and efficient. **Calgary Transit** operates both buses and streetcars ("C-Trains"). Buses run all over the city and cost $1.25. You need only call 276-7801 to find out how to get where you want to go. Though they cover less territory, C-Trains are free in the downtown zone (along 7th Ave. S.; between 10th St. SW and City Hall); you pay the $1.25 fare only when you leave downtown. Though you can get on the trains without a ticket, be careful: the C-Train honor code is occasionally enforced by "spot checks" which can cost you $25 and a lot of humiliation. Most of what you'll need—lodging, food, and sights—is within the C-Train's free zone anyway. Hitchhiking is illegal within the Calgary city limits; and, like the C-Train honor code, it is policed.

Accommodations

Cheap rooms in Calgary are rare only when packs of tourist Stampede into Calgary's hotels—reserve ahead for July.

Calgary International Hostel (IYHF), 520 7th Ave. SE (269-8239). Conveniently located several blocks south of downtown with access to C-train and public buses. Complete with snack bar, meeting rooms, cooking and barbeque facilities, laundry, and a cycle workshop. Disabled access. Discount tickets for the Calgary Tower can be purchased by showing your hostel card at the Tower. Lockout 10am-4:30pm. Curfew Tues.-Wed. midnight, Thurs.-Mon. 2am. Members $10, nonmembers $15. Sept.-April members $8, nonmembers $13.

University of Calgary, 3330 24th Ave. (220-3203), in the NW quadrant of the city. A little out of the way, but easily accessible via bus #9 or the C-Train. If you can't make the Olympic squad, at least you can sleep in their beds—U of C was the Olympic Village home to 1988 competitors. Olympian-sized rooms for competitive prices. There's also a cafeteria and a pub on this serene campus. Room rental office is located across the campus in the Kananaskis Building, a 12-minute walk from the train stop (open 24 hr.). Virtually unlimited supply of rooms in the summer, fewer rooms available in winter (but do inquire). With student ID singles $15.75, shared rooms $10.50. Without student ID singles $22, doubles $30; breakfast included.

YWCA, 320 5th Ave. SE (263-1550). As luxurious as a "Y" can be, and in a fine, quiet neighborhood. A range of rooms. The security makes for a somewhat lifeless lodging. Cafeteria open all day. Women only. Singles $22, with bath $29.50. Dorm beds $15.

York Hotel, 636 Centre St. SE (262-5581). More central location, larger rooms, and a notch up from the St. Louis. Bath and cable TV included. Singles $58. Doubles $68. 20% discount for senior citizens.

St. Louis Hotel, 430 8th Ave. SE (262-6341), above the St. Louis Tavern. Depending on your point of view, the location means either excitement or danger. Location not recommended for women. The few grim-looking long-term residents generally keep to themselves. Friendly management. Singles $16, with TV $19, with TV and bath $21. Doubles with TV and bath $26. Prices increase during Stampede (about $3). Daily first come, first serve; no reservations.

Regis Hotel, 124 7th Ave. SE (262-4641). Friendly management and clean rooms, though the lobby of this old, dingy hotel has the feel of an old dingy hotel. Singles $29.40, with TV $32.55, with TV and bath $40. If you're looking for some solitary confinement, try "the sleeping room"—a closet-like single with no TV, bath, or windows $24.15.

Food

Finding food is relatively easy in Calgary. Ethnic and cafeteria-style dining spots line the **Stephen Ave. Mall,** 8th Ave. S between 1st St. SE and 3rd St. SW, and the indoor mini-malls nearby. Good, cheap food is also readily available in the **"Plus 15" Skyway System.** Designed to provide indoor passageways during bitter winter days, this bizarre mall connects the second floors of dozens of buildings throughout the city. You can join the system at any "participating" building; just look for the blue and white "Plus 15" signs on street level.

For more expensive, trendy restaurants, go to the **Kensington District,** along Kensington Rd., between 10th and 11th St. NW. Take the C-train to Sunnyside or use the Louise Bridge to reach this area. Other good and lively café-restaurants are on 4th St. SW. This area can be reached most easily by taking the #3 or 53 bus.

City Hall Cafeteria, (268-2463) in the City Hall Municipal Building at the intersection of 7th Ave. SE and Macleod Trail (2nd St.), or take the back entrance to City Hall. Backpackers and briefcasers guzzle cheap coffee (40¢) and gobble muffins (70¢). Early birds with time for a more balanced morning meal can feast on the breakfast buffet ($2.45, 7-8am). Open Mon.-Fri. 7am-4pm.

Hang Fung Foods Ltd., 119 3rd Ave. SE (269-5853), located in the rear of a Chinese market with the same name. Enormous bowl of plain *congee* (rice broth) $1, with abalone and chicken $3. A heaping plate of barbecue duck and steamed chicken on rice is $4.25. Bring your own silverware if you haven't mastered chopsticks. Open daily 8:30am-9pm.

4th Street Rose, 2116 4th St. SW (228-5377). California cool pervades this fashionable restaurant on the outskirts of town: high ceilings, tile floors, and oh-so-casual waiters. Sit at the bar and watch TV or chow down at a table and chow down. Gourmet pizzas, homemade pasta, and fresh salads ($2.75-6). Take bus #3 or 53 and avoid the long hike. Open Mon.-Thurs. 8am-1am, Fri. 8am-2am, Sat. 10am-2am, Sun. 10am-midnight.

Pasta Frenzy, 2120 4th St. SW (245-1888). If 4th St. Rose is either too loud or too crowded, go to Pasta Frenzy next door. Open-air seating and relaxed pace, with similar airs and graces (both restaurants are owned by the same people). A sophisticated Italian assortment includes pizza ($6-8), pasta, and salads ($2-5); good desserts too. Open Mon.-Sat. 11:30am-midnight, Sun. 11am-11pm.

Picadilly Grill, 216 7th Ave. (261-6699). A pleasant restaurant/cafe in the heart of downtown with pink and green tables, a checkered floor and mirrored walls. They didn't film *Grease* here, but they could have. Burgers and sandwich entrees $5-6. "Big Affair" entrees (steak, linguini, etc.) $7-10. Take out or sit down. Open Mon.-Fri. 6:30am-10, Sat. 8am-10pm, Sun. 10am-8pm.

Take Ten Cafe, 304 10th St. NW (270-7010). Light dining in Kensington with a German accent. Und evreesing is under $4.50. The *wienerschnitzel* ($4.45) includes gravy, vegetable, and fries. ½-lb. basket of curly fries with gravy $1. Hungarian ghoulash $4. Homemade cakes and muffins. Lunch special from 11am-2:30. Open Mon., Thurs.-Sat. 8am-5pm, Tues. and Wed. 8am-4pm, Sun. 10am-4pm.

Bohemia Bistro, 124 10th St. NW (270-3116), near Kensington Rd. (tucked away on 2nd floor). Perhaps the most unusual of the Kensington district restaurants. An eclectic menu features unkosher "kosher" sandwiches ($6-7) and pastas with original combinations ($7-8.50). Lunch is a good buy at $4-6. Indulge in a chocolate truffle on the way out ($1). Open Tues.-Thurs. 11:30am-midnight, Fri.-Sat. 11:30am-1am.

The Roasterie, up the street from the Bohemia Bistro. No meals here, just cookies, muffins, and about 20 kinds of coffee, ranging from Rioberry ($1.75) to HiTest ($1) to Vietnamese Iced Coffee ($2)—all served in giant cups. Before you leave, play the "tip game" by pelting coins into the tip cup from behind the counter (a 10-ft. jumper). Hot chocolate ($1) and tea (60¢). Open Mon., Thurs. 8:59am-midnight; Tues., Fri. 9am-midnight; Wed., Sat. 9:01am-midnight; Sun. 9:01am-6pm.

Krono's Pizza and Steak Place, 506 10th St. NW (283-0939 or 283-3111). About a block up from The Roasterie, with formica tables, vinyl couches and junior jukeboxes, this classic pizzeria is too normal for the Kensington District. The menu includes an incredible variety of pizzas (small $7-8, large $10-12) and not half-baked pasta ($7-8). The heated pizza sub with ham, salami, tomatoes, meat-sauce, and mozzarella cheese ($6) is *magnifico*. Open Mon.-Thurs. 11am-1am, Fri. 11am-2am, Sat. 4pm-2am, Sun. and holidays 4pm-11:30pm.

Under the Sunbrella Cafeteria, 610 8th Ave. SE (262-6342), on the 2nd floor of the Golden Age Club. Very convenient to the hostel, this center for the retired welcomes the hungry of all ages. Patio furniture and bright lights create a cheerful, relaxing atmosphere. Daily hot lunch and dinner specials ($4.45) include potato, vegetable, and roll plus coffee or tea, reminding many of the corporal punishment of their grade-school days. Open Mon.-Fri. 8am-6pm; last hot meal 5:30pm, Sat. 10am-2pm.

Sights

Don't just gaze at the **Calgary Tower** (266-7171), 101 9th Ave. SW, ride an elevator to the top ($3, children $1.25; discount if you present your hostel card) for a spectacular view of the Rockies on clear days. The 190m tower also affords a 360° view of the city. Xybots, Pacmania, and other video games in the video arcade (presumably the highest in Central Alberta) will keep vidiots amused when clouds obscure the view. The revolving **Panorama Dining Room** atop the tower can be expensive, but the "Breakfast in the Sky" special, a full morning meal for $9.50 (children $5.25), includes a free elevator ride in the price (elevator pass is valid throughout the day). (Rides Mon.-Sat. 7:30am-11:30pm, Sun. 8am-10:30pm.)

The **Glenbow Museum,** 130 9th Ave. SE (264-8300), just across the street from the Tower, is a nexus of cultural pride in this boomtown. There's something for everyone amidst the odd mix of modern art, military artifacts, and mineral samples, including an assortment of edifying exhibits for schoolchildren (who often stampede through the museum on weekday mornings). At the entrance are five cases of Olym-

LET'S GO Travel

1991 CATALOGUE

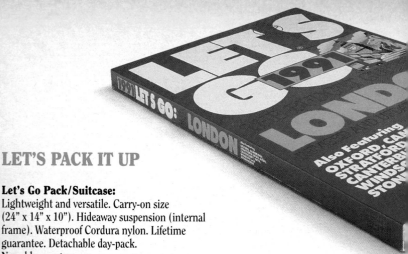

LET'S PACK IT UP

Let's Go Pack/Suitcase:
Lightweight and versatile. Carry-on size
(24" x 14" x 10"). Hideaway suspension (internal
frame). Waterproof Cordura nylon. Lifetime
guarantee. Detachable day-pack.
Navy blue or grey.
10014 Suitcase $144.95
Free shoulder strap and
Let's Go travel diary.

Passport/Money Case:
Zippered pouch of waterproof nylon.
71/2" x 41/2". Navy or grey.
10011 Passport Case $6.50

Undercover Neck Pouch:
Ripstop nylon and soft Cambrelle. 61/2" x 5".
Two separate pockets. Black or tan.
10012 Neck Pouch $6.95

Fanny Pack:
Pack cloth nylon. Three compartments.
Charcoal or Marine Blue.
10013 Fanny Pack $13.95

Let's Go Travel Books:
Europe; USA; Britain/Ireland;
France; Italy; Spain/Portugal/Morocco; Gree
Israel/Egypt; Mexico; California/Hawaii; Pac
Northwest; London; New York City.
1016 Specify USA; Europe $1
1017 Specify Country $1
1018 Specify New York or London $
This is $1.00 off the cover price!

**International Youth Hostel Guide for
Europe and the Mediterranean:**
Lists over 3,000 hostels. A must.
10015 IYHG $1
FREE map of hostels worldwide.

Sleepsack: (Required at all hostels)
78" x 30" with 18" pillow pocket. Durable
poly/cotton, folds to pouch size. Washable.
Doubles as a sleeping bag liner.
10010 Sleepsack $1

LET'S G⊕ Travel
We wrote the book on budget travel

1991-1992 American Youth Hostel Card
(AYH): Recommended for every hosteler, this
card is required by many hostels and brings
discounts at others. Applicants must be US
residents. Valid internationally.

10022	**Adult AYH (ages 18-55)**	**$25.00**
10035	**Youth AYH (under age 18)**	**$10.00**
10023	**Plastic Case**	**$0.75**

FREE directory of hostels in the USA.

'’S SEE SOME I.D.

International Student
ification Card (ISIC): Provides
nts on accommodations, cultural events,
es and, this year, increased accident/
al insurance. Valid from 9/1/90–12/31/91.
0 ISIC **$14.00**
“International Student Travel Guide”
surance information.

International Teacher Identification
(ITIC): Similar benefits to the ISIC.
4 ITIC **$15.00**
“International Student Travel Guide” and
nce information.

Youth International Education
nge Card (YIEE): Similar benefits
ISIC. Available for non-students under
e of 26. Valid by calendar year.
4 YIEE **$14.00**
“Discounts for Youth Travel.”

Eurail Pass: the best way to travel Europe.

First Class

10025	15 Day	**$390.**
10026	21 Day	**$498.**
10027	1 Month	**$616.**
10028	2 Months	**$840.**
10029	3 Months	**$1042.**

Flexipass

10030	5 Days within 15	**$230.**
10031	9 Days within 21	**$398.**
10032	14 Days in 1 month	**$498.**

Eurail Youth Pass (Under 26)

10033	1 Month	**$425.**
10034	2 Months	**$560.**
10036	15 days in 3 months	**$340.**
10037	30 days in 3 months	**$540.**

Child Passes (age 4-12) also available.

All Eurail Pass orders include FREE: Eurail Map,
Pocket Timetable and Traveler's Guide.

LET'S G🖐® Travel
One source for all your travel needs

LET'S GET STARTED

PLEASE PRINT OR TYPE. Incomplete applications will be returned.

International Student/Teacher Identity Card (ISIC / ITIC) application enclose

❶ Dated proof of current FULL-TIME status: letter from registrar or administrat
or copy of transcript or proof of payment.

❷ One picture (1 1/2" x 2") signed on the reverse side.
Applicants must be at least 12 years old.

Youth International Exchange Card (YIEE) application enclose:

❶ Proof of birthdate (copy of passport or birth certificate).
Applicants must be age 12 – 25.

❷ One picture (1 1/2" x 2") signed on the reverse side.

❸ Passport number _____ ❹ Sex: M   F

Last Name_____First Name_____

Street_____
Continental U.S. Addresses only. We do not ship to P.O. Boxes

City_____State_____Zip Code_____

Phone (   )_____—_____Citizenship_____

School/College_____Date Trip Begins_____/_____/____

ITEM NUMBER	DESCRIPTION	QUAN-TITY	UNIT OR SET PRICE		TOTAL P
			Total Price		
			Total Shipping and Handling		
			Optional Rush Handling (add $9.95)		
			Mass. Residents (5% sales tax on Gear, Books & Maps)		
				TOTAL:	

Shipping and Handling			Please allow 2-3 weeks for delivery.
If your order totals:		Add	**RUSH ORDERS DELIVERED WITHIN**
Up to 30.00		$2.00	**ONE WEEK OF OUR RECEIPT.**
30.01 to 100.00		$3.25	Enclose check or money order payable to
Over 100.00		$5.25	Harvard Student Agencies, Inc.

LET'S G® Travel

Harvard Student Agencies, Inc. Thayer Hall–B Cambridge, MA 02138
(617) 495-9649   1-800-5LETSGO

pic pins, the most extensive collection in this Olympic-pin-collecting town. (Open daily 10am-6pm. Admission $3, senior citizens $1, students and children $2, under 12 free; free on Sat.) Less than a block northeast of the museum, the **Olympic Plaza** still attracts crowds on sunny days. The site of the medal presentations during the Winter Games, this open-air park now hosts a variety of special events, from the Kids' Fest to the Calgary Jazz Festival (both in June). For an update on Olympic Plaza programming, call 268-5207 during business hours. One of the park's most interesting features, the **walkway**, was constructed out of more than 20,000 bricks, each purchased for $20-30 and engraved with the name or personal message of the patron. Try to decipher such cryptic, possibly Satanic, messages as "NGF 1959 BN B IN YYC."

Five blocks down 8th Ave. to the west is home of **Devonian Gardens.** Located on the fourth floor of Toronto Dominion Sq. (8th Ave. between 2nd and 3rd St. SW), this 2.5-acre indoor garden contains fountains, waterfalls, bridges, and over 20,000 plants, including 138 different local and tropical varieties. After a few hours of wading through shopping oceans in the downtown malls, make yourself dizzy watching a school of goldfish swim in circles. If you wish absolute privacy, Devonian Gardens can be yours for the low, low price of just $650 per hour. (Open daily 9am-9pm. Free.)

A few blocks to the northwest, the **Energeum**, 640 5th Av. SW (297-4293), in the lobby of the Energy Resources Building, is Calgary's shrine to fossil fuel. A film in the upstairs theater of this small but informative oil museum re-creates the mania following Alberta's first oil find. Displays and short video segments downstairs subject oil drilling to the latest miracles of representation. You can put the tar-like substance right up to your nose, and run your hand (gloved, of course) through a pile of the oozing glop. (Open Sun.-Fri. 10:30am-4:30pm; Sept.-May Mon.-Fri. 10:30am-4:30pm. Free.)

Farther west, roughly 4.3 light-years from Alpha Centauri, is the **Alberta Science Centre and Centennial Planetarium** (221-3700, 11 St. and 7th Ave. SW in earth-speak, near the Greyhound Bus Terminal). Gloved-hands-on experiments here test the laws of physics, while a simple pendulum and a few descriptive plaques explain how the elder Foucault determined that the earth rotates on its own axis. Planetarium shows disclose that Jupiter's Great Red Spot could swallow three Earths and still have room for Take Ten Café's ghoulash. Out back there are three life-size models of aircraft from World Wars I and II. (Science Centre open Wed.-Sun. 1-9pm. Most planetarium shows are after 6pm. Laser shows on weekend evenings. Admission to both planetarium and Science Centre $5, children $2.50; Science Centre only $2, children $1.50.)

Just a stroll away from the Science Centre is **Prince's Island Park,** which can be reached by footbridges from either side of the Bow River. The park contains biking and fitness trails, playground equipment, and a snack bar. Although usually quiet, the park sometimes hosts loud events, such as the Caribbean Cultural Festival in June.

Calgary's other island park, **St. George's Island,** is accessible by the river walkway to the east and is home to the marvelous **Calgary Zoo.** Try to visit in the late spring when many of the animals give birth to new attractions—the Australian mothers seem to be especially prolific. After you've observed all the animals and learned why the giraffe has the highest blood pressure of any animal (too much booze and smokes), take a relaxing walk through the **botanical garden.** The zoo also includes a **prehistoric park,** which takes you back in time some 65 million years, and a **children's zoo.** (Open daily at 9am; closing time is seasonally adjusted. For more information, call Zooline, 232-9300. Admission $6, senior citizens and ages 12-17 $3.50, under 12 $2.50. "Tuesdays are special:" adults $3, senior citizens free.)

The nearby **Fort Calgary Interpretive Centre** (290-1875) offers an exhibit hall and a comprehensive film which maps out Calgary's evolution from cowtown to oiltown. Take a scenic walk on one of the riverside interpretive trails that begin from the center and explore the remains of a 19th-century fortress set up by the Royal Canadian Mounted Police and torn down by developers. (Open daily 9am-

5pm. Free.) The center is on 9th Ave. SE, just east of downtown; grab bus #1 ("Forest Lawn") eastbound.

Although the actual Olympic flame has long since extinguished in Calgary, retailers continue to carry the torch, offering hundreds of different official Olympic merchandise, most, of course, at fire-sale prices (the market for 1988 Olympic memorabilia has evidently peaked). The more important legacies of the Games are several newly built, world-class athletic facilities—not only great arenas for recreation but also fascinating architectural sights. The two most impressive are the **Olympic Oval,** an indoor speed-skating track on the University of Calgary campus (hours vary from season to season; call 220-7890 for more information), and **Canada Olympic Park,** the site of the bobsled, luge, and ski jumping competitions. A guided tour of Olympic Park will cost you $6 (senior citizens and children $3), but go for it—the one-hour trip around the facilities includes a chance to stand in the bobsled track and to glance down the slope from atop the 90m ski jump tower. The **Olympic Hall of Fame** (268-2632), also located at Olympic Park, exalts the Olympic ideology with displays, films, and videos. (Open daily 10am-5pm. Admission $3; senior citizens, students, and children $2.)

For non-vicarious downhill excitement, turn to the slopes of **Nakiska at Mount Allan** (591-7777), a newly carved ski area on Hwy. 40 in Kananaskis Country (see Near Calgary). (Lift tickets $27 per day, children $7, students $19; $18 per half-day, children $8. Senior citizens and the disabled, $8 for the whole day. Children under 8 free.) Nordic skiers receive an even better deal—they can tread where Olympians once trod for free at the **Canmore Nordic Centre** (678-2400), in Kananaskis Country just outside the town of Canmore. Of the 56km of trails, one is designed for beginners; the rest are all Olympic level. If you have brought along your biathlon association membership card and a rifle, you are cordially invited to use the shooting range and, in summer, the roller-ski course.

The Stampede

Even people who think that rodeo is grotesque and silly have trouble saying "Calgary" without letting a quick "Stampede" slip out. Somehow, it seems as though everyone envisions the city as wedded to "The Greatest Outdoor Show on Earth," but Calgarians themselves are perhaps the most guilty of perpetuating this relationship. Every year around Stampede time, the locals throw free pancake breakfasts and paint every ground-level window downtown with cartoon cowboy figures offering misspelled greetings ("Welcum, y'all"). Underneath ten-gallon hats, locals command tour groups to yell "Yahoo" in the least likely of circumstances. Simply put, the entire city of Calgary flips out.

And why not? Any event that draws millions from across the province, the country, and the world deserves the hoopla—and your attention. Make the short trip out to **Stampede Park,** just southeast of downtown for a glimpse of steer wrestling, bull riding, wild cow milking, and the famous chuckwagon races, where canvas-covered, box-shaped buggies whiz by in a chariot race that defies the laws of aerodynamics. (Tickets $9-31.) The Stampede also features a **midway,** where you can perch yourself atop the wild, thrashing back of a roller coaster.

Parking is ample, but the crowd is always more than ample in July—take the C-Train from downtown to the Stampede stop. In 1991, the Stampede will run from July 5-14. For official information and ticket order forms, write Calgary Exhibition and Stampede, Box 1060, Station M, Calgary T2P 2K8, or call 800-661-1260. If you're in Calgary, call 261-0101 or visit Stampede Headquarters, 1410 Olympic Way.

Stampede Park still has sights to amuse and educate year-round. The **Olympic Saddledome** (261-0455) startles the area with its unique architecture. Site of hockey and figure skating events for the Winter Olympics, the Saddledome now hosts concerts, Calgary 88s basketball, horse racing, and Calgary Flames NHL hockey. Groups can book a free tour; call 261-0400. Aspiring agronomists will not want to miss Alberta Wheat Pool's **Grain Academy** (263-4594) on the second floor of the Roundup Centre in Stampede Park. Not quite as thrilling perhaps as watching Broncobuster Billy-Boy-Bob, you can use the meter-tall model of a grain elevator as your mobile textbook as you observe the intricate model train display that traces the route that the harvested grain takes from Alberta's prairie to Vancouver's international ports. (Open Mon.-Fri. 10am-4pm, Sat. noon-4pm. Free.)

Those who prefer their sports participatory should jog over to **Lindsay Park Sports Centre,** 2225 Macleod Trail S. (233-8393), across from Stampede Park. This Venusvillian bubble, often mistaken for the Saddledome, offers four swimming pools, an indoor track, numerous basketball courts, a weight room, and aerobics. Built in 1983 for the Western Canada Summer Games, Lindsay Park is primarily a "competition and training" facility for Canadian athletes of all levels. Call ahead to be sure it is open to the public on a particular day. (Admission $5, children $1.55. Open Mon.-Fri. 5:30am-10pm, Sat. 6am-9pm, Sun. 9am-9pm.)

Entertainment

After a long, hard day pounding barrels of local crude, many young Calgarians like to pound bottles of local brew along **"Electric Avenue,"** the stretch of 11th Ave. SW between 5th and 6th St. Swimming in neon, this avenue juices up every night, blasting music with such gusto, you'll think all the clubs run their speakers through the same turntable. Beware of Electric Avenue during hockey playoff time: they close off the street and lines wind around the block. Last call in Calgary is theoretically at 1:45am.

Bandito's, 620 11th Ave. SW (266-6441). A current favorite, but any of the joints along 11th Ave. will do. Drinks $3-4. Lively DJs. Most open for lunch around 11am and stay open until somewhere past 2am, depending upon business.

Ranchman's Steak House, 9615 Macleod Trail S. (253-1100). One of Canada's greatest honkytonks. Experience Calgary's Wild West tradition firsthand, on the dance floor stomp to the tune of live C&W tunes or in the not-so-subtle flavor of Calgary Stampede beer. Open Mon.-Sat. 7pm-2am.

St. Louis Tavern, 430 8th Ave. SE (262-6341). Cheaper drinks and more character than most places on 11th Ave. Open Mon.-Tues. 10am-midnight, Wed.-Thurs. 10am-1am, Fri. 10am-2am, Sat. 10am-1am.

O'Brien's Pub & Restaurant, 636 Centre St. S (262-5581). Located in the core of downtown, this bar serves great drinks and cheap food. Billiards in the back room, dancing out front. What a party. Open Mon.-Sat. 11am-2am.

Dinero's, 310 Stephen Ave. Mall (264-6400). Popular as a place for drinks after work, this Tex-Mex outpost serves up plenty of *cerveza.* No Corona on tap, but keg upon keg of Molson and Coors ($3), not to mention Heineken ($3.25). Happy hour Mon.-Fri. 4-7pm. On Wed., Margueritas are $2.50. Bar open daily 11am-2am.

The Stadium Keg, 1923 Uxbridge Dr. NW (282-0020). Where the "Dinos" from the nearby University of Calgary eat, drink, and be merry. Good rock'n'roll blasted at a level which still allows you to hear yourself think. Two large TVs. Drink specials nightly 6-9pm. Mon., Thurs.-Fri. 12-oz. drafts $1.50. Chicken wings 25¢ per basket on Thurs. Hi-balls $1.49 on Fri. Open daily 4:30pm-2am-ish.

Calgary has many movie theaters, including one in the Stephen Ave. Mall. The **Centre for Performing Arts,** 9th Ave. and 1st St. SW (294-7444), hosts part of the Calgary Jazz Festival, ballet concerts, and the Calgary Philharmonic Orchestra. Most tickets $10-20. Call to find out if senior citizen and student discounts apply.

Near Calgary

You won't lose the crowds by going to the **Tyrrell Museum of Palaeontology** (pronounced TEER-ill), near Drumheller, but you will lose all sense of self-importance. The world's largest display of dinosaur specimens reminds you that humanity is a mere crouton in the Caesar salad of Earth's history. From the Big Bang Theory to the Quarternary Period (that's us), Tyrrell covers it all with a dizzying array of displays, educational computers, and videos. And if you're not slide-tackled by a hyperactive, class-trip runaway, you may just be able to build your own "Sillysaurus" on one of the nine computers in the museum.

The museum is on Secondary Hwy. 838, a.k.a North Dinosaur Trail, 6km from Drumheller. From Calgary, it's a 90-minute drive via Hwy. 2 N. to Hwy. 72 and 9 E. (Check out **Horseshoe Canyon**, about 20 minutes west of Drumheller, as you approach—and then learn how it was formed when you walk though the museum.) As with many tourist attractions in Alberta, Tyrell is not directly served by public transportation, but you can ride **Greyhound** from Calgary to Drumheller (2 per day, one way $12.25) and hoof it out to the museum. The museum's cafeteria food is surprisingly inexpensive and tasty. Grab a seat beneath an umbrella on the patio and beat the heat (but not the flies) with a breakfast or lunch special (about $4). (Open daily 9am-9pm; Labor Day-Victoria Day Tues.-Sun. 10am-5pm. Donations $2, senior citizens and young adults $1.50, families $5.)

Those yearning for a stroll in the Badlands will enjoy Tyrell's free 90-minute **interpretive walks** through Dinosaur Country (offered 11am, 3pm on weekends and holidays only). Midland Provincial Park staffers lead these tours two or three times per day during the spring and summer. Check the information desk at the museum (where the tours start) for exact times.

Tyrell lies within **Midland Provincial Park,** one of the newest and most underdeveloped parks of its kind in Canada. Only about 10% of the park's 1500 acres have been developed, and the park's facilities are still only open for day use. Nonetheless, tourists on their way to Tyrell should not be deterred from making a stop at **McMullen Island** for a quick picnic, or at the site of the **Old Midland Mine Office** (823-1754 or 823-1749), 2km east of the museum. This renovated coal miner's credit union now dispenses a map of the park and ideas on how to explore the area. Most of the park facilities are open only in summer. For camping in town, two options are available: **Shady Grove Campground** (823-2576), located in Drumheller on Hwy. 9 N. just off the north side of the bridge, and **Dinosaur Trailer Court** (823-3291) at the intersection of Hwy. 9 N. and Dinosaur Trail North.

Those who prefer to observe non-extinct scaly vertebrates should visit **Reptile World** (823-TOAD) on Hwy. 9, a 10-minute walk from Drumheller. The legacy of the flea market which used to occupy this space lingers on as you can purchase many of the "zoo's" animals. Hands-on displays (hold a boa) accompany interesting facts (a snake can swallow prey twice as wide as its head) at this self-touted "largest collection of live reptiles in Canada." (Open daily 10am-10pm; in winter 10am-6pm. Admission $3.75, senior citizens and children $2.50.)

Drumheller itself is certainly an unenticing tourist destination, but if you spend too much time at Tyrell you should consider spending the night at either the newly renovated **Alexandra Hotel** (823-2642) or the **Waldorf Hotel** (823-2623), both on Railway Ave. in the center of town. There are pleasant rooms at both establishments. Singles at the Alexandra cost $25, doubles $30. The Waldorf charges similar rates: singles $20, doubles $30. Make sure your room's air conditioner functions. For those who want to get away from the downtown Drumheller, try the **Riverside Inn Crawford's Bed and Breakfast,** 501 Riverside Drive West (823-4746). Singles $35, doubles $40. Large color TV, VHS, delicious breakfast, and genuine hospitality. Call beforehand. Chow down at the **Corner Grill** (823-4888), at the corner of 3rd Ave. and Centre St. (Open daily 7:30am-midnight). Or for the friendliest service and highest quality food in town, head to **The Old Grouch's** (823-5755), 175 3 Ave. W. Stop into this mom-and-pop establishment for an immense, homemade muffin (90¢) or gorge yourself on a super sub ($8), enough meat, cheese, and hot peppers to satisfy even the hungriest Stegosaurus. Beware of long lunch lines in the summer; but when they're not busy, Mr. and Mrs. Grouch will chat with you over coffee and a freshly-baked cookie. (Open Mon.-Sat. 10am-10pm, Sun. noon-10pm.) If you're short on time and money, visit the **Burger Barn** (823-8866) at 305 4 St. W. for a quick ¼-pounder ($2). The drive-thru window at this barn-turned-burger-joint is reminiscent of a million other fast food restaurants, but nothing the Golden Arches offers could match the Barn's Super Backbacon Burger (with fries and a small soda $5). (Open daily 10am-10pm.)

The area's dinosaur fetish persists at **Dinosaur Provincial Park,** 118km southeast of Drumheller. Actually the main field station for the Tyrrell Museum, the park sits amid the Canadian Badlands of eastern Alberta near **Brooks.** The **Field Station** (378-4342) 48km east of Brooks, contains a small museum that complements Tyrrell, but the main attraction is certainly the **Badlands Bus Tour,** which runs four to 10 times per day between Victoria Day and Labor Day. For $1.50, you get chauffered into the restricted archaeological hot spot for dinosaur discoveries. Many fossils still lie within the ever-eroding rock; you might make some kind of discovery yourself at one of the stops on the tour. Unfortunately, all you can take home are your memories and your Polaroids. If you point out your discovery to the knowledgeable guide, you can also take home the coveted "Fossil Finder Certificate." The **campground** in the park is shaded from the summer heat (unlike the rest of the park), and grassy plots cushion most campsites. The campground stays open year-round but is fully serviced only in summer. (Sites $5. Park open Victoria Day-Labor Day daily 9am-9pm. After Labor Day, you must make an appointment for a tour.) Call or write the Field Station, Dinosaur Provincial Park, Box 60, Patricia T0J 2K0. From Drumheller, follow Hwy. 56 S. for 65km, then take Hwy. 1 about 70km to Brooks. Once in Brooks, go east along the well-marked Hwy. 873 and 544. Bikers should be especially cautious since much of the route from Brooks is paved only in loose gravel.

Kananaskis Country

Tucked away between two of Alberta's most conspicuous tourist magnets, Kananaskis Country recently celebrated its tenth anniversary. South of the Trans-Canada Highway and midway between Calgary and Banff, K-Country is a 4000-square-kilometre conglomeration of three provincial parks—**Bow Valley, Peter Lougheed,** and **Bragg Creek**—and several recreational areas (**Spray Lakes** and **Highwood/Cataract Creek** are two of the largest). Preservation and development of K-Country began in 1978, yet even in high season, tourists are sure to find this wilderness tranquil and unspoiled.

For outdoor types, Kananaskis Country offers skiing, snowmobiling, windsurfing, golfing, biking, and hiking. Eager staff members at the five park information centers can help design itineraries for park visitors. Expect to be showered with topographical maps and elaborate brochures on your activity of choice. A **Park Visitor Centre** lies within or nearby each of the three provincial parks. The Alberta parks system operates out of a center in **Bow Valley,** just north of Hwy. 1 between Seebe and Exshaw (673-3663; open daily 8am-7pm); another in **Elbow Valley** on Hwy. 66 near **Bragg Creek** (949-4261); and a cozy, chalet-style office, complete with a fireplace and a wooden deck overlooking Pocaterra Creek, in **Peter Lougheed Park,** on the Kananaskis Lakes Trail (591-7222; hours vary from season to season). The parks system also runs a more central office on **Barrier Lake,** near the junction of Hwy. 40 and 68 (673-3985; open daily 9am-7pm, 9am-5pm in winter). **Travel Alberta** maintains an especially helpful office in **Canmore,** just off Hwy. 1A near the northwest border of K-Country (678-5277; open Sun.-Thurs. 9am-6pm, Fri.-Sat. 8am-8pm).

Kananaskis' hiking trails accommodate many different kinds of nature lovers. Those with limited time or endurance will enjoy the interpretive hour-long hikes. The Canadian Mt. Everest Expedition Trail (2.4km), for example, provides a majestic view of both Upper and Lower Kananaskis Lakes. More serious hikers will find Gillean Dafferns' *Kananaskis Country Trail Guide* the definitive source on area trails, detailing 337 hikes (published by Rocky Mountain Books). For additional hints and trail updates, ask a staff member at an Information Centre. Bikers will also find the park staff helpful for planning treks along the untraveled highways and trails.

If you are traveling by bus, relinquish any hopes of visiting K-Country; buses do not service the area directly. If you are bound for Kananaskis Country or bust, you can take one of the frequent buses to Banff which will drop you off about 20km from the region's northwestern boundary at Canmore (see Calgary Practical Information). Once in Kananaskis, **hitchhiking** is difficult but possible.

No less than 3000 campsites are accessible via K-Country roads, and camping is unlimited in the backcountry as long as you set up camp at least 1km from a trail. Established campsites in Kananaskis cost at least $7 per night. The **Ribbon Creek Hostel** (591-7333), near the Nakiska Ski Area, 24km south of the Trans-Canada Hwy. on Hwy. 40, accommodates 48 people. The hostel's private family rooms hold four beds each, and its living room has a fireplace. (Members $6, nonmembers $10. Closed 9am-5pm and all day Tues.) **William Watson Lodge** (591-7227), a few km north of the Information Centre in Peter Lougheed Park, accommodates disabled people. Although only Albertan disabled people and senior citizens may make reservations to stay in the cabins, the main lodge is open year-round and anyone may drop by to enjoy the highly accessible local trails.

Southern Alberta

While central Alberta churns relentlessly toward post-modernity, propelled by the rivalry between oil-rich Calgary and Edmonton, southern Alberta remains a revolution or two behind the times. Living over oil-free land, most southern Albertans farm, ranch, and mine coal. Some of North America's best-preserved and - exhibited Native archeological sites are in the parks of this region, including Head-Smashed-In Buffalo Jump (with its new $10 million interpretive center). And people touring the region in search of large-scale cataclysms should make a point of visiting Crowsnest Pass, where you can visit the sites of two massive mining mishaps.

Lethbridge

Lethbridge seems out of place in southern Alberta—and not only because its main tourist attraction is a lush, green Japanese garden. Amidst the miniscule prairie towns that dot the region, the city of 60,000 is home to two universities and one of Canada's most interesting historical and recreational parks. The expanding urban development and the frequent gusty winds that plague the city may make Lethbridge seem like a sort of light-weight Chicago. Nonetheless, Alberta's third largest city manages to retain the tempered rustic pride characteristic of the surrounding villages.

Practical Information and Orientation

Visitor Information: Chinook Country Tourist Association, 2805 Scenic Dr. (320-1223), at the intersection of Scenic and Mayor Magrath Dr. Staff will gladly help you plan a tour of southern Alberta. Maps, brochures, and guides to the city and the entire region. Open May-Labor Day daily 8am-9pm; Labor Day-Oct. 15 9am-5pm; Oct. 16-April 8:30am-4:30pm. A newer **Information Centre,** located on Brewery Hill, on 1 Ave. S. off Hwy. 3 (320-1222), provides the same maps and pamphlets and features an intoxicating vista of Brewery Gardens, formerly a disposal site for coal ashes. Open May-Labor Day daily 8am-9pm; Labor Day-Sept. 9am-5pm.

Greyhound: 411 5th St. S. (327-1551). 3 buses daily to Calgary ($19.45) and Edmonton ($41.45). Open Mon.-Sat. 8am-7pm, Sun. 8-11:30am and 1-7pm.

Buses: Lethbridge City Transit runs 9 routes that will take you anywhere within the city. You can catch the buses at the intersection of 4th Ave. S. and 6th St. S. Fare $1, students (to grade 12) 75¢, senior citizens and children 60¢. For more information call 320-3885.

Taxi: Lethbridge Cabs, 327-4005. $1.80 plus $1 per km thereafter. Senior discount 10%. 24 hr.

Car Rental: Rent-A-Wreck, 3230 24th Ave. S. (328-9484). Must be 21 with credit card. $30 per day with 100 free km. 11¢ per additional km. Open Mon.-Sat. 8am-5:30pm.

Weather: 320-7623.

Women's Shelter: Harbour House, 604 8th St. S., run by the YWCA (320-1881, phone staffed 24 hr.).

Sexual Assault Crisis Line: 327-4545 or 800-552-8023.

Police: 444 5 Ave. S (328-4444).

Post Office: 704 4th Ave. S. (820-7133). Open Mon.-Fri. 8:30am-5pm. Postal Code: T1J 0N0.

Area Code: 403.

Lethbridge lies along Highway 3, the Crowsnest Highway. Highways 4 and 5 run into the city from the south. From Calgary or Edmonton, drive south on Hwy. 2 until it intersects Hwy. 3, then go about 50km east. In the city, avenues run east-west and streets north-south. The Canadian Pacific Railroad passes through the center of the city, dividing it into north and south sections.

Accommodations

The reputable motels along Mayor Magrath Dr. cost about $40, and in summer hotels invariably flash vacancy signs. Unless your coffers are hollow, stay away from the sleazy, ultra-cheap hotels in the city center. Try to bed down at either the **University** or the **YWCA.**

University of Lethbridge (329-2584), across the Oldman River from the city but easily reached by bus #7 and 8. In summer, the residence office—Room C-442 in University Hall—rents rooms to almost anyone. Clean sheets, good security, friendly neighbors, and a convenient location offset spartan dorm rooms and shared bathrooms. Singles $17. Shared rooms $13. With student ID singles $15.80, shared rooms $11.60, large singles $17.80.

YWCA, 604 8th St. S. (329-0088). Very safe for women traveling alone. Comfortable, homey place complete with shared kitchenette. Singles $20. Shared rooms $18.

Parkside Inn, 1009 Mayor Magrath Dr. (328-2366), next to the Japanese Gardens, Heritage Lake, and the golf course. Take bus #1 from downtown. At the high end of the totem pole. The recently remodeled rooms are "big and plush"; each includes A/C, cable TV, and bathroom. Singles $36. Doubles $44.

Henderson Lake Campgrounds (328-5452), at Henderson Lake in the southeast corner of the city. Shaded and peaceful sites for tenters, virtual driveways for RVs. The RVs have the last laugh, though—when it rains the lower tenting area floods in biblical proportions. Tent sites $10, with hookups $15.50.

Food

Those travelers who become addicted to the common Canadian $2.99-or-less breakfast special might find Lethbridge is unable to satisfy their early-morning habit. Lethbridgians are careful when choosing words to describe the cost of local cuisine—it's always "moderate" or "reasonable," rarely "cheap." Budget travelers can either spend the extra few dollars and enjoy local meals or suffer the wrath of Mayor McGrath Dr.'s McDonaldses, A&Ws, Bonanzas, and Kentucky Frieds. More of the same cluster near the City Centre. Several inexpensive eateries line the second floor of the Lethbridge Centre Mall.

The Shasta, 329 5 St. S. (329-3434). Ignore the gaudy lamps and wallpaper and explore the long list of luncheon specials, like a grilled cheese and mushroom sandwich with salad and fries for $3. Great Caesar's Ghost—the steak and Caesar salad dinner special includes garlic toast and potato for $8. Budget burgers ($3-5). Open Mon.-Thurs. 11am-10pm, Fri.-Sat. 11am-11pm.

Top Pizza and Spaghetti House, 11 St. and 4 Ave. S. (327-1952). Good pizza at good prices. Small pizzas start at $5.30. A medium pie with pepperoni and mushroom costs $8; large dish of spaghetti with meatballs $6.25. A triple-decker club is $3.50. Open Mon.-Thurs. 11am-1am, Fri.-Sat. 11am-3am, Sun. noon-midnight.

The Duke of Wellington, 132 Columbia Blvd. W. (381-1455), in the West Village Mall. Students and encumbered nobility dine here infrequently; it's close to the university but somewhat expensive. Daily sandwich specials (under $5) include soup and fries. Open Mon.-Sat. 11am-10pm.

Sights

Fort Whoop-Up (329-0444), located in **Indian Battle Park** on the east bank of the Oldman River, is a replica of the notorious whiskey trading outpost which originally stood some 10km from present-day Lethbridge. Dressed in period costumes, the guides working out of the **Interpretive Centre** explain the history of the whiskey and fur trade from the days of the fort's construction. Europeans introduced the Native Americans to make-shift whiskey—pure grain firewater flavored with tobacco, lye, dirt, or whatever else was handy at the time—and in the process took advantage of the local tribesmen. Numerous incidents of violence and disorder occurred between the two trading partners until 1874, when the Mounties galloped into the fort. A well-balanced slide show is projected regularly; a film shown by request. (Interpretive Centre open daily 10am-6pm; Labor Day-May 15 10am-4pm.) For an additional 50¢ hop aboard the **Whoop-Up Wagon Train,** a motorized modern-day stagecoach which will take you on a 20-minute tour of the park and the Oldman River valley.

A stop that young children and naturalists alike will appreciate is the **Helen Schuler Coulee Centre and Nature Reserve** (320-3064), a section of Indian Battle Park consecrated for the protection of local vegetation, prairie animals, and the occasional porcupine. (Open Sun.-Thurs. 10am-8pm, Fri.-Sat. 10am-6pm; Labor Day-Victoria Day Tues.-Sun. 1-4pm.) Here you can learn about creepy crawly creatures and the tremendously talented toad. One of the trails leads outside the Reserve to the **Coal Kiosk,** an information-packed outpost that sketches the progress of the coal mining industry in Lethbridge from the first excavation in 1881 through Lethbridge's incorporation as a city in 1906. Behind the outpost are two authentic (closed-off) mines. The kiosk lies beneath the spectacular **High-Level Bridge,** the longest and highest of its kind in the world. The black steel skeleton opened to trains in 1909 and is still in use today, supporting traffic many times heavier than its designers envisioned.

The **Nikka Yuko Japanese Garden** (328-3511) in the southeast corner of town is the most trumpeted of the city's attractions. Constructed and reconstructed (just to be safe) in Japan, then dismantled and shipped to Lethbridge for another reconstruction, the main pavilion blends surprisingly well into the Albertan placidity. An informative Japanese-Canadian hostess appears at each point of interest to guide you through the garden. Don't neglect to ring the Japan-Canada peace bell, or to remove your shoes upon entering the pavilion. (Open May 15-June 20 daily 9am-5pm; June 21-August 9am-8pm; Sept.-Oct. 4 9am-5pm. Admission $2.50, seniors and ages under 17 $1.25.) Adjacent to the Japanese Garden is **Henderson Lake;** this manmade reservoir is the nucleus of a city park in the southeast corner of Lethbridge. The park offers boat rentals (rowboats $6, canoes $7) and a trail around the lake perfect for a morning run or an evening stroll. Take bus #1 to both the garden and the lake. For more information call 320-3020. Boat rental available May-Aug. (Open Mon.-Fri. noon-10pm, Sat.-Sun. 10am-10pm.)

The University of Lethbridge displays $14 million of **art** downtown in an old Eaton's department store (4401 University Dr., 329-2690). The works range from 20th-century Canadian painters to pop artists of the 50s. (Open in summer Mon.-Fri. 1-4:30pm, in winter noon-4:30pm.)

Near Lethbridge: Fort Macleod

Fort Macleod witnessed a rare instance of European benevolence toward Native Americans. In 1873, alarmed by the lawlessness, violence, and exploitation caused by the whiskey trade, the Northwest Mounted Police (NWMP) dispatched 300 of its men to clean up this den of debauchery. In a performance worthy of the Keystone Cops, the Mounties got lost en route, giving Fort Whoop-Up's whiskey traders time to escape south of the border down Montana way. When the force finally arrived, it was greeted not by a hail of gunshots but by the sole remaining liquor vendor. Unable to purchase the fort from the conniving moonshiner, the mounted police moved on to found Fort Macleod and to keeping whiskey traders out of Native Canadian territory.

The **Fort Macleod Museum** (553-4703) at 219 25 St., in a 1957 replica of the 1874 fort, exhibits typical NWMP uniforms, guns, tools, and furniture; stop by only if you're a real Mounties fan. The Interpretive Centre at Fort Whoop-Up in Lethbridge presents a much better synopsis of the area's history for no charge. (Fort and museum open May-June 14 daily 9am-5pm; June 15-Sept. 7 9am-7pm; Sept. 8-Oct. 15 9am-5pm. Off-season tours by appointment only. Admission $3, ages 13-18 $1, under 13 50¢.) Try to visit in July or August when the real spectacle unfolds. Four times daily during these peak tourist months, the Fort Museum's **Mounted Patrol Musical Ride** takes its song-and-dance to the streets. If you cannot catch the real thing, check out the picture of the Mounties in similar formation on the back of the $50 bill.

For nighttime fun in Fort Macleod, the **Great West Summer Theatre** (553-4151) puts on a summer-long production at the **Empress Theatre**, on Main St. If you like bad jokes, plotlessness, zany madcap antics, and off-key singing, you'll just love it. Even if you don't, it's the only thing to do at night anyway. (Tickets $8, under 13 $6.) If you are compelled to spend the night in Fort Macleod, the friendly **DJ Motel** (553-4011) at 416 24 St. has 15 comfortable rooms with bath and cable TV. Singles start at $30, doubles at $32. You can pick up a $2 coupon at the Head-Smashed-In Interpretive Centre here.

Greyhound (265-9111 or 800-661-8747) runs to Fort Macleod from Lethbridge (3 per day, $3.60 one way). Step into the bus station for a bite to eat at the **Java Shop** (533-3063). A sleepy crowd of townsfolk congregates here for the quick and filling breakfast special—sausage and two eggs ($4). The cinnamon rolls are as big as a house. (Open daily 6am-8pm; sometimes open until 1am if there's a late bus getting in.) Just around the corner you can order up a more sophisticated morning meal at the **Continental Bake Shoppe and Lunch Counter** (553-4124). An omelette with coffee, hash browns, and toast costs $3.75. Those with more petite appetites will enjoy a hot sausage roll ($1.05) or a homemade muffin. (Open Mon.-Sat. 7:30am-5:30pm.) For supper, head on over to **Luigi's Pizza and Steak House**, on Main St., 1km east of the Greyhound depot. (Small specialty pizza $5.50, medium $8, baked pasta $5.)

Head-Smashed-In Buffalo Jump

Coveted as a source of fresh meat, sustenance, tools, and shelter, the buffalo became the victim of one of the most innovative forms of mass slaughter in history: the buffalo jump. Agile Blackfoot tribesmen wearing coyote skins would slither behind a herd, skillfully force it into a "gathering basin," and then spook some 500 nearly-blind bison into a fatal stampede over a 10m cliff. For over 5500 years, Native Americans in Southern Alberta created buffalo supermarkets with this technique. No buffalo jump site is as well-preserved as the Head-Smashed-In Buffalo Jump, named about 150 years ago after a young thrill-seeking warrior was drowned by a waterfall of buffaloes as he watched the event from front row seats at the base of the cliff.

Although UNESCO will fine you $50,000 if you forage for souvenirs in the 10-meter-deep beds of bone, you can learn about buffalo jumps and local Native American culture at the **Interpretive Centre** (553-2731), a $10-million, 7-story, brand-new facility built into the cliff itself. The center also shows films of a reenactment of the fatal plunge, which, to the relief of the SPCA, used frozen buffalo to hurl off the cliff. Two km of walking trails, both above and below the cliff, serve as venues for the fascinating and free guided tours. (Open daily 9am-8pm; Labor Day-Victoria Day 9am-5pm. Free.)

There is not yet any public transportation to this unique North American hunting ground. Rent a car or arrange a ride from Lethbridge or from Fort Macleod, which is 18km southeast of the buffalo jump along Secondary Rte. 785.

Crowsnest Pass

Crowsnest Pass is an easy daytrip from Lethbridge and an irresistable stopover for disasterophiliacs en route to southern Alberta via British Columbia or Montana. Named for Crowsnest Mountain, the mesa-like peak that dominates the valley, Crowsnest Pass actually comprises five tiny towns: **Coleman, Blairmore, Frank,** Hillcrest, and **Bellevue.** In its days of glory nearly a century ago, the Pass was heralded as the promising "Pittsburgh of Canada." Entrepreneurs and immigrants flocked to the mountains with dreams of digging a fortune—or simply a month's good pay—from the abundant coal deposits. But as tragedies obliterated sites and underground mining became obsolete, the putative Pittsburgh perished. The mining communities have disappeared, but their legacy remains hewn in (and strewn across) the unlucky hills of the Pass.

You might have to spend the night in the Pass, especially if you're coming from central British Columbia, but try to make this only a daytrip. The four towns wilt quickly with the setting of the sun.

Accommodations, Camping, and Food

Grand Union International Hostel, 7719 17th Ave. (562-8254), in downtown Coleman. Has the feel of an over-a-tavern motel, but rooms are clean and the crowd is "interesting." 64 beds distributed into 26 rooms. Laundry facilities, recreation room, and a restaurant next door (the Mineshaft Café). Members $9, non-members $13, youths (6-15 years) $4.50, children under 5 free. Check-in 8am-11pm.

Turtle Mountain Motor Inn, on Hwy. 3 just west of Frank (562-2412). Worn but cheap. Singles $24. Doubles $26.

Stop Inn Motel, on Hwy. 3 in Coleman (562-7381). A classic non-franchised motel: drive-up rooms and kitchenettes ($3 extra). Singles $30. Doubles $33.

Chinook-Allison Campground. Follow Hwy. 3 west from Coleman for 9km, then follow the signs up Allison Creek Rd. Free camping virtually inaccessible to the foot traveler. Bring a sleeping pad to cushion the 70-odd stony sites.

Crowsnest Campground (562-2932), just off Hwy. 3A in Blairmore. More commercial than most in the Pass, this campground offers hot showers, a heated pool, and 110 sites for RVs or tenters.

Chris and Irvin's Café, 7802 17 Ave. (563-3093), in downtown Coleman. Serves up a chicken burger ($2.25) and the miner's deluxe ($4). Fantastic homemade fries $1.50. Open Mon.-Fri. 6am-10pm, Sat. 7am-10pm, Sun. 8am-8pm.

Sights and Activities

Start your day at the **Leitch Collieries** (562-7388), on Hwy. 3 at the east end of the Pass, for a good introduction to the history of the Pass. Nineteenth-century miners put their picks to the wall inside the hills about 2km from the road, but the coal was later processed in a complex of buildings right where Hwy. 3 passes today. Most of the company's remaining buildings are weed-covered ruins, but the power house and mine manager's house are well preserved. Ask one of the casually clad interpreters who roam the area to decipher the coal miner's lingo on the signs. (Open May 15-Sept. 15 daily 9am-5pm; off-season tours can be arranged. Free.)

Heavy mining turned Crowsnest Pass into a modern Pompeii in 1903, when one-too-many tunnels brought Turtle Mountain tumbling like a giant sandcastle. Ninety million cubic feet of stone spilled into the town of Frank, burying 70 people and their houses in less than two minutes. Today, a decapitated mountain and a mile-long river of boulders are all that remain of the incident. The large grey rocks serve as a massive cemetery, as none of the bodies or houses have been excavated. The

Frank Slide Interpretive Centre, also on Hwy. 3 (562-7388), gives you a notion of what Frank was like before Turtle tumbled; its award-winning multimedia presentation details the lives, origins, and attitudes of the miners. For a close look at a mining ghost town, inquire about guided hiking tours to **Lille,** inaccessible by auto. (Centre open daily 9am-8pm; Labor Day-Victoria Day 10am-4pm. Free.)

An equally thrilling disaster befell **Hillcrest** in 1914 when methane in the mine shafts ignited, killing 189 miners. According to the interpretive film, the lesson to be learned is that "you're only as safe as the stupidest guy in the mine." Their memorial cemetery is hard to find but worth the effort (and free). Many of the gravestones within the mass burial area are inscribed in Slavic tongues—testimony to the popularity of the risky mining career to new immigrants at the turn of the century. Follow the Hillcrest access road off Hwy. 3 until the road forks; take the right fork and immediately make a sharp right down a gravel road to the fence-enclosed cemetery.

For a historical overview of the entire Crowsnest Pass region, pack your lunchbox and go to school—to Coleman High School, that is, in downtown Coleman. The high school was transformed into the **Crowsnest Museum** after the Crowsnest Historical Society purchased it for $1 in 1983 (talk about budget-minded). Exhibits highlight the Pass community near the turn of the century with displays depicting traditional school rooms and barber shops. (Open daily 10am-noon, 1-4pm; Labor Day-Victoria Day Mon.-Fri. only. Free.) In winter, the **Allison Lake Recreation Area** operates an extensive network of cross-country ski trails in the shadow of Crowsnest Mountain. Take Hwy. 3 west from Coleman for 9km, then follow the signs up Allison Creek Rd. Also, crazy-Ian MacGregor types can hike up with their skis to the top of the Frank slide to enjoy the silver lining of this tragic-accident-turned-ski-slope.

Waterton-Glacier International Peace Park

Waterton-Glacier transcends international boundaries to unite two of the most unspoiled (but relatively accessible) wilderness areas on the continent. Symbolizing the unobtrusive peace between the United States and Canada, the park provides a haven for bighorn sheep, moose, and mountain goats—and for tourists weary of the more crowded woodlands farther south. In autumn, the parks play host to the hundreds of bald eagles that gather to feast on salmon in McDonald Creek near West Glacier.

Despite its idealistic ambitions, Waterton-Glacier is for all intents and purposes, two distinct areas: the small Waterton Lakes National Park in Alberta, and the enormous Glacier National Park in Montana. Each park charges its own admission fee (Waterton CDN$4, Glacier US$5), and you must exit the greater park boundary—and go through customs—to pass from one to the other.

Many of the dates given below are approximate, and with good reason: snow melt is an unpredictable process. To find out which areas of the park, hotels, and campsites will be open when you visit, contact the headquarters of either Waterton or Glacier (see Practical Information). As a general rule, the parks are in full swing from late May to Labor Day.

Glacier National Park, Montana

Practical Information and Orientation

Park Headquarters and Information: Superintendent, Glacier National Park, West Glacier, MT 59936 (888-5441). Open Mon.-Fri. 8am-4:30pm.

Visitor Information: St. Mary's, at the east entrance to the park (732-4424), shows different short films (such as *Time of the Grizzly*) every day. Open daily May 26-June 16 9am-5pm, June 16-Labor Day 8am-9pm, Sept. 3-Sept. 30 9am-5pm. The center at **Apgar,** at the west park entrance, leads children's programs from June-Nov. Open daily May 26-June 15 8am-

4:30pm, June 16-Labor Day 8am-9pm, Sept. 4-Nov. 17 8am-4:30pm. There is a third visitors center at **Logan Pass** on Going-to-the-Sun Rd. Open mid-June to late summer daily 9am-6pm.

Border Crossing Stations: Chief Mtn., Open May 18-May 31 9am-6pm; June 1-Sept. 14 7am-10pm. Closed in Winter. **Piegan/Carway,** May 16-Oct. 31 7am-11pm; Nov. 1-May 15 9am-6pm. **Trail Creek:** June 1-Oct. 31 9am-5pm. Closed in winter. **Roosville,** open 24 hr. year-round.

Emergency: West side of park (888-5407). East side (732-4401). Many Glacier area (732-5532).

Post Office: At Lake McDonald Lodge, in the park. Open Mon.-Fri. 9am-3:45pm. General Delivery ZIP Code: 59921.

Area Code: 406.

Glacier National Park's layout is simple: One road enters through West Glacier on the west side, and three roads enter from the east (at Many Glacier, St. Mary, and Two Medicine). West Glacier and St. Mary are the two main points of entry into the park, and are connected by **Going-to-the-Sun Road** (known as "The Sun"), the only road that traverses the park. Fast-paced **U.S. 2** runs between West and East Glacier along 82 mi. of the southern park border. Look for the "Goat Lick" signs off Rte. 2 near **Walton.** Mountain goats often descend to the lick for a salt fix in June and July.

Amtrak (800-872-7245) traces a dramatic route along the southern edge of the park. Daily trains serve West Glacier from Seattle, WA (one-way $114) and Spokane, WA ($57); Amtrack also runs from Stanley, ND to East Glacier ($97). Greyhound can get you as far as Great Falls, MT, over 100 mi. southeast of East Glacier on Rte. 89. A car is the most convenient mode of transport to the park, a virtual necessity once there.

Accommodations and Camping

The beautiful scenery and high prices conspire against anyone who plans to stay indoors in Glacier. If you feel you must have a roof over your head, be prepared to part with at least $50 per night.

You'll need to make reservations if you want a real bed in the park. **Glacier Park, Inc.,** handles reservations for all the lodges. From mid-September to mid-May, contact them at Greyhound Tower Station, 5185, Phoenix, AZ 85077 (602-248-6000); from mid-May to mid-September at East Glacier Park 59434-0147 (406-226-5551, in MT 800-332-9351). The company operates seven lodges, which open and close on a staggered schedule. The Apgar Village Inn opens first, in late May, with rooms starting at $50. The other six lodges open in mid-June.

Camping offers a cheaper and more picturespue alternative to indoor accommodations. All developed campsites are available on a first-come, first-served basis for $6-8; the most popular sites will fill by noon. However, "Campground Full" signs sometimes mean "full now," sometimes "full three days ago," so scan carefully for vacancies. Firewood can be sparse, so bring a stove.

There are 15 campsites accessible by car, and all are easy to find (for example, Many Glacier Campground is at Many Glacier and Two Medicine Campground at Two Medicine). Just ask for the handout **Auto Campgrounds** at any visitors center and follow the map you're given when you enter the park. **Avalanche** campsite is open to hard-sided units only, due to the possibility of bear attack. One of the most peaceful campgrounds is **Sprague Creek** on Lake McDonald. There are only 25 sites, so arrive early. Three sites at Sprague are reserved for bicyclists; towed units are prohibited altogether. Campgrounds without running water in the national forests surrounding the park usually offer sites for $5. Check at the Apgar or St. Mary's Visitor Center for up-to-date information on conditions and vacancies at established campgrounds.

Sights and Activities

Backcountry trips are the best way to appreciate the pristine mountain scenery and the wildlife for which the park is famed. The **Highline Trail** from Logan Pass is a good day hike and passes through prime bighorn sheep and mountain goat territory. The visitors center's free *Backcountry* pamphlet has a hiking map marked with distances and backcountry campsistes. All travelers who camp overnight must obtain a free wilderness permit from a visitors center or ranger station. Backcountry camping is allowed only at designated campgrounds. The **Two Medicine** area in the southeast corner of the park is less traveled, and the trek to **Kintla Lake** rewards you with a fantastic double vision of nearby peaks reflected in Two Medicine Lake.

Before embarking on any hike, familiarize yourself with the precautions you should take to avert a run-in with a bear. Ask for information on bears at any visitors center or ranger station. Don't be foolish: The bears in Glacier, mainly grizzlies, can grow up to eight feet tall and 300 pounds, and can run twice as fast as Carl Lewis. Learn about the bears and steer clear of them. Rangers will be happy to instruct you on the finer points of noise-making and food storage to keep Yogi from feasting on your picnic basket (or you). For safety tips, see Camping in the General Introduction.

Every year, the Kokanee salmon (which were introduced into western Montana 70 years ago) swim upstream to spawn and die along the shores of McDonald Creek below the lake. Somehow the bald eagles got wind of this, and they now show up in the hundreds every autumn to chow down. The family reunion begins in late September, and their numbers peak around the beginning of November. You can view the birds through a telescope on the bridge over McDonald Creek, but you have to keep your distance so you don't disturb them.

Going-to-the-Sun Rd. may be the most beautiful 50 mi. stretch of road in the world. Even on cloudy days, the consistently stunning Alp-like peaks will have you struggling to keep your eyes on the road. Snow keeps the road closed until late June; check with rangers for exact dates.

Although The Sun is a popular **bike route,** only experienced cyclists with appropriate gear should attempt this grueling stint. The occasional disappearance of the shoulder on the road creates a potentially hazardous situation for bikers. From June 15 to Labor Day, bike traffic on The Sun is prohibited from 11am to 4pm between the Apgar turn-off at the west end of Lake McDonald and Sprague Creek Campground, and also from Logan Creek to Logan Pass. The east side of the park has no such restrictions.

Boat tours operate on all of Glacier's large lakes. At Lake McDonald and Two Medicine Lake, 55-minute tours leave throughout the day ($5, children over 6 $2.50). The tours from St. Mary and May Glacier (75 min.) provide access to Glacier's backcountry ($6, children over 6 $3). The $5 sunset cruise is a great way to see the daily phenonemon, which doesn't occur until about 9pm in the middle of the summer.

You can also rent canoes ($4 per hr.), rowboats ($5 per hr., $18 for 10 hr.), and outboards ($10 per hr., $40 for 10 hr.) at Apgar, Lake McDonald, Many Glacier, and Two Medicine. All require a $50 deposit. Fishing is excellent in the park—cutthrout trout, lake trout, and even the rare Arctic Grayling challenge the angler's skill and patience. No permit is required—just be familiar with the fishing limits of the park, explained by the pamphlet *Fishing Regulations,* available at all visitors centers.

Trail Rides leave from the Many Glacier Hotel and the Lake McDonald and Apgar corrals. A two-hour ride costs $15; a trip to one of the chalets may cost up to $37. **Glacier Raft Co.** in West Glacier (800-322-9995 or 888-5454) has full- and half-day trips down the middle fork of the Flathead River, near West Glacier. A full-day with lunch included is $48; half-day trips leave in both the morning and the afternoon ($25). Call for reservations.

While in Glacier, don't overlook the interpretive programs offered by the rangers. Inquire at any visitors center for the day's menu of guided hikes, lectures, birdwatching walks, and children's programs.

Waterton Lakes National Park, Alberta

Waterton is only a small fraction of the size of its American neighbor, but offers much of the same scenery and activities. While a trip North is not essential, a hike in the backcountry offers a less crowded alternative during Glacier's peak tourist season (mid-July to August).

Practical Information

Visitor Information: **Waterton Information Office** (859-2445). When you arrive at the park entrance, drive 5 mi. south toward Waterton Townsite; the information office is clearly marked on the right. At the office, grab a copy of the monthly *Waterton-Glacier Guide* for its detailed information of local services and activites. Open 8am-9pm daily.

Park Headquarters and Information: Superintendent, Waterton Lakes National Park, Waterton T0K 2M0 (859-2224). Open Mon.-Fri. 8am-4pm.

Border Crossing Stations: See Glacier National Park Practical Information.

Canadian Customs Information: In Lethebridge, AB (328-2603).

Bike Rental: **Pat's Texaco and Cycle Rental,** Mount View Rd., Waterton Townsite (859-2266). Mountain bikes $7 per hr., plus $20 "damage deposit."

Emergency: **Royal Canadian Mounted Police** (859-224).

Post Office: Fountain Ave. at Windflower, Waterton Townsite, AB T0K 2M0. Open Mon.-Fri. 8:30am-4:30pm.

Area Code: 403.

Accommodations, Camping, and Food

You don't have a choice: once you've entered Waterton Lakes, all you can do is drive five mi. south to **Waterton Townsite,** a town that comes out of its winter hibernation to greet the summer sun- and sight-seekers with exorbitant prices. Take a look at the dominating **Prince of Wales Hotel** (859-2231), which maintains a proper distance from the pedestrian Townsite. Have tea at the hotel and enjoy the royal view of majestic Waterton Lake, but don't stay there unless the prince himself is treating. Instead, pitch your tent at the **Townsite Campground** at the south end of town. If you must stay indoors, drop by **Dill's General Store,** on Waterton Ave. (859-2345), and ask to sleep in one of the nine rooms of the Stanley Hotel. Rooms will take $35 out of your pocket (singles or doubles), but you'll still be without a private bathroom or a shower.

Waterton is sorely lacking in budget restaurants; the most attractive option in the Townsite is the **Zum Burger Haus,** which serves decent cheeseburgers for $5 on the pleasant patio. (Open daily 7am-10pm).

Activities

On four wheels, drive either the **Akamina Parkway** or the less-traveled **Red Rock Canyon Road.** Both leave the main road near the Townsite and end at the heads of popular backcountry trails. If you've brought only your high-tops to Waterton, set out on the **Crypt Lake Hike,** which stretches four mi. from Waterton Townsite; you'll feel entombed as you pass through a natural tunnel bored through the mountainside. Those fleeing the Canadian authorities should choose the **International Hike,** which puts you in Montana some four mi. after leaving the Townsite. To camp overnight you must obtain a free permit from the information office or the park headquarters. A one-an-a-half-hour boat tour of Upper Waterton Lake leaves from the **Emerald Bay Marina** in the Townsite (admission $10, ages under 13 $5). If you'd prefer to get some exercise on the lake, you can rent a rowboat at Cameron Lake for $6 per hour. **Alpine Stables,** 2½ mi. north of the Townsite (859-2462, in winter 653-2449), conducts trail rides of varying lengths. (One-hr. ride $9.50, all-day $46.)

ALASKA

Alaska is a land of many names. To the native Aleuts, the beautific and enormous expanses of "Alashka"—"The Great Land"—reflected their remarkable culture and history which thrived in the harsh Aleutian chain for millenia. To the Europeans who boldly set forth into Alaska's uncharted wilderness in search of gold, furs, and eventually oil, Alaska was the "Last Frontier." For the tourist, Alaska is the "Land of the Midnight Sun," where in the summer months it is possible to read outdoors 24 hours a day.

Physically, Alaska is truly the "Great Land." One-fifth of all of America's land mass—586,000 square miles—is in this one state. In a span from Ketchikan to the Southeast to stormy Attu at the end of the Aleutian Chain, Alaska encompasses four time zones. There are 33,000 mi. of coastline, which if stretched out in a single line would reach from New York to San Francisco 11 times over. There are over 3 million lakes larger than 20 acres, nearly all of which abound with grayling, arctic char, and steelhead trout. Alaska is home to Wrangell-St. Elias National Park, the largest national park in America, comprising an area of 13 million acres (twice the size of Massachusetts). There are an astonishing 19 peaks over 14,000 ft., and several glacial ice fields larger than the state of Rhode Island. In addition, there are several collossal mountain ranges, such as the Wrangell Mountains, the Chugach Mountains, the Brooks Range, and the McKinley topped Alaska Range.

Alaska is so big and diverse that it has several distinct geographic zones located within its border. In the archepelago of the Southeast, where the state capital of Juneau resides upon its own isle, the numerous fjord-scarred islands contain verdant rainforests and primordial swamps (known as *muskeg*). It is here that the greatest

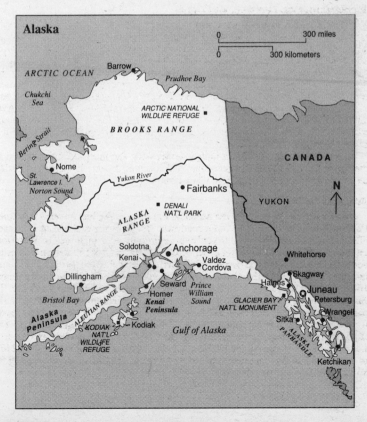

collection of bald eagles gather every year to discuss politics, filling the sky like sparrows.

Southcentral Alaska, most notably Kodiak Island, the Kenai Peninsula, and Prince William Sound, is even more wild than the jungles of the Southeast. Average rainfalls in the sound and Kodiak often exceed 170" per year, accounting for an abundance of wildlife. Kodiak is host to the largest carnivore in North America, the Kodiak brown bear, which can exceed 1500 pounds in bulk, due largely to the overflowing plethora of salmon which spawn in the island's rivers. The warm waters of this region support countless marine mammals such as humpback whales, orcas, sea lions, sea otters, and seals.

Farther north, in the Interior, there exists a land of harsh and beautiful extremes. The landscape is dominated by the towering Mt. McKinley (at 20,320 feet above sea level, the tallest mountain in North America), while much of the surrounding area is interminable flatlands. In the summer, the sun remains above the horizon for some 20 hours a day, resulting in a dry 90°F average temperature, while in the winter, scant sunshine rarely raises the mercury above a bone-chilling -50°F. And in the extreme north, amid the Arctic Circle, perpetual sunlight in the summer is countered by a three month long winter. It is here that polar bear, fur seal, and walrus cavort upon the forzen tundra beneath the glow of the dancing *Aurora Borealis.*

The first humans visited these lands over 20,000 years ago, passing over the Bering Land Bridge from Siberia to Alaska. Today, four distinct native ethnic groups remain in Alaska. The Southeast is inhabited by the Tlingit (pronounced KLINGit) people, who are renowned for their magnificent totem poles and the highly defendable wooden forts, from which they almost staved off the Russians in the 19th century. The Interior and Southcentral regions are inhabited by the Athabaska nation, and the tectonically active region of the Aleutian Island Chain was and is still largely populated by the Aleuts, a gentle people who were enslaved by the Russians for fur trapping. Eskimos inhabit almost exclusively the northern rim of Alaska, the area within the Arctic Cirlce. Linguistically speaking, Alaskan Eskimos share a common heritage with the Native Siberians across the Bering Strait, and in recent years, Soviets have begun interacting with Eskimos and Aleuts.

Alaska was "discovered" by the Danish (though Russian sponsored) explorer Vitus Bering, who landed on Kayak Island of Prince William Sound on July 2, 1741. The Russian Company soon began a massive colonization of the Alaskan wilderness, inspired by the lucrative fur trade. Russian bases for operation were located primarily in the Southern coastal region, which bears the unmistakable mark of Slavic influence even today. Within a century of Russian exploitation, the once bountiful supply of fur-bearing animals was nearly exhausted, and they welcomed the American bid for the "dead land."

In the Russian-American capital of Sitka, on October 18, 1867, the United States purchased Alaska for $7,200,000, or approximately 2¢ per acre. Critics nicknamed the transaction "Seward's Folly," after the Secretary of State who negotiated the deal. But before the end of the century, James Seward was vindicated when large deposits of gold were unearthed, causing a rush of greedy sourdoughs. And in 1968, decades after the largest gold mines had been stripped, a huge oil field was discovered on the shore of the Beaufort Sea in the Arctic Ocean. In 1981, four years after the Trans-Alaska pipeline was installed, $7,200,000 worth of crude oil flowed from the Arctic oil field every four-and-a-half hours, forever silencing the critics of "The Folly."

Despite her gifts, Alaska has a love-hate relationship with Mother Nature. Located at the edge of the Pacific Plate on the "Ring of Fire" and almost due north of the Hawaiian volcanic chain, the Aleutian Islands are perpetually racked by earthquakes and active volcanoes. From Kenai, one can gaze across Cook Inlet at Mt. Augustine, which is constantly puffing ash and soot into the air. In Valdez and Cordova, it is not unusual to wake up in the morning and discover that volcanic ash has turned the snow brown.

Alaskans scoff at the Californian preoccupation with earthquakes; many long-time residents have lived through the Good Friday quake, which was more than ten times stronger than the "love tap" which interrupted the 1989 World Series. This earthquake, which occurred on March 27, 1964 and registered 8.6 on the Richter Scale was centered in Miner's Lake (located between Whittler and Valdez) and lasted eight long minutes. Its aftershocks contunued for several days. Many coastal towns, including Kodiak and Whittier, were demolished by a tsunami which followed immediately afterwards. According to one survivor in Valdez, "We saw every drop of water drain from the Bay, and we got scared. Nobody knew what was going on, but we all ran like hell for the hills. When the tidal wave came in, it wiped out everything that was in its way—ships, cars, houses, and people." Valdez was completely destroyed and had to be rebuilt on a new site.

Not all of Alaska's misfortunes have been inspired by Nature, however. Exactly 25 years to the day after the '64 earthquake, the Exxon tanker *Valdez* ran aground in the early morning of Good Friday, 1989, spilling over 250,000 barrels (at 40 gallons per barrel) of syrupy crude oil into the clear waters of Prince William Sound. Spreading out from Bligh Reef, where the tanker collided, the oil was carried in an ever-widening arc which reached the shores of Kodiak Island several hundred miles to the south. The immediate effects were devastating, as thousands of marine mammals and birds suffered horrible deaths. Clean-up crews were completely unprepared, negligently underfunded and grossly undermanned—the first wave of beach-scrubbers were armed only with plastic cheerleader's pom-poms for use as oil mops.

Yet despite the immediate damage of the spill, it is clear that the press painted a picture which was largely disproportional to the crisis. Only 10% of the Sound suffered from oil poisoning, and less than 2% of Alaska's total coastline was touched with oil. Though by the summer of 1990 no oil was visible to the casual observer, the long-term effects of the spill are uncertain at best; in 1990 several orca pods normally located in the sound were missing.

The Spill notwithstanding, a trip to Alaska is guaranteed to be a high point in any accomplished traveler's life. For outdoorsmen, Alaska is a paradise. Hunting abounds with wilderness full of caribou, bear, moose, Dall sheep, and even scattered mountain goats. Fishermen will find themselves perpetually enticed by the millions of spawning salmon, off-shore halibut which can weigh over 500 pounds and exceed nine feet, and countless unnamed and rarely, if ever, fished interior lakes and streams overflow with trophy-sized grayling and trout. And for those who simply enjoy hiking and camping, Alaska provides unequaled opportunities. More than half of all the world's glaciers are in Alaska, and many are accessible by road. Only one-fifth of Alaska can be reached by highway, and the rest can only be attained by floatplane, snow mobile, or dogsled. Because of this isolation, the true bushwacker will find endless opportunity for backcountry exploration in practically virgin forest.

Practical Information

Emergency: 911.

Capital: Juneau.

United States Customs Service: 202-566-8195. This Washington, DC office will connect you with the Canadian Customs and Excise office for information regarding the rules and regulations of traveling through Canada.

Avalanche and Mountain Weather Report: 271-4500.

State Troopers: 269-5511 in Anchorage, 452-2114 in Fairbanks.

Time Zones: Alaska (most of the state; 4 hr. behind Eastern); Aleutian-Hawaii (Aleutian Islands; 5 hr. behind Eastern).

Drinking Age: 21.

Postal Abbreviation: AK.

Area Code: 907.

Impractical Information

Nicknames: The Last Frontier and Land of the Midnight Sun.

Population: 523,048.

Motto: North to the Future.

Flower: Forget-Me-Not.

Bird: White Ptarmigan.

Year of Incorporation: Jan. 3, 1959 (49th state).

Area: 586,412 square mi.

Tourist Information

Alaska Division of Tourism, 605 W. 4th Ave. You can also write them at P.O. Box E, Juneau 99811 (465-2010). Open Mon.-Fri. 8am-4:30pm.

Alaska Public Lands Information Center, Old Federal Bldg., Anchorage 99510 (271-2737 or 258-PARK for a recording). Help in traversing any and all wilderness areas. Open daily 9am-8pm. Branch office in Fairbanks; others under construction in Ketchikan and Tok.

Alaska State Division of Parks, Pouch 7-001, Anchorage 99510 (762-2617). Open Mon.-Fri. 8am-4:30pm.

United States Forest Service, P.O. Box 1628-ATD, Juneau 99802 (586-8806). General information regarding national parks and reserves. Open Mon.-Fri. 8am-4:30pm.

National Park Service, Parks and Forests Information Center, W. 4th Ave, Anchorage 99503 (271-2737). Open Mon.-Fri. 8am-5pm.

Alaska Department of Fish and Game, P.O. Box 3-2000, Juneau 99802. Get your hunting and fishing regulations here.

State Employment Service, P.O. Box 3-7000, Juneau 99802. For those hunting for jobs, instead of game. Branch offices in Anchorage, Ketchikan, and Petersburg.

Legislative Information Office, 3111 C St. (561-7007), Anchorage 99501. For those who would like to delve into Alaska's ever-juicy political debates. Or call the Alaska State Government General Information service at 465-2111.

Anyone venturing onto Alaska's roads should buy a copy of the *Milepost,* published by the Alaska Northwest Publishing Company, 130 2nd Ave. S., Edmond, WA 98020 (for information, call 907-563-1141, Mon.-Fri. 8:30am-4:30pm). The *Milepost* ($15) is packed with information about Alaskan and Canadian communities as well as up-to-date ferry schedules and maps of the highways and roads.

Getting There and Getting Around

The **Alaska Highway** is a rocky inroad from British Columbia; friendly RV drivers are the distinct majority on the largely unpaved route. The **Alaska Marine Highway** navigates an extensive ferry system from Bellingham up through the scenic islands of the Panhandle and alongside the glaciers of the central coast. No matter how you come to Alaska, make your plans well in advance because of the exorbitant cost of travel both to and within the state. One excellent way to compensate for money lost in transportation is to make full use of Alaska's free state campgrounds.

Air Travel

Flying to Alaska is the quickest and often the cheapest way to escape northward, usually directly to Anchorage from the Lower 48. As of August 1990, round-trip fares from Boston to Anchorage ran $623 (with 2-week advance purchase). Check with the major domestic carriers serving Alaska: **Western, Northwest, United,** and **Alaska Airlines** (800-426-0333, in WA 800-654-5669). In Anchorage, try **Lifeco Travel Center** (266-6600) or **Polaris Travel Service** (279-7461).

One in 36 Alaskans has a pilot's license, and for a good reason: Alaska lacks an extensive road or rail network. Given Alaska's size, air travel is often a necessity. Several intrastate airlines transport passengers and cargo to virtually every village in Alaska: **Alaska Airlines** (to larger Bush towns and Cordova); **Mark Air** (to larger Bush towns, Kodiak, and the Aleutians; 800-426-6784); **ERA Aviation** (southcentral; 243-0822); **Southcentral Air** (southcentral; 561-4193); **Reeve Aleutian Airways** (Aleutians; 243-4700); and **Ryan Air Service** (practically anywhere in the Bush; 561-2090). Many other charters and flight-seeing services are available. Check the *Milepost* (see Tourist Information), or write **Ketchum Air Service Inc.,** North Shore Lake Hood, Anchorage 99503 (243-5525), to ask about their charters. One-day flights and overnight or weekend trips to uninhabited lakes, mountains, and tundra range upwards from $165. Although expensive, they are a great way to get away from the tourist centers, see wildlife, and perhaps catch some of Alaska's famous fish.

Railroad Travel

In 1984 the **Alaska Railroad** became one of the last nationally owned railroads in the country to be sold. This frontier railroad, the northernmost in North America, covers 470 miles of land, much of it inaccessible by road or boat. For some folks in isolated cabins, the train is the only link to civilization. The train connects Seward and Whittier in the south with Anchorage, Fairbanks, and Denali National Park.

Service runs from Anchorage to Fairbanks ($88) daily in the summer, once per week in the winter. Given advance notice in the winter, the engineer will drop cargo or passengers along the way. On the way to Fairbanks, trains stop at Denali National Park. Southbound from Anchorage, the train is the only land route to Whittier (one way $36). The short 30-minute ride ducks under two tunnels and runs from Portage several times per day to coincide with the schedule of the M.V. *Bartlett.* Passenger service to Seward was recently reintroduced for summer visitors. Advance reservations are required for all except Whittier trips. Write **Alaska Railroad Corporation,** Passenger Services, P.O. Box 7-2111, Anchorage 99510-7069. (Call 265-2494 for schedules, fares, and reservations.)

On the Panhandle, the 90-year-old **White Pass and Yukon Route** carries passengers over an old Klondike Gold Rush trail from Skagway to Bennet, BC. Motorcoach service continues on from there to Whitehorse. For more information, contact the White Pass and Yukon Route, P.O. Box 435, Skagway 99840 (983-2217 or 800-343-7373).

Bus Travel

Although Greyhound doesn't run beyond Whitehorse, YT, scheduled bus services connect British Columbia, Whitehorse, and Haines with central Alaska, including Anchorage. The **Alaskon Express** P.O. Box 100479, Anchorage 99510 (277-5581), a subsidiary of **Gray Lines of Alaska,** runs two buses per week in summer from Whitehorse to Anchorage. The one-way fare is about $140; you'll also need to pay for overnight accommodations (about $85). Service from Haines is also available twice per week. One-way fare is $173, plus overnight accommodations. Several enterprising van owners run small operations from Haines to Anchorage, synchronized with the ferry. Fares can be as low as $105, but service is often unreliable. Gray Lines's charters and tours often appear expensive, but many include meals, lodging, and sights otherwise difficult to reach. **Gray Line Tours,** 547 W. 4th Ave., Anchorage 99501 (277-5581), offers a round-trip two-day excursion from Anchorage to Valdez that includes a sail across the Prince William Sound, a piggy-back van-on-a-train ride from Whittier, and one night's accommodations, all for $259.

Driving in Alaska

Juneau is the only state capital in the nation that cannot be reached by automobile. In fact, roads reach only a quarter of the state's area. The highways that traverse the southern part of the state are narrow, often gravely ribbons extending from point to point with few services.

In 1942, the U.S. Army Corps of Engineers built an in eight months an astonishing 1500-mi. road from British Columbia to Fairbanks, in order to provide supply lines for Alaska's far-flung military bases. The Alaska Highway, as it is now called, runs from Dawson Creek, BC, to Fairbanks. Anchorage can be reached via the Tok Cut-off. The interminable Canadian stretch of the road is poorly maintained, dragging out the entire drive to three to five days. Only hardsiders should attempt this; lodgings en route are hard to come by. Winter and summer travelers alike are advised to let a friend or relative know of their position along the highway several times in the course of a trip.

To the embarrassment of most residents, many major roads in Alaska are still in deplorable condition. Dust and flying rocks are a major hazard in the summer, as are the road construction crews who seem to interrupt long-distance trips with miserable 10- to 30-mile patches of gravel. Radiators and headlights should be protected from flying rocks with a wire screen, and a fully functioning spare tire is absolutely essential. Winter can actually offer a smoother ride. Active snow crews keep roads as clear as possible, and the packed surface and thinned traffic permit easy driving without summer's mechanical troubles. At the same time, the danger of avalanches and ice are cause for major concern. Check the road conditions before traveling; in Anchorage call 243-7675 (winter only), or simply tune in to local radio stations.

Hitchhiking

Many people hitchhike instead of depending on buses in Alaska. Note that it is not legal everywhere, and hitchers must beware of being stranded on lightly traveled stretches of road. A wait of a day or two is not unusual on certain stretches of the Alaska Hwy. Luckily, Alaskans are a friendly and cooperative group, and most rides last at least a day. Campgrounds and service stations make the best bases for hitching, providing an opportunity for mutual inspection before a long journey.

Catching a ride into Alaska on the Alaska Hwy. involves passing the Alaska-Yukon "border" check, which is a series of routine questions about citizenship, residency, insurance, contraband, and finances, followed by an auto inspection. In the event that a hitchhiker is turned back, it is the driver's responsibility to return the hitchhiker to the "border." Hitchers should walk across the border to avoid hassles.

A popular alternative to hitching the entire length of the Alaska Hwy. is to take the Marine Hwy. to Haines and hitch a ride from there with cars off the ferry. Often the competition in summer is heavy; it may be easier to remain on the ferry to Skagway, take a bus or train to Whitehorse in the Yukon, and hitch the Alaska Hwy. from there. Always carry extra money, food, and warm sleeping gear. The next town or ride could be days away.

Alaska Marine Highway

The Alaska Marine Highway consists of two *unconnected* ferry systems administered by one bureaucracy. The southeast system runs from Bellingham up the coast to Skagway, stopping in Juneau, Ketchikan, Haines, and other towns. The southwest network serves Kodiak Island, Seward, Homer, and the Prince William Sound. Practically none of southeast Alaska (the Panhandle) is accessible by road; these areas can be reached only by plane or on the Marine Highway.

The full trip from Bellingham to Skagway takes three days and costs $241 (ages 6-12 near ½-price, under 6 free). The route is vision-quenching, peppered with whales, bald eagles, and the majesty of the Inside Passage. (The *Love Boat's* Alaskan voyages took this trip.) All southeast ferries have free showers, cafes, lectures on history and ecology, and a heated top-deck "solarium" where cabinless passengers can sleep (bring a sleeping bag!). These ferries are a great way to travel. **Cabins** costs at least $175 from Bellingham to Skagway, and are unnecessary—everyone, young and old, sleeps in the solarium. **Vehicles** up to 40 feet can be taken aboard (van from Juneau to Ketchikan costs $85). Spaces for vehicles are very limited; reservations are crucial and often necessary months in advance in summer. Cabinless passengers rarely need reservations, however.

The ferries in the southwest are more expensive and less plush than those in the southeast. They lack showers, the food is worse, and the solariums are smaller. They also ride the open sea, where navies of seasickness bugs love to rock your vessel to and fro.

The ferry schedule, a function of tides and other navigational exigencies, is a byzantine maze. Write ahead; for all schedules, rates, and information, contact Alaska Marine Highway, P.O. Box R, Juneau 99811 (800-642-0066 or 907-465-3941). On all ferries, senior citizens sail free if they travel standby (space is usually available). Disabled travelers can do so as well (permits are issued by mail).

Employment

Finding work in Alaska depends largely on being there, being energetic, and being persistent. Alaska's booms in construction, fishing, and lumber are not wholly fictitious. As more people head to the state each year in search of employment, however, jobs become harder to find. Summer is the best season for job hunting, as the state makes the most of good weather before winter closes many industries down. It is best to come with a return ticket in hand.

Cannery and fish processing jobs are currently the most popular forms of summer employment. Many processing plants in the southeast, on Kodiak Island, and in the Aleutians have long waiting lists. Nearly two-thirds of their employees are hired through company offices in Washington, Oregon, or California, but canneries that need help often have jobs on short notice. You can obtain a list of processors from the **Alaska Department of Fish and Game,** Division of Commercial Fisheries, P.O. Box 3-200, Juneau 99802 (465-4112; open Mon.-Fri. 8am-4:30pm). Inquiries about the current employment outlook should be addressed to the **Alaska Department of Labor,** P.O. Box 1149, Juneau 99811 (465-4839; open Mon.-Fri. 8am-4:30pm).

To some, the continued popularity of cannery work is baffling. The work (gutting fish by hand) is difficult, boring, and unpleasant. Pay in July 1990 averaged about $6 per hour, with time-and-a-half for overtime. Most workers do a great deal of overtime, thereby making better than average wages.

The job market for Fairbanks and the Interior differs greatly from the rest of the state. However, seasonal jobs are available. For more information, call and sign up with the **Private Industry Council** (456-5189; open Mon.-Thurs. 8am-noon and 1-4:30pm). Also, keep in mind Forestry Service jobs. Though usually low-paying, they are often easy to acquire, and the chance to see Alaska's wilderness makes them truly worthwhile.

Camping

The **U.S. Forest Service** maintains more than 178 **wilderness** log cabins for public use: 142 in **Tongass National Forest** in Southeastern Alaska, and 36 in **Chugach National Forest** in Southcentral Alaska. The cabins are scenic and well maintained. User permits are required along with a fee of $10 per party (no limit in size) per night. Reserve several months in advance. Most cabins have seven-day use limits, except hike-in cabins (3-day limit May-Aug.). Cabins sleep six, and are usually accessible only by air, boat, or hiking trail. Facilities at these sites rarely include more than a wood stove and pit toilets. Some cabins provide skiffs (small boats). For maps or further information write to the U.S. Forest Service (see Tourist Information). For information about free cabins within wildlife ranges, contact the **U.S. Fish and Wildlife Service,** 1011 E. Tudor Rd., Anchorage 99504.

State-run campgrounds are always free. They usually offer toilets and drinking water, but no showers. For information on state campgrounds and waysides, contact the Alaska State Division of Parks (see Tourist Information).

Four **federal agencies** control and manage park lands in Alaska: the U.S. Forest Service (USFS), the Bureau of Land Management (BLM), the National Park Service, and the U.S. Fish and Wildlife Service. The USFS maintains numerous campgrounds within the Chugach and Tongass National Forests (sites $4-5), and strictly enforces a 14-day maximum stay. The BLM runs about 20 campgrounds throughout the state, all free except the Delta BLM campground on the Alaska Highway. The National Park Service maintains campgrounds in Denali National Park, Glacier Bay National Park, and Katmai National Park and Preserve. Camping fees usually range from $4 to $6. The several campgrounds managed by the U.S. Fish and Wildlife Service are confined to the Kenai National Wildlife Refuge, P.O. Box 2139, Soldotna 99669. Government campgrounds in Alaska rarely have dump stations or electrical hookups.

Remember to leave an itinerary at the offices of parks, hotels, state troopers, and guides. It is an important safety measure that takes little time to prepare.

For additional information about hiking and camping in Alaska, consult *Adventuring in Alaska,* written by Peggy Wayburn and published by the Sierra Club. Successful hiking and camping adventures require advance planning. After reading about the area you plan to visit, stop by the Forest Service office in Anchorage (2525 Gampbell, #107) or chat with the local Forest Service employees.

Southcentral Alaska

The regions of southcentral Alaska—Anchorage, Prince William Sound, the Kenai Peninsula, and Kodiak Island—are each separate and self-contained. What ties them together is a network of well-maintained roads, a rare convenience not to be taken lightly in the northland. The roads merge the economies of these areas, keeping prices reasonably close to those in the Lower 48.

Southcentral Alaska epitomizes the state's uncorrupted beauty—towering snow-coated peaks, rivers churning with fish, and a catalogue of animal life that rivals a full season's showing of *Wild Kingdom.* After a spell in the great outdoors, Anchorage, Alaska's largest city by a factor of ten, provides all the usual satisfactions of American civilization.

Anchorage

Perhaps the most remarkable fact about Anchorage is that just about everything—from the glass and steel of the buildings to the food and merchandise of the supermarkets and department stores—arrived here the same way people do: over 1500 mi. of tortuous road, on an expensive air journey, or by barge or container ship across one of the roughest seas in the world. The city has an aroma of prefabrication—John McPhee has called it "condensed, instant Albequerque." "Los Anchorage," as some rural residents prefer, is as close to "big city" as Alaska gets. Approximately half the state's population—some 250,000 people—live here. A decentralized jumble of fast-food joints and discount liquor stores, Anchorage also supports semi-professional baseball and basketball teams, frequent performances by internationally known orchestras and pop stars, dramatic theater, and opera.

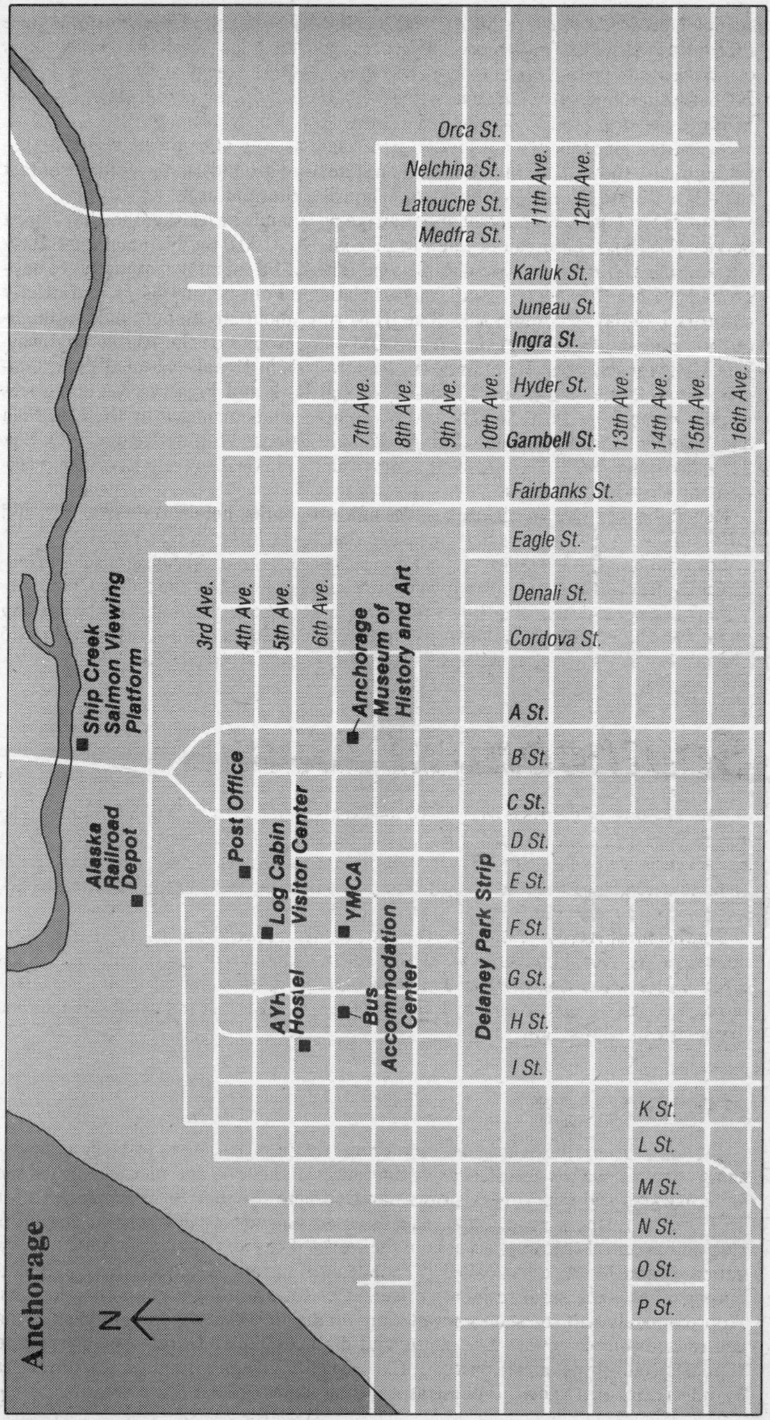

Anchorage

N ←

Ship Creek
Salmon Viewing
Platform

Alaska
Railroad
Depot

Post Office

Log Cabin
Visitor Center

AYh
Hostel

YMCA

Bus
Accommodation
Center

Anchorage
Museum of
History and Art

Delaney Park Strip

3rd Ave.
4th Ave.
5th Ave.
6th Ave.
7th Ave.
8th Ave.
9th Ave.
10th Ave.
11th Ave.
12th Ave.
13th Ave.
14th Ave.
15th Ave.
16th Ave.

Orca St.
Nelchina St.
Latouche St.
Medfra St.
Karluk St.
Juneau St.
Ingra St.
Hyder St.
Gambell St.
Fairbanks St.
Eagle St.
Denali St.
Cordova St.
A St.
B St.
C St.
D St.
E St.
F St.
G St.
H St.
I St.
K St.
L St.
M St.
N St.
O St.
P St.

The *Anchorage Daily News* recently won a Pulitzer Prize for its reporting on suicide and alcoholism in the region.

Anchorage's history is anomalous for Alaska: no one ever struck gold here, Baranof and the Russians didn't stop by, its location is not a natural travel hub. But the Alaska Railroad's decision in 1914 to move its headquarters to a small rail camp turned Anchorage into the state's Grand Central Station. While Juneau remained the state's capital, Anchorage became the organizational headquarters and staging area for the massive buildup in Alaska by national authorities during and after WWII. Today Anchorage's international airport is among the world's busiest, serving passengers en route to the Far East.

Downtown Anchorage, centered on 4th Avenue, was until recently a red neon, adult bookstore district. But the state has hosed down the filth with a quick spray from the petrodollar hydrant. New Federal and state buildings pass aesthetic muster before even the most fastidious tourist. While the area between A and Fairbanks St. is still strewn with bars and pull-tab joints, it's difficult to maintain a nocturnal netherworld in a city where the night may last for as little as one hour.

Practical Information and Orientation

Visitor Information: Anchorage Convention and Visitors Bureau, 201 E. 3rd Ave. (274-3531). **Log Cabin Visitor Information Center,** W. 4th Ave. at F St. (274-3531). Open daily 7:30am-7pm; Oct.-April 8:30am-6pm. The Log Cabin is generally crammed with visitors and a staff of volunteers. Plenty of maps and brochures. The **All About Anchorage Line** (276-3200) runs a recorded listing of each day's events. For information on fine arts and dramatic performances, call the **Artsline** (276-2787). Smaller visitor information outlets are located in the airport's domestic terminal near the baggage claim, in the overseas terminal in the central atrium, and in the Valley River Mall, first level.

Alaska Public Lands Information Center, Old Federal Bldg. (271-2737), 4th Ave. between F and G St. An astounding conglomeration of 8 state and Federal offices (including the **National Park Service, U.S. Forest Service, Division of State Parks,** and the **U.S. Fish and Wildlife Service**) under one roof provides the latest information on the entire state. You will find animal displays, a computerized sportfishing map, and an interactive trip-planning video unit. Films daily at 12:15pm and 3:30pm, or upon request. Open daily 9am-7pm.

Airport: Alaska International Airport, P.O. Box 190649-VG, Anchorage 99519-0649 (266-2525). Serviced by 7 international carriers, including **British Airways** (248-1803) and **Japan Airlines** (274-3551); 5 interstate carriers, including **Delta** (249-2110), **Northwest Airlines** (266-5636), and **United** (241-6522); and 3 intrastate carriers. Nearly every airport in Alaska can be reached from Anchorage, either directly or through a connecting flight in Fairbanks.

Alaska Railroad: P.O. Box 107500, 2nd Ave., Anchorage 99510-7500 (265-2494), at the head of town. To: Denali ($68), Fairbanks ($98), and Seward ($35). Ten-day unlimited mileage railpass $209. For more information write to Passenger Service, P.O. Box 107500, Anchorage 99510. Office open daily 8am-8pm; may be closed if no trains are arriving.

Alaska Marine Highway: 333 W. 4th St. (272-4482), in the Post Office Mall. No terminal, but ferry tickets and reservations. Open Mon.-Fri. 8am-5pm.

Buses: Alaska Intercity Line, 614 W. 4th Ave. (800-478-2877 or 279-3221). One-way to: Kenai/Soldotna ($27.50), Homer ($37.50), Seward ($37.50), Valdez ($65), and Denali (tour packages only, prices vary). **Alaska-Denali Transit,** P.O. Box 4557, 701 W. 58th Ave., Anchorage 99510 (561-1078 or 273-3331). Daily to Denali National Park ($35), pickup at hostel (7th and H), at 8am. To Haines ($115) leaves from hostel Sat. 8am, arrives Sun. 8am.

People Mover Bus: 343-6543, in the Transit Center, on 6th St. between G and H St., just up the street from the hostel. Buses leave from here to all points in the Anchorage Bowl 5am-midnight. Cash fare 85¢, tokens 75¢ (the hostel sells them for 60¢). The Transit Center office is open Mon.-Fri. 9am-5pm.

Taxi: Yellow Cab, 272-2422. **Checker Cab,** 276-1234.

Airport Shuttle: Dynair Charter Service (243-3310 or 243-3144). Service from airport to downtown ($5).

Car Rentals: Allstar Rent-A-Car, 512 W. International Airport Rd. (561-0350). $39 per day with 150 free mi., 25¢ per each additional mi. Reserve 6-7 days in advance. Open Mon.-Fri. 7am-10pm, Sat.-Sun. 9am-5pm.

Road Conditions: 243-7675.

Bicycle Rental: at the **Clarion Hotel** (243-2300), on Spenard just east of Minnesota. Close to the Coastal Bike Trail. $5 for the 1st hr., $2.50 each additional hr., $20 per day. **Scooters** are available in front of the Federal Bldg. $10 per hr. 8-11am and 1-7pm, $7 per hr. 11am-1pm.

Weather: 936-2525. **Motorists Forecast:** 936-2626. **Marine Weather Forecast:** 936-2727.

Camping Equipment: Recreational Equipment, Inc. (REI), 2710 Spenard (272-4565), at Minnesota (bus #60). High-quality equipment includes packs, clothing, tents, stores, and dried food. Open Mon.-Fri. 10am-9pm, Sat. 9:30am-6pm, Sun. noon-5pm. The **Army-Navy Store,** on 4th Ave. across from the Post Office Mall, offers even lower prices. Open daily 10am-7pm.

Laundromat: K-Speed Wash, 600 E. 6th St. (264-2631). Take bus #60 or 3. Open Mon.-Sat. 9am-10pm.

Crisis Line: 276-1600. 24-hr. hotline with referral services. **Rape Crisis:** 276-7273.

Visitor Language Assistance: 276-4118. Preprogrammed assistance in languages from Laotian to Finnish. Anchorage also shelters **consulates** from most Western European countries and Japan.

Handicap Access Line: Challenge Alaska, 563-2658. The Log Cabin (see above) is equipped with a TTY for the communicatively disabled.

Hospital: Humana, 2801 De Darr (276-1131).

Emergency: 911.

Post Office: W. 4th Ave. and C St. (277-6568), on the lower level in the mall. Open Mon.-Fri. 10:30am-5pm, Sat. 9am-3pm. General Delivery ZIP Code: 99510. The state's central post office is located next to the international airport. It does not handle general delivery mail, but is open 24 hr.

Area Code: 907.

Anchorage dominates the southcentral region of Alaska from its perch 114 mi. north of Seward on the Seward Hwy., 304 mi. west of Valdez on the Glenn and Richardson Hwy., and 358 mi. south of Fairbanks on the George Parks Hwy. It is due north of Honolulu, and equidistant from Atlanta and Tokyo.

Anchorage can be reached by road, rail, or air. **Anchorage International Airport,** a few miles southwest of downtown off International Airport Rd., is served by all the Alaska airlines, as well as by major American and international airlines. The People Mover Bus runs only three times per day from the airport to downtown, but the visitors center near the baggage claim can direct you a short distance from the terminal to more frequent routes. Airporter vans run 24 hr. to downtown ($5); a cab ride will set you back about $13.

The downtown area of Anchorage is laid out in a regular grid pattern. Numbered avenues run east-west, and addresses are designated East or West from **C Street.** North-south streets are lettered alphabetically west of **A Street,** and named alphabetically east of A Street. The rest of Anchorage spreads out along the major highways. The **University of Alaska-Anchorage** campus lies on 36th Ave. off Northern Lights Blvd.

Accommodations

Although Anchorage is blessed many times over with affordable lodgings, few Good Samaritans built their inns downtown. The best option is, as usual, the hostel. Several bed and breakfast referral agencies operate out of Anchorage. Try **Alaska Private Lodgings,** 1236 W. 10th Ave., Anchorage 99511 (258-1717), or **Stay With a Friend,** P.O. Box 173, 3605 Arctic Blvd., Anchorage 99503 (344-4006). Both can refer you to singles from $45 and doubles from $55.

Anchorage Youth Hostel (AYH), 700 H St. (276-3635), 1 block south of the Transit Center downtown. Excellent location, clean rooms, common areas, kitchens, showers, and laundry. Large enough to offer family rooms and hardly ever be full. Lockout 9am-5pm. Members $10, nonmembers $13. Not to be confused with the Alyeska Youth Hostel, and certainly not to be confused or associated with the Dog Patch Hostel.

Alyeska Youth Hostel, P.O. Box 10-4099, Anchorage 99510 (783-2099 or 277-7388). Rustic 6-bed hostel near a ski slope, about 25 mi. southeast of downtown in the Alyeska Ski Area. Members $8, nonmembers $11. Reservations required. Don't be surprised if you're the only person there, especially in the summer. In winter, it's packed with skiers.

Qupqugiaq Bed & Breakfast, 3801 Lois Dr. (562-5681) at the corner of Spenard Rd. and Lois Dr., a 5-min. drive from the airport. (How do you spell that?) Clean, comfortable rooms, with a full breakfast. Singles $18. Doubles $28.

Heart of Anchorage Bed and Breakfast, P.O. Box 5042, 4025 Hillcourt Dr. (279-7066 or 279-7703), off Dimond St. near June Lake. Convenient to downtown and to the airport. Singles $45. Doubles $55. Call ahead for reservations.

Midtown Hotel, 604 W. 26th (258-7778), off Arctic Blvd. Cheapness attracts long-term residents. All rooms share baths. Singles $37.80. Doubles $43.20.

Samovar Inn, 720 Gampbell (277-1511), at 7th. Plush rooms equipped with jacuzzi-style bathtubs. King-sized doubles only $67.50.

Northern Lights Thrift Apartments, 606 Northern Lights (561-3005). The clean rooms are not much bigger than the queen-sized beds. Singles and doubles $35.

Arctic Inn Motel, 842 W. International Airport Rd. (561-1328), at Arctic Ave. Not exciting, but a free taxi zips the mile between motel and airport. Family-run, with a home-style restaurant and bar. All rooms $54.

Anchor Arms Motel, 433 Eagle St. (272-9619), near the 4th Ave. strip (the bad part of downtown, even after the petrohydrant treatment). Grim outside but cozy inside. All rooms have kitchen and bath. Singles $55.

Camping

The two camping areas within the city are both equipped for tents and RVs. Many free campgrounds lie just outside the city limits, maintained by the State Division of Parks and Outdoor Recreation. These campgrounds have some of the state's best sites, with water and toilets. Most sites hide along dirt roads off the highway. Bring your own food and supplies. Among the best of the state campgrounds are **Eagle River** and **Eklutna** (pronounced EE-cloot-nah), which are 12.6 mi. and 26.5 mi. (respectively) south of Anchorage along Glenn Hwy. For more information on these and other campsites, contact the Alaska Division of Parks, 3601 C St., 10th Floor, Pouch 7-001, Anchorage 99510 (561-2020), or the Anchorage Parks and Recreation Dept., 2525 Gampbell St., #404 (271-2500).

Centennial Park, 8300 Glenn Hwy. (333-9711), north of town off Muldoon Rd.; look for the park sign. Take People Mover Bus #3 or 75 from downtown. Facilities for tents and RVs. Showers, dumpsters, fireplaces, pay phones, and water. 7-day max. stay. Check-in before 6pm in peak summer season. Sites $12, for seniors $8.

Lions' Camper Park, 5800 Boniface Pkwy. (333-1495), south of the Glenn Hwy. In Russian Jack Springs Park next to the Municipal Greenhouse; 4 blocks from the Boniface Mall. Take People Mover Bus #12 or 45 to the mall and walk. Connected to the city's bike trail system. 10 primitive campsites with water station, fire rings, and showers. Self-contained vehicles only. 7-day max. stay. Sites $12. Open May-Sept. daily 10am-10pm.

John's RV Park, 3543 Mt. View Dr. (277-4332). Only 2 mi. from downtown. Full hookups $16.75.

Food

By virtue of its size and largely imported population, Anchorage's culinary fare is extraordinarily diverse. Within blocks of each other stand greasy spoons, Chinese restaurants, and classy hotel-top French *maisons*. The city's finer restaurants line the hills overlooking Cook Inlet and the Alaska Range. The closest grocery to the hostel is the **Family Market,** 1301 I St., at 13th Ave. (272-4722; open Mon.-Sat. 7am-10pm, Sun. 8am-6pm).

Tito's Gyros (279-8961), on 4th St. near McDonald's. Pizza by the slice ($2), a rarity in Alaska. Juicy gyro sandwich ($5.25), and the best ice cream downtown (single scoop $1). Open Mon.-Sat. 11am-10pm, Sun. 2am-9pm.

Downtown Deli, 525 W. 4th Ave. (274-0027), across the street from the Log Cabin visitors center. Slightly more elegant and expensive (entrees $5-9) than your basic Lower 48 deli. The Monte Cristo sandwich ($7) is unacCountably delicious. Owned by Anchorage's former mayor, Tony Knowles. Open daily 6am-11pm.

Wing and Things, 529 I St. (277-9464), between 5th and 6th. Unbelievably good chicken wings barbecued amidst wing memorabilia and inspirational poetry. Ten wings for $5. Open daily 11am-9:30pm.

Burger Jim's, 704 4th St. (277-4386), at Gampbell near the Alaska Native Medical Center. Jim takes his work literally. Burger, fries, and a coke $3. Open Mon.-Sat. 10am-8:30pm.

Blondie's Café (279-0898), on D between 4th and 5th. Jazzy atmosphere with poor ventilation. Reuben sandwich more successful than Debbie Harry's solo career (and at $6.50, cheaper than an album). Breakfast menu available all day. Open daily 11am-8pm.

Thai Cuisine, 444 H St. (277-8424). Above-average Thai fare in a cozy environment. Huge bowl of soup $4. Lunch specials include entree, soup, and salad ($6). Open Mon.-Sat. 11am-10pm, Sun. 5-10pm.

Sack's Café, 625 *5th Ave.* (274-3546). Tasty but expensive vegetarian vegetarian food. Salads $8. Portions are decent sized, that is if you're a rabbit. Carnivores might starve here. Open Mon.-Thurs. 11am-9:30pm, Fri.-Sat. 11am-11pm, Sun. 11am-2:30pm.

Cyrano's Book Store and Café (274-2599), on D between 4th and 5th. Come here to ghost-write love letters and rest your schnozz. Classical music, a current *Wall Street Journal,* tall glass of lemonade, and an excellent bowl of chicken gumbo $6. Nutritious sandwiches $4.50. Sat. night is open-mike night. The best book store in the state proves that Anchorage has come a long way since the days remembered by John McPhee when books were sold for 47¢ per lb. Open Sun.-Thurs. 11am-9pm, Sat. 11am-2am.

Kumagoro Restaurant, 533 4th St. (272-9905). The combination of Alaskan fish and Japanese efficiency results in an excellent, reasonably priced sushi restaurant. Daily lunch specials, such as Halibut Teriyaki with soup, rice, and vegetables ($6). At night, Alex Tylers ham it up at the live mike. Bar open daily 10am-2am, restaurant open daily 10am-10pm, although food is available until closing time.

Old Anchorage Salmon Bake, 251 K St. (279-8790), in the Bluff at 3rd and K. $17 buys an all-you-can-eat dinner of salmon, halibut, reindeer sausage, and crab legs, plus salad, beans, and (still hungry?) sourdough rolls. Smaller, *cheechako* meals also available. Salmon and all-you-can-eat salad $13. The light lunch includes salad bar and beans with such orders as the salmon burger ($6.25) or Rudolph-the-Reindeer-dog ($5.50). Open May-Sept. daily 11am-2pm and 4-10pm.

Simon and Seafort's Salon and Grill, 420 L St. (274-3502). Down a few beers and a bowl of great clam chowder ($3.50) in the salon. Prices are steep (dinner $12-20), but the incredible view of Cook Inlet and delectable seafood and pasta keep people flocking in. Open Mon.-Fri. 11:15am-2:30pm and 5-10:30pm, Sat. noon-2pm and 5-10:30pm, Sun. 5-10:30pm. Salon open daily 11:30am-11:30pm. Reservations recommended.

Skipper's, at 5 locations: 3960 W. Dimond Blvd. (248-3165), 702 E. Benson Blvd. (276-1181), 5668 DeBarr Rd. (333-4832), 601 E. Dimond Blvd. (349-8214), and 3611 Minnesota Dr. (563-3656). This is a chain. Skipper's all-you-can-eat specials guaranteed to stuff the hungriest of sailors. Only $5.29 for all the fishfries, chowder, and cole slaw you can ram down your gullet (with shrimp $8). Open daily 11am-11pm.

Sights and Seasonal Events

Watching over Anchorage from Cook Inlet is **Mount Susitna,** known to locals as the "Sleeping Lady." For a fabulous view of Susitna, as well as of the other mountains (including, on a clear day, even **Mt. McKinley**) that tower over Anchorage's ever-growing skyline, drive out to **Earthquake Park** at the end of Northern Lights Blvd. Once a fashionable neighborhood, the park now memorializes the disastrous effects of the Good Friday earthquake in 1964, a day Alaskans refer to as "Black Friday." Registering at 8.6 on the old Richter scale (9.2 on the current scale), the quake was the strongest ever recorded in North America.

A four-hour walking tour of downtown begins at the visitors center. Interesting street-corner signs describe the history of the locale, and you can absorb the tour in smaller segments while wandering about downtown. For guided walking tours, contact **Historic Anchorage Inc.,** 542 W. 4th Ave. (562-6100, ext. 338), on the second floor of the Old City Hall. Tours leave Monday through Friday at 10am ($2, seniors $1). **Grayline** (277-5581) offers a 3½-hour Anchorage City tour, leaving daily at 8am and 3pm ($20, children under 12 $10).

Public and private museums fill downtown Anchorage. The public **Anchorage Museum of History and Art,** 121 W. 7th Ave. (264-4326), on the corner of 7th Ave. and A St., is without a doubt the best. The museum features permanent exhibits of Alaskan Native artifacts and art, as well as a Thursday night Alaska wilderness film series (7pm). (Open Mon.-Sat. 10am-6pm, Sun. 1-5pm; Sept.-May Tues.-Sat. 10am-6pm, Sun. 1-5pm. Admission $3.) The **Alaska Wildlife Museum,** 844 W. 5th St. (274-1600), has informative, if uninnovative, displays on Alaskan wildlife but charges a wolfish $5. (Open daily 9am-9pm.) Your museum dollar may be better spent at the **Imaginarium,** 725 5th Ave. (276-3179), a hands-on "science-discovery center" recreating aurora borealis, glacier formation, and other scientific oddities of the north. (Open Mon.-Sat. 11am-6pm. Admission $4, under 12 $3.) The aesthete can examine the **Visual Arts Center,** 5th and G St. (274-9641), which showcases the best Alaskan artists north of Homer. (Open Mon.-Sat. 10am-6pm. Admission $1.) The menacing black-glass **Arco Tower** (263-4545), on G between 6th and 7th, the tallest building in Alaska, shows oppressively propagandist films on Alaskan industry in the lobby and maintains a quiet art gallery in the tower. Artists present their work on weekdays at 2 and 3pm. (Free.) The **Heritage Library** (276-1132), in the National Bank of Alaska Office Bldg. at Northern Lights Blvd. and C St., contains a display of rare books and Native artifacts. (Open Mon.-Fri. 1-4pm. Free.)

If you wish to see real Alaskan wildlife in the comfort of an urban setting, visit the **Alaska Zoo,** Mile 2 on O'Malley Rd. (346-3242) where you can say hi to Binky the Bear and other orphaned Alaskan beasts. Call **Rideline** (343-6543) for information on bus service. (Open daily 9am-6pm. Admission $5, senior citizens $4, ages 13-18 $3, ages 3-12 $2, children under 3 free.) **Star the Reindeer** lives in a fenced-in courtyard close to downtown on 10th and I. He has paced this tiny plot for 25 years, becoming Anchorage's mascot in the process. You can feed him carrots if you so wish.

Shopping

If you want to shop where the air literally reeks of authenticity, head to the close confines of the nonprofit gift shop at the **Alaska Native Medical Center,** 3rd and Gampbell. Because many Natives pay for medical services with their own arts and handicrafts, the Alaska State Museum in Juneau has sent buyers here to improve its exhibitions. Walrus bone *ulus* (knives used by Natives; $15-60), fur moccasins, Eskimo parkas, and dolls highlight the selection. (Open Mon.-Fri. 10am-2pm.) There are also several somewhat tamer shops downtown. **David Green Master Furrier,** 130 W. 4th Ave. or 423 W. 5th Ave. (277-9595), offers parkas and other fur garments stripped from the backs of dead Alaskan animals. The merchandise is expensive but tours are free; call ahead. (Open daily 9am-6pm.)

Craftworks from Alaska's Bush country, similar to those on display at the Museum of History and Art, are sold at the **Alaska Native Arts and Crafts Showroom,** 333 W. 4th Ave. (274-2932). Birch baskets start at $10, beadwork and other jewelry at $20, ivory carvings at $30. (Open Mon.-Fri. 10am-6pm, Sat. 10am-5pm.) Local craftsmen carve ivory, weave baskets, and work on animal skins at the **Gingham House,** corner of K St. and 6th Ave. (Open Mon.-Sat. 10am-4pm.) **Bering Sea Originals,** in Dimond Mall, 800 E. Dimond Blvd. (349-3322), and in Northway Mall, 3101 Penland Pkwy. (274-7126), features all sorts of Alaskan handicrafts. *Ulus* start at $10 and ivory carvings at $25. (Both locations open daily 10am-9pm.)

Entertainment and Seasonal Events

The **Alaska Experience Theater,** 705 W. 6th Ave. (276-3730), is where brown bears and Native dances come alive on the inner surface of a hemispherical dome. Lighting show almost as professional as Brett and Mike's soon-to-be-internationally known K&A Co. (The 40-min. film shows hourly Sun.-Thurs. noon-8pm, Fri.-Sat. noon-9pm. Admission $6, children $4.) Yearning for a touch of Arctic Broadway? The **4th Avenue Theatre,** 628 4th Ave., 1 block west of the Log Cabin visitors center and 5000 mi. west of New York City, offers summer shows such as *West Side Story.*

Anchorageans of all shapes and tax brackets party at **Chilkoot Charlie's,** 2435 Spenard Rd. (272-1010), at Fireweed. The bar has a rockin' dance floor and a quiet lounge. Ask about the nightly drink specials; otherwise you'll end up paying an outrageous amount to subsidize those who do. That's why Chilkoot Charlie's motto is "We screw the other guy and pass the savings on to you!" Take bus #7 or 60. A rival hotspot is **Darwin's Theory** (277-5322), located on 426 G. St. downtown. The "theory" here is that "a smart monkey doesn't monkey around with another monkey's monkey!" Less crowded and more interesting is **Mr. Whitekey's Fly-by-Night Club,** 3300 Spenard Rd. (279-7726), a "sleazy bar serving everything from the world's finest champagnes to a damn fine plate of Spam." The Monty-Pythonesque house special gives you anything with Spam at half-price when you order champagne (free with Dom Perignon). Try Spam nachos or Spam and cream cheese on a bagel ($2-6). Nightly entertainment ranges from rock to jazz to blues. (Open 3pm-2:30am.) The motto-less Midnight Express, 2612 Spenard Rd. (279-1861), hosts rock-and-roll bands Tuesday through Saturday; music starts at 9pm. (Open Sun.-Thurs. 10am-2:30am, Fri.-Sat. 10am-3am.) Downtown bars get nastier around C St., but the **Frontier Club** on 4th and H St. is quiet, inexpensive, and filled with garrulous, cribbage-playing Alaskans.

For more spontaneous entertainment, watch for annual events celebrated Alaska-style. Call the **event hotline** (276-3200) to see what's coming up. The **Campbell Creek Classic** in early June is, according to the visitors bureau, a "zany race covering approximately 4 miles . . . on almost anything that floats." The longest day of the year (June 21) brings dancing to the streets and runners from all over the world to the inspirational **Mayor's Marathon.** The **Iditarod Race** (notice the letters I-D-I-O-T), a grueling 1049-mi. sled dog competition traversing two mountain ranges, 150 mi. of the Yukon River, and the ice pack of the Norton Sound, begins in Anchorage on the first weekend in March. Twelve to 18 days later, the winner (and, with luck, some of the other competitors as well) arrives in Nome. The tortuous route commemorates the heroic journey of mushers in Anchorage's early days who carried serum to halt Nome's diptheria epidemic. The **Fur Rendezvous,** held the second week of February, brings back the time when fur trappers gathered to whoop it up. Today, affectionately referred to as "Fur Rondy," it includes the world sled dog championship races, a grand prix, and snowshoe softball games.

Near Anchorage: South

Driving south on the Seward Hwy. one follows the **Turnagain Arm** of the Cook Inlet. Miles of the arm are uncovered at low tide only to drown under 10-ft. high "bores," waves created as the 15mph riptide races in. **Warning:** although you might be tempted to stroll around on the exposed sand at low tide, *don't do it.* The arm is fed by glacial streams carrying fine silt, and you wouldn't be the first person to die in the resulting quicksand-like substance. The water in Cook Inlet is so cold, that if you got caught in the incoming tide, you wouldn't survive for more than five minutes.

Fifteen miles down the arm sits the **Potter Section House Historical Site** (345-2631), the last standing original roadhouse for the Alaska Railroad. The site now houses a ranger station for Chugach National Forest and a small railroad museum. (Open daily 9am-6pm.) Off of Seward Hwy. lies the **Alyeska Ski Resort,** proposed site of the 1998 Winter Olympics (Alyeska received the U.S. bid for 1994, but was rejected by the World Olympic Committee). The resort is open November to April for skiing, and June 14 to September 14 from 10:30am to 5pm for sight-seeing chair-lift rides ($10, children $5, 4-person family ticket $25). While in Alyeska, stay at the **Alyeska International Youth Hostel (AYH)** (see Anchorage Accommodations). Turn left onto Alyeska Blvd. off Seward Hwy., right on Timberline, then right on Alpina.

Just up Crow Creek Rd. is **Erickson's Mine,** a national historic site with eight original buildings and an active gold mine run by New Yorker Cynthia Toohey and her children. (Admission $4 for goldpanners, $2 for sight-seers.) This strike predates even the Klondike and Fairbanks ones, and the site is the un-reconstructed real McCoy. Campsites are available for $5. As you leave Crow Creek Rd., stop in at the **Double Muskie** (783-2822), set back from the road in the trees. The "Muskie" deserves its reputation as the best restaurant in Alaska. If you can't swing the spicy cajun-style dinner ($14-25), at least treat yourself to a drink or dessert (the Double Muskie Pie, a blend of chocolate and pecans, defies description). (Open Tues.-Thurs. 5-11pm, Fri.-Sun. 4-11pm.)

Portage Valley

Four roadside glaciers lounge over the Portage Valley, grinding channels through the earth in an ice-age-old tradition. As the glaciers gradually recede, frozen chunks fall into Portage Lake, leaving huge blue icebergs within a snowball's throw of shore. Perched on the lakeside, the **Begich, Boggs Visitors Center** has the strangest name and most modern displays of any Alaskan information outlet. The center's exhaustive glacial exhibitions and historical movie ($1) attract plenty of visitors. (Open daily 9am-6pm.) Take the five-mi. (10-min.) detour off Seward Hwy., south of Alyeska along the well-paved Portage Highway.

Three state-run campgrounds on Portage Hwy. have excellent sites with pan-oramic glacial views (sites $5). **Beaver Pond, Black Bear,** and **Williwaw** all provide water and toilets; Williwaw adds a short hiking trail and a viewing ledge overlooking salmon-spawning areas (salmon season late July-Aug.). Naturalists introduce trav-elers to the few easy hiking trails that begin from the visitors center. For more infor-mation on the hikes and trails, call the **Anchorage Ranger District Office** (345-5700), or write to Chugach National Forest, Anchorage Ranger District, 201 E. 9th Ave., #206, Anchorage 99501 (271-2500).

Portage is 45 minutes from downtown Anchorage by car along Seward Hwy. Hitchhiking is easy (see Kenai Peninsula for tips). In addition, every tour group and its mother runs day trips to Portage. The cheapest may be the one given by **Grayline** (277-5581), which conducts a six-hour tour of Portage Glacier, including stops at the Begich-Boggs Visitor Center and at Alyeska ski resort (daily tours at 8:30am and noon; $28, children under 12 $14).

Near Anchorage: North

To counteract urban claustrophobia, head for the summit of **Flattop Mountain** in the "Glenn Alps" of the Chugach Range near Anchorage. The excellent view of the city and (if it's clear) sun-soaked Mt. McKinley is well worth the hour-long hike. The hike is deceptively difficult, due to its steepness and slippery shale, but is manageable even for a novice. Wear long pants, as you may find yourself sliding down on your bum. And when climbing, remember—bears have the right-of-way. If Flattop can't satisfy your craving for wilderness, head for **Chugach State Park,** which covers 495,000 acres east and south of the city. The **Eagle River Visitors Center** (694-2108) is at Mile 12.7 on Eagle River Rd., off Glenn Hwy. The wildlife displays, hiking trails, and other facilities are spellbinding. (Open Thurs.-Mon. 11am-7pm; in winter Fri.-Sun. 10am-6pm.)

Due north is **Matanuska Valley,** an area settled by Scandinavian farmers in 1935 as part of a New Deal program. President Roosevelt wanted to transplant families from the depressed Midwest to experiment with agriculture in Alaska. The idea was never popular enough to create the exodus that Roosevelt hoped for, but the project did result in growth the President never dreamed of—namely, 75-lb. cabbages. Long summer daylight has turned garden-variety vegetables into mastadon-sized meals. Fist-sized strawberries are popular snacks. In summer, fresh produce is available (in bulk) from roadside stands along Glenn Hwy. between its junction with George Parks Hwy. and the town of Wasilla.

Perhaps the valley's biggest event is the **Alaska State Fair,** on the fairgrounds at Mile 40.2 on Glenn Hwy. This 11-day event, ending on Labor Day, includes parades, rodeos, livestock, and agricultural sideshows starring the aforementioned cabbages. (Open daily 10am-10pm. Admission $6, senior citizens $2, ages under 13 $1.)

But wait—there's more to the Matanuska than vegetables borrowed from the set of *Sleeper*. Relive the pleasant days when dog sleds carried medical supplies across miles of subfrozen (−40°F) tundra at the **Knik Museum and Mushers Hall of Fame,** at Mile 14 on Knik Rd., which features mushing memorabilia and famous dog sleds in its Canine Hall of Fame. (Open June 15-Sept. 15 Wed.-Sat. 11am-5pm, Sun. 1-6pm. Call Vi Reddington at 376-5562 for visits at other times.) Twenty-two miles from downtown Wasilla, **Independence Mine State Historic Park** (745-5897), in Hatcher Pass, features hiking, hang gliding, fishing, restored mine buildings, and a lodge. Take either Glenn Hwy. to Mile 50 and the Fishhook-Willow Rd. to the park, or Parks Hwy. to Mile 71, Fishhook-Willow Rd.'s other end.

Head to **Big Lake** (Mile 52 on Parks Hwy.) and **Nancy Lake** (Mile 67.5 on Parks Hwy.) for excellent camping, lodging, canoeing, fishing, and more. Or splash in whitewater on the lower **Matanuska River** for as little as $40. (Call collect 745-5753, or write NOVA, P.O. Box 1129, Chickaloon 99674.) Check *The Milepost* for an extensive list of hunting and fishing lodges and campgrounds in the area.

Torrents of brochures will entreat you to join hunting expeditions, river floats, sea-plane excursions, or combinations of all three. **Ketchum Air** (243-5525), the most persistently advertised, charges $120-1000 for custom-tailored adventures. But **NOVA** (745-5753) and other companies can toss you about in the whitewater for $50.

Palmer

Palmer has long been the major educational and commercial center south of Anchorage—extraordinary, considering that it is actually located to the north of Anchorage. Learn more about its history at the **visitors center** (745-2880), a log cabin downtown, across the railroad tracks on South Valley Way at E. Fireweed Ave. (Open May-Sept. daily 9am-6pm.) The **Alaska Historical and Transportation Museum,** at Mile 40.2 on Glenn Hwy. (745-4493), is only a mile from the town center. The museum encases implements from the loggers, miners, fishermen, and farmers of Alaska's past. (Open daily 8am-4pm. Admission $3, ages under 12 $1.50.) For a closer gander at Alaska's modern agriculture, tour the dairy facilities and gardens of the **University of Alaska Experiment Station** (745-3257), on Trunk Rd., ½ mi. north of the junction of Glenn and Parks Hwy. (Tours June-Aug. daily.)

A few miles off Parks Hwy. on Hatcher Pass Rd. lies the world's only domesticated **Musk-Ox Farm.** Neither bovine nor perfume producers, these beasts are actually hairy nephews of the buffalo. Natives weave their locks into scarves and hats. The musk-ox *was* indigenous to Alaska but hunted to extinction by Natives centuries before European arrival. Today's herds have been transplanted from the Eurasian continent across the Arctic Circle.

Fall asleep to the distant moans of these furry behemoths at the **Denali Park Campground,** on Denali St. off Arctic Ave. near the visitors center. The state-run park has 100 spots, with sewage disposal facilities and showers.

Wasilla

Taste a chunk of "real Alaska" down the road in Susitna Valley, between Wasilla and Lucille Lakes. Wasilla, which means "breath of air," shares Palmer's agricultural heritage. Despite its location only 42 mi. north of Anchorage on the Parks Hwy., the town lives in the wild outback of rough frontier days—a fact reflected by the nearby Dog Musher's Hall of Fame. If you want to see if dog mushing is your calling, call **Mush Alaska,** P.O. Box 871752, Wasilla 99687 (376-4743). Half-hour excursions start at $15 per person.

Take in the **Wasilla Museum** (376-2005) and the town's **visitors center,** on Main St. off the Parks Hwy. Behind the museum is **Frontier Village,** complete with Wasilla's first school, sauna, and ferris wheel. (Open daily 10am-6pm. Admission $1, children under 13 free.)

Anchorage's **Stay-With-A-Friend B&B** (344-4006) projects its sphere of influence north to Wasilla. Singles start at $40, doubles $50. Campers should continue south toward Anchorage for another 13 mi. to **Eklutna Campground,** a state-run spot with free water and toilets. For more information on the area, contact the **Wasilla Chamber of Commerce,** P.O. Box 871826, 1801 Parks Hwy., #A-8, Wasilla 99687 (376-1299).

Prince William Sound

Of all of Alaska's natural attractions, few can rival the Prince William Sound. Glaciers as large as eastern states, soaring ice-capped mountains, and majestic fjords all serve as a backdrop for Alaska's largest accessible natural playground. The Sound is filled with humpback whales, orcas, cavorting sea lions, and sea otters, as well as millions of birds which pass through the **Copper River Delta** on their annual migration.

In recent decades, the Sound has made headline news world-wide; not as a result of its inherent wonders and vast natural reserves, but rather because of the grave catastrophes which have assaulted them. The Good Friday Earthquake of 1964 caused an estimated $750 million in property damage, lowering downtown Anchorage by several feet and virtually wiping Valdez off the map. Then, 25 years later—also on Good Friday—the Exxon *Valdez* released 11 million gallons of pure crude oil into the Sound's unsuspecting waters, marring the shores and killing thousands of marine animals.

Originally settled by the Chugach, the most southerly of the North American Eskimos, Prince William Sound was a cultural center of prehistoric Alaska. All four major native ethnic groups crossed paths here, to trade, socialize, and sometimes fight. Then in 1741, the first Europeans to land in Alaska came to the Sound's Kayak Island. Russian explorer Vitus Bering landed here, shortly before establishing the Russian-Alaskan capital at Sitka, and he was followed by a multitude of treasure seekers from Spain, Portugal, France, America, and England. In 1778, enterprising British explorer Captain James T. Cook sailed into the Sound in search of the legendary Northwest Passage through the Arctic. In doing so, he claimed the entire region in the name of Prince William Henry, the future King William IV of England.

The Sound is 15 times larger than San Francisco Bay, and is the northernmost warm-water embayment in North America. Most of the Sound has been subsumed under the Chugach National Forest, a 5.9 million-acre preserve. Local industry is based upon the rich natural reserves located within Chugach, including timber, fish and wildlife, abundant minerals, and inexhaustible recreational possibilities. Tourism has only recently become important, and for this reason the Sound is perhaps one of the few places in Alaska where you can still peek in on "true" Alaskan communities at work.

Whittier

The site Whittier now occupies serves as a rest stop between Prince William Sound and the Turnagain Arm of Cook Inlet (see Anchorage). Native and Russian fur traders bivouacked here before crossing the 13 mi. isthmus known as the Portage Pass. In the late 19th and early 20th centuries, this pass was heavily traveled by gold seekers and mail carriers.

Whittier is hedged on all sides by massive glaciers and waterfalls, making it a town of beauty as well as of convenience. The town itself is named for one of the nearby glaciers, which was named after the poet John Greenleaf Whittier. It was not until WWII, when the U.S. Army drilled a railroad tunnel connecting the Sound's ice-free seaport with the Alaska railroad, that Whittier became a permanent community. Today, with more boats in the harbor than there are residents, Whittier serves as a staging ground for pleasure seeking Alaskans and tourists.

Practical Information and Orientation

Visitor Center: P.O. Box 747 (472-2379), located in the center of town, slyly camouflaged next to the railroad tracks in a refurbished railroad car. Organized information on hiking, boating, camping, and fishing available. Open daily 10am-6pm.

Harbor Master Office: P.O. Box 608 (472-2320 or 472-2330), in small boat harbor. 330-boat capacity, landing 25¢ per linear ft. Showers available ($2.50). Open 24 hr. in summer, daily 8am-midnight in winter.

Alaska Railroad: (265-2494 for a person, 265-2607 for a machine). Six round-trip runs between Portage and Whittier every day in summer ($7.50 each way). Bus service from Anchorage to Portage twice daily, leaving from the train depot on 2nd St. in Anchorage ($17.50).

Alaska Marine Highway: (272-4482), located ½-mi. east of town, next to the small boat harbor. To: Valdez ($54), Cordova ($54) with a detour to view the Columbia Glacier. Cordova/Whittier direct (i.e. without detour) $32.

Kayak Rental: Price William Sound Kayak Center (562-2866 or 472-2452). Single boats $35 per day, double $55 per day.

Laundromat: Sportsman Inn (472-2357), on Eastern Ave.

Medical Services: Whittier Clinic (472-2303 or 911). Serves as Whittier's pharmacy, hospital, medical emergency center (472-2340), and ambulance dispatcher. Over-the-counter pharmaceuticals available at the Anchor Inn (472-2354).

Police: 472-2340.

Post Office: On 1st floor of Begich Towers. Open Mon., Wed., Fri. 11:30am-5:30pm. General Delivery ZIP Code: 99693.

Population: 300.

Area Code: 907.

Whittier, Portage, Billing's, and Maynard Glaciers encompass the town of Whittier, which lies 63 mi. southeast of Anchorage, and 105 mi. west of Valdez. Whittier is also 3690 mi. from Tokyo, 2998 mi. due north of Honolulu, and 3855 mi. from Soddy-Daisy, TN.

Accommodations and Camping

There are two public campgrounds in Whittier, the **Whittier Camp Grounds,** located behind Begich Towers next to the Horsetail Falls, and **Smitty's Cove,** near the U.S. Army fuel dock. Both are free and have limited facilities. Whittier Camp Ground has running water and a picnic table, but don't keep any food in your tent; the summer bear trail passes right through camp. Smitty's Cove has no running water and no sideboard, but provides great opportunities for scuba diving and fishing.

There are also two hotels in Whittier. The **Sportsman Inn,** on Eastern Ave., near the Army Dock (472-2461), provides clean, comfortable rooms at reasonable prices (singles $43, doubles $49). The **Anchor Inn** (472-2354) has dingier rooms at slightly higher prices. Singles $45, with bath $55. Doubles $50, with bath $60.

Food

Although Whittier is not known for its culinary delights, you can still enjoy standard Alaskan seafood meals at standard Alaskan seafood prices. The Anchor Inn is the best place for groceries, but buyer beware: a box of cereal can run a nightmarish $5.

Hobo Bay Trading Company, in Harbor Area (472-2374). Aunt B., the proprietor and "pro-piemaker" has been dishing out Mexican goodies since before you were born. Try a hearty taco ($2) or make an attempt at B.'s heaping nachos ($5). Open Thurs.-Tues. 11am-8pm.

Swiftwater Seafood ("ain't got no phone"), in the Triangle. Superior fried seafood. Fish n' chips $7, and daily lunch specials. Open daily 11am-8pm.

Irma's Outpost, in the Triangle (472-2461). Jumbo sandwiches ($6). Scrumptios muffins and pie slices ($1.45). Also the only liquor store in town. Yeah Irma. Open daily 10am-10pm.

Sportsman Inn, on Eastern Ave. (472-2461). Tasty salmon salad sandwich with fries and soup ($5.25). Easily the most pleasant restaurant in town. Open daily 7am-9pm.

Sights

According to the town's advertising slogan, Whittier is "unique even to Alaska," and this is undeniably true. Social-life (as well as everything else in this condensed town) centrifuges around **Begich Towers,** the refurbished officers' quarters where 85% of the town's residents now live. The Towers also house the **Whittier Museum,** which contains some rare shellfish specimens, 1964 earthquake memorabilia, and even an orca's skull. (Open daily in summer 1-5pm.) At the top of the Towers is a **sun room,** with an outstanding view of the surrounding glaciers and waterfalls. With several stores on the the lower floors, the residents of these modern miracles need never set foot out-of-doors. At night, residents head to Whittier's two bars, located in the (you guessed it) Sportsman Inn and Anchor Inn.

Hiking opportunities are abundant, with some of the best hikes being to the **Portage Glacier** (via the **Portage Pass**), the **Horse Tail Falls,** and the **Second Salmon Run,** down Shotgun Cove Rd. Head to Smitty's Cove, right off the State Ferry dock, or (alternately) to the **First** and **Second Salmon Runs,** for coves of salmon just dying to be eaten. The visitors center has information on trails.

Near Whittier, tour boats operate daily. **Phillips' Cruises and Tours** (800-544-0529 or 276-8023) conducts a popular 26-glacier cruise ($119). **Honey Charters** (344-3340) hires out boats for personalized tours ($29 per person for 2-hr. cruise; $150 per person for an 8 to 11-hr. cruise). A nice day trip is a cruise up the nearby **College Fjord,** to see the **Harvard** and **Yale Glaciers.** The Harvard Glacier is the bigger of the two. Of course.

Valdez

Lasting evidence of Mediterranean influence in Alaska, Valdez was named by explorer Don Salvador Fidalgo after the Marine Minister for Spain, Valdes y Basan. Before coming under American control in 1867, Valdez was governed by Russian fur traders. Although not nearly as famous as the Klondike Trail, it was from Valdez in 1897-98 that gold-seekers struck out to find the "all-American route" into the Alaskan interior's newly-tapped gold deposits. Ironically, Valdez today has become the terminus for wealth, rather than the start of the trail for goldpanners, as the Trans-Alaska Pipeline deposits its "Black Gold" into waiting oil tankers. With high-tech big business and sculpted peaks perched upon snow-sealed mountains, Valdez is known as the "Little Switzerland" of Alaska. The **Columbia Glacier,** the second largest tidewater glacier in North America, is only a few hours away by boat, and along with Mt. McKinley is perhaps the greatest single natural wonder in Alaska.

Practical Information and Orientation

Tourist Information: Valdez Convention and Visitor Bureau, P.O. Box 1603-B (835-2984), on the corner of Fairbanks and Chenega St. Information on sights, accommodations, hiking and camping. Movies on the devastating 1964 earthquake, and a documentary on the Pipeline (shows every 2 hr. daily 10am-6pm; admission $3, children $1.50). Open daily 8am-8pm.

Fishing Information: U.S. Fish and Game, 337 Fairbanks Dr., Valdez 99686 (835-2562). Numerous canneries in Valdez attest to the abundance of fish in the Valdez Arm.

Airport: Valdez Airport, serviced by **MarkAir** (800-478-0800) and **Alaska Airlines** (800-426-0333), as well as local charters. One way to Anchorage $88.

Buses: Greyline Pipeline Tours (276-8866). Guided tours of the Alyeska Pipeline Terminal (daily 10am and 7pm, $16). Both **Grayline of Alaska** (835-2357) and **Alaska Inter-City Line** (800-478-2877) provide daily service to Anchorage ($58).

Alaska Marine Highway: P.O. Box 647 (835-4436), located in the City Dock at the end of Hazelet Ave. To: Whittier ($54), Cordova ($26), and Seward ($54).

Taxis: Valdez Yellow Cab (835-2500).

Car Rental: Valdez-U-Drive, P.O. Box 852 (835-4402), at the airport. $39 per day with 50 free mi., plus 15¢ per additional mi. **Avis** (835-4774), also at airport. $46 per day with 100 free mi., plus 35¢ per additional mi.

Bike Rental: Beaver Sports (835-4727).

Kayak Rental: Keystone Raft and Kayak Adventure, P.O. Box 1486V (835-2606). Valdez is within easy reach of superb whitewater, ranging from class II to IV. $25 per hr., $125 per day. Make reservations at least 1 day in advance.

Laundromat: Sparkle Laundry, 124 Hazelet Ave. (835-5777). $2 per *warsh,* dryer $1.50. Open daily 10am-8pm.

Weather: National Weather Service—Valdez, 835-4505.

Crisis Line: 835-2999.

Pharmacy: Valdez Drug and Photo, 321 Fairbanks Dr. (835-4956). Open Mon.-Fri. 9:30am-6:30pm, Sat. 11am-2pm.

Hospital: 835-2249.

Emergency/Ambulance: 911.

Police: 835-4560.

Post Office: corner of Galena St. and Tatitlek St. (835-4449). Open Mon.-Fri. 9am-5pm, Sat. 10am-noon. General Delivery ZIP Code: 99686.

Population: 3,000.

Area Code: 907.

Valdez resides at the head of the Valdez Arm, in the northeast corner of Prince William Sound. Valdez is 304 mi. (as the hiker hitches) east of Anchorage, and is connected by the spectacular **Richardson Highway,** which intercepts the Glenn Highway to Anchorage in Glennallen. The Richardson Highway is one of the most scenic drives in Alaska.

Accommodations and Camping

The South Harbor Dr. Campground, home to many of Valdez's transient cannery workers, is the best place for transient budget travelers as well. The Visitors Bureau also lists over 70 bed and breakfasts, which generally charge about $50 for singles and $55 for doubles.

South Harbor Drive Campground (835-2531), (not surprisingly) on S. Harbor Dr., overlooking the small boat harbor. 50 sites with wooden tent platforms, water, toilets. No showers. Sites $5, rarely collected.

The Garden House Bed and Breakfast, 708 Cottonwood Dr. (835-2957). Take Hazelet Rd., left, left, left onto Klutina Rd., right onto Copper Dr., left onto Cottonwood Dr. Nice rooms, homemade breakfasts, and a great view of nearby Mineral Creek. Singles $50. Doubles $55.

Chalet Alpine View Bed and Breakfast, 1147 Mineral Creek Dr. (835-5223), also overlooking Mineral Creek. Private rooms and continental breakfast buffet. Singles $50. Doubles $55.

Totem Inn, P.O. Box 648, Valdez 99686 (835-4443), on Richardson Hwy. The least expensive of Valdez's ridiculously over-priced hotels. (Stay in a B&B!) Singles $89. Doubles $94.

Sea Otter RV Park, P.O. Box 947 (835-2787) on N. Harbor Dr. Call ahead for reservations, as this park is often full. Full hookups $14, tenters $12. Showers free for guests, $2.50 otherwise.

Valdez Glacier Campground (835-4314), located 5 mi. east of town on the Richardson Hwy., next to the airport. Site of the town which was destroyed in the 1964 earthquake, this campground is difficult to reach without a car or bicycle. View of the awesome glacier.

Food

The bustling-est town on Prince William Sound, Valdez supports several excellent restaurants. For those who must stick to tight budgets, there's always the **Shop-Rite** on 113 Egan Rd. (835-4496; open daily 7am-midnight.)

Alaska Halibut House, corner of Meals Ave. and Pioneer Dr. (835-2788). Everybody, local cannery worker and intrepid tourists alike, orders the fried seafood. Don't let the fast-food atmosphere dismay you, the Halibut Basket with Fries ($5.75) is amazing. Open daily 6am-11pm.

Totem Inn, corner of Richardson Hwy. and Meals Ave. (835-4443). The quality of the chow is diametrically opposed to the value of the Inn's overpriced hotel rooms. Whopping eggs, hash browns, toast, and sound cup of strong coffee $4. Open daily 5am-11pm.

No Name Pizza, on Egan Dr. (835-4419). Pizza to make Goldilocks smile—8" Baby ($6), 12" Mama ($11), and 16" Papa ($16), each with up to 3 ingredients. The pizza bomb ($7.50), however, is just right. Open daily 8am-1am.

Fu Kung, 203 Kobuk St. (835-5255). Fine Chinese dinners $7-11, some incorporating local seafood. Open daily 8am-10pm.

Sights

After an 800-mi. journey from the oil fields of Prudhoe Bay, the oil in the **Trans-Alaska Pipeline** is deposited in Valdez. Located across the bay from town, the monolithic terminal dumps millions of gallons of rich crude oil every day into the maws of awaiting tankers. **Greyline Pipeline Tours** (835-2357 or 276-8866) will take you the 14 mi. to the terminal and explain how the Play-doh-like substance is transported and processed. Even staunch environmentalists will be impressed. To see the other side of the oil business, head to the offices of the **Prince William Sound Conservation Alliance,** 310 Egan Drive, #218, a non-profit organization dedicated to public education and political action. Inside, view the excellent "Oil and the Marine Environment" exhibit for a closer look at the Exxon *Valdez* oil spill. Even hardcore industrialists will be impressed. (835-2799; open daily 9am-5pm.)

In town, head to the **museum** on Egan Dr. Inside, you'll see Valdez's original 1907 Ahrens steam fire engine, and a posterboard covered with works by America's best cartoonists in their attempts to rub salt in Exxon's wounds. (Open daily 9am-7pm. Free.) On rainy days—and Valdez has many—the town's **library,** 200 Fairbanks Dr., is a good place to spend a few idle hours. (Open Mon. 10am-6pm, Tues.-Thurs. 10am-8pm, Fri. 10am-6pm, Sat. noon-6pm.) Valdez is also home to **Prince William Sound Community College,** which displays works, including fabulous 10-ft. carved heads, by the renowned Native sculptor **Peter Toth** (no, he's not a reggae singer).

The area around Valdez produces abundant natural attractions. **Hiking** opportunities abound, but can be rough going as there are few developed trails. **Mineral Creek,** just north of downtown, which follows a magnificent gorge through uninhabited backcountry is a good place to begin (but look out for bears). By boat, helicopter, or plane, you can investigate two of the Sound's most prized possessions: **Columbia** and **Shoup Glaciers. ERA Helicopter** (835-2595) will give you a one-hour flightseeing tour of both ($139 per person).

In an attempt to spice up small-town life and milk tourists, Valdez created the **Gold Rush Days** celebration, held in August. The month-long fundraiser includes a fashion show, banquet, dance, and even an 1890s Casino Night. But beware of the traveling Jail, which picks up aimless tourists and makes them drink gallons of warm beer. If you can't get yourself incarcerated, head to the **Pipeline Club** (835-4332) on Egan Dr.

Cordova

The most isolated of the Sound's three main towns, Cordova marks the convergence of four ecological systems: forest, delta, estuary, and ocean. The town is also within easy reach of the Copper River Delta, which plays host to the majority of North America's migratory bird species. Fortified by rugged mountains of volcanic rock and by salmon filled-seas, nature-lovers and fishermen who "visit" this pleasant area have been known to stay indefinitely.

Practical Information

Visitor Information: Cordova Chamber of Commerce, P.O. Box 99, 622 1st St. (424-7260), next to the bank. Information on accommodations, transportation, and attractions. Open Tues., Thurs., Sat. 1-4pm. **USDA-Chuguch National Forest District**, Cordova Ranger District, Box 280 (424-7661), corner of 2nd and C St. Excellent information on hiking trails and fishing.

Fishing Information: U.S. Fish and Game (424-3213).

Airport: 13 mi. east of town on the Copper River Hwy. Serviced by **Alaska Airlines** (800-426-0333 or 424-3278). One way to: Juneau ($144), Anchorage ($82), and Kodiak ($205).

Alaska Marine Highway: P.O. Box 1689, Cordova 99574. (800-642-0066 or 424-7333), 1 mi. north of town on Ocean Dock Rd. One way to Valdez ($26), Whittier ($54), Seward ($54), and Port Lions ($86).

Buses/Tours: Copper River Express, P.O. Box 724 (424-5463). Dowie Ferguson takes you on a personalized tour of glaciers and the "Million Dollar Bridge." (4 hr., $25).

Taxis: D & L Taxi (424-3456) and **Imperial Cab Co.** (424-7575).

Car Rental: Imperial Car Rental (424-3201), across from the Killer Whale Café. $50 per day, unlimited mileage. Best deal in town, but with only 2 cars, you should call ahead. **Reluctant Fisherman Inn** (424-3272). $50 per day, 50¢ per mi.

Camping Equipment: Flinn's Clothing & Sporting Goods Store, on 1st St. (424-3282). Open daily 9am-6pm.

Laundromat: Club Speedwash (424-3201) in the Prince William Motel. Open daily 8am-10pm.

Weather: 424-3333.

Crisis Line: 424-8300.

Pharmacy: Cordova Drug Co., P.O. Box 220, on 1st St. (424-3246). Open Mon.-Sat. 9:30am-6pm, Sun. 10am-1pm.

Ambulance: 424-6100.

Hospital: 424-8000.

Emergency: 911.

Police: 424-6100.

Post Office: corner of 2nd St. and Browning Ave. (424-3564). Open Mon.-Fri. 9am-5:30pm. General Delivery ZIP Code: 99574.

Population: 3500.

Area Code: 907.

Orientation

Cordova is located on the east side of Prince William Sound on Orca Inlet, connected to the rest of the world only by boat or plane. A road connecting Cordova with Valdez was under construction, but was destroyed in the 1964 earthquake. Plans to resume work on this road are uncertain.

Accommodations

Cordova township maintains no public campgrounds, though there are Forest Service campgrounds along the Copper River Highway. There is, however, a privately owned "campground," affectionately known as "Hippy Cove," where people can crash for free.

Hippy Cove, 2 mi. north of town on Orca Road. With its own unique social life, Hippy Cove is guaranteed to keep you entertained. Most of its inhabitants are short-term cannery workers, although there are some lifers left over from the Psychedelic Era. Evil Kneivel-types will not want to miss the **rope swing**, which sweeps you from a steep river bank out over a rainforest-like gorge, and then returns you in one breath. There is also a redwood **sauna**, which town members and Cove dwellers share. The dress code requires a birthday suit. Hippy Cove is free and has drinking water.

Alaskan Hotel and Bar, P.O. Box 484, on 1st St. (424-3288). Small rooms with color TVs. Bottom floors a teensy noisy at night because of the bar. Singles $35, with bath $45.

Cordova House Hotel, 1st St. (424-3388). Small, oddly-shaped rooms with color TV and nice bathrooms. Singles $52. Doubles $62.

Reluctant Fisherman Inn, 407 Railroad Ave. (424-3272). The nicest rooms in town. Singles $75. Doubles $85.

Prince William Motel, 501 1st St. (424-7772), in the alleyway across from the Killer Whale Café. Nice rooms. Laundromat available. Singles $75. Doubles $85. Seniors stay for $67.60.

Chugach National Forest (424-7661). The Forest Service maintains 19 cabins on the Copper River Delta, as well as a campground at **Cabin Lake,** Mile 12.1 on Copper River Hwy. Obtain information on cabins at the USDA (see Practical Information).

Food

Restaurants are quite good in Cordova, but budget travelers can get their Ramen at **Davis' Super Foods** on 1st St. (Open Mon.-Sat. 8am-8pm, Sun. 10am-3pm.)

Sourdough Café, on 1st St., near the museum (424-5494). No Alaskan town would be complete without a "Sourdough Cafe," and Cordova is no exception. Excellent food and hefty portions. 2 sourdough pancakes, 2 eggs, and a juicy ham steak ($6.75). Open Mon.-Sat. 6am-11pm, Sun. 7am-11pm.

Ambrosie Restaurant, on 1st St. across from the Sourdough (424-7175). Good Italian fare—scarf your own mini-pizza ($6). Open Mon.-Sat. noon-midnight, Sun. 4pm-midnight.

Killer Whale Café, on 1st St. (424-7733), across from Flinn's Clothing Store. Killer sandwiches $6-$8. Delicious homemade muffins 85¢. Open Mon.-Sat. 7:30am-4pm.

Reluctant Fisherman, 407 Railroad Ave. (424-3272). Excellent local-seafood dinners ($18-27). A good place to test out a loved one's credit cards. Open daily 6am-10pm.

Sights

The two greatest sights in Cordova are the **Childs Glacier** and the **Million Dollar Bridge.** Both are suspended at the end of the Copper River Highway, 50 mi. from town. The bridge was built in 1906 by Michael J. Heney (who also built the White Pass and Yukon Railway), and was an engineering marvel due to its placement between two active glaciers. The bridge collapsed during the 1964 earthquake, and no attempts have been made to rebuild it. The Childs Glacier is one of the more active tidewater glaciers, especially on hot summer days. Under the heat of the sun, the glacier constantly creaks and groans, calving chunk after chunk of indigo ice into the green water with a roar. Some icebergs are so large that they create "tidal waves" of several feet which sweep out into the stream, often depositing bewildered salmon onto the opposite shore. You can keep whatever fish you find on the beach, but be careful since bears play this game as well.

Closer to town along the Copper River Hwy. is the vast expanse of the **Copper River Delta,** a preserve which covers an area of over two million acres. **Fishing** here is superb as all five species of Pacific Salmon spawn seasonally in the Copper River. The Delta is alive with bears, moose, foxes, wolves, coyotes, eagles and even sea otters. **Hiking** in the Delta is often wet, tough work, but the neighboring Chuguch Mountains provide excellent hiking and climbing opportunities. An easy hike from town is the 2.4 mi. **Crater Lake Trail,** which can be reached via Power Creek Rd., 1.5 mi. north of Cordova. The **USDA Forest Service** has excellent information on other trails, as well as maps (see Practical Information).

Once back from town, stop by the **museum** and **library** both located in the same building on 1st St. Inside the museum you'll find Cordova's answer to *Dune:* real iceworms (*Mesenchytraeus Solifugus*) which live inside the glaciers. Less exciting is the ancient Haida Kayak. Every Saturday at 7:45pm, the Cordova Historical Society screens a 30-minute **movie** called the "*Cordova Story*" in the library. (Library open Tues., Wed., Fri. 1-5pm, Thurs. and Sat. 7-9pm).

For the past 30 years, Cordova residents have had an annual **Iceworm Festival** in order to honor the semi-legendary creature and defeat cabin fever. The celebrations break loose the first week in February, and include the parade of a 100-ft. Iceworm propelled by Cordova's youngsters down frozen 1st Street. Like most coastal towns in Alaska, Cordova also hosts an annual **Salmon Derby** in August. At other times of the year, locals seek solace from the rainy nights at the **Alaskan Hotel and Bar** (424-3288), which still houses the original oak barfront dating back to 1906. (Open Mon.-Fri. 8am-2pm, Sat.-Sun. 8am-4am.)

Kenai Peninsula

Life on the Kenai Peninsula has always been as rough as the Alaskan terrain. For centuries, the Kenaitze tribe fed off the land's fish and game. In the late 1700s, seeing a chance to profit from the sources of Kenaitze subsistence, Russian fur trappers established some of Alaska's first white settlements here. Their zest for capturing the coveted sea otters nearly drove the animal to extinction by the mid-19th century, depleting the area's wildlife population and allure for trappers. The United States arrived in 1867, and salmon fishermen rapidly replaced the fur traders—today nearly 40% of Alaska's sport fishing is done in the Kenai's lakes and rivers. Vigorous stocking programs conducted by the U.S. Fish and Wildlife Service ensure that the Kenai's waterways will teem with salmon for years to come. The Kenai Peninsula still shows vestiges of its colorful history. Many of the original Native American and Russian names remain, as well as old Russian Orthodox log churches. And the Kenai Peninsula's residents still depend on the region's natural resources for their livelihood.

The **Seward-Anchorage Highway** to the Kenai Peninsula winds south from Anchorage along the Turnagain Arm and the Chugach Mountains, which rise 12,000 feet straight up from Cook Inlet. The two forks of the highway terminate at Seward and Homer, small fishing communities of exceptional beauty. On the way to Homer the road passes Kenai (site of one of Alaska's first oil discoveries), and the small towns of Soldotna, Clam Gulch, and Ninilchik. Across Kachemak Bay from Homer sits Seldovia, site of an old Russian church. **Hitching** from Anchorage is not difficult in the summer, especially on weekends. Take bus #9 from Anchorage as far south as it will go and ask the driver to point you in the direction of the Seward-Anchorage Hwy.; from there, motorists are often willing to help. The peninsula's rivers and inlets afford fabulous fishing opportunities. If you plan to fish, make sure to ask locals for tips—everyone's an expert. They know where the fish are and how to catch them.

The Kenai is where Alaskans vacation, especially those from Anchorage and the Interior. They avoid all the towns save Homer. You'll find a state park or USFS **campground**—such as those at Bird and Quartz Creeks—about every eight mi. along the highway. Freshwater streams are also common along the highway and throughout the peninsula, but in summer so are "combat" fishermen (the banks are lined with crazies with hooks, sometimes only a few feet apart). Good camping can be found outside designated areas; great spots are hidden in the brush near every town. **Showers** are available near most harbors for a minimal fee; check with the harbormaster. For more information on hiking, hunting, fishing, camping, and other recreational opportunities, as well as regulations, contact the following: **Kenai Fjords National Park** (see Seward); **Alaska Maritime National Wildlife Refuge** (see Homer); **Kenai National Wildlife Refuge** (see Soldotna); **Chugach National Forest,** 201 E. 9th Ave., #206, Anchorage 99501 (261-2500); **State of Alaska, Division of Parks and Outdoor Recreation,** P.O. Box 1247, Soldotna 99669 (262-5581); and **State of Alaska, Department of Fish and Game,** P.O. Box 3150, Soldotna 99669 (262-9368).

Kenai

Kenai (pronounced keen-EYE), the second oldest white settlement in Alaska, is the largest and fastest-growing town on the peninsula. First a Native community, it became a Russian village with the building of Fort St. Nicholas in 1791, and then an American garrison when the U.S. Army built Fort Kenay in 1889. Kenai finally became known as the "Oil Capital of Alaska" with the 1957 discovery of oil in Cook Inlet. Remnants of each era are scattered throughout town: Native artifacts, a Russian Orthodox church, and American military installation, and oil rigs stationed in the inlet. During the summer months, Kenai becomes home to the largest collection of Beluga whales in Alaska, which chase spawning salmon through the mouth of the Kenai River.

Practical Information and Orientation

Visitor Information: Chamber of Commerce and **Visitors Center** 402 Overland St. (283-7989), in "Moosemeat John" Hedburg's Cabin at the corner of Main St. and Kenai Spur Rd., behind the metal grizzly bear (oh, that crazy frontier flavor). Open Mon.-Fri. 9am-5pm, Sat.-Sun. 10am-4pm. **Nikiski,** an unincorporated area just north of Kenai, has its own visitors center at the Nikishka Shopping Mall (776-8825), P.O. Box 8209, Nikiski 99635. Open Mon.-Fri. 8am-5pm.

National Park Service: 502 Overland Dr. (283-5855), P.O. Box 2643, Kenai 99611. Best source of information on **Lake Clark National Park and Preserve,** located across Cook Inlet from Kenai.

Airport: 1 mi. north of downtown. Take Kenai Spur Rd. to Willow St., follow signs for Airport Loop. Serviced by **Southcentral Air** (283-5404), **ERA** (283-3168 or 283-9091), and **Mark Air** (800-478-0800). One way to Anchorage ($49) and Kodiak ($98).

Taxi: The Cab Co. (238-7101).

Car Rental: Allstar Rent-a-Car (283-5005), at the airport. $35 per day, 100 free mi., 28¢ per additional mi. **Avis** (283-7900). $40 per day, 100 free mi., 35¢ per additional mi. **Hertz** (283-7979). **National** (283-9566).

Buses: Alaska Intercity Line (262-9445) One way to Anchorage ($27.50). Hourly shuttle between Kenai (pickup at airport) and Soldotna (pickup at **Klondike Sal's**; $4).

Tours: Kahtnu Tours, 2679 Bowpicker Ln. (283-7152). $15 for a good 3-hr. tour.

Pharmacy: Kenai Drug Inlet Pharmacy, 1135 Kenai Spur Hwy. (283-3714), in the Benco Bldg. Open Mon.-Fri. 10am-6pm.

Crisis Line: 283-7257.

Women's Resource Center: 335 S. Spruce St. (283-7257).

Hospital: Central Peninsula General Hospital, 250 Hospital Pl. (262-4404), Soldotna.

Emergency: 911.

Police: 283-7879.

Post Office: on Fidalgo Way. Open Mon.-Fri, 8:45am-5:15pm, Sat. 9:30am-1pm. General Delivery Zip Code: 99611.

Population: 6500.

Area Code: 907.

Kenai, on the western Kenai Peninsula, is about 148 mi. from Anchorage and 81 mi. north of Homer. It can be reached via Kalifornsky Beach Rd., which joins Sterling Hwy. from Anchorage just south of Soldotna, or Kenai Spur Rd., which runs north through the Nikishka area and east to Soldotna. Both roads show off the peninsula's lakes and snow-capped peaks: on a clear day, you can also see the 10,000 ft. **Mt. Redoubt Volcano** from across Cook Inlet.

Accommodations and Camping

Remember that all along the highway are recreational campgrounds. Kenai city campground is mosquito infested, loud, and a bit of a haul from the center of town—but free for three days. Take Kenai Spur Rd. to Forest Dr. and turn towards the ocean. Stake a spot close to the water for a great view. There are also several B&B's in Kenai; obtain a list at the Visitors Center.

Katmai Hotel, 10800 Kenai Spur Rd. (283-6101), 1 block from downtown. Small rooms, worn but neat. Singles $69. Doubles $79.

King Oscar's Motel, P.O. Box 1080 (238-6060), on the corner of Kenai Spur Hwy. and Airport Way. Singles $79.50. Doubles $89.50.

Uptown Motel, 47 Spur View Dr., P.O. Box 1886 (283-3660). Nice rooms. Cable TV. Singles $79.50. Doubles $89.50.

Irene's Lodge Bed and Breakfast, 702 Lawton Dr. (283-4501). Comfy rooms and homemade breakfasts. Singles $62.50. Doubles $100.

Kenai Riverbend Campground, Porter Rd. (283-9489, 262-5715, or 262-1068). Take Kalifornsky Beach Rd. off Spur Hwy. Rooms as well as campsites with full hookups. In summer fishermen descend to the Kenai Riverbend, one of the best salmon fishing holes in the world: one hooked the 1985 world record King salmon (97 lbs.) just a few minutes upstream. Riverbend has it all: boat launching and rentals, rods and tackle, bait, laundry, and showers. Singles $60. Doubles $65. Camping sites $12; RVs $18, with hookups $20. Reservations often necessary, especially during King Salmon runs.

Overland RV Park, P.O. Box 326 (283-4227), and **Kenai RV Park,** P.O. Box 1913 (283-4648), both in Old Kenai. Full hookups $6.

Food

Carr's Grocery (283-7829), in the Kenai Mall on Kenai Spur Rd., has a great deli and sandwich bar. (Open 24 hr.; deli closes at 8pm.)

Pizza Paradisio, on Kenai Spur Rd. (283-7008), across from the Kenai Mall. Thick pizza with plenty of toppings (large from $11) and other Italian food. Spaghetti dinners run $8. Or go with the gyro and french fries ($7). Open daily 11am-11pm. Free delivery.

Thai House, 106 S. Willow St. (283-7205) Tantalizing buffet $6, with salad bar $7.50. Spicy hot curries $7-9. Open Mon.-Fri. 11am-9:30pm, Sat.-Sun. 11am-10:30pm.

Harry Gaines Bar-B-Q Express, (283-3018), in the Kenai Mall. Southwestern specialties. Try "the Cowpoke" (sandwich, beans, and drink) $4, with ribs and bread $6. Open Mon.-Thurs. 9am-7pm, Fri.-Sat. 9am-8pm, Sun. noon-5pm.

Louie's Restaurant (283-3660), in the Uptown Motel on Kenai Spur Hwy. 3 pieces of "broasted" chicken, fries, and garlic bread ($9). Open daily 6am-11pm.

Windmill Restaurant, 145 Willow St. (283-4662). Where Kenai goes Dutch. Try the seafood *Quiche Zuider Zee* ($7). Good sandwiches ($4.50-$7.25). Dinners a bit expensive ($15-25), but the steaks are exceptional. Open Mon.-Sat. 11am-11pm.

Sights and Activities

The grandest sight in Kenai is **Cook Inlet,** a frame for miles of white sand, two mountain ranges, and volcanic Mt. Augustine and Mt. Redoubt. Photograph all this as well as beluga whales, salmon, and gulls from the overlook at the end of Forest Dr., or from the bluff at Alaska and Mission Ave. A small caribou herd roams the flatlands between Kenai and Soldotna, and can often be spotted along Kenai Spur Hwy. or Kalifonsky Beach Rd.

The town itself is an unimpressive jumble of highways, intersections, and shopping malls, having more in common with the suburban sprawl of New Jersey than with Alaska's frontier towns.

There is a worthwhile self-guided walking tour of Old Kenai, which begins at the Visitors Center. Here you will find **Ft. Kenay** and the **Kenai Historical Museum.** Though they do their best to lure tourists, the museum is threadbare, and the fort a cheap replica of the original 1868 structure. Both are on Overland Dr. and Mission St. (283-7294; open Mon.-Sat. 10am-5pm). Across the RV park from the fort is the **Holy Assumption Russian Orthodox Church,** the oldest building in Kenai. Originally built in 1846 and rebuilt in 1896, this national historic landmark contains a 200-year-old Bible. Call the priest at the rectory (283-4122) for a tour ($2 mandatory "donation"). The **Kenai Library** on Main St. Loop, next to the courthouse, shows free films on the area at 2pm. (Open Mon.-Sat. 8:30am-8pm.)

Recreational opportunities in the Kenai area abound. Check at the Chamber of Commerce for fishing charter information (prices are comparable to those in Soldotna), or with the Forest Service for canoeing and hiking opportunities. The **Captain Cook State Recreation Area,** 30 mi. north of Nikiski at the end of Kenai Spur Rd., offers swimming, fishing, and free camping, and canoe landing points on the Swanson River. Contact the Kenai Chamber of Commerce for rules and regulations.

Soldotna

Soldotna, once merely a fork in the road on the way to Homer, Kenai, or Seward, has become the center of government and recreation in the Kenai Peninsula. Soldotna, which means "soldier" in Russian, is the peninsula's premier fishing spot. World-record salmon are caught regularly in the Kenai River, a few minutes from downtown. Kenai Riverbend Campground, halfway between Soldotna and Kenai (see Kenai Accommodations) is offering a $10,000 reward to the person who catches a salmon weighing more than the current record of 97 pounds. Even in Alaska, ten thousand dollars goes a long way toward paying for a budget vacation.

Practical Information and Orientation

Visitor Information: Visitors Center, P.O. Box 236 (262-1337), between Miles 95 and 96 on Sterling Hwy., just across the river from downtown. Modern facility with photo displays and stairs down to the river. The world-record king salmon is here on permanent display. Open mid-May to Labor Day daily 9am-9pm. **Chamber of Commerce,** P.O. Box 236, Soldotna 99669 (262-9814), next door to the visitors center. Open Mon.-Fri. 9am-5pm.

Division of Parks and Outdoor Recreation: at Mile 85, Sterling Hwy. P.O. Box 1247 (262-5581), on Morgans Rd. Information on campgrounds and fishing.

Airport: Soldotna does not maintain its own airstrip, but an hourly shuttle connects downtown with the Kenai Airport (see Kenai Practical Information.)

Car Rental: Ford Rent-A-Car, (262-5491). $30 per day, 100 free mi., plus 10¢ per additional mi. Also **Hertz** (262-5857), in King Salmon Motel and **A-1 Auto Rental** (262-5593), 44761 Sterling Hwy., Soldotna.

Buses: Alaska Intercity Line, 44619 Sterling Hwy. (262-9445). To Anchorage ($27.50), Homer ($27.50), and Kenai (shuttles run every hr., $4).

Taxi: AAA Taxi (262-1555). **The Cab Co.** (262-7101).

Laundromat: Alpine Laundromat, on Sterling Hwy., next to the Dairy Queen. Open Mon.-Sat. 8am-10pm, Sun. 9am-10pm.

Crisis Line: 283-7257.

Pharmacy: Soldotna Professional Pharmacy, 245 Binkley St. (262-3800). Open Mon.-Fri. 9am-6:30pm, Sat. 10am-3pm.

Ambulance: 262-4500.

Hospital: Central Peninsula General, 250 Hospital Pl. (262-4404).

Emergency: 911.

Post Office: corner of Corral and Binkley St., downtown. Open Mon.-Fri. 9am-5pm, Sat. 9am-1pm. General Delivery ZIP Code: 99669.

Population: 3200.

Area Code: 907.

Soldotna is 140 mi. southwest of Anchorage on Sterling Hwy., at its junction with Kenai Spur Rd. Take the Seward Hwy. south from Anchorage and turn right onto Sterling at the only fork in the road.

Accommodations and Camping

Soldotna caters to both ends of the bed market: backpackers with tents and anglers with cash. The former can stay at nearby campgrounds and shell out $2 for hot, clean showers at the **River Terrace RV Park** on the river, while the latter can stay directly across the highway at the **Kenai River Lodge,** 393 Riverside Dr. (262-4792), for $85 per night (fishing guides extra).

The Duck Inn, Mile 3 on Kalifornsky Beach Rd., by the Red Diamond Mall(262-5041). All rooms with private bath. Singles and doubles $49.50. No reservations.

Soldotna Inn, 35041 Kenai Spur Hwy. (262-9169), just north of downtown. P.O. Box 565, Soldotna 99669. Luxurious high-priced rooms, with a snazzy restaurant downstairs. Singles $64. Doubles from $74.

Lake Country Bed and Breakfast (283-9432), 2 mi. out of town. HC-2 Box 584, Soldotna 99669. Large home with sun deck, library, and recreation room. Rooms $39-69.

Swiftwater Park Municipal Campground, south on Sterling Hwy. at Mile 94, and **Centennial Park Municipal Campground,** off Kalifornsky Beach Rd. near the visitors center, are both in the woods and have boat launches. Conveniently located on the river, the campgrounds have excellent fishing. There are even tables set aside for cleaning fish. One-week maximum stay. Sites $7, but these are considered "unofficial" sites and are sometimes used for hunting—be sure to avoid being shot.

Food

The Kenai-Soldotna area has boomed within the past 20 years, attracting swarms of fast-food joints. Although the weekend warriors storming down from Anchorage in search of king salmon may favor a Big Mac or Frosty over real food, there are many good local restaurants for true budget travelers who can't stomach another "kangaroo burger." Groceries can be procured at the **Safeway** downtown, located on Sterling Hwy. (Open 24 hr.)

Sal's Klondike Diner, 44619 Sterling Hwy. (262-2220), ½ mi. from the river and several hundred miles from the Klondike. Best diner in town. Menu "loded" with gold rush trivia. Superb "fisherman's buffet" breakfast (daily 4am-11am, $5). Sandwich with salad and fries $4-6. Open daily 4am-10pm.

Four Seasons, 43960 Sterling Hwy. (262-5006), just north of the Soldotna Y. Some of the best homestyle food in all Alaska. Hearty quiche (an oxymoron perhaps, but true), solid salad and sourdough bread ($5.50). Immense dinners $11-19. Great sausage lasagna and vegetable skewers. Open Mon.-Sat. 11am-3pm, 5:30pm-10pm.

Black Forest Restaurant, 44278 Sterling Hwy. (262-5111). Nostalgic foreign travelers should stop in, as the owner is gregarious in English, French, and Phillipino and loves swapping stories. Whopping ½-lb. cheeseburger ($4.25). 12" submarine sandwiches $4.50-$5. Open daily 11am-9pm.

Bull Feathers (262-3844) in the Peninsula Center Mall, on Sterling Hwy. Substantial ½-lb. burgers, with a packed "fix-in's burger bar" ($5). Very tasty "Jo Jo's" (deep-fried potato slices). Open Mon.-Fri. 9am-9pm, Sat. 9am-7pm, Sun. 11am-5pm.

China Sea Restaurant (262-5033), on the upper level of the Blazy Mall, ¼ mi. from the river. Chinese and American food. All-you-can-eat buffet for lunch (11:30am-1:30pm, $7) and dinner (5-10pm, $9). Dishes are unexciting, but edible. Hungry travelers should take advantage of the buffets. Open Mon.-Fri. 11:30am-9pm, Sat.-Sun. noon-9pm.

J.B. Supper Club (262-9887), 5 mi. south on Sterling Hwy. Meat and potatoes at basic prices. Friday night dinner special (with steak, soup, fries, and garlic bread) $9. Live music on weekends, featuring local rock n' roll bands. Open Tues.-Sat. noon-midnight.

Bunk House Inn, 44701 Sterling Hwy. (262-4584). Delicious breakfast buffet, with great biscuits n' gravy ($5). Spicy cajun chicken with salad bar ($12). Open daily 5am-midnight.

Sights and Activities

The **Damon Memorial Historical Museum,** at Mile 3 on Kalifornsky Beach Rd., holds artifacts from native burial grounds and a large diorama. (Open Mon.-Fri. 9am-5pm. Admission $1.) The **Kenai National Wildlife Refuge Visitors Center** (262-7021), off Funny River Rd. at the top of Ski Hill Rd., directly across from the Soldotna visitors center, is a great source of information on this 197-million-acre refuge for moose, Dall sheep, and other wild animals. It also shows dioramas and victims of taxidermy. A ½-mi. nature trail is nearby. (Open Mon.-Fri. 8am-6pm, Sat.-Sun. 10am-6pm; Labor Day-Memorial Day Mon.-Fri. 8am-4pm, Sat.-Sun. 10am-5:30pm.)

The **Kenai River** wriggles with wildlife of the slippery kind. Pink, king, red, and silver salmon glide through at various times during the summer, and steelhead and dolly varden multiply all summer long. Numerous **fishing charters** run the river, usually charging $100-125 for a half-day of halibut or salmon fishing, or $150 for both (contact the visitors center for more information). There is no need to spend so much, however. The downtown area is loaded with equipment rental shops that will fully outfit you with everything from bait to licenses for under $25 per day, and you can angle from the shore. The best places to throw in a line are in areas where the current runs slowly (e.g. near a bridge) since salmon often rest here on their journeys upstream.

Fast-paced river sports weave into the **Kenai National Wildlife Refuge** and dozens of one- to four-day long **canoe routes** wind their way through the forest. A few places in town, including the Riverbend Campground, will rent you boats. **The Sports Den** has canoes for $25 per day, $50 for a long weekend. Boats are also available on the highway: more than one resident puts his vessel in the front yard and hangs a "for rent" sign on it. Boat rentals are far from inexpensive, but the experience of gliding through some of the nation's most remote waterways is well worth it. For free canoe route maps, write the Refuge Manager, Kenai National Wildlife Refuge, P.O. Box 2139, Soldotna 99669 (262-7021).

The end of July brings **Soldotna Progress Days,** still in celebration of the completion of a natural gas line in 1961. Activities include a parade, a rodeo, and an airshow.

Ninilchik and Clam Gulch

Ninilchik is yet another small town (pop. 845) with spectacular fishing and fantastic scenery. Its strong Russian heritage, however, distinguishes it from other small peninsula towns. The only real sight-seeing attractions are the old **Russian fishing village** on Village Rd. north of town, and the **Holy Transfiguration of Our Lord Orthodox Church** (built in 1901). Both overlook Cook Inlet. The church and cemetery are still in use, but the Russian village is overshadowed by the huge wolverine mascot staring at the highway from the high school's façade.

The **Deep Creek Recreation Area,** nearby, is one of the most popular on the peninsula. Locals say it has the world's best salt-water King salmon fishing. Silver and pink salmon, dolly varden, and steelhead trout often swim by. Ninilchik's "Biggest Little Fair in Alaska," the **Kenai Peninsula State Fair,** is held each August. It's similar to a county fair in the Midwest—horse show, 4-H exhibits, livestock competition, arts and crafts, . . . the usual suspects. (For more information, contact the Fair Association, Box 39210, Ninilchik 99639.)

Groceries can be bought at the **General Store** on Sterling Hwy. (567-3378). **R&R's Burger Bar,** next door, has great cajun chicken ($6). Open daily, hours vary.

If you decide to stay in town for the night, the **Beachcomber Motel and RV Park,** on Village Rd. (567-3417), offers the cheapest rooms. Each room has a shower, full kitchenette, TV, and a great location on the beach. (Singles $45. Doubles $58. Full hookups for RVs $15.) For campers the choice is obvious: stay at one of the **state campgrounds** near town—each with water and toilets ($5). Superb sites in **Ninilchik State Recreation Area** are less than 1 mi. north of the library. There are RV hookups closer to town at **Hylea's Camper Park,** Mile 135.4 on Sterling Hwy. (567-3393).

The library's **Visitor Information** section is more informative than the local visitors center. They also shows free films on Alaska every Wed. at 7pm (567-3333; open Mon.-Sat. 11am-4pm).

Come to nearby **Clam Gulch** (pop. 141) to see what all the clamor over clams is about. Clamming requires a sports fishing license and there is a daily limit of 60 clams per person. Rubber gloves and waterproof footgear are highly recommended, as well as a clam-digging shovel, which you can pick up at any sporting goods store in Kenai for $5-10. Clam Gulch claims only one cot-cluttered corner store, the **Clam Shell Lodge,** Mile 118.3 (262-9926). The lodge has clean hotel rooms, RV parking with electricity, a bar/restaurant, and showers. The cook's specialty? Clam chowder, of course. Other good places for madcap clammers are Deep Creek, Ninilchik, and Homer Spit.

Homer

At first glance, Homer appears no different from any other lively college town in America. There are several sunny outdoor cafés, small movie theaters specializing in foreign films, health food grocery stores, and a number of used book stores and art supply houses. Yet Homer is different in one important aspect—it has no college. This Shangri-la is the happy product of a large artists' enclave combined with a solid fishermen's community

Homer owes its inherent attractiveness of Homer to its location. Surrounded by 400 million tons of coal, Homer rests on **Kachemak** (smoky) **Bay,** named after the mysteriously burning coal deposits that the first settlers came upon. Homer is split into two parts: the town and the Spit, a 3.5-mi. sandbar jutting into Kachemak Bay. Across the Bay from the Spit is the stupendous **Kachemak Bay State Park,** where the southern end of the **Kenai Mountains** reaches the sea. Astride this magnificent mountain range lies the **Harding Icefield,** a mass of glacial ice with a surface area greater than the state of Rhode Island. Even from 40 miles away, in downtown Homer, the edge of this massive icefield can be seen peeking over the rim of the Kenai mountains in the form of huge glacial fingers.

Practical Information and Orientation

Visitor Information, halfway down the Spit (235-7740 or 235-5300). Offers the epic work *250 Ways to Enjoy Homer,* covering everything from rockhounding to a day-long llama trek ($3.50). Open daily 7am-10pm. In town, go to the **Pratt Museum,** 3779 Bartlett St. (235-8365), for brochures. Open daily 10am-5pm.

Park Information: Kachemak Bay Visitor and Convention Association, P.O. Box 1001, Homer 99603 (235-6030). **Alaska Maritime National Wildlife Office,** 202 Pioneer Ave. Wildlife exhibits, marine photography, and helpful advice on backcountry adventures in Kachemak Bay. Videos about the region, including one on the oil spill, are loaned out upon request. Open Mon.-Fri. 8:30am-5pm, Sat.-Sun. 10am-5pm.

U.S. Fish and Game: 235-8191.

Intercity Bus: Alaska Intercity Line (800-478-2877 or 235-4235). From Anchorage $37.50.

Local Bus: Homer Shuttle runs the 6 mi. between downtown and the Spit ($3). May 28-Sept. 5 daily 10am-8pm. Check at the tourist office for a schedule. Service is unreliable at best; be prepared to get around another way.

Alaska Marine Highway: P.O. Box 355, Homer 99603 (235-8449), terminal at the end of the Spit. The M.V. *Tustumena* sails into Homer several times per week from Valdez or Cordova ($126), Seward ($86), and Kodiak ($42).

Taxis: A-Smile Taxi, 235-6995. **Lynx Taxi** (235-8101).

Bike Rental: Quiet Sports (235-8620), 144 W. Pioneer Ave., across from Don José's. Mountain bikes (½ day for $10, full day for $15). Also rents **kayaks** (single $30-35 per day, double $50 per day). They also have the best selection of **camping equipment** in town.

Laundromat: Homer Cleaning Center, Main St. (235-5152), downtown. Open Mon.-Sat. 8am-10pm, Sun. 9am-8pm.

Employment Center: Job Service, 349 E. Pioneer Ave, Homer 99603 (235-7791).

Hospital: 235-8101.

Women's Crisis Line: 235-8101.

Emergency: 911.

Police: 235-3150.

Post Office: 235-6125. On Homer Bypass near Kachemak Way. Open Mon.-Fri. 9am-5pm. General Delivery ZIP Code: 99603.

Population: 4000.

Area Code: 907.

Homer sits cozily on the southwestern Kenai Peninsula on the north shore of Kachemak Bay. The Sterling Hwy. links it with Anchorage (226 mi. away) and the rest of the Kenai Peninsula.

Accommodations and Camping

Of Homer's two **municipal campgrounds,** one is in town and one is on the Spit. To get to the former, take Pioneer to Bartlett St., go uphill, and take a left at the hospital entrance on Fairview St. The campground on the Spit covers most of the Spit's edges out 2 mi. Both sites are $5, usually uncollected. Spit sites can be windy.

The tourist office has a list of B&Bs, starting at $45 per night.

Heritage Hotel, 147 W. Pioneer (235-7787 or 800-478-7789 in AK), in the middle of downtown. A large, log cabin building with 3 types of accommodations: rooms with shared baths, rooms with private baths, and suites. Rooms are spacious and sterile. Prices start at $54.50 and rise to $64.50.

Driftwood Inn, 135 W. Bunnell (235-8019), a short walk from downtown. Take the Homer Bypass, turn right on Main St., then right again on Bunnell. Rustic and family-run with barbecues on the large porch. Originally Homer's first schoolhouse. Courtesy van. Rooms $54-69.

Ocean Shores Motel, 300-TAB Crittendon (235-7775), off Sterling Hwy. 1 block from downtown. Excellent views of mountain and ocean. Singles from $45.

Lakewood Inn, 984 Ocean Dr. #1 (235-6144), on the corner of Ocean Dr. and Lake St. Spitting distance from the Spit. Singles $65. Doubles $70. Rates $15 less during winter months.

Nancy's Nap Bed and Breakfast, P.O. Box 1934 (235-6788) at 265 E. Pioneer Ave. Great backyard with deck perfect for sunning or a nap. Rooms $45-55, with shared bath.

Brass Ring Bed and Breakfast, 987 Hillfair Court (235-5450). Take the Homer Bypass to Lake St., then turn right on Hillfair Court. Five bedrooms share 2 bathrooms, but laundry facilities, nice decor, and friendly owners combine to make a very attractive B&B. No smoking. Singles $60. Doubles $65.

City Camping, Parks and Recreation Dept., 600 Fairview Ave.

Spit Camping, Harbormaster's Office, 4350 Spit Rd. (255-3160).

Homer Spit Campground (235-8206), at the end of the Spit. Tent sites $6, hookups $13. Free showers.

Homer Cabins, 3601 Main St. (235-6768). All units with double beds, cable TV, kitchens. Rustic little log cabins cost $55 per night.

Food

Homer has many grocery stores, ranging from the **Smoky Bay Cooperative,** 248 W. Pioneer Ave., which carries only health food (235-7252; open Mon.-Sat. 8am-8pm, Sun. 10am-6pm) to the 24-hr. **Eagle Quality Center,** 436 Sterling Hwy. (235-2408).

On the Spit, you can buy fresh seafood for campfire cookouts directly from fishermen or at one of the large retail outlets: **Icicle Seafood Market,** 842 Fish Dock Rd. (235-3486), near the mouth of the harbor; or **The Exchange** (235-6241), just up the road.

Café Cups, 162 Pioneer Ave. (935-8330). A gathering ground for artists and young travelers. Tasty, unusual sandwiches ($4-5). Excellent coffee $1. Spaces outside, with chessboards and cribbage sets available. Open Mon.-Fri. 7am-11pm, Sat. 8am-midnight, Sun. 9am-4pm.

Fresh Sourdough Express Bakery and Coffee Shop, 1316 Ocean Dr. (235-7571), on the main drag to the Spit. Dine indoors or out on the deck, or just pick up some fresh-baked goods. Try the all-you-can-eat breakfast buffet ($8) for some real food. Open daily 6am-10pm. **The Sourdough Connection** (253-8701), its affiliate on the Spit next to the Salty Dawg, serves sandwiches and coffee and specializes in charter lunches ($5.75-7.50).

Boardwalk Fish 'n' Chips (235-7749), at the end of Cannery Row Boardwalk across from the harbormaster's office. A local favorite. Truly excellent halibut with chips $5.75. Open daily 11:30am-10pm.

Pizza Nick's, on Pioneer Ave. (235-6921 or 235-7312), downtown. 17" pizza $14.50-22. Great Mexican dinners $8.75-13. Open daily 11am-11pm.

Duncan House, 412 Pioneer Ave. (235-5344). Specializes in breakfast and local seafood lunch platters ($5-8.75). Open Mon.-Sat. 7am-3pm, Sun. 8am-2pm.

Addie's Big Paddies (235-8132), on the Spit. Conveniently located near the boat harbor for the early fisherman, and near the **Salty Dawg** for the late night partier. The food's a little greasy, but is guaranteed to fill you up. Big sandwiches and burgers ($5-6). Open 24 hr.

Blue Dragon Chinese Restaurant, 3858 Lakeside Mall #1 (235-8523), in the Lakeside Mall on Pioneer Ave. Filling daily lunch specials including entree, soup, and fried rice ($5.50). Open daily 11am-10pm.

Lands End Resort, P.O. Box 273 (235-2500 or 235-2525), as the name would suggest, at the end of the Spit. The poshest on the peninsula, the food is justifiably expensive. Lunch specials $7.50-9.25, dinner specials $10-20. Or just sit on the patio sipping cocktails to watch the sea otters cavort. Open Mon.-Fri. 7am-10pm, Sat.-Sun. 6am-10pm.

Sights and Seasonal Events

The **Pratt Museum,** 3779 Bartlett St. (235-8635), is probably the best museum on the peninsula. Historical exhibits and an excellent gallery of local art have recently been joined by a permanent exhibit on the Exxon *Valdez* oil spill. If you're at the Pratt on a Friday afternoon, be sure to help feed the resident octopus. (Admission $3, seniors $2, ages under 18 free. Open daily 10am-6pm.)

Nearly everyone who comes to Homer spends some time on the **Homer Spit.** Here one can admire the view and wonder how in the world geology created and preserved the 3.5-mi. strip of sand jutting into the unruly Pacific. The Spit is lined with fishing charter services and typical boardwalk candy and ice-cream stores. Several times throughout the summer, the high tide fills a fishing lagoon with incoming salmon. When the tide goes out, the salmon are trapped, and the banks are lined with hungry fishermen angling for supper.

Homer has any number of **art galleries,** such as **Homer Artists** at 564 Pioneer, and two good **theaters:** the **Family Theater** (235-6728), on Main and Pioneer, and the **Pier One** (235-7333), halfway down the Spit. The Pier One features concerts as well as plays (admission $7).

Homer never sleeps; nightlife ranges from beachcombing at low tide in the midnight sun to investigating whether the sawdust and sourdough-filled **Salty Dawg**

Saloon under the log lighthouse at the end of the Spit ever actually closes (open 11am-whenever, as the sign says). The Dawg is covered with business cards from all over the world—adventurous travelers should see if they can find the 1991 *Let's Go* researcher/writer's blood donor's card behind the bar. **Land's End Resort,** at the very end of the Spit, has an expansive if expensive view of Kachemak Bay; for cheaper spirits head to **Alice's Champagne Palace,** 196 Pioneer Ave. (235-7650), a wooden barn with honky-tonk music as well as nickel beers and dollar tacos on Monday nights.

Since Homer is often billed as the halibut capital of the world, it should perhaps come as no surprise that a pair of halibut derbies are the town's most popular annual events. The **Homer Jackpot Halibut Derby** offers prizes from $500 to $10,000 for the biggest fish and the tagged fish. The smaller **Rescue 21 Halibut Derby** is held in July. But Homer celebrations are for more than just the halibut: the annual **Winter Carnival,** held the first week in February, features sled dog races and snow mobile competitions. In March, Homer's small artist population exhibits at the **Art Rondy.**

Near Homer

For a closer look at the bay and its wildlife, hike or boat into **Kachemak Bay State Park.** Within the park, trails are rough and visitors facilities limited. (For park regulations and precautions call 262-5581 in Soldotna, or write the State of Alaska Department of Natural Resources, Pouch 7-0001, Anchorage 99510.) **Charter boats** are another great way to tour (and fish in) the bay. Over 80 charter companies operate out of Homer, offering sightseeing, salmon fishing, halibut fishing, and clam digging excursions. Fishing trips generally cost $100-125 for a full day, though specials are sometimes available. Several charters have offices on the boardwalk across from the Salty Dawg Saloon, although there are other offices located up and down the Spit from there. **Rainbow Tours,** Box 1526, Homer 99603 (235-7272), located on the Cannery Row Boardwalk, offers sightseeing "adventures" ($15-30). **Central Charters Booking Agency,** 4241 Homer Spit Rd., Homer 99603 (235-7847), offers $30-78 sightseeing runs, $60-105 salmon runs, and $105 halibut runs. (Open daily 10am-6pm.) **South Central Sports,** 1411 Lakeshore Dr. (235-5403), runs a shuttle service convenient for backpackers, with non-scheduled stops across Kachemak Bay. (Round-trip fares $35-40.)

Halibut Cove, an artists' community and fishing village, is accessible from Homer only by boat or plane. The cove has some of the best bird watching in the region. Check out the octopus-ink paintings at **Diana Tillion's Cove Gallery** (open until 8pm). The **Saltery** (296-2223) is the cove's only restaurant. Specialties include chowder and sushi rolls. (Open daily 2-9pm. $5-12 per person; reservations recommended.) Make this a daytrip—the only places to stay in town are **Halibut Cove Cabins,** Box 1990, Homer 99603 (296-2214), which charges $55 for singles and $65 for doubles (bring your own bedding and food), and the **Quiet Lodge Bed and Breakfast** (296-2212), which charges $100 for doubles in separate cabins.

The easiest way to see the sloping bluffs that rise behind Homer is to cruise **Skyline Drive,** which runs along the rim of the bluffs. The wildflowers (mostly fireweed, accompanied by scattered bunches of geranium, paintbrush, rose, etc.) bloom from June to September. On a clear day, the view of the Kenai Mountains is unrivaled.

Proudly billing itself as the most westerly. point on the U.S. Highway System, the otherwise obscure village of **Anchor Point** lies 16 mi. northwest of Homer on the Sterling Hwy. The town is quickly becoming a suburb to Homer. Like the next town, it has its **Salmon Derby,** in mid-May. If you decide to spend the night, go to the **Anchor River Inn** (235-8531), just off Sterling Hwy. in front of the bridge (Mile 157). Rooms from $30; groceries 24 hr. The town's **visitors center** is in **Kyllonen's RV Park** (235-6435), on River Rd. (P.O. Box 610, Anchor Point 99556).

Visitor-shy but extremely interesting is **Nikolaeusk,** perhaps the only village in the U.S. where Russian is the primary language. Nikolaeusk's Old Believers are Russian Orthodox schismatics who in the past 200 years have lived variously in China, Brazil, Oregon, and Kenai, venturing ever farther from decadent, *pagoni* influences. Today, the backward town is dirt poor and rife with schism over whether to accept a priest trained in Rumania. The economy survives on fishing and a shop selling the handmade traditional Russian clothing that the village's inhabitants regularly wear. To find Nikolaeusk, take North Fork Rd. (in the center of Anchor Point) east to the Nikolaeusk post office. Go down the gravel road at the post office until you get to the village. *Don't* hitchhike, because you'll never get out, and don't act like a tourist—the Believers have other things on their mind besides serving visitors.

Seldovia

Right across Kachemak Bay from Homer, this small town has been virtually untouched by the ideology of progress prevailing on the rest of the peninsula. The Russians named Seldovia for its herring, but today the year-round king crab industry keeps the town afloat. Stop by the small **museum,** 206 Main St. (234-7625), sponsored by the Seldovia Native Association (open Mon.-Fri. 8am-5pm). The **Pacific Pearl Fish Processing Plant** (234-7680) will give visitors the unheard of privilege of touring the facility. On a hill overlooking the water, the **St. Nicholas Orthodox Church** was built in 1891 (open daily 1-2pm).

Nearly everything in town can be covered on foot, but taxis are available (234-7859). **Rainbow Tours** (235-7272) offers a daily tour of Seldovia ($30). As part of the AK Marine Highway System, twice per week the ferry M.V. *Tustumena* runs between Homer and Seldovia ($28 round-trip). Enjoy the post-midnight sun on the Tuesday 2:45am ferry, or book a saner crossing; the Wednesday morning ferry departs at 11:45am and returns three hours later, leaving time to see the town. If you miss the ferry, you can sleep on **Outside Beach,** 2 mi. out of town. Public rest rooms, water, and showers can all be found at the harbormaster's office. To avoid roughing it in the sand, make reservations before you leave Homer at the **Bayview Lodge** (234-7633; singles $40, doubles $60) or the **Boardwalk Hotel** (234-7816; singles $44, doubles $48).

Seldovia triples in size on Independence Day. The old-fashioned celebration draws visitors from all over the peninsula and includes parades, log-rolling, a naked baseball game, and (presumably non-naked) greased pole climbing, as well as a potluck picnic.

Seward

Seward traces its origins to a Russian shipyard built somewhere nearby by the ubiquitous Russian explorer Alexander Baranof in the 1830s. The present town was built in 1904 as the southern terminus of the Alaska railroad, and it was from here that the famous Iditarod Dogsled Trail to Anchorage and Nome began. Today, Homer is also accessible by road, via the Seward Highway—the only nationally designated *Scenic Byway* in Alaska.

Like Homer, Seward is divided into two parts of interest to outsiders, one near the ferry dock and one near the small-boat harbor. The streets in Seward are named after the U.S. Presidents from Washington to Van Buren. A, B, C, and D Streets usurp the rightful place of John Quincy Adams, Andrew Jackson, and Jimmy Carter, however.

Practical Information and Orientation

Visitor Information: Chamber of Commerce, 3rd and Jefferson St. (224-3094), in the railroad car *Seward.* Pick up a map with a self-guided walking tour on it, and (yawn) mark your own hometown on the Chamber's world map. Open Memorial Day-Labor Day daily 11am-4pm.

National Park Service Visitor Center: 1212 4th Ave. (224-3375), at the small-boat harbor. Information on and maps of the spectacular Kenai fjords. Listings of tours and kayak rentals. Open daily 8am-7pm; Labor Day-Memorial Day Mon.-Fri. 8am-noon and 1-5pm. **Seward Ranger Station, Chugach National Forest (USFS),** 334 4th Ave., at Jefferson. Extensive trail information, maps, and advice on trails close to town, as well as the complete Iditarod route. Cabin reservations. Open Mon.-Fri. 8am-5pm.

Alaska Department of Labor: Seward Employment Center, 5th and Adams, P.O. Box 1009, Seward 99665 (224-5276).

Harbor Air: Seward Airport (224-3133 in Seward, 243-1167 in Anchorage), 2 mi. north of town on the Seward-Anchorage Hwy. Flights to and from Anchorage daily (one way $52). 45-min. flight tours $50 per person.

Alaska Railroad: (224-5550 or 265-2494). Depot at northern edge of town. Train daily to Anchorage at 6pm ($35).

Seward Bus Line: P.O. Box 1338, Seward 99664 (224-3608 or 278-0800). 550 Railway Ave., near the Ferry Dock. To Anchorage daily at 9am ($25).

Alaska Marine Highway: (224-5485). The M.V. *Tustumena* serves: Kodiak (one way $48), Seldovia (one way $90), Homer (one way $86), and Valdez (one way $54). Call for schedule.

Trolley: 224-8075, ext. 03210. Just wave it down and it will go anywhere in town for $1.

Taxi: Independent Cab, 224-5000. **Yellow Cab,** 224-8788.

Car Rental: National, 217 5th Ave. (224-5211), at New Seward Hotel. From $56 per day with 100 free mi., each additional mi. 33¢. Must be 21 with major credit card. Make reservations at least 1 week in advance.

Laundromat: Seward Laundry, 4th and C St. Showers $2. Open Mon.-Sat. 10am-9pm, Sun. 11am-6pm.

Pharmacy: Seward Drug, P.O. Box 127, Seward 99664 (224-8989), on 4th Ave. Open daily 9:30am-8pm.

Hospital: Seward General, at 1st Ave. and Jefferson St. (224-5205).

Emergency: 911.

Police: 244-3338.

Post Office: 5th and Madison. Open Mon.-Fri. 9:30am-4:30pm, Sat. 10am-2pm. General Delivery ZIP Code: 99664.

Population: 3000.

Area Code: 907.

Seward is located on the southeast side of the Kenai Peninsula, in **Resurrection Bay.** Anchorage, due north, connects via the 127-mi. long **Seward Hwy.** Seward, Nebraska is 4135 mi. to the southeast.

Accommodations

Seward has some nice, cheap rooms. This is a good place to stay in a hotel and give you and your tent a rest.

Van Gilder Hotel, 308 Adams St. (224-3525), just off 3rd. A well-preserved National Historic Site that could be the setting of any frontier Western. Elegant bar. Clean rooms. Singles $50, with bath $60. Doubles $60, with bath $85. You must make reservations.

The Korner House Bed and Breakfast, 501 Ash St. (224-3231). Turn west at Mile 2.1 off Seward Hwy. onto Ash. It's tough to find a better-kept room in Seward. Singles $38. Doubles $55. Breakfast included.

The New Seward Hotel and Saloon, 217 5th Ave. (224-8001). Ask to stay in the original hotel, not the addition. Fantastic bar downstairs. Singles $48, with bath $74. Doubles $58, with bath $87.

Tony's Hotel, Bar, and Liquor Store (224-3045), on Railway and 4th. Surprisingly clean, safe rooms considering it's on top of a gin joint. Singles $38. Weekly: singles $100.

Camping

Seward's municipal campgrounds are clean and inexpensive, though there are private alternatives which offer more solitude.

Municipal Campgrounds: City Greenbelt Camping Area, off 7th Ave. along the beach north of Jefferson. Grassy tenting area with water, fireplaces, and clean toilets. Strategically located on Resurrection Bay. **City RV Parking,** on 4th Ave. at Van Buren, by the small-boat harbor and beyond the ball park. Toilets and water. **City Campground,** Mile 2 of Seward Hwy., by Forest Acres. 22 sites. 14-day max. stay. All sites $4.25.

Kenai Fjords RV Park, 4th Ave. and D St. (224-8779). Gravel parking near the boat harbor. Sites $9, full hookups $4.50.

Bear Creek RV Park (224-5725). Turn off Seward Hwy. at Mile 6.6 and take Bear Leg Rd. ½ mi. Slightly off the beaten path. Laundry and hookups. No tents. RVs $12. Hot showers $2.

Food

Downtown Seward has oodles of seafood restaurants, hamburger joints, and pizza parlors. Pick up groceries at **Bob's Market,** 207 4th Ave. (Open Mon.-Sat. 9am-7pm, Sun. noon-6pm.)

Bob's Kitchen, on corner of 4th Ave. and Washington St. Don't miss "Bob's Special" breakfast, it may be the biggest, best Alaskan breakfast you'll ever have—2 eggs, 2 bacon strips, 2 sausage links, toast, hash browns, biscuit with gravy, and coffee ($5). Now that's a meal. Open daily 6am-8pm.

Seward Salmon Bake and Bar-B-Q (224-7051), in municipal boat harbor, across from the National Park Center. Although the salmon is well worth the price ($10), its the barbecue which deserves praise; by far the best ribs and chicken in Alaska (served with homemade cole slaw; platters $5-6.75) Try the homemade cole slaw. Open daily 11am-9pm.

Breeze Inn, in the small-boat harbor (224-5298). Not your average hotel restaurant. Breeze in for the huge all-you-can-eat buffet (lunch $8, dinner $11). Breakfasts on the "2-2-2"-plan (2 each of eggs, bacon, and pancakes, $5). Great view of harbor and bay. Open daily 6am-9pm. Live music (country and rock) on weekend nights.

Peking, 338 4th Ave. (224-5444), at Jefferson St. Tasty lunch specials, with rice and soup ($5.45-6.45). Open daily 11:30am-10pm.

Harbor Dinner Club, 240 5th Ave. (244-3012), across from the New Seward Hotel. A local favorite. Try the Champion Burger—cheese, onions, mushrooms and peppers heaped onto a ¾-lb. fresh beef pattie ($7). Open daily 11am-2:30pm, 5pm-11pm.

Ray's Waterfront Bar & Grill (224-5606), on 4th Ave. next to the Coast Guard Station. The finest restaurant in Seward, next to the small boat harbor. Dinners are expensive ($16-20) but the portions are immense. Bar is open until 2am, and a special (cheaper) bar menu is available. Open daily 11am-11pm.

Sights and Seasonal Events

The walking tour of Seward printed on the map available at the Chamber of Commerce passes many homes and businesses that date back to the early 1900s. A complete tour takes two to three hours. The **Resurrection Bay Historical Society Museum,** in the basement of City Hall (corner of 5th and Adams), exhibits Native artifacts and implements used by pioneers. See the cross-section of a 353-year-old tree, which sprouted in the same year that Harvard University was founded in Cambridge, Massachussetts. (Open June 15-Labor Day daily 11am-4pm. Admission 50¢, children 25¢.) From June 15 to Labor Day you can see *Seward's Burning* (the "Earthquake Movie," as residents call it) at the **Seward Community Library,** 5th Ave. and Adams St. (224-3646). No, it doesn't star Charlton Heston, Ava Gardner, or even Charo; rather, this movie shows actual footage of the 1964 Good Friday earthquake (with a supporting cast of fires and tidal waves), which destroyed much of Seward when it hit southcentral Alaska. (Library open Mon.-Fri. 1-8pm, Sat. 1-6pm. Screenings Mon.-Sat. at 2pm. Donations $1.)

Seward is a great place for **day hikes.** Nearby **Mt. Marathon,** scaled by locals in a race every July 4, offers a great view of the city and ocean. From the corner of 1st and Jefferson, take Lowell St. to its very end to reach the trail. **Exit Glacier,** billed as Alaska's most accessible glacier, is 9 mi. west on the road that starts at Seward Hwy. Mile 3.7. From the ranger station, take the steep and slippery 4-mi. trail to the magnificent Harding Ice Field above the glacier. Although you can get near the face of the glacier, the rangers will prevent you from actually touching it (or getting within 50 ft. of it, for that matter) as chunks of ice weighing several tons are continually breaking off. This hike is only for the intrepid. Check the ranger station (see Practical Information) for other trails if you are not intrepid.

Known as the "gateway to Alaska" because of its position as the southern terminus of the railroad, Seward is also the point of entry to the **Kenai Fjords National Park.** Much of the park consists of a coastal mountain system packed with wildlife. The best way to see this area is from boats in the bay; pick up the list of charters at the Park Service visitors center or from shops along the boardwalk next to the harbormaster's office. Most run $70-100 per day, $45-50 per half-day. For more information, contact **Kenai Fjord Tours** (224-8068 or 224-8069), **Mariah Charters** (243-1238), **Kenai Coastal Tours** (224-7114) or **Quest Charters** (224-3025; open in summer 6am-10pm).

Fishing is heavenly in the Seward area. Salmon and halibut can be caught in the bay, grayling and dolly varden right outside of town. Charters are available for both halibut and salmon throughout the summer; prices run from $90-100, with all gear provided. Call Quest Charters or Mariah Charters (see above). You can also fish for free on the docks.

The **Silver Salmon Derby** opens each year on the second Saturday in August and closes eight days later. Prizes go for the largest fish (up to $5000) and the tagged fish (up to $10,000 for the fish specifically marked by officials prior to the event). Seward's other big event is the **Mountain Marathon** on the 4th of July. Alaska's oldest footrace began when one sourdough challenged a neighbor to make it up and down the 3022-ft. peak in less than an hour. That was in 1915, and the guy couldn't do it. Last year, the winners of the men's race (45 min.) and the women's (55 min.) demonstrated that humankind is on the move. The race has been joined by a parade, the governor, and hundreds of enthusiasts running, sliding, falling, and bleeding down the steep mountain to the shores of Resurrection Bay. Thousands of sadistic spectators set up lawnchairs anywhere in town and watch the race with binoculars.

Near Seward: Moose Pass

Known, barely, for Ed Estes' waterwheel (an alleged "internationally known landmark"), tiny Moose Pass began as a flag-stop for the Alaska Railroad and now isn't much of anything. Moose Pass offers a **Solstice Festival** on the weekend nearest every solstice with lots of beer, a carnival, and other fun for kids and adults. Located at Mile 29 on Seward Hwy., the town has four campgrounds with excellent fishing: **Primrose** at Mile 18, **Ptarmigan Creek** at Mile 23, **Trail River** at Mile 24, and **Wye** at Mile 36. All are run by the Chugach National Forest; write **Alaska Public Lands Information,** 605 W. 4th, Anchorage 99501 (271-2737). There is a hotel, the **Moose Pass Inn** (288-3110), at Mile 30. Rooms are expensive ($65 and up) and reservations often necessary.

Kodiak Island

Nearly 100 miles off the Kenai Peninsula lives Kodiak Island, perhaps the harshest and most majestic area of southern Alaska. In this century, the island has been rocked by earthquakes, washed over by *tsunamis,* and covered in two feet of volcanic ash. Rain falls on Kodiak about half the year. Kodiak aptly takes its name from the Kodiak brown bear, the fiercest creature of the Alaskan wild.

The magnitude of Kodiak's roughness is equalled by its beauty and the wealth of its resources. The island is ringed by glacially sculpted fjords. Rugged mountains and lush flora cover its 3670 square mi. The fishing port is the third most productive in the U.S.

Kodiak

Kodiak was the first capital of Russian Alaska (1792-1804), before Alexander Baranof moved the Russian-American Company headquarters to Sitka. It was here that the Russians carried out their worst atrocities, enslaving Aleut natives and using them to hunt the sea otters to near extinction.

The area has been subject to natural tragedies. In 1912 Mt. Katmai erupted, covering Kodiak Island with 18 inches of ash and obliterating much of the area's wildlife; plots of ash remain in the forests today. In 1964 the biggest earthquake ever recorded in North America shook the area, creating a tidal wave that destroyed much of downtown Kodiak, including 158 homes. There was $24 million worth of damage in total. The Army Corps of Engineers and local resourcefulness turned Kodiak back into a thriving fishing port, but one wrecked 200-ft. vessel, *The Star of Kodiak,* was cemented into the ferry dock and converted into a cannery.

Practical Information and Orientation

Visitor Information: Information Center (486-4070), at Center St. and Marine Way, right in front of the ferry dock. Hunting and fishing information, charter arrangements, and a self-guided walking tour map. Open Mon.-Fri. 8am-5pm. **Chamber of Commerce,** P.O. Box 1485, Kodiak 99615 (486-5557), in the same building.

Sport Fishing Division: Alaska Department of Fish and Game, Box 686, Kodiak 99615 (486-4791). Information on fishing regulations and seasons.

Airport: Mark Air (800-478-0800 in Alaska, or 800-426-6784) and **ERA** (800-426-0333). Round-trip $185 if booked 2 weeks in advance, otherwise one way $123. If you're lucky, your visit will coincide with periodic price wars (with trenches as low as $49 one way fares).

Alaska Marine Highway: The M.V. *Tustumena* (486-3800) sails to Kodiak May-Sept. 3 times per week; Oct.-April less frequently. To: Homer ($42), Seward ($48), Whittier ($108), and Valdez or Cordova ($86). Week-long run to Dutch Harbor once every 3 weeks ($176).

Car Rental: National (486-4751), on Rezanof Hwy., downtown. $45 per day, unlimited mileage. **Hertz** (487-2661). $45 per day, 50 free mi., 40¢ per additional mi. **Rent-A-Heap,** 513 Carolyn St. (486-5200). $24 per day, 24¢ per additional mi.

Taxis: Ace Mecca, 486-3211.

Camping Equipment: Mack's Sports Shop, 117 Lower Mill Bay (486-4276), at the end of Center Ave. Open Mon.-Sat. 9am-6pm, Sun. 10am-3pm.

Laundromat: Ernie's, 218 Shelikof (486-4119), across from the harbor. Drop-off available. Shower $2. Open Mon.-Sat. 7am-10pm, Sun. 8am-8pm.

Weather: Aviation Forecasts (487-4338), **Local Forecasts** (487-4313), **Marine Forecasts** (487-4949).

Hospital: Kodiak Island, 1915 E. Rezanof Dr. (486-3281).

Emergency: 911

Post Office: on Lower Mill Bay Rd. Open Mon.-Fri. 9am-5:30pm, Sat. 10am-4pm. General Delivery ZIP Code: 99615. Substation in **Kraft's Grocery,** 111 Rezanof. Open Mon.-Sat. 10am-6pm.

Population: Kodiak Island 14,375. Kodiak township 6686.

Area Code: 907.

The city of Kodiak is on the eastern tip of Kodiak Island, roughly 200 mi. south of Homer. The airport is 4 mi. south of town, while the ferry terminal is downtown. If you are traveling to and from the Kenai by ferry, study the schedule carefully or you might find yourself stranded on Kodiak for longer than you would like.

Accommodations and Camping

If you want to stay in a hotel in Kodiak, *make a reservation* before the summer begins. The hotels are generally filled, and finding a room becomes almost impossible when the airport shuts down due to bad weather, which is often.

Kodiak has just built a tent city 2 mi. west on Rezanof Hwy. to accommodate cannery workers. Called **Sandy Beach Park,** the place looks and feels like a gravel parking lot, and smells like fish. It's only $3, and has free, hot showers. Two miles farther up Rezanof is the prettier and less smelly **Buskin River Recreation Area.** Contact Mary Monroe at **Kodiak Bed and Breakfast,** P.O. Box 1729, 308 Cope St.,

Kodiak 99615 (486-5367), for a local referral of rooms in private Kodiak homes.
Rooms start at $40.

Shelikof Lodge, 211 Thorsheim Ave. (486-4141), behind the McDonalds at the end of Center
Ave. Comfortable rooms with cable TV. Singles $55. Doubles $60.50.

Star Motel, 119 Brooklyn Terrace (486-5657). Dreary exterior masks equally dreary rooms.
All rooms $55.

Northland Ranch/Resort, P.O. Box 2376 (486-5578). 30.3 Mile Chiniak, 40 mi. from downtown, near the USAF . Northland can set you up horseback riding, hunting, or fishing on
the ranch. The attached restaurant is excellent. Rooms $35-75. Horseback riding $15 per
hr.

Sandy Beach Campground (Tent City), 2 mi. from ferry terminal. From terminal take Center
St. to Rezanof, and turn left. After 2 miles turn left on Sandy Beach Rd. Raised platforms
for tents, hot showers, toilets, drinking water. Siter $3, not strictly enforced.

Fort Abercrombie State Park Campground, 4 mi. northeast of town on Rezanof-Monashka
Rd. Water, shelters, and outhouses. No RV hookups; designed for campers. WWII ruins,
a trout fishing lake, and spectacular sunsets. 7-night max. stay. Sites $5.

Buskin River State Recreation Site, 4½ mi. southwest of the city. Water and toilets. Over
50% of Kodiak's sport fishing is done on the river. 7-night max. stay. Sites $5.

Pasagshak State Recreation Site, 40 mi. from the city at the mouth of the Pasagshak river.
Water and toilets. Noted for King salmon fishing. 14-day max. stay. 7 sites. Free.

Food

Kodiak has an odd dearth of restaurants. **Kraft's Grocery,** 111 Rezanof, is a big,
everything-you-might-ever-need kind of place. **City Market,** on Lower Mill Bay Rd.
(also called Rezanof East St.), is very low-budget and stocks inscrutable frozen
goods. Try a *Daing na galung-gong* for 65¢.

Kodiak Café, 203 Marine Way (486-5470), between the boat ramp and the "Star of Kodiak."
A fishermen's diner with fare to match. Enormous burgers with fries $5.25-7.50. Hot cakes
from $2.75. Open 24 hr. in summer.

Fox Inn, 211 Thorsheim (486-4141), in the Shelikof Lodge. Straightforward country specials
from burgers to chicken. Halibut dinner $10.75. Open Tues.-Sat. 7am-9:30pm, Sun. 8am-
9pm.

Out to Lunch (486-4868), in Bakery Mall on Rezanof and Center. Trying to be an upscale
deli, but let's face it, New York City is over 5000 miles away. Excellent desserts; try the pecan
pie ($2) and don't be afraid to ask for whipped cream if you really want it.

China House, 202 Rezanof St. (486-8288). Authentic Chinese food. Daily lunch specials, including rice and soup ($4.49). Dinner $9-13.

Sights and Seasonal Events

Built in 1793 as a storehouse for sea otter pelts, the **Baranof Museum,** 101 Maine
Way (486-5920), is the oldest Russian structure standing in Alaska, as well as the
oldest wooden structure on the entire West Coast. The museum displays Russian
and native artifacts. Check out their small library of period photos and literature
ranging from the Russian colony to the 1964 earthquake. (Open Mon.-Fri. 10am-
3pm, Sat.-Sun. noon-4pm. Admission $1, children under 12 free.) The **Russian Or-
thodox Church,** not far from the museum, houses the oldest parish in Alaska (1794).
Its elaborate icons date back to the early 19th century, and its old church bells are
still rung by hand. (Tours given by appointment. Call 486-3854.) Alaska's only outdoor theater, **The Frank Brink Amphitheater** on Minashka Bay, presents the historical play *Cry of the Wild Ram* every year on August weekends. The play covers
30 years of the life of Alexander Baranof, the Russian settler who established the
first colonies on Kodiak and the Kenai Peninsula. Dress warmly and bring a good
book to read. (Admission $10, seniors and children $5. Contact Land 5 Travel Service, P.O. Box 221, Kodiak 99615, or call 486-3232 for reservations.)

Beautiful **Fort Abercrombie State Park,** 3½ mi. north of town, was the site of the first secret radar installation in Alaska. The fort is also the site of a WWII defense installation; some bunkers and other reminders of the Alaskan campaign remain. In fact, several islands in the Alentian chain were attacked by Japanese *zeros*, and American military minds tensely assumed that Kodiak would be the next target. The real attack, however, hit Pearl Harbor, not Alaska. Six and a half miles southwest of Kodiak is an old naval station, now the base for the Coast Guard's North Pacific operations.

Home to the largest commercial fishing fleet in Alaska, Kodiak Island also has very popular sport fishing. Try Cascade Lake for trout, Buskin River or Saltery Creek for dolly varden, crab, and salmon. The **Pasagshak River** is also teeming with red salmon which can be snagged directly from the shore. For information on regulations and seasons, contact the Sport Fishing Division (see Practical Information).

At the end of Rexanof Hwy., at the southeast tip of Kodiak near **Ugak Island,** there is a large bison herd. The animals were transplanted onto the island and have defended themselves against marauding Kodiak bears. The imported cattle herds have not fared so well.

Fifty-four miles north of Kodiak is **Shuyak Island State Park,** an undeveloped area with ample hunting, fishing, and kayaking. There are four **cabins** available to the public for $15 per night. Reserve ahead at the Division of Parks and Outdoor Recreation, SR Box 3800, Kodiak 99615, or call 486-6339 for more information.

The **Kodiak Crab Festival,** held for one week in late May, celebrates the area's major industry with parades, a seal skinning contest, kayak and crab races, and a blessing of the fleet. **St. Herman's Day,** August 9, celebrates the first saint of the Russian Orthodox Church in North America (canonized in 1970). The **Great Buskin River Raft Race,** in June, is a rousing affair—five beer breaks are part of the rules. The **State Fair and Rodeo,** in mid-August, includes crafts and livestock.

Kodiak National Wildlife Refuge

The Wildlife Refuge, on the western half of Kodiak Island, was inaugurated in 1941 and has grown to nearly two million acres. An estimated 2400 Kodiak bears live on the island along with a variety of other mammals and several hundred bald eagles. The bears are usually seen in July and August, when they fish in streams. They hibernate from December to April, bearing cubs in February and March. Though the bears are half-vegetarian and usually avoid contact with humans, be careful. The largest and most powerful carnivore in North America, Kodiaks can easily kill humans with one claw tied behind their back. Because of their relatively small numbers, hunters are permitted to kill only one bear apiece every four years.

Other mammals native to the area are red foxes, land otters, weasels, tundra moles, and little brown bats. These are found in many other parts of Alaska as well. Deer, snowshoe hares, beavers, muskrats, Dall sheep, mountain goats, and red squirrels have been transplanted from other parts of the state to Kodiak. The 800 mi. of coastline in the refuge are home to thousands of waterfowl and about 20 seabird species. Off the coast, whales, porpoises, seals, sea otters, and sea lions frolic.

For those who want to get close to the animals, the refuge has 12 **cabins.** It is difficult to reach the refuge without paying a lot of money, however. Air charters should be booked in advance and cost upwards of $275. Boats can also take you to the refuge; inquire at the information center in Kodiak. The cabins are free, but they are invariably full. Make advance reservations, then cross your fingers and hope that you are one of the lucky few selected in the drawing held every three months. For information about the park as well as cabin reservations, contact the Kodiak National Wildlife Refuge Managers, 1390 Buskin River Rd., Kodiak 99615 (487-2600). If you're in town, drop by the **U.S. Fish and Wildlife Headquarters and Visitor Center,** just outside Buskin State Recreation Site, 4 miles southwest of town, for wildlife displays and more information. (Open Mon.-Fri. 8am-4pm.)

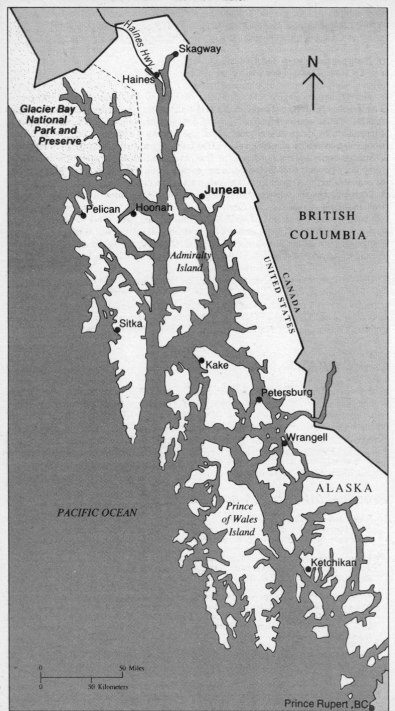

Southeastern Alaska (The Panhandle)

The Panhandle is flung 500 miles from the Gulf of Alaska to Prince Rupert, BC. The Tlingit (KLING-kit) and Haida (HI-duh) tribes have left a deep mark on the region, which forms a loose network of islands, inlets, and deep saltwater fjords, surrounded by deep valleys and rugged mountains. Temperate rain forest conditions, 60-odd major glaciers, and 15,000 bald eagles distinguish the Panhandle.

Southeastern Alaska is one of the few places in the world where the blast of a ferry boat heralds the day's important event. The 1000 islands and 10,000 miles of coastline in the Alexander Archipelago are connected to each other and to Seattle by ferries run by the Alaska Marine Highway. While the Interior and the Southcentral regions of Alaska have experienced great urban sprawl (by Alaskan standards), the communities of Southeastern Alaska cling to the coast. While Gold Rush days haunt such towns as Juneau and Skagway, others, like Sitka and Wrangell, hearken back to the era of the Russian occupation. Petersburg, on the other hand, is a busy fishing depot with strong ties to its Norwegian heritage; Ketchikan is a charming mill town.

The cheapest, most exciting way to explore Southeastern Alaska is on the Alaska Marine Highway system. The state-run ferries connect Seattle, Ketchikan, Petersburg, Wrangell, Sitka, Juneau, Haines, and Skagway, as well as some smaller Native and fishing communities. You can avoid the high price of accommodations in smaller communities by planning your ferry trip at night and sleeping on the deck.

Ketchikan

A Ketchikan proverb claims that "If you can't see the top of Deer Mountain, it's raining, and if you *can* see the top, it's about to rain." Indeed, about 164 inches per year marinate this good-sized fishing and lumber town of 14,600, cradled at the watery base of the mountain; locals have to ignore the rain, or nothing would ever get done. The southernmost city in Alaska, Ketchikan is also the first port for ferries and cruise ships visiting the state. Elevated walkways and numerous staircases between multi-leveled streets keep tourists—the most important source of the town's income—high and dry.

Practical Information and Orientation

Visitor Information: Ketchikan Visitors Bureau, 131 Front St. (225-6166), across from the cruise ship docks downtown. Offers map of a good walking tour, along with friendly advice. Open daily, in conjunction with docked cruise ships.

United States Forest Service: Ranger District Office, Federal Building (747-6671 or 225-2148), on Stedman at Mill. Information on cabins and trails. Films of the Ketchikan area are a worthwhile escape from the rain, if nothing else.

Airport: A small ferry transports people to a dock 3 mi. north of downtown on N. Tongass Ave. ($2.50). The Alaska Marine Highway terminal is only a short walk from the airport ferry dock. **Alaska Airlines** (225-2141), in the Ingersoll Hotel, at the corner of Front and Dock St. provides flight information from Ketchikan. Open daily 8am-5pm. Daily flights to Juneau $103.

Alaska Marine Highway: At the far end of town on N. Tongass Hwy. (225-6181). Buses run into town until 6:45pm; after that you might want to hitch a ride to avoid paying a $7 cab fare.

Buses: Fare $1, under 11 and senior citizens 75¢. Frequent stops (about every 3 blocks). Buses run every ½-hr. Mon.-Sat. 6:45am-6:45pm.

Taxis: Sourdough Cab, 225-6651. **Alaska Cab,** 225-2133. **Yellow Cab,** 225-5555.

Car Rental: All-Star Rent-A-Car, airport office (225-2232) or 2828-V Tongass Ave. (225-5123 or 800-426-5243). Free local pick-up and delivery. $40 per day, plus 50 free mi. 25¢ each additional mi. Open daily.

Alaska State Employment Office: 2030 Sea Level Dr. (225-3181), at the west end of town. Open Mon.-Fri. 8am-4:30pm.

Laundromat: Suds and Duds, 325 Bawden (225-9274), near the hostel. Open daily 8am-8pm.

Sexual Assault/Rape Crisis Line: W.I.S.H. (225-9474).

Pharmacy: Race Drug, 300 Front St. (225-3144). Open Mon.-Fri. 9am-5pm.

Post Office: Main office next to the ferry terminal. Open Mon.-Fri. 9am-5pm. General Delivery ZIP Code: 99901. Substation in the back of The Trading Post, on the corner of Main and Mission St.

Population: 14,300.

Area Code: 907.

Ketchikan sits on an island 235 mi. south of Juneau, 90 mi. north of Prince Rupert, BC, and 600 mi. north of Seattle, WA. The Parks and Recreation Center, 345 Main St., will store your backpack free Mon.-Fri. 9am-5pm.

Accommodations

Except for hostels, housing in town is relatively expensive. However, the **Ketchikan Bed and Breakfast Network,** Box 3213, Ketchikan 99901 (225-8550), provides rooms from $35 to $65.

Ketchikan Youth Hostel (AYH), P.O. Box 8515, Ketchikan 99901 (225-3319). On the corner of Main and Grant St. in the United Methodist Church. Although there are no beds, 4" thick foam mats on the floor are quite comfortable with sleeping bags. Clean kitchen, common area, and two showers. Very friendly houseparents. Lockout 8:30am-6pm. Lights off at 10:30pm, on at 7:00am. Members $4, nonmembers $7. No reservations. Open June 1-Sept. 1.

Union Rooms Hotel, 319 Mill St., Ketchikan 99901 (225-3580). Built shortly after the turn of the century, this unattractive hotel provides inexpensive and reasonably clean rooms for $26.50 and up. $10 key deposit required.

Pioneer Hotel and Bar, 118 Front St., Box 8535, Ketchikan 99901 (225-2336). Hotel manager is also bartender. Singles with bath $40. $10 key deposit.

Ingersoll Hotel, 303 Mission St., Ketchikan 99901 (225-2124). Quaint, clean rooms. Located downtown on the waterfront. Some rooms face onto the Tongass Narrows for a spectacular view. Make reservations at least 1 month in advance for summer. Singles $69. Doubles $79. Oct. 1-March 31, singles $58. Doubles $69.

Camping

Signal Creek Campground, 6 mi. north on Tongass Hwy. from the ferry terminal. A U.S. Forest Service campground on the shores of Ward Lake. Water and pit toilets. 25 units. Sites $5. Open in summer.

Last Chance Campground, 2 mi. north of Ward Lake's parking lot entrance. 25 sites, predominantly for RVs. Water, pit toilets. Sites $5. Open in summer.

Three C's Campground, ½-mi. north of Signal Creek. Four units for backpackers. Water, pit toilets, firewood.

Ketchikan RV Park, (225-6166). Parking for 19 RVs in town, next to Sea Mart supermarket. No hookups, but water and trash facilities. Sites $5.

Clover Pass Resort, P.O. Box 7322-V, Ketchikan 99901 (247-2234), 14 mi. north of Ketchikan. 35 complete RV hookups with electricity, sewer, water, laundry, and a dump station.

Food

The supermarket most convenient to downtown is **Tatsuda's,** 633 Stedman at Deermount St., just beyond the Thomas Basin. (Open daily 7am-11pm.) **Bayside Grocery,** on Stedman near the docks, has a smaller selection but is open 24 hr.

Harbor Inn, 320 Mission St. (225-2833). Generous portions in a friendly fishermen's hangout. Three eggs, gravy, hashbrowns, and bacon $6.25. Hearty portion of sizzling Red Snapper $7.95. Open 24 hr.

Jimbo's Korner Kafe, 307 Mill St. (225-2240), across from the cruise ship docks. Try a 1-lb. Alaskan burger for $7.95. Open 24 hr., but may klose early on Sundays. Pretty krazy, eh?

Chico's, Dock and Edmond St. (225-2833). Tortellini meets the tortilla. Zesty Mexican/Italian decor and music. Spicy dinners $8-11. $4.50 for tons of spaghetti. Open daily 10am-11pm.

Pioneer Pantry, 124 Front St. (225-3337), across from the visitors bureau. The decor fails to thrill, but the food is filling. Sandwiches come with salad, fries, or soup ($4.25-7). Breakfast specials $5. Open daily 8am-6pm.

Anchor Inn, 834 Water St. (225-4545), a few hundred meters past the tunnel from downtown. Frequented by fishermen from the docks across the road. Eggs, hashbrowns, bacon, and toast $4.95. Soup and sandwich lunches $5.50.

Ketchikan Cafe, 314 Front St. (247-CAFE). Among the best Ketchikan has to offer. Entrees vary from local seafood dishes to 10-oz. New York steak. Homemade bread. Superb view of the Tongass Narrows, tasteful decor, and melodious classical music make this restaurant a pleasant escape from an often hectic town. All dinners include soup, salad, and dessert ($14.95). Open daily 8am-9pm.

Sights

The best way to see the sights in Ketchikan is to follow the excellent walking tour map offered by the visitors bureau. Fortune-seeking prospectors turned Ketchikan into a mining boom-town, and a little bit of its history is preserved on **Creek Street,** a thriving red light district until 1954. Creek St. was notorious as the only place where both sailors and salmon went upstream to spawn. Revel in the sordid past of **Dolly's House,** 24 Creek St. (225-6329), a former brothel-turned-museum opened by its enterprising madam. There are countless antiques from the 20s and 30s, set amidst bawdy colors and secret caches. Hours vary; call ahead. (Admission $2.)

Also on the walking tour is the **Totem Heritage Center,** 601 Deermount St., which houses 33 well-preserved totem poles from Tlingit and Haida villages. (Open Mon.-Sat. 8am-5pm, Sun. 9am-5pm. Admission $2, under 18 free; Sun. afternoon free.) The **Tongass Historical Museum,** on Dock St., explains the strange interaction of natives, rain, salmon, and prostitutes. (Open mid-May to Sept. Mon.-Sat. 8:30am-5pm, Sun. 1-5pm. Admission $1, under 18 free; free Sun.) Next door to the museum, the scenic chairs of the **Ketchikan Library** are the best place to pass a rainy day. (Open Mon. and Wed. 10am-8pm, Tues. and Thurs.-Fri. 10am-6pm, Sat. noon-5pm.) All those obsessed with the sex-lives of fish will be enamored of the **Deer Mountain Hatchery,** in the city park off Fair St. The hatchery is free and open sporadically.

The best and largest totem park in the world is 2½ mi. southwest of Ketchikan on Tongass Hwy. in the **Saxman Native Village.** The native village has a tribal house, native dancers, and an open studio where artisans carve new totems. (Open daily 9am-5pm and on weekends when a cruise ship is in.) Thirteen-and-a-half mi. north of Ketchikan on Tongass Hwy. is **Totem Bight,** featuring 13 totems. Entry to both parks is free, and visitors are welcome during daylight hours. For those interested in purchasing authentic native art, the **Scanlon Gallery,** 310 Mission St. (225-4730), has the best pieces in town.

A good day-hike from Ketchikan is up **Deer Mountain.** Walk past the city park on Fair St. until it becomes a gravel road. Follow this up to the trailhead. In 2½ hr. you'll reach a spectacular outlook of Ketchikan and Prince of Wales Island.

The magical **Misty Fjords National Monument** lies 30 mi. east of Ketchikan and is accessible by boat or float plane. This 2.2-million-acre park offers excellent camping, guided summer tours, and year-round workshops. Call the Ketchikan Visitors Bureau or the Misty Fjords Visitor Center, on Mill St., for information about tours to the park (plan on spending at least $120 for a day trip). In town, the **Frontier Saloon** (225-4407), at 127 Main St., has live music Tuesday though Sunday in summer. (Open daily 10am-2am.) The **Arctic Bar** (225-4709), on the other side of the tunnel is the place fishermen haunt when on terra firma. (Open Sun.-Wed. 9am-midnight, Thurs.-Sat. 9am-2am.)

Wrangell

An isolated fishing and logging town on the Alaska Marine Highway, Wrangell (RANG-uhl) thrives upon its own small-town atmosphere. In 1986, the hamlet defeated a U.S. Postal Service attempt to install rural delivery—the townspeople didn't want to lose the communal endeavor of picking up their own mail. Surrounded by forests and snow-capped mountains, the small city was founded by miners seeking gold on the Stikine River. Their descendants host Alaska's largest Independence Day celebration; the $30,000 blowout includes speedboat racing, log rolling, and fireworks. Whew hah!

Practical Information

Visitor Information: Wrangell Visitors Bureau, P.O. Box 49 (874-3901 or 874-3770), in the A-frame building at Outer Dr. and Brueger St., next to the large totem pole. Open May-Sept. Mon.-Fri. 10am-4pm, Sat.-Sun. if a cruise ship is in port.

United States Forest Service: Ranger District Station, 525 Bennet St. (874-2323), past 2nd Ave. about 10 min. from downtown. Helpful advice on wilderness expeditions to the Stikine River and the LeConte Glacier. Open Mon.-Fri. 8am-5pm.

Alaska Marine Highway: Terminal in town (874-2021 or 874-3711). Generally 1 northbound or southbound ferry per day. To: Ketchikan ($20), Sitka ($32), and Juneau ($48).

Taxi: Star Cab, 874-3622. **Porky's Cab Co.,** 874-3603.

Car Rental: All-Star Rent-a-Car, P.O. Box 1349, Wrangell 99835 (800-426-5243 or 874-3322), located in the Thunderbird Hotel on Front St. $40 per day plus 50 free mi. 25¢ per extra mi. Must be 21.

Laundromat: Thunderbird Hotel Laundromat, (874-3322). Wash $1.75, driers 25¢ per 5 min. Open daily 7am-8pm.

Pharmacy: Wrangell Drug, 202 Front St. (874-3422). Open Mon.-Sat. 9am-5pm.

Emergency: 874-2000.

Police: Public Safety Building, Zimovia Hwy. (874-3304).

Post Office and Customs House: On Church St., 3 blocks from ferry terminal. Open Mon.-Fri. 9am-5:30pm, Sat. 11am-1pm. General Delivery ZIP Code: 99929.

Population: 2,500.

Area Code: 907. When calling within town limits, you need only dial the last 4 numbers of the 7-digit code.

Accommodations and Camping

Backpackers can sleep for free in **city park,** two mi. from the ferry. From the terminal, take 2nd St. until it becomes Zimovia Hwy.; keep going until the cemetery. The park is behind the cemetery, next to the ballpark. Bathrooms and picnic tables available. However, there are no level sites, no showers, and usually no neighbors, so don't plan on staying too long if you can help it. (The 24-hr. limit is unenforced.)

Harding's Old Sourdough Lodge, P.O. Box 1062, Wrangell 99929 (874-3455). On the other side of town from the ferry terminal. Follow Case Ave. until it ends, then go down the dirt road about 50 yards. A quiet, family-run hotel. Laundry facilities. Singles $45-56. Doubles $53-64. Charters, skiff rentals available through the hotel.

Thunderbird Hotel, P.O. Box 110, Wrangell 99929 (874-3322). In the center of town, 3 blocks down Front St. Large, clean rooms with private baths and cable TV. In summer, try to reserve a room at least 1 month in advance. Single $50. Double $57. In winter all rooms $50.

Stikine Inn, P.O. Box 990, Wrangell 99929 (874-3388). Centrally located at the end of Front St., on the way into town from the ferry terminal. Wrangell's oldest and largest inn, with great oceanfront rooms. Sun.-Thurs. singles $65, doubles $70; Fri.-Sat. singles $40, doubles $45.

Clark Bed and Breakfast, 732 Case Ave., P.O. Box 1020, Wrangell 99929 (Mon.-Fri. 10am-5pm, tel. 874-2125; Mon.-Fri. 7-9pm and Sat.-Sun. 10am-9pm, tel. 874-3863). Only 2 rooms. Singles $35. Doubles $45. $25 deposit required.

RV Camping: Shoemaker Bay, 5 mi. south of downtown on Zimovia Hwy. Water tap; holding tank dump but no electrical hookups.

Food

Get groceries at **Benjamin's** (874-2341), between Front St. and the town harbor. The deli section has big turkey sandwiches for $2.79. (Open Mon.-Sat. 8am-6pm.)

Maggie's and Son Pizza, corner of Front and Lynch St. (874-2353). Large portions, friendly service, and a great view of tourists bustling off cruise ships make Maggie's a local favorite. Excellent hot sausage sandwich $2.75. Delicious ice cream. Open Mon.-Fri. 11am-8pm, Sat.-Sun. 11am-9pm.

Diamond C Café, Front St. (874-3677). Cozy luncheonette with colonial character. Large club sandwich $6. Open Mon.-Sat. 6am-4pm, Sun. 6am-3pm.

J & W's, 1 block down Front St. (874-2120). An archetypal burger stand—astroturf carpeting and yellow picnic benches. Cheeseburger $3.05. Open Mon.-Thurs. 11am-8pm, Fri.-Sat. 11am-10pm, Sun. noon-8pm.

The Dockside, (874-3388), in the Stikine Inn. Good for breakfast or lunch. 3-egg omelette with ham or bacon $6.25. Soup and sandwich $5.25. Open Mon.-Sat. 6am-10pm, Sun. 7am-10pm.

Sights

Wrangell's **waterfront** supports a steady trickle of fishing trawlers and log booms plying through the large channel. Walk down **Front Street** past the false-fronted buildings, for a taste of the town and the harbor. You can take rubbings of ancient **petroglyphs,** the wall drawings of Bering Strait immigrants, on display just outside town. Take a left from the ferry terminal on the old Airport Rd., walk 15 min. along the road, and then follow the signs to the beach. Halfway between the petroglyphs and downtown is **"Our Collections" Museum,** a privately-owned accumulation of family items, furniture, tools, and other Alaskan memorabilia. Admission is free, and hours coincide with cruise ship landings. The **Wrangell Museum** (874-3770) illustrates the history of the local Tlingit tribes and of the city's development. (Open in summer Mon.-Sat. 1-4pm and when a cruise ship is in town. Admission $1, 16 and under free.)

Farther down Front St., towards the harbor, **Totem Park** features the work of local native artists. The park is free, and well-situated boulders provide a good place for eating lunch while observing the magnificently carved totems. **Chief Shakes Island and Bear Tribal House** (874-3505), on the harbor, draws most of Wrangell's few visitors. If the tribal house is closed, you can always walk around the island and view the seven outstanding totems. (Open Tues. 3:30-6:30pm, Wed. 10am-1pm and 3:30-6:30pm, Sat. 1-2:30pm and 3:30-6:30pm.)

Motorists should explore some of the logging roads outside town. Hiking near the city is also quite good, and **Loop Road** is a locally touted three mi. walk through the scenic and mossy **muskeg** (bog). Be careful: bears, moose, mink, and beavers govern the areas outside the city limits. Wrangell's immense **salmon bake** in early June raises money for a July 4th celebration but is a party in itself. The **Tent City Festival,** held in February, fêtes the logging industry.

Ten float-plane minutes from Wrangell is **LeConte Glacier,** the southernmost active tidewater glacier in North America. Trips cost upwards of $50. Try **Sunrise Aviation** (874-2319) for good, cheap tours of the glacier and the **Stikine River,** as well as charter flights to cabins in **Tongass National Forest.**

Petersburg

Proud port of the largest halibut fleet in the world, Petersburg became a boomtown in the late 70s, when someone discovered an insatiable Japanese appetite for salt-soaked halibut eggs. One of the most strikingly beautiful and now one of the wealthiest towns in Southeast Alaska, Petersburg's inhabitants have not lost their friendly, down-to-earth character, nor have they forgotten their Scandinavian heritage. Everyone in town claims to be descended from Peter Buschmann, a Norwegian immigrant who built the first cannery here, and *rosemaling* (a Norwegian form of decorative painting) adorns many buildings.

Practical Information

Chamber of Commerce/Visitor Information: P.O. Box 649, Petersburg 99833 (772-3646), in the Harbormaster Bldg. Helpful staff. Open Mon.-Fri. 8am-5pm.

U.S. Forest Service: Petersburg Ranger District Office, P.O. Box 309, Petersburg 99833 (722-3871), upstairs in the Post Office Bldg. on Nordic Dr. at Haugen. Supervises the Stikine Area of the Tongass Forest (write for information on wilderness cabins in the area). Information on trails. Open Mon.-Fri. 8am-5pm.

Airport: Alaska Airlines (772-4255), 1 mi. from the Federal Bldg. on Haugen Drive. Helicopter and float planes available for sight-seeing ($70 per person).

Alaska Marine Highway Terminal (772-3855), at mile 0.9 on the Mitkof Hwy., 1 mi. from the center of town. To: Ketchikan ($32), Sitka ($22), Wrangell ($14), and Juneau ($38).

Taxi: City Cab (772-3003). $3 per person (when sharing the ride) from ferry to Tent City, the campground owned by the cab company. **Chris West Cab** (772-9378).

Car Rental: Allstar Rent-A-Car, (772-4281), at the Scandia House Hotel. $40 per day with 50 free mi. 20¢ extra per mi. Also rents 18' boats ($150 per day).

Employment: Petersburg Job Service, Haugen Dr. and 1st St. All 4 canneries hire through this agency. Cannery or deckhand openings posted in the window. Open Mon.-Fri. 8am-noon and 1-4:30pm.

Laundromat: Glacier Laundry, downtown on Nordic and Dolphin. Will clean sleeping bags. Open daily 8am-8pm.

Pharmacy: The Drug Store, downtown Nordic Dr. Open Mon.-Fri. 9:30am-6pm, Sat. 9:30am-5pm, Sun. noon-3pm.

Hospital: Petersburg General Hospital (772-4291), on Fram and N. 1st St.

Emergency: City Police (772-3838). **State Troopers** (772-3100).

Post Office (772-3121), on Haugen and Nordic Dr. Open Mon.-Fri. 9am-5:30pm, Sat. 9am-noon. General Delivery ZIP Code: 99833.

Population: 3,500.

Area Code: 907.

Accommodations

The only place for backpackers is Tent City, an amiable community of student cannery workers. A stagnant swamp makes camping closer to Petersburg impossible, and the next nearest campground is 17 mi. away.

Tent City, on Haugen Dr. past the airport, 2.1 mi. from the ferry. Originally built by the police department and now managed by City Cab, Tent City provides a unique opportunity for backpackers to camp in one of Alaska's most facinating terrains: muskeg swamp. Sound wooden platforms and interconnected walkways keep tenters high and dry, while the virtually uninterrupted ecosystem flurries aound them. Toilets, covered picnic tables, community fire, but no showers. $5 per night. Credit available for "permanent" tenters.

The Narrows (772-4284), across from the ferry. Extremely narrow but clean rooms. 25 units. Singles $55. Doubles $65. Call for summer reservations before June.

Jewels By the Sea, 1106 Nordic Dr. (772-3620), ¼ mi. north of the ferry terminal. Small B&B with a great view of the **Wrangell Narrows.** Bicycles available. Airport or ferry pickup. Cozy place for honeymooners. Singles $45. Doubles $50. Only 3 rooms, so make reservations before the summer.

Scandia House, 110 Nordic Dr. (772-4281), between Fram and Gjoa St. Exceptionally clean rooms. Boat and car rental offices based here. Anyone can reserve the hot tub and spa for $7.50 per hour, $6 per person for two or more. Showers $3.15. Open 6am-midnight. Singles $50, with bath $65. Doubles $55, with bath $70.

LeConte RV Park, P.O. Box 1548, Petersburg 99833 (772-4680), at 4th and Haugen. One mi. from ferry, 3 blocks from downtown. Full hookup. Rates vary.

Ohmer Creek Campground, Mile 22 Mitkof Hwy. 15 sites. 14-day max. stay.

Food

Petersburg is one of the best towns in all of Alaska for fresh seafood, and most of the restaurants procure their catches directly from local fishermen. **Hammer and Wikan,** on Nordic Dr. (772-4246), has a huge selection of groceries and also sells camping gear and insect repellent. (Open daily 8am-6pm.)

Homestead Café (772-3900), Nordic Dr. at Excel, across from the general store. A quality restaurant for good ol' American grub. Ham n' Eggs $6.50. Roast beef sandwich, soup, and fries $4.75. Open Mon. 6am-midnight, Tues.-Fri. 24 hr., Sat. midnight-10pm.

Helse-Health Foods and Deli (772-3444), on Sing Lee Alley off Nordic Dr. With flowers, ferns, little wooden stools, and plenty of Reggae, this earthy place is perfect for a stoned soul picnic. "Island Mermaid Sandwich"—tuna, avocado, and cheese $5.75. Open Mon.-Fri. 9am-5pm, Sat. 10am-3pm.

Harbor Lights Pizza, Sing Lee Alley (772-3424), overlooking the harbor. Decent pizza. 16" cheese pie ($14.25) and bountiful salad bar ($2). Come here for an incredible view of the dock and $6-7.50 pitchers of beer. Open Sun.-Thurs 11am-11pm, Fri-Sat. 11am-midnight.

Pellerito's Pizza (772-3727), across from the ferry. 85¢ per scoop of ice cream. "Louisiana Torpedo" sandwich $3.65. Open daily 7am-11pm.

The Quay (772-4600), 1103-C S. Nordic Dr., across from the ferry. This newly opened restaurant has quickly become the hottest spot for local seafood connoiseurs. Broiled or fried halibut $13.95. All seafood is local and fresh. Catch it while you can. Open daily 6am-10pm.

Sights

This is the best place in the Panhandle to see a fishing town at work. Although none of the town's three canneries were previously open to the public, at least one cannery is beginning to give tours. Consult Visitor Information for location, price, and times.

To understand the development of this pristine Norwegian village, head to the **Clausen Memorial Museum,** on 2nd Ave. and Fram St., which shows native artifacts and an inspiring history of fishing techniques. You've heard of the big fish in a little pond, but their world-record 126½-lb. king salmon beats all. Outside the museum is the stunning **Fisk Fountain**, dedicated to the fish on which Petersburg thrives. (Open Mon.-Thurs. 11am-4:30pm, Fri.-Sat. noon-5pm. Admission $1.)

Petersburg is surrounded on all sides by rewarding hiking trails and fishing sites. Pick up a free guide to local trails at the **Petersburg Ranger District** (see Practical Information and Orientation), as well as a comprehensive pamphlet on sport fishing near Petersburg. Adjacent to Tent City, a **boardwalk** has been constructed through the dense muskeg jungle, leading to the sea; a one-mi. walk each way provides a glimpse into Alaska's endless expanse of flora and fauna. A common, though somewhat foolhardy, dusk activity for Tent City campers is to follow Nordic Dr. one mi. north to the city dump, a gourmet restaurant for local wildlife, especially black bears. This can be extremely dangerous as the hungry bears here no longer fear humans, and can be unpredictably brazen.

On the weekend closest to May 17, Petersburg joins its international brethren in joyous celebration of Norwegian independence from Sweden. During the **Little Norway Festival,** mock Vikings are as plentiful as halibut eggs. And on Independence Day, the entire town gets a little crazy and celebrates in true American style with a parade and fireworks.

On the opposite side of Kupreanof Island from Petersburg, the weather clears for the tiny and peaceful settlement of **Kake**, home of the world's largest totem pole (132' 6"). Kake is a permanent village of the Tlingit, comprising 85% of the 600 inhabitants. Across the channel a large population of brown bears roams the outskirts of **Angoon**, another Native village. Except for commercial fishing, the inhabitants have renounced modernization. Though the economy remains at the subsistence level, they have steadfastly clung to their ancient customs. There are no campgrounds in Angoon, but two hotels provide 18 units of housing for visitors. **Tenakee Springs** on Chichagof Island is a community of wooden houses erected on stilts and connected by plank walkways. Tenakee is best known for its hot springs, which have been attracting bathers since the *fin-de-siècle.*

Sitka

Dominated by the snow-capped volcano of Mt. Edgecumbe, Sitka was the center of Alaskan history until the early 20th century. Russian explorer Vitus Bering made the first modern landfall in Alaska in 1741 on nearby Kayac Island, and in the same year, the Russians settled at Sitka. Decades of bloody fighting between the Russians and the native Tlingits ensued, which culminated in the heroic last stand battle of 1804, where the Tlingits stood and when Alexander Baranof, the manager of the Russian-American Company, lasted. He consolidated his spoils by making Sitka the capital of Russian Alaska and the symbol of Russian supremacy on both sides of the Bering Straits—the "Paris of the Pacific" for the next 63 years, larger than either San Francisco or Seattle. After the transfer of Alaska to American hands in 1867, Sitka became the territory's capital from 1884 until 1906. Travelers from all nations came here to profit from the trade in sea otter pelts and to enjoy the trappings of a glittering society life. The legacy of this cultural preeminence in the Northwest remains, as Sitka currently is the fifth largest city in the state and a center for the arts in Southeast Alaska.

Practical Information and Orientation

Chamber of Commerce/Visitors Bureau, Centennial Bldg., 330 Harbor Dr. (747-8601 or 747-5940). New Archangel Dancers and Isabel Miller Museum located in the same building. The Visitor's Bureau is extremely organized. Open Mon.-Sat. 8am-5pm.

U.S. Forest Service: Sitka Ranger District, Tongass National Forest, 204 Siqinaka Way, Sitka 99835 (747-6671), off Katlian St. Open Mon.-Fri. 8am-5pm. Pick up a copy of *Sitka Trails* at the **information booth** in front of the Centennial Bldg. at Lincoln St. Donation $1. Open May-Sept. daily 8am-5pm.

Airport: Alaska Airlines (800-426-0333 or 966-2266). Regular service to Seattle, Anchorage, Juneau, Ketchikan, Wrangell, and Petersburg. To Juneau ($71) or Ketchikan ($103).

Alaska Marine Highway: 7 Halibut Rd. (747-8737 or 800-642-0066), 7 mi. from town. To: Ketchikan ($48), Petersburg ($22), and Juneau ($22).

Buses: Sitka Tours (747-8443) runs a shuttle bus and tour guide service from the ferry terminal, whenever the ferries are in port. Ride into town $2.50; tours $8.

Taxis: Arrowhead Taxi, 747-8888. **Baranof Taxi,** 747-3366. **Sitka Taxi,** 747-5001. **Tlingit and Haida Cab,** 747-6621.

Car Rental: All-Star Rent-A-Car, 600 C Airport Rd. (800-426-5243 or 966-2552). $35 per day with unlimited mileage. **Avis** (966-2404), in airport as well. Similar rates.

Laundromats and Shower Facilities: Homestead Laundromat, 619 Katlian Ave. (747-6995). Wash and dry $1.75, showers $2. Open daily 8am-8pm. **Duds n' Suds Laundromat,** 908 Halibut Point Rd. (747-5050), near hostel. Wash and dry $1.50. Shower $1.25. Open Mon.-Fri. 7am-8pm, Sat. 8am-8pm, Sun. 9am-10pm.

Pharmacy: Harry Race Pharmacy, 102 Lincoln St. (747-8666), by Castle Hill. Open Mon.-Sat. 9am-6pm, Sun. 10am-3pm.

Post Office: 1207 Sawmill Creek Rd. (747-3381), far from downtown. General Delivery ZIP Code: 99835. In town, try the **substation,** 407 Lincoln (747-6286), in the back of Bayview Trading Co. on Harbor Dr. Both open Mon.-Fri. 9am-5pm.

Population: 8,300.

Area Code: 907.

Sitka inhabits the western side of Baranof Island, 95 mi. southwest of Juneau and 185 mi. northwest of Ketchikan. The O'Connell Bridge connects downtown to Japonski Island and the airport. Sitkas is the only major town in southeastern Alaska with direct access to the Pacific Ocean.

Accommodations and Camping

AYH has finally succeeded in establishing a permanent hostel in Sitka. Camping facilities are decent, but are at least five mi. from town. Sitka also has nine **bed and breakfasts** from $35 a night up. The Centennial Building Chamber of Commerce office has rates and phone numbers for all.

Sitka Youth Hostel (AYH), 303 Kimshan St., Box 2645, Sitka 99835 (747-8356). In the United Methodist Church on Edgecumbe and Kimsham St. Find the McDonalds, a mi. out of town on Halibut Point Rd., and walk 25 yd. up Peterson St. to Kimsham. A small hostel with army cots. Kitchen facilities. Friendly houseparents with endless traveling lore. One chore required. Lockout 9am-6pm. Curfew 11pm. Members $5, nonmembers $8.

Potlatch House, 713 Katlian St., Box 58, Sitka 99835 (747-8611). Clean and modern. Singles $59. Doubles $67.

Sitka Hotel, 118 Lincoln, Sitka 99835 (747-3288). Cheap; clean, quiet rooms. The building itself is a little dingy. 60 units. Singles $37.80, with bath $43.20. Doubles $43.20, with bath $48.60. Seniors get a discount.

Super 8 Motel, 404 Sawmill Creek Blvd. (747-8804). Lousy location, but allows pets and has wheelchair-accessible rooms. Singles $61. Doubles $65.

Sawmill Creek Campground, 13 mi. SE of the ferry terminal, 6 mi. out of town. Take Halibut Point Rd. to Sawmill Creek Rd. junction, in Sitka. Follow Sawmill Creek Rd. to pulp mill, then take left spur for 1.4 mi. Unmaintained 9 unit campground. No water or showers. Picnic tables, fireplaces, 2 outhouses. Good fishing in nearby Blue Lake. 14-day max. stay. Free.

Starrigaven Creek Campground, at the end of Halibut Point Rd., 1 mi. from the ferry terminal, 8 mi. from town. A USFS campground. 30 sites, pit toilets. 14-day max. stay. Sites $5.

Sealing Cove. From ferry go south on Halibut Point Rd. to Lake St. Follow Lake St. across the bridge to Sealing Cove. 26 RV spots. Water and electricity. Sites $5.

Food

Do your grocery shopping at the **Market Center Grocery,** Sawmill Creek and Baranof St., uphill from the Bishop's House (open Mon.-Sat. 10am-8pm, Sun. noon-

6pm), or close to the hostel at **Lakeside Grocery,** 705 Halibut Point Rd. (Open Mon.-Sat. 9am-9pm, Sun. 11am-7pm.) You can also pick up fresh seafood from fishermen along the docks or at **Sitka Sound Seafood** on Katlian St., which occasionally offers surplus fish for retail sale.

Staton's Steak House, 228 Harbor Dr. (747-3396), across from the Centennial Bldg. Delicious, well-sized portions. Lunch special includes deep-fried halibut and heaps of french fries ($7). Sandwich with soup $5.75. Open Mon.-Thurs. 11:30am-2pm, Tues.-Sat. 5-9pm.

Coffee Express, 104 Lake St. (747-3343), in downtown. Excellent coffee 80¢, and filling soup and sandwich $6. Cinnamon rolls rolled big and buttery ($1.75). Open Mon.-Fri. 7am-5:30pm, Sat. 8am-5pm, Sun. 8am-2pm.

The Bayview Restaurant, 407 Lincoln St. (747-5440), upstairs in the Bayview Trading Company. Everything from *russkia ribnia blyood,* a Russian fish delicacy ($7.25) to a Mousetrap sandwich (grilled cheese, $4). Edible burgers. A spectacular view of the harbor. Open Mon.-Sat. 11am-7pm.

Lane 7 Snack Bar, 331 Lincoln St. (747-6310), next to the Cathedral. Chomp on hotter 'n hell chili dogs ($2.75) and lip-smacking hot fudge sundaes ($2.50) while you bowl some turkeys (games $2.25, senior citizens $1.25) in your tour of downtown Sitka. Open Mon.-Sat. 11am-11pm, Sun. 11am-10pm.

Sitka Café, 116 Lincoln St., next to Sitka Hotel. Mexican, American, and Oriental fare. Chicken burger, fries, and a salad $4.50. Nachos $4.50. Crowded when it opens for breakfast at 6am. Open daily 6am-9pm.

Channel Club, 2906 Halibut Point Rd. (747-9916), 3 mi. from downtown. The restaurant every Sitkan will recommend. Fantastic salad bar with over 30 items. Open Sun.-Thurs. 6-11pm, Fri.-Sat. 6pm-midnight.

Sights

Modern Sitka treasures its rich Russian heritage, and the most lasting symbol of Slavic influence is the onion-domed **St. Michael's Cathedral.** The church was built in 1848 by Bishop Innocent. In 1966, however, fire claimed the original structure, though Sitka's quick-witted citizens saved the majority of priceless artifacts and paintings. The Cathedral was promptly rebuilt, in strict accordance with plans for the first building, and today its haunting icons gleam on its walls. Among the Cathedral's most valued works are the *Sitka Madonna* the *Pantocrator,* both by Russian master Vladimir Borbikovsky, as well as several neo-Italian paintings, from the movement supported by Catherine the Great. Services are open to the public, and are conducted in English, Tlingit, and Slavonic (old Russian). (Open Mon.-Sat. 11am-3pm, though these hours may be extended when a cruise ship is in port.)

Two blocks farther down Lincoln is the **Russian Bishop's House,** home of Ivan Veniaminov, the builder of St. Michael's Cathedral. The cathedral was such a success he was canonized as St. Innocent in 1977. Restoration of the building to its original 1842-3 condition has recently been completed for a whopping $9 million. The house is one of four remaining Russian colonial buildings in the Americas, and it has been refurbished with the exact materials, colors, and patterns with which Veniaminov himself decorated his home. Upstairs is a magnificent chapel, dedicated to the Annunication of the Virgin Mary, and adorned with beautiful gold and silver icons (which, unlike those in St. Michael's, may be photographed). For history and architecture buffs, this sight is a must. (Open 9am-5pm, tours every ½-hr.)

The **Sheldon-Jackson Museum** (747-8981), located at the east end of Licoln St., is perhaps one of the best museums in the state for native artifacts and history. Many collections date back to the 1880s and represent all four major native ethnic groups—Athapaskan, Aleut, Eskimo, and Tligit. (Open daily 8am-5pm. Admission $2, free with student ID.) For naturalists, the **Alaska Raptor Rehabilitation Center,** in Island Community College on Sawmill Creek Rd. (747-8662), has a fantastic collection of recovering wildlife. Volunteers staff the center and give tours.

The other side of town from the college is a repository of local history. Historic **Castle Hill,** site of Baranof's Castle and Tlingit forts, grants an incredible view of Mt. Edgecumbe, the inactive volcano known as the "Mt. Fuji of Alaska." Castle

Hill also saw the sale of Alaska to the United States in 1867 (open daily 6am-10pm). Stroll down the enchanting, manicured trails of the **Sitka National Historic Park** (Totem Park, as locals call it), at the end of Lincoln St. (747-6281), 1 mi. east of St. Michael's. The trails pass by many restored totems on the way to the site of the **Tlingit fort,** where hammer-wielding chieftain Katlian almost held off the Russians in the battle for Alaska in 1804. The park **visitors center** offers audiovisual presentations and the opportunity to watch Native artists work at the Native American Cultural Center. There is also a small museum here, which is dedicated entirely to the local Kiksadi Tlingits. (Open daily 8am-5pm.)

Sitka's economy today is built upon its commercial fisheries. Wander up Katlian St. to view the processing, or clamber down to the docks at Crescent or Thomsen Harbors. Jobs are available through most canneries directly, though employment is not easy to come by. (As in all Alaskan summer jobs, it helps to pursue them aggressively, as well as be in the right place at the right time.) A better taste of local life can be found at the **Pioneer Bar** on Katlian St. (747-3456), whose walls are covered with planks left over from local boats and southeast shipwrecks.

There are excellent **hiking** opportunities in the Sitka area—make sure to pick up the thick booklet *Sitka Trails* at the USFS information booth or office (free). The outstanding trails include the Indian River Trail, an easy 5.5-mi. trek up the valley to the base of **Indian River Falls,** and the three-mi. uphill trail to the top of **Gavan Hill.** Make sure to bring waterproof clothing when hiking on rainy days, as Sitka is immersed in a virtual rain forest. A fine three-mi. trek from downtown crosses the runway at the Japonski Island airport to the old WW II causeway that heads past abandoned fortifications all the way to **Makhanati Island.**

The June **Sitka Summer Music Festival** ranks as one of the state's most popular events and draws world-renowned musicians to play chamber music. The concerts, held in the Centennial Building on Tuesday, Friday, and some Saturday evenings, can be crowded—reservations are a good idea (all shows $10, $60 seasonal passes are available). Contact the visitors bureau for information and advance ticketing (747-8601). The **All-Alaska Logging Championships** take place the weekend before Independence Day.

Juneau

Built on a tiny strip of land at the base of noble Mt. Juneau, Alaska's capital city is the only one in the nation inaccessible by highway. This so-called "little San Francisco" mixes and matches Victorian mansions, log cabins, Russian Orthodox churches, "Federal" style *quonset* huts, and simple frame houses with shutters painted with Norwegian *rosemaling*. This potpourri of styles hints at the richness of Juneau's history.

Tlingit Chief Kowee led Joe Juneau and Richard Harris to the gleaming "mother lode" in the hills up Gold Creek in October, 1880. By the next summer, boatloads of prospectors were at work in the already-claimed mines. Twenty-five years later, Juneau superseded Sitka as capital of the territory of Alaska.

Mining ended in Juneau in 1941, but by then fishing, lumber, and legislation had filled in to support Juneau's economy. Today, Juneau exists for the government and tourists, but it remains a city of energy and beauty.

Practical Information and Orientation

Visitor Information: Davis Log Cabin, 134 3rd St., Juneau 99801 (586-2284), at Seward St. Excellent source for pamphlets on walking tours, sights, and the natural wonders in the vicinity. Open Mon.-Fri. 8:30am-5pm, Sat.-Sun. 10am-5pm; Oct.-May Mon.-Fri. 8:30am-4pm. **Marine Park Kiosk,** Marine Way at Ferry Way (no phone), right by the cruise ship unloading dock. Manned by enthusiastic volunteers armed with pamphlets and information. Open May-Sept. daily 9am-6pm.

U.S. Forest and National Park Services: 101 Egan Dr. (586-8751), in Centennial Hall. Helpful staff and extensive pamphlets provide information on hiking and fishing in the Juneau area, as well as particulars pertaining to USFS cabins in Tongass Forest. Write here for Ton-

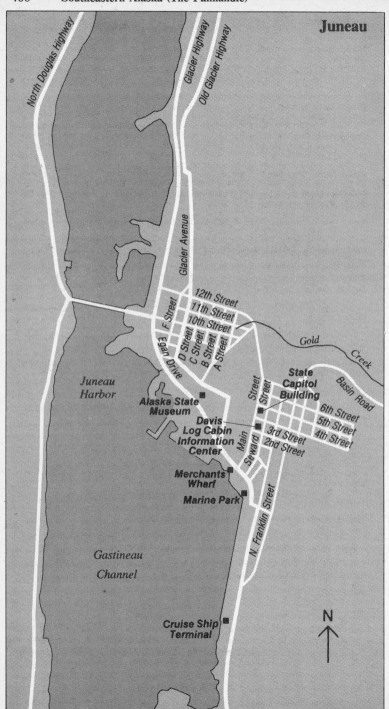

Juneau

North Douglas Highway

Glacier Highway

Old Glacier Highway

Glacier Avenue

12th Street
11th Street
10th Street

F Street
Egan Drive
D Street
C Street
B Street
A Street

Gold

Creek

Basin Road

State
Capitol
Building

6th Street
5th Street
4th Street

Street
Street

Juneau
Harbor

Alaska State
Museum

Davis
Log Cabin
Information
Center

3rd Street
2nd Street

Main
Seward

Merchants
Wharf

Marine Park

N Franklin Street

Gastineau

Channel

Cruise Ship
Terminal

N

gass reservations. Free, informative 20 min. films are shown every hour, describing areas such as Glacier Bay. Open daily 9am-6pm; Labor Day-Memorial Day Mon.-Fri. 8am-5pm.

Juneau International Airport: 9 mi. north of Juneau on Glacier Hwy. Serviced by Alaska Air, Delta Airlines, and local charters. **Alaska Air** (789-0600 or 800-426-0333), on Franklin St. at 2nd St., in the Baranof Hotel. One-way to: Anchorage ($195), Sitka ($71), Ketchikan ($103). Flights every morning and afternoon. Check Log Cabin Visitors Center for schedules and routes of all airlines.

Buses: Capital Transit (789-6901). Runs from downtown to Douglas, the airport, and Mendenhall Glacier. Leaves Marine Park for airport and glacier 5 min. after the hr. every hr. 7am-3pm. From 3-10pm, leaves Marine Park 35 min. after the hr. The fare is 75¢ to all points. **Eagle Express Line** (789-5720) runs vans to the airport ($5) and offers atour of Mendenhall Glacier, Juneau, and Douglas City (2½ hr., $19, children $9.50). Tours to the glacier alone (1½ hr., $8).

Alaska Marine Highway: P.O. Box R, Juneau 99811 (800-642-0066 or 465-3940). Ferries dock at the Auke Bay terminal at Mile 13.8 Glacier Hwy. To: Bellingham, WA ($200, car and driver $680), Ketchikan ($66, car and driver $221), Sitka ($22, car and driver $70) and Haines ($18, car and driver $54).

Taxis: Capital Cab (586-2772) and **Taku Taxi** (586-2121). Both conduct city tours as well as runs to Mendenhall ($50 per 1½ hr.).

Car Rental: Rent-A-Wreck, Airport Blvd. (789-4111), $28 per day with 100 free mi. 15¢ per extra mi.

Bike Rental: S. Franklin St., across from the Marine Park Garage (586-2277). All-terrain bikes $5 per hr., $25 per fun-filled day (8am-8pm). Open daily 8am-8pm.

Kayak rental: Alaska Discovery, 369 S. Franklin St. (586-1911 or 463-5500). Single kayak $30 per day, $45 for weekend. Open daily in summer 10am-5pm.

Camping Equipment: Foggy Mountain Shop, 134 Franklin St. (586-6780), at 2nd. High-quality but expensive gear. Open daily 10am-5pm.

Fishing Hot Line: 465-4116. For non-emergencies, call the Department of Fish and Game at 465-4180.

New Kids on the Block Hotline: 900-NEW-KIDS.

Laundromat: The Dungeon Laundrette, 4th and Franklin St. (586-2805). Open daily 8am-8pm. Hostel also has facilities.

Weather: 586-3997.

Crisis Line: 586-HELP (586-4337). Lines open 7-11pm.

Pharmacy: Juneau Drug Co., 202 Front St. (586-1233). Open Mon.-Fri. 9am-9pm, Sat. 9am-6pm, Sun. noon-6pm.

Hospital: Bartlett Memorial, 3½ mi. off Glacier Hwy. (586-2611), north of downtown.

Emergency and Ambulance: 911.

Police: 210 Admiral Way (586-2780), near Marine Park. Visitors can pick up a permit here to allow 48 hr. parking in a 1-hr. zone. RVs need no such permits.

Post Office: 709 W. 9th St. (586-7138). Open Mon. 8:30am-5pm, Tues.-Fri. 9:30am-5pm. General Delivery ZIP Code: 99801.

Population: 29,946.

Area Code: 907.

Juneau stands on the Gastineau Channel opposite Douglas Island, 650 mi. southeast of Anchorage and 900 mi. north of Seattle. **Glacier Highway** connects downtown, the airport, the residential area of the Mendenhall Valley, and the ferry terminal.

Accommodations

If you can't get into Juneau's hostel, the **Alaska Bed and Breakfast Association,** P.O. Box 3/6500 #169, Juneau 99802 (586-2959), will provide information on rooms in local homes year-round. Most Juneau B&Bs are uphill, beyond 6th St., and offer singles from $40 and doubles from $45. Reservations recommended.

Juneau Youth Hostel, 614 Harris St. (586-9559), corner of 6th and Harris. Clean, friendly, and properly managed. Showers ($1), laundry, and kitchen facilities. 24 extra squeaky metal-frame bunk beds (bring some oil or earplugs). Lockout 9am-5pm. Members $7, nonmembers $10. Make reservations before the summer for expected stays in July and August.

Alaskan Hotel, 167 Franklin St. (586-1000 or 800-327-9347 in the lower 48). A handsome hotel built of dark wood, right in the center of downtown. Has been restored to its original 1913 decor. Singles $40, with bath $55. Doubles $45, with bath $61. Hot tubs noon-4pm $10.40, after 4pm $20.80.

Driftwood Lodge, 435 Willoughby Ave., Juneau 99801 (586-2280). Behind the State Office Building. Courtesy van will whisk you to and from the airport, and sometimes out to Mendenhall Glacier. Singles $49. Doubles $62. With kitchen units $59-62.

Camping

Both campsites within Juneau's vicinity are carefully groomed by the Forest Service (see Practical Information). Both have a 14-day limit.

Mendenhall Lake Campground, Montana Creek Rd. Take Glacier Hwy. north 9 mi. to Mendenhall Loop Rd.; continue 3½ mi. and take the right fork. A cool view of the glacier, with trails that can take you even closer. 61 sites. Fireplaces, water, pit toilets. Sites $5.

Auke Village Campground, on Glacier Hwy., 15 mi. from Juneau. 11 sites. Fireplaces, water, pit toilets. Sites $5.

Food

Juneau tries to accommodate those seeking everything from fresh salmon to Big Macs. Buy groceries at the **Foodland Supermarket,** 631 Willoughby Ave., past the Federal Building and near Gold Creek. (Open Mon.-Sat. 9am-7pm, Sun. 10am-6pm.) Seafood lovers haunt **Merchants Wharf,** next to Marine Park. **Taku Smokeries,** 230 S. Franklin St. (463-3474), has the best lox this side of Zabar's ($13 per lb.).

Armadillo Tex-Mex Cafe, 431 S. Franklin St. (586-1880). Fantastic food, always packed with locals and tourists alike. Hunker down to "BBQ Hot Link Sausages" ($6.95) and a heaping plateful of T. Terry's Nachos ($4.50). Open Mon.-Sat. 11am-10pm, Sun. 4am-10pm.

Fiddlehead Restaurant and Bakery, 429 W. Willoughby Ave. (586-3150), ½-block from the State Museum. Fern-ishings for the sprouts-lovin' set. Lures mobs with its beef, salads, seafood, exquisite desserts, and fresh Alaskan sourdough. Great sandwiches and burgers on Fiddlehead buns with soup or salad ($8-10). Dinner $9-20. Open Mon.-Fri. 6am-10pm, Sun. 7am-10pm.

Heritage Café and Coffee Co., Franklin St. (586-1088), across from the Senate Bldg. A great place to escape for an hour or two from Juneau's often wet and tourist-ridden streets. Large sandwiches ($4.95) and excellent bottomless cup of coffee ($1). Open Mon.-Wed. and Fri. 7am-11pm, Thurs. 7am-7pm, Sat. 8am-11pm, and Sun. 9am-11pm.

Federal Building Cafeteria, Federal Building, 2nd floor, on Willoughby Ave. Although this eating place provides little in the way of decor, it won't leave you with a budget deficit (filling lunch for under $5).

Vito 'n' Nicks, 299 N. Franklin (463-5051), at 3rd. Large, gooey Chicago-style cheese pizza ($15) easily feeds 3 people. Grinder $6.25. Homemade cinnamon rolls $2. Open Mon.-Thurs. 7:30am-8pm, Fri. 7:30am-9pm. Sat. noon-8pm.

The Grubstake, E. 3rd St. (586-6414), up the steep dirt hill at the end of 3rd, underneath the Bergman Hotel. A local miners' favorite, this subterranean steakhouse serves stout meals for reasonable prices. "The Grubber"—8-oz. N.Y. sirloin, potatoes, carafe of wine, $12.95. Open Mon.-Fri. 11am-2pm, daily 6pm-10pm.

Silverbow Inn, 120 2nd St. (586-4146), downtown. French and American cuisine served on antique oak tables in a country-inn atmosphere. Rotating menu. Lunch $7-13, dinner $12-24. Reservations recommended. Open Mon.-Fri. 11:30am-2pm, Sat.-Sun. 9am-2pm; daily 5:30pm-9:30pm.

Gold Creek Salmon Bake, on Basin Rd. (586-1424), 10 min. drive from downtown in the historic Last Chance Basin. Beside crystal-clear Gold Creek and the ruins of the original A-J Gold Mine. All the salmon you can eat with all the fixings for $19. Live local music nightly. A free bus leaves the Baranof on N. Franklin daily at 6pm. Open daily Memorial Day-Labor Day 5:30-9pm.

Sights

Three thousand years ago, the "Little Ice Age" froze much of what is now Southeastern Alaska, creating the thousands of glaciers which still exist in this region today. Of these, the most visited is the **Mendenhall Glacier,** about 10 mi. north of downtown Juneau. Mendenhall is only one of 38 glaciers in the Juneau Ice Field, which covers an area of over 1,500 square mi. At the glacier visitors center, rangers will explain everything you could possibly want to know about the glacier. (Open daily 9am-6:30pm.) The rangers also give an interesting ecology walk everyday at 10:30am. The best view of the glacier without a helicopter is from the three-and-a-half mi. **West Glacier Trail**. To reach the glacier, you can either hitchhike from anywhere along Glacier Hwy. or take the local public bus (75¢) down Glacier Hwy. and up Mendenhall Loop Rd. until it connects with Glacier Spur Rd. From here it's less than a half-hour walk to the visitors center. **Eagle Express Line** runs excellent tours (see Practical Information and Orientation), though a tour is by no means necessary to appreciate this hulking mass of ice.

In Juneau itself, the **Alaska State Museum,** 395 Whittier St. (495-2901), is a good introduction to the history, ecology, and native cultures of "The Great Land." The museum's exhibits are unusually informative on the cultures of Alaska's four main native groups: Tlingit, Athabaskan, Eskimo, and Aleut. It also houses the famous "First White Man" totem pole, on which the artist carved the likeness of Abraham Lincoln. (Open May 15-Sept. 15 Mon.-Fri. 9am-6pm, Sat.-Sun. 10am-6pm; off-season Tues.-Sat. 10am-4pm. Admission $2, students free.) The **Juneau-Douglas City Museum,** 114 W. 4th St. (586-3572), provides unrivaled insight into Juneau's history. There are displays on mining, hand-woven quilts, native crafts, and a flattering antique scale which knocks a few pounds off of your actual weight. Open daily 9am-5pm, admission free.

The unimpressive **state capitol** building is located at 4th and Main. Tours are offered daily from 9am to 5pm in the summer, but your time is better spent wandering uphill to check out the **St. Nicholas Russian Orthodox Church** on 5th St. between N. Franklin and Gold St. Built in 1894, the church is the oldest of its kind in southeastern Alaska. Services are conducted in English, Slavonic (old Russian), and Tlingit. Open to the public. One block farther uphill on 6th St. is a 45-foot **totem pole** carved in 1940. The **State Office Building** (affectionately called the S.O.B. by locals) has an observation platform on the eighth floor overlooking the downtown, Douglas Island, and the Channel.

Farther downhill along N. Franklin, the **Historic Senate Building** shelters an atrium with specialty shops, including authentic Russian and Irish gift stores. In nearby **Marine Park,** rambunctious children play as young lovers picnic, and watch the lazy passage of ships through the **Gastineau Channel.** Free concerts are held Friday nights, from 7 to 8:30pm.

Finding the best view of downtown is simply a matter of walking to the end of 6th St. and then up the trail to the summit of **Mt. Roberts** (3576 ft.)—a steep 4-mi. climb. Miners flocked to "them thar hills" in the 1880s after Joe Juneau and Dick Harris found treasure in Gold Creek. Though mining is no longer an active industry in Juneau, the mines are still active as tourist sights and frequently host salmon bakes. The **Alaska-Juneau Mine** was the largest in its heyday. **Last Chance Basin,** at the end of Basin Rd., is now Gold Creek's mining museum.

Juneau is one of the best hiking centers in Southeast Alaska. In addition to the ascent of Mt. Roberts, **Perseverance Trail,** which leads past the ruins of the historic **Silverbowl Basin Mine** behind Mt. Roberts makes for a pleasant day trek. For more details on this as well as several other area hikes, drop by the state museum bookstore, the park service center, or any local bookstore to pick up *Juneau Trails,* published by the Alaska Natural History Association ($2). The rangers provide copies of particular maps in this book at the Park Service Center. (See U.S. Forest and National Park Service under Practical Information.)

During winter the slopes of the **Eaglecrest Ski Area** on Douglas Island (contact 155 S. Seward St., Juneau 99801, 586-5284 or 586-5330), offer good skiing. ($19 per day, children up to 6th grade $10, grades 7-12 $14. Rental of skis, poles, and boots $17-18, for children $14.) In summer, the Eaglecrest "Alpine Summer" self-guided nature trail is a good way to soak in the mountain scenery of virtually untouched Douglas Island.

At night, tourists head to the **Red Dog Saloon** (463-3777), on S. Franklin. The Red Dog may not be authentic, but who cares, it's still a fun place to visit. Live music on weekends. Locals hang out farther up Franklin. The **Triangle Club** (586-3140), on Front St., attracts the more hard-drinking set, while young people (as well as the cruise ship crowd) congregate at the **Penthouse,** on the fourth floor of the Senate Building. The **Lady Lou Revue** (586-3686), a revival of Gold Rush days, presents weekly toe-tappin' musicals. A large family attraction, the Revue is performed in the Perseverance Theatre in Merchants' Wharf, 2 Marine Way. Tickets ($14, children $7) can be purchased at the door or in local bookstores.

Near Juneau: Glacier Bay National Park and Preserve

In 1879, when naturalist John Muir became the first white man to see what nature had uncovered in Glacier Bay, he wrote, "These were the highest and whitest mountains, and the greatest of all the glaciers I had yet seen." He wasn't kidding. Crystal boulders float in the 65-mi.-long fjords of Glacier Bay, while humpback whales glide smoothly past. **Glacier Bay National Park** encloses 16 tidewater glaciers, as well as Mt. Fairweather of the Saint Elias Range. Here you can see with your own eyes what you've probably only glimpsed on *Mutual of Omaha's Wild Kingdom:* gigantic icebergs tumbling off glaciers and plunging dramatically into the icy blue water. Charter flights, tours, and cruise ships all make the spectacular voyage into Muir Inlet, offering close-up views of glaciers, rookeries, whales, and seals.

Because of the sensitive wildlife in the area, the number of people allowed into the park is limited. Visitors should contact the park superintendent, Glacier Bay National Park and Preserve, Gustavus 99826 (697-2230). Wilderness camping and hiking is permitted throughout the park, and tour-boat skippers drop passengers off at points designated by the park service; you'll have to make arrangements to be picked up later.

Any visit to this park will be expensive. The least costly way to get to the island is by **Alaska Airlines** (800-426-0333), which flies daily to Gustavus for $70 round-trip. Gustavus is only ten mi. from the park, and it's an easy hitch to Bartlett Cove, though a bus is available ($15 round-trip). An **information center** is maintained in **Bartlett Cove** by the park service. (Open June-Sept. daily 8am-7pm. In winter, call 697-2232 Mon.-Fri. 8am-4:30pm.) Once at Bartlett Cove, backpackers can stay in the free state campground, which has 25 sites and is rarely full. However, in order to see the most impressive part of the park, the **West Arm,** it is necessary to take a boat tour.

The best tourboat is the *Spirit of Adventure,* which conducts an eight-hr. tour of the glaciers for $142. For an extra $23.50, the boat will drop off campers or kayakers, and pick them up again at pre-arranged times. The *Spirit* is owned by the Glacier Bay Lodge (800-622-2042), next to Bartlett Cove, which has top quality rooms (singles $99, double $126). **Puffin Travel, Inc.** (907-789-9787) runs a bed and break-fast, providing free bicycles and transfers to and from the airport. (Singles $35. Dou-bles $50, each additional person $10.) They also operate a travel booking service for other accommodations, as well as sight-seeing, fishing, and photography tours. Write for more information to Puffin Travel, Inc., Box 3-LG, Gustavus, AK 99826.

Cruises into the park are also available, though they are quite expensive. **Alaska Sightseeing Tours** (800-426-7702) operates a three-day, two-night trip from Juneau, which includes both the east and west arms of the Bay ($399-$599 per person). The cruise sails from May 28 to September 3 every Monday, Wednesday, and Friday at 4pm.

Northern Panhandle

North of Juneau, the inside passage grows in magnificence: the mountains become bigger and snowier, the whales and eagles friendlier. The **Alaska Marine Highway** can take you up to Haines ($14 from Juneau, ages 6-11 $8; vehicle up to 15 ft. $35). Sleep on the ferry or stay up all night traveling through this land of many glaciers and soaring peaks.

Haines

In the early 1890s, adventurer Jack Dalton improved an old Indian Trail from Pyramid Harbor up to the Yukon. The investment paid off during the Gold Rush from 1897 to 1899, when stampeding gold-seekers paid outlandish tolls on the quickest road to the Klondike. Thanks to the army's further refinements to the road during World War II, the **Haines Highway** is now the most traveled overland route into the Yukon and the Interior from southeastern Alaska.

The area's star attraction is the convergence of over 3000 bald eagles (more than double the town's human population) on the Chilkat Peninsula's "Council Grounds" from November to January each year. Haines is perhaps the most attrac-tive of the southeast fishing villages, where granite coastal range sets the graceful white walls of Victorian Ft. Seward. For outdoors enthusiasts, Haines provides su-perb hiking, biking, and fishing opportunities. While Haines lacks the energy of Ju-neau and Ketchikan or the history of Sitka, it is worth a trip for the scenery alone.

Practical Information

Visitor Information Center: 2nd Ave. near Willard St. (766-2234, 766-2202, or 800-458-3579). Information on accommodations, hiking around town, and the surrounding parks. Make sure to pick up the free pamphlet *Haines is for Hikers*. Free coffee and a place to stash your pack inside. Open June-Sept. Mon.-Sat. 8am-8pm, Sun. 10am-7pm.

State Park Information Office: 259 Main St. (766-2292), above Helen's Shop. Legendary Ranger Bill Zack can tell you all you need to know about camping in the area, the dangers of bears, and the Chilkat Bald Eagle Preserve. Open Tues.-Sat. 8-8:30am and 4-4:30pm.

Buses: Alaskan Express, on 2nd Ave. Box 574 (766-2030 or 800-544-2206), across from the Visitor's Center in the **Wings of Alaska** office. Buses leave Haines along the Haines Hwy. on Tues. and Fri. To: Anchorage ($173), Fairbanks ($149), and Whitehorse ($71). Open Mon.-Sat. 7am-7pm. **Alaska-Denali Transit,** 701 W. 58th Ave., P.O. Box 4557, Anchorage 99510 (561-1078). Van service to: Anchorage ($115), Fairbanks ($99), Denali ($105), and Tok ($65), every Tues. at 8am from Bear Creek Camp in Haines. Call ahead for ticketing and pick-up information. Open Mon.-Fri. 8am-5pm.

Alaska Marine Highway Terminal: 5 Mile Lutak Rd. (766-2111), 4 mi. from downtown. You can easily hitch into town or take a taxi for $7.

Taxi: Haines Taxi 766-3138.

Car Rental: Avis, in the Halsingland Hotel (766-2733), $50 per day, with 100 free mi., 35¢ per each additional mi..

Laundromat: Susie Q's, Main St., just up from the harbor and across from the museum. Open Mon.-Fri. 8am-8pm, Sat.-Sun. 8am-5pm.

Health Center: 766-2521.

Mental Health Center: 766-2177

Ambulance and Emergency: 911.

Police: 766-2121.

Post Office: corner of 2nd Ave. and Haines Hwy. Open Mon.-Fri. 9am-5:30pm. General Delivery ZIP Code: 99827.

Population: 1200 in the town of Haines, 3000 in Haines Borough.

Area Code: 907.

Both the U.S. and Canada have **customs offices** at Mile 42 Haines Hwy. (767-5511 and 767-5540, open daily 7am-11pm). Travelers must have at least $150 or credit card, as well a valid form of ID as proof of citizenship to cross into Canada, although it is up to the whim of border officials to decide when this requirement should be enforced.

Accommodations and Camping

Rather than wander three mi. out of town to the hostel, campers should crash in **Port Chilkoot Camper Park** down 2nd Ave. in front of Ft. Seward.

Hotel Halsingland, Box 1589MD, Haines 99827 (800-542-2525 or 766-2000). Dollar-for-dollar the best hotel in Haines. Located in the old Ft. Seward officers' quarters. 60 rooms. Rooms $30, with bath $63. Some rooms have fireplaces or claw-footed bathtubs. Avis car rental located here.

Summer Inn Bed and Breakfast, 247 2nd Ave., P.O. Box 1198, Haines 99827 (766-2970). Nice rooms, full breakfast, and great view of the Lynn Canal and surrounding mountains. Singles $45. Doubles $60.

Bear Creek Camp & Hostel (AYH), Box 1158, Haines 99827 (907-766-2259), on Small Tract Rd. almost 3 mi. outside of town. From downtown, follow 3rd Ave. out Mud Bay Rd. to Small Tract Rd. 22 beds. Kitchen facilities. No curfew. Call ahead for ferry pickup. Members $10, nonmembers $12. Cabins $30. Showers $2.

Port Chilkoot Camper Park, Box 473, Haines 99827 (766-2755). 60 neat campsites for tents ($5.50) and RVs (full hookup $9). Laundromat, showers, telephone available.

Campgrounds: Chilkat State Park, 7 Mile Mud Bay Rd. (32 sites), **Chilkoot Lake,** 10 Mile Lutak Rd. (33 sites). **Mosquito Lake,** 27 Mile Haines Hwy. (7 sites). **Portage Cove Wayside,** .75 mi. from town on Beach Road. Backpackers only. All sites have water and toilets, $5.

Haines Hitch-Up RV Park, P.O. Box 383, Haines 99827 (766-2882). ½ mi. west of town on Main St. 92 full-hookup units, $14.

Food

Those wishing to forgo restaurant fare can hit **Howser's Supermarket** on Main St. (open Mon.-Sat. 9am-8pm, Sun. 10am-7pm). The store has a great salad bar with a large pasta selection ($2.49 per lb.), and a deli counter with surprisingly good chow. Golden 3-piece fried chicken, 5 Jo-Jos (deep-fried potato wedges) and a soda $5.

Porcupine Pete's, Main and 2nd Ave. (766-9199). Great sandwiches, such as a large French Dip, $5. Slice of pizza and soup $3. Excellent ice cream, single scoop $1. Open daily 11am-10pm.

Chilkat Bakery and Restaurant, 5th Ave., near Main (766-2920). Family-style restaurant with healthy portions. The *best* baked goods: bread loaves $1.70, cinnamon rolls $1. Friday night Mexican all-you-can-eat buffet ($10.49) locally favored. Open Mon.-Fri. 7am-8pm, Sat. 7am-6pm.

Bamboo Room, 2nd Ave. near Main St. (776-9109), next to the Pioneer Bar. Great breakfast spot, always crowded with fishermen on their way out to the nets. Hot cakes and coffee $3.75, omelettes from $4. Open daily 6am-10pm.

Port Chilkoot Potlatch, at the Tribal House of Ft. Seward (766-2000). All-you-can-eat salmon bake with all the trimmings ($17.50). Although the Potlatch is undoubtedly a tourist trap, the salmon is unbeatable. Reservations recommended since tickets are pre-sold to cruise ships. Served nightly 5-8pm.

The Lighthouse Restaurant, corner of Front and Main St. (766-2442). Large daily lunch specials $6.75. Filling deluxe cheeseburger with fries $5.50. Excellent salad bar with locally-caught seafood dinners $15-18. Open daily 7am-10pm.

Sights

Fort William Seward, on the west side of town, was once the only army barracks in Alaska, and now serves as the center of activity in Haines. In the middle of the fairgrounds sits a **Totem Village,** complete with a tribal house. On selected nights, the **Port Chilkoot Dancers** perform traditional native dances here (766-2160; Mon. and Sat. at 8pm, Wed. at 6:45pm and 7:45pm. Admission $7, students $4, children under 5 free. Tribal House open Mon.-Fri. 9am-5pm, weekends if a cruise ship is in.) Crossing to the far side of the fairgrounds takes you to the **Alaska Indian Arts Center.** Inside, visitors are welcome to watch native artisans in their workshops and marvel at the craft of totem pole carving. (766-2160; Mon.-Fri. 9am-noon, 1-5pm.)

In town, the **Sheldon Museum,** 25 Main St., houses Native art and artifacts downstairs and exhibits on the history of Haines upstairs. Movies about Haines are shown at 2pm. (Open daily 1-5pm. Admission $2.) The museum serves free Russian tea. Haines is also something of an artists' colony. Check out the works of local artists like Jenny Lyn Smith, Jenny Lyn Bader, and Tresham Gregg III in galleries near the visitor center. Some of the better galleries include the **Northern Arts Gallery,** the **Sea Wolf Studio,** the **Art Shop,** and **Chilkat Valley Arts.**

The **Haines Highway.** winds 40 mi. form Haines through the **Chilkat Range** and up through the Yukon Territory in Canada. Natural magnificence practically avalanches onto the highway. **Chilkat State Park,** a 19-mi. drive up the highway, protects the largest population of bald eagles in North America—3500 of 'em. From November through January, travelers can see great numbers of eagles perched on birchwoods in the rivers or flying overhead. **Chilkat Guides** (766-2409), P.O. Box 170, leads four-hour raft trips in eagle season down the Chilkat River. ($70, rubber boots and ponchos provided.) Haines is also home to the **Southeast Alaska State Fair** and the **King Salmon Derby** in late August. The **Winter Carnival** and **Alcan 200 Snowmobile Races** liven up February considerably for those in the area.

Skagway

In 1896, George Carmack, Skookum Jim, and Tagish Charley made an accidental discovery in a tributary off the Klondike River and uncovered gold lying thick between slabs of rock—"like cheese in a sandwich." Within two years, Skagway became the major staging area for the Klondike Gold Rush, and the placid settlement was beseiged by legions of crazed gold-seekers. The mounted police called the town "little better than a hell on earth . . . about the roughest place there ever was."

Today, the town itself has been restored wholesale by the National Park Service to its original 1898 condition. Skagway visitors come from miles around to revel in this zany history as well as the living wilds which surround the town. The one-hour ferry ride from Haines to Skagway is considered to be one of the most impressive stretches on the entire Inside Passage.

Practical Information and Orientation

Visitor Information: Klondike Gold Rush National Historical Park Visitor Center, 2nd and Broadway (983-2921). Walking tours daily at 11am and 3pm. Ranger talks daily at 10am and 2pm. Also shows on the hour a film on the gold rush, an excellent introduction to Skagway's history. Open June-Aug. daily 8am-8pm; May and Sept. 8am-6pm. **Skagway Convention and Visitors Bureau** (983-2854), in the City Bldg., 1 block off Broadway on 7th. P.O. Box 415. Open Mon.-Fri. 9am-6pm.

Alaska Marine Highway: 983-2941. Ferries daily to Haines ($12) and Juneau ($22).

Flights: Skagway Air Service (983-2218). Four flights per day to Juneau ($65).

Trains: White Pass and Yukon Route, 1 block off Broadway on 2nd., P.O. Box 435 (800-343-7373 or 983-2217). 3 hr. round-trip excursion to White Pass Summit, on one of the steepest railroad grades in North America. (Trains leave daily at 9am. $69, under 13 $34.50.) Motor-coach service to and from Whitehorse, YT. (Trains leave daily from Skagway at 7:45am. $89 one way, under 13 $44.50.)

Buses: Alaskan Express, in the Westmark Inn, 3rd St. between Broadway and Spring (800-544-2206 or 983-2241). Overnight travel to Anchorage ($185) and Fairbanks ($169). Tues. and Fri., at 7:30.

Taxi: Pioneer Taxi (983-2623). Tour of town $10. Ferry to Broadway $2.

Car Rental: Avis, in the lobby of the Westmark Inn (983-2247). $40 per day, 100 free mi., plus 35¢ per each additional mi.

Tours: Frontier Tours (983-2512). Takes backpackers to Dyea for $5 per person (3-person min.). **Skagway Sourdough Tours** (983-2521). White Pass Summit Tour $12.

Laundromat: Klothes Rush Laundry, Broadway and 5th (983-2370). Open Mon.-Sat. 9am-10pm, Sun. 10am-10pm.

Post Office: Broadway and 6th, next to the bank. Open Mon.-Fri. 8:30am-noon and 1-5pm. General Delivery ZIP Code: 99840.

Area Code: 907.

On the same latitude as Stockholm, Skagway is the terminus of the Alaska Marine Hwy., at the northernmost tip of the Inside Passage. From here, travelers on wheels can connect to the Alaska Hwy. by taking Yellowhead Hwy. 2 to Whitehorse via Carcross. Haines is located only 12 mi. away by water, but 359 mi. away by road. Hitchers would do best to spend $12 on the ferry to Haines and try the more heavily traveled Haines Hwy. to the Interior.

Accommodations

The bunkhouse in Skagway has been usurped by an art gallery. Campers can either shell out $6.25 for sites at **Hanousek Park** on 14th at Broadway or head out for the Chilkoot Trail in Dyea, 9 mi. from Skagway, to stay at the free ranger-staffed campground there. Reservations at least one month in advance are wise at all Skagway hotels.

Hanousel Park, on Broadway and 14th (983-2768), 1.9 mi. north of the ferry terminal. Drinking water, toilets, fire rings, sewer dump, but no showers. Sites $6.

Dyea Camping Area, 9 mi. southwest of Skagway on the Dyea Rd. This free campground is near the base of the **Chilkoot Trail,** and contains 22 sites. Pit toilets, fire rings, but no drinking water nor showers.

Mary's Bed and Breakfast, 10th and State St. (983-2875). Includes full breakfast and ferry pickup. Single $40. Double $50.

Skagway Inn, P.O. Box 500, Skagway 99840 (983-2289), on Broadway at 7th. Built in 1897 as a brothel, the inn is now respectably refurbished. All rooms with shared baths. Singles $48. Doubles $55. Breakfast included.

Golden North Hotel, P.O. Box 343, Skagway 99840 (983-2294), on 3rd Ave. and State St. A splendid hotel, the oldest operating in the state. Each room restored differently to period style, some with canopy beds, claw-footed bathtubs, and the like. Singles $60. Doubles $70.

Sergeant Preston's Lodge, P.O. Box 538, Skagway 99840 (983-2521), at 6th and State. Barracks-like exterior belies such interior luxuries as comfortable rooms and cable TV. Singles $45, with bath $55. Doubles $55, with bath $65.

Wind Valley Lodge, 22nd and State St.(983-2236). Courtesy car pick-up and spa available for guests. All private baths. Singles $48. Doubles $58.

Pullen Creek Park Campground (983-2768) on the waterfront, by the small boat harbor. 42 sites with full hookup. Sites $13.50.

Hoover's Campground, 4th and Main (983-2454), ¼ mi. north of ferry terminal. 15 RV sites, full hookup. Sites $12.

Food

Campers can pick up last-minute groceries for the Chilkoot trail at the **Fairway Supermarket** at 4th and State. (Open Mon.-Sat. 9am-8pm, Sun. 9am-6pm.) The majority of restaurants in Skagway are located in the Historic District, on Broadway between 2nd and 7th St.

Sourdough Café, on Broadway between 2nd and 3rd (983-2291). Cafeteria atmosphere vastly improved by the delectable spaghetti dinner with meatballs, salad, and garlic bread ($6). Delicious halibut calzone ($6). Open daily 11am-8pm.

Northern Lights Café (983-2225), on Broadway in the Historic District. The best prices on the block—try the "Mermaid Burger" (halibut sandwich with fries, $5.50) or the tower of sourdough pancakes ($3). Open daily 6am-10pm; Oct.-April 7am-8pm.

Sweet Tooth Saloon, on Broadway between 2nd and 3rd (983-2405). Sandwiches and soup or salad $3.20-5.50. This saloon scoops a mean ice cream cone ($1.25). Open daily 6am-6pm.

Pack Train Inn, on Broadway at 4th Ave. Blue-ribbon-hog-sized ham sandwich with split pea soup $6. Open Sat.-Thurs. 10:30am-5:30pm.

Dee's Restaurant, on 2nd Ave. (983-2200). Fresh Alaskan salmon and (more) halibut barbecued on an open pit, with a bountiful salad bar $13. Open daily 11am-9pm.

Sights

Most of Broadway (which is most of town) is preserved in pristine 1898 form as the **Klondike Gold Rush National Historic Park.** Check out the hourly film *Days of Adventure, Dreams of Gold* at the Park's **Visitor Center** (see Practical Information). Then wander down Broadway to peep at the **Red Onion Saloon,** on 2nd Ave., Skagway's first bordello. In the good ol' days, each lady marked her availability by placing one of the dolls on the rack downstairs in the appropriate position—vertical or prostrate. Farther down Broadway is the 1899 **Arctic Brotherhood Hall,** Alaska's first gold-mining fraternity. Twenty thousand pieces of driftwood cover the facade of the Hall, which is an excellent example of Victorian rustic architecture.

True gold rush buffs can mine for pleasure at the **Trail of '98 Museum,** on the second floor of City Hall, at 7th Ave. and Spring St. (Open June-Sept. daily 8am-8pm; May 9am-5pm. Admission $2, students $1.) The **Corrington Museum,** on 5th and Broadway (983-2580), contains an intriguing display of carved bone and ivory pieces, most of which are on sale at reasonable prices (that is, if you've managed to strike gold recently yourself). (Open daily 8:30am-7:30pm. Free, until you buy something.)

At night, go to the Red Onion to hear live jazz (no cover) and then to the *Skagway Days of '98* show in the **Eagles Dance Hall** at 6th and Broadway. The show, in its 65th year, features song and dance, play money gambling by the audience, and audience-actor interaction—definitely worth your the price. (983-2234; shows daily in summer, 8pm gambling, 9pm show).

Built as the gold craze calmed in 1900, the **railroad cars** of the White Pass & Yukon Route, have been resurrected from the locomotive graveyards of the West and now run from Skagway to the summit of White Pass and back. The scenery of this narrow passage is overwhelming. (Trains run May 24-Sept. 27 daily at 9am. Irregular service before May 24. Fare $67, ages under 13 $32.50.) On the east side of town, the tracks pass by the **Gold Rush Cemetery,** where Frank Reid is honored for giving his life to cleanse the streets of local crimelord "Soapy" Smith. Beyond the cemetery and farther out of town **Reid Falls** gently cascade 300 ft. down the mountainside.

Near Skagway: The Chilkoot Trail

In the winter of 1898, nine out of every ten stampeders-to-the-Klondike slogged through Skagway, every one somehow transporting one ton of gear in the harsh weather. Formerly an Indian footpath, the Chilkoot Trail extends 33 mi. from the ghost town of Dyea to the shores of Lake Bennett over the precipitous Chilkoot Pass. The three-to-five-day hike is littered with wagon wheels, horse skeletons, and other ballast the prospectors left behind, as well as commemorative plaques placed by the National Park Service.

The Chilkoot is considered the best hiking trail in Alaska, but it is extremely demanding. Weather conditions change rapidly, especially in the Summit area; avalanches are not uncommon even well into June. Be sure to check with the ranger at the visitors center in Skagway for current trail conditions before you leave. Rangers are also usually at the trailhead in Dyea daily from 5-7pm. If you are planning to continue into the Yukon Territory, be sure to call Canadian customs (403-821-4111) before leaving Skagway (Dyea has no phones), and have proof of solvency ($150 or a credit card, plus a valid photo ID) before crossing the border.

To return to Skagway, leave the trail between Lake Bennett and Bare Loon Lake and follow the White Pass railroad tracks back to the Klondike Hwy., where hitching is fairly easy in summer.

The Interior

Between the Alaska Range to the south and the Arctic Brooks Range to the north sprawls Alaska's vast Interior, blanketing 166,000 square mi. with the nation's wildest and most startling terrain. Most of the Interior alternates between low, flat patchworks of forest and marshy, treeless tundra. The drainage of four great rivers has created the sloughs, inlets, lakes, bogs, and swamps that sustain the world's largest waterfowl population. Moose, grizzlies, wolves, caribou, Dall (bighorn) sheep, lynx, beavers, and hares all become game for the would-be hunter. The unofficial state bird, the mosquito, outnumbers all other animals in the summer by over 1000:1. (Natives love to joke that there is not a single mosquito in the state of Alaska—they are all married and have kids.) Excepting Fairbanks (the state's second-largest city), the region is sparsely inhabited.

Interior Alaska is the home of Athabaskan Native Americans, many of whom still trap, hunt, and fish along the Interior's network of waterways. These nomadic hunters traditionally covered an area much larger than the Eskimos did, following the migration of caribou and the spawning cycles of salmon. Unlike Native Americans in the Lower 48, Athabaskans have not been confined to reservations; instead they own their own land, a result of the Alaska Native Land Claims Settlement Act. Although many have left their remote villages and traditional lifestyle for Fairbanks and Anchorage, their pride in their physical endurance, as well as their unique cultural heritage, lives on in their stories and games. Today Athabaskans still compete in dog-sled races and the annual World Eskimo-Indian Olympics, where thousands of spectators thrill to the sight of pain and endurance, such as races involving 10-lb. weights tied to participants' earlobes.

Mt. McKinley towers even above its 14,000-ft. neighbors in the Alaska Range, and in the summer can be spotted as far away as downtown Anchorage 300 mi. to the south. In the winter, long days are replaced by eternal night, and the vision of Mt. McKinley is replaced by the **Northern Lights**. Natives believed the lights were caused by the spirits of the dead.

Denali National Park

Established in 1917 to protect wildlife, Denali National Park just happened to include within its boundaries the highest mountain in North America. Athabaskan Native Americans have long called this mountain Denali, or "The Great One." One can only hope the Princeton-educated prospector who renamed the peak after Republican presidential nominee William McKinley in 1896 was not trying to translate its original name. From base to summit the greatest vertical relief in the world, Denali stands 20,320 ft. above sea level and 18,000 ft. above the meadows below. Denali is so big it manufactures its own weather—it is visible for only about 20% of the summer. You can experience the glories of Denali without seeing it, though—the park's tundra, taiga, wildlife, and lesser mountains make any trip worthwhile.

Practical Information and Orientation

Visitor Information: Visitor Access Center (683-1266), 7 mi. from Rte. 3. The terminus of the shuttle bus service; registration here for the park ($3) includes unlimited bus service once inside. Maps, free shuttle-bus schedules, free backcountry permits for overnight hiking, and information on campsites, wildlife tours, sled dog demonstrations, and campfire talks. All travelers are asked to stop here for orientation. Denali Park's indispensable publication, the *Alpenglow,* is also available (free). Open in summer for information and bus tokens daily 5:45am-8pm; for campground registration and backcountry permits daily 8am-8pm. The center is new, and has installed a backcountry simulator which provides uselful information for novice wilderness hikers. **Eielson Visitors Center,** another shuttle-bus stop 66 mi. into the park, is staffed by helpful rangers who post day-to-day sightings of the mountain. Open in summer daily 9am-8pm. Write **Denali National Park and Preserve,** P.O. Box 9, Denali Park 99755 (683-1266), for information on the park or consult the **Public Lands Information Center** (see Anchorage Practical Information).

Alaska Railroad: Traffic Division, Pouch 7-2111, Anchorage 99501 (683-2233). Stops at Denali daily in summer on its way to Fairbanks (one way $35; 4 hr.) and to Anchorage (one way $66; 7 hr.).

Buses: Alaska-Denali Transit, P.O. Box 4557, Anchorage 99510 (561-1078 or 273-3331). Daily shuttle from Anchorage ($35).

Denali Shuttle Bus: leaves Visitor Access Center daily 6am-7:10pm. Tokens ($3), unlimited passage. Annual pass $15.

Medical Clinic: 683-2211, in Healy. Open Mon.-Fri. 9am-5pm.

Emergency: 683-2295.

Post Office: next to Denali National Park Hotel, 1 mi. from the VAC Open Mon.-Fri. 8:30am-noon and 1-5pm, Sat. 9:30-11:30am; Oct.-May Mon.-Fri. 9:30-11:30am. General Delivery ZIP Code: 99755.

Area Code: 907.

Denali Park opens to the road, the railroad, and aircraft. The park entrance is 237 mi. north of Anchorage, and 121 mi. south of Fairbanks, along the scenic **George Parks Highway.** The 90-mi. gravel **Denali Highway** connects McKinley with Paxson, a town located midway between **Delta Junction** and **Glennallen.** Although there is no winter access, this bouncy stretch of road is among Alaska's most breathtaking, skirting the foothills of the Alaska Range amid countless lakes and streams with countless grayling, trout, and arctic char. Denali Park is located in the geographic center of the state, and at over five million acres is slightly larger than the state of Massachusetts.

Accommodations and Camping

Any hotel room in or near the park will be expensive. **ARA Outdoor World, Ltd.,** 825 W. 8th Ave., #240, Anchorage 99501 (276-7234), runs the park's tourist services, including the **Denali National Park Hotel** (683-2215), which more closely resembles Grand Central Station' than a wilderness outpost. Nearby are the railroad station, airstrip, nature trails, park headquarters, grocery store, and gas station (all of which, of course, are ridiculously overpriced). You pay for the railroad station theme and accessibility to tourist services. (Open May 20-Sept. 10. Singles $93. Doubles $105. Reserve early.) More rustic accommodations deep inside the park near Wonder Lake are somewhat less expensive. The best is **Kantishna Roadhouse** (radio phone 345-1160 WQH 23; $70 per night).

Hardsiders are going to have a hard time in Denali. There are few hookups or dump stations, and driving is allowed on only 12 mi. of Denali Park Rd. RVs can pay $10 per night to park at **Riley Creek Campground** in the middle of it all—the hotel, the visitors center, the train depot—or park on **Denali Road** outside the park behind the yellow trash cans for free.

Backpackers are assured a space for free in **Morino Campground,** next to the hotel, while they wait to get an inside-the-park site or a backcountry permit. Sites inside the park are distributed on a first-come, first-served basis, so arrive at the visitors center as early as possible in the morning. A wait of several days to get an inside-the-park permit is not uncommon: be patient and make sure you've brought along plenty of food.

The Happy Wanderer Hostel, Mile 238.6 Parks Hwy. (683-2690 or 683-2360), a 30-min. walk from the VAC. Eight beds, kitchen facilities, lockers. Reserve at least 1 mo. in advance. $15.

Denali Grizzly Bear Cabins and Campground, Mile 23 Parks Hwy. (683-2696), 7 mi. south of the VAC. Wide range of immaculate, restored wood cabins from Fairbanks gold mines of the 20s and 30s. For more information, write P.O. Box 7, Denali National Park 99755, or call 488-3932. In winter, write to 5845 Old Valdez Trail, Salcha 99714, or call 488-3932. Doubles from $49. Triples from $60. Quads from $67. Sites $12, tent cabins $16, electrical and water hookups $5.

Denali Cabins, P.O. Box 229, Denali National Park 99755 (683-2643), 1 mi. south of Denali Grizzly Bear Cabins and Campground. More rustic cabins, though hot tubs are included. No baths. Check-out 11am. Cabins sleeping 1-4 people $72. Reservations required.

Lynx Creek Campground, 2 mi. north of the entrance (683-2548). The closest private campground. RV sites $14.50, with hookups $18.75. Open May 20-Sept. 17.

Morino Creek, Mile 2.4 on Denali Park Rd., a ¼-mi. trail from Riley Creek. The backpackers' staging area. Bear-resistant food locker. Closest water at Chevron station ¼ mi. away. Pit toilets. No vehicles. Just walk in and pitch a tent. As many sites as needed. Free.

Wonder Lake, Mile 85 on Denali Park Rd. You are a happy camper indeed if you reach the park and Wonder Lake is not full. Spectacular views of Mt. McKinley. Piped water, flush toilets. No vehicles allowed. Tents only. Sites $10.

Riley Creek, Mile ¼ on Denali Park Rd. Often has the only open sites by mid-morning. Piped water, flush toilets, and a sewage dump. Sites $10. Open year-round.

Savage River, Mile 12 on Denali Park Rd. Flush toilets and water. Accessible only by shuttle bus or by a vehicle with a permit. Sites $10.

Sanctuary River, Mile 22 on Denali Park Rd. River water and pit toilets. Accessible only by shuttle or by a vehicle with a permit. Sites $10.

Teklanika River, Mile 29 on Denali Park Rd. Piped water and pit toilets. Accessible only by shuttle or by a vehicle with a permit (sound familiar?). Sites $10.

Igloo Creek, Mile 34 on Denali Park Rd. River water and pit toilets. Accessible only by shuttle. No vehicles allowed. Tents only. Sites $10.

Food

Groceries in Denali are available at the **Mercantile,** next to the Chevron, for shamefully high prices—a small jar of peanut butter costs $4.50. *Bring groceries into the park with you.* The hotel has an expensive restaurant and an unappealing snack shop. **Lynx Creek Pizza,** 1.5 mi. north of the park entrance, serves excellent and reasonable Mexican food and pizza. This is the place to go after spending several grueling days in the backcountry. Taco salad that would satisfy even Steve "Carnivore" Cohn ($6.75). Open daily 11am-midnight.

Sights and Activities

Denali accommodates hardcore and fledgling hikers alike. **Shuttle buses** from Riley Creek visitors center leave every ½-hour to various points in the park, including all campsites, Eielson visitors center, and Wonder Lake at the end of the line. Tokens ($3) are available at Riley Creek 24 hr. in advance. (A shuttle bus for wheelchair users leaves the center Tues.-Sun. at 9:30am.) Although the 10-hour, 170-mi. round-trip bus tour is an excellent way to see the wilds, it's nonetheless an awfully long time to ride along a bumpy road in a crowded school bus. In fact, these school buses were designed with negligible legroom and high backs to prevent horseplay. Visitors, especially those with small children, would be wise to opt for either the seven- or five-hour trips leaving from the same point. Once the tour begins, don't stay glued to your seat. The shuttles make frequent stops. The first shuttles leave Riley Creek at 6am. The earlier one departs, the better one's chances of seeing wildlife.

Those wishing to get off the roads can take the shuttle anywhere for a day hike. If you plan to spend the night in the park, you must either obtain a campsite for $10 or a free **backcountry permit** from the visitors center at Riley Creek. Only 2 to 12 hikers can camp in each of the 43 zones, so select a few different areas in the park in case your first choice is booked. Usually, however, the rangers will leave two or three zones open to unlimited backcountry camping, so that you can always hike the wilderness if you *really* want to. No matter where you camp, you must keep within the zone you signed up for, and you have to pitch your tent completely out of sight of the road (so as not to spoil the view for others). To keep from getting lost, you can also obtain topographic maps ($2.50) at Riley Creek. Many zones require you to carry a black, cylindrical bear-resistant food container, available free at Riley Creek. Set up your camp in the form of a triangle, 100 yards on a side. Place your tent at one point, the food container at another point, and do all of your cooking at the third point. Bears are a serious threat—don't even keep toothpaste or soap in your tent. Bears do not normally associate human scent with food, but if one should happen to come upon your sleeping-bag wrapped body while searching for the twinkies stashed under your pillow, it's burrito time!

Catching a glimpse of both the majestic peak and its many creatures takes perfect timing and better luck. You can increase your chances of seeing Denali's denizens by watching for them in their specific habitats. Dall sheep generally flock near the Igloo and Cathedral Mountains as well as along Primrose Ridge near Savage River in the summer; look for them near Polychrome Pass in the fall. Caribou congregate in alpine meadows in summer, and move to the hills between the Eielson visitors center and Wonder Lake in the fall. Moose meander everywhere, but are especially common during early mornings and late evenings near the Riley Creek Campground, in Savage River, and between Teklanika and Igloo campgrounds. Grizzly bears are everywhere; 200 to 300 live in Denali Park. Though no one has ever been killed by a bear in Denali, you know what they say.

If you meet a bear, rangers advise *slowly* backing up and talking slowly and loudly to the bear. Wave your arms and let it know that you're a human being, since bears are notoriously near-sighted. Whatever you do, don't imitate it. The bear will think you're making fun of him or that you want to challenge him, which you shouldn't and don't. Running is a recipe for disaster. Rangers also advise hikers to travel in small groups and to talk while hiking to alert bears to your presence. They advise solitary campers to wear bells, which are available at Riley Creek for 50¢. Singing is okay too, but don't whistle—you'll sound like the grizzly's favorite snack, ground squirrels.

The best times to see Mt. McKinley, which emerges only about once every three days, are evenings in the late fall (Sept.-Oct.); during the summer, fog usually shrouds "the Weathermaker." In any season, your best chance to view the mountain is to stick to the Wonder Lake Campground. Otherwise, take a shuttle to the Stony Hill Overlook, the Eielson visitors center, or the overlook near the Savage River Campground (at the rise in Sable Pass). The most impressive visions of the mountain materialize in the morning and late in the evening. A climb to the summit takes 30 days round-trip and costs thousands of dollars. Bush plane operators from Anchorage, Fairbanks, and Talkeetna can get you close to the summit faster and cheaper, though the price is almost as steep (about $100 per person). The Denali Park Hotel will set you up with a pilot. Scheduled flights from the hotel leave at 4 and 7pm daily, last an hour, and cost $105 per person.

Several rafting companies run the rapids of the Nenana River. **Owl Rafting** (683-2215) runs both a fast-action canyon run and a scenic float. (Both 2 hr. $32. Must be 12. Departures at 9am, 3pm, and 7pm.) They also run a special raft at 5:45pm to the McKinley Resort. The $40 ticket includes a dinner of salmon and ribs as well as a "show" at the end. (Tickets available at hotel front desks.)

The Park's **Ranger Headquarters**, ½ mi. down Denali Park Rd. from VAC, schedules nature hikes and lectures. Lectures take place in the auditorium of the Denali Park Hotel most nights at 7pm. Check the *Alpenglow* for information.

Fairbanks

At the end of the 19th century, thousands of Italian immigrants flocked to America's cities in search of streets "paved with gold." But Felix Pedro, an Italian miner, decided to start from scratch and headed to the largely unexplored Alaskan Interior. On July 22, 1902, on the banks of the Chena River, Pedro unearthed a shiny fortune. Within a year of his discovery, thousands more would-be treasure hunters had Rushed to the Interior, and Fairbanks soon arose as the commercial and cultural center of Alaska's northern reaches.

Today, the Trans-Alaska Pipeline carries far more riches through Fairbanks than the gold-laced pebbles of mountain streams. The city is now—as it was at the century's start—largely a service and supply center for the surrounding Bush. To the north, the lonely highway escorts the pipeline to Prudhoe Bay. Hitchhiking up this "highway" (actually a dirt road) all the way to the Arctic Ocean is not for everyone, but may prove one of the most memorable experiences of your Alaska adventure (see Prudhoe Bay). And to the south, the needles of black spruce and sheets of permafrost roll out a green and gold carpet for Mt. Denali and the Alaska Range.

Practical Information and Orientation

Visitor Information: Convention and Visitors Bureau Log Cabin, 550-Q 1st Ave., Fairbanks 99701 (456-5774). Free 1-hr. walking tours of the city with friendly and knowledgeable guides. Pick up their free pamphlet *Visitor's Guide: Fairbanks and Alaska's Interior,* listing tourist offices, transportation services, maps, annual events, activities, and shops. Open daily 8am-6:30pm; Oct.-April Mon.-Fri. 8am-5pm.

Alaska Public Lands Information Center (APLIC): 3rd and Cushman St. (451-7352). Exhibits and recreation information. Free daily films. Staff welcomes requests for information about hiking; write to 250 Cushman St., #1A, Fairbanks 99701. Open daily 8:30am-9pm; in winter Tues.-Sat. 10am-6pm. Come after 5pm to avoid the tourist busloads.

Fairbanks Information Hotline: 456-INFO. 24 hr. recording of festivals and events.

Airlines: Delta (474-0238) flies to the Lower 48. **Alaska Air** (452-1661) goes to Anchorage ($135) and Juneau ($195). **Mark Air** (474-9166) flies to larger Bush towns. Round-trip to Barrow $564.

Alaska Railroad, 280 N. Cushman (456-4155), next to the *Daily News-Miner* building. An excellent way to see the wilderness. One per day May-Sept. to Nenana ($17), Anchorage ($98), and Denali National Park ($35). Ages 5-11 ½-price.

Buses: Alaska Sightseeing Tours (276-7141). $299 to Prudhoe Bay. **Gray Line of Alaska,** 1980 Cushman (456-7742). Similar rates to Bush towns.

City Bus: MACS, 6th and Cushman (456-3279). Three routes through downtown Fairbanks and the surrounding area, as well as one to the North Pole area. Fare $1.50, senior citizens,

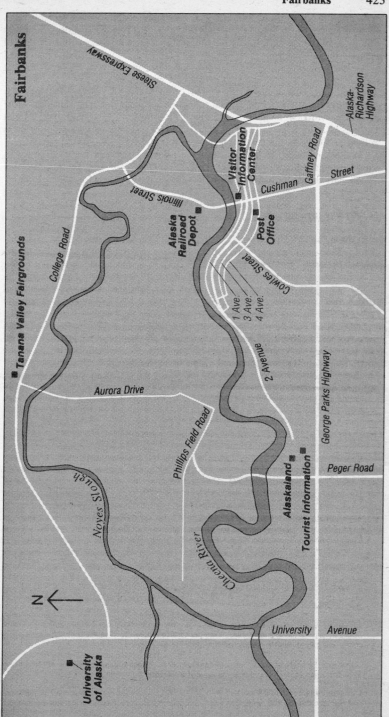

Fairbanks

Steese Expressway

Alaska-Richardson Highway

Gaffney Road

Visitor Information Center

Cushman   Street

Illinois Street

Post Office

Alaska Railroad Depot

Cowles Street

1 Ave.
3 Ave.
4 Ave.

College Road

Tanana Valley Fairgrounds

2 Avenue

George Parks Highway

Aurora Drive

Phillips Field Road

Alaskaland

Tourist Information

Peger Road

Noyes Slough

Chena River

N

University   Avenue

University of Alaska

ages 5-18, and disabled people 75¢, under 5 free. Day pass $3. Pick up a schedule at the convention and visitors bureau.

Taxi: Golden Nugget Cab (451-8294). **Northern Lights Taxi Co.** (456-2557).

Car Rental: Avis Rent-A-Car (800-331-1212 or 474-0900), at the International Airport. $40 per day, 100 free mi., 35¢ per each additional mi. Also **Budget** (474-0855), **Hertz** (452-4444), **Holiday Payless Car Rental** (474-0177), and **Allstar Rent-A-Car** (456-3213).

Road Conditions: 456-ROAD.

Camping Equipment: Clem's Backpacking Sports, 315 Wendell (456-6314), near the visitors bureau. **Rocket Surplus,** 1401 Cushman (456-7078). The latest in camouflage fashions. **Apocalypse Design, Inc.,** 101 College Rd. (451-7555), at Illinois. Fast repairs on zippers and straps.

Laundromats: B & C, at University and College (479-2696), in Campus Mall. Open Mon.-Sat. 8am-midnight, Sun. 9am-midnight. Also at 3rd and New Steese (452-1355), in Eagle Mall. Open Mon.-Sat. 8am-10pm, Sun. 9am-noon. Both have shower facilities ($2, with towel $2.50).

Weather: 452-3553.

Help Lines: Rape Emergency, 452-7273. **Poison Control Center,** 456-7182. **North Star Council on Aging,** 452-1735. **VD Hotline,** 474-6000. **Traveler Rescue Service,** 451-0544.

Crisis Line: 452-4357. Also provides contacts with gay and lesbian support groups.

Senior Citizens Center: 1424 Moore St. (452-1735).

Hospital: Fairbanks Memorial, 1650 Cowles St. (452-8181).

Alaska State Troopers: 452-1313.

Post Office: 315 Barnette St. (472-0722). Open Mon.-Fri. 9:30am-5:30pm, Sat. 10am-2pm. General Delivery ZIP Code: 99707.

Population: Fairbanks City, 27,000; Greater Fairbanks Borough, 74,000.

Area Code: 907.

Fairbanks is centrally located, and serves as the supply and culture nexus for most Bush and Arctic communities. The city lies 882 mi. northwest of Ketchikan and 508 mi. north of Kodiak Island; Anchorage is 358 mi. away via the **George Parks Hwy.,** and Prudhoe Bay can be reached by 516 mi. of the gravelly **Dalton Highway.**

Accommodations

Cheap accommodations limp in the far reaches of town and are often unsavory. Stick to the hostel or the hotels listed below and avoid flophouses in the outskirts. For referrals to private homestays, track down the **Fairbanks Bed and Breakfast,** P.O. Box 74573, Fairbanks 99707 (452-4967), which provides singles for $36, doubles for $48. Write ahead for reservations.

Fairbanks International Youth Hostel (AYH), P.O. Box 7-2196, Fairbanks 99707 (456-4159), in the quonset hut behind the farmer's market, on the corner of College Rd. and Aurora Dr. Truly an oasis in the desert of anal-retentive American youth hostels. The friendly atmosphere breeds immediate commeraderie, since the intrepid travelers who make it this far north all share a bond of adventurous spirits. In the evenings, perhaps the best social activity in Fairbanks gathers around the blazing nightly bonfire, often extending into the wee hours of the (sunny) night. The proprietor, Paul Shultz, has a wealth of information about the area and is always willing to point hostelers toward adventure (including Prudhoe Bay). 16 beds, 2 recreation rooms, cooking stove, hot showers, and outdoor barbecue pit. No curfew, no lockout. Members $5.25, nonmembers $7.25, or just set up your tent anywhere on hostel property for $4.25. Open May-Sept.

Gaffney Motel, 741 Gaffney Rd. (452-3534). The Cushman St. side of the schitzophrenic hotel is a windowless cinderblock wall—the other side is paneled with wood and has sliding glass doors and balconies. Singles $70. Doubles $75.

Cripple Creek Resort Hotel, P.O. Box 101, Ester 99725 (479-2500), 8 mi. south of Fairbanks off Parks Hwy. Pleasant atmosphere with an old-style saloon next door. Management takes pride in the fact that the rooms are cleaner than in the old days. Singles $40. Doubles $45. Triples $50.

Alaska Motor Inn, 419 4th Ave. (452-4800). Big rooms with cable TV and very nice bathrooms. Spotlessly clean. Singles $54. Doubles $64.80.

Camping

Private campgrounds are overpriced, but you can avoid them either by resorting to public state campgrounds, or by pitching a tent on the Youth Hostel grounds ($4.25).

Tanana Valley Campground (456-7956), next to the hostel. Tanana has the least expensive commercial sites in town, but some of them resound with noise from the fairground and busy street nearby. Caters to RVs. Free showers, laundromat, and grocery store down the street. Sites $10.

Chena Lake Recreation Area, University Ave. Take Airport Way west from the Richardson Hwy., right on University. The most popular place in town, and invariably full. Arrive early—no reservations. Water, toilets, and picnic tables provided. Sites $6.

John Alfonsi Sr. Memorial Campground (474-7355), at the university. Full facilities, with 15 drive-in and 15 walk-in campsites. Sites $2 per day or $7.50 per week for UAF students, $4 per day or $15 per week for non-UAF students.

Food

Fairbanks throbs with fast-food joints and pleasant, expensive, outdoor bistros. There is little in between. Groceries are available round the clock at **Safeway,** University and Airport Way, and at **Pay 'n' Save,** on the other side of town at Cushman and Airport. **Green Gopher Produce,** at College and Antoinette, sells the cheapest fresh fruit in town during the summer. (Open Mon.-Sat. 8am-8pm, Sun. 8am-7pm.) Get the best homemade ice cream in Alaska at **Hot Licks,** located in the Campus Corner Mall at the intersection of College and Farmer Loop Rd. (Open daily 9:30am-10:30pm.)

Souvlaki (452-5393), across the bridge from the visitors center. Succulent grape leaves 3 per $1. Lamb casserole and soup lunch specials $4.50. Open Mon.-Fri. 10am-8pm, Sat. 10am-6pm.

Café de Paris, 244 Illinois St. (456-2800). Delightful for an outdoor lunch or breakfast. With a name like this, it's got to be expensive: Chicken Kiev $9. Open Mon.-Sat. 10am-3pm.

Hunan Golden Restaurant, 513 4th Ave. (456-8844). 14-item lunch buffet $6.75, available Mon.-Fri. until 2:30pm. Open Mon.-Fri. 11:30am-11:30pm, Sun. 5-10pm.

Gordo's Restaurant, 126 N. Turner Dr. (456-7593). $8 Mexican lunch buffet. Excellent nightly dinner specials $7.75. Open Mon.-Sat. 11am-9pm.

Food Factory, 36 College Rd. (452-3313), and at 18th and Cushman (452-6348), both downtown. Caters to the Alaskan appetite ("Food just like Mom used to send out for!"). Cheesesteaks $5.75-7. Their forte is beer (106 varieties from around the globe). Open Mon.-Thurs. 10:30am-11pm, Fri.-Sat. 10:30am-1am, Sun. noon-10pm.

Speedy Submarine Sandwich Shop, 542 3rd Ave. (451-8305). Speedy's is straight from Chicago and makes the best foot-long subs in Fairbanks ($3.75-5.75). Open Mon.-Fri. 10am-6pm, Sat. 11am-5pm.

Royal Fork Buffet, 414 3rd St. (452-5655), at Steese Hwy. Part of a national chain of all-you-can-eat restaurants dedicated to overstuffing gluttonous patrons with cafeteria food. Different menu each day. Dinner $8.35, Sunday breakfast $6.75. Open Mon.-Thurs. 11am-8pm, Fri.-Sat. 11am-9pm, Sun. 9am-8pm.

Alaska Salmon Bake, Airport Way and Peger Rd. (452-7274), inside Alaskaland. One of the best salmon bakes in town. $14 buys enough salmon, halibut, ribs, and fixin's to satisfy a pioneering appetite. Tues. $3 off on halibut. Open May-Sept. daily 5-9pm.

Cripple Creek Resort, 8 mi. south of Fairbanks, in Ester. The restaurant offers a $9 buffet-style, all-you-can-eat halibut and caribou stew meal. Mmmm. Open daily 5-9pm.

Sights

One of Fairbanks's proudest institutions is the **University of Alaska-Fairbanks,** at the top of a hill overlooking the flat city. The **University of Alaska Museum,** 907 Yukon Dr. (474-7505), on West Ridge Hill, presents an excellent jumble of exhibits on subjects ranging from the formation of coal to Russian Orthodox vestments to Native baskets—all in the same room. (Open daily 9am-7pm; May and Sept. 9am-5pm; Oct.-April noon-5pm. Admission $3, senior citizens and students $2.50, families $10. Oct.-April Fri. free.) Another interesting stop at the university is the **Agriculture Experimental Station** where, with the aid of the long summer days, cabbages grow to the size of large subwoofers. Also at the university, the **Large Animal Research Station** offers tours on Tuesdays and Saturdays at 1:30 and 2:30pm ($2; think carefully about the cabbages before venturing here). The Student Activities Office in the **Wood Campus Center** posts listings of movies ($3-5), outdoor activities, and occasional music fests.

Alaskaland, P.O. Box 1267, Fairbanks 99707, on Airport Way, is a poor man's Arctic Disneyland. What it lacks in rides, it makes up for with gift shops, faux can-can shows, pioneer homes, gunfights, a sternwheel riverboat, and a pioneer museum. Feel the chills running up and down your spine? The quintessential tourist trap. But hey, at least it's free.

View a technological wonder of the world, the **Trans-Alaska Pipeline,** on the Steese Hwy. heading out of Fairbanks. The pipeline was elevated to protect the tundra's ecological system. (Overcome by his new-found passion for the environment, President George Bush noted that caribou love the pipeline so much they even rub themselves up against it.) Or take the **Riverboat Discovery** (479-6673) on a four-hour tour down the Chena River to the Tanana River past Athabaskan summer fish camps. During the trip, the captain and his crew unleash a flood of Fairbanks history. The riverboat leaves the docks on Dale Rd. (off Airport Way) at 8:45am and 2pm daily. (June-Aug.; fare $25, ages 12-18 $22.50, under 12 $17.)

Fairbanks harbors many art galleries but few artists. **Artworks,** 3677 College Rd. (479-2563), **Fine Arts Center,** Art Dept., #307 (456-7015), and **New Horizons Gallery,** 815 2nd Ave. (456-2063), all rise above the Elvis-on-velvet genre, but only by degrees. None dares charge admission.

Outside town lie all sorts of trivialities. The **Dog Mushers Museum,** at Mile 4 Farmer Coop Rd. (457-6528), is the canonic statement on the subject. **Pedro's Monument** marks the original site of Pedro Felix's 1902 gold discovery at Mile 16 Steese Hwy., five mi. north of Fox.

Entertainment

With nothing but black spruce to keep them company in the surrounding tundra, Fairbanksans turn to the bars at night. Expect stiff drinks and boisterous rugged-types fresh from the North Slope oil fields. UAF students head for the **Howling Dog Saloon,** 11½ mi. down Steese Hwy. (457-8780), for the live rock 'n' roll scene. (Open Tues.-Sun. 5pm-5am.) At some of the downtown bars, rowdiness flirts with violence.

Sunset Inn, 345 Old Richardson Hwy. (456-4754). Looks like a warehouse, but since Fairbanksans need only the bare necessities (drinks, dance floor, pool tables), it's usually jam-packed. Live top-40 dance music. Open Wed.-Thurs. and Sun. 10pm-3:30am, Fri.-Sat. 9:30pm-4am.

Senator's Saloon, Mile 1.3 on Chena Pump Rd. (479-8452), in the Pump House Restaurant. The only oyster bar in Fairbanks. Take drinks out to the deck and watch float planes land and river boats whiz by. Open Sun.-Thurs. 11am-1am, Fri.-Sat. 11am-2am.

Fox Roadhouse and Motherlode, Mile 11.5 Steese Hwy. (457-7461), across from the Howling Dog. Don't be surprised if you see horses hitched up to the post out front, and try not to stare when they collect shotguns at the front door. Open daily 9am-2am.

Seasonal Events

The best time to visit the city is in July—citizens don Gold Rush rags for **Golden Days,** a celebration of Felix Pedro's discovery of gold in July 1902. The week of July 12-21 sparkles with parades, sales, and many other gala events. Watch out for the traveling jail; if you haven't purchased the silly-looking button commemorating the event, you may be taken prisoner, and sometimes you pay a steep price to get out. (Most stores and businesses in town sell the buttons.) But the adventurer might as well stay on board the paddywagon—it's a free ride and it goes all over Fairbanks. For details, write the Fairbanks Chamber of Commerce, P.O. Box 74446, Fairbanks 99707 (452-1105). Make hotel reservations several months in advance.

The **Tanana Valley Fair** (452-3750), in the second week of August, features many shows and competitions as well as a bona fide rodeo. Follow the line of cars down College Rd. to the fairgrounds. (Admission $4, senior citizens $3, ages under 12 $2; $25 family pass covers all family members each day of the fair.)

For a sports spectacular with native flavor, see the **World Eskimo-Indian Olympics,** P.O. Box 2433, Fairbanks (452-6646). At the end of July, Natives from all over Alaska compete in shows of strength and endurance, all the while entertaining one another with ancient stories and traditional dances.

On June 22, the **Yukon 800 Marathon Riverboat Race** sends 20 lunatics in 16-ft. trawlers 800 mi. up and down the mighty Yukon, beginning and ending in Fairbanks. For contestant information and race time, contact Fairbanks Outboard Association, P.O. Box 340, Fairbanks 99707 (452-6347). The **Nochalawogya Festival** presents three days of fascinating Athabascan culture beginning on June 6 (Estelle Day). Contact Tanana Native Council, P.O. Box 91, Tanana 99777 (366-7160), for more information.

Baseball fanatics should come watch the Fairbanks Goldpanners strut their stuff. The Goldpanners have won five minor league National Championships since 1970, and always have a number of hot new rookies on their starting line-up. Games are at **Growden Memorial Park,** near Alaskaland (451-0095, admission $4). Don't be afraid to sneak in a few beers; the entire bleacher section tends to whoop it up.

Near Fairbanks

Fairbanks is, culturally speaking, a C-major triad amid the tritones of the deep Interior wilderness. If you seek a break from city life and have already conquered Mt. McKinley, dangle your feet in the plentiful lakes and hot springs nearby. Since many of the recreational lakes are continually restocked with fish, casting lines can be a fully predictable "sport."

Two major roads lead south of Fairbanks. George Parks Hwy. heads southwest by Denali National Park, and Richardson Hwy. runs to Valdez in the Prince William Sound. Take George Parks Hwy. 60 mi. south to the state's **agricultural areas.** Exciting grain crops planted on land bought from the state for next to nothing thrive on the healthy soil and long summer sun.

Lakes

The **Chena River Recreation Area,** at Mile 26-51 on Chena Hot Springs Rd., covers 254,080 acres of fishing, hiking, canoeing, and camping around the Upper Chena River and Chena Lakes. Rent the necessities right on the lake: canoes $6 per hour, rowboats $8 per hour, sailboats $10 per hour, fishing rods $2 per day. The 78 campsites, some of which offer disabled access (off Laurence Rd.), are free. Hiking trails include: **Granite Tors** (trailhead at Mile 39 campground), a 12-16 mi. round-trip hike to granite rocks—great for overnight campouts; **Angel Rocks** (starting at Mile 48.9 campground), an easy 3½-mi. trek through exquisite wilderness; and **Chena Dome Trail** (beginning at Mile 15.5), a more remote 29-mi. adventure overlooking the river valleys. There is also a shooting range at Mile 36.5. (Admission $1 per person, $3 per vehicle.)

Harding Lake (Mile 42 on Richardson Hwy.), **Birch Lake** (Mile 48 on Richardson Hwy.), and **Quartz Lake** (Mile 86.2 on Richardson Hwy.) are Sunday anglers' dreams. The state stocks the lakes with salmon and trout. Boat ramps are provided at each lake, and small boats can be rented at Quartz and Harding. ($7 per hr.) Campsites are free and available only at Harding and Quartz Lakes.

Hot Springs

Fifty-seven miles northeast of Fairbanks on Chena Hot Springs Rd., the **Chena Hot Springs Resort** allows you the chance to go soak your head—or body. Expect fine fishing near this inn once the water temperature drops from the spring snow melt. Handsome hiking trails are nearby. The chalet accommodations are a bit steep (singles with half-bath $48, with full bath $58; doubles $68-78), although pool admission is included. Non-patrons may use the hot pool for $5.50, children under 13 $4.50. There are also tent and RV campsites in the area. (Sites $5. For reservations, write 110 Antoinette St., Fairbanks 99701, or call 452-7867. Open Mon.-Fri. 10am-3pm.) On the way to the hot springs stands the **Two Rivers Lodge and Restaurant,** Mile 16 Chena Hot Springs Rd. (488-6815). Set in a rustic cove of pine trees near a scenic pond, this restaurant grills up succulent ribs and Alaskan specialties. (Open Wed.-Sun. 6-11pm.)

The **Arctic Circle Hot Springs** (520-5113), discovered in 1893, are three hours north of Fairbanks on Steese Hwy. The **hostel** on the fourth floor charges $15 for bunk accommodations, $35 for a room. Several **campgrounds** line Steese Hwy. nearby, where the scenery is stunning. Or just camp directly on the banks of the virile Yukon. Gaze up at **Eagle Summit** between diving into the Olympic-sized swimming pool and indulging yourself at the ice cream parlor. On June 21 and 22, those on the peak can watch the midnight sun cha-cha across the horizon without ever setting.

Cripple Creek Resort

Seven miles south of Fairbanks (Mile 351.7 on the George Parks Hwy.) lies the drunkard's dream of Cripple Creek Resort, a reconstructed turn-of-the-century village built with all the creature comforts of the 1990s. This quiet little town with reasonable prices and a measure of authenticity (the general store sells fresh reindeer meat) comes as welcome relief from the gift shops of Alaskaland.

A bus makes the circuit of 10 Fairbanks hotels before heading south to the resort. To make the necessary reservations (round-trip $4), call 479-2500. The all-you-can-eat buffet ($12, with crab $18) lines up such local delicacies as reindeer stew (sorry, Rudolf) and Alaska Dungeness Crab. Dinner is served under the roof of a charming hotel designed to resemble an old miners' bunkhouse. (Singles $33. Doubles $38. Triples $43. Continental breakfast included.) After-dinner entertainment is scarce. The *Crown of Light,* a film shown twice per night in the Firehouse Theatre, projects the aurora borealis onto a giant 30-ft. screen while symphonic music plays over the speakers. After the film, sidle through the swinging doors onto the sawdust floor of the **Malemute Saloon,** and watch the can-can dancers strut their stuff-stuff. The cost of buffet dinner and show, including drinks, gratuity, and transportation, is $24 per person. What a party.

Campers can park their RVs a minute's walk from the saloon for $5 per night. A sewage dump and water are available.

Although not nearly as lively as some of the downtown Fairbanks bars, Cripple Creek is the place for a pleasant, more relaxed evening. Call or write for reservations at least two days in advance (Cripple Creek Resort, P.O. Box 109, Ester 99725; 479-2500).

North Pole

Yes, Vanessa, there is a town called North Pole. It's just 13 mi. south of Fairbanks on Richardson Hwy., and its post office (ZIP Code 99707) receives thousands of letters each Christmas. Unfortunately for Santa and the elves, the town's population has doubled in the last four years. Four shopping malls now bestride the landscape, and a monstrous overpass guards Badger Road from the perils of the highway.

The only place of any interest to most tourists is **Santa Claus House** (488-2200), just off (you guessed it) Santa Claus Lane. The world's largest statue of St. Nick guards the door. The house is packed with expensive trinkets and souvenirs, so stay outside and marvel at the colorful Christmas murals. (Open May-Dec. daily 8am-7pm.)

At Mile 11 on Richardson Hwy., **Apple Joe's Supper Club** (488-6611), offers unbeatable prime rib and lobster (it's anybody's guess how they swam all the way to the North Pole). Joe's entrees start at $10.50.

Nenana

Nenana (pronounced nee-NAN-nuh) lies 53 miles south of Fairbanks on George Parks Hwy. Once the end of the Alaska Railroad, and situated at the confluence of the Tanana and Nenana Rivers, the town is now famous for the **Nenana Ice Pool.** Alaskans and residents of the Yukon Territory, bored out of their skulls during the long winter months, bet on the exact minute when the ice will give out, thereby dislodging a large tripod ceremoniously stuck there. The pot regularly amounts to over $115,000. Today this tradition is just one of the events at the **Nenana Ice Classic,** a festival that attracts people from far and wide. Even in the summer you can see the famous tripod that houses the timing device for the big event. Beware of locals who try to sell you a ticket, trip, or Ice Bridge in advance. For more reliable information on the event, write P.O. Box 272, Nenana 99760 (832-5446). The town's nightlife revolves around the two ornery-looking corner bars next to the train station. No hotels are of note, and the nearest campgrounds are another 20 mi. south on George Parks Hwy. The **Alaska Railroad** stops here on its way to Anchorage.

Steese National Conservation Area

Steese is home to an abundance of wildlife, and has some of the best grayling fishing in the Interior. Simply take **Steese Highway** until it ends at Circle, and start walking. Make sure to get detailed topographical maps from ALPIC (see Fairbanks Practical Information) before you go. Climb the **Crazy Mountains,** or see if you can find the legendary **Windy Creek Hot Springs** on the south side of **Ketchikan Dome.** However, beware of bear and moose, and be careful about wandering around on a sourdough's gold mine. There are plenty of **cabins** throughout the woods, which you are free to stay in so long as they don't appear to be currently inhabited and aren't locked.

Delta Junction

For years farmers and buffalos duked it out at Delta Junction, 97 mi. south on Richardson Hwy., but the scuffle has since been settled as a draw. Today, the farmers' barley and the buffalo (brought here in the early part of the century) have been relegated to opposite sides of the central road. Planting programs, studies of bison chips, and continuous work by the government and farmers have worked toward keeping the bison on their side of the street. Meanwhile, the **Delta Agriculture Project,** grown to over 50,000 acres, will harvest its eleventh major crop in 1991. The **Delta Youth Hostel (AYH)** is located 3 mi. off the road from Mile 272. (Open May-Sept. For information, call 895-5074 Mon.-Fri. 9am-5pm. Members $5. Nonmembers $7.) **Big Delta Historic Park,** near Delta Junction, is the home of **Rika's Roadhouse,** a restored roadhouse full of genuine pioneer spirit.

Tok

At Delta Junction, the Alaska Hwy. breaks off from Richardson Hwy. on its way toward the Yukon and British Columbia. One hundred miles southeast of Delta, the town of Tok (pronounced TOKE) puffs away at Alaska Hwy.'s Anchorage turn-off. Historically a trading center for Athabaskans, today Tok is primarily of interest to travelers on the Alaska Hwy. who are deciding whether to head for Fairbanks or Anchorage. Make your decision at the **Tok Youth Hostel (AYH),** one mi. south along Pringle Dr. from Mile 1322 of the Alaska Hwy. (Members $5.50, nonmembers $8.50. Open May-Sept.) The hostel is in fact just a big canvas tent. The **Stage Stop Bed and Breakfast** rents a great cabin and free stables for your horses for $35. (Write P.O. Box 69, Tok 99780, or call 883-5338.) **Fast Eddy's Pizza** warms decent pizza (from $13) but better showers and washing machines. (Mile 1313; 883-2382). **Christochina's Trading Post** (822-3366), Mile 32.7 Tok Cut-off, has full RV hookups, *free* tenting, and great sourdough. (Post open daily 6am-11pm.) While in Tok, you can walk the **Eagle Trail,** a great short hike just two mi. from downtown, or pay homage to the powerful **Tanana River** only one mi. away. Tok's **visitors center** is on the highway; it shares the 883-5667 line with the hostel.

In the summer of 1990, Tok made national news as over 40,000 acres of surrounding woodlands burnt to the ground in the largest of many fires sweeping Alaska. Luckily, the town itself was spared, but only by the providential, unseasonal rain storms which doused the flames. If you're seeking summer employment in Alaska and have a fire fighter's red card, you're hired.

The Bush

Nome, Bristol Bay, Kotzebue, Bethel—all Alaskans know of these places, few have seen them. This is the Alaska where polar bears still ride the icefloes. This is the Alaska where cannery workers and oil drillers swarm to earn money, and then have nowhere to spend it. This is the Alaska of which documentaries are made. Known variously as the Country, the Wilderness Rim, and the Bush, this vast expanse of frozen tundra and jagged coastline is only occasionally smudged with small Native settlements, narrow landing strips, and other insignificant signs of human presence. Millions of acres of this intriguing and harsh country occupy the northeast, northwest, and southwest quadrants of the state.

Each area of the Bush has its own distinctive features. The Southwest is characterized by lakes, ponds, and sloughs, and by amazing Bristol Bay, where the breeding salmon draw brown bears in droves. Nome, on the Bering Sea, is a gold town on the tundra. Arctic Alaska is hard with permafrost, supporting polar bears, walrus, caribou, bowhead whales, and monster mosquitoes. This is a trip for the hardy, serious traveler. Adventure is a key concept; most towns won't spend time entertaining guests. Wherever you go, be prepared for rough and inhospitable country. And remember, bears have the right-of-way.

Transportation through much of this region is expensive. Tour outfitters abound, ready and willing (for a steep price, of course) to lead you into the wilds to fish, hunt, canoe, kayak, camp, photograph, and explore. "Fly-in" fishing trips (usually $100-300) include round-trip airfare, accommodations, meals, fishing license, and equipment. A one-day tour to Barrow from Anchorage runs $399; a two-day tour to Nome and Kotzebue $442. Contact **Mark Air,** P.O. Box 196769, Anchorage 99519 (243-6275) or **Gray Line of Alaska,** 547 W. 4th Ave., Anchorage 99501 (277-5581). Regular air service is more expensive and entails planning your own itinerary and finding lodgings. Reserve in advance for supersaver fares. In addition to Mark Air, **Alaska Airlines** (243-3300 in Anchorage) and **Reeve Aleutian** (243-4700) fly into most of the larger Bush communities; **Ryan Air Service** (248-0695) serves a number of the smaller towns. Hanging around small airports such as Merrill Field in Anchorage is another possibility for finding a flight.

Some of the best places for making big Alaskan money are in the Bush; Bristol Bay canneries, Unmak Island trawlers, and Barrow's oil base among them. It is common practice for employers (except small-time commerical fishermen) to fly employees to these areas once they have hired them in Anchorage or Fairbanks. Anyone who offers you a job in the Bush without transportation is probably playing a mean practical joke.

Southwest Alaska

Southwestern Alaska's Bering Sea coast, inaccessible by road, comes to life in a few small, coastal Native villages. The immense flatland is the home of the Aleut and Eskimos, who live off the land as their ancestors did. The area's thousands of lakes, ponds, and sloughs, and the great **Bristol Bay**, provide most of the world's sockeye salmon. Thousands of commercial fishermen from around the world converge here in June and stay until the salmon run ends in early August. The villages offer many opportunities for working in canneries.

Dillingham, on the northern shore of Bristol Bay, and **King Salmon** are good bases for exploration. King Salmon is the gateway to **Katmai National Monument,** an area scarred by the second greatest volcanic eruption in recorded history. Surrounded by spectacular ocean bays, fjords, and volcanic crater lakes, the ash-covered valley still jets columns of steam into the air, earning the sobriquet "Valley of Ten Thousand Smokes." Mark Air flies to King Salmon, the staging area for Katmai treks, twice weekly (round-trip from Anchorage $241 with 30-day advance purchase). **Bethel,** farther north on the Yukon Delta, is the commercial center of the area. Once among the largest Native villages in Alaska, Bethel is now home to more non-Natives than Natives. Mark Air flies to Bethel (round-trip from Anchorage $241 with 30-day advance purchase).

Nome

One of the largest Bush towns, Nome boomed during the 1897-98 gold rush, and some folks still dig ore today. Visit the **Carrie McLain Museum** on Front St. (443-2566) when it's too cold to venture into the Bush. There are exhibits on the Bering Land Bridge, Eskimo culture, and the Gold Rush, as well as a fine collection of photographs of northwestern Alaska dating from the beginning of the century. (Open Tues.-Sat. 11am-3pm and 6-8:30pm.)

The 1000-mi. **Iditarod Trail** from Anchorage is not the easiest way to reach Nome, but in February, the traffic thickens for the arduous Iditarod Trail Dog Sled Race. Following the trail of a musher who once carried life-saving serum to combat an epidemic in Nome, the race currently attracts participants from all over the world. The **Midnight Sun Festival** in June includes Eskimo dancing, baby contests, a waterskipping competition, and the daffy Nome River Raft Race. For more information or explanations of these events, contact the **Nome Convention and Visitors Bureau,** P.O. Box 251, Nome 99762 (443-5535; open Mon. 8:30am-5pm, Tues.-Fri. 8:30am-6:30pm, Sat. 10:15am-6:30pm). Alaska Airlines flies to Nome (round-trip from Anchorage $310 with 30-day advance purchase).

Arctic Alaska

Arctic Alaska coldly embraces everything north of 66°30'. This inhospitable environment rests gingerly on the deeply frozen ground. Lakes dapple the land, the result of snowmelt puddling on top of the impenatrable permafrost. The region's sand dunes, deserts, and tundra-bred wild flowers may shatter your preconceptions about the Arctic.

The population of Arctic Alaska is almost entirely Native. Contemporary society has made its mark in the powerful Native-owned corporations (at least one has made the Fortune 500), formed in 1971 by the statewide Alaska Native Land Claims Settlement Act. Membership in a corporation has allowed many Natives to maintain their way of life without the economic pressures that have affected Native Americans elsewhere.

Barrow is the world's largest Eskimo village and a focal point for Native-rights action. It may be a modern city in the Alaskan sense of the word, but the Eskimos have not forgotten their customs. In April and May, villagers carry on the tradition of the whale hunt, both to preserve the culture and to eat. The entire community participates, some hunting, some hauling, others carving up the whale (a bowhead whale can feed entire villages, even today).

East of Barrow lies **Prudhoe Bay,** where the crude oil from the north slope begins its 800-mi. journey down the pipeline to Valdez. South and east of Prudhoe Bay is the huge **Arctic National Wildlife Refuge,** home of grizzly, black, and polar bears, along with caribou, moose, and other citizens of the ice republic.

While **Dalton Highway** runs along the pipeline from Fairbanks to Barrow and Prudhoe Bay, it is only open for the general public to Disaster Creek (Milepost 211). Permits needed to travel farther are available from the Dept. of Transportation, 2301 Peger Rd., Fairbanks 99701 (451-2209). Those who need to say they've entered the Arctic can drive 8 hours from Fairbanks to **Coldfoot** (678-9301), Mile 175, the only hotel on the Dalton and 60 mi. past the Circle. Rooms and full RV hookups are predictably expensive. Guests do, however, get the chance to meet Dick Mackey, hotel proprietor and winner (by one minute) of the 1987 Iditarod. The lifting and falling course of the Dalton periodically brings into sight phantasmagoric configurations of river, pipeline, and pump station.

Kotzebue is the commercial center of a 43,000-square-mi. area in western Alaska. It is also the home of the tundra-covered **Kotzebue National Forest** (comprising only one tree). The **Ootukahkuktuvik Museum** ("place having old things") presents old whaling guns, old Russian beads from trading history, and other old things.

Prudhoe Bay

At the northern boundary of Alaska, the **north slope** of the **Brooks Range** gradually descends into the Beaufort Sea. It was on these grassy flatlands, literally the edge of North America, that oil was discovered in 1968. Prudhoe Bay, once just another inconsequential landmark along the mostly uninhabited ring of the Arctic Ocean, is now the largest single source of domestic oil in America.

Within 10 years of this landmark discovery, the 800-mi. long **Trans-Alaska Pipeline** had been strung between Prudhoe Bay and the warmwater port of Valdez. Manufactured in Japan of 48" stainless steel pipe sections, each measuring 60 ft. in length, the pipeline winds its way in and out of the Arctic soil through seemingly eternal stretches of uninhabited tundra. Approximately 1.8 million barrels of crude oil (72 million gallons) gush through the Valdez terminal every day, and this continual flow is assured by a number of interspersed **pump stations,** which maintain the enormous velocity of the 160°F crude. By 1981, an estimated $7,200,000 dropped into awaiting tanks every 4½ hours, returning the equivalent of "Seward's Folly" over five times a day.

Construction of the pipeline began in 1974, bringing a boom to Alaska's already strong economy the likes of which had not been seen since the Gold Rush of '98. State revenues from oil taxation have created a trust fund in the name of the people of Alaska, providing the government with enough money to operate without the need for any additional private taxation. In fact, Alaskan residents receive a yearly subsidy check of $1000 from the government, courtesy of the oil companies.

Practical Information

Visitors Information, although there is no visitor's center, any of the hotel desks or travel agencies can provide you with information. The **Goodyear,** at the end of the TAPS-Haul Rd., is a good place to get information, as well as spare parts for your busted automobile. (Open daily 24 hr.)

Airport: serviced by **Alaska Airlines** (659-2567 or 800-426-5292) and Mark Air (659-2717 or 800-478-0800). One way to Anchorage ($283) and Fairbanks ($210).

Pharmacy: **Prudhoe Bay General Store,** Pouch 340007, Deadhorse 99734 (659-2425), near the North Star Inn. Open daily 8am-9pm.

Medical Clinic: 659-5300.

Fire and Ambulance: 659-5300.

Security: East Camp: 659-5631. **West Camp:** 659-5289. **P.B.O.C.:** 659-5634. Prudhoe Bay bans firearms.

Post Office: Deadhorse (659-2669). Located in the **General Store.** Open daily noon-3pm, 6:30-9pm. General Delivery ZIP Code: 99734.

Area Code: 907.

Orientation

Prudhoe Bay is 516 mi. north of Fairbanks, at the end of the Dalton Highway, alternatively known as the TAPS (Trans-Alaska Pipeline System) Highway or what truck drivers refer to as the "haul road." Prudhoe Bay is the farthest point north accessible by road in North America, and is 350 mi. north of the Arctic Circle. Because of the dangers surrounding oil production, Prudhoe Bay along with the camp at Deadhorse is a dry town: alcohol and firearms are strictly *verboten.* Be forewarned that there are no such things as roads here—civilization just exists wherever they decided to build it.

Accommodations and Food

All of the hotels in Prudhoe Bay are run by the same corporation, the **Northwest Alaska Native Corporation (NANA).** These "hotels" are aimed more at providing room and board for pipeline employees than at entertaining tourists. All hotels charge the same price for rooms. All of the rooms look the same, as each hotel was built out of rectangular trailors which were stacked together like Legos. The rooms are small, but neat, with shared baths. (Singles $90. Doubles $75 per person.) In addition, there are no restaurants, merely cafeterias in each hotel that serve surprisingly good buffet meals three times daily. There are always fruit and drinks available. Technically, meals are $19 and all-you-can-eat, but pipeline employees eat for free. Employees must sign in before each meal, but the security guard really has no idea who anyone is, due to the constant influx of new workers.

The Deadhorse Hotel, P.O. Box 34-0086 Deadhorse 99734 (659-2940), on the Spine Rd.

NANA Hotel, P.O. Box 340112, Prudhoe Bay 99734 (659-2840).

Arctic Caribou Inn, Pouch 340112, Deadhorse 99734-0112 (659-2368).

Prudhoe Bay Hotel, Pouch 340004, Prudhoe Bay 99734 (659-2449).

Sights

There really is no "town" in this town; rather, everything exists for and because of the oil. Spend a few hours, look around a bit, and then head back to Fairbanks. Seven mi. from town are the **Arco** and **British Petroleum** oil fields. Public access is denied, but if you hitch a ride with an employee you can penetrate the camp. Special clearance is needed to actually enter the pumping station, but once inside you can just walk around or head down to the beach on the Arctic and skip stones or swim. **Arctic Caribou Inn,** Pouch 340112, Deadhorse 99734-0112 (659-2368), of Prudhoe Bay and Deadhorse, conducts tours which include the necessary clearance to enter the pump station proper. (Tours, with a guided walk on the Arctic beach and 1 buffet meal in addition to the Arco oil field stop, cost $65; similar trips from Fairbanks include transportation for $299.)

Although the process of oil production is fascinating, the real reward of a trip to Prudhoe Bay is in the adventure. The Dalton Hwy. is now open to public transit (with permits) all the way to Prudhoe Bay, but there are few services along the way. Don't attempt the drive unless you have a four-wheel drive vehicle, spare food, spare gas, and spare supplies. Plan on going through at least two spare tires, as well, as the road is unpaved and terribly bumpy.

The best way to get to Prudhoe Bay is by hitchhiking. Hundreds of trucks make the 1000-mi. round-trip between Prudhoe Bay and Fairbanks every day. Due to the excesses of liability insurance, most truck drivers are unwilling to take passengers, but have patience and you'll eventually get a ride. The best place to hitch is from the **Hilltop Café,** Mile 4.2 Steese Hwy., 16 mi. north of Fairbanks (open 24 hr.) Simply sit inside and strike up a conversation with every truck driver that comes in. The chances are good that if they're going north, they're going straight through to Prudhoe Bay. Although you'll meet with reluctance to take you along, they all have interesting stories to tell and are usually very impressed that you're dedicated (crazy) enough to hitchhike this far.

No road anywhere in the world can compare with the Dalton Hwy. The first segment of the trip passes through the **Arctic Circle** at 66°33' N. Latitutde, 185 mi. north of Fairbanks. 160 mi. north of Fairbanks is the town of **Circle,** which is nothing more than a big circle on the northern side of the **Yukon River.** The terrain bristles with dense forests of stunted spruce trees (their root systems never fully develop because of the permafrost) interspersed with innumerable glacial streams and lakes.

Beyond the Arctic Circle, the road begins to rise towards the magnificent **Brooks Range.** At a point just before the mountains there is a small sign next to a scraggly tree, signifying this shrub as the northernmost spruce tree in Alaska. Beyond this point, the terrain is entirely tundra. In the foothills is the "town" of **Coldfoot,** which boasts the northernmost truck stop in North America, the **Coldfoot Café** (678-9301; open 24 hr.). Afterward, the road continues to ascend until it reaches the splendid **Chandalar Shelf.** The 12 mi. shelf features sheer cliff faces, stunning gorges, and a large number of Dall sheep, moose, and bear.

The Brooks are finally breached at **Atigun Pass** (elev. 4752 ft.), and the north slope begins its 200 mi. descent into the Arctic. Surprisingly, the last 100 mi. to Prudhoe Bay are almost completely flat. Here, the marshy tundra plays host to thousands of caribou, which range at will across millions of acres of knee-high brush. It is not uncommon to be forced to wait for up to an hour on the road, as an entire caribou herd meanders past. Caribou can often be seen roaming right through town.

In the winter, eternal night brings temperatures of less then -60°F to miserable Prudhoe Bay, which is blanketed in snow and ice until the May thaw. The Beaufort Sea freezes completely, and the Arctic wildlife returns to the land after spending the summer out at sea on the Arctic ice floes. Indeed, it is not uncommon for polar bears to roam into town in search of seals (or perhaps a hapless ARCO employee).

For those who are unwilling to take the inherent risks of hitchhiking to Prudhoe Bay, there are more expensive alternatives. **Alaska Airlines** (659-2567 or 800-426-5292) conducts day tours of Prudhoe Bay, including transportation from Anchorage, for $299. **Mark Air,** P.O. Box 196769, Anchorage 99519-6759 (243-6275 or 800-426-6784), offers overnight tour packages starting at $362 from Fairbanks or $459 from Anchorage. There is also a Barrow-Prudhoe Bay overnight tour ($529).

INDEX